LSE MONOGRAPHS IN INTERNATIONAL STUDIES

The Law of War

The changing nature of modern warfare provides the immediate context of this major new survey of *The Law of War* by Ingrid Detter De Lupis. This is the first substantive treatment in the English language since 1952. Vital developments in, for example, the restriction of weaponry and the human- itarian treatment of individuals are subjected to detailed analysis. The whole concept of warfare is extended beyond traditional inter-state conflicts to include internal struggles of certain dimensions. There is thus particular emphasis in this new work on the position of liberation and guerilla move- ments in modern warfare.

Every important feature of the subject is covered, including the territorial application as well as the effects and enforcement of the rules of warfare. A vast amount of evidence from various legal sources and in many different languages is assembled and analysed in support of the author's arguments. *The Law of War* should become the standard working guide to the subject for students of international law, as well as of international relations and politics, for many years to come.

LSE MONOGRAPHS IN INTERNATIONAL STUDIES

PUBLISHED FOR THE CENTRE FOR
INTERNATIONAL STUDIES, LONDON SCHOOL OF
ECONOMICS AND POLITICAL SCIENCE

The Centre for International Studies at the London School of Economics
and Political Science was established in 1967 with the aid of a grant from
the Ford Foundation. Its aim is to promote research and advanced training
on a multi-disciplinary basis in the general field of international studies.

To this end the Centre sponsors research projects and seminars and
endeavours to secure the publication of manuscripts arising out of them.

*Whilst the Editorial Board accepts responsibility for recommending the inclusion of a
volume in the series, the author is alone responsible for views and opinions expressed.*

ALSO IN THIS SERIES

China's Policy in Africa, 1958–1971 – Alaba Ogunsanwo
Hitler's Strategy 1940–1941: The Balkan Clue – Martin van Creveld
The Totalitarian Party: Party and People in Nazi Germany and Soviet Russia –
Aryeh L. Unger
Britain and East Asia, 1933–1937 – Ann Trotter
Britain and the Origins of the New Europe, 1914–1918 – Kenneth J. Calder
The Middle East in China's Foreign Policy, 1949–1977 – Yitzhak Shichor
The Politics of Soviet Cinema, 1917–1929 – Richard Taylor
The End of the Post-War Era: Documents on Great-Power Relations, 1968–75 –
edited by James Mayall and Cornelia Navari
*Anglo-Japanese Alienation 1919–1952: Papers of the Anglo-Japanese Conference on
the History of the Second World War* – edited by Ian Nish
Occupation Diplomacy: Britain, the United States and Japan 1945–1952 – Roger
Buckley
*The Defence of Malaysia and Singapore: The Transformation of a Security System
1957–1971* – Chin Kin Wah
The Politics of Nuclear Consultation in NATO 1965–1980 – Paul Butenx
British Policy towards Greece during the Second World War 1941–1944 – Procopis
Papastratis
*Détente and the Nixon Doctrine: American Foreign Policy and the Pursuit of Stability
1969–1976* – Robert S. Litwak
*The Second Baldwin Government and the United States, 1924–1929: Attitudes and
Diplomacy* – B. J. C. McKercher
America's Commitment to South Korea: The First Decade of the Nixon Doctrine –
Joo Hong Nam
The Politics of Oil in Indonesia: – Khong Cho Oon Foreign Company – Host
Government Relations

THE LAW OF WAR

INGRID DETTER DE LUPIS

*Barrister-at-Law of the Middle Temple and Lincoln's Inn; Senior Associate Member,
St Antony's College, Oxford*

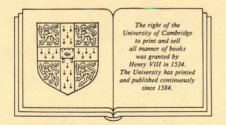

The right of the
University of Cambridge
to print and sell
all manner of books
was granted by
Henry VIII in 1534.
The University has printed
and published continuously
since 1584.

CAMBRIDGE UNIVERSITY PRESS

Cambridge

New York New Rochelle Melbourne Sydney

Published by the Press Syndicate of the University of Cambridge
The Pitt Building, Trumpington Street, Cambridge CB2 1RP
32 East 57th Street, New York, NY 10022, USA
10 Stamford Road, Oakleigh, Melbourne 3166, Australia

First Published 1987

Printed in Great Britain at the University Press, Cambridge

British Library cataloguing in publication data
De Lupis, Ingrid Detter
   The law of war.-(LSE monographs in
   international studies)
   1. War (International law)
   I. Title   II. Series
341.6   JX4511

Library of Congress cataloguing in publication data
Detter De Lupis, Ingrid, 1936–
   The law of war.
   (LSE monographs in international studies)
   Bibliography.
   Includes index.
   1. War (International law)   I. Title   II. Series.
JX4511.D47   1987   341.6   86–34349

ISBN 0 521 34337 2 hard covers
ISBN 0 521 34838 2 paper back

CS

To my son Nicholas

CONTENTS

ABBREVIATIONS

ABM	Anti-ballistic missile
AD	*Annual Digest*
AFDI	*Annuaire français de droit international*
AJIL	*American Journal of International Law*
AöR	*Archiv für öffentliches Recht*
ASAT	Anti-satellite (weapons)
ASBM	Air-to-surface ballistic missile
ASDI/SJIR	*Annuaire suisse de droit international/Schweizerisches Jahrbuch für internationales Recht*
ASIL	American Society of International Law
AVR	*Archiv für Völkerrecht*
BFSP	*British and Foreign State Papers*
BWs	Biological weapons
BYIL	*British Yearbook of International Law*
CanYIL	*Canadian Yearbook of International Law*
CBWs	Chemical and biological weapons
CCD	Committee of the Conference on Disarmament
CD	Conference on Disarmament
CICR	*Comité international de la Croix Rouge*
ColLR	*Columbia Law Review*
CWs	Chemical weapons
EFTA	European Free Trade Association
GAOR	*General Assembly Official Record*
GA Res.	General Assembly Resolution
GYIL	*German Yearbook of International Law*
HC	*House of Commons Debates*
IATA	International Aviation Transport Association
IC	*International Conciliation*
ICAO	International Civil Aviation Organisation
ICJ	International Court of Justice

ICLQ	*International and Comparative Law Quarterly*
ICRC	International Committee of the Red Cross
IHEI	Institut de Hautes Etudes Internationales
ILC	International Law Commission
ILM	*International Legal Materials*
ILR	*International Law Reports*
IMT	*International Military Tribunal*
IRRC	*International Review of the Red Cross*
ITU	International Telecommunications Union
IYHR	*Israeli Handbook of Human Rights*
JIR	*Jahrbuch für internationales Recht*
JO	*Journal officiel*
LJ	*Law Journal*
LNOJ	*League of Nations Official Journal*
LNTS	League of Nations Treaty Series
LQ	*Law Quarterly*
LQR	*Law Quarterly Review*
LR	*Law Review*
MBFR	Mutual Balanced Force Reductions
MilLR	*Military Law Review*
NedTIR	*Nederlands Tijdschrift voor Internationales Recht*
NordTIR	*Nordisk Tidskrift for International Ret*
NRGT	Nouveau Réceuil Général de Traités
NZWR	*Neue Zeitschrift für Wehrrecht*
ÖZöR	*Österreichische Zeitschrift für öffentliches Recht*
PCIJ	Permanent Court of International Justice
RBDI	*Revue belge de droit international*
RCADI	*Récueil des Cours de l'Academie de droit international de la Haye*
RDH	*Revue de droit de l'homme*
RDI	*Revue de droit international*
RDILC	*Revue de droit international et de législation comparée*
RDP	*Revue de droit public*
RDPC	*Revue de droit pénal et de criminologie*
RDPMDG	*Revue de droit pénal militaire et droit de la guerre*
REDI	*Revista española de derecho internacional*
RGDIP	*Revue générale de droit international public*
RHDI	*Revue hellénique de droit international*
RIAA	*Reports of International Arbitral Awards*
RICR	*Revue international de la Croix Rouge*

RILC	*Revue international de législation comparée*
RivDI	*Rivista di diritto internazionale*
RMS	*Revue militaire suisse*
RSCDPC	*Revue de science criminelle et de droit pénal comparée*
SFDI	Société Française pour le Droit International
SIPRI	Stockholm International Peace Research Institute
SLBM	Sea-launched ballistic missile
SöFM	*Sveriges överenskommelser med främmande makter*
SOU	*Sveriges offentliga utredningar*
TIAS	United States, Treaties and Other International Agreements Series
TransGrotSoc	*Transactions of the Grotius Society*
UKTS	United Kingdom Treaty Series
UNSCOR	*United Nations Security Council Official Record*
UNTS	United Nations Treaty Series
UPU	Universal Postal Union
WHO	World Health Organisation
YHR	*Yearbook of Human Rights*
YWA	*Yearbook of World Affairs*
ZaöRVR	*Zeitschrift für ausländisches öffentliches Recht und Völkerrecht*
ZVR	*Zeitschrift für Völkerrecht*

PREFACE

> The cosmic dust...changes the colours of the sky...colours the
> sunlight with a bloody line...penetrates our dwellings and our
> lungs...[and] acts injuriously upon living organisms.

This is not a description of any nuclear holocaust. The words are
those of an author, writing 87 years ago, about the nature of the 'wish
for war' which pervades the mind of statesmen like 'penetrating cos-
mic dust'.[1]

The known horrors of war do not have to be described; but one
should remember that they are the implementation of an at least
oblique wish for war, or, since many wars are generated spontaneously and may appear 'unavoidable', a wish to *allow* war. Others hold
that wars have ceased to exist, now that they are theoretically outlawed. Whatever disturbances that now occur must, they say, therefore be given another name, such as armed conflicts.

But conflicts that are factually very similar to traditional war still
occur in the international society. It is important to regulate the
behaviour of parties to any such conflict. Efforts have been made to
this effect in various fields. Numerous treaties and conventions have
been concluded and certain general and specific rules can be discerned.

There is no modern treatise on these rules. Older works cannot be
used by simple updating as the very nature of war has changed,
especially in view of increased number of internal conflicts. The present work attempts to fill that gap. However, the work covers an
immense area of problems and must necessarily balance the importance of different subjects by stringent selection.

The title of this work, 'The Law of War', using a singular rather

[1] I. S. Bloch, *Modern Weapons and Modern War*, London, 1900, lxiii.

than the more common term 'laws of war', is intended to indicate that there is now a homogeneous body of rules applicable to the modern state of war. The term 'laws of war', as applied to the subject as a whole, tends to convey an image of fragmentary regulation of matters of diverging nature and importance. The 'Law of War' comprises such different matters and provides the framework inside which problems and rules can be systematically ordered.

However, the expression 'laws of war' will also be used in this work, but to refer to the various components of the law, for example the various legal instruments, declarations and treaties which form part of the legal system devised for war.

The contents and the ambit of the Law of War have changed drastically in modern times, particularly in the last few decades. Matters which were once at the centre of attention in warfare are now of less pertinence. For example, blockade was always assumed to be of paramount importance to naval warfare but, in recent naval conflicts, few close or long-distance blockades have been imposed and the strategy of blockades has fallen into disuse. Furthermore, the law of prize represents another area of declining importance in modern warfare, and can perhaps now, along with angary, be more conveniently viewed as a derogation from the protection that property might otherwise enjoy in hostilities, rather than a practice specially pertinent to naval warfare.

Because of this change, this work has devoted proportionally less space to relevant rules in fields such as these than earlier textbooks and sought to deal more with problems of modern importance. Some topical problems concern the extension of the application of the Law of War to internal disputes which will be discussed in detail in various contexts throughout the book. For the reader to be aware of the place of such modern problems in a coherent system of law, this book will, albeit briefly, set out the conceptual framework of the law of prohibition of force in general in international society in Part I. Rules on belligerence and humanitarian rules will be analysed in Part II and Part III is devoted to the effects of war and various methods of securing, or avoiding, the application of the Law of War. The present book attempts, in its conclusions, to evaluate the contemporary Law of War in legal and political terms.

I

GENERAL PRINCIPLES

1 THE CONCEPT OF WAR

A. THE NATURE OF WAR

Is war a dispute between men rather than between States? The question has often been asked with regard to traditional wars between States, as wars are *fought* by individuals. There is no other area where greater duties are imposed on individuals and no other activity in which they are exposed to more personal suffering. Many traditional inter-State wars may have been fought by men filled with patriotic ardour; in others, individuals have not had such firm belief in any cause; other wars, again, have been fought by professional mercenaries whose allegiance could be bought.

One may detect a different pattern of commitment in civil wars, internal conflicts and other disputes where one party is not a State. Members of at least one party in such armed conflicts, usually the non-State party, almost by definition fight for a cause, whereas members of the other party sometimes lack this motivation. Contrary to what Ulpian claimed when he said there are no real enemies in civil wars,[1] internal wars and similar disputes where citizens take up arms against fellow citizens are probably more fiercely fought than inter-State wars. In internal wars individuals may thus be more directly confronted.

Traditional inter-State wars are sometimes held to be waged between States, whereas individuals are only 'incidentally' enemies. During the time of the consolidation of national sovereignty one could expect writers to underline that war is a relationship between States, especially in the light of Bodin's theory of internal and external sovereignty.[2] With the entrenchment of the idea of sovereignty

---

[1] *Dig.* 1, XLIX, t. xv, I, xxi: 'In civilibus dissentionibus, quamvis saepe per eas respublica laedatur, non est tamen in exitium discedat, vice hostium non sunt eorum inter quos jura captivatum aut post liminorum fuerint.'

[2] *Six livres de la republique*, Paris, 1577; for comments on the double and sub-aspects of sovereignty, see my *International Law and the Independent State*, London, 2nd edn, 1987, 3ff.

such attitudes were perpetuated. Rousseau considered that war is not a matter of a relation 'man to man' but only between 'State and State', as individuals are only enemies by accident, not as men, not even as citizens but as soldiers; not as members of the fatherland but as its defenders.[3] But Vattel claimed[4] that when the head of State, the sovereign, declares war against another sovereign, it is the whole nation which declares war on another nation, for the sovereign acts on behalf of the whole society. This view seems to indicate that it is really the individuals who are at war. This passage has often been quoted in English cases[5] and courts in other countries have taken similar views.[6] In one case the Supreme Court of the United States underlines that 'war between nations is war between their citizens'.[7] But, when courts affirm the view of Vattel, it is not because they disagree with Rousseau's idealistic view of men being forced to be enemies, but because they are concerned precisely with the relationship in law between individuals, the effects of war on their contracts, property or other rights. Inter-State wars and non-State wars are, as will be demonstrated,[8] indistinguishable in this respect: both affect legal relationships of individuals elsewhere and both are, in the final analysis, fought by individuals.

Why, then, should, as many suggest, different rules apply in the two types of conflict? Is it the exaggerated sovereignty view that a State has the right to any 'police action' in its own territory?[9] It will be investigated later to what extent various laws of war are applicable inside the internal sphere of States. But at this stage it may be remarked that Vattel suggested that similar rules *ought* to apply in the two types of conflict.[10] This applies, in the first place, to all rules of warfare including humanitarian law. For the laws of war benefit individuals. Secondly, for the sake of equality in unequal conflicts, similar rules of warfare ought to apply.

[3] J. J. Rousseau, *Du contrat social*, 1762, i, c. 4: 'La guerre est donc point une relation d'homme à homme, main une relation d'état à état, dans laquelle les particuliers ne sont ennemies qu'accidentellement, non point comme hommes, ni même comme citoyens, mais comme soldats; non point comme membres de la patrie, mais comme ses défenseurs.'

[4] 3 *Droit des gens*, 1758, iii c. 5, s.70.

[5] E.g. *Janson* v. *Driefontein Consolidated Mines*, (1901) AC 493.

[6] For United States courts, see e.g. *The Benito Estenger*, 176 US 568.

[7] *Sutherland, Alien Property Custodian* v. *Mayer*, (1926) 271 US 372.

[8] Below, pp. 303ff.   [9] See below, pp. 171ff.

[10] *Droit*, iii c. 5, s.70: 'Mais toutes les fois qu'un parti nombreux se croit en droit de résister au souverain, et se voit en état de venir aux armes, *la guerre doit se faire entre eux de la même manière qu'entre deux nations différentes*' (emphasis added).

This does not preclude that the State is the normal war-waging machine.[11] Nor will the application of rules of the Law of War to individuals lessen or erode the State's sovereignty. There are numerous clauses in many relevant documents to the effect that provisions granting rights to individuals or to 'peoples' will not affect the sovereignty of States.[12] And Protocol II of 1977 to the Geneva Conventions of 1949[13] adds that its provisions do not affect the sovereignty of States, nor its 'legitimate means to maintain or re-establish law and order in the State or to defend national unity or territorial integration of the State'.[14]

War is thus essentially a relationship by armed force between individuals, subjected in varying degree[15] to the Law of War. It must now be investigated what other characteristics contemporary war presents in order to arrive at a tentative definition.

B. THE DEFINITION OF WAR

To prevent war one must analyse the war phenomenon.[16] Furthermore, as war entails certain legal consequences it is important to ascertain when a state of war has become effective. If, for example, a legal state of war existed between the United States and North Vietnam, a blockade of Haiphong would be a belligerent right; but if there was no war a blockade would be of 'doubtful legality'.[17] In this way, the state of war determines the legitimacy of counter-measures.

A state of war is also relevant to the question of whether treaties have been abrogated or suspended. It will also be important to establish whether contracts of individuals have been affected by frustration or impossibility and whether insurance or export finance policies are effective.

When there is a situation of war other highly detailed rules also enter into operation: for example, rules concerning the behaviour of

---

[11] See below, p. 103.
[12] See documents on self-determination, below, pp. 26ff. But on the decline of the State paradigm in international law, see my *Concept of International Law*, Stockholm, 1987, 18ff.
[13] See further below, p. 170.
[14] Article 3(1).   [15] See below, p. 106.
[16] G. Bouthoul, *La guerre. Eléments de polémologie*, 6th edn, Paris, 1978.
[17] G. E. Carlisle, 'The interrelationship of international law and United States naval operations in South East Asia', 22 *JAG Journal of US Navy*, 1967, 11, stating that there was no state of war. On change of attitude in 1972 when a blockade was imposed see D. P. O'Connell, *Influence of Law on Sea-Power*, Manchester, 1975, 94, and below, p. 269.

belligerents such as rules on permissible weapons, targets and means of warfare, as well as humanitarian rules. Other rules which apply in traditional state of war situations concern prohibition of trade with the enemy.

i. Traditional views

Clausewitz's statement that war is an act of force to compel our enemy to do our will[18] concerns the *motive* of war, answering the question *why* a war is waged, assuming that there is a 'will' with which another State does not comply voluntarily. The 'definition' does not provide criteria for when war actually exists. Equally, his statement that war as an instrument of policy implies the 'continuation of political intercourse with the addition of other means'[19] concerns the *function* of war, addressing the question of *how* war is waged, assuming that a foreign policy cannot be implemented in any ordinary way but has to be supplemented by special forceful means.

Some call war 'the state of force between States with suspension of peaceful relations'.[20] Sometimes it has been held that *all* peaceful relations must have been severed for a war to exist: it has been claimed that the distinction between war, even if now supposedly outlawed, and peace is that only peaceful situations, or at least situations of non-war, including situations of acute international tension and perhaps even armed conflict, are 'legal'. The distinction, in turn, between war and peace is that in war all peaceful relations are disrupted.[21] That is to say, States can engage in hostilities of warlike dimensions but as long as they preserve or display the intention of preserving some rudimentary peaceful relations there is, legally, no

---

[18] C. von Clausewitz, *On War*, ed. M. Howard and P. Paret, Princeton, 1976, Bk. 1, ch. 1, 75. For earlier definitions see, for example, H. Rettich, *Zur Theorie und Geschichte des Rechts zum Kriege*, Stuttgart, 1888, 14.

[19] *Ibid.*, 605; cf. 88.

[20] A. Verdross, *Völkerrecht*, 5th edn, Vienna, 1964, 432: 'Zwischenstaatlichen Gewaltstand unter Abbruch der friedlichen Beziehungen'. For Grotius' view, see *De jure belli ac pacis* (1625; Edition London, 1923), 1, ch. 1, 2; at apparent variance with earlier commentators, Grotius held that war was a condition rather than an activity. O. Grob, *The Relativity of War and Peace*, New Haven, 1949, 81, considers Grotius' definition to be a 'mistake'. Cf. A. D. McNair, 'The legal meaning of war and the right to reprisals', 11 *TransGrotSoc* 1926, 29; see C. Eagleton, 'The attempt to define war', *IC*, 1933, 235.

[21] *Dalmia Cement Ltd* v. *National Bank of Pakistan, ICC, Arbitral Award*, (1976) by Professor Pierre Lalive, 67 *ILR* 611.

'war'. By this reasoning Arbitrator Lalive held that there was no war between India and Pakistan during the hostilities in 1965.[22]

Others require the suspension of the law of peace, rather than of peaceful relations, for a state of war to exist,[23] thus importing, as a condition for the existence of war, one of its potential legal effects. Similarly, rupture of diplomatic relations is also a consequence rather than a criterion for any state of war.[24]

Some call war 'a contention between two or more States through their armed forces, for the purpose of overpowering each other and imposing such conditions of peace as the victor pleases'.[25] But the last few words alone may indicate that such a definition must be obsolete: a victor is no longer entitled to impose whatever conditions he wishes. And, furthermore, the concept of war cannot depend on its own consequences. The same writer adopts unacceptable views when he contends that wars are not, even nowadays, necessarily designed to correct a suffered wrong.[26] War has also been called 'a legal condition of things in which rights are or may be prosecuted by force'.[27] But if this definition is accepted, there can be wars without hostilities, for example if the option of prosecution is not exercised – or would there exist a 'potential war'? Some wars have, in the past, been declared and not fought, for example by the Latin American States during the Second World War.[28] Some States have sought to take part in a war, by declaring war and attempting to join hostilities, but have still not qualified as belligerents because they did not fully participate or their hostilities did not imply sufficient force.[29] In other cases there have been considerable hostilities without there being a war, at least according to the parties.[30] And in other situations it has been held that since not all peaceful relations were suspended, there was no war.[31]

---

[22] *Ibid.*

[23] F. Berber, 2 *Lehrbuch des Völkerrechts, Kriegsrecht*, Munich, 1969, 3.

[24] Cf. Ch. Rousseau, *Le droit des conflits armés*, Paris, 1983, 35.

[25] Oppenheim, 2 *International Law, War and Neutrality*, 7th edn, ed. H. Lauterpacht, London, 1952, 202.

[26] *Ibid. Contra*, Vattel, 3 *Droit*, 1, whom he criticises, alleging that States may have been 'driven' into war for political reasons 'only', *ibid.*

[27] 7 Moore 1907, 153.

[28] See H. W. Briggs, *The Law of Nations*, 2nd edn, London, 1953, 972 n. 16.

[29] See, on expeditionary forces sent by Brazil during the Second World War, A. A. Cancado Trindade, *Repertorio pratica brasileira do direito internacional*, Brasilia, 1984, 329.

[30] On the Sino–Japanese War in 1937 see 3 Hyde 1687; on the Vietnam War, see Carlisle, 'International and United States naval operations', and O'Connell, *Influence of Law on Sea-power*, 93ff.

[31] See above, on the *Dalmia Cement Case*, p. 6.

There are also cases where 'war' is used as a figure of speech. The 'wars of assassination'[32] merely denote a unilateral method to dispose of political enemies. Colonialism has been called a 'frozen war' to denote hostile policies and unilateral resentment. And, of course, the 'Cold War' implies a war of minds, without physical hostilities.[33]

ii. Relevance of a declaration of war

In spite of the diverging attitudes illustrated above, it is often assumed that there is little uncertainty as to whether or not a state of war exists. The question arises whether a declaration of war, as some writers claim, is relevant to the existence of a state of war.

Grotius claimed that such a declaration was a necessary condition which must be fulfilled before 'formal' war could exist. Grotius' rule was intended not so much to preclude treacherous attacks by one State on another in cases where there had been no preceding conflict of any proportion and where the attacked State had no means of preparing itself; it was above all necessary to ensure that war was waged by the clear decision of both parties.[34]

It was well accepted in the doctrine[35] that war might well start, and often did, without any formal declaration. Sometimes a declaration of war was useful as a final threat which itself was helpful in preventing an actual outbreak of hostilities.[36] But, in the opinion of international lawyers, there was no general obligation to make such a declaration.[37] And in practice there were many occasions without a declaration of war, especially if there had been demands for amends.[38]

However, since an attack with modern weapons could be executed with greater speed than before, a body of opinion advocated, around

[32] J. F. Murphy, *The United Nations and Control of International Violence*, Manchester, 1983, 175.

[33] On 'frozen war', see A. A. Masrui, 'The contemporary case for violence and the international system', 81 *Adelphi Papers*, 1971, 18. Some claim there is, in the 1980s, a 'second' Cold War, see e.g. F. Halliday, *The Making of the Second Cold War*, London, 2nd edn, 1986.

[34] *De jure belli ac pacis*, Bk. III, ch. iii, V and XI. Grotius divided wars into declared wars (that were legal) and undeclared wars (that were not necessarily illegal). The law of nations would neither support nor oppose the latter category (Oxford edn, at 171).

[35] E.g. Bynkershoek, *Quaestiones Juris Publici*, i. c. 2;

[36] Vattel, *Droit*, iii, 3.

[37] G. F. Martens, *Précis du droit des gens modernes de l'Europe*, 1789, 274.

[38] For example, Gustavus II Adolphus' note to Emperor Ferdinand II; Zouche, *Juris et juridicii feciales sine jure inter gentes et questionum et eodem explicatio*, 171.

the turn of the century,[39] making declarations of war obligatory, as
swift attacks were almost synonymous with treacherous attacks.[40]
Therefore, a conclusive declaration of war was needed by one of the
parties, and war would exist as soon as such a declaration had been
issued. Hague Convention III of 1907 included an obligation to
make declarations of war. This Convention prescribed that hostilities
must not commence without 'previous and explicit warning' in the
form of a declaration of war or of an ultimatum.[41] The inclusion of
this rule was mainly due to the widespread disapproval of the use of
torpedo boats by Japan to attack Russian warships without a declaration of war in 1904, although there had been some earlier trends in
requiring declarations of war.[42] As declarations of war became required by law there were even specific rules on their form.[43] There
were also settled rules on the function and form of an ultimatum.[44]

A declaration of war, even a unilateral one, was usually sufficient
evidence that a state of war existed. Such a declaration was held to be
an instrument with definite legal consequences and no 'mere challenge' which could be 'accepted or refused at pleasure'.[45] But in the
world of unequal States such a declaration was sometimes ignored by
a more powerful State even if there were continuing hostilities.[46]

On the other hand, formal requirements of declarations of war
were soon relaxed to include also conclusive behaviour from which an
animus belligerendi, i.e. an intention to wage war, could be inferred. An

[39] But still in *Janson* v. *Driefontein Consolidated Mines*, (1902) AC 484, 497, it was held
that as long as a State 'abstains from declaring or making war, there is peace'.

[40] Cf. *Institut de Droit International*, 21 *Annuaire* 1906, 283.

[41] Hague Convention III Relative to the Opening of Hostilities, 1907, 3 NRGT, 3
série, 437, article 1.

[42] On earlier practice L. J. D. Feraud-Giraud, 'Des hostilités sans déclaration de
guerre', *RILC*, 1885, 19; A. de la Pradelle, 'Des hostilités sans déclaration de guerre',
RDP, 1904, 846; L. de Sainte-Croix, *La déclaration de guerre et ses effets immédiats*, Paris,
1892.

[43] H. Steinlein, *Die Form der Kriegserklärung*, 1917; C. Eagleton, 'The form and function of the declaration of war', *AJIL*, 1938. It has been held that there are still rules on
form in situations where a declaration is relevant: it must be a communication by one
State to another directly, so a radio broadcast announcement would not be sufficient,
see the *Dalmia Cement Case*, 67 *ILR* 751. This is a surprising opinion in view of practice
during the Second World War to accept such form.

[44] H. Johann, *Begriff und Bedeutung des Ultimatums im Völkerrecht*, Berlin, 1967.

[45] *The Eliza Ann*, (1813), 1 Dodson 244.

[46] For example, the United States claimed in 1914 that a state of war did not exist
with Mexico although the Mexican Foreign Minister had stated that he regarded his
country to be at war with the United States because of the hostilities, US For. Rel.
1914, 493.

example of an act which suggested such an *animus* existed was, for example, a demand on third States to observe the laws of neutrality.[47]

According to many writers, a State had a certain liberty in deciding whether war existed: if a State was attacked by armed force it could either treat the attack as war or respond with force outside the ambit of war.[48] Some suggested a State could 'elect' to treat acts as having introduced a state of war, almost by analogy to attitude to breach in the English law of contract.[49] Declarations could even be retroactive,[50] and thus introduce the legal effects of war with retrospective effect.

At the root of the rules on declarations of war was the 'state of war' doctrine, i.e. the doctrine of '*de jure* war' or the doctrine of 'war in the legal sense'. This doctrine linked the state of war to the intention of the parties to the conflict concerned or at least to the intention of one of them.[51] Such a doctrine is obviously 'absurd',[52] but it was adopted by statesmen. The doctrine makes the existence of war depend on the mere subjective will of a party who may admit, or not admit, that war exists irrespective of objective circumstances. Any such doctrine is designed to be misused by States which may avoid the use of the term 'war' either to avoid time-consuming constitutional procedures imposed in time of 'war', or simply in order not to offend pacific feelings of some of its citizens; there were often political advantages in applying armed force against another State without upgrading this action to 'war'.[53]

Later, as war became outlawed in international society, declarations of war became politically awkward. How could a State, bound by the Covenant of the League of Nations or by the Briand–Kellogg Pact of 1928,[54] make any declaration of war when it was illegal to wage war? The reluctance to use the term 'war' dates from around this time.[55] But conflicts and war still occurred and States again began to commence war without declarations. And States now saw

[47] J. L. Brierly, 'International law and the resort to armed force', 4 *Cambridge LJ*, 1932, 308, 311–12.
[48] McNair, 'The legal meaning of war', 29, 38.
[49] Brierly, 'Resort to armed force', 311.
[50] L. Delbez, 'La notion étique de la guerre', 57 *RGDIP* 1952–3, 193.
[51] 7 Moore 153.
[52] I. Brownlie, *International Law and the Use of Force by States*, Oxford, 1963, 26.
[53] Cf. *ibid.*, 27.   [54] On prohibition of war, see further below, pp. 54ff.
[55] However, some writers emphasised that war was still allowed in certain circumstances and one should then speak of 'war' rather than of 'use of force', Ö. Undén, *Om begreppet anfallskrig*, Uppsala, 1930, 11.

great merit in treacherous attacks, as they would take the enemy unguarded.[56]

But even after the first steps of outlawing war, many still claimed that States could decide that war existed (or did not exist) by a subjective test, perhaps coupled with a test as to whether a state of war was 'recognised' by third States.[57]

It was thus accepted for a long time that it was States' intentions rather than the nature of their acts that decided whether a state of war existed.[58] But the provisions of the Covenant forbidding its members to resort to war[59] were at least occasionally interpreted in practice to imply that war should be assessed in the objective sense, i.e. regardless of the views of the parties involved. This was, for example, the case when Italy invaded Abyssinia in 1935 and the parties to the conflict both denied that a state of war existed between them. But the Council of the League decided that Italy had resorted to war.[60]

On the other hand, there were numerous situations when the Council of the League of Nations allowed the subjective notion of war to prevail. In the Sino–Japanese conflict, for example, the Council held, on that ground, that no state of war existed between the parties in 1933.[61] Numerous other conflicts were also, for similar reasons, held not to amount to any state of war.[62]

Declarations of war, depending as they did on the subjective will of States, made clear that war 'in a formal sense' existed, i.e. war existed in the 'opinion' of one or more of the parties to a conflict. But the dichotomy of a state of war in a formal sense, relying on subjective criteria, and actual war in the material sense is now probably obsolete.[63]

Thus war will no longer exist *merely* because of the subjective will of one of the parties to a conflict. In spite of this development, in doc-

[56] The invasion of Abyssinia by Italy in 1935 took place without any declaration of war, see further below, p. 55. So did the German invasion of Poland in 1939 and the Japanese attack on the United States in 1941.

[57] Q. Wright, 'When does war exist?' 26 *AJIL* 1932, 362. On the subjective test see also J. Fischer Williams, 'The Covenant of the League of Nations', in *Some Aspects of the Covenant of the League of Nations*, London, 1934, 298.

[58] See, for example, the Secretary General of the League of Nations, 1927, Doc. 14, V. 4, 83.

[59] Article 12. But the article did not prohibit the use of force in general, see below, p. 55.

[60] League of Nations, 1935, Doc. No. C. 411.

[61] LNOJ, 1933, Spec. Suppl., 122, 22.

[62] On fighting between Japan and China in 1937, see Brownlie, *Force*, 387–8; and between Colombian and Peruvian 'bands', see *ibid.* and below, p. 18.

[63] Cf. E. Castrén, *The Present Law of War and Neutrality*, Helsinki, 1954.

trine and in practice the subjective view is still occasionally put forward and it is claimed that war subsists only if there is an armed conflict between two or more States and at least of one of them considers itself at war.[64]

In the *Dalmia Cement Case*[65] it was held that it is necessary that at least one party has an *animus belligerendi*, but the Arbitrator relaxed other criteria. Certain other statements also indicate that declarations of war have become irrelevant.[66] On the other hand, a declaration of war may *clarify* that war exists, especially if there are accompanying actual hostilities to warrant this assessment. Arbitrator Lalive examined all the circumstances together with a declaration of war in the form of a broadcast[67] by Ayub Khan. The Arbitrator found that the 'declaration' was not a communication by one State to another. Nor were there other circumstances to corroborate the existence of war.[68]

There is an apparent subjective view in the Geneva Conventions of 1949[69] where article 2 provides that the Conventions 'apply to all cases of declared war or any other armed conflict which may arise between two or more of the High Contracting Parties, even if the state of war is not recognized by one of them'. This wording could lead to a conclusion that the Conventions would not apply if both (or all) parties deny the existence of war. But most admit there was a drafting error,[70] and that there must be an objective test.

Later instruments bearing on rights of individuals deviate more emphatically from subjective opinions of States or other parties to a conflict. The Draft Code of Offences Against Peace and Security of Mankind[71] thus refers, for its ambit of application, to situations of

---

[64] Sweden, *Krigets Lagar*, SOU: 1984, 48; cf. J. Spiropoulos, 'Sur l'existence de l'état de guerre entre la Grèce et l'Albanie', 1 *RHDI* 1948, 375.

[65] (1967) 67 *ILR* 751 and above, p. 6.

[66] See, for example, Resolution XI of 21st ICRC Conference, Istanbul, 1969, which referred to 'parties to a conflict' without mentioning declarations of war as relevant, nor indicating that parties have to be 'recognised' units.

[67] On this see above, p. 6.   [68] See the *Dalmia Cement Case*, 751.

[69] Misc. No. 4, 1950, Cmd. 8033.

[70] ICRC, 1 *Commentary* 32 and 3, *ibid.*, 23. The drafting history of the article shows that the original proposed words were 'by parties concerned', ICRC, *Report on 1947 Conference*, 272. Cf. D. Bindschedler-Robert, *A Reconsideration of the Law of Armed Conflict*, Geneva, 1969, 49; J. Gutteridge, 'The Geneva Conventions of 1949', 26 *BYIL* 1949, 298. Brownlie is led to the conclusion that the article clearly dispenses with subjective tests by relying on an inaccurate text where 'one of them' has been replaced by 'any of them', *Force*, 394 n. 2.

[71] ILC, 1 *Yearbook* 1951, 73, 224; 2 *ibid.*, 136.

armed conflict even if recognised by 'none' of the parties, a wording which has also been adopted by the 1954 Hague Convention for the Protection of Cultural Property.[72]

There is no reason why this should not be assessed regardless of the attitudes of the parties to the dispute, for example by third States.[73] The position now appears to be that war may well exist although there has been no declaration of war. It is obviously desirable to devise objective, rather than subjective, criteria as a guide to whether there is a state of war or armed conflict.

But subjective criteria will always be relevant, albeit in different stages and layers, and can, it is submitted, never be completely eliminated, at least not until some impartial, possibly judicial, body is entrusted with the task of identifying the existence of a war. Even the assessment of third States cannot be wholly independent of their subjective opinions and will inevitably depend on information available to them as well as on their political attitudes.

It will also often remain a matter of subjective assertion to establish the scale at which skirmishes transgress from the field of 'intermittent disturbances' to cross the threshold into the realm of 'war' or 'armed conflict'.

Although some contend that, to define war, one would have to resort to organic, psychological, material and teleologic material,[74] there is probably greater merit in allowing for a common-sense meaning. Such a method could be used to decide the effect on contracts of private parties by examining what the parties understood by the reference to war,[75] and it could be extended to other situations when certain objective elements are present.[76]

There are good reasons why one may condone a variety of definitions of war or armed conflict to enable such definitions to be used for different purposes,[77] for example to allow rules of war protecting

---

[72] 249 UNTS 240.

[73] Brownlie, *Force*, 401; E. Borchard, 'War and peace', 27 *AJIL* 1933, 114–17.

[74] xxx, 'La notion juridique de la guerre, le critérion de la guerre', 57 *RGDIP* 1953, 177. Cf. L. Kotzsch, *The Concept of War in Contemporary History and International Law*, London, 1956.

[75] Cf. *Kawusaki Kisen Kabushiki Kaisha of Kobe* v. *Bantham Steamship Co.*, (1939) 2 KB 544.

[76] Cf. *Re Al-fin Corporation Patent*, (1970) Ch. 160 on United Kingdom being 'at war' with North Korea, a 'non-recognised' entity.

[77] Thus Grob, *The Relativity of War and Peace*, 177. Cf. A. C. Gialdino, *Gli effeti della guerra sui trattati*, Milan, 1959, 251, and below, p. 300 on the effect of war on treaties and contracts.

individuals the widest possible application. Geneva Convention III on Prisoners of War[78] specifies[79] that there need be no fighting for the Convention to apply: it is sufficient for persons to be captured.[80]

Sometimes the term 'war' has been construed to have a narrow meaning, depending, still, on a formal declaration of war which, in the event, enabled an administratrix of a deceased employee of the United States Navy to recover a fine.[81] In other cases bearing on insurance[82] it was held that 'time of war' is an expression which must be held 'against' the insurance company and thus be construed to give maximum benefit to the insured. Consequently, the court held that there was no 'war' in Vietnam and double indemnity payment was due.[83] Other cases too, have construed 'war' in a wide sense for the purpose of payment of insurance monies.[84]

But in cases turning on military discipline the attitude of courts has been different. Here, courts have normally construed 'war' to cover precisely what a soldier might have understood himself to be involved in for the purpose of discipline, for example with regard to desertion.[85] Courts have then underlined that 'war' for the purpose of 'military law' must include also *de facto* war where there has been no declaration of war by the competent body.[86]

It may be suggested that courts have to some extent been guided by what the effect of a specific definition of 'war' would have on the rights and duties of the parties in the particular litigation. In particular there appears to be a sharp distinction between cases concerning the potential impact on rights of civilians and on the duties of members of the armed forces; in the latter case it is not unlikely that the question of example of military discipline and general preventive aspects influenced the courts.

[78] See below, p. 281.   [79] Article 4.

[80] Cf. E. David, *Mercenaires et volontaires internationaux en droit des gens*, Brussels, 1978, 370.

[81] *Robb* v. *United States*, (1972) 456 F 2nd 768.

[82] *Hammond* v. *National Life and Accident Insurance Co.*, (1971) La. App. 243 SO 2nd 902.

[83] The Court might have been influenced also by the fact that there had been no accident in action: the deceased had been killed by a fire on his ship started by carelessness by his own crew.

[84] E.g. *Western Reserve Life Insurance Co.* v. *Meadown*, (1953) 20 *ILR* 578.

[85] *Broussard* v. *Patton*, (1972) 566 F 2nd 816. Cf. *United States* v. *Bancroft*, (1953) 20 *ILR* 586.

[86] See *Broussard* v. *Patton*, above, where there had been no declaration of war by Congress in the Vietnam War.

The definition of 'war' became even more complex when the incidence of civil and internal wars, i.e. non-State wars, increased. Units that are not States are not competent to make declarations of war, so the issue of such declarations was not relevant. Bearing in mind the complexities of internal war and, in particular, the hazy area when a territorial unit or population group emerges from the grasp of the sovereignty of one State to form its own independent entity, it can now be said that, in such situations too, declarations of war are obsolete. There is still, in inter-State as well as in internal relations, a need for fair warning before attacks lest such attacks appear treacherous. On the other hand, the whole essence of guerilla warfare is based on terrorist tactics and surprise attacks, the only way rebels can outweigh the structural power supremacy of the organised State.

However, the treacherous hazards to the established State in such warfare are, to some extent, compensated by the fact that at least once the first attack has occurred, the State has as much fair warning of future attacks as a declaration of war would have implied.

Parties which engage in war do not have to be recognised as States by their enemy. A country, nation or group can be a belligerent in spite of non-recognition.[87] Conversely, the application of the treaties of the Law of War, for example the Geneva Conventions, does not imply any 'recognition'[88] of a party to a dispute as a 'State'. This is often made abundantly clear by forceful pronouncements of States, for example by General Gowon when he agreed to apply the Geneva Conventions in the war with Biafra: such action certainly did not imply any recognition of Biafra.[89]

Decisions in the United Nations on, for example, Korea indicate that conflicts either involving a newly organised territorial unit or two distinct territorial units, which can be expected to be 'relatively permanent', are 'to be treated as conflicts between established States'.[90] Similar attitudes were apparent in the case of Vietnam.[91]

---

[87] *The Fjeld*, (1950) Prize Court of Alexandria, 17 *ILR* 1950, 345; *Diab* v. *Attorney General*, (1952) Supreme Court of Israel, 19 *ILR* 1952, 550.
[88] Below, p. 161.
[89] ICRC, 1967, 37, and below, p. 37.
[90] M. S. McDougal and L. Feliciano, *Minimum World Public Order*, Princeton, 1961, 221.
[91] J. N. Moore, 'The lawfulness of military assistance to the Republic of Vietnam', 61 *AJIL* 1967, 1ff.

iii. *Distinction between war and other hostilities*

a. *War and armed conflict*

It has been said that between war and peace there is 'nothing'.[92] This is apparently correct in legal terms[93] although there may, of course, be a crisis verging upon war.[94] There is now a trend to prefer the term 'armed conflict' to that of 'war', almost as if it were a third category. Some States have often denied that they are at 'war'[95] and preferred to call a conflict something different. Thus the United Kingdom underlined in the Korean War that 'We are not engaged in a war but in an action of the United Nations Forces in lawfully resisting aggression under the United Nations Charter.'[96] Some writers have chosen the term 'armed conflict' as opposed to the traditional type of 'formal war'.[97] It may be convenient – and there are certainly many eminent authors[98] who prefer to take this line – to avoid using the term 'war' and include internal wars under 'armed conflict' so as to explain the extension of the laws of war to such internal conflicts. But it is equally, and possibly more, convenient to extend the notion of 'war' to include non-State armed conflict as well. After all, scholars, may define terms as they wish, provided they are clear and consistent; and there is little merit in a term 'armed conflict' *per se*, especially if this term in many languages comes across as an artificial expression.[99] Furthermore, Clausewitz prescribed as the main criterion of war 'an act of force to compel our enemy to do our will',[100] and it may then seem adequate to use the term 'war' for the problems dealt with in this work.[101]

---

[92] Grotius, *De jure*, Bk. III, ch. xxi, 1, i, quoting Cicero, 8 Phillipan Speeches, ch. 1.

[93] A. D. McNair and D. V. Watts, *The Legal Effects of War*, 4th edn, Cambridge, 1966, 45: this is also the position in English law: *Janson* v. *Driefontein Consolidated Mines*, (1902) AC 484, at 497; The 'status mixtus' suggested by G. Schwarzenberger, *The Frontiers of International Law*, London, 1962, 242, probably obscures rather than clarifies by introducing an unnecessary category: Brownlie, *Force*, 401 n. 3.

[94] R. N. Lebow, *Between Peace and War, the Nature of International Crisis*, Baltimore, 1981.

[95] On a similar position with regard to declaration of war, see above, p. 8.

[96] The Foreign Secretary's Statement in the House of Commons, 11 June 1952, *Hansard*, col. 202: 'we are not engaged in a war with the Republic of North Korea because we do not admit that there is such a state. What we are engaged in is an action of the United Nations Forces?'

[97] Bindschedler-Robert, *Reconsiderations*, 5ff.

[98] Apart from Bindschedler-Robert, see Rousseau, *Conflits armés*.

[99] For example, 'bewaffnete Konflikten' in German and 'beväpnade konflikter' in Swedish.   [100] Clausewitz, *On War*, Bk. 1, ch. 1, 75.

[101] Especially as Clausewitz qualified 'force' by requiring it to be 'physical', thus eliminating economic warfare, which is not dealt with in the present work.

But Clausewitz's requirement of force by a sovereign power has to be discarded for the purpose of modern regulation of war; as we shall see, even new treaties on the Law of War recognise the status of rebels and several instruments envisage such groups as parties to treaties.[102]

A further, probably erroneous, reason for a distinction between war and armed conflict is the claim that only States can wage wars. One can no longer say that only States are 'entitled' to engage in wars since they are not so legally empowered. But to many there are still some remnants of the privilege states used to enjoy: wars are, to them, by definition inter-State wars. Entities which are not States may be engaged in qualified wars such as civil wars and armed conflicts, but not in wars properly so called. These views are probably due to the traditional and nowadays inaccurate notion of the State as the only war-waging machine.[103] In numerous recent hostilities belligerents have often been units other than States.

But if we were to admit that units other than States can wage wars, then certain other criteria for war mentioned above[104] would fall: it serves little to distinguish war from armed conflict by assessing whether or not the parties have broken off all peaceful relations or not if one of the belligerents is not a State. A rebel unit can, by definition, not have had peaceful relations, or any other 'official' relations, with his opponent. He may wish to establish such peaceful relations once his goal has been won and he represents his own State, but, until such time, there will not have existed any peaceful relations which can be partially or totally broken.

A further confusion has also been created by the use of the new term 'armed conflict'. Which is the larger concept, war or armed conflict? Some have considered whether armed conflict is short of war or includes war.[105] And is aggression short of war or does it include war?[106] Is aggression an act of war or is war a type of aggression?

Many members of the Institut objected to any exaggerated importance of definitions.[107] It may be questioned whether discussions on the meaning of terms like these are fruitful in the absence of obvious

---

[102] Below, p. 102.   [103] See below, p. 105.   [104] See above, p. 6.
[105] Cf. Institut de Droit International, Preliminary Report by Broms, 59 *Annuaire* 1981, 204.
[106] See below, p. 57.
[107] See Briggs, in Institut de Droit International, 59 *Annuaire* 1981, 248; Verosta, *ibid.*, 254; McDougal, *ibid.*, 251. *Contra*, Zourek, *ibid.*, 258.

logic or in the absence of common agreement on the definition of a term. It may be better to allow for some flexibility of meaning.

But most writers and commentators use the term 'armed conflict' to denote something less than war, assuming thus that war is the larger concept implying a more intense or full-scale situation than armed conflict.

For the purpose of this work, however, the general term 'war' has been chosen to include certain armed conflicts of certain dimensions.[108] Naturally not all armed conflicts amount to war, so armed conflict may or may not be war. Since the subjective meaning of war has been abandoned,[109] there is a similar problem with regard to war: a conflict may be war or it may not be war. But nothing will be solved by preferring a particular term to another as both concepts require a certain threshold to apply according to contemporary practice. Yet, the distinction between war and armed conflict is not really fruitful and is not one of type but one of scale and degree.

b. War, raids and expeditionary forces

There must obviously exist a *de minimis* rule to distinguish war and other forms of armed conflict from raids. Sporadic operations fall outside the concept of 'armed attack'[110] unless 'powerful bands of irregulars' are involved in a 'coordinated and general campaign'.[111] It will be a considerable problem to decide *in casu* whether the required 'intensity of coercion'[112] has come about for there to be actual armed conflict. All might agree that it must be a dispute of a certain 'magnitude',[113] but it remains for decisions in each individual case to draw the relevant line. And who is to decide?

What is clear, again in principle rather than by detailed criteria, is that no international conflict will exist if raids are carried out by expeditionary forces which do not represent their government,[114] or by other units for which a State is not responsible,[115] or for which it

[108] See above, on definition of war.
[109] See above, p. 12.   [110] Brownlie, *Force*, 278.
[111] *Ibid.*, 279. For there to be a 'war' there must be a 'substantial measure of organisation on both sides' and a 'clear line of command', see E. Luard, *War in International Society, a Study in International Sociology*, London, 1986, 6.
[112] Institut de Droit International, 59 *Annuaire* 1981, i, 251, comments by McDougal.
[113] Cf. *ibid.*, 258, comments by Zourek.
[114] *Eastern Carrying Insurance Co.* v. *National Benefit Life and Property Insurance Co.*, (1919) 35 TLR; *Pesquerias* v. *Beer*, (1947) 80 Lloyd's Rep. 318.
[115] E.g. the incursions by Jameson and his 800 men into Transvaal in 1895–6, N. Gelsvik, 'Militaert forsvar eller civil vern', *Syn og Segn*, Oslo, 1930, 4.

declares that it is not responsible, and for which no other State assumes responsibility.[116] In cases where it is clear that one State is responsible for such raids[117] there may still not be any international armed conflict if fighting is not extended. But a war of another type may exist in such a case between the group responsible for the incursions and the attacked State, provided, again, that hostilities do not fall within the *de minimis* rule.

But nothing prevents individual volunteers[118] from joining other forces, provided they are not mercenaries.[119] Furthermore, neutral powers do not incur any responsibility if persons on their territory cross the frontier to offer their services to one of the belligerents.[120]

On the other hand, State-encouraged or State-sponsored participation may be prohibited as assisting strife in another country; the limits and implications of such assistance will be discussed later.[121]

Yet, unless incursions by groups sponsored by a State or self-sponsored groups are of prolonged and intensive nature, they will fall under the *de minimis* rule and will not constitute war.

c. War and terrorism

Many writers suggest that 'terrorism' has something to do with the Reign of Terror during the French Revolution.[122] But suppression by a State of its own subjects in its own territory on a scale of 'terror' dimensions is better referred to by other terms.[123]

There is no convenient definition of terrorism, and it may be useful

[116] On Pakistani raids into Kashmir in 1965, see UNYB 1965, 159; on Indonesian raids into Malaysia in 1964–5, see 5 *IRRC* 1965, 71.
[117] On e.g. United States raid at the Bay of Pigs in Cuba see 10 *Digest of International Law*, 236.
[118] See below, pp. 109ff.
[119] See below, p. 118.
[120] Hague Convention V 1907 on Rights and Duties of Neutral Powers and Persons in War on Land, 3 NRGT, 3 série, 504, article 6; Hague Convention XIII 1907 on Rights and Duties of Neutral Powers and Persons in Maritime War, *ibid.*, 713, article 8.
[121] See below, p. 66.
[122] R. Friedlander, 'Terrorism and international law: what is being done', *Rutgers Camden Law Journal*, 1977, 41; J. J. Paust, 'Non-protected persons or things', in A. E. Evans and J. F. Murphy (eds.), *Legal Aspects of Terrorism*, Lexington, 1978, 341, on 'system of general terrorisation' in Belgium during the Second World War.
[123] Geneva Convention IV on Civilians also uses 'terrorism' to signify measures taken by a State. Thus 'collective' penalties (against the civilian population) and likewise all measures of intimidation or of terrorism are prohibited, see article 33. Cf. A. Roberts, 'Terrorism and international order', in L. Freedman *et al.* (eds.), *Terrorism and International Order*, London, 1986, 10.

to attempt to define the concept for the purpose of drawing a line between terrorism and war, and especially between terrorism and guerilla warfare, where the line may not be too clear.

(1) State terrorism. One type of terrorism is perpetrated by the State, not against its own subjects in its own territory as discussed above, but against other States and other citizens in furtherance of its own interests. Such State terrorism may be divided into two groups. One of these concerns assassination missions against undesirable persons in other States, for example the elimination of certain Libyan citizens in other countries.[124] Another group concerns acts of a more random character against targets in some way representing or connected with a 'hostile' or disliked country. An example of this type of act is the Libyan attack in 1986 on a West German disco used by American soldiers or the Syrian-backed attempt to sabotage an Israeli jet plane at Heathrow, also in 1986.

(2) Group terrorism. The more common kind of terrorism is not perpetrated by a State but precisely directed against it. It may be carried out either by groups of the State's own subjects, like the Baader Meinhof Gang, and later the Red Brigade, in Germany, or by groups whose political headquarters are based in another country, like the IRA in Ireland, or, on a different scale, the Tamils taking action in Sri Lanka and India. The 'cause' for which such groups may take action is usually political, but covers a wide spectrum, ranging from the declared objective of 'anarchy' in the case of the Baader Meinhof Gang, to the quest for self-determination of a province, as in the case of the IRA, or for greater autonomy without necessarily claiming independence, like the Tamils in Sri Lanka. Sometimes the 'cause' concerns general dissatisfaction with the political and economic structure of a country and action is taken from within against specific targets who are thought to be representative of that structure. As one example of this pattern one may mention the activities of Action Directe in France.

(3) Prevention of terrorism. There is now a series of international conventions to suppress international terrorism, for example in the

---

[124] On 'wars of assassination', see above, note 32.

form of hijacking[125] or kidnapping of diplomats.[126] Some other general conventions have also been concluded,[127] but none of them contain any useful definition of terrorism. Nor does the current literature on terrorism[128] provide much clarification.

(4) Definition of terrorism. What are the hallmarks of terrorism? Actions against specific targets are not new in history and leaders of States and, indeed, public figures have had to accept certain dangers that go with their profession. We may therefore leave aside the assassination missions either by States or by groups. But the 'new' type of terrorism that has flourished in recent years has another element: it is basically and predominantly exercised against 'random' targets, often innocent civilians. This type of terrorism invariably implies a demand that certain acts be taken by someone else. The demand may be clearly expressed or merely assumed to be understood by whoever is empowered to take the acts requested. Terrorism is thus basically 'extortionate' as its perpetrators seek to obtain certain ends by force. Normally there will be political demands; but there is very little difference in technique between this type of politically extortionate terrorism and the type for private ends.[129]

[125] The 1963 Tokyo Convention of Offenses and Certain Other Acts Committed on Board Aircraft, 704 UNTS 219; the 1970 Hague Convention for the Suppression of Unlawful Seizure of Aircraft, TIAS 7192; the 1971 Montreal Convention for the Suppression of Unlawful Acts Against the Safety of Civil Aviation, 10 *ILM* 1151.

[126] The Organization of American States (OAS) Convention to Prevent and Punish Terrorism Taking the Form of Crimes Against Persons and Related Extortions that are of International Significance 1971, TIAS 8413; 65 *AJIL* 898; the United Nations Convention on the Prevention and Punishment of Crimes Against Internationally Protected Persons Including Diplomatic Agents 1973, TIAS 8532; 13 *ILM* 41; the UN Convention Against the Taking of Hostages 1979, 18 *ILM* 1456.

[127] The 1977 Strasburg Convention (Council of Europe) on Suppression of Terrorism, 15 *ILM* 1979, 1972; the 1980 Dublin (EEC) Convention on Suppression of Terrorism, 19 *ILM* 1980, 325; cf. the 1978 Bonn Declaration on International Terrorism, 17 *ILM* 1285.

[128] For recent works on terrorism, see Y. Alexander and J. M. Gleason, *Behavioural and Quantitative Perspectives on Terrorism*, Oxford, 1981; M. H. Livingston, L. B. Kress and M. G. Wanck (eds.), *International Terrorism in the Contemporary World*, London, 1978; Y. Alexander *et al.* (eds.) *Terrorism: Theory and Practice*, Boulder, Colorado, 1979; J. Lodge (ed.), *Terrorism: A Challenge to the State*, Oxford, 1981; C. Rozakis, 'Terrorism and the internationally protected persons in the light of the ILC's Draft Articles', *ICLO*, 1974, 32; L. A. Sobel, *Political Terrorism*, vol. 1, New York, 1975, vol. 2, New York, 1979; Evans and Murphy, *Terrorism*; Y. Alexander and A. O'Day, *Terrorism in Ireland*, London, 1984.

[129] For example, the type whereby an individual is kidnapped and a demand for money is made to a bank which employs him.

But the second hallmark, which has not been noticed by commentators, is that the force or the threat of force applied by terrorists is not normally against the persons who can grant the wishes of the terrorists but against some other person(s) or authority. For example, terrorists hijack an aeroplane or kidnap an ambassador to apply force against a 'connected' State to release certain persons from custody; or terrorists plant bombs which kill or maim innocent citizens in a large city, thereby applying force against their government to grant certain claims to independence. Guerilla warfare, on the other hand, is usually aimed directly at the 'enemy'. But, in common with peacetime terrorism, it is carried out by 'treacherous' means.

If the demands are made by persons in one State against others in that same State for acts to be performed in the same territory, this still does not mean that terrorism is intra-State and non-international. It must be investigated whether the demands made concern the granting of independence for, if they do, we may speak of international terrorism. The terrorists wish to set up their own State and the situation is thus potentially international. Secondly, in this case there is often outside support, in one form or another, which is another aspect which may internationalise an otherwise national situation.[130] Thirdly, even in situations which do take place within the national layer acts of terrorists as well as treatment of terrorists by the authorities may no longer be a matter for domestic jurisdiction alone if there is a convention restricting the power of the territorial State,[131] and perhaps also in other cases.[132] The way in which terrorist acts are carried out often implies attacks directed against either important and valuable assets such as aircraft or, as in the *Achille Lauro* incident in 1985, a ship; or against persons who, as representatives of their government, are particularly 'valuable', such as diplomats, as in the attack against West German Ambassador Spreti in Guatemala in 1973; or against other instrumentalities of the attacked State, the armed forces, as in the attacks on the Guards in Hyde Park and Regent's Park in London in 1983; or finally – and this is the type which most leads to public indignation and which furthermore may be the least 'effective' type –

---

[130] See on such assistance below, pp. 66ff.
[131] As, for example, under the European Convention of Human Rights, e.g. the *Ireland* v. *United Kingdom* case, (1978) European Court of Human Rights, *Pleadings*, vol. 23, 1 and 2.
[132] On the power of a State as limited in its own territory, see my *International Law and the Independent State, passim*.

against completely unconnected and innocent members of the civilian population, as in the bomb attack at Harrods in London in 1984.

The intermittent time factor is another typical feature. There is often a lull in the activities of terrorists so that the next attack is gauged to when no one expects it: this forms the backbone of treacherous attacks by surprise.

The aim of terrorists may be to create chaos so that new repressive measures introduced by the government will make the population inclined to revolutionary change when the terrorist movement could become a guerilla movement.[133] But these last remarks may also indicate that terrorism is conceptually to be conceived as a preliminary step of unconventional warfare.[134]

A definition may be ventured in spite of the obvious problems in covering a somewhat hazy area:

International terrorism implies either isolated assassination and 'hostility' missions or the intermittent use or threat of force against person(s) to obtain certain political objectives of international relevance from a third party.

But the 'isolation' or 'intermittent' factor, which is a hallmark of terrorism, excludes it, at the same time, from constituting *per se* a war. As will be shown, however, terrorist 'tactics' may be adopted in war[135] for the purposes of guerilla warfare.

d. A specific definition of war

It may be realistic to admit the following: (1) war still occurs; (2) the belligerents are often non-States; (3) the distinction between war and armed conflict can be used only loosely to indicate the scale of hostilities.

All types of war are fought by individuals, with different allegiance to different entities, and these entities are not always States. War remains essentially sustained struggle between individuals by armed force. In a war individuals will be organised to pursue their hostile or defensive acts for a group, either the traditional nation State, or for another unit such as a 'people' of ethnic, religious, cultural or political unity and/or for an organisation with specified goals, usually including the realisation of its own statehood.

But not every group can be belligerent; and not every type of fighting constitutes war. With regard to the organisation of a group, there must be certain requirements regarding its structure to warrant

---

[133] See further R. Clutterbuck, *Guerillas and Terrorists*, London, 1977.
[134] See below, p. 51.   [135] Below, pp. 50ff.

the status of belligerent. Rules adopted by recent conventions[136] for the status of combatant can be applied *mutatis mutandis* to identify groups of *belligerents*. It should thus be required that members of the relevant group wear uniform, and that they are subject to military discipline.

If such criteria are adopted we evade the illogical situation of which many now approve, at least by acquiescence, namely that there are combatants recognised as such by international conventions[137] but who do not fight on behalf of a belligerent, as only States according to these authors can wage wars. It may be impossible to answer with absolute certainty which acts bring about a state of war.[138] But at some given point, which may not be possible to define *a priori*, the scale of hostilities may reach the point when it can be reasonable to speak of war.

With regard to the intensity of hostilities, fighting must pass a certain threshold in order to constitute war, according to the *de minimis* rule. There will almost always be some latitude for uncertainty in this respect and a certain reliance on subjective criteria is inevitable.

War is thus a sustained struggle by armed force of a certain intensity between groups, of a certain size, consisting of individuals who are armed, who wear distinctive insignia and who are subjected to military discipline under responsible command.

Such a definition is the natural consequence of the concept of combatant.[139] For if combatant is defined as someone who distinguishes himself from the civilian population, carries arms openly[140] and is subjected to an internal disciplinary system, he must also act on behalf of a belligerent. That belligerent, a State or another party, is thus a party to war. Hence, war must be a conflict between groups of combatants, as those have been defined in the contemporary Law of War.[141]

C. CHANGES IN INTERNATIONAL SOCIETY

i. Democratisation of international society

The right of unrecognised groups to wage war is the result of a sudden and intense development in international society, a development which probably started around the end of the First World War.

---

[136] Below, p. 103.   [137] Below, p. 108.
[138] Guggenheim, *Traité du droit international public*, Geneva, 1952, 350.
[139] Below, p. 103.   [140] Below, p. 114.
[141] Below, p. 106, for details on requirements of combatancy.

The change has first of all to do with territorial context. It is to a State that the allegiance of individuals is tied by their nationality. In recent years increased attention has been focused on other ethnographic concepts than States. For example, the peace treaties after the First World War offered *options* for the choice of nationality by individuals based on ethnic rather than on geographical criteria[142] coupled with protection for minorities – in all a development showing the loosening of the State from its territorial base[143] or at least a loosening of the ethnic groups from the framework of the territorial State.

On the other hand there was a marked trend, for example the practice of the United States, of requiring popular support for a government before it was recognised: conditions of plebiscites were often made before recognition was forthcoming.[144] This is another way of placing individuals in the foreground and it marks an important, and not often analysed, change in international relations. The concern for minorities on the one hand and the requirement for popular consent on the other mark the advent of democratisation of international society.

The majority of international lawyers insist that only States, and perhaps international organisations, are 'subjects' of international law, i.e. are capable of assuming international rights and duties. The system they present is increasingly incoherent and illogical as they refuse to accept that, at least in modern times, the individual, and certain groups of individuals, can also be bearers of such rights and duties.[145] New ideas in other fields, such as politics and international relations studies, have, however, had their impact on the system of international society, although few theorists of law have seen any reason to adapt their static view that the system, as they see it, essentially applies between States.

One idea, taken up by writers on international relations, as well as by the United Nations and by certain statesmen, especially those representing the Third World, is that of 'democracy', as a new imperative rule in the international community rather than merely representing an alternative form of government. It appears that it is no longer possible for States to argue that the way they organise their internal

---

[142] E.g. Versailles Treaty on 'Czechs' and 'Poles' of 'German nationality', see articles 85 and 91 respectively, *AJIL*, 1919, Suppl., 193 and 200.
[143] Cf. W. Schätzel, 3 *Internationales Recht*, Bonn, 1962, 180–6.
[144] 1 Hackworth 30.
[145] For a new theory on the role of subjects/creators/actors in international law and on the formation of rules, see my work on *The Concept of International Law, passim.*

affairs is merely a concern for themselves. One result that flows from this new idea of 'compulsory' democracy is that of self-determination.

Self-determination means that individuals have the right to determine the social rules that are to bind them.[146] Self-government to some would mean 'moral' or 'social' consensus and would rely on many ideas of, for example, Rousseau.[147] But problems arise when assessing which individuals shall have such right of self-determination. Some take the extreme view that it is literally a question of a right of single individuals.[148] The Marxists say the right belongs to a 'class' of people. Others claim that it is a right enjoyed by a 'people'. A President of the United States even used those two terms as interchangeable when he stated, at the time of the Russian Revolution, that 'No people must be forced under sovereignty under which it does not wish to live.'[149]

In recent days the problem of self-determination has attracted considerable attention from scholars and statesmen. From a modest concern for the protection of minorities,[150] it is now claimed that certain liberation movements, whether or not representing such minorities, should have the right of self-determination.

There were early resolutions on self-determination in the United Nations[151] culminating in 1960, at the beginning of the massive decolonisation phase, in Resolution 1514 (XV) on the Granting of Independence to Colonial Countries and Peoples. The Resolution was later supplemented by a supervisory mechanism to ensure[152] implementation.[153] Numerous specific resolutions emphasised the importance of the right of self-determination in specific territories.[154]

---

[146] J. Lively, *Democracy*, Oxford, 1980, 136.

[147] For criticism, see A. Cobban, *Rousseau and the Modern State*, 2nd edn, London, 1964, 47.

[148] D. Rowen, *The Quest for Self-determination*, New Haven, 1979, 54–5.

[149] Message from President Woodrow Wilson on 16 May 1917 to Russia, see S. B. Baker and W. E. Dodd, *War and Peace, Presidential Messages, Addresses and Public Papers 1917–1924 of Woodrow Wilson*, New York, 1927, i, 50.

[150] See Capotorti, in UN E/CN.4. Sub. 2, 384 and Adds. 1–7.

[151] GA Res. 421 D (V) 1950; 545 (VI) 1952; 637 A (VII) 1952.

[152] This implies, from the point of theory of international institutions, an interesting control of the execution of a technically unbinding resolution; but cf. the 'sanctioned' recommendations in EFTA, see my 'Aspects institutionnels de l'Association Européenne de Libre Echange', *AFDI*, 1960.

[153] See Resolutions 1654 (XVI) 1961 on the creation of a Special Committee charged with special duties with regard to implementation; 1810 (XVII) 1962, on its membership; 1815, 1817 (XVII) 1962 and 1970 (XVIII) 1963 on its functions; 35/118 1980 on a Plan of Action for Full Implementation; 36/52 and 37/82 on further implementation.

[154] For Rhodesia/Zimbabwe see GA Resolutions 1747 (XVI) 1962; 2024 (XX) 1965; 2151 (XXI) 1966; 2262 (XXII) 1967; 2383 (XXIII) 1968; 2505 (XXIV) 1969; 2652 (XXV) 1970; 2769 (XXVI) 1971; 2945 and 2946 (XXVII) 1972; 3115 and 3116

The General Assembly Resolution on Friendly Relations and Cooperation of States in 1970[155] specified the modes of implementing the right of self-determination, and listed the ensuing rights to establish a sovereign and independent State, associate or integrate with another, or to merge into 'any other political status freely determined by a people' with a corresponding duty of States to 'refrain from any forcible action' which would deprive peoples of such a right. But the resolution contains a caveat that it must not be construed to authorise or encourage any action which would dismember or impair the territorial integrity, or political unity, of a sovereign State *if that State has complied with the principle of equal rights and self-determination and if that State has a government representing the whole people*. The Resolution thus states that the right of self-determination does not include any right of secession from a parent State which has safeguarded the rights of all and which has a democratically elected government. Yet, that part of the resolution has been largely discarded by many liberation movements which claim that the paramount objective of their work is precisely to establish their own State, in order to safeguard rights which they claim were never respected by the former parent State.

However, it is important to distinguish between movements which are hoping to establish their own State, or to join with another State than the one where they are present, and the movements which seek to enhance the protection of minorities which they represent. The liberation movements aiming for their own new States must also be distinguished from certain movements like, for example, certain action groups in Brazil, which merely seek to improve their social conditions but which do not wish to secede from any State.

(XXVIII) 1973; 3297 and 3298 (XXIX) 1974; 3396 and 3397 (XXX) 1975; 31/154 A and B 1976; 32/116 1977; 33/38 A and B 1978; 34/192 1979; cf. SC 216 and 217 1965; 221 and 232 1966; 253 1968; 277 and 288 1970; 314, 318 and 320 1973; 388 1976, 403, 406, 409 and 415 1977; 423 and 437 1978; 445, 448 and 460 1979; and 463 1980; for Namibia, GA Res. 65 (I) 1946; 2145 (XXI) 1966; 2248 S-V 1967; 31/147 1976; 34/92 A 1979; 35/227 1981; 30/121 C 1981; 37/233 C 1982; 37/233 C 1982 (continuing); cf. SC 245 and 246 1968; 264 and 269 1969; 276, 283 and 284 1970; 301 1971; 309, 310, 319 and 322 1972; 342 1973; 366 1974; 385 1976; 431, 432, 435 and 439 1978; 447 1979; 475 1980 (continuing); on Palestine GA Res. 2535 B (XXIV) 1969, 2628 and 2672 (XXV) 1970 (on equal rights and self-determination), 2787 and 2792 (XXVI) 1971; 2963 (XXVII) 1972; 3236 and 3237 (XXIX) 1974; 3376 (XXX) 1975 on the establishment of a Committee on Self-determination, to 37/86 A 1982 (continuing); cf. SC 446 1979; on East Timor GA Res. 37/30 1982; on Western Sahara, GA Res. 34/37 1979 and 37/28 1982.
[155] Resolution 2625 (XXV). See further my *International Law and the Independent State*, 8ff.

The Resolution on Friendly Relations also clarifies that an entity may not necessarily exercise self-determination on its own by forming its own independent State but may wish to merge with another State. This implies also that an entity may prefer to stay with a parent country. For example, the United Kingdom argued in the Falklands War that the right of the Falklanders to stay under British rule was an expression of the principle of self-determination.[156] In other situations it has been found that the 'ties' between one State and a certain people were not sufficiently strong to bring the rule of self-determination into application for the purpose of affiliating that people to that State.[157] The rule of self-determination has now been said to be a 'strong' rule, ousting competing claims based on other legal ties with a people.[158] But in other examples, especially in earlier practice, the right of self-determination was denied, and, in spite of entrenched and undisputed ties with a State, a people could be denied the right to merge with that country. That this could happen and be endorsed by other States as well as by the world organisation was amply illustrated in the Aland Island referendum.[159] However, there is now a marked change of attitude. The rule of self-determination has been treated with such priority that it is often held to be more important than individual rights. It has been inserted as article 1 of the United Nations Covenants on Human Rights of 1966.[160] Some claim that the whole doctrine is the result of an ideological intrusion of a notion invented by or for the Third World and supported by the Soviet Union.[161] But, as has been shown above,[162] it is ample evidence in practice that there has been a long development, not least supported and encouraged by the United States, to bring into focus the notion of 'popular support' for a government and it is this, more than anything else, which is at the root of the rule of self-determination.

Other implications of the rule of self-determination are, of course, that indigenous populations, separated from a colonial country by great distance, should obtain self-rule and independence. Most of the decolonisation process, carried out mainly in the 1960s, is now com-

[156] Cf. Murphy, *The United Nations*, 71.

[157] *Western Sahara Case*, (1975) ICJ, Advisory Opinion, *Reports*, 1975, 68.   [158] *Ibid.*

[159] See my *Independent State*, 183ff. Cf. E. Castren, 'Die Selbstsverwaltung Alands', *Internationales Recht und Diplomatie*, 1957, 107.

[160] 6 *ILM* 360; 6 *ILM* 368.

[161] A. Khol, *Der Menschenrechtkatalog der Völkerrechtgemeinschaft*, Vienna and Stuttgart, 1972, 46.

[162] Above, p. 26.

plete. But there are some territories left of which European powers have not wished to rid themselves. French attitudes have recently been described as incompatible with the rule of self-determination.[163] On the other hand, it has been claimed that it is precisely the exaggerated views expressed in the United Nations with regard to self-determination which have contributed to the growth of undesirable liberation wars.[164]

Individuals may have numerous rights and duties under international law. However, to join international society and to be able to act as a unit *vis-à-vis* other States, conclude treaties with them and fully act as spokesman for its members, a liberation movement must establish itself as a State. The state-centric paradigm may have been abandoned in some international relations theory but, in practice, the State still remains a most important focus of imputation and a most important power structure.

Even those who see States as mere 'clusters of systems and parts of systems within geographical areas controlled and integrated in some degree by politically created administrative systems'[165] accept that new members admitted to international society are units called States. But within those States self-determination must be granted to certain groups and units so that they, in turn, can become 'States'.

Difficult problems of definition arise. What is a people or a nation? Surely any fragmentation into minute units cannot be condoned.[166] However, it is possible to distinguish certain liberation movements which appear to represent a considerable part of the population in a State and which, according to currently accepted ideas, ought to have a right of secession from the central government.[167] Even if there is agreement as to the required constituent hallmarks of a State, it is admitted that there are units in the contemporary system which lack

---

[163] A. Oraison, 'Quelques réflexions critiques sur la concession française du droit des peuples à disposer d'eux-mêmes à la lumière du différend franco-comorien sur l'île de Mayotte', *RBDI*, 1983, 655ff.
[164] Cf. L. C. Green, 'The legitimation of terrorism', in Alexander (ed.), *Terrorism: Theory and Practice*, 175ff.
[165] J. W. Burton, *Systems, States, Diplomacy and Rules*, Cambridge, 1968, 27.
[166] See my *Independent State*, 17. Cf. 13ff.
[167] See General Assembly Resolutions 637 (VII) of 1952 on self-determination, 1514 (XV) of 1960 on Independence of Colonial Countries and Peoples and 2625 (XXV) of 1970 on Friendly Relations and Cooperation Among States, which states that a territory of a colony or other 'non-self-governing territory' has, under the Charter, a 'status separate and distinct from the territory administrating it'; cf. article 21 of the Universal Declaration on Human Rights; article 1 of the International Covenant on Economic, Social and Cultural Rights and on Civil and Political Rights.

some of these features and which are yet allowed very much the same prerogatives of a State: there are liberation movements which have become so consolidated that they are accepted, by States and by international organisations, as full-scale actors in the society. They send 'representatives', if not ambassadors;[168] they conclude agreements which are certainly akin to treaties; they 'adhere' to State treaties[169] and they even wage war, the traditional monopoly of the State.

There is a considerable problem in reconciling the modern attitude *vis-à-vis* liberation movements and the rules of the reserved domain. Under traditional international law, especially as entrenched in article 2(4) of the United Nations Charter, no other State and no international organisation may scrutinise what is happening inside a State unless it has the full consent of the territorial State. These attitudes are nowadays most vehemently put forward in the context of verification techniques where, naturally, States are most jealous of their territorial integrity. However, in other fields, there has certainly been some relaxation of the firm rule: there is virtually universal agreement that any maltreatment of citizens is a matter in which other States and organisations may take legitimate interest and even stipulate a changed course of action, possibly sanctioned by severe economic measures. For example, only a changed view of the reserved domain can explain how it was possible, and legitimate, to put pressure on Rhodesia, a State by any of the traditional tests, to change its minority rule policy or on South Africa to change its apartheid policy; or on certain Latin American States to restore 'democracy'.

Self-determination is thus the main field of focus when it comes to assessing the 'democratic' rights of peoples in other States, but, as has been shown, there are also other incidental rights, such as the right not to be subjected to apartheid, which are now lifted up to the level of international rights, that is to a level of international, and not merely national, concern.

There is another aspect to the democratisation of international society. Not only is there a firm trend to allow groups in other States to be granted their independence, and to seek international protection of certain vulnerable groups even if these do not wish their independence. There is also a trend towards allowing more multiplication of States from underrepresented areas of the world into international society. It

---

[168] Below, p. 46.   [169] Below, p. 158.

is thus normally admitted that the 'democratisation of foreign policy' implies the admission into international society of more Third World States.[170]

Democratisation of international society thus means several different things. For example, it describes how international law, especially regarding rules on democracy, human rights and humanitarian law, operates inside States. Furthermore, the notion implies that the way a State organises its society is no longer a purely internal matter: rights of individuals must, at all times, be respected. It also indicates that a government may no longer be legitimate if it does not have popular support. The concept furthermore indicates that, within States, new units may have the right to split from the parent state if there is considerable popular support for a liberation movement. Finally, democratisation of international society also implies that Third World States should have more influence on international affairs than the traditional pattern admitted and be the equals of the older or more developed States. These aspects have never been systematically studied or analysed by international lawyers, who traditionally consider international law as a system concerned only with the relationship between States and, possibly, international organisations.[171]

In the context of this work on the Law of War the most relevant aspect of the democratisation of international society is the increased application of rules pertaining to this system inside States and to units other than States, and to 'States' in the making.

ii. The cross effects of practices in different wars

Because States have recently had to adapt to warfare by insurgents, freedom fighters and guerillas, they have adopted new methods themselves, and developed new weapons, which in all probability will be carried over into the realm of inter-State wars. There have already been many examples of this development. It is not only the State involved in guerilla warfare that learns to modify its contingent arsenal for potential inter-State wars. Other States and groups have studied, observed and learnt from the strategy and adaptation of methods of more 'experienced' States, and in some cases have adopted similar modifications, often entailing a deterioration in the ethics of war.[172]

---

[170] J. W. Burton, *International Relations, a General Theory*, Cambridge, 1965, 109ff.
[171] Cf. above, p. 25. For criticism see my *Concept*, 18ff.
[172] On the concept, see below, p. 134.

The United States changed to completely new methods to combat Vietnamese guerillas, who were much helped by the jungle, their natural environment. From the point of view of method, the United States resorted to more flexible and mobile warfare. It was decided to employ airborne troops, not parachutists, as had been the practice during the Second World War, but helicopter-airborne troops who could be landed and picked up with the speed required for quick, mobile guerilla warfare.[173]

With regard to weapons, the United States resorted to new types, many of questionable legality, such as napalm,[174] gas[175] and Agent Orange, a defoliant weapon.[176]

In the Iran–Iraq War, an inter-State war, there have been persistent reports of the use of gas.[177] Such weapons were not used in the Second World War – at least there was no evidence of such practices. It may perhaps be assumed that recent warfare, in certain internal wars, has lowered the standard of ethics with regard to biological and chemical weapons.[178]

Conversely, the adoption of new or outlawed weapons by States in their inter-State disputes entails a danger that the use of such weapons may be carried over – and back – into the realm of internal conflicts, especially if it can be argued that non-States are not bound by prohibitions contained in treaties concluded by States.[179] Guerillas are also often obliged to resort to primitive weapons and methods, many of which are cruel,[180] because of their lack of access to 'sophisticated' weapons. As a result, counter-guerilla tactics have been developed, sometimes using similar means.[181]

Apart from such cross-effects in the use of weapons and methods, there is also a fundamental connection between inter-State and internal war. It may be argued that the whole situation of inter-State war will encourage a spiral of internal wars by its very existence, and by its impact will produce tensions inside States.[182] On the other hand,

---

[173] On guerilla tactics, see below, p. 51.
[174] See below, p. 188, on the legality of incendiary weapons.
[175] See below, p. 211 on the legality of biological and chemical weapons.
[176] See below, p. 226 on the legality of environmental weapons.
[177] See *Report by the Secretary General of a Mission*, S/16962, 19 February 1985.
[178] See below, p. 211 on these weapons and recent prohibitions by treaty.
[179] See below, p. 154 on that argument.   [180] Below, p. 50.   [181] Below, p. 51.
[182] For example, the external wars of Russia contributed to the October Revolution in 1917; cf. J. N. Rosenau, *International Aspects of Civil Strife*, Princeton, 1964, 49–50. Cf. L. B. Miller, *World Order and Local Disorder: the United Nations and Internal Conflicts*, Princeton, 1967, 35, on internal disputes caused by Cold War tension.

internal war situations may, in turn, increase the likelihood of international war.[183]

D. TYPES OF WAR

i. Geographical war

Wars can be classified according to their geographical ambit and thus fall into two broad groups of inter-State wars and civil wars, and other wars which are 'internal' to a State.

a. Inter-State war

Traditional inter-State war is war *par excellence*, with the wealth of refined detailed rules that history can provide only in an area where violence has so often rewarded State interests.

There is a vast literature on traditional inter-State war and on classical warfare.[184] But in the contemporary world such wars are but one type, and perhaps no longer the most common type, of war. Yet, as the State remains the main war-waging machine,[185] the characteristics of inter-State wars are important. It may be sufficient here, in an area of the most prolific writings in international law and politics, to mention only a few areas where inter-State war has changed.

The main changes in inter-State war concern new tactics and strategies adopted initially to combat guerillas:[186] these practices are likely to be adopted in inter-State wars. Other recent changes in inter-State warfare concern the potential use of indiscriminate weapons,[187] involving, almost by definition, attacks on illegitimate targets[188] and other swift or comprehensive types of attacks, eliminating the earlier distinction between the theatre or region of war and areas outside the battle zone.[189]

The pattern of other wars has not always copied the strategies and idiosyncrasies of State war, which has sometimes had to renew its own methods because of developments in modern weapons[190] and in response to tactics deployed by guerillas.[191]

[183] But the relationship between domestic and international security is complex and by no means 'one to one', see R. Rosecrance, *International Relations: Peace or War*, New York, 1973, 1964, 11.
[184] For some of these works, see above, pp. 5ff.   [185] Above, p. 17, and below, p. 105.
[186] Above, p. 31 on cross-effects of practices in different wars and below, p. 52 on guerilla warfare.   [187] Below, p. 136.   [188] Below, p. 232.
[189] Below, p. 139.   [190] Below, p. 51.   [191] Below, p. 53.

b. Civil war

The traditional notion of a war as an inter-State conflict is no longer prevalent. Nowadays, wars frequently occur 'within the national layer of society, with or without external participation'.[192] This is said as if civil war was something new. It may be that there has been a period of relatively few such wars, but the development must be seen in an accurate historical light. It was *because* there were so many civil wars, or perhaps one *bellum omnium contra omnes*, in the Middle Ages, that the rise of the nation State in the sixteenth and seventeenth centuries came about, precisely to put an end to such strife.[193] Thus, the very reason for the State, which is now seeing its monopoly of war-waging encroached upon by civil wars (and other internal wars),[194] was the extent of civil unrest and civil disturbances of clear warlike dimensions earlier in history. It is in this historical context that we must see modern internal wars.

It is not sufficient to dismiss the *Staatsraison* as 'pathological'.[195] One may as well, for the sense of equality, dismiss 'guerilla raison' as equally 'pathological'. For it is the guerillas who, when their demands for self-determination or other rights are not met, resort to arms against the State; and the State then takes violent counter-measures to suppress them, whereupon a full-scale war often ensues. The 'fault' often lies with the State for not having given some leeway to the demands of the internal movements. But the violence nearly always starts on the side of the insurgents.

For the more traditional category of internal war, usually termed 'civil war', specific rules developed once such wars started again within the consolidated nation State. In these wars citizens of one State become belligerents against their own State. These wars were often the

---

[192] G. Modelsky, *Principles of World Politics*, New York, 1972, 304.

[193] G. Weill, *Théories sur le pouvoir royal en France pendant les guerres de religion*, Paris, 1892; F. Meinecke, *Die Idee der Staatsraison in der Geschichte*, 4th edn, Berlin, 1957; C. J. Friedrich, *Constitutional Reason of State*, Providence, RI, 1957; G. Botero, *Della Ragione di Stato*, Turin, 1948; A. J. M. Cornelissen, *De strijd om de moderne staatsidee*, Nijmwegen, 1946; G. Muller, 'Zur Grundlegung von der Lehre von der Staatsallmacht in der politischen Theorie des 17. Jahrhunderts', in *Geschichte in Wissenschaft und Unterricht*, GWU, 3, 1952; H. J. Laski, *The Foundation of Sovereignty and Other Essays*, New York, 1921; B. de Jouvenel, *De la souveraineté*, Paris, 1955; F. A. v.d. Heydte, *Die Geburtsstunde des souveränen Staats*, Frankfurt, 1952; K. Kraus, 'Die absolute Monarchie und die Grundlegung des modernen Staats', in *Geschichte in Wissenschaft und Unterricht*, GWU, 8, 1957; on earlier 'private wars' or *Faustrecht* see E. Nys, *Le droit de la guerre et les précurseurs de Grotius*, Brussels, 1882, 54ff.

[194] Below, p. 105.

[195] E. Krippendorff, *Staat und Krieg*, Frankfurt, 1985, 16ff.

result of the disintegration of sovereignty, and in turn such wars enhanced the undermining of central authority. Because of the limited geographical scope of civil wars, and often because of their limited impact, such wars have been called *Kleinkriege*, i.e. 'small wars' in German.[196] By tradition, the status of insurgents has been subjected to a number of formal rules,[197] for example the rules on recognition.[198] Thus, it has been claimed, even in modern textbooks, that the legal situation changes fundamentally once insurgents have been recognised. For example:

There is no doubt that a foreign State commits an international delinquency by assisting insurgents in spite of being at peace with the legitimate Government. But matters are different after recognition. The insurgents are then a Belligerent Power and the civil war is then a real war. Foreign States can either become a party to the war or remain neutral ...[199]

Thus, insurgency can be distinguished, it is said, from belligerency.[200]

According to classical theory and practice, laws of war can apply only once a State has recognised, by its discretionary decision, the insurgents as belligerents. Only then would the laws of war, or whatever part thereof the State considered appropriate, become applicable to the situation.[201]

Explicit declarations were rare, one of the few examples being the declaration of the American Congress of 4 July 1861 that a state of war existed between the Union and eleven Southern States.[202] The Nigerian Government's declaration of war against Biafra on 12 August 1967 is another example.[203] Perhaps also the declarations of blockade by Madrid in July 1936 of Spanish Morocco and the Canary Islands can be counted in this category, but there are diverging views on the effect of this declaration.[204]

---

[196] Cf. below, p. 50 on the meaning of 'guerilla'.
[197] On the historical aspects see R. R. Oglesby, *Internal War and the Search for Normative Order*, The Hague, 1971.
[198] See H. Lauterpacht, *Recognition in International Law*, Cambridge, 1948, 270.
[199] 2 Oppenheim 660.
[200] E.g. W. W. Wilson, 'Recognition of insurgency and belligerency', *AJIL*, 1937 (ASIL) 136.
[201] E. Castrén, *Civil War*, Helsinki, 1966, 135, 139. Cf. F. Castberg, 'Folkerettslige spörsmål omkring den spanske borgerkrig', *Nord TIR*, 1938, 162: there was only a 'rebellion' against the lawful government, *ibid.*, 165; recognition of the 'government' of the insurgents would even violate international law, *ibid.*, 165.
[202] Cf. C. Zorgbibe, 'De la théorie classique de la reconnaissance de belligérance à l'article 3 des Conventions de Genève', in Centre Henri Rolin (ed.), *Droit humanitaire et conflits armés*, Brussels, 1970, 84.
[203] *Ibid.*   [204] Cf. *ibid.*, 25.

There can also be other forms of implicit recognition of insurgents.[205] Third States can explicitly[206] or by implication[207] recognise insurgents in civil war as belligerents.

If such recognition, explicit or implicit, were effective, the Law of War in its entirety would become applicable. Indeed, some claim that the whole dispute automatically becomes 'international' and *therefore* the laws of war become operative.[208] This is particularly evident, it is claimed, as article 2(3) of the 1949 Geneva Conventions provides for the applicability of the Conventions to non-parties; this did not, some claimed, necessarily mean third States, but would also cover recognised belligerents in civil war.[209] Others argue that only common article 3 becomes operative in civil war.[210]

Many cling to the exclusive State paradigm, asserting that even 'recognised insurgents' are by no means subjects of international law: only States can have that claim.[211] But it must be admitted that recognised belligerents, for example in the Spanish Civil War, necessarily had some rights and duties under international law.[212]

Recognition was a traditional requirement for the application of the Law of War in a civil war. Recognition thus had constitutive effects for entities which were not States, and which even after recognition were not States. Of course, recognition of belligerence must be distinguished from recognition of statehood or government.[213] Adherence by the insurgents to the Geneva Conventions or to other parts of the laws of war did not imply that they had become, or were on the way to becoming, States.[214] On the other hand, recognition of insurgents by other States had a retroactive effect insofar as acts taken within their own territory were concerned. Numerous cases after the Russian

---

[205] R. J. Wilhelm, 'Problèmes relatifs à la protection de la personne humaine par le droit international dans des conflits armés ne présentant pas un caractère international', 137 *RCADI* 1972, iii, 330; Castrén, *Civil War*, 86, 153.

[206] See, for example, recognition by the United Kingdom of the belligerency of the American Confederate States in 1861, 51 BFSP 165; recognition by the United Kingdom, France, Italy and the United States of belligerency of Czechoslovaks, A. Hobza, 'Questions de droit international concernant les religions', 5 *RCADI* 1922, iv, 387.

[207] On recognition by 'conduct' by the United Kingdom in the Spanish Civil War, see e.g. H. A. Smith, 'The problems of the Spanish Civil War', 18 *BYIL* 1937, 22ff.

[208] 2 Oppenheim 370–1.   [209] *Ibid.*, 371.

[210] This would imply the application of only some basic rules. On the meaning and ambit of article 3, see below, p. 167.

[211] See CICR, *Rapport d'une commission d'experts* (Rapport Pinto), Geneva, 1962. For criticism of the traditional theory of subjects, see my *Concept, passim*.

[212] Cf. Zorgbibe, 'De la théorie', 93, 86.   [213] 2 Oppenheim 212, n. 2.

[214] See below, p. 161.

Revolution authorised, as it were, *ex post facto* acts taken by the Revolutionary Government, from a date *before* other States had given actual recognition. Courts in these countries treated transactions as having certain legal effect in the light of such retroactivity.[215] The constitutive effects could be abolished, retroactively even, in case the insurgents did not succeed in their task.[216]

For example, the Nigerian Government recognised Biafra as a belligerent,[217] but since Biafra eventually lost its fight for self-determination, the constitutive elements of recognition were abrogated retroactively. Or, in an alternative analysis, the constitutive elements operated only for a limited function, that of belligerency.

A requirement of recognition means that the legal personality of insurgents fluctuates during the dispute, contrary to an international dispute where the two parties in fact and in law remain the same.[218]

Some distinguish between recognition of belligerency and recognition of insurgency. If hostilities inside a State reach such proportions that it cannot be regarded as one of 'mere' insurgency, the relationship between the parties to a dispute becomes like that between two disputing States.[219] In other words, recognition of belligerency 'internationalises' the dispute.[220] The consolidation of insurgents into 'belligerents' seems a reasonable criterion for the entry into application of the laws of war,[221] but what was not clear was how there could be such a marked difference between the position of recognised insurgents and unrecognised insurgents when there was no duty to recognise them. Recognition was often withheld, not least as it often showed a 'sign of weakness', indicating that the government was inclined to give way to the claims by the insurgents; recognition was the first 'concession' to insurgents of perhaps many to come.[222]

It was long claimed that recognition of belligerency was indispens-

---

[215] But retroactive effects would be allowed only for acts of the recognised entity in its own territory: *Lehigh Valley Railway Co.* v. *Russia*, (1927) 21 F 2nd 396.

[216] But monies collected for an unsuccessful revolutionary government do not necessarily devolve on a subsequent *de jure* government: *Irish Free State et al.* v. *Guaranty Safe Deposit Co. et al.*, (1927) 222 NYS 182. What constitutes a *de jure* or a *de facto* government is a question for the Courts: *Lehigh Valley Railway Co.* v. *Russia*, (1927), 21 F 2nd 396.

[217] Above, p. 35.

[218] J. Siotis, *Le droit de la guerre et les conflits armés d'un caractère non-international*, Paris, 1958, 23: 'la personnalité juridique du partie insurgé change constamment à partir du moment ou son existence est consacrée par le droit positif, tandis que celle des deux parties dans un conflit international reste toujours le même'.

[219] McNair, *Legal Effects*, 32–3. [220] 2 Oppenheim 370, n. 1. [221] See below, p. 105.

[222] M. Greenspan, *The Modern Law of Land Warfare*, London, 1959, 19.

able for the application of the laws of war and that recognition of insurgents was indispensable for the application of even minimum humanitarian rules.[223]

The act of recognition places insurgents in a category distinct from other rebels under a theory still defended by many.[224] But courts have not been too concerned with whether insurgents have been recognised or not when dealing with disputes between individuals. Even if no recognition of belligerency – or of statehood – had come forth from the parent State or any other State, Courts may apply laws and regulations of insurgent governments insofar as they are 'just and equitable' and if the 'morality of the proceedings satisfies ... a Court of Equity'.[225]

Nowadays, it appears that at least some rules of the Law of War enter into effect automatically once there is a civil war, or indeed any other form of internal conflict of the relevant type and scale. It shall be investigated later whether the threshold of intensity required for such upgrading from dispute to war can be identified and to what extent the laws of war become applicable in such internal situations.

Some writers still consider civil war as more comprehensive or more intense than other internal conflicts.[226] But 'civil war' is not a term of art. It could possibly be defined as the traditional type of conflict when insurgents have been 'recognised' as belligerents.[227] What purpose does such a definition serve when such recognition is rarely forthcoming in modern practice? The term 'civil war' is even thought to reflect occurrences in the past, above all referring to the Spanish Civil War or the American Civil War. The term was used in the Nigerian–Biafran conflict but it is rarely used today. Instead 'internal conflicts' and 'liberation wars' have been given more prominence. But it may be underlined in this context that, conceptually, 'internal armed conflict' and 'internal war' include, for the purposes of this work, the 'traditional' type of civil war. Internal war is thus a wider term.

---

[223] McNair, *Legal Effects*, 32–3, on application of article 3 of the Geneva Conventions, and below, p. 271.
[224] Castrén, *Civil War*, 135. Cf. A. Rosas, *The Legal Status of Prisoners of War*, Helsinki, 1976, 244. But *contra*, see Ti-Chiang Chen, *The International Law of Recognition*, London, 1951, 303: A. Ross, *Laerebog i folkeret*, 4th edn, Copenhagen, 1961, 141; F. Seyersted, *United Nations Forces in the Law of Peace and War*, Leiden, 1966; H. Blix, 'Contemporary aspects of recognition', 130 *RCADI* 1970, ii, 615.
[225] *Fred S. James & Co.* v. *Rossia Ins. Co. of America*, (1928) 160 NE 364.
[226] E.g. 1 Hyde 253.   [227] Above, p. 35.

c. Internal war

Lately it has become more common to speak of 'internal war' rather than 'civil war'. The latter expression still conveys a need for elaborate rules on recognition, on clear consolidation and other characteristics that are not always present in modern conflicts.

The world has changed. There are few civil wars with explicit recognition of belligerency along traditional lines. Do the rules of war then not apply in modern internal unrecognised conflicts? It is important to answer this question in some detail, as the most serious violations of the laws of war are often committed in internal, not in international, wars.[228] There are also a large number of these internal wars, many of them affecting the Third World: of 147 armed conflicts after the Second World War over 90 involved developing countries.[229]

The parties to armed conflicts since 1945 in intra-State situations numbered at least 120 in the period from 1945 to 1976,[230] and by 1985 there had been well over 150 such conflicts.[231]

One new type of entity which appears to be able to wage war is the unrecognised but organised liberation movement or freedom fighting group. The terms given to these groups vary and are not uninfluenced by political attitudes; by their own side they are likely to be called freedom fighters, whereas the enemy side may be more inclined to refer to them as rebels, insurgents or terrorists.[232] The right of these bodies to be belligerents is evidenced in contemporary political reality. Present practice is in sharp contrast with the outmoded techniques for civil war and it is to be noted that, although textbooks still insist on the requirements of recognition of belligerency,[233] this now appears as an obsolete formality.

Many observers claimed that the Korean War was internal. So it appeared to the Soviet Union, as there was, in its opinion, only one

---

[228] Siotis, *Le droit de la guerre*, 13. It would be a spurious argument to claim that, because 'no one' is bound by the laws of war in internal conflict, there cannot be any violations.

[229] Lugano Report, 39.

[230] J. Kunde, *Peace Research*, 1978, reprinted in A. Eide and M. Thee (eds.), *Problems of Contemporary Militarism*, New York, 1980, 261.

[231] Study of Secretary General on Conventional Disarmament, A/39/348, 1985. For a study of some rebellions, see D. E. H. Russell, *Rebellion, Revolution and Armed Force*, London, 1974; for United Nations attitudes to and actions in internal conflicts, see O. Schachter, 'The United Nations and internal conflict', in J. N. Moore (ed.), *Law and Civil War in the Modern World*, Baltimore and London, 1974, 422ff.

[232] Cf. above, p. 23, and below, p. 116.

[233] Above, p. 35.

legitimate government.[234] Whatever may be said about the legality of the international enforcement action, or its nature as a UN action,[235] it would seem incontrovertible that the Korean conflict implied an international war and a war of some dimension.

The Vietnam War was also held to be 'internal' for a long time.[236] We may either call it, like the Korean War, an internal major war with outside participation, or an international war fought within the territory of one particular State.[237] But it becomes artificial and constrained to view such major outbreaks as the Korean and Vietnam wars as 'internal' war, however modified. In many cases courts did not hesitate to name these disputes 'wars'.[238]

d. Internationalised war

But the traditional distinction between inter-State wars and civil or internal wars no longer suffices. Some internal wars will 'count' as international wars; they are, so to speak, 'internationalised' internal wars, a heavy but realistic expression.

The question arises whether internal war in a State should be qualified as 'international' in cases where there is outside support from other States. If such support is given, the conflict will inevitably intensify and there will be international repercussions. It is well known that the Spanish Civil War would not have escalated to its actual level if Italian legionnaires and the German Condor division had not assisted Franco, and the Soviet Union and numerous volunteers, on the other hand, had not come to the assistance of the Government.

Some claim that, because of this outside involvement, the Spanish Civil War, as also the revolt in East Pakistan where India gave military support to the rebels, were 'international wars'.[239] The United States openly funds, by what is termed 'covert aid', guerillas in Afghanistan and 'Contras' in Nicaragua.[240]

Writers have sought to establish criteria which will assist in the identification of an 'international' as opposed to a 'non-international' dispute. For example, it has been suggested that assistance given by another State to the government side would 'internationalise' a

---

[234] Siotis, *Le droit de la guerre*, 29. Cf. above p. 36.
[235] Below, p. 78.   [236] See below.
[237] At least before the division of the country. On international and internal wars see above, p. 33.
[238] Above, p. 14, and below, p. 305.
[239] T. Wulff, *Handbok i folkrätt under krig, neutralitet och ockupation*, Stockholm, 1980, 74–5.
[240] Below, p. 46.

conflict.[241] Others suggest that any assistance, to either side, internationalises an armed conflict.[242] And some even visualise different sets of rules applying between a government and insurgents, and between an intervening State and insurgents, only the latter relationship bringing in international law.[243]

The question is complicated by the fact that most apparently 'internal wars' do, in fact, receive some kind of outside support. Insurgents usually need help in obtaining weapons and ammunition. The question then arises whether a distinction should be made between outside military support and outside financial support. There will always be considerable difficulty in proving what support has been given by outside sources.

It may be that certain types of conflicts, defined by a teleological criterion, i.e. what we call programmatic wars,[244] are to be considered as 'international'. This is what has been done according to a statement by the General Assembly in the case of 'liberation wars'.[245] Even if these types are now largely historical[246] there will be others that will be 'internationalised' because of outside support.[247] Which conflicts will cease to be internal and merit being called 'internationalised' does not merely depend on geographical implications. It is rather a question of intensity and degree of outside participation and ensuing spread of causes and effects of the war. The question may also be asked about the type of intervention that would entail such 'internationalisation', but this question is impossible to answer *a priori*. As often happens in international relations, there is a question of scaling measures into differentiated types of acts and these types can then be used for different situations. In other words, various types of intervention can engender consequences which render an internal war 'international'.

The two sides of a conflict may have different views on whether or not the conflict is international. The views of outside observers (or supporters and objectors) may differ as well, as, for example, in the Korean War, when the Soviet Union claimed there was an internal

---

[241] Zorgbibe, 'De la théorie', 50; cf. E. Suy, in Centre Henri Rolin, *Droit humanitaire et conflits armés*, 53. Cf. Wilhelm, 'Problèmes relatifs à la protection de la personne humaine', 358.
[242] E.g. Centre Henri Rolin, S. McBride in *Droit humanitaire et conflits armés*, 49; T. Farer, 'The humanitarian laws of war in civil strife: towards a definition of "international armed conflict"', in *ibid.*, 53.
[243] H. Meyrowitz, 'Le droit de la guerre dans le conflit de Vietnam', AFDI, 1967, 156.
[244] Below, p. 42.   [245] GA Res. 3103 (XXIII) 1973.   [246] Above, p. 28.
[247] On the effect of assistance, see below, p. 69.

war as there was only one legitimate government, and the Western powers took a different line.[248] One involved government side may even have two different attitudes with regard to the conflict, depending on whether they focus their attention on outside support or on the nationality of the rebels. For example, in the Yemen conflict of 1962–70 the royalists considered the conflict international in relation to Egyptian forces and internal *vis-à-vis* the rebels.[249]

But it is difficult to lay down objective criteria to distinguish international wars and internal wars and it must be undesirable to have discriminatory regulation of rules of the Law of War for the two types of conflict.

ii. *Programmatic war*

Wars can be classified according to a teleological criterion, i.e. according to the purpose of the war. Such a criterion is not always congruent with the geographical extension of a war. Thus, one type of war for a 'purpose', or what we call 'programmatic' war, is the liberation war. Some such wars of national liberation may be internal and perhaps this is most often the case. But sometimes liberation wars are not so localised, as for example the wars in which the Palestine Liberation Front (PLO) has been involved. It is not internal to any one State and has little but the broad basis of its programme in common with other liberation movements.

Thus, the geographical classification of wars tells us little about their scope except in a purely territorial way. A 'civil' or 'internal' war may or may not be a liberation war. It certainly has a 'purpose' or it would not be waged; but one does not know, even by presumption, what that purpose may be.[250] But programmatic wars are waged for a specific purpose. An important observation must be made. Inter-State wars might occasionally have been programmatic in the days when aggressive war was permitted. Many writers assume that this is still the case, although they express themselves in a rather more cumbersome way

[248] Cf. Siotis, *Le droit de la guerre*, 29. But the forces in the Korean War were probably 'collective' units of the participating States rather than UN forces, see my *Law Making by International Organisations*, Stockholm, 1965, 60–1.
[249] K. Boals, 'The relation of international law to the internal war in Yemen', in R. A. Falk (ed.), *The International Law of Civil War*, Baltimore, 1971, 306.
[250] But note R. D. S. Higham (ed.), *Civil War in the Twentieth Century*, Lexington, 1972, who in his introduction claims that civil wars are 'the work of right-wing reactionaries', thus imputing, without much foundation, a programmatic nature to civil wars.

by explaining war as 'a continuation of foreign policy by other means'. This phrase they have borrowed from Clausewitz,[251] who no doubt was justified in referring to such wars in the days when the military force of States was unrestrained. But the point is that such wars are rare among States in modern times, and perhaps even earlier, as wars often result from a host of different factors,[252] which, by coincidental juxta-position and timing, favour the outbreak of a war. Yet, some insist that certain inter-State wars result from 'rational'[253] or even 'cold'[254] decisions.

The only programmatic type of war likely today is the non-State war. Non-State groups may not have a 'foreign policy', in its tradi-tional form, to extend into war. But this is nevertheless what seems to happen: it is the guerillas and rebels who fight for a 'cause'[255] and who are motivated to attain it. These groups are perhaps too small to fall victim to 'accidental' wars, the wars into which States have drifted in the past by being overwhelmed by the complexity of predisposing coincidentals. The wars waged by the insurgents and guerillas do appear as programmatic in the sense described and, because they lack enough coherence to have a foreign policy like States, it may be useful to adopt a new adjective to denote the specific type of some of their wars.

a. Liberation war

(1) General characteristics. Liberation wars have, by a gradual development in international society, been thought to constitute a category distinct from civil war and other internal conflicts.

There has been a series of resolutions in the General Assembly on the legal character of liberation wars, stating that national liberation wars, involving a 'struggle against colonial and alien domination, and against racist regimes',[256] are 'to be regarded as international armed

---

[251] *On War*, 605.
[252] Cf. M. Howard, 'Reflections on the First World War', in M. Howard (ed.), *Studies in War and Peace*, London, 1970, 109. Cf. below, p. 85, note 2.
[253] J. Bernard, 'The sociological study of conflict', in J. Bernard, I. H. Pear and R. Aron (eds.), *The Nature of Conflict: Studies of the Sociological Aspects of International Tensions*, Paris, 1957, 40.
[254] R. E. Osgood and R. W. Tucker, *Force, Order and Justice*, Baltimore, 1967, 9.
[255] Above, p. 3.
[256] See the wording e.g. in article 1(4) in Protocol I of 1977 and below, p. 161. Such criteria are probably not cumulative.

conflicts in the sense of the 1949 Geneva Conventions'.[257] Some Declarations of the General Assembly carry great weight, although technically speaking they are devoid of binding force.[258] The view that liberation wars are international conflicts, a qualification which will lead to increased protection for those involved in such wars, has not been adopted by Protocol I of 1977 to the Geneva Conventions in its much discussed article 1(4).

Article 1(4) of Protocol I expressly states that the Protocol shall apply to 'armed conflict in which peoples are fighting against colonial domination and alien occupation and against racist regimes in the exercise of their right to self-determination'.[259] The reference to national liberation war implies, by the cross-reference to article 2 of the Geneva Conventions, that liberation wars are to be put on an equal footing with war or other armed conflict between States.[260] However, Protocol I does not expressly say that liberation wars are 'international', although the conclusion of reading the articles is that liberation wars are 'equated' with full-scale international conflict *for the purpose of the application of the Protocol*. However, some delegates considered the effect of article 1(4) to be very much the same as of the above-mentioned resolutions of the General Assembly and, since the resolutions are not binding, article 1(4) would create 'new law'.[261]

To consider liberation wars as being of an 'international character' had become something of an 'idée fixe' of the Third World, but only with regard to war fought against colonial regimes and not within socialist or Third World States themselves.[262]

By a simple unilateral declaration[263] a liberation movement can now formally adhere to Protocol I of 1977,[264] to the Geneva Conventions of 1949, and to the Conventional Weapons Conventions of

[257] Resolution 3103 (XXVIII) 1973; cf. Resolution 2592 (XXIV) 1960. Much of the wording of this resolution was incorporated in article 1(4) of Protocol I of 1977; see below, p. 161. Cf. earlier resolutions of the General Assembly, e.g. on Independence of Colonies 1514 (XV) 1960; on Racial Discrimination 1965; (on separate personality) 2446 (XVIII) 1968; 2625 (XXV) 1970 on Friendly Relations; cf. above, p. 28.
[258] See my *Law Making*, 207–13, and my *Concept*, 95–105; 61–91, 73–5.
[259] The article then refers to the principles of the Charter of the United Nations and to the Resolution on Friendly Relations and Cooperations among States, see above, note 257.
[260] Article 1(4) read together with 1(3) of Protocol I and common article 2 of the Geneva Conventions.
[261] United Kingdom, CDDH/1/SR.46; France, *ibid.*, 49.
[262] G. Best, *Humanity in Warfare*, London, 1980, 321.
[263] Under article 96(3).
[264] Below, p. 258.

1981,[265] and in these important respects liberation movements are put on the very same footing as States.

The extended notion of international conflict, comprising armed conflicts involving liberation movements, has also been adopted in the Convention on Limitation of Certain Conventional Weapons which Cause Traumatic Effects.[266] Some claim that the cross-reference in this Convention to Protocol I may create problems for States which wish to ratify the 1981 Convention but which have not accepted the Protocol, as there are no provisions for reservations in the Convention.[267] The fact that there are no provisions for reservations, however, does not necessarily mean that reservations cannot be made,[268] as long as the reservations are in line with the general objectives of the Convention.[269] Naturally, it is desirable for humanitarian conventions not to include reservations as such conventions are designed to ensure the homogeneous application of a protective regime. Occasionally 'reservations' to such instruments do not constitute 'true' reservations in the sense that they restrict the application of a treaty, but contain political announcements, e.g. that the ratification of a treaty by another State does not mean that that State 'exists',[270] or that a treaty-making party lacks competence to conclude international treaties.[271] If reservations actually extend the protection afforded by the instrument, no objections can be made by those who wish to promote humanitarian law. For example, the Eastern bloc made 'reservations' to the Genocide Convention[272] and some of these reservations *extended* the application of the Convention to non-self-governing territories. These 'reservations' can be seen as a part of the trend, albeit not always implemented by their authors, to grant 'international' status to liberation movements in non-self-governing territories and subject them to the protection of international instruments.

[265] Under article 7(b); see further below, p. 258.
[266] Article 1, see below, p. 180.
[267] Cf. Ph. Bretton, 'La Convention du 10 avril 1981 sur l'interdiction ou la limitation d'emploi de certaines armes classiques qui peuvent être considérées comme produisant des effets traumatiques excessifs ou comme frappant sans discriminations', *AFDI*, 1981, 127.
[268] E.g. my *Essays on the Law of Treaties*, London, 1967, 62ff.
[269] *Genocide Case*, Advisory Opinion, (1951) ICJ *Reports*, 25.
[270] E.g. reservations to the Protocols of 1977 by Oman, 29 March 1984; by Israel, 2 August 1984; by Syria, 14 November 1983; by Israel, 4 January 1984.
[271] E.g. the challenge of the competence of the United Nations to conclude treaties with respect to Namibia, see reservation by South Africa of 24 February 1984 to the Geneva Conventions and Protocols.
[272] See 78 UNTS 278.

(2) Political affiliations of liberation movements. Some liberation movements are firmly linked to East or West. The 'Contras' in Nicaragua and the guerillas in Afghanistan are openly supported by the United States.[273] The liberation front AZAPO in South Africa is, being 'anti-capitalistic', supported by the Eastern bloc.[274]

In recent conflicts in Africa, China and the Soviet Union have supported different factions. China thus sided with ZANU against ZAPU, with UNITA and GRAE against the MPLA; and with SWANU against the ANC; and in all these cases the Soviet Union took the party of the other side.[275] One liberation movement may support another such movement in another geographical area, for example AZAPO in South Africa supports the PLO.[276] In such a case there is a certain solidarity shown between movements, as if they share the same objectives and goals. Similar solidarity has been shown when liberation movements attend international conferences, especially if such conferences negotiate treaties which will bear upon the rights of liberation movements.

(3) Participation of liberation movements in international conferences. Liberation movements are often able to attend international conferences on a very similar footing to States, provided the conference is thought to 'concern' them. Thus, the PLO is a non-State member of the Group of 77[277] and has taken part in General Assembly meetings and in sessions of many other international organisations.[278]

When the Protocols to the 1949 Red Cross Conventions were negotiated in 1977, there were eleven liberation movements which took part in the Diplomatic Conference elaborating the Additional Protocols.[279] This participation caused numerous States to make 'declarations' as to the presence of these movements which were not 'States'. Some said that it was only because of the humanitarian character of the instruments to be drafted that it could be conceded that liberation movements could attend.[280] Others said that their participation might lead

[273] Cf above, p. 40.   [274] *Sunday Times*, 13 January 1985.
[275] W. Laqueur, *Guerilla, Historical and Critical Study*, London, 1977, 373.
[276] *Sunday Times*, 13 January 1985.
[277] K. P. Sauvant, *The Group of 77*, New York, 1981, 3.
[278] C. Lazarus, 'Le statut des mouvements de libération nationale à l'ONU', *AFDI*, 1974, 173.
[279] However, only the PLO and SWAPO took part in all the four sessions, see M. Bothe, K. J. Partsch and W. A. Solf, *New Rules on Victims of War*, The Hague, 1982, 8.
[280] E.g. statement by Germany, CDDH/54, vol. 5, 251. Cf. France, *ibid.*, 25.

to 'greater respect for law and concern for basic principles of humanity in the conduct of the armed conflicts in which these movements are taking part',[281] thereby indicating that the improvement of humanitarian standards must also be respected by the liberation movements themselves.[282] Some Third World countries insisted that only 'recognised' liberation movements should be allowed to take part, in particular those which had been 'recognised' by regional organisations such as the Organisation for African Unity or the League of Arab States.[283] In fact, failure to support such 'recognised' liberation movements may well, according to other Third World countries, be 'tantamount to encouraging slavery and racism'.[284] However, liberation movements had been admitted as observers on numerous occasions in the past, even before the General Assembly declared, in 1974, that there must be an opportunity for the liberation movements to express their views and to propose changes to ensure that new rules 'meet the needs of the time'.[285]

The Diplomatic Conference on the reaffirmation and Development of Humanitarian Law Applicable in Armed Conflict decided at its First Session in 1974 not to invite the Revolutionary Republic of South Vietnam and, in response to a questionnaire on government attitudes, the ICRC decided not to amend the Rules of Procedure to allow its participation. There was much criticism of this decision, especially as the Revolutionary Government was a party to the Geneva Conventions at this time. Some delegates also underlined that the decision was contrary to the Paris Agreement and the Final Act of the International Conference on Vietnam.[286]

At the Lucerne Conference there were several liberation movements, for example the PLO, the Seychelles Peoples United Party (SPUP), the African National Congress (South Africa) (ANC); the Zimbabwe African Peoples' Union (ZAPU); the Pan African Congress of Azania (South Africa) (PAC) and the South West African Peoples' Organization of Namibia (SWAPO). These movements all appear in the list of 'experts' attending the Conference.[287]

During the Conference on the 1977 Protocols to the Geneva Con-

---

[281] United States, *ibid.*, 260; cf. Spain, *ibid.*, 256.
[282] See further below, under 'reciprocity', p. 339.
[283] Indonesia, CDDH/54, vol. 6, 62–3.   [284] Madagascar, *ibid.*, 190.
[285] PLO-Observer, A/C.6/37/SR.19, 5, 18.   [286] *Lucerne Report*, 1975, 1ff.
[287] *Lucerne Report*, 1975, 94–5. On the other hand, during the second session of the Conventional Arms Conference in Lugano in 1976 no liberation movement attended. The League of Arab States, which had not been at the Lucerne Conference, sent a representative, *Lugano Report*, 225.

ventions there was some question as to whether liberation movements would be allowed to attend. The General Assembly insisted in Resolution 3102 (XXVIII) that liberation movements be invited to attend. Although it is questionable whether the General Assembly has power even to recommend who attends a State conference, the Rules of Procedure of the Conference were eventually amended to allow for the presence of liberation movements, although it was emphasised that only States would have the right to vote.[288]

Liberation movements also attended the final Conference on Conventional Weapons of 1981,[289] not only as observers but as future potential parties to the Treaty, which, like Protocol I of 1977,[290] provided for the possibility of accession by liberation movements.[291]

But the attendance of liberation movements is often accompanied by a series of protests from States who do not support their cause, similar to those declarations which are usually lodged to object to the attendance of an unrecognised State. Complaints can concern the mere form of address to a party invited to attend a Conference. An invitation by the ICRC to the conference in Delhi in 1956 was addressed to the 'Government of Taiwan'. That country protested and was strongly supported by the United States in its attempts to allow for the 'official name'. When the amendment had duly been carried by a special resolution, thirty other delegates, including the Indian host representatives, walked out in protest.[292]

Attendance at conferences, or even adherence to treaties, does not mean that an entity is recognised as a 'State'. But by being allowed to accede to treaties, now specifically foreseen by the Law of War,[293] certain non-State groups are gradually being given very similar rights and duties as States with regard to treaty making.

b. Resistance or partisan war
A group of citizens may organise themselves to combat an invader from within an occupied territory. They may use guerilla tactics,[294]

---

[288] CDDH/22, 1.3.1974, SR.7.
[289] Below, p. 180.   [290] Below, p. 161.   [291] Below, p. 182.
[292] J. A. Joyce, *Red Cross International and the Strategy of Peace*, New York, 1959, 210–11.
[293] On provisions to this effect in the Weaponry Convention, see below.
[294] Note that L. E. Cable, *Conflict of Myths, the Development of American Counterinsurgency Doctrine and the Vietnam War*, New York and London, 1976, 198, makes a distinction between 'guerilas' and 'insurgents', assuming that the first category has support from outside. But such a definition is not common, or essential, in contemporary terminology. Cf. below, p. 61 on assistance in internal war.

and they sometimes call themselves guerillas, but the war waged is programmatic insofar as it is an inherent objective of the war to oust the occupying power and to force that party to give up the territory. These wars are thus a special form of liberation war.

Many resistance activities may fall short of war by the *de minimis* rule,[295] by constituting merely sporadic and unilateral attacks. But other resistance, such as the partisan movement in Yugoslavia during the Second World War, has led to full-scale prolonged hostilities.

c. Revolutionary war

Another type of programmatic war is revolutionary war. Revolutionary war means that the purpose of the war is to overthrow the existing government and replace it by another, led by the rebels. Most often the revolutionary war type is associated with Marxist–Leninist teachings, and revolutionary warfare is therefore essentially a class war in military terms.[296]

d. Separatist war

Dissident groups may not wish to overthrow the government, as in revolutionary warfare, but may have a more limited aim, often with regard to independence sought for a particular territory. In this type of conflict the groups acting against the government do not seek to challenge the authority of that government over the country as a whole, but merely with regard to a portion to which they claim they have better rights.

Such separatist, or secessionist, wars are thus fought to obtain sovereignty over a part of the territory, but not to question the powers of the legitimate government in their totality.

e. Preemptive war

Preemptive or preventive war takes an intermediate position as not being fully programmatic for the achievement of any positive aim but

---

[295] Above, p. 18.
[296] See, e.g., C. E. Black and T. Thornton, *Communism and Revolution*, Princeton, 1964; R. Thompson, *Revolutionary War in World Strategy 1945–1969*, New York, 1970; C. Johnson, *Autopsy on People's War*, London, 1973; Johnson, *Revolution and the Social System*, Stanford, 1964; Johnson, *Revolutionary Change*, London, 1966; C. Leiden and K. Schnitt (eds.), *The Politics of Violence: Revolution in the Modern World*, Englewood Cliffs, New Jersey, 1968; T. Arnold, *Der revolutionäre Krieg*, Pfaffenhofen, 1961; C. Delmas, *La guerre révolutionnaire*, Paris, 1959; G. Tanham, *Communist Revolutionary Warfare*, New York, 1961. Some have called typically revolutionary wars 'peasant wars', see E. Wolf, *Peasant Wars in the Twentieth Century*, London, 1971.

to preclude some other action being taken. Preemptive war has much in common with anticipatory force,[297] for it often implies an assumption that another party is about to resort to war or to some other hostile or unfavourable course of action. A war is thus started in the belief that, because of acute danger, action provides the only safe route.[298]

iii. Unequal war

Wars can also be classified according to the relative strength or standing of the belligerents. Not that States, or other parties, to a war can ever be equal.[299] But a war waged by a group which is not a State, against the traditional war-waging machinery of the State, is possibly, by nature, an unequal war. It is not only the resources that differ on the two sides and the fact that only the State is likely to have warships, aeroplanes or nuclear weapons. But the whole structure of international society based on the State as the accepted geographical and political unit will place the non-State party in a war in a particularly unequal situation, due to its lack of standing in the international community.

Important trends are beginning to erode the differences between warfare among States and warfare involving groups.[300] A particularly important development is that allowing groups to adhere to treaties on the Law of War,[301] as this is important to abolish the other unequal idiosyncrasy: that States are bound by obligations under the Law of War by treaties, but groups, because of their inequality, are not.

iv. Methodological war: guerilla war

Some wars can be classified according to the methods they employ. Guerilla war[302] is characterised by small units, great mobility, often rudimentary organisation and certain tactics not often used in other warfare. The natural environment often sets the limits and provides

---

[297] Below, p. 60.
[298] J. Stracey, *On the Prevention of War*, London, 1962, 78.
[299] On the distinction between political equality and forensic equality, see my 'The problem of unequal treaties', *ICLQ*, 1966, 1086; on unequal treaties see my *Independent State*, 194–223.
[300] Above, p. 24 on democratisation.   [301] Below, p. 158.
[302] The term is technically a tautology but has been adopted in common use: guerilla means 'small war'; cf. above, p. 35, on 'Kleinkrieg'; the persons fighting such a wars are 'guerilleros', a word rarely used nowadays. On distinction between guerillas and insurgents see above, note 294.

the facilities for guerilla operations, either as partisans in the hills, or as units in the jungle.

Guerilla warfare[303] has often been thought to involve particularly perfidious methods of warfare.[304] Observers comment that cruel practices invariably accompany guerilla warfare.[305] Guerillas have had to compensate for their lack of sophisticated weapons by devising and improvising methods of combating forces stronger and better equipped than themselves. But these methods, which perhaps originally were not that cruel or inhuman, soon made State parties take counter-measures[306] to overpower guerillas in their natural habitat, in the jungles or in the hills, and such measures often involved defoliant weapons[307] or other chemical[308] or biological weapons,[309] so that the type of warfare used to combat the guerillas escalated to proportions unknown even in the Second World War.

In their motivation some guerillas are influenced by Marxist–Leninist thinking or by Trotskyite factions and this sometimes influences their warfare techniques.[310] Some guerillas are associated with anti-colonialist movements,[311] others with more limited activities.[312]

Certain types of guerilla operations are confined to prewar situations: 'urban' guerillas[313] thus carry out activities similar to those of

[303] M. Veuthey, *Guérilla et droit humanitaire*, 2nd edn, Geneva, 1983; P. W. Barrett and L. Nurick, 'Legality of guerilla forces under the laws of war', *AJIL*, 1949, 563; I. P. Trainin, 'Questions of guerilla warfare in the law of war', *AJIL*, 1946, 534; G. I. A. D. Draper, 'The status of combatants and the question of guerilla warfare', 45 *BYIL* 1971, 173; C. Atala and F. Groffier, *Terrorisme et guerilla*, Ottawa, 1973.
[304] According to Roberts' definition guerilla units operate in a 'concealed or semi-concealed way' with the aim to harass the opponent and wear him down slowly, rather than openly confront large concentrations of his military forces', A. Roberts, *Nations in Arms*, 2nd edn, London, 1986, 35. Note that he includes in guerilla war what we have called 'programmatic wars', for example revolutionary war and partisan war, as well as 'insurgency' and 'irregular warfare'. *Ibid.*, 36.
[305] P. C. Mayer-Tasch, *Guerillakrieg und Völkerrecht*, Baden-Baden, 1972, 21; W. Hahlweg, *Guerilla:Krieg ohne Fronten*, Stuttgart, 1968, 47.
[306] See on counter-tactics, J. J. McCuen, *The Art of Counter-revolutionary War*, Harrisburg, 1966.
[307] Above, p. 32.   [308] Above, p. 32.   [309] Above, p. 32.
[310] Laqueur, *Guerilla*, 326ff, 357ff, 374ff and 341. On more or less adept attempts to justify partisan and guerilla warfare by Marxist doctrine, see E. Tomaon, *Kriegsbegriff und Kriegsrecht der Sowjetunion*, Berlin, 1979, 154ff.
[311] Rousseau, *Conflits armés*, 78–9.
[312] J. Niezing (ed.), *Urban Guerilla Studies on the Theory, Strategy and Practice of Political Violence in Modern Societies*, Rotterdam, 1974.
[313] R. Moss, *Urban Guerillas*, London, 1972.

terrorists[314] but may, after successful rebellions, expand their activities to full-scale guerilla warfare.[315]

Mao Tse Tung visualised guerilla warfare as an intermediate position and a provisional way of deploying armed forces. The characteristics of guerilla warfare are, he says, irregularity, i.e. decentralisation, lack of uniformity, absence of strict discipline and simple methods of work.[316] But such features must be eliminated to make the armed forces reach 'higher stages' when they must become more centralised, more unified, more disciplined and more thorough in their work, for the guerilla features stem from the 'infancy' of the armed forces[317] and are no longer appropriate.

The other hallmark of guerillas, mobility, will, on the other hand, often be useful.[318] Other advice is limited to strategic exhortations like 'do not hit out in all directions',[319] recommendations on finding success by 'joining with minority nationalities',[320] or calls for keeping up production in guerilla zones during intervals between fighting.[321]

Che Guevara's writings, on the other hand, are of a more practical nature for the individual guerilla fighter. Here there are clear instructions to guerilla fighters on how to survive in the bush, how to make improvised weapons and how to organise small groups to avoid detection by the enemy from the air. But, at the same time, there is some concern for innocent lives and special attention is drawn to the difference between terrorism and sabotage. Whereas the latter method can be useful to guerillas, the former 'often makes victims of innocent lives that would be valuable to the revolution'.[322] Terrorism, says Che

---

[314] Above, p. 23.
[315] D. E. H. Russell, *Rebellion, Revolution and Armed Force*, London, 1974, 103.
[316] Mao Tse Tung, People's Publishing House (ed.), 1 *Selected Works of Mao Tse Tung*, Peking, 1977, 243; the following writings, many of them included in the *Selected Works*, are particularly relevant: *Mao on People's War*, Peking, 1967; Mao, *Concentrate on Superior Force to Destroy the Enemy Forces One by One*, Peking, 1968; Mao, *The Concept of Operation for the Huiai-Hai Campaign*, Peking, 1969; Mao, *The Concept of Operation on the Peiping–Tientsin Campaign*, Peking, 1969; Mao, *Problems of Strategy in China's Revolutionary War*, 2nd edn, Peking, 1965; cf. M. Rejai (ed.) *Mao on Revolution and War*, Garden City, 1969; cf. also J. Ch'en, *Mao Papers*, London, 1970.
[317] 1 *Selected Works*, 243.
[318] *Ibid.*, 200ff, 248; Mao, 'Mobile warfare, guerilla warfare and positional warfare', 2 *ibid.*, 170.
[319] 1 *Selected Works*, 35.   [320] *Ibid.*   [321] *Ibid.*, 247.
[322] Ernesto ('Che') Guevara, *Guerilla Warfare*, London, 1969, 26; see the original version, *La guerra de guerillos*, Havana, 1960; cf. *Pasajes de la guerra revolucionaria*, Mexico, 1969; V. Ortiz (trans.), *Reminiscences of the Cuban Revolutionary War*, London, 1968.

Guevara, must be used only to 'put to death some noted leader of the oppressing forces'.[323]

SWAPO made a statement at a Colloquium in Brussels in 1970 to the effect that

One of the aspects of this war is the difference in attitude to military ethics between us and our enemy. The South African Government ... treat [guerilla fighters] as ordinary prisoners ... Our guerillas are under instruction not to attack the civilian population in any given area except in case of self-defence, not to attack churches and missionary establishments ... and not to attack or in any other way harm defenceless women and children ... With regard to the treatment of prisoners of war, SWAPO adheres strictly to the Geneva Conventions of 1949.[324]

So guerillas emphasise that they abide by the rules of the Law of War and it is their enemy who violates them.[325] As will be shown, guerillas are clearly bound by the Law of War[326] and something might be gained by further dissemination of knowledge as to their obligations under this legal system.

There is no doubt that guerillas have developed their own tactics and style of combat, largely by improvisation using the means at their disposal. In this sense, their warfare is what might be called 'methodological', but there is no obvious political content in it. The tactics, known throughout the history of warfare, were developed in modern days in partisan warfare[327] in the Second World War, when small units sought the protection of the natural environment to give them an advantage in combat. Later other guerillas, in Latin America and in Vietnam, adopted similar techniques. But guerilla warfare is not necessarily, although it often is, linked to communist aims. Similar techniques have been adopted by the 'Contras' in Nicaragua and by the 'resistance movements' in Afghanistan.

The situations in which guerilla wars are waged range from sustained attempts to fight an invading or occupying power[328] to military activities to oust a colonial regime or a legitimate government.

---

[323] *Guerilla Warfare*, 26. On terrorism, see above, p. 19.
[324] Centre Henri Rolin, *Droit humanitaire et conflits armés*, 251–2.
[325] Cf. below, p. 293.   [326] Below, p. 347.
[327] See, e.g. C. Loverdo, *Les maquis rouges des Balkans 1941–1945*, Paris, 1967.
[328] Above, p. 48.

2 PROHIBITION OF WAR

A. LIMITATION OF THE USE OF FORCE

i. *Rules prohibiting war*

Rules restraining war and the use of force in international society are usually coupled with a positive duty to solve disputes by peaceful means. Such positive duties preceded the complete prohibition of war. Hague Convention I of 1899 on Pacific Settlement of Disputes[1] and the similar Convention I of 1907[2] obliged the parties to seek a peaceful solution to their disputes before resorting to hostilities. The Treaties for the Advancement of Peace, the so-called Bryan Treaties of 1913–14, prohibited declarations of war or the opening of hostilities until an arbitral commission had examined the merits of the dispute.[3]

By article 10 of the Covenant of the League of Nations members of the League pledged that they would 'respect and preserve, as against any external aggression, the territorial integrity and existing political independence' of other States. This implied a system of guarantees to which some of the Great Powers, like the United Kingdom, have taken exception in the drafting of the Covenant.[4] But the obscure article 10 was coupled with articles 12–15 which prescribed certain procedures for the pacific settlement of disputes. Above all, article 12 prescribed a cooling-off period of three months after an arbitral award attempting to regulate the dispute; but after that war could be commenced. But war was not outlawed by the Covenant. The Covenant thus introduced a distinction between legal and illegal wars;

---

[1] 26 NRGT, 2 série, 920.   [2] 3 NRGT, 3 série, 360.
[3] See, for example, the Treaty with Italy, *AJIL*, 1916, Suppl., 288; 33 *AJIL* 1939, Suppl., 86. Numerous bilateral treaties were concluded, see Brownlie, *Force*, 23ff. 57.
[4] F. S. Northedge, *The League of Nations: its Life and Times 1920–1926*, Leicester, 1986, 43.

the latter category comprised conflicts where the formal procedure laid down had not been followed. However, not even aggression was completely forbidden by article 10 as that article was subordinate to some of the subsequent articles, in particular 15(7) which allowed certain wars to enforce legal rights. Therefore, an invasion could take place in the context of a 'legal' war under article 15 and then not violate article 10.[5]

Article 12 of the Covenant thus restricted the right of the members of the organisation to resort to war. The League of Nations condemned Italian aggression against Abyssinia in 1935[6] as well as the operations of Soviet forces in Finland in the Winter War in 1939[7] as violations of article 12.

But article 12 prohibited only 'war' (before a certain time had elapsed), which gave rise to problems if there was any doubt whether hostilities amounted to such a state of affairs. The way war was defined at the time[8] left considerable scope for belligerents to avoid disputes being classified as 'wars' if they so wished, regardless of objective circumstances. Furthermore, once article 12 restrained the right to go to war, there was another reason for not admitting that war existed, in that States wanted to avoid criticism for taking 'illegal' action.

Until Hague Convention II of 1907 on Limitation of the Employment of Force for the Recovery of Contract Debts[9] came into force, it had not been unusual for States to recover payment of money by armed force or to take reprisals. For example, when France failed to pay instalments on the spoliation claims under a treaty of 4 July 1831, President Jackson stated on 1 December 1934 that the United States should insist upon prompt execution of the treaty and in the case of refusal 'take redress into their own hands'.[10] Article 10 of the Covenant of the League of Nations restrained the use of force to a certain extent in a limited area. There was also some tentative regulation of the use of force in the Draft Treaty of Mutual Assistance of 1923,[11] the Geneva Protocol of 1924[12] and the Locarno Treaty of 1925.[13]

[5] Cf. D. H. Miller, 1 *The Drafting of the Covenant*, New York, 1928, 170. For other interpretations see Brownlie, *Force*, 63. On the other hand the Covenant did outlaw war against a State which was abiding by an arbitral award, see article 13(4); on the contradiction between this article and article 12, see Northedge, *The League*, 56.

[6] *LNOJ*, 1935, 1223–6 and above, p. 11.   [7] *LNOJ*, 1939, 539.

[8] See above, p. 5.   [9] 3 NRGT, 3 série, 414.

[10] *Richardson's Messages*, III, 97, 106, and *ibid.*, 147, 152–61.

[11] *LNOJ* 1923, Spec. Suppl., 16.   [12] 188 LNTS 53.   [13] 154 LNTS 290.

But the comprehensive regulation of war and the use of force was still to come. The Briand–Kellogg Pact in 1928[14] finally outlawed not only aggressive war but all types of war for the solution of international controversies or as an instrument of national policy.[15] The prohibition of war was coupled with a corresponding duty to settle disputes by peaceful means.

One method of reinforcing the prohibition in the Briand–Kellogg Pact was by the doctrine and practice of non-recognition as put forward in the Stimson doctrine of 1932.[16] According to this statement situations created by force would not be recognised by the United States.[17]

Other landmarks in the prohibition of war and the use of force in the international community were a series of Latin American treaties, e.g. the Treaty to Avoid or Prevent Conflicts between the American States of 1929[18] and the Treaty of Non-Aggression and Conciliation of 1933, the Savedra–Lamas Pact.[19] Some of these treaties were not limited to American States but were ratified by some European States as well.[20] A number of bilateral treaties of friendship built up a further network of obligations to renounce war and the use of force.[21]

With the establishment of the United Nations the prohibition of the use of force, and threat thereof, became entrenched in the Charter's article 2(4). The Inter-American Treaty of Reciprocal Assistance, the Rio Pact, of 1947[22] also reiterated the prohibition of the use of force and the threat of force.

Much has been written about the ambit of article 2(4) of the United Nations Charter;[23] there is above all an area of doubt as to whether the article covers economic force.[24] However, there is cer-

[14] 94 LNTS 57.
[15] But some dismissed the Act as being 'without value' in international law, see Ö. Undén, *Idén om krigets kriminalisering*, Uppsala Universitets Årsskrift, 1929, 22.
[16] See, in detail Q. Wright, 'The Stimson Note of January 7, 1932', 26 *AJIL* 1932, 342.
[17] Cf. the Chaco Declaration by the League of Nations Assembly of the same year, 1932, with similar contents, signed by 19 American States, and 6 Hackworth 45.
[18] 33 LNTS 26.
[19] 163 LNTS 393. This treaty was replaced as between the American States by the Treaty of Bogota of 1948 which established the Organization of American States, 30 UNTS 55.
[20] See the Savedra–Lamas Pact, which was ratified by Bulgaria, Czechoslovakia, Romania, Spain and Yugoslavia, as well as by a series of Latin American States.
[21] See, further, Brownlie, *Force*, 101–5.   [22] 21 UNTS 77.
[23] See e.g. C. M. H. Waldock, 'The regulation of the use of force by individual states and international law', *RCADI*, 1952, ii, 455.
[24] M. P. Doxey, *Economic Sanctions and International Enforcement*, Oxford, 1971. Cf. E. Sciso, 'L'aggressione indiretta nella definizione dell'Assemblea Generale delle Nazioni Unite', *RivDI*, 1983, 253; J. Barber, 'Economic sanctions as a policy instrument',

tainly no doubt that any form of armed force is forbidden under the Charter, if it is directed against the territorial integrity or political independence of any State *or* if it is inconsistent with the purposes of the United Nations.[25] But there are legitimising factors undermining the general prohibition.[26] The Agreement on Prevention of Nuclear War between the United States and the Soviet Union in 1973,[27] a treaty concluded for 'unlimited duration',[28] provides in article I that the 'Parties agree they will act in such a manner as to prevent the development of situations capable of causing a dangerous exacerbation of their relations, as to avoid military confrontation and as to exclude the outbreak of nuclear war between them and between either of the Parties and other countries'. Article II provides that 'each Party will refrain from threat or use of force against the other Party, against Allies of the other Party and against other countries in circumstances which may endanger international peace and security'. Such a treaty, essentially reiterating obligations already existing under the Charter, possibly reinforces the duty to refrain from the use of force.

Specific acts of force are now forbidden, *inter alia* acts that were earlier often referred to as 'acts of war'. The prohibition of aggression and intervention, highly relevant to the status or existence of war, will be examined briefly.

ii. Rules prohibiting aggression

'Aggression' did not always have negative connotations. There was a time when the concept also covered 'defensive aggression',[29] although this seems a contradiction in terms, now that 'aggression' has such a pejorative ring.

Some commentators claim that aggression is specific to the international community, as municipal law never uses aggression as a basic concept or any other notions of 'that character'.[30] But the whole of municipal criminal law, in most legal systems, rests on restraints of force and violence between citizens. Such restraints regulate 'attacks'

International Affairs, 1979, 367; R. St J. Macdonald, 'Economic sanctions in the international system', *CanYIL*, 1969, 69. On similar discussion bearing on the use of force, including economic force, and treaties, see my *Independent State*, 145–63; D. Leyton-Browne, *The Utility of International Economic Sanctions*, London, 1986.

[25] G. Tunkin, *Sila i pravov mezhdunarodnoe sisteme*, Moscow, 1983, 37.
[26] Below, p. 71.   [27] 917 UNTS 86.   [28] Article VII.   [29] Brownlie, *Force*, 351.
[30] J. Stone, *Aggression and World Order, Critique of United Nations Theories of Aggression*, London, 1958, 119.

or 'assaults' by citizen on citizen, which is surely behaviour similar to that of a State attacking another State. But it is not so clear, in the voluminous international discussions on a definition of aggression, that aggression merely implies 'attacks', although this would probably be the common-sense approach.

Numerous attempts to define aggression have been made, not only by writers but, above all, by statesmen in declarations or conventions and by the General Assembly of the United Nations. There have been considerable difficulties in defining aggression and one may wonder why this task, carried out as it has been in such intricate detail, has been thought so important. Some acts may well be 'typical' of aggression and such 'typical acts' may include armed attack, invasion, occupation, annexation, blockade; such acts would also constitute what was often previously called 'acts of war'.[31] But it is questionable whether one can progress further than providing some illustrative examples, for a notion of which we, *a priori*, can have only a general idea but which, *in casu*, may express itself in acts which may be classed as illegal. There are the same difficulties, on the whole, as if we set out to define 'force'.

The first attempt of any significance may have been the Agreement for Pacific Settlement of Disputes, the Geneva Protocol, in 1924.[32] Later the more elaborate Soviet Declaration of Aggression followed in 1933.[33] There were other attempts to define aggression, for example in the Convention for the Definition of Aggression the same year,[34] the Buenos Aires Convention of 1936,[35] the Saafabad Pact of 1937,[36] the Harvard Draft Convention on Rights and Duties of States,[37] and a series of bilateral agreements, for example a treaty between the Soviet Union and Finland in 1932,[38] the Soviet Union and Poland in 1932[39] and the Soviet Union and China.[40] But the value of the definitions, often relying on enumerative examples,[41] may be limited.

The Security Council of the United Nations is empowered under

---

[31] E. Aroneanu, *La définition de l'agression, exposé objectif*, Paris, 1958, 85ff.

[32] C. G. Westman, *Kring Genèveprotokollet*, Stockholm, 1924; Eagleton, 'The attempt to define war', 599ff; cf. R. Erich, *Några folkrättsliga synpunkter hänförande sig till sanktionsproblemet*, Uppsala, 1936, 11; Ö. Undén, 'Quelques observations sur la notion de guerre d'agression', *RDILC*, 1931, 5.

[33] League of Nations for Reductions and Limitations of Armaments, Series B, 2, 236.

[34] 147 LNTS 71.   [35] 6 Hudson 361.

[36] 190 LNTS 21, between Afghanistan, Iraq and Turkey.

[37] 33 *AJIL* 1939, Suppl., 821.   [38] 157 LNTS 395.   [39] 136 LNTS 38.

[40] 181 LNTS 102.   [41] See further Brownlie, *Force* 359ff.

article 39 of the Charter to identify an aggressor in the international community.[42] Such action presupposes a clear general notion of what aggression implies. Attempts to define the notion of aggression in the United Nations date back to the early 1950s,[43] when it was thought important, for the application, for example, of article 39, to have a definition of what aggression means.

The Soviet Union proposed a Draft Resolution in 1950 in the First Committee,[44] which the General Assembly referred to the International Law Commission for comment.[45] The ILC produced no definition, but after the Sixth Committee considered its Report, several States volunteered definitions, usually enumerative,[46] but occasionally attempting general definitions.[47]

General Assembly Resolution 599 (VI) of 1952 further emphasised the desirability of a definition.[48] A series of Special Committees was set up.[49] The fourth Special Committee[50] held seven sessions and produced a Report which it submitted to the General Assembly, proposing a definition of aggression. On the basis of this Report the Sixth Commimttee approved a Draft Resolution which it recommended the General Assembly to accept.

But a definition may, in the opinion of many States,[51] be inappropriate: it is still for the Security Council to determine *in casu* whether aggression has taken place.[52] Many have argued that the Charter is deliberately silent to allow leeway for the exercise of this discretionary power of the Security Council[53] and, it must be noted, Resolution 3314 (XXIX) of 1974 indicates[54] that nothing within the adopted

[42] The General Assembly may acquire similar powers if the Security Council remains inactive and there is a threat to the peace, see the Uniting for Peace Resolution 377 (V) 1950; cf. my *Law Making*, 38ff.
[43] See further B. B. Ferencz, *Defining International Aggression, the Search for World Peace, a Documentary History and Analysis*, New York, 1975, for chronological data and on the extensive literature.
[44] A/C.1/608.   [45] GA Res. 378 B (V) 1950.   [46] USSR, A/C.6/1.208.
[47] Bolivia, A/C.6/L.211.
[48] On comments by the Sixth Committee, see Stone, *Aggression*, 54ff.
[49] A Special Committee was set up by General Assembly Resolution 688 (VII) of 1952 and given a mandate to define aggression; a second Special Committee, established by General Assembly Resolution 895 (IX) in 1954, then took over; a third Special Committee was formed under General Assembly Resolution 1181 (XII) 1957; and finally a fourth Special Committee by General Assembly Resolution 2330 (XXII) in 1967.
[50] For reference, see the previous note.
[51] For example, for the United States, see statement by Truman, *Whiteman Digest*, 740.
[52] Cf. Sixth Committee views in 1952, A/C.6/L.206.
[53] See Murphy, *The United Nations*, 85.   [54] See the fourth Preamble paragraph.

definition shall affect the scope of the powers of the United Nations organs under the Charter.

A definition of aggression is certainly riddled with difficulty. The United Kingdom delegation had pointed out that the 'desirability' of a definition depended on whether such a definition is at all possible.[55] But the great difficulty is not to phrase a definition but to apply that definition to fact.[56]

In 1974 the General Assembly passed Resolution 3314 (XXIX), which had adopted the proposed wording. The resolution provides a definition of aggression, based largely on an enumeration of certain acts which, together or by themselves, would amount to aggression.

The resolution defines aggression as

the use of armed force by a State against the sovereignty, territorial integrity or political independence of another State, or in any other manner inconsistent with the Charter of the United Nations, as set out in this Definition.[57]

The text then goes on to exemplify certain typical acts of aggression:

(a) The invasion or attack by the armed forces of a State of the territory of another State, or any military occupation, however temporary, resulting from such invasion or attack, or any annexation by the use of force of the territory of another State or part thereof;

(b) bombardment by the armed forces of a State against the territory of another State or the use of any weapons by a State against the territory of another State;

(c) the blockade of the ports or coasts of a State by the armed forces of another State;

(d) the attack by the armed forces of a State on the land, sea or air forces, or marine and air fleets of another State;

(e) the use of armed forces of one State which are within the territory of another State with the agreement of the receiving State, in contravention of the conditions provided for in the agreement or any extension of their presence in such territory beyond the termination of the agreement;

(f) the action of a State in allowing its territory, which it has placed at the disposal of another State, to be used by that other State for perpetrating an act of aggression against a third State;

(g) the sending by or on behalf of a State of armed bands, groups, irregulars or mercenaries, which carry out acts of armed force against another State of such gravity as to amount to the acts listed above, or its substantial involvement therein.[58]

The resolution thus suggests[59] that there is certain anticipatory

---

[55] A/AC.77/SR.7, 8.

[56] For early comments along these lines see League of Nations, 'Commentary on the definition of a case of aggression', *LNOJ*, Spec. Suppl., 16.

[57] Article 1.   [58] Article 3.   [59] Article 2.

force which is not in violation of the Charter. The text provides that the first use of armed force by a State, in contravention of the Charter, shall constitute prima facie evidence of aggression. However, the Security Council may take certain 'relevant circumstances' into account to find anticipatory force devoid of features of aggression. Thus the first use of armed force by a State may be legitimised by the opinion of the Security Council, a method which surely undermines even the general prohibition of force in article 2(4) of the Charter.

Another controversial passage deals with assistance by 'armed bands, groups, irregulars or mercenaries, which carry out acts of armed force' as it is highly uncertain what level of 'involvement' would entail State responsibility under this heading.[60] Assistance in internal strife, to which this article clearly applies, is one of the most important areas for regulation[61] and it would have been desirable for the resolution to contain some more detailed criteria.

The resolution of 1974 may have some value in drawing attention, for example, to the nature of acts of assistance to belligerents, as some such acts will also be held to constitute aggression, for example the sending of armed bands.[62]

The value of the attempt of definition may be questioned. The State-centric view, which is entrenched in the resolution, limits the scope of the definition considerably, for only States can commit aggression.

The notion of aggression needs to be reconsidered in the light of contemporary warfare, which often involves guerilla warfare movements whose members are recognised by numerous international conventions as 'combatants'[63] and therefore, logically, as belligerents.[64]

But because of the way that the prohibition of aggression is phrased in international documents like the Resolution of 1974 on Aggression, wars waged by groups and aggression carried out by groups are not covered. Even if this limited ambit of the resolution is justified in the view of many, it will be investigated whether and to what extent the laws of war apply to groups and entities which are not States.

iii. Prohibition of certain intervention

a. The relative notion of intervention

Intervention is a loose term which has been used in a number of ways. It may mean virtually any type of 'interference' in the affairs of

---

[60] Sciso, 'L'aggressione', 253. Cf. Y. N. Rybakov, *Voorozhennaya agressia, tiagchaishe mezhdunarodnoe prestuplennye*, Moscow, 1980, 63ff.
[61] Below, p. 66.   [62] Cf. below, p. 68.   [63] See below, p. 108.   [64] See above, p. 124.

another State, from acts ranging from those similar to aggression[65] to milder acts by, for example, political[66] or economic pressure;[67] sometimes the mere presence of warships offshore[68] or the discussion of affairs in another State, for example in the United Nations,[69] has been thought to constitute intervention.

The purpose of intervention is usually to make a State do something it would not otherwise do.[70] A State can be 'made' to do this forcibly or not, directly or not and openly or not.[71] As intervention presupposes an act against the will of a State, the term cannot be used for UN action in a territory.[72] As for aggression, it may not be suitable, or possible, to provide a definition of intervention, especially in view of ideological differences.[73] But perhaps certain 'intervening' acts can be discerned which infringe the sovereignty of States.

The basis for the protected area into which other States may not intervene is found in article 2(7) of the Charter of the United Nations, which deals with what has become known as the 'reserved domain'[74] and which specifies that States have certain spheres of 'domestic jurisdiction'.[75]

States bound by the Charter[76] would, to some extent, have renounced their exclusive domestic jurisdiction, for example in the case of threat to the peace, and would, in such rare cases, be obliged to abide by any enforcement action. This would mean, in the eyes of a few, that United Nations action would be 'illegal' if it concerned a

[65] Above, pp. 6off.   [66] For example, the practice of propaganda, below, p. 262.
[67] See above, p. 56 and note 24. Cf. R. Higgins, 'Intervention and international law', in H. Bull (ed.), *Intervention in World Politics*, New York, 1984, 30.
[68] P. Calvocoressi, *World Order and New States*, London, 1962, 17.
[69] For protests regarding discussions of human rights, see R. J. Vincent, *Non-intervention and International Order*, Princeton, 1974, 15.
[70] C. C. Hyde, *1 International Law*, Boston, 1922, para. 69; cf. S. Hoffman, 'The problem of intervention', in Bull, *Intervention*, 9.
[71] H. Bull, in *Intervention*, 1.
[72] E. Luard, 'Collective intervention' in Bull, *Intervention*, 160. To such action the States have already given their abstract consent, see my *Law Making*, 322.
[73] C. Thomas, *New States, Sovereignty and Intervention*, London, 1985, 9. Of course Hoffman is right when he says that 'In its widest sense, to be sure, every act of State constitutes intervention', Hoffman, 'The problem of intervention', 8. For a wide concept of intervention see J. N. Rosenau, *International Politics and Foreign Policy*, New York, 1969, 161.
[74] E.g. M. S. Rajan, *United Nations and Domestic Jurisdiction*, 2nd edn, London, 1961.
[75] Cf. the Declaration on the Inadmissibility of Intervention in the Domestic Affairs of States and the Protection of Independence and Sovereignty, GA Res. 2131 (XX) 1966.
[76] By virtue of their 'abstract consent' see my *Law Making*, 322ff, and below, p. 76. On relevance of consent as a legitimising factor, see below, p. 75.

non-member State of the United Nations,[77] for such a State would have preserved the totality of its domestic jurisdiction. However, even in such cases it would seem likely that the United Nations could extend its actions to a third State.[78]

Among acts of political pressure the practice of non-recognition may be mentioned as one which has often been referred to as intervention. For example, Senor Guardia, Special Agent of President Tinoco of Costa Rica in Washington, stated in 1917, when the United States had refused to recognise the government, that 'the fact that the Washington Government refuses to recognise the legally constituted Government of Costa Rica, and seeks to justify its refusal by invoking a principle that is no part of international law [that of popular will freely expressed], will probably be interpreted as unjustified intervention'.[79]

Many thus focus on the object, the type of affair into which interference takes place. They thus classify as intervention any activity which affects the 'domestic' affairs of another State.[80] But the prohibition of intervention becomes meaningless if intervention is understood to consist in any form of involvement or interference.[81] Other writers concentrate more on the aspect of coercion, that is the act of interference itself. But the two elements, coercion and involvement in domestic affairs, operate together. Some writers have thus suggested that any activity which interferes coercively in the domestic affairs of another State constitutes intervention.[82] This definition, even though slightly circular, at least limits intervention to action taken by force.

Some commentators have suggested that intervention is permissi-

---

[77] A. V. Thomas and A. J. Thomas, *Non-intervention*, Dallas, 1956, 226.

[78] Cf. my *Essays*, 100ff on effect on third parties.   [79] 1 Hackworth 235.

[80] For example, 'covert' intervention to influence the internal affairs of other nations. For a discussion of this definition (allegedly of the CIA), see *ASIL*, 1975, 192, The element 'domestic' will, of course, always be essential to an act of 'intervention' albeit in conjunction with other factors. Cf. Hoffman, 'The problem of intervention', 10: 'Intervention should be restricted to acts which try to affect not the external activities but the domestic affairs of a State.'

[81] Vincent, *Non-intervention and International Order*, 13. On the relevance of 'power' relationships in intervention situations, see H. J. Morgenthau, 'To intervene or not to intervene', 45 *Foreign Affairs* 1967, 425; on 'coercion' in intervention see M. Beloff, 'Reflections on intervention', *Journal of International Affairs*, 1968, 198; Strupp-Schlochauer, 2 *Wörterbuch* 145. But some claim that the coercion must not amount to 'war' as intervention can take place only in peacetime: they claim that the requirement of peace is 'an element in the definition of intervention': Thomas and Thomas, *Non-intervention*, 73.

[82] A. Piradow-Starnscheko, 'Das Prinzip der Nichteinmischung im modernen Völkerrecht', in R. Arzinger (ed.), *Gegenwartsprobleme des Völkerrechts*, Berlin, 1962.

ble if another State has already illegally intervened. Thus, John Stuart Mill wrote on internal disturbances and insurgency that 'Though it be a mistake to give freedom to a people who do not value the boon, it cannot but be right to insist that if they do value it, they shall not be hindered from the pursuit by foreign coercion.'[83] Thus, if the Russians sought to stop the Hungarian insurgency by lending support to Austria, England would have been entitled to intervene too, to assist the Hungarian insurgents. That would, said Mill, be construed as 'intervention to enforce non-intervention' and that was always 'lawful', although it was more questionable whether first action could be taken.[84] But any extended right of 'counter-intervention' or subsequent intervention, in response to earlier interventionary action, is bound to escalate any conflict and must be viewed with extreme caution.

Many commentators have argued that intervention in an internal conflict is always unlawful. The Vietnam War was, for a considerable time,[85] classified as an 'internal conflict' and some scholars claim, as we have seen, that no other State had the right to interfere in collective self-defence under general international law or under the Charter of the United Nations.[86]

This work is concerned with the use of armed force and therefore we shall limit our attention to two main types of intervention, intervention by direct armed force and intervention by offering assistance to another State, or to non-State groups in another State, in an armed conflict.

There is a clear conceptual connection between intervention and war. For if intervention is an act by force to make a State do what it would otherwise not do, war is a magnification of this situation when a State seeks to force an enemy to do its will.[87]

Intervention may have become a synonym for violence, force and egoism.[88] It is indeed intervention, and not the principle of non-intervention, that needs explanation.[89] But insofar as it involves direct military force there is no question that it has been outlawed, and similar statements may be made with respect to this type of interven-

[83] John Stuart Mill, 'A few words on non-intervention', *Fraser's Magazine*, 1859.
[84] *Ibid.*   [85] See above, p. 40.
[86] Moore, 'The lawfulness of military assistance to the Republic of Vietnam', 1.
[87] Clausewitz, *On War*, 75, and above, p. 6.
[88] P. A. Massourides, *Le principe de non-intervention en droit international moderne*, Athens, 1968, 83.
[89] R. Little, *Intervention, Involvement in Civil Wars*, London, 1975, 32.

tion as were made in respect of war and the use of force in general. Instruments forbidding the use of force often specifically mention intervention as a prohibited act.[90] Even in the case of instruments which do not specifically mention intervention, such acts can normally be subsumed under the prohibition of the use of force. Other instruments focus on intervention and introduce further prohibitions,[91] but, in turn, such agreements often also refer to a general prohibition of the use of force as well.

Intervention by direct military action is thus merely a specific method of employing armed force against another State. The alleged cases for permissible intervention of this type, humanitarian intervention and what in this book is called 'patronising intervention', will be discussed later.

The second type of intervention, which implies the assistance to a State or group involved in a conflict, can be subdivided into two main groups: intervention which assists a State engaged in a traditional inter-State war; and intervention which assists a State, or groups within that State, when there is a war of non-State character. In the first case, assistance may often be given to a State under some defence pact or alliance treaty and such treaties will furnish sufficient title for legitimate intervention by military troops or by giving financial or other aid. The treaties which furnish the competence for such intervention can be replaced, *in casu*, by the more or less formal *ad hoc* consent of a State.[92]

Apart from such intervention in war a State may assist a State involved in a non-State conflict in a *third* State. Furthermore, assistance may be given to a State, or to groups within that State, in an internal conflict. It is the last-mentioned type which creates the greatest difficulty in practice from the point of view of assessing legitimacy: when is it 'right' to assist a government to suppress groups seeking self-determination and when is it 'right' to assist insurgents who are rising against the legitimate government?

[90] See in particular, the United Nations Charter, article 2(7).
[91] For example, the Montevideo Convention on Rights and Duties of States 1933, 165 LNTS 19; the Buenos Aires Convention for the Maintenance, Preservation and Re-establishment of Peace with Additional Protocol Relative to Non-intervention. 1936, 188 LNTS 9; the Bogota Charter of OAS 1948, 30 UNTS 55.
[92] On the relevance of consent, see my *Independent State*, 197, and below, p. 71 on legitimising factors. The supply of arms to Iran by the United States during the Iran–Iraq War in 1986 in exchange for hostages in the Middle East is one example of assistance in an inter-State war by a third party.

b. Assisting the government in internal conflict

Intervention has been condemned as a form of aggression by the General Assembly if it leads to 'fomenting civil strife'.[93] Some writers have questioned whether it is ever permissible for a State to request or receive outside military assistance in internal conflicts.[94] But the section of the United Nations Definition of Aggression[95] forbids assistance in the form of bands, groups or irregulars who will carry out acts of armed force against another State. Thus, 'the sending by or on behalf of a State of armed bands, groups, irregulars or mercenaries, which carry out acts of armed force against another State of such gravity as to amount to the acts listed above [such as invasion, bombardment, blockade] or its substantial involvement therein'[96] will amount to aggression. Can one then, by an *e contrario* deduction, conclude that assistance in other forms to another government is permissible? In other words, even if a State is not allowed to dispatch, for example, irregulars, can it send official forces?

There are some indications that it may no longer be permissible to lend any assistance, by irregular or regular forces, to governments in such situations and some support for this contention may be found in the UN General Assembly Resolution on Friendly Relations,[97] which forbids 'organizing, instigating, assisting or participating in acts of civil strife or terrorist acts in another State or acquiescing in organized activities within its territory, directed towards the commission of such acts, when the acts referred to in the present paragraph involve a threat or use of force'. It has been claimed that the Friendly Resolution of 1970, which gives a wider scope to the prohibition of intervention, is an 'authoritative' interpretation of article 2(4) of the Charter.[98] This may not be accurate, as the General Assembly does not have the power to make such 'authoritative' interpretations.[99] Yet it may be correct to state that there is a presumption of illegality of intervention.

But, in spite of presumptions of illegality in general, military assistance by regular forces may be offered to the government under the provisions of a treaty. For example, the Havana Treaty of 1928 provides specifically that arms may be provided to a requesting gov-

[93] GA Res. 380 (V) 1950. Cf. Rosenau, *International Aspects of Civil Strife*.
[94] 1 Hyde 182, 253.   [95] Res. 3314 (XXIX) 1974; above, p. 60.
[96] Article 3(g), for comments see Ferencz, 2 *Defining International Aggression*, Sciso, 'L'aggressione', 253.
[97] Res. 2526 (XXV) 1970.   [98] Above, p. 56.
[99] *UN Study on the Naval Arms Race*, 26 July 1985, 85.

ernment until belligerency is recognised.[100] The Batista Government of Cuba complained when the United States ceased arms supplies and demanded further assistance under this treaty.[101] The general provisions of the Rio Treaty of 1947 on Inter-American Reciprocal Assistance[102] also appear to leave room for such assistance.

There may even be assistance provided by intervention in order to save the operations of a treaty. For example, the Customs Receivership Convention between the United States and the Dominican Republic of 1907[103] was jeopardised by a revolution in 1913. The Secretary of State of the United States, through the Minister in Santo Domingo, informed the new government that, above, all, the Dominican Republic was not allowed to increase its debt by costs for a revolution under the aforementioned Convention without the consent of the United States. Subsequently, the United States sent 'advisers' to the Dominican Republic to bring about the election of another President; a candidate was approved and recognised by the United States the following year.[104]

In addition military assistance may also be given in individual cases under informal security arrangements with allied governments, even if there is no specific treaty on the matter. Some writers claim that, if such agreements with for example the United States are to remain 'credible', the United States must at least maintain a 'viable and perceivable *capability* to intervene'.[105]

c. *Assistance to insurgents*
There have been statements to the effect that assistance to insurgents especially if furnished by the export of arms by individuals rather than by direct State support, is not illegal under international law. The United States emphasised that duties of neutrality do not necessarily imply that arms exports, either to governments or insurgents, have to be prohibited, especially if legislation has to operate extraterritorially in order to be effective.

---

[100] Above, p. 35. On recognition of belligerency in civil war, see below, p. 105.
[101] E. E. T. Smith, *The Fourth Floor*, New York, 1962, 91.
[102] Article 6; for reference see above, p. 56, note 22.
[103] 1 Malloy 418.   [104] 1 Hackworth 240–1.
[105] J. R. Picket, 'Airlift and military intervention', in E. P. Stern (ed.), *The Limits of Military Intervention*, Beverly Hills, 1977, 137. Specific consent may also be given *in casu*: see below, p. 71 on legitimising factors and cf. my *Law Making*, 64 and 74 on specific consent to United Nations operations in the Congo. Cf. L. Doswald-Beck, 'The legal validity of military intervention with the invitation of the government', *BYIL*, 1985, 189.

When the Mexican Government asked the United States to prevent arms supplies from Texas to rebels in Mexico, the United States
Government replied initially that the arms supplies were not illegal
under United States law. When a joint Resolution of Congress was
subsequently passed to enable the President to prohibit arms exports
if and when he identified, in any American country, 'conditions of
domestic violence ... which are promoted by the use of arms or
munitions of war procured from the United States'[106] it was emphasised by the Secretary of State, in a note to Mexico, that

> This action was taken not because of any obligation so to do resting upon the
> Government by reason of the rules and principles of International Law,
> which obligations were already far more than met by the existing so-called
> neutral status of the United States, but solely from a sincere desire to promote
> the return of peace to Mexico and the welfare of a neighbouring nation.[107]

Assistance in the form of military support to insurgents appears now
to be outlawed by the instruments mentioned above, the General
Assembly Resolution 3314 (XXIX) of 1974 as well as by the earlier
Resolution 2625 (XXV) of 1975, which reflect general international
law on these issues.[108] However, assistance is not usually given by
overt military support but more often by financing guerilla or resistance operations or revolutionary warfare. Figures and data are obviously not easily accessible in this sector, but certain assistance has
been given quite openly. Thus the State Department of the United
States announced in 1984 that it had set aside 'aid' of some $280
million for Afghan guerillas for 1985 and $21 million to support
Nicaraguan 'Contras'.[109] In spite of the openness of such support to
forces opposing their government, the United States classifies such
support as 'covert aid'.[110]

d. *Assistance to groups in other non-State conflicts*
With regard to assistance to non-State parties in liberation wars,
similar comments may be made with regard to assistance to insurgents
and other belligerents in internal wars. In the case of a non-State
party, physically present and organised with headquarters or miliary
installations in the territory of another State, it would seem, however,
that any assistance to that body would have to have the consent of the
territorial State.

---

[106] 1 Hackworth 29–30.   [107] *Ibid.*, 30.
[108] On the effect of General Assembly Resolutions, see my *Law Making*, 207ff.
[109] *Sunday Times*, 30 December 1984.   [110] *Ibid.*

Such general rules might be relevant to assistance, for example, to the Palestine Liberation Organization (PLO), engaged in a war which is neither an inter-State war nor an internal war.[111] For example, the situation in the Middle East is highly complex and it is at times unclear which State or group is a belligerent. But it is fairly settled that the PLO is a belligerent, alone or in conjunction with other parties. As has been shown above,[112] the PLO is engaged in one of the few disputes still classified as liberation wars. For the purposes of numerous Conventions, such wars are held to be 'international', but since the PLO has no territorial base, it cannot be considered a State, and the conflict is therefore technically a non-State war. On the other hand, it is not an internal war, for it is not fought by citizens against their own government.

e. The effect of assistance to either party
At the root of the problem lies the fact that, if assistance from outside is stopped, the conflict may cease. There are obligations, for example under the Havana Convention on Duties and Rights of States in the Event of Civil Strife, 1929[113] for States bound by the Convention to prevent persons on their territory, nationals or aliens, from crossing the border to start or promote civil strife. States have only occasionally agreed to refrain from assisting either side in internal wars.

One example of this rare practice was the Spanish Civil War. Specific non-intervention agreements were concluded, involving parallel instructions to diplomatic, consular and naval authorities of other States in Spain. The parties to these agreements were the United Kingdom, the United States and a number of European powers. The United Kingdom had taken the initiative in an agreement with Germany[114] and invited others to join.[115] The United Kingdom and France exchanged notes on non-intervention and 27 other States made 'similar' declarations.[116]

Non-intervention, in these agreements and declarations, implied initially the prohibition of arms exports coupled with a system of information on implementation of this obligation. In 1936 a Non-Intervention Committee was created and, gradually, prohibitions were introduced on the recruitment of volunteers and other restrictive

---

[111] Cf. above, p. 39.   [112] Above, p. 47.   [113] For reference, see above, p. 56.
[114] 65 BFSP 769.
[115] N. Padelford, *International Law and Diplomacy in the Spanish Civil Strife*, New York, 1939, 54ff.
[116] *Ibid.*, 57.

measures were agreed between the members of the Committee. An Observation Scheme was started in 1937 round the frontiers of Spanish territory to verify that the Agreement was being observed. Eight international agencies were established to supervise and administer the obligation of non-intervention.[117]

The Evacuation Plan of the Powers in 1938 received consent by both sides in the war; earlier there had been certain protests that observation officers unsurped the sovereign rights of Spain.[118]

There are good reasons why this practice of non-intervention should be applied in other internal conflicts. The obligations to refrain from lending assistance in internal wars are not very different from the duties that flow from the status of neutrality in inter-State wars. In such wars third parties readily accept that they must be 'impartial'; they furthermore readily undertake to punish those of their nationals who in any way breach a blockade or carry contraband.[119]

Why should not similar duties accrue to third States and their nationals in the event of internal war? We have adopted a wider concept of war than other writers, mainly to avoid the artificialities of the ambiguous concept 'armed conflict'.[120] However, not *every* armed conflict or disturbance will constitute internal war. Third States and their citizens are not likely to be in any real doubt as to whether war exists. Insurance companies are not, as we shall see, guided by any technical difference between inter-State or internal war: the question is whether there is a 'war-risk area'.[121]

The consequences of accepting the wider notion of war, covering internal war also, will not have any substantial negative repercussions for third States. What must be emphasised is that without outside assistance the strife might well die out. Even in Vietnam this possibility existed before the United States intervened.[122]

The asymmetry which always exists in a non-State conflict will be exaggerated if assistance to governments, but not to insurgents, is allowed. Assistance in any form given to States or to groups in internal

[117] Apart from the International Non-Intervention Committee itself, these were the International Board for Non-Intervention, two Chief Administrators, the Group of Administrators and Deputies, the Corps of Observation Officers, the Naval Patrol, the International Fund, and the Accounts Officer. The implementation of these tasks was funded (apart from the patrol) by a common pool of participating States: Padelford, *Spanish Civil Strife*, 79ff.
[118] *Ibid.*, 113, 115.   [119] 2 Oppenheim 673ff.   [120] Above, p. 16.   [121] Below, p. 319.
[122] L. E. Cable, *Conflict of myths, the Development of American Counterinsurgency Doctrine and the Vietnam War*, New York and London, 1986; Q. Wright, 'Legal aspects of the Vietnam situation', 60 AJIL 1966, 750.

disputes or other non-State wars may, on the other hand, internationalise the dispute and, in this way, give it new dimensions.[123] If this happens, the once 'internal' dispute may become classified as 'international', with the repercussions this may have for the application of international conventions and other legal rules.

B. LEGITIMISING FACTORS

The question whether an act implies illegal use of force, aggression or intervention is often a question of fact. There are limited opportunities for assessing a situation by an impartial entity and, even in cases where such examination is available by, for example, the International Court of Justice, political reasoning may override legal arguments. This situation is amply illustrated in the recent *Nicaragua* v. *United States Case*.[124] The United States had previously accepted the Court's jurisdiction by the Optional Clause of the Court's Statute,[125] albeit with reservations.[126] But in the *Nicaragua Case* the United States decided not to continue its attendance before the Court.

There are a number of factors which, at least in the opinion of the acting State, may legitimise[127] forceful behaviour which, if it were not for these factors, would be clearly illegal under international law.

i. Recovery

It has been said that article 2(4) of the United Nations Charter which forbids force would be inapplicable if a State 'recovers' territory under foreign 'illegal' domination. Arguments like these were used[128] by India with respect to Goa[129] and by Argentina in the case of the Falklands Islands.[130]

---

[123] Above, p. 40. But it may not be possible, as Dunér claims in *Military Intervention in the 1970s*, London, 1986, to express the likelihood of escalation in a mathematical formula.
[124] (1984) and (1986), ICJ *Reports*, 1984 and 1986.
[125] On the Optional Clause, see C. H. M. Waldock, 'The decline of the optional clause', 32 *BYIL* 1956, 244.
[126] On the United States reservation, see H. Briggs, 'Reservations to the acceptance of compulsory jurisdiction of the International Court of Justice', 93 *RCADI* 1958, 229.
[127] Tunkin conceives the prohibition of force as concerning only aggressive force and therefore dispenses with legitimising elements, see *Sila*, 37.
[128] Cf. O. Schachter, 'General course in public international law', 178 *RCADI* 1982, v, 142.
[129] 16 UNSCOR 987.
[130] GA, A/37/PV, 51 (1982). J. F. Gavelle, 'The Falkland (Malvina) Islands: an international law analysis of the dispute between Argentina and Great Britain', 107 *MilLR* 1985, 5ff.

Borders are often disputed and the very notions of aggression or other types of force then become even more relative.[131] But some borders are more entrenched than others: for example, some borders are 'internationally recognised'. A Draft of the UN Resolution on Aggression[132] suggested that any use of force to alter 'internationally agreed lines of demarcation' should be specifically prohibited.[133] This Draft was not adopted. However, there are indications that international borders that have obtained recognition either by express agreement or by long-standing practice are specially protected from alterations by force. For example, the General Assembly Resolution on Friendly Relations[134] also forbids the use of force or threat to violate international lines of demarcation.

On the other hand, the exceptional case must be allowed for: there could be a situation when borders have been wrongly assessed.[135]

ii. Hot pursuit

Raids will not, even if intense,[136] constitute hostile acts which amount to acts of war if they are carried out in hot pursuit. There are numerous historical examples to illustrate this rule, which applies to land, air and sea.[137] For example, General Jackson followed Indians into Spanish Florida after they had attacked American positions in Georgia[138] and Pancho Vilas was pursued into Mexico after he and his men had made incursions into American territory.[139]

Hot pursuit often comes, as a legal category, near self-defence or even anticipatory force. One example of this inter-relationship is the incident in 1919 when the United States sent armed forces to put an end to rebels shooting from Ciudad Juarez into American territory.[140]

[131] J. Stone, 'Hope and loopholes in 1974 definition of aggression', AJIL, 1977, 226.
[132] Res. 3314 1974 and above, p. 60.
[133] Article 4(2) of the Six-Power Draft, A/AC.134/L.17.
[134] Res. 2625 1970, and above, p. 27. On the role of prescription as the main function of the otherwise vague notion 'customary law', see my *Concept*, 60, 63, 104.
[135] For a discussion, see *Temple of Vihar Case*, ICJ *Reports*, 1962, 6.
[136] On the intensity criterion, above, p. 18.
[137] Cf. N. Poulantzas, *The Right of Hot Pursuit in International Law*, Leiden, 1969; not all agree that the maritime notion of hot pursuit can be applied analogously to land and air situations; but the notion is derived from law as between neighbour (*droit de voisinage* or *Nachbahrrecht*) and there are good grounds for allowing an extensive application, especially in view of State practice. For the historical background see Institut de Droit International, 13 *Annuaire* 1894, 330; 34 *Annuaire* 1928, 759.
[138] 2 Moore para. 215.   [139] 2 Hackworth 291.   [140] 2 Hackworth 299.

iii. Self-defence

As self-defence is authorised in article 51 of the Charter, it follows that it will also constitute a legitimising factor for certain acts of force which would otherwise be forbidden. There is a question whether article 51 limits the right of self-defence in two respects.

First, it appears to limit a wider right of self-defence under international law by referring to an 'armed attack'.[141] But 'armed attack' is probably now understood to be a wider concept.[142] It has been suggested that the right of self-defence may exist even in cases where there has been no previous use of force,[143] although the normal functioning of self-defence is obviously to repel by force another act of force.[144]

Secondly, article 51 appears to restrict the right of self-defence under general international law by introducing a time element: States have the right to resort to force only until the Security Council takes the necessary measures to 'maintain' international peace and security. There was a question, for example, in the Falklands War when and if a time limit for action by the Security Council expired and when a State can take action on its own without awaiting decisions of the Security Council.[145] Some writers point out that the fact that the Security Council has a matter under its jurisdiction does not preclude the exercise of the right of self-defence under article 51. Consequently, Resolution 502 of the Security Council in the Falklands War was not necessary as authorisation for British action, as it is clear that a State retains the right to defend itself regardless of such formalistic criteria concerning handling by UN organs. If States did not retain that freedom they would soon hesitate to refer any matter to the Security

---

[141] S. C. Khare, *Use of Force under UN Charter*, New Delhi, 1985, 83, 123. On earlier meaning of 'armed attack' see Brownlie, *Force*, 365–8.

[142] Cf. my 'Foreign warships and immunity for espionage', *AJIL*, 1984, 72; cf. Khare, *Use of Force*, 85ff.

[143] R. Taoka, *The Right of Self-defence in International Law*, Osaka, 1978, 173.

[144] See, in detail, D. W. Bowett, *Self-defence in International Law*, Manchester, 1958, *passim*, and on the rule *vim vi repellere omnia jure permittunt*, at 3; cf. H. Kelsen, 'Unrecht und Unrechtsfolge im Völkerrecht', *ZaöRVR*, 1932, 270, and Kelsen, *Law of the United Nations*, New York, 1964, 269ff; Waldock, 'The regulation of the use of force by individual states', 455ff. On older law under the Covenant of the League of Nations, see E. Giraud, 'La théorie de la légitime défense', *RCADI*, 1934, iii, 858; Gallus, 'Des amendements au Pacte de la Société des Nations en vue de le mettre en harmonie avec le Pacte de Paris', *RGDIP*, 1930, 30.

[145] For the Falklands War, see below, p. 75.

Council.[146] In some cases the right of self-defence may even come near the right to act by necessity.[147]

As in the case of all situations involving what has been called here 'legitimising factors', much will turn on the facts. But the argument of self-defence has been used in numerous recent conflicts even when the nature of the action seemed unlikely to warrant such qualification and when it could perhaps have been justified under another heading. Vietnam argued to the Security Council that its invasion of Kampuchea in 1978 was an 'action in self-defence after border skirmishes started by the Pol Pot clique'.[148]

The special problem of anticipatory self-defence is notoriously difficult to tackle. It is a field riddled with relative concepts where proportion and questions of fact may legitimise forceful action to preempt a concrete and overhanging threat of aggression. But since the notion has been resorted to in a number of conflicts as a cloak for drastic incursions, bombardments and attacks of alleged 'guerilla strongholds' or 'subversive centres' in the territory of other States,[149] it must be emphasised that anticipatory force falls under the prohibition of force in article 2(4) of the Charter, entailing a *presumption* that it is illegal. A mere threat of attack does thus not warrant military action.

It may be questioned under what circumstances, if any, a right to anticipatory force may be exercised. If it does exist in some form as a right, it also appears that it is a right which can be forfeited: a state which itself does not have 'clean hands' cannot take such actions. For example, the Security Council condemned South African raids into Angola even though Angola had allowed SWAPO considerable freedom to use its territory for guerilla attacks into Namibia.[150]

iv. Reprisals

Reprisals[151] provide, according to traditional notions, a legitimate ground for applying force against another State. This right presupposes a previous violation of the rights of a State followed by the refusal

[146] See, for a discussion, Murphy, *The United Nations*, 69–70.
[147] R. Y. Jennings, '*The Caroline and McLeod Case*', *AJIL*, 1938, 85.
[148] SC Res. 511 (1982); 512 (1982). Cf. below, p. 109 and p. 79 on the status of volunteers and on humanitarian intervention.
[149] B. Crozier, 'Terrorism: the problem in perspective', in US Dept. of State, *Conference on International Terrorism*, Washington, DC, 1976; cf. Khare, *Use of Force*, 110–22, 130.
[150] SC Res. 454 (1979).
[151] On the current confusion between reprisals against States and reprisals against individuals, see below, p. 254.

on the part of the violating State to make amends. The offended State is then entitled to take 'proportionate' reprisals.[152] As illustrated in the litigation concerning the frozen assets in 1980,[153] the right of reprisals subsists as a right to impose economic measures to force another State to comply with international law. When the American diplomats and other personnel had been taken into custody by Iran, the United States froze Iranian assets in all American banks to bring about the release of the hostages.

It is, however, questionable whether, after the establishment of the United Nations, the right to take reprisals still exists: the right of self-defence probably does not include the right of reprisal[154] and it may be that all claims should be channelled through the United Nations to be legitimate. On the other hand, if that organisation is slow to act, as it was in both the Iranian and the Falklands affairs, an at least temporary right of action may revert to the member States.

v. The consent of a State

The traditional view is that no international conflict will exist because of an attack if the territorial government has given its consent to a particular act of force. Some even claim that the difference between intervention and war is precisely that an intervening State has the 'acquiescence' of the other State.[155] That is, of course, not necessarily true, as there are numerous cases of interventions where the 'other' State did not consent or acquiesce but, nevertheless, the situation never escalated into war.[156] But consent of a State, if freely and properly given, can legitimise an intervention which otherwise would have been unlawful. United States assistance, for example, in suppressing raids of bandits and revolutionaries in Texas between 1911 and 1914 was probably made lawful by the consent of the Government of Mexico.[157]

Consent is certainly at the root of many rights States enjoy and,

---

[152] *Naulilaa Arbitration* (1928) 2 *RIAA* 1013; *Air Services Agreement Arbitration* (1963), 16 *RIAA* 5; cf. J. Stone, *Legal Controls of International Conflict*, Sydney, 1954, 2nd edn, New York, 1973, A. E. Hindmarsh, *Force in Peace*, Cambridge, Massachusetts, 1933.
[153] This case, which was prepared in the High Court in London, was settled out of court when the hostages were released by Iran.
[154] R. Higgins, *The Development of International Law through the Political Organs of the United Nations*, London, 1963, 217; cf. D. Bowett, 'Reprisals involving recourse to armed force', 66 *AJIL* 1972, 1.
[155] Thomas and Thomas, *Non-intervention*, 73.
[156] On the threshold, above, p. 18.   [157] 2 Hackworth 282.

conversely, of many burdens a State may suffer in international society. Different degrees of consent may even be required for certain situations where a State allows another State a right to act in its territory.[158] Consent may thus deprive an action of its illegality by the rule *volenti non fit injuria*. Consent may be given *in casu* in case of, for example, raids, but also in some general form in advance,[159] for example in a treaty allowing for intervention in certain circumstances. It may be added that one treaty which does allow for such right of intervention is the United Nations Charter itself, which authorises, for example under article 41, organs of the organisation to intervene in the internal affairs of a State.

By using the theory of 'abstract consent'[160] we may explain that the authorisation of the United Nations – which could have constituted a separate legitimising factor – can conveniently be subsumed under the present subheading: the parties to the Charter, and those who acceded to it later, agreed, beforehand and in the abstract, to certain actions by the UN, and such actions include, for example, sanctions[161] which may involve military action, possibly with UN Forces; because of the 'abstract consent' such action cannot be held to be in contravention of any rules prohibiting force. There is an overriding presumption that UN action is compatible with international law.

But individual States who apply force to another State have to accept a different presumption: that of deviating from a compelling rule prohibiting force unless they can show, *inter alia*, clear consent on the part of the State they 'assist' by military force. Sometimes formal consent by the government is not sufficient if that government, for example, has no 'popular support'.[162]

Thus, assistance lent to a 'puppet' government, or to a government controlled by the intervenor (or by some other State) will always be illegal. The rule on democratic consent demands that the 'people' wish for assistance. In theory, this is quite clear. In practice, there are often insurmountable problems in assessing the evidence on which legality depends. Soviet writers claim that the Soviet Union was requested to intervene in Afghanistan by the legitimate government[163] and the United States claims that 'assistance' was sought by Nicaragua, if not

---

[158] For a theory of 'continuous consent' for e.g. military bases, see my *Independent State*, 197ff.
[159] For a theory of 'abstract consent' by a previous authorising treaty, see my *Law Making*, 322ff; cf. the previous note.
[160] See the previous note.   [161] Under articles 38, 41 and 42.
[162] Cf. above, p. 25 on democratisation of international society and below, p. 80 on patronising intervention; cf. 1 Hackworth 175.
[163] Rybakov, *Agressia*, 147.

by the government, by a faction that should have formed the government.[164] In both these situations the intervening State seems not to have discharged a duty of showing the international society that the interventions had popular support. In neither case has the intervenor rebutted the strong presumption that, on the face of it at least, he has committed a violation of the rule of internatonal law which protects territorial integrity.

It has been argued that outside support of the Soviet Union in Mongolia in 1921 and in Manchuria to suppress counter-revolutionaries in 1929 was legitimate as the consent of the rightful government of the Soviet Union had been obtained.[165] A similar situation was that of British assistance by bombardment following attacks of armed bands on Aden,[166] although in this case self-interest was even more obvious in the assistance given.

But the situation is more complex if one considers the effect of consent, or lack thereof, in the case of assistance given or offered to insurgents.[167] This is an area where problems bearing on intervention, recognition and the effect of consent of the legitimate government converge.

It could validly be argued that the requirement of consent of the legitimate government is irrelevant and, *per se*, a legal and factual impossibility in respect of any act offered to assist insurgents. It has been claimed that matters radically change after recognition,[168] when other States may become parties to the war.[169] But it has also been demonstrated[170] that this is probably not correct in view of contemporary State practice, which rejects the formalistic notion of war in favour of a functional criterion whether substantial hostilities are actually taking place.[171]

vi. *Non-responsibility*

A State has a duty to suppress injurious acts against foreign States and a particular duty to prevent any hostile military expeditions. This is an old rule in international law.[172] For a long time a distinction has existed with regard to the fitting out of military expeditions and the

[164] *Nicaragua* v. *United States Case*, (1984) and (1986), ICJ *Reports*, 1984 and 1986.
[165] I. Brownlie, 'International law and the activities of armed bands', *ICLQ*, 1958, 732. On assistance to government in internal disputes, see above, p. 66.
[166] Brownlie, 'Armed bands', 725.
[167] On assistance to insurgents in general, see above, p. 67.   [168] See above, p. 35.
[169] So 2 Oppenheim 660.   [170] See above, p. 13.   [171] See above, p. 24.
[172] R. E. Curtis, 'The law of hostile military expeditions as applied by the United States', *AJIL*, 1914, 1.

venture of individuals. The former, but not the latter, was prohibited by Hague Convention V in 1907[173] and by many preceding national legislative Acts.[174]

There were many borderline cases between fitting out expeditions and the expeditions of volunteers, for example in the Spanish Civil War, when volunteers left *en masse*. Other cases difficult to categorise were the expeditions of volunteers of the People's Republic of China in Korea.[175] Some writers had raised the argument that volunteers, for whom a State is not responsible under international law, could never be allowed to act in a situation when the United Nations was taking 'enforcement action'. But the situation was complicated by a number of uncertain issues, above all concerning whether there was really a United Nations 'enforcement action' in Korea. There were clear indications that it had been a collective security action only of certain States, as there was no actual UN authorisation for the action.[176]

States have often sought to justify the use of force against another territory by claiming that attacks or incursions were carried out by units of volunteers for which the State was not 'responsible'.[177] Responsibility may, it has been claimed, be diminished to the point of complete exoneration if State control of territory is weakened or hampered by disturbances or civil war.[178] Sometimes a State claims that it has simply 'no knowledge' of the expedition.[179] In recent practice this line was taken by Vietnam to justify, in conjunction with other arguments,[180] their invasion of Kampuchea in 1978.[181]

Today, when the use of force and aggression has been outlawed, the duty to prevent any military incursions by persons into foreign territory is enhanced. Whereas formerly a duty of this kind existed only *vis-à-vis* 'friendly nations',[182] it is now extended to all nations and, it may

---

[173] For reference see p. 19, note 120, above.

[174] E.g. the UK 1870 Foreign Enlistment Act, 33 & 34 Vict. c. 90, applied in *R.* v. *Sandoval*, (1887) 56 LTR 526 and in *R.* v. *Jameson*, (1896) 2 QB 425.

[175] GAOR, 5th sess., 1st Committee, 1950, 401.

[176] S. Bastid, *Cours de droit international public*, Paris, 1951–2, 340; cf. my *Law Making*, 60.

[177] Cf. above, pp. 19 and 61.

[178] Statement to the Chief of the Swiss Federal Political Department to the Swiss National Council, 14 June 1971, concerning Jordanian liability for hijacked planes diverted to Jordan by the PLO, *Annuaire suisse*, 1972, 249.

[179] See *St Alban's Claim, 4 Moore 4042*, on a secret mission sent from Canada to the United States.

[180] Below, p. 79 on humanitarian intervention.

[181] Cf. Murphy, *The United Nations*, 61; cf. SC Res. 611 (1982) and 512 (1982).

[182] Cf. *The Alabama, United States* v. *United Kingdom, 7 Moore 1059*; but even then there was a question of special duties under a treaty, the Treaty of Washington of 8 May 1871.

be assumed, imposes a demand for even greater control by the State even of volunteers' activities.[183]

vii. Humanitarian intervention[184]

States have often claimed that they have resorted to humanitarian intervention and that therefore their actions are compatible with international law, assuming that 'humanitarian' motives justify acts of force. Even in the most implausible situations such defences have been put forward. There was little to substantiate any such legitimising circumstances in the Grenada invasion,[185] apart from the fact that even if there had been, there was a lack of proportion between the need and the size and intensity of action.

It is difficult to find a 'pure' case of humanitarian intervention. In the complex situation of a military intervention, however, it may be that humanitarian motives can be pleaded 'in mitigation'.[186] Humanitarian intervention provided the basis of legitimacy for Tanzania's invasion of Uganda in 1979. This action could hardly be construed as self-defence, in spite of some such claims, in response to armed border incursions by Amin troops, as the reponse in that case was grossly disproportionate.[187] But the incident raises an interesting question: does the attacking State itself have to state that it is taking humanitarian intervention? Tanzania had not done so and yet, because of the nature of Amin's rule in Uganda, there were no voices raised against the invasion.

Humanitarian intervention must be allowed rarely and with caution. In the past there has been much misuse of this title for unlawful intervention and a cloak for a number of unrelated activities. On the

---

[183] Cf. below, p. 109 on the status of volunteers in war.
[184] On general aspects of intervention see above, p. 61.
[185] See, on the Grenada invasion, W. Gilmore, *The Grenada Intervention*, London, 1984.
[186] T. Schweisfurth, 'Operation to rescue nationals in third states involving the use of force in relation to the protection of human rights', 23 *GYIL* 1980, 159; on forfeiting the character of 'humanitarian' intervention when other motives are present, see T. E. Behuniak, 'The law of humanitarian intervention by armed force, a legal survey', 79 *MilLR* 1978, 157; B. Simma, 'Zur bilateralen Durchsetzung verträglich verankerte Menschenrechte', in C. Schreuer (ed.), *Autorität und internationale Ordnung*, Berlin, 1979, 129; H. S. Fairley, 'State actors, humanitarian intervention and international law: reopening Pandora's box', 10 *Georgia Journal of International and Comparative Law*, 1980, 29; T. Franck and N. Rodley, 'After Bangladesh: the law of humanitarian intervention by military force', *AJIL*, 1973, 275; I. Brownlie, 'Humanitarian intervention', in J. N. Moore (ed.), *Law and Civil War in the Modern World*, Baltimore, 1974, 217.
[187] On proportionality in self-defence, see above, p. 74.

other hand, there must be cases where the unilateral use of force is 'less wrong than to turn aside'. One possible such case might have been the Vietnamese invasion of Kampuchea after the Pol Pot reign of terror.[188]

viii. Patronising intervention

There is a type of intervention, practised in both East and West, which could perhaps be conveniently termed 'patronising intervention'. This form of intervention is most affected by political attitudes and particularly by the doctrine of 'spheres of influence' which, contrary to some views, is still current in State practice. Although not always carried out by military means, this kind of intervention is often accompanied by forceful action which the acting State claims is legitimate, albeit having its roots in an exaggerted view of what may legally follow from a geographical/political concept like the 'sphere of influence'.

This is thus not a new type of intervention.[189] It may be new to call it 'patronising'; such a term would seem to sum up best the action when States intervene to bring about 'what is best' for another country. Sometimes a State may refer to its action as being legitimised because of 'State interests', or some other vague term, which does not confer any legitimising effect in international law, although it may explain the desirability of an action in political terms. A State may announce that action to 'destabilise' a foreign government may be 'taken in the best interests of the countries concerned'.[190] Sometimes a State may refer to self-defence or collective self-defence[191] although the whole tenor of the action would be more readily explained by a concept like 'patronising intervention'.

---

[188] Murphy, *The United Nations*, 63–4. But on more spurious claims on the basis of self-defence, see above, p. 74.
[189] Cf. the Monroe Doctrine 're-applied' for Cuba, Q. Wright, 'The Cuban Quarantine', 57 *AJIL* 1963, 546; M. S. McDougal, 'The Soviet Cuban Quarantine and self-defence', 57 *AJIL* 1963, 597; E. Giraud, 'L'interdiction du recours à la force, la théorie et la pratique des Nations Unies', 67 *RGDIP* 1963, 503; on the Eisenhower doctrine, announced on 9 March 1957, on the Lebanon see, for a critique, J. Delivanis, *La légitime défense en droit international public moderne*, Paris, 1971, 131–2; for the Truman and Nixon doctrines on a firm stand by the United States against 'communist aggression' and on Soviet views in response to 'imperialist aggression' see C. Alibert, *Du droit de se faire justice dans la société internationale depuis 1945*, Paris, 1983, 321, 336, 363ff; for the Brezhnev doctrine see, e.g., D. Frenzke, *Die Rechtsnatur des Sowjetblocs*, Berlin, 1981, 204.
[190] Statement by President Ford, 16 September 1974, reprinted in Falk, 'An alternative to covert intervention', ASIL, *Proceedings*, 1975, 195.
[191] Cf. above, p. 73.

When asked whether States have a right to 'destabilise' a constitutionally elected government of another country, President Gerald Ford stated in 1974 that 'It is a recognized fact that historically as well as presently such actions are taken in the best interests of the countries concerned'.[192]

The most striking case in recent times is the action of the United States in mining the ports of Nicaragua and taking other 'paramilitary' action against that State. The United States claimed that 'United States actions are in the exercise of the right, indeed the duty, to engage in collective self-defence with the other Central American States in response to Nicaragua's acts.'[193] The International Court of Justice decided by an injunction in 1984 that the United States should cease such activities,[194] but the United States claimed that it was entitled to pursue certain other measures. The United States then decided to withdraw from the Court proceedings and discontinued its acceptance of the Optional Clause.[195] However, even if a State claims to be entitled to take action by force in the interest of another State, such interference violates not only the rule prohibiting force, but also the right of self-determination.[196]

ix. Self-determination: revival of 'just war' theories

There is no shortage of commentaries on the medieval and post-medieval theories on 'just war'.[197] This century, and in particular during the last few decades, there has been a noticeable revival of just war theories, using such theories not only to justify wars for the pursuit of just causes in religious terms[198] but to find a legal justification for 'liberation' wars against 'domineering' larger or stronger States.

Even early writers who condemned inter-State wars still saw justification of wars of international liberation, insisting that they must be

[192] Statement, 16 September 1974; Falk, 'Covert intervention', 195. Cf. Fatouros, 'Remarks on covert intervention and international law', ASIL, *Proceedings*, 1975, 192. See discussion on covert intervention to influence the internal affairs of another State in *ASIL*, 1975, 192.
[193] Verbatim Record, CR/84/17, 74.
[194] ICJ *Reports*, 1984, p. 169, on the interim measures.
[195] ICJ *Reports*, 1986, p. 15, and cf. above, p. 76.   [196] See my *Independent State*, 3ff.
[197] M. Keen, *The Laws of War in the Later Middle Ages*, Oxford, 1965, 63ff; F. H. Russell, *The Just War in the Middle Ages*, Cambridge, 1975; J. T. Johnson, *Just War and the Restraint of War: a Moral and Historical Inquiry*, Princeton, 1981.
[198] For example, cf. the activities of Hezbolla soldiers in the Lebanon; and cf. on 'jihad' in the Moslem world A. Rechid, 'L'Islam et le droit des gens', 60 *RCADI* 1937, ii, 375; cf. also below, p. 127 on alleged *jus ad bellum*.

more 'just' and legitimate than any international wars.[199] According to Marxist writers a war against 'suppressors' and 'enslavers' of peoples will always be lawful within a capitalist society.[200] Thus, use of force to attain 'self-determination' is permissible[201] and, it is claimed, liberation wars by 'dominated' small or new States do not violate any legal rules.

The rule of self-determination has been used as a justification for measures of coercion. It has been argued that it could not be 'wrong' or 'illegal' to start wars for national liberation on the basis of such a rule of self-determination. Some Soviet writers hold that 'nations' who are not States can resort to national liberation wars.[202] Other Soviet commentators deny that 'nations' whose 'personality' is just emerging can participate in inter-State relations.[203] In this way, the 'new' concept of liberation wars as 'international' wars[204] is logically difficult to reconcile with the view that liberation movements are cut off from inter-State relations. But then liberation wars are not necessarily on such an inter-State footing but concern more immediately the attainment of self-determination.

The desire to defend liberation movements and their goals has led some writers to condemn 'repressive' force applied by lawful governments to any such movements.[205] The few who sought to apply the principle of self-determination without any corollary of a 'right to fight' at the Conference on Conventional Weapons made their suggestions in vain.[206]

There has been an increasing body of opinion suggesting that war waged by liberation movements would have special features and constitute 'just war'.[207] At least according to views put forward by the Third World itself 'emancipation wars' would have this standing.[208]

At the Diplomatic Conference elaborating the 1977 Protocols it was also suggested, for example by the Chinese delegation, that national

---

[199] A. Rougier, *Les guerres civiles et le droit des gens*, Paris, 1903, 160.
[200] Cf. Lenin, 8 *Werke*, Berlin edn, 1958, 568.   [201] Tunkin, *Sila*, 40.
[202] N. A. Ushakov, *Soviet Yearbook of Internationl Law*, 1964–5, 74.
[203] Lukachuk, 2 *Mezhdunarodnogo pravo*, Kiev, 1968, 9.   [204] Above, p. 40.
[205] N. Ronzitti, 'Resort to force and wars of national liberation', in A. Cassese (ed.), *Current Problems of International Law*, Milan, 1975, 320.
[206] A/CONF.95/8, Annex II, Appendixes B and C (Germany).
[207] See below, p. 126, on the historical background.
[208] E.g. H. Meyrowitz, *Le principe d'égalité des belligérants devant le droit de la guerre*, Paris, 1970, 100. Cf. H. Weber, *Der Vietnam Konflikt – Bellum Legale? Die Rechtspflichten der Staaten unter dem Gewaltgebot der UN-Charta*, Hamburg, 1970; J. T. Johnson, *Can Modern Wars be Just?*, London, 1984; M. Walzer, *Just and Unjust Wars*, London, 1978.

liberation wars are just and should therefore be 'supported' by all countries that uphold justice.[209] But some representatives rebutted this idea as an 'archaic' concept.[210] Some insisted that the right to wage wars need not follow from the rule of self-determination. Germany objected at the 1980 UN Conference on Conventional Weapons that it would be inappropriate to include a reference in the Preamble to the 'right to fight for national liberation' but suggested that instead a reference to the right to self-determination be adopted.[211]

Some individuals have sought to benefit from the concept of just war by claiming that they would be exempt from any duty to fight in any venture which is not 'just'.[212]

Even if the Third World occasionally attempts to revive the obsolete theories of the just war which may be conceptually and practically unacceptable in these days when all war has been outlawed, it must be emphasised that such theories lack any legal basis. Yet, even if a war is 'just' in the eyes of some developing countries, the warfare must still be subjected to stringent laws of warfare and humanitarian rules, and in this sense the Law of War will uplift any armed conflict to a higher 'civilised' standard, whether or not it is claimed that the conflict or war is 'just'.[213]

Those who instigate liberation wars may violate the *jus ad bellum* which exists no more,[214] but States must still not exempt belligerents of liberation movements from the *jus in bello*. For there is often a temptation for States 's'opposant à un violateur du *jus ad bellum* de vouloir soumettre ce belligérant illégal à un régime discriminatoire sur le plan du *jus ad bello*'.[215] Just war theories are defunct and liberation movements must seek other means to attain statehood for their people. The normal legitimising factor is then the rule of self-determination which undoubtedly furnishes a legal title for resisting (but not for starting to employ) use of force in contemporary international society. Naturally, it is difficult to determine when and who 'starts' to use force. But, if it is a 'clear' question of 'second' use, it may be legitimised under modern international law, not as self-defence but under the heading of self-determination. Once an armed conflict has developed, there must be

[209] CDDH/SR.12, vol. 5, 120.   [210] Ibid., 123.
[211] A/CONF.95/8, Annex II, Appendixes B and C.
[212] *US* v. *Mitchell*, (1967) 386 US 972.
[213] Cf. J. C. Bluntschli, *Das moderne Kriegsrecht der zivilisierten Staaten*, 2nd edn, Nordlingen, 1874, para. 519: 'Das Kriegsrecht zivilisiert den gerechten und den unrechten Krieg ganz gleichmässig.'
[214] Below, p. 126.   [215] Meyrowitz, *Le principe*, 401.

safeguards to ensure that certain minimum rules of the Law of War are respected by all sides in a conflict. Liberation movements are thus undoubtedly bound by the Law of War.

The rules of self-determination are particularly relevant to questions of legality of resistance, of partisan or guerilla war, especially when a country is occupied by a foreign State. There is necessarily a conflict between the 'rights' of an occupying power and the 'rights' of resistance. Some have claimed that resistance against an occupying force is illegal by an *e contrario* conclusion of what follows from the right of a *levée en masse*,[216] whereas others consider all population to have a right to rise against an occupier.[217] Soviet writers have asserted a right to resistance if occupation is not 'effective',[218] although it is not clear who is to assess the effectiveness. Certain cases also indicate that a right to rise against an occupier exists, at least against an occupier who himself does not respect the laws of war.[219]

[216] F. Castberg, *Soldater, partisaner og franktirörer*, Oslo, 1954, 16, 23; J. Andenaes, 'Var hjemmefrontens kamp folkerettsstridig?' *Festskrift J. H. Andresen*, Oslo, 1948, 6; R. R. Baxter, 'The duty of obedience to the belligerent occupant, 27 *BYIL* 1950, 266.
[217] F. Bauer, *Krigsförbrytarna infoör domstol*, Stockholm, 1944; H. Brandweiner, 'Das Partisanenproblem und die Genfer Konvenetionen von 12. August 1949', 72, *Juristische Blätter* 1950, 263, speaking of a '*Jus insurrectionis*'.
[218] See references in Kulski, 'Some Soviet comments on international law', *AJIL*, 1951, 347.
[219] *The Flesch Case*, (1948) Norwegian Supreme Court, Retstidende, 1948, 80.

3 PREVENTION OF WAR

A. DOUBLE NATURE OF RELEVANT FACTORS

Treaties on restraining force and/or providing for pacific settlements of disputes constitute complementary negative and positive obligations which lessen the danger of actual war.

Apart from such conventional[1] obligations, certain factors also reduce or increase the likelihood of war. Conversely, favourable social conditions may entrench security and prevent war.

It is a formidable task to indicate the causes of war,[2] as these are often found in complex interrelationships of immediate goal-settings, structural imbalances and coincidentals. For example, social conditions may give rise to conflicts and become the origins of a dispute.[3]

B. UNDERMINING FACTORS

Experts in the field of sociology and psychology analyse specific reasons for tensions and conflict in international society.[4] In the syllabus for students of Peace Studies at Columbia University there is even a literature of aggressive behaviour of animals.[5] Many circumstances

---

[1] 'Conventional' is used here to denote that the source of obligation derives from a convention; this adjective is common in the terminology of international law but must, of course, be distinguished from 'conventional' (implying 'traditional') warfare as opposed to guerilla warfare; see above, p. 50; and from 'conventional' (meaning 'non-nuclear') weapons as opposed to nuclear weapons; below, p. 180.

[2] The leading work is M. Howard, *The Causes of War and Other Essays*, London, 1983; cf. G. Blainey, *The Causes of War*, London, 1973; J. G. Stoessinger, *Why Nations Go to War*, New York, 1978. For works on causes of specific wars, see H. W. Koch (ed.), *The Origins of the First World War*, 2nd edn, London, 1984; E. Robertson, *The Origins of the Second World War*, London, 1971; J. R. Gainsborough, *The Arab–Israeli Conflict*, London, 1986, 129ff on the causes of the Six Day War.

[3] See above, p. 49 on revolutionary war.

[4] See numerous studies by SIPRI, the Stockholm International Peace Research Institute.

[5] For the study of 'biosociopsychological' bases of war, the course refers to Hamburg's article on 'Aggressive behaviour of chimpanzees and baboons in natural habitat', 8 *Journal of Psychiatric Research* 385.

which contribute to increased risk of conflict, such as, for examples, militarism and militarisation,[6] are largely unquantifiable. There are problems even in identifying exact causes of a specific war and it is still more difficult to suggest general causes of war. Naturally, territorial ambitions, claims to 'Lebensraum' or to territory which has been wrongfully lost[7] always play a part. Ideological aspirations, sometimes disguised as measures necessary to 'national security' to protect a socio-economic system, are increasingly important. Economic ambitions are also relevant although economic factors are thought to be relatively unimportant by some commentators.[8]

The risk of war is increased and prolonged if there is general 'hostility' towards another country, either on a neighbour scale or in terms of East–West polarisation. Among neighbours there may be long-standing disagreement about borders or demarcation lines or even a divergence of 'culture' which makes States, like brothers, more hostile to those who are near than to those much further away. Between East and West there is a gradually entrenched ideological gap where mutual suspicion and prejudice play an ever increasing part in exacerbating tension.

In addition to other causes of war, the lack of condemnation may furnish a further reason to start hostilities. States may resort to force, or continue to use force, if there is no outright condemnation by other States. Declarations by the United Nations are no substitute for clear positions taken by individual States in this respect.

When, on 22 September 1980, Iraq started invading Iran, both the United Kingdom and France remained 'neutral' and did not speak up against the war. The reason for this silence was heavy investment by both the United Kingdom and France in both belligerent countries and this was thought to be a sensitive question.[9] As a result, the Security Council – whose action would anyway not have been a substitute for pronouncement by States – did little.[10]

Another important cause of war is the failure of the judicial system. The United States argued in the *Nicaragua Case*[11] that the Interna-

---

[6] A. Eide and M. Thee, *Problems of Contemporary Militarism*, London, 1980.

[7] See above, p. 72.

[8] Q. Wright, *Study on War*, 2nd edn, Chicago, 1965, 1293; this was also Hitler's view, *Mein Kampf*, Berlin, 1939, 199.

[9] Cf. Murphy, *The United Nations*, 65.

[10] But see the Draft Resolution on control of the Shatt el Arab waterway, *ibid.*, 65.

[11] *Nicaragua* v. *United States (Jurisdiction)*, ICJ *Verbatim Records*, 84/18, 64; cf. *Nicaragua* v. *United States (Merits)*, ICJ *Reports*, 1986.

tional Court of Justice is not able to consider matters reserved for the Security Council. However, it was clear in the *Iranian Hostage Case*[12] that the United States considered the Court to have precisely that function. The *Corfu Channel Case*[13] had also clearly showed that the Court is competent to consider questions bearing on the use of force. And the *Expenses Case*[14] had indicated that the Court can also consider 'political' issues.

But rules restraining force will naturally be undermined if a State considers that the International Court lacks the competence to consider the legality of coercive measures, potentially involving war, or giving rise to actual war.

In the *Iranian Hostage Case* it was evident that Iran thought little of the Court, not presenting itself before it, and ignoring the Interim Order. In the *Nicaragua Case* it is obvious that the United States, when it comes to its own national interests, does not have much respect either for the Court's authority, abandoning the proceedings midway.

C. STABILISING FACTORS

It is, of course, impossible to provide any detailed indication of factors which preserve peace. This is not because this work is not the appropriate place for any lengthy analysis but rather that such factors escape identification, except by large patterns, as it is not the factors individually that are important as much as their juxtaposition with other factors. Any development which links States together is likely to contribute to peace if acts are carried out universally. In other words, world-wide attempts to promote, for example, trade or cultural exchanges are likely to lessen the danger of war. Restrictions of trade in arms will also reduce the possibility of war.[15] On regional levels there is always a danger of bloc-building and eventual antagonising of groups. But, generally speaking, certain formations will assist in the peace-keeping effort.

i. Alliances

Alliances, according to traditional theory, stabilise the balance of power,[16] at least as long as the members all perceive one common

[12] *United States* v. *Iran*, ICJ *Reports*, 1979, 7, and 1980, 3.
[13] ICJ *Reports*, 1949, 4.   [14] ICJ *Reports*, 1962, 246.
[15] See, e.g., J. C. Martinez, 'Le droit international et le commerce des armes', in Colloque de Montpellier, *Le droit international et les armes*, Paris, 1982, 93ff.
[16] Cf. I. Claude, *Power and International Relations*, New York, 1962; M. Wight 'The

outside threat. Alliances restrain violence between the members of that particular pact[17] but may, on the other hand, contribute to tension *vis-à-vis* another powerful alliance. Such polarisation may be mitigated by special negotiations between such blocs, as in the case of multilateral negotiations on nuclear disarmament[18] or other talks specifically between military alliances, like the Mutual Balanced Forces Reductions talks between NATO and Warsaw Pact States.[19]

ii. Coordination of foreign policy

The harmonisation of foreign policy may be inherent in alliances. Beyond the realm of military alliances, there is also considerable scope for coordination as a result of similar political ideologies. Occasionally such similarities are evident only when confronted with another major bloc, inspired by different ideas. Thus, in spite of diverging foreign policies in Western Europe, such policies are sufficiently homogeneous to form the subject matter of a Treaty on Coordinated Foreign Policy, concluded on 3 December 1985 within the framework of the EEC.[20]

iii. Disarmament

It is important to assess briefly the role of disarmament in the context of stabilisation.[21]

A sharp, albeit often unwarranted, distinction is often made between arms limitation or arms control, disarmament and the laws of war. By arms limitation or arms control one normally understands any measure of restraint of testing, manufacturing, possessing or de-

---

balance of power', in H. Butterfield and M. Wight (eds.), *Diplomatic Investigations: Essays in the Theory of International Politics*, London, 1966; A. Wolfers, *Discord and Collaborators: Essays on International Politics* Baltimore, 1962.

[17] S. Verosta, *Theorie und Realität von Bundnissen, 1897–1914*, Vienna, 1971; P. Barendon, *System der politischen Staatsverträgen seit 1918*, Berlin, 1937, 211; J. R. De Orue y Arregui, 'Le régionalisme dans l'organisation international', 53 *RCADI* 1935, iii, 1. But note the rift in NATO when Greece and Turkey supported different communities in Cyprus in the hostilities of 1974.

[18] Below, p. 90.   [19] Below, p. 94.   [20] EEC News Release, 3 December 1985.

[21] There is a vast literature on disarmament. See, for example, L. Freedman, *Arms Control in Europe*, London, 1981; N. Sims, *Approaches to Disarmament: an introductory analysis*, 2nd edn, London 1979; for UN studies, see UN, *The Relationship between Disarmament and International Security* 1982, E.82, ix.4; UN, *Study on All Aspects of Regional Disarmament*, 1981, A/35/416. Cf. UN, *Comprehensive Study on Confidence Building Measures*, 1982, A/36/474.

ploying of a specific type of weapon. Disarmament, on the other hand, implies the reduction in, or renunciation of, a type of weapon.

But 'arms limitation' may obviously imply far-going rules which inevitably entail the 'reduction' or 'renunciation', at least with regard to certain types, or certain types of uses, of weapons. Conversely, disarmament may involve specified control of use of a weapon, as in the En-mod Convention.[22] Treaties of either of these categories have been thought so irrelevant to the laws of war that they are not even included in the ordinary collection of texts on the laws of war. Yet, there is little difference in structure and function between, for example, the En-mod Convention and the Geneva Gas Protocol, or between the Biological Weapons Convention and the 1868 St Petersburg Declaration. It appears unjustified to group texts of clear relevance to the conduct of modern war in different groups. All texts concerning disarmament are of essential importance to the laws of war.

a. Early attempts

There were some early efforts towards disarmament, for example the treaty between Argentina and Chile in 1902 whereby the parties undertook to cancel orders for construction of warships and notify each other of any new construction.[23] The Washington Conference on the Limitation of Armaments in 1921–2 introduced some restrictions on large warships in the final treaty.[24] Some measures were quantitative and constituted 'the most direct means of limiting and reducing the competitive accumulation of arms'.[25] Others were qualitative and gave rise to problems, as technological improvement was difficult to verify.[26]

Other restrictions, again, in other treaties[27] implied 'geographic' or 'mission restraints'. Others concerned the limitation of certain types of naval deployment, for example prohibiting permanent stationing of arms on the high seas.[28] Furthermore, the London treaty of 1930 introduced similar restrictions on warships.[29]

[22] Below, p. 227.
[23] The Treaty worked for about six years: UN, *Study on the Naval Arms Race*, Geneva, 1985, 140.
[24] Treaty of Washington of 6 February 1922, below, p. 267.
[25] There was a freeze on manufacturing, on numbers and on the introduction of new systems; UN *Study on the Naval Arms Race*, 141.
[26] *Ibid.*, 142.
[27] For example, the Rush Bagot Treaty of 1817; the Montreux Convention 1936 on the demilitarisation of areas; cf. below. p. 142.
[28] *Ibid.*, 144; cf. the 1982 Law of the Sea Convention, below, p. 147.
[29] Treaty of 22 April 1930.

b. The contemporary position

Plans by the Soviet Union for a complete disarmament treaty (CDT) were presented to the Geneva Conference in 1962. The United States responded to this proposal by plans for staged elimination. The 10th Special Session of the General Assembly in 1978 (SSD) was devoted to the disarmament question. The first session on disarmament set out a 'disarmament strategy',[30] discussed further in a second session in 1982.

At present, there is little hope of achieving anything but partial disarmament in certain specific areas. Talks have been carried out at different levels: between the superpowers at intermittent summit meetings; on a multilateral level at the Disarmament Conference in Geneva; and, again on a multilateral basis, but limited to confidence-building measures, in Stockholm and Vienna. The Stockholm Conference on Confidence and Security Building Measures and Disarmament in Europe (CDE), established under the Helsinki Accords in 1975, finally led to the adoption of a 'Document'[31] but, in the other fora, talks continue.

Advances on disarmament depend on negotiations as well as on other factors such as budgetary restraints. If there is no agreement, there may be factual restraints, at least for certain types of weapons.[32]

(1) Nuclear disarmament Nuclear weapons attracted early attention in the disarmament negotiations after the war.[33] There has also been, and still is, much discussion on the legality of such weapons.[34] A presumption of illegality of nuclear weapons is clearly conducive to further advances in nuclear disarmament.

Public fears of hazards from nuclear pollution were probably one

---

[30] GA Res. 5–10/2, 3 *United Nations Disarmament Yearbook*, 1978. On measures 'collateral' to general disarmament, see A. Gotlieb, *Disarmament and International Law*, Toronto, 1965, 44ff.

[31] CDE, Document of 19 September 1986, and below, p. 94.

[32] The United States Congress deleted allocations for further chemical weapons from the defence budget of 1983 and, in spite of certain pressure from the Reagan administration, has not yet reallocated funds. For a commentary, see N. Sims, 'Chemical weapons, control or chaos?' *Faraday Discussion Paper No. 1*, London, 1984, 14.

[33] Note efforts by the Commission for Conventional Disarmament 1946–52; the Disarmament Commission (for both nuclear and conventional weapons) 1953–7, with an important five-power subcommittee; the Ten Nations Disarmament Committee (TNDC), expanded into an 18-power committee (ENDC) in 1962; the Committee of the Conference on Disarmament (CCD), an even larger body, 1969–79, in turn transformed and amplified into the Conference on Disarmament (CD) in 1979.

[34] Below, p. 201.

of the reasons for the Partial Test Ban Treaty (PTB)[35] in 1963.[36] The important factor of public opinion also contributed to inducing France to make a unilateral declaration that it would cease testing nuclear weapons after having been taken to the International Court of Justice by Australia and New Zealand.[37]

Certain preventive treaties have been concluded between the superpowers in the form of bilateral treaties. Some such agreements are the ABM Treaty of 1972,[38] the SALT Interim Agreement,[39] the Agreement on Basic Relations,[40] the Agreement on Basic Principles of Negotiation on the Further Limitation of Strategic Offensive Arms,[41] the Agreement on Prevention of Nuclear War,[42] the Threshold Test-Ban Treaty (TTBT)[43] and the Treaty on Underground Nuclear Explosions.[44] There is also a series of bilateral agreements on warning systems between the United States and the USSR.[45]

Other relevant treaties have been negotiated on a bilateral basis between the United States and the USSR but resulted in a multilateral instrument. This is the case of the Non-Proliferation Treaty of 1968.[46]. This Treaty imposes restrictions on non-nuclear States (not to acquire nuclear weapons), but not on the superpowers. It also obliges States to negotiate 'in good faith' for further disarmament; it would seem to break at least the spirit of the Treaty if they do not only fail to do this but actually build up further arms arsenals.

The Sea-Bed Treaty of 1971 also introduced certain limitations for

---

[35] 480 UNTS 43. Cf. endorsement in the General Assembly, Res. 1910 (XVIII) 1963. In 1985 there were 110 parties, including most militarily significant States, except for China and France.

[36] *Brandt Commission Papers*, 1981, 373.

[37] *Nuclear Test Cases*, ICJ, Reports, 1974, 253.

[38] 1972, 11 ILM 784. The agreement restricts missile defences to two sites (later one site) with 100 missiles allowed at each site.

[39] 1972, Interim Agreement on Certain Measures with Respect to the Limitation of Strategic Offensive Weapons, 11 *ILM* 791. The Agreement limits the number of ICBM and SLBM launchers; it lapsed in 1977 but was extended by mutual consent.

[40] 1972, 11 *ILM* 756.   [41] 1973, 12 *ILM* 897.   [42] 1973, 12 *ILM* 903.

[43] 1974 Treaty on the Limitation of Underground Nuclear Tests, 13 *ILM* 906.

[44] 1976, 15 *ILM* 891.

[45] Memorandum on a Direct Communication Link, 1963, 2 *ILM* 793 (the Hot Line Agreement); Agreement on Measures to Improve the Direct Communication Link, 1971, 10 *ILM* 1174; Agreement on Measures to Reduce the Risk of Outbreak of Nuclear War, 1971, 10 *ILM* 1173; and the Agreement on the Prevention of Incidents on and over the High Seas, 1972, 11 *ILM* 778.

[46] 729 UNTS 161. At present there are 130 parties (1985). For a summary of various non-proliferation policies, see J. Goldblat, *Nuclear Proliferation, Guide to the Debate*, London (SIPRI), 1985, and Goldblat, *Non-proliferation: the Why and the Wherefore*, London, 1985.

the emplacement of nuclear weapons,[47] but its ambit of application is not quite clear.[48] Other relevant treaties are, for example, the Outer Space Treaty of 1967,[49] the Antarctic Treaty of 1959,[50] the Treaty of Tlatelolco of 1967[51] and the Treaty of Rarotonga of 1985.[52] The Enmod Convention[53] prohibits the use of nuclear weapons for modification of the environment.

The numerous relevant multilateral treaties play an important part in strengthening the operation of the bilateral treaty network between the superpowers.[54]

(2) Conventional and other arms control and disarmament Some progress has been made by outlawing certain conventional weapons in the 1981 Convention.[55] Other weapons, the use of which conflicts with the basic principles of the laws of war,[56] may be tainted by illegality. Such a state of affairs may prompt the adoption of further agreements, which may confirm such illegality.[57]

Attention has also been focused on massive scientific research and development research (R and D), which could be directed to either civil or military application. Attempts are being made to prohibit weapons at the research stage so that the use of prohibited weapons will be made even more unlikely.[58]

(3) Verification problems Verification, in itself a vast problem which has given rise to a considerable literature,[59] is usually perceived as a slowing down problem factor in disarmament. Naturally,

---

[47] UKTS 1973 13; TIAS 7337; cf. endorsement by the UN General Assembly in Res. 2660 (XXV) 1970. There are 74 parties (1985).
[48] See below, p. 91 on naval mines.
[49] 610 UNTS 205, and below, p. 147. There are 85 parties (1985).
[50] 402 UNTS 71, and below, p. 142.
[51] With two Protocols, 634 UNTS 326 and below, p. 148.
[52] *ILM*, 1985, 1085, and below, p. 149.   [53] Below, p. 226.
[54] See Draft Comprehensive Programme on Disarmament, 1986, CD/732, 131; cf. Arms Race in Outer Space, *ibid.*, at 107; and on Nuclear Weapons, *ibid.*, at 18.
[55] Below, p. 180.   [56] Below, p. 207.
[57] On the creation of rules by 'recognition' or 'adoption', in agreements or otherwise, see my work on *The Concept of International Law*, Stockholm, 1986, 103ff.
[58] See United Nations, *Study by the Secretary General on Conventional Disarmament*, New York, 1985, A/39/348, 25.
[59] E.g. K. Tsipis, D. W. Hafemeister and P. Janeway (eds.), *Arms Control Verification: the Technologies that Make it Possible*, Oxford, 1986; I. Bellany and C. D. Blacker (eds.), *The Verification of Arms Control Agreements*, London, 1983. *Cf.* A. McKnight, *Atomic Safeguards: a Study in International Verification*, New York, 1971; A. S. Krass, *Verification: How Much is Enough?* London (SIPRI), 1983.

States are reluctant to allow, for example, on-site inspections by national or international bodies to verify compliance with agreement on disarmament or arms control, although there have been recent signs of increased willingness to allow such procedures.[60] But sophisticated reconnaissance defence systems play a role, at least for some weapons. There are already extensive photoreconnaissance programmes,[61] electronic reconnaissance[62] and early warning satellites.[63] And certain arms control agreements are now coupled with rudimentary verification rules.[64]

(4) Diffusion of tension by talks Negotiations, either within the framework of the United Nations or outside in other forms, contribute to the diffusion of tensions between States, especially between blocs and in the field of arms control and disarmament. The United Nations provides a useful forum for discussion even in cases when specific conventions are being negotiated, but the entrenchment of lengthy negotiations in a permanent body of the United Nations, for specific purposes, tends to exacerbate tensions. This has, for example, been the effect of the negotiations in the Conference on Disarmament, CD, as well as in its predecessors CCD and ECDC.[65] CD now has important feedbacks to and from the General Assembly and transfers its functions, complete with national delegations, to the sessions of the General Assembly every October.

Other important talks, which are of particular relevance for the diffusion of tension, are the discussions within the Conference for European Security (CSCE) under the Helsinki Accords of 1975.[66] The Conference on Confidence and Security Building Measures and Disarmament in Europe (CDE) in Stockholm was established under the Helsinki Act in 1975.[67] The act itself is often thought to lack legal

[60] E.g. Statement by President Gorbachev, 15 January 1986, TASS Release on CW, below, p. 225.
[61] Extensive programmes exist, *inter alia* in the United States, the USSR and Japan; France operates its SAMRO (Satellite Militaire de Reconnaissance Optique) based on the civilian Spot (Systeme probatoire d'observation de la terre) system.
[62] Like the US ELINT Cosmos satellites, normally launched from the 'Big Bird' photoreconnaissance satellite, which monitor missile test signals; or US EORSAT (Ocean Surveillance Satellites) and USSR RORSAT (Robot Ocean Surveillance Satellites).
[63] Like the US Test Ruby infra-red sensors.
[64] See below, p. 220.   [65] See above, p. 90.
[66] For subsequent discussions see meetings in Madrid and Ottawa in 1985.
[67] Under a mandate of 6 September 1984.

obligation,[68] but the British Foreign Office regards at least one provision as 'binding'.[69] That is the stipulation that military manoeuvres involving more than 25,000 men shall be notified to other States.[70]

After 32 months of negotiations an agreement, the 'Stockholm Document',[71] was reached on 21 September 1986 whereby both NATO and Warsaw Pact powers will provide notification of all manoeuvres surpassing this numerical limit. It may well be that this agreement, couched in euphemistic terms as a mere 'document', is of unparalleled importance in diffusing tension, at the low and practical level of military manoeuvres, between East and West. The document reduces the notifiable level of troops to the lower figure of 13,000.[72]

The possibility of a direct communication link under the 'Hot Line' Agreement[73] may also reduce tensions in an acute crisis and may, to some extent, eliminate the chances of a war by 'accident'.

Other talks are the Negotiations on Mutual Reductions of Forces and Armaments and Associated Measures in Central Europe in Vienna, between NATO and Warsaw Pact States.[74] Such 'associated measures' concern so-called 'confidence and security building measures' and verification. Problems are caused by lack of data regarding the actual strength and number of forces and arms on the opposite side as well as by problems of verification. Measures have thus been discussed which will reduce these uncertainties. To the Western powers there was more interest in commencing talks on reduction of forces rather than armaments, but both matters were finally included. The Vienna talks are usually referred to as discussions on Mutual and Balanced Forces Reductions, which is really only a Western expression and not the official name; the USSR preferred the term 'equal' reductions. These talks may have shown little progress but may, as they attempt to discuss reduction of the size of armed forces and conventional armaments in Central Europe, contribute to maintenance of peace by their very protraction.

[68] See my *Concept*, p. 103.

[69] UK Foreign and Commonwealth Office, *Defence and Disarmament Issues*, no. 17, July 1985.

[70] The provision does not apply to the 'wester-most' 250 kilometres of the area of the Soviet Union.

[71] CDE 19 September 1986; this Draft was adopted.

[72] Or the involvement of 300 battle tanks, *ibid.*, at 31.1.1.

[73] Above, note 43.

[74] E.g. J. G. Keliher, *The Negotiations on Mutual and Balanced Force Reductions*, New York, 1980.

(5) Restraint of arms trade Restricting trade in weapons will also have a clear effect on the number of parties of war-waging capability.

When on 2 December 1939 the United States President condemned bombing of civilians from the air[75] he added that he hoped that American manufacturers and exporters of aeroplanes, aeronautical equipment and materials 'would bear this in mind before negotiating contracts for export of such articles to nations obviously guilty of unprovoked bombing'.[76] Restraint of the arms trade reduces the likelihood of certain local armed disputes. Conversely, the more ready access States or other parties have to arms supplies, the more likely it is that they will resort to them in time of conflict. Against this many argue that States have a definite interest in purchasing arms for legitimate defence interests and it is not for other States to comment on their purchases. Much is needed for defence purposes and it is impossible to distinguish between what is purchased for legitimate defence purposes and what exceeds such needs. There is also concern about the potential conversion of use of nuclear material and technologies from peaceful activities to military use and also about the overall standards in nuclear trade. In spite of IAEA efforts to promote safeguards for nuclear activities, materials which could be transformed into non-peaceful use are often exported without much control. The NPT Review Conference in 1985 urged countries exporting nuclear material or technology to demand that the importing State ensured adequate safeguards of operation. But Argentina accepted an offer for a nuclear reactor from Germany with no safeguard conditions rather than a cheaper offer from Canada demanding full safeguards on the nuclear industry.[77]

Trade in conventional arms presents different problems from trade in nuclear material. It is probably only in conventional weapons that States have a clearly legitimate interest in purchasing arms for defence interests. It may no longer be possible to arrive at international treaties restricting access to arms in certain regions.[78]

International society has an interest in ensuring that the arms trade does not expand into furnishing too many breakaway groups

---

[75] 6 Hackworth 267.   [76] *Ibid.*   [77] *New Scientist*, 3 October 1985, 26.
[78] E.g. the 1890 Brussels Act prohibited imports of certain firearms into certain areas of Africa; the 1906 Act of Algeçiras prohibited the import of firearms into Morocco; the 1919 St Germain Draft Convention on Control of Arms Trade, the 1925 Geneva Draft Convention on Arms Trade, and the 1929 Draft Convention on International Supervision of Arms Manufacturing laid down rules for export licences for arms and other restraining rules; none of the latter Draft Conventions came into force.

with ready access to arms. When arms are sold to the Third World, industrialised States are indeed often content that such arms sales will bring in foreign exchange and enhance employment. SIPRI surveys transfers to the Third World of 'major' weapons, for example aircraft, missiles, armoured vehicles and ships. But there is a clear connection between the arms trade and the risk of armed conflict in areas to which the arms have been imported.[79]

However, there is, as yet, little State control of the arms trade. Even when sanctions are imposed for all goods to a particular country, as in the case of Rhodesia, arms find their way there, often through several third parties ostensibly indicated on the letters of credit and bills of lading and other title documents. Some collective undertakings, for example the Ayacucho Agreement of 1974,[80] concern the limitation of arms and provide for an end to the acquisition of arms for offensive purposes on a regional basis. But the agreement concerns only arms supply exceeding what is needed for defence purposes and poses, as such, many problems of identification.[81]

iv. *Peaceful settlement of disputes*

Direct negotiations are often the most effective way of solving a dispute,[82] especially by preventing the escalation of problems, tackling issues as they arise.

If a dispute grows in proportion a third State or the Secretary General of the United Nations may offer their *bona officia*[83] to assist

---

[79] Cf. the activities of the US Arms Control and Disarmament Agency (ACDA). For trade in conventional weapons see J. Turner, *Arms in the '80s*, Stockholm (SIPRI), 1986, and R. Yakemchouk, 'Le transit international des armes de guerre', RGDIP, 1979, 350. But other problems arise as arms production in the Third World increases; many States will not then rely on arms imports, see M. Brzoska and T. Ohlson, *Arms Production in the Third World*, London (SIPRI), 1985; for new enrichment methods facilitating nuclear arms production, see A. S. Krass, P. Boskma, B. Elzen and W. A. Smit, *Uranium Enrichment and Nuclear Weapon Proliferation*, London (SIPRI), 1986. On suggestions that arms transfers should be conditional on training in the Law of War see the discussion of the Lieber Group in *ASIL*, 'The responsibility for training foreign military personnel', *ASIL*, 1984, 1.

[80] Between eight Latin American States, Argentina, Bolivia, Chile, Colombia, Ecuador, Paraguay, Peru and Venezuela.

[81] Above, p. 95.

[82] Cf. S. L. Kass, 'Obligatory negotiation in international organisations', *CanYIL*, 1965, 36ff.

[83] V. Pechota, *The Quiet Approach: a Study of the Good Offices Exercised by the United Nations Secretary General in the Cause of Peace*, New York, 1972; D. Bindschedler-Robert, 'Les bons offices dans la politique étrangère de la Suisse', in *Handbuch der Schweizerischen Aussenpolitik*, 1975, 679.

the reaching of an agreement, normally by approaching each party separately to discuss a potential solution of the problem.

The third party may also take part by consulting with the two parties and proposing solutions to the negotiating parties; such assistance is usually referred to as 'mediation'.[84] The two methods can be combined, as in the border war between Kenya and Somalia in 1967 when President Nyerere of Tanzania offered a venue for talks in Arusha by good offices and President Kaunda of Zambia mediated.

A more institutionalised system of investigation is also used. When the dispute is about questions of fact, a fact-finding commission may be useful to ascertain the background objectively.[85] Sometimes such commissions are entrusted with both the task of fact-finding and with mediation and thus perform what is commonly called conciliation services.[86]

Hague Conventions I of both 1899[87] and of 1907[88] both provided for the solution of disputes by *bona officia* and mediation and the parties agreed to attempt such a solution before resorting to any armed force. Contracting parties also agreed that efforts by third parties to settle their disputes by such negotiation would not be regarded as any unlawful intervention. The Convention of 1907 also provided for assistance by fact-finding commissions, without any obligations for the parties, however, to refer disputes to such bodies.

A number of bodies have been established for conciliation purposes, for example under the Bryan Treaties[89] and under the auspices

---

[84] W. Schücking, *Das völkerrechtliche Institut der Vermittlung*, Kristiania, 1923; N. Politis, *'L'avenir de la médiation'*, RGDIP, 1910, 130; L. L. Randolph, *Third Party Settlement of Disputes in Theory and Practice*, New York, 1973; D. R. Young, *The Intermediaries, Third Parties in International Crises*, Princeton, 1967; cf. J. Burton, *Conflict and Communication in International Relations*, New York, 1969. See below, p. 325 on mediation for the purpose of ensuring implementation of treaties on the Law of War.

[85] See, e.g., W. J. Shore, *Fact-finding in the Maintenance of Peace*, Dobbs Ferry, New York, 1970; N. Politis, 'Les commissions internationales d'enquête', RGDIP, 1912, 149; T. Bensalah, *L'enquête international dans le règlement des conflits*, Paris, 1976.

[86] J. P. Cot, *La conciliation internationale*, Paris, 1968; H. Wehberg, 'Die Vergleichkommissionen im modernen Völkerrecht', in *Festgabe Makarov*, Stuttgart, 1958, 551; G. Revel, 'Rôle et caractère des commissions de conciliation', RGDIP, 1931, 564; J. Efremoff, 'Organisation de la conciliation comme moyen de prévenir la guerre', 59 *RCADI* 1937, i, 103; F. S. Hamzeh, *International Conciliation*, Amsterdam, 1965; D. Schindler, *Die Schiedgerichtbarkeit seit 1914*, Zurich, 1937, 176ff; F. M. van Asbeck, 'La tâche et l'action d'une commission de conciliation', *NedTIR*, 1956, 1; F. Castberg, *Mellemfolkelig Rettspleie*, Oslo, 1925, 86; E. Hambro, *Folkerettespleie*, Oslo, 1956, 68; C. C. Hyde, 'The place of commissions of inquiry and conciliation treaties in the peaceful settlement of international disputes', BYIL, 1929, 96.

[87] Above, p. 54.   [88] Above, p. 54.   [89] Above, p. 33 *AJIL*, 1939 suppl., 861.

of the League of Nations.[90] The Charter of the United Nations provides ample provisions for the peaceful settlement of disputes.[91]

Arbitration[92] and judicial settlement, as encouraged by the Hague Conventions of 1899 and 1907,[93] are other normal ways of settling disputes peacefully[94] and have grown in importance in modern times. Arbitration has developed into a much used method of resolving disputes.[95] There are obvious reasons for referring disputes to the International Court of Justice,[96] although the recent lack of respect for the Orders and Judgments of the ICJ has given cause for concern.[97]

v. Pacts against war

The numerous treaties which forbid the use of force and bind parties not to resort to war[98] also play their part in the peace-preserving process. By making war illegitimate such treaties will restrain some State action. But conventions on prohibitions of force will assist little in the reduction of internal war as the non-State party is not bound by any of the agreements forbidding war and cannot conceive of its behaviour as illegitimate under international law as the traditional version of this system normally[99] does not recognise insurgent groups, as 'international persons'.

[90] But note that many 'conciliation' commissions set up under peace treaties are really concerned with claims, for example regarding property; on such commissions, with quite different functions, see 14 *RIAA* 1965, 13 (Anglo-Italian Commission); *ibid.*, 67 (US–Italian); 16 *ibid.*, 1969, 183 (French–Italian) and *ibid.*, 228, 300 (Netherlands–Italian), and cf. D. Vignes, 'La commmission de conciliation franco-italienne', *AFDI*, 1955, 212.

[91] Articles 24, 35–37 for the Security Council; articles 11, 12 and 14 for the General Assembly. See Stone, *Legal Controls*, 185ff; A. S. Lall, *International Negotiations*, New York, 1966.

[92] See, e.g., A. M. Stuyt, *Survey of International Arbitrations 1794–1970*, Leiden, 1972; J. L. Simpson and H. Fox, *International Arbitration: Law and Practice*, London, 1959; K. S. Carlston, *The Process of International Arbitration*, New York, 1946; P. Chapal, *L'arbitrabilité des différends internationaux*, Paris, 1967; L. B. Sohn, 'The function of international arbitration to-day', 108 *RCADI* 1963, i, 1.

[93] Above, p. 54.

[94] L. Delbez, *Les principes généraux du contentieux international*, Paris, 1962; H. J. Hallier, *Internationale Gerichte und Schiedsgerichte*, Cologne, 1961: see also the European Convention for Peaceful Settlement of Disputes, 320 UNTS 243, which widens the scope of reference to the ICJ.

[95] For example, numerous cases between Iran and the United States are currently dealt with by the Permanent Court of Arbitration in the Hague.

[96] See, e.g., S. Rosenne, *The Law and Practice of the International Court*, 2 vols., Leiden and New York, 1965.

[97] Above, p. 71.   [98] Above, p. 54.   [99] But see below, p. 158.

vi. Interaction by trade and loans

Strong economic interdependence may not be a guarantee against war[100] but it normally has a stabilising effect. Much could be said about the intricate effects of international trade and concessional finance as peace-preserving factors. For example, trade is, at least in the West, usually perceived as the *primus motor* of détente and conducive to prevailing concerns about peaceful activities. As regards the relationship between the Western States themselves, it may be sufficient to point at the activities of GATT,[101] the International Monetary Fund (IMF)[102] and the World Bank[103] on a geographically wider level. On the regional level, customs unions and free trade areas also contribute to linking States together by trade.[104] Many of these organisations also fill a function by institutionalising cooperation.[105] But much is achieved by general world trade to stabilise international patterns, although new trends of 'economic nationalism' may be undermining.[106] Investment finance mechanisms and supplementing machinery for the solution of investment disputes are also important factors in the peace-preserving effort.[107]

vii. Institutional factors

The United Nations may play a role in several different ways in international armed conflicts, using one or more of the mechanisms mentioned above. It has been suggested that the UN will be particularly helpful in opening up issues by public debate; assisting by 'quiet diplomacy', good offices and conciliation; offering inquiries and reports; ascertaining the 'will of the people'; carrying out on-the-spot observation and surveillance; contributing to consensual peace-keeping and policing; offering economic assistance and technical coopera-

[100] E.g. between Germany and other European States in 1939, see J. M. Keynes, *The Economic Consequences of Peace*, New York, 1920, 17.
[101] K. W. Dam, *The GATT Law and International Economic Organisation*, Chicago, 1970; T. Flory, *Le GATT, droit international et commerce mondial*, Paris, 1968; J. H. Jackson, *World Trade and the Law of GATT*, Indianapolis, 1969.
[102] See, e.g., D. Carreau, *Souveraineté et coopération monétaire internationale*, Paris, 1970.
[103] See, e.g., A. Broches, 'International legal aspects of the World Bank'; 98 *RCADI* 1959, 301.
[104] For a survey, see my *Ekonomisk integrationsrätt*, Uppsala, 1973.   [105] Below, p. 100.
[106] J. Mayall, 'Reflections on the "New Economic Nationalism"', 10 *Review of International Studies* 1984, 313.
[107] See my *Finance and Protection of Investments in Developing Countries*, 2nd edn, London, 1987, 133ff.

tion; determining which governments are entitled to be represented on the United Nations; taking sanctions and enforcement measures; elaborating norms and criteria of conduct.[108]

The only item on this useful list which does not quite square with our problem concerning liberation wars and internal wars is perhaps the one concerning representation of governments at the United Nations; for in view of the participation of non-State bodies in treaties on the Law of War[109] and in view of their part in the warfare itself, the participation of 'States' rather than emerging 'nations' in the world organisation is sometimes an anomaly. There is little harm liberation movements could do were they to take part in debates. On the contrary, they might derive some benefit themselves and become more aware of the obligations incumbent upon them. But the world has been too worried to give liberation movements any 'standing' or any particular 'status', almost forgetting that, in reality, certain movements already behave very much like State entities and often, so far, without the entailing duties.[110]

Some international organisations were created precisely to constitute stabilising factors to ensure peace, in a more technical, more precise and probably more effective way than the general methods of the United Nations. This was the case of the European Coal and Steel Community,[111] although this is often forgotten in the maze of contemporary economic regulations. This organisation was established to create a common market, with free circulation of goods, manpower and capital, for the two main base industries of war: coal and steel. No member of the Community can start armaments production without the knowledge of the other parties. The second objective was to create a balancing factor between the two superpowers and to introduce Europe as a third unit, along the lines suggested by Immanuel Kant and Abbé de St Pierre.[112] Later, when nuclear power was thought viable and important as another base industry for war, the European Community for Atomic Energy was formed in 1957, creating a common market for fissile material.[113] The general common market, the European Economic Community, supplemented these two by deep economic integration of the member

---

[108] Schachter, 'The United Nations and Internal Conflict', 409.
[109] Below, p. 158.   [110] Below, p. 165.
[111] P. Reuter, *La Communaute européenne du Charbon et de l'Acier*, Paris, 1952.
[112] On these theories, and for references, see my 'Problem of unequal treaties', 1086.
[113] On the vast literature on the origins of the Communities, see my *Bibliography of International Law*, New York and London, 1976, 523ff.

States. This customs union, with external tariffs to third States, would also effectively reduce any risk of war, at least between the members themselves.

Certain other institutional arrangements greatly contribute indirectly to the prevention of violence and ensuing war. Technical organisations play a much underrated role in this respect. States are interlinked and deeply interdependent on technical cooperation through organisations like the specialised agencies of the United Nations, especially the Universal Postal Union (UPU), the International Telecommunications Union (ITU), the World Health Organization (WHO), the World Meteorological Organization (WMO) and the International Civil Aviation Organization (ICAO). States are inhibited from resorting to violence if it implies the disruption of all the activities of these organisations in their country. It is awkward to be outside the postal or telecommunication networks (under UPU and ITU), or without cooperation in health matters (under WHO), and it would be hazardous to continue civil aviation operations without the rules of the ICAO.[114]

Another peace-preserving factor is the vertical displacement of representatives of States in organisations: it is not normally the foreign ministries who send delegates to the technical organisations, but the post offices, telecommunications departments, health ministries and meteorological departments. This means that the integrating network ties together State administration at a level lower than that of normal external contacts, i.e. lower than the *niveau* of the foreign ministries. A consequence of this is the integration on a wider organisational basis within member States of organisations. Seen together with common rules of simple majority votes, or 'contracting out' procedures, dispensing with any further form of State approval,[115] the new law of organisations represents substantial technical peace-preserving guarantees.

[114] On the activities and powers of these organisations, see my *Law Making*, 217–329.
[115] For a detailed analysis of these rules and State practice, see *ibid.*, *passim*.

4 THE WAR-WAGING MACHINERY

A. THE RESOURCES OF STATES

States have permanent forces and assets which are put at their disposal in war. Other belligerents lack these resources and this explains why, for example, guerilla wars are fought on land, and not at sea or in the air; for guerillas do not have warships or aeroplanes.

States use their forces, military aeroplanes[1] and other transport and equipment. It is particularly important to set out what a warship implies as such ships form an important part of the war-waging machinery.

There is, with regard to ships, a problem similar to that of distinction between civilians and combatants.[2] Ships operated by navies are of two kinds. First, there are fighting ships, including auxiliary cruisers and converted merchantmen. Secondly, there are auxiliary ships of all descriptions. These ships are public ships. They are all commanded by commissioned officers of the fighting fleet, manned by a crew subject to military discipline, bear external marks distinguishing their nationality, listed in the list of warships of the belligerent nations and, finally, they observe the laws and customs of the Law of War.[3]

Merchantmen can be converted into warships on the condition that they comply with all the characteristics of fighting ships.[4] Conversion can, according to French doctrine, take place on the high seas,[5] although this has been contested elsewhere.[6] By being absorbed

---

[1] On the importance of identification markings, see my 'Foreign warships and immunity for espionage', 65.

[2] Below, p. 106.

[3] Cf. Convention 1982 on the Law of the Sea, article 29. See further on the status of warships, my 'Foreign warships', 60ff.

[4] Hague VII 1907, articles 1–6; *The Kronprinz Wilhelm, AD*, 1929–30, 510.

[5] Rousseau, *Conflits armés*, 223.

[6] On the conversion of the Russian merchantmen *The Smolensk* and *The Petersburg* in the Red Sea in the Russian–Japanese War see 'Chronique, Communication de F. Rey', *RGDIP*, 1909, 401 at 509.

in the navy of a State converted ships are in a different class from privateering ships, which under special *lettres de marque* had formerly been authorised to attack enemy merchant vessels.[7] A third group of ships often employed by navies is composed of merchant ships under charter which carry out services, like carrying provisions and supplies, for a limited time. Such ships are usually held to remain private ships.[8]

Merchantmen may carry defensive armament but, in order not to be classified as converted vessels, such armaments must be light.[9] However, in earlier German doctrine at least, any armed ship is considered as a warship[10] although this is probably contrary to generally accepted opinion.[11]

B. BELLIGERENTS AND COMBATANTS

The State is, say some writers, the sole source of the 'right' to use violence.[12] It is certainly the traditional war-waging machine.[13]

If war is defined as a state of armed conflict between States it follows, to those who accept this definition, that the 'subjects' of belligerence can only be States.[14] But even traditionalists admit, on reflection, that groups of citizens, for example those recognised as belligerents in civil war,[15] can wage war. Even other groups, of some consolidated structure,[16] can be belligerents, as has been amply demonstrated in contemporary warfare in Korea, in Vietnam or in the Middle East.

International organisations can also be belligerents. Some writers hold that it is somehow incompatible with the tasks of the United Nations to claim that the organisation is involved in a war.[17] But

---

[7] Privateering was forbidden by the Declaration of 1856, below, p. 265. On the practice see G. G. Wilson, 'Conversion of merchant ships into warships', 2 *AJIL* 1908, 271.

[8] *The Princess Alice*, 6 Hackworth 447; 23 *AJIL* 673; but *The Locksun*, a collier ship, was held not to be a merchantman, *ibid.*

[9] Cf. Scott, 'The execution of Captain Fryatt', 10 *AJIL* 1916, 865.

[10] Strupp-Schlochauer, *Wörterbuch des Völkerrecht*, 1920, 503.

[11] Rousseau, *Conflits armés*, 226.

[12] M. Weber, 'Legitimacy, politics and the state', in H. Gerth and C. W. Mills (eds.), *From Max Weber: Essays in Sociology*, New York, 1958, 77, reprinted in W. E. Connolly (ed.), *Legitimacy and the State*, Oxford, 1984, 33.

[13] Above, p. 33, and below p. 105.

[14] F. Berber, 3 *Lehrbuch des Völkerrechts, Kriegsrecht*, Munich, 1977, 5.

[15] Above, p. 35.   [16] On the threshold, see above, p. 18.

[17] A. D. McNair and D. V. Watts, *The Legal Effects of Wars*, 4th edn, Cambridge, 1966, 45.

surely the peace-keeping efforts of the United Nations[18] do not alter the factual situation in which the United Nations intervenes and it would seem illogical to impute any special character to a conflict because of an intervention by the UN when that situation already exists.

On the other hand, there might be wars in which the United Nations only *appeared* to intervene but where the organisation was not really a belligerent. This was, for example, the case in Korea where the UN appeared as an umbrella for collective State action.[19] There have been other cases where the distinction is sometimes difficult to draw between collective action and action by an organisation. For example, the Inter-American Peace Force in the Dominican conflict in 1965 consisted of units from States and was probably a collective body for intervention purposes.[20]

Some claim that international organisations in general lack the competence to wage wars, with the notable exception of the United Nations.[21] The reason for this exception would be that article 42 of the Charter expressly foresees forceful action by the Security Council which might involve the use of armed forces of the organisation.[22]

There is no reason why other organisations could not be belligerents and no *a priori* reason why such entities should be excluded as subjects of the laws of war. For example, the planned European Defence Organisation was to have had an army of its own.[23] The forces of NATO, too, are subjected to the laws of war. NATO forces may be recruited on a collective basis from the participating members. However, there is no doubt that the organisation has 'international personality', even by the stringent traditional tests.[24] And the troops that NATO has at its disposal gradually lose their national ties, as do the contingents to the UN forces, in favour of allegiance to the unified command. The same, perhaps to a lesser extent, may be said for the troops of the Warsaw Pact.[25] The troops operating under

[18] On the Peace-Keeping Forces, see R. Higgins, *United Nations Peace-Keeping Forces, Documents and Commentary*, 4 vols., Oxford, 1976–81; Seyersted, *United Nations Forces in the Law of Peace and War*, D. W. Bowett, *United Nations Forces: a Legal Study of UN Practice*, London, 1964.

[19] See S. Bastid, *Cours de droit international*, Paris, 1951–2, 340; R. R. Baxter, 'Constitutional forms and some legal problems of international military command', 29 *BYIL* 1952, 335. Cf. my *Law Making*, 60ff; Alibert, *Du droit de se faire justice*, 62–8.

[20] 5 *IRRC* 1965, 303.   [21] *Ibid.*   [22] *Ibid.*

[23] See B. Burrows and G. Edwards, *The Defence of Western Europe*, London, 1982; cf. R. Aron and D. Lerner, *La querelle de la CED*, Paris, 1956.

[24] CLBV, 'La personalité juridique de l'OTAN', *AFDI*, 1955.

[25] L. Gelberg, 'Uklad Warszawski', *Studium prawno miedzynarodowe*, Warsaw, 1957.

the United Nations aegis in Korea may fall into a slightly different category, not being forces of the United Nations – as the decision to take action had been taken against the veto of the USSR. The units were probably troops of the collective operation of the Western powers, but, as such, were detached from their respective home States and placed under a collective command which, at least on an *ad hoc* basis, functioned as an international organisation.[26]

The most important newcomers among belligerents are the internal groups, liberation movements and other non-State conglomerates. Insurgents may always have existed and there may always have been rules for their treatment: insurgents would in many States be tried for treason for their acts against the State. Over the years some rudimentary rules for their protection have evolved by the mechanisms of 'recognised belligerency'[27] There is no doubt that the present-day evolution of internal warfare has subsequently brought about further considerable changes both in the substance of the law and in its ambit.

The rise of the nation State in the fifteenth and sixteenth centuries may originally have put an end to numerous civil wars;[28] today it may be that the unwillingness of many States to grant equal rights to citizens, or to allow consolidated ethnic groups their own territory or minimum rights, actually contributes to an increase in the occurrence and intensity of civil strife. Although a practice of recognition of belligerents in civil war has existed,[29] it was later accepted that entities which have not received such formal recognition may also qualify as belligerents: non-recognition of groups, fronts or entities has not affected their status as belligerents nor the ensuing status of their soldiers as combatants.[30]

It is thus indisputable that States are not the only war-waging agents, or 'war machines', today: internal groupings and non-State entities have also acquired this quality. For more obvious peace-preserving objectives, the United Nations can also take part in war, as might other organisations, whether in their own name or as an umbrella for collective State action.

In inter-State wars the belligerents will be States and the combatants the members of their armed forces. Other entities described above are also potential 'belligerents' and the members of their

---

[26] Cf. above, p. 104.   [27] Above, p. 35.   [28] Above, p. 34.   [29] See above, p. 35.
[30] *The Fjeld*, (1952) (Prize Court of Alexandria) 17 *ILR* 1950, 345; *Diab* v. *AG*, (1952) (Supreme Court of Israel), 19 *ILR* 1952, 550.

armed forces are potential 'combatants'. Thus, it is the combatants who fight on behalf of a belligerent. But even if the members of the armed forces of the various entities are 'potential combatants' they do not become 'actual combatants' for the purposes of the application of the laws of war unless there are hostilities of a certain intensity. It is, for the ambit of the laws of war, of principal importance to have a clear notion of who is, and who is not, a combatant.

C. THE NOTION OF 'COMBATANT'

i. *The principle of distinction*

It is important to have clear criteria to distinguish the civilian population from combatants.[31] Any confusion of the division between the two groups will inevitably endanger protection granted under the Law of War. National manuals on warfare rely on the distinction as an important notion.[32]

ii. *Qualifications for combatant status*

a. *Potential combatants*

(1) Regular forces One distinguishes traditionally between regular troops,[33] whether or not including militia corps,[34] and other

---

[31] On the principles of distinction, see E. Rosenblad, *International Humanitarian Law of Armed Conflict, Some Aspects of the Principle of Distinction and Related Problems*, Geneva, 1979, 61ff.

[32] E.g. United Kingdom, *Manual of Military Law, the Law of War on Land*, pt. 3, article 284; United States, *Laws of Warfare*, 1956, paras. 39–42; France, *Règlement de discipline générale dans les forces armées*, ch. 4, article 34; ch. 2, article 5; Federal Republic of Germany, *Verordnung*, 1961, paras. 64, 68; Switzerland, *Manual des lois et coutumes de la guerre*, 1963, ch. 2, article 25.

[33] See Greenspan, *Modern Law of Land Warfare*, 68; M. S. McDougal and F. P. Feliciano, *Law and Minimum World Public Order: the Legal Regulation of International Coercion*, New Haven, 1961, 544.

[34] As for example in Switzerland. The question of the compostion of regular troops is a matter for municipal law: Hague Regulations, article 1(2); cf. 2 Oppenheim 255. The British Home Guard would probably be considered as part of the regular troops: Stone, *Legal Controls*, 568. If a State incorporates semi-military organisations or police forces in the regular troops it must inform other parties to a 'conflict': Protocol 1, Article 43(3). On civil defence personnel, see *below*, p. 251. Cf. Sweden, Committee on International Law, *Folkrätten i krig, Rättsregler under väpnade konflikter – tolkning, tillämpning och undervisning*, Sveriges offentliga utredningar (SOU), 1984: 56, 76. Yet national conditions can only supplement and not override requirements of international law.

forces. The regular troops form the core of the 'lawful combatants'. Women may form part of such regular troops and enjoy equal privileges.[35] The regular forces also include soldiers of foreign nationality.[36] An ambiguous provision in article 3 of the Regulations provided that armed forces may consist of combatants as well as non-combatants. The latter group consists of members of the armed forces not taking direct part in the hostilities.[37] Article 4(A)1 of 1949 Geneva Convention II eliminates this ambiguity by referring only to 'armed forces'.[38]

The Hague Regulations provide that

The laws, rights, and duties of war apply not only to armies, but also to militia and volunteer corps fulfilling the following conditions:
1. To be commanded by a person responsible for his subordinates;
2. To have a fixed distinctive emblem recognisable at a distance;
3. To carry arms openly; and
4. To conduct operations in accordance with the laws and customs of war.[39]

The 1949 Geneva Conventions also deal with certain similar criteria which distinguish civilians from combatants. Thus, to be a combatant, a person would have to be

(a) ... commanded by a person responsible for his subordinates;
(b) ... having a fixed distinctive sign recognizable at a distance;
(c) ... carrying arms openly;
(d) ... conducting their operations in accordance with the laws of customs of war.[40]

The same requirements applying to irregular forces are presumably also valid for members of regular units.[41] However, this is not clearly spelt out: there is no textual support for the idea that members of regular armed forces should wear uniform. On the other hand, there is ample evidence that this is a rule of law which has been

---

[35] 2 Berber 143.

[36] On the question whether foreign nationals can be forcibly called up, as in the United States during the Vietnam War, see Rousseau, *Conflits armés*, 71.

[37] On the distinction in the Hague Regulations, article 3, between combatants and non-combatants as part of armed forces, see S. E. Nahlik, 'L'extension du statut de combattant à la lumière du Protocole I de Genève de 1977', 164 *RCADI* 1979, iii, 171, 191, 193.

[38] *Ibid.*, 201.   [39] Article 1; 3 NRGT, 3 série, 464.

[40] Article 13 of Geneva Convention I; cf. article 13 of Geneva Convention II, article 4 of Geneva Convention III, and articles 4, 13, 27–34 of Geneva Convention IV.

[41] Similar requirements to those in the Geneva Convention are found in national war manuals for regular forces, e.g. 3 *British Manual of Military Law, The Law of Land Warfare*, 1958, para. 94; US Army, FM 27–10, *Law of Land Warfare*, 1956, 27–8.

applied to a number of situations to ascertain the status of a person.[42] Any regular soldier who commits acts pertaining to belligerence in civilian clothes loses his privileges and is no longer a lawful combatant.[43] 'Unlawful' combatants may thus be either members of regular forces or members of resistance or guerilla movements who do not fulfil the conditions of lawful combatants.[44]

Regular forces of belligerents may include 'militia or volunteer corps'; the Hague Regulations[45] as well as the Geneva Conventions[46] all recognise that such units may be incorporated in the regular forces.

Protocol I of 1977 to the Geneva Conventions,[47] on the other hand, does not rely on 'understood' criteria for regular forces but stipulates that all

combatants are obliged to distinguish themselves from the civilian population while in preparation for or engaged in an attack; even in situations where owing to the nature of the combat an armed combatant cannot distinguish himself, he shall retain his status as a combatant, provided that, in such situations, he carries his arms openly:
(a) during each military engagement, and
(b) during such time as he is visible to the adversary while he is engaged in a military deployment preceding the launching of an attack in which he is to participate.[48]

The Protocol phrases these difficult criteria[49] mainly in order to cover operations of liberation movements,[50] but it enlarges, on the other hand, the notion of 'regular' forces. It defines thus the 'armed forces' of a party to a conflict as

all organized armed forces, groups and units which are under the command responsible to that Party for the conduct of its subordinates, even if that Party is represented by a government or an authority not recognized by an adverse Party. Such armed forces shall be subject to an internal disciplinary system which, *inter alia*, shall enforce compliance with the rules of international law in armed conflict.[51]

---

[42] Cf. below, p. 112.   [43] Cf. my 'Foreign warships', 61 ff.

[44] See R. R. Baxter, 'So-called unprivileged belligerency: spies, guerillas and saboteurs', 28 *BYIL* 1951, 322.

[45] Hague Regulations, article 1 *in fine*; for reference above, p. 107.

[46] Geneva Convention I, article 13(1); Geneva II, article 13(1); Geneva III, article 4(1).

[47] For reference, see above, p. 12. See Schindler and Toman, *Documents*, 2nd edn, 619; A. Roberts and R. Guelff, *Documents on the Laws of Law*, Oxford, 1982, 387. For background to the Protocols, see K. Suter, *An International Law of Guerilla Warfare*, London, 1984.

[48] Article 44.   [49] See below, p. 110 on interpretation.   [50] Below, p. 113.

[51] Article 43(1).

Members of such forces are combatants and 'have the right to participate directly in hostilities'.[52] Although the language is more flexible
than that of the 1949 Conventions, the requirements for combatancy
remain, in spite of what other commentators have suggested,[53] at
least if the various parts of the text in the Protocol are read in context.

(*2*) *Irregular forces* International law has gradually allowed combatant status to those who are not members of regular forces. Under
the Geneva Conventions of 1949 regular forces are thus supplemented by irregular forces, such as other militia or volunteer corps
not forming part of regular troops,[54] as well as members of resistance
movements, which will be considered lawful provided their members
meet certain requirements. These requirements have shifted through
history but may today be of greater importance than ever before,
given the nature of contemporary warfare.

(*i*) *The special position of volunteers* As has been shown, militia and
volunteers may form part of the regular army and they are then part
of the regular forces. In other situations, perhaps more common,
militia and volunteers are separate from the regular forces and form
the core of what is called 'irregular forces'.

The Hague Regulations[55] have already recognised the extension
qualification of 'regular' belligerents to cover militia and volunteers.
As has been shown,[56] the main characteristics of a 'combatant',
which were used to apply to members of the regular forces as well,
were initially designed precisely to cover *certain* irregular forces which
merited inclusion under the ambit of the laws of war.[57] There were
conditions, however: their actions would be connected with their own
State, they had to be headed by a responsible leader, fight openly,
carry a distinctive sign and observe the laws of war.

But there was little certainty about the necessary size of units of
volunteers and whether, in an actual case, a 'volunteer' would be
considered as a 'combatant' or as a 'war criminal'.[58]

'Clandestine' movements, including volunteers, would, in earlier
practice, not qualify as combatants. But citizens who take up arms

[52] Article 43(2).   [53] Above, p. 107.   [54] Cf. above, p. 106.
[55] Article 1; for reference, above, p. 107.   [56] Above, p. 103.
[57] See above, p. 107, on the Hague Regulations, p. 108 on the Geneva Conventions.
[58] In the *List Case*, (1948) US Military Tribunal, *AD*, 1948, 640, the Nuremberg
Military Tribunal held that a civilian who takes part in hostilities is guilty of a crime
against the laws of war and is a 'war criminal'.

against the enemy may be considered a combatant in a *levée en masse*.[59] Under the Armistice Agreement between France and Germany in 1940[60] the French Government undertook to forbid all Frenchmen to fight against Germany on the side of any of Germany's enemies. Those who did not obey this provision would be punished as illegal militia ('franc-tireurs').[61] But other risings against an occupier or invader have been held to be 'legal' and, at times, the persons acting in such events have been considered as combatants if they fulfilled the requirements of the Hague Regulations.

When Geneva Convention III introduced the four requirements for combatant status, it became apparent that 'partisans' and resistance movements would be recognised as belligerents. The new rules were much criticised as they would put an occupying power 'under considerable strain'.[62] But many emphasised that the conditions of the Geneva Convention were adequate as only 'secret and disguised' forces presented any threat to occupying powers.[63]

Protocol I of 1977 to the Geneva Conventions altered the ambit of the category previously considered as 'irregular' by widening the notion of regular forces or, alternatively, by eliminating the distinction between the two concepts.[64] Whether or not the traditional criteria for a combatant, or the new rules, are applied, it is still difficult in practice to ascertain who is a lawful volunteer.

National case law confirms that certain resistance movements are considered as regular troops.[65] But it is uncertain what distinction subsists between such movements and other types of guerilla groups. The former category, for example the French resistance movements, all involve a certain degree of organisation but some, for example the *maquis*, are not associated with 'open' activities as required for regular combatants.[66] On the other hand, certain groups are so consolidated and of such a nature that they are even classified as regular troops. Apart from certain incidents, some involving serious violations of international law, the members of Free French Forces (Forces fran-

---

59   But see below, p. 111, on *levée en masse*.
60   The Agreement of 22 June 1940; see Rousseau, *Conflits armés*, 73.
61   On the meaning of 'franc-tireur', see *ibid.*, 75.
62   Castberg, *Soldater, partisaner og franctirörer*, 13.
63   2 Oppenheim 215.   64   Above, p. 108.
65   *The Bruns Case*, (1946) Norway, Eidsivating Lagmannsrett, 13 *AD* 1946, 391. The case emphasised two of the traditional conditions for such status, i.e. the forces would be held to be regular provided they act openly and obey the laws of war.
66   Above, p. 107.

çaises libres, FFL) were treated as regular belligerents during the Second World War. And, in spite of its undoubtedly clandestine work, some commentators have also placed the *maquis*, the French Interior Forces (Forces françaises de l'intérieur, FFI), or other types of highly organised partisan movements, in a similar category.[67]

(ii) Levée en masse One group which has traditionally been held to be exempt from any requirements imposed on other forces is the civilian population when it rises against an invader as a *levée en masse*.[68] If the population rises spontaneously there is no need to be organised or to wear emblems, although it is required of civilians in such a *levée* to carry arms openly and to comply with the laws of war. Yet, if they do, they should not be treated as marauders or criminals for all they have done has been to spring to the defence of their country.[69] Except for the situation of a *levée en masse*, civilians are considered as non-combatants. They are not entitled to take part in belligerency or to use arms, even in self-defence, against the enemy. In return they enjoy protection under international law.

The spontaneous rising against the enemy has less importance in modern war where the gradual taking of villages, towns and land is not the predominant pattern. But even in traditional situations, the right is very limited: the Hague Regulations[70] indicate that it can be exercised only *before* occupation and some commentators claim that citizens must use their right to *levée* even before an invasion.[71] The right has even been called an 'anomaly' in modern international law.[72] Yet the right to *levée en masse* undoubtedly still exists and may be considered as an expression of the patriotism of the ordinary citizen to repel the enemy.[73]

(iii) Problems relating to the Geneva requirements During the preparatory work of the Geneva Conventions it was not indicated which weapons had to be carried openly and commentators have assumed that the requirement concerned personal hand weapons.[74] But the

[67] Rousseau, *Conflits armés*, 74–5.
[68] See article 2 of Hague Convention IV; Geneva I, article 13(6); Geneva II, article 13(d); Geneva III, article 4A(b). For historical examples, and for the special type where the *levée* is ordered by the government, see Rousseau, *Conflits armés*, 72–3.
[69] Hague Regulations 1(2). Cf. *British Manual*, para. 95.
[70] Article 2.   [71] 2 Oppenheim 258.   [72] Baxter, 'Spies', 335.
[73] F. Bauer, *Krigsforbrytarna infor domstol*, Stockholm, 1944, 1.
[74] Sweden, *Folkrätten i krig*, 82.

conditions imply several relative concepts: at what distance must the weapons be visible? And how far must the 'distance' measure at which distinctive emblems can be seen? In the *List Case*[75] the Soviet star in a cap was not considered sufficiently visible at a distance.

Naturally, the criteria would, in practice, cause considerable problems. Scarcely any of the Second World War resistance movements would have qualified as combatants under the four stringent criteria of the Geneva Conventions.[76] But the criteria cannot be too strictly applied and, as we have seen,[77] certain movements have been treated in practice as belligerents. After all, the hallmark of any resistance movement is concealment.[78] It is probably only in peacetime that there is a clear distinction between civilian and military forces.[79] Yet the principle of distinction between combatant and civilian is at the root of the Law of War.[80]

(iv) Guerillas and the new combatant status There are two separate questions to be considered in the context of guerilla war. One is whether it is legal under international law to conduct war against the established government, as may be the case against an occupier. The second question concerns whether, or under what conditions, the participants in guerilla war, the guerilleros themselves, deserve to be treated as 'combatants' and entitled to any rights as such under international law.

With regard to the first question, we have touched upon relevant problems of legitimacy in a section on revolutionary and resistance wars.[81] It remains to investigate whether individual members of resistance or guerilla forces are 'combatants' under modern international law.

[75] 8 *Trials of the Major War Criminals*, Nuremberg, 1947, 55–9.
[76] Cf. J. Pictet, 'The new Geneva Conventions for the protection of war victims', 45 *AJIL* 1951, 462 at 472. Cf. Baxter, 'So-called unprivileged belligerency', 323.
[77] Above, p. 103.   [78] Cf. G. Best, *Humanity in Warfare*, London, 1980, 327.
[79] Colombia, CDDH/SR.41, vol. 6, 180.
[80] Cf. Rosenblad, *Humanitarian Law*, 61; Cf. Resolutions of the General Assembly of the United Nations 2444 (XXIII), and of the Vienna Conference of the ICRC 1963, Resolution XXIII, 3rd principle. For comments on earlier practice, see L. Nurick, 'The distinction between combatant and non-combatant in the law of war', *AJIL*, 1945, 680; G. I. A. D. Draper, 'Combatant status, the historical perspective', 2 *RDPMDG* 1972, 135ff; M. Veuthey, 'Comportément et statut des combattants', 12 *RDPMDG* 1973, 47; on recent changes in the notion of combatant see W. T. Mallinson and S. V. Mallinson, 'The juridical status of privileged combatant under the Geneva Protocol of 1977', 42 *Law and Contemporary Problems* 1978, 4; Nahlik, 'L'extension', 171.
[81] Above, p. 48.

The principle of distinction[82] is of importance. If a person fulfils the requirements for combatant status he is entitled to the 'rights' of a soldier, notably to enjoy prisoner of war status if captured; if he does not fulfil the requirements, he is an 'unlawful combatant' and may be shot. Even a third position has been suggested in case law: resistance fighters may, if they do not wear uniform or carry their arms openly, still be 'lawful' provided they use no forbidden weapons and act in accordance with the laws of war. But it has been suggested that, although their activity is permitted by international law, they may still not be entitled to any rights as 'soldiers' and may therefore be shot if captured.[83] In the view of such anomalous repercussions, it is of little comfort to the resistance fighter to know that his activity is 'lawful'.

During the Vietnam conflict it was argued that the conditions for combatants ought to be changed so that the FLN guerillas could more easily comply with the requirements for combatants: as the rules stood they were unable to follow them and therefore 'lost' their potential protection under international law.[84] According to a suggestion made in 1970,[85] one method which could be chosen for allowing combatant status to guerillas would imply the use of relevant criteria for *levée en masse*.[86] This was not the path chosen; instead the problem was tackled in the 1977 Protocols.

Protocol I of 1977 recognises guerillas as belligerents[87] provided they act under responsible command and provided they are subject to discipline which enforces relevant rules of international law. Protocol I of 1977 even recognises that it is not always possible for guerillas to distinguish themselves from the civilian population and provides that they will still retain the status of combatants provided they carry arms openly during each military engagement and during such time as they are visible to the adversary while engaged in military operations preceding an attack.[88] But Protocol I does not really reduce the four conditions in the Geneva Conventions[89] but rephrases them. The requirement of distinctive military signs is still applicable; to

---

[82] Above, p. 106.
[83] Norway, *The Bruns Case*, (1946) (Eidsivating lagmansrett) 13 *AD* 1946, 391, in this part not reversed on appeal; the Supreme Court did not comment on this curious reasoning.
[84] Sweden, *Folkrätten i krig*, 80.
[85] G. I. A. D. Draper, 'The legal classification of belligerent individuals', in Centre Henri Rolin, *Droit humanitaire et conflits armés*, 149.
[86] Cf. above, p. 111.   [87] Articles 43(1) and 44(3).
[88] Article 44(3).   [89] Above, p. 108.

wear some rudimentary form of uniform[90] has, by tradition, been a
hallmark and a condition of combatant status[91] and for prisoner of
war status.[92] Only in exceptional circumstances may a combatant
not distinguish himself from the civilian population. Due to the difficulties caused by the application of the Geneva Conventions with
respect to the requirement of 'openly' carried arms,[93] this condition
has now been revised to imply that arms must be carried openly
during actual fighting. Although hailed, and criticised, as an innovation, this is not an unusual rule in the Law of War: warships have
often been thought to have a right to use false flags until they engage
in action.[94] The suspension of the duty of distinction applies to combatants only in extreme cases, whereas permission to allow warships
to fly false flags was the normal rule.

But some question these rules and claim that marks of insignia and
a duty to carry arms openly are obligations which put the guerilla
fighter at a grave disadvantage. Besides, the very nature of partisan
warfare is against such practice.[95]

The Protocols have not been ratified by an overwhelming number
of States and a number of militarily important States are still missing
from the list of those which are bound.[96] However, the Protocols may
in many respects reflect what the existing law already is and then, in
those parts, be binding, not by virtue of the obligation of the Protocols as treaties, but by virtue of the underlying obligation in previously accepted rules.[97] But with regard to the new combatant status
it must be questioned whether the requirements have actually been
relaxed by Protocol I. It is submitted that similar rules to those of the
Geneva conditions still apply for the status of a combatant, and,
correspondingly, for prisoner of war status.

[90] But a star in a cap is not sufficient, see above, p. 112.

[91] On the transformation of a reconnaissance soldier without a uniform into a common spy see my 'Foreign warships and espionage', 62ff.

[92] *Koi* v. *DPP*, (1968) 2 WLR 723 (PC); *Ali* v. *DPP*, (1968) 3 All ER 488 (PC); Cf.
R. Baxter, 'The Privy Council on the qualifications of belligerents', *AJIL*, 1969, 290; S.
Elman, 'Prisoners of war under the Geneva Convention', 18 *ICLQ* 1969, 178.

[93] Above, p. 111.   [94] See below, p. 260, also for criticism of this way of warfare.

[95] I. P. Trainin, 'Voprosy partizanskoi voiny v meshdunarodnom prave', in *Izvestija
Akademii Nauk SSSR*, 1945, 4, 1; Trainin, 'Questions of guerilla warfare in the law of
war', 534; F. I. Koshevnikov and V. A. Romanov, *Meshdunarodnoe pravo*, Moscow,
1966, 614.

[96] States have ratified the Protocols (1987); of the major powers, France has ratified
Protocol II. On declarations on non-applicability to nuclear weapons, see below,
p. 201. On application of the Protocols in internal wars, see further below, p. 170.

[97] Cf. my *Concept*, 104 and *Essays*, 117, on an underlying basis of obligation.

The combatant still has to be subjected to internal discipline under a system which applies the rules of war. Some writers claim that guerillas must act under some 'responsible quasi-governmental authority' in order to enjoy protection under Protocol I.[98] Naturally, the application of these rules will inevitably cause numerous problems in practice. There is, for example, little in Protocol I which prevents guerillas from living as civilians.[99] The ICRC itself had argued that 'openness' must be a *conditio sine qua non* for privileges of belligerency, i.e. unless guerillas behaved 'openly' they could not enjoy privileges of combatants. Some commentators have supported this view, dismissing any alternative regulation.[100]

It is a specific feature of guerilla warfare that members of guerilla groups merge, intermittently, with the civilian population.[101] As late as the Nuremberg trials it was thought that guerillas and resistance movements would not be privileged, as members of resistance forces 'must accept the increased risks involved in this mode of fighting'.[102] Germany sought to deny the status of combatants to de Gaulle's Free French forces and claimed that they were no more than a camouflage to overthrow the legitimate government of Marshal Pétain.[103]

It may be correct to assume that protection of the civilian population must be undermined if there is no clear distinction between civilians and combatants. However, guerilla movements have often in the past acted to safeguard the civilian population, together with whom they often have a common cause, by, for example, staying away from a village to save inhabitants from victimisation.[104] Occasionally they have considered tactics which are not related to any inhabited area.[105]

There has been a gradual confusion of the concepts resistance/ guerilla/terrorist movements. The term chosen sometimes merely indicates the attitudes of the beholder. What is important to assert, however, is that the Protocols of 1977 afford protection to both resistance

[98] Y. Dinstein, 'The new Geneva Protocols: a step forward or backward?' *YWA*, 1979, 267.
[99] Best, *Humanity in Warfare*, 327.
[100] Y. Dinstein, 'Another step in codifying the laws of war', *YWA*, 1974, 285.
[101] See F. O. Miksche, *Secret Forces, the Technique of Underground Movement*, London, 1950, ch. 2.
[102] *US* v. *List*, 8 *Trials of the Major War Criminals*, 1949, 34, 58.
[103] Best, *Humanity in Warfare* 239. Cf. R. Miller, *The Law of War*, Lexington, 1975, 31.
[104] Best, *Humanity in Warfare*, 242.
[105] P. Boissier, *Histoire du Comité International de la Croix-Rouge de Solferino à Tsoushima*, Paris, 1963, 116.

movements and to guerilla action insofar as members of both these types of forces will have the status of lawful belligerents, under certain conditions, and therefore qualify for prisoner of war status, for example. It appears possible to comply with the provisions on combatant status under the Protocols of 1977 without significantly reducing the protection of civilians.[106]

Protocol I of 1977 affords no protection for terrorists,[107] nor does it authorise soldiers to conduct military operations disguised as civilians. In practice it is obviously difficult to identify terrorists and distinguish them from lawful combatants: surely members of resistance and guerilla movements often use precisely terrorist tactics and could easily be subsumed under a terrorist concept by their adversary. However, Protocol I does give members of forces operating in occupied territory an 'incentive' to distinguish themselves from civilians when preparing to carry out an attack.[108]

The French delegation wished to extend protection to resistance movements even beyond the actual limits of Protocol I and claimed, during the Diplomatic Conference leading up to the 1977 Protocols, that even such resistance members who are not ever distinguishable from the civilian population, the true 'underground' workers, should be protected too and not only the more established 'maquis', 'partisan' or resistance movements.[109]

Some have forcefully criticised the provisions on guerillas of Protocol I, claiming that 'Giving quarter to a handful of guerilleros who camouflage themselves as civilians may have its merits, but the outcome will be counterproductive from a humanitarian standpoint if, as a result, a multitude of civilians be subjected to the rigours of total war.'[110] Yet the provisions on guerilla warfare in Protocol I must be seen in the context of both the extremely limited ambit of article 1(4) to which the Protocols apply[111] and in relation to the increased protection the civilian population enjoys, in any event, against reprisals.[112]

Protocol II, which has as its particular focus internal conflicts, appears to adopt even fewer criteria for combatant status. The Protocol applies to conflict between the armed forces of a contracting party and 'dissident armed forces or other organised armed groups which,

[106] United States, CDDH/SR.41, vol. 6, 149.   [107] Above, p. 19.   [108] *Ibid.*
[109] CDDH/III/SR.33–36, Annex, vol. 14, 537. The statement is ironic in view of France's final conclusion that Protocol I violates a State's right to self-determination, see further below, p. 201.
[110] Dinstein, 'Another step in codifying the laws of war', 284–5.
[111] See below, p. 161.   [112] See below, p. 254.

under responsible command exercise such control over a part of its territory as to enable them to carry out sustained and concerted military operations and to implement this Protocol'.[113] The question of the threshold of application of Protocol II will be dealt with later,[114] but at this stage one may note that the result of the actions of a dissident army, for example that they control territory and are able to carry out sustained military operations, does not indicate what criteria shall be applied to combatant status. In the absence of specific requirements one is either obliged to revert to the basic conditions of the 1949 Conventions or, by analogy, to apply the provisions in Protocol I.

Even if the more liberal rules of Protocol I were to be applied for guerillas to qualify as combatants there would, in practice, be considerable problems. On balance, however, protection of guerillas would uplift the overall level of humanitarian law.

There is no doubt that the new definition in Protocol I of 1977 will remedy a defective law.[115] It was unsatisfactory to have a lack of symmetry, for example, between the concept 'prisoner of war' and 'combatant': for example, Geneva Convention III[116] defined the former concept without referring to the latter term.

On the other hand, the criteria of a combatant are still vague and difficult to apply in practice. There is no doubt that there is still confusion as to who is a combatant and who is a civilian due to the lack of stringent criteria for qualification as a combatant.[117]

Another case for erosion of the important fundamental rule of distinction is the emergence of weapons of mass destruction which assume that everyone is a target and thus involved in the war.[118] For rather than allowing such weapons to change the concept of distinction, the presumption should be that such weapons are incompatible with international law.[119]

The requirement of uniform, or some form of military insignia, as required by earlier and contemporary practice, is essential for combatant status in conjunction with other requirements retained by the 1977 Protocols.[120]

[113] Article 1(1).   [114] See p. 170ff
[115] G. Abi-Saab, 'Les mécanismes de mise en oeuvre du droit humanitaire', 82 *RGDIP* 1978, 177.
[116] Article 4; for reference see above, p. 12.
[117] Cf. M. F. Furet, *La guerre et le droit*, Paris, 1979, 129ff.
[118] Rousseau, *Conflits armés*, 81.   [119] Below, p. 195.
[120] See comments above, p. 114.; cf. definition of war, above, p. 23.

(3) Mercenaries A category which is exempt from protection is that of mercenaries.[121] However, the definition of mercenaries is so narrow that many will fall outside its ambit:[122] For example, only those who, having been recruited in another country join military forces for 'personal gain'. But who will decide what motivates a man?

Third World States felt strongly about prohibiting mercenaries, if possible, 'throughout the world'.[123] Many such States held that the text of the Protocols should have been 'stronger', to oblige States to forbid recruitment and training as well.[124] Angola even made a special Declaration on ratification that, in the opinion of that State, anyone who trains or recruits mercenaries will be considered as a mercenary criminal as well as States which allow such activities to take place in the territory under their jurisdiction.[125] One should remember that 'the historical experience of many peoples bears witness to the fact that mercenaries violate all international laws concerning human rights'[126]

A few States emphasised that even mercenaries should enjoy some protection under the Protocol.[127] Later, other commentators pointed out that it is hardly compatible with the rules of the Law of War to single out a group like mercenaries, who after all constitute a category taking part in traditional warfare, for unequal and unprotective treatment.[128] Presumably mercenaries are entitled under the fundamental rights of the Protocol[129] to, for example, fair judicial process. To exempt them, however, from all substantive provisions, for example concerning prisoner of war status, does appear to be contrary to the demands of modern humanitarian law. On the other hand, the category as defined by the Protocol is so narrow that many will, in practice, still fall into protected categories as their motivation cannot be assessed by others. There is, however, a danger that parties to conflicts will assume that a soldier is motivated, for example, by 'personal gain' when he is not, and therefore exempt an entitled person from due protection under the Protocol.

---

[121] Article 47.   [122] Cf. Best, *Humanity in Warfare*, 375, and note 83.
[123] Afghanistan, CDDH/SR.41, vol. 6, 175. Cf. USSR, *ibid.*, 203.
[124] Senegal, *ibid.*, 177; Cf. Mozambique, *ibid.*, 193, referring to the Angola Trials in 1976 which 'shed new light on the scope and the criminal nature of the system of mercenaries'.
[125] See Declaration on ratification, 20 September 1984, to the Depository of the Swiss Government (unpublished), Annex III.
[126] Libya, CDDH/SR.41, vol. 6, 199.   [127] Australia, *ibid.*, 175.
[128] P. de la Pradelle, 'Le droit humanitaire des conflits armés', *RGDIP*, 1978, 28.
[129] Article 75.

(4) Spies Another group exempted from prisoner of war status is spies,[130] whether or not they have acted as combatants. Traditionally, international law attaches decisive importance to whether or not a person is wearing a uniform.[131] A soldier who is not wearing uniform runs the risk of being treated as a spy.[132]

A new distinction is made in Protocol I of 1977 between spies and those members of the armed forces who gather information in occupied territory where they are resident. Such persons will not be considered as spies provided they do not employ false pretences or act through clandestine means.[133] It appears that even spies may claim certain fundamental guarantees under the Protocol such as due process of law.[134]

D. LEGAL EFFECTS OF COMBATANT STATUS

The main effect of being a lawful combatant is entitlement to prisoner of war status.[135] Unlawful combatants, on the other hand, are a legitimate target for any belligerent action but, if they are captured, they are not entitled to any prisoner of war status. They are also personally responsible for any action they have taken and may thus be prosecuted and convicted for murder if they have killed an enemy soldier. They are often summarily tried and enjoy no protection under international law.[136]

Combatants are entitled to privileged status even if they belong to a State which has not been recognised.[137] During the Conferences in 1907 it was argued by the Great Powers that there was only need for one distinction: that between regular forces and civilians. Regular forces would, they said, be entitled to far-reaching privileges under international law, whereas resistance movements and other irregular movements would not be protected. Such attitudes would naturally lead to weaker resistance in countries under occupation. Smaller States claimed, at the Conferences, that civil defence units and resistance movements also play an important role in the defence of the State and that they, too, ought to be considered as combatants.[138] But, as has been shown,[139] state practice recognised certain irregular

[130] Article 46(1).   [131] See my 'Foreign warships', 53.   [132] *Ibid.*   [133] Article 46(2).
[134] Article 75.   [135] See further below, pp. 281ff.   [136] Cf. my 'Foreign warships', 62.
[137] Geneva Convention III, article 4A(3). See below on liberation movements, pp. 282ff.
[138] T. Wulff, *Handbok i folkrätt under krig, neutralitet och ockupation*, Stockholm, 1980, 77.
[139] Above p. 108.

soldiers during the Second World War. After the amendments and clarification of the law in the Geneva Conventions of 1949 and in the 1977 Protocols, it is now fairly established that guerillas also, under certain conditions, may acquire combatant status. However, as long as ratifications of Protocol II are not forthcoming in any number and from any major States, it is questionable to what extent guerillas, or 'detainees' when captured, may acquire prisoner of war status.[140]

[140] Cf. below, p. 281.

5 THE NATURE OF THE LAWS OF WAR

A. THE HISTORICAL BACKGROUND

There is evidence that some ancient civilisations prohibited certain methods of warfare; agreements on the treatment of prisoners of war were concluded in Egypt around 1400 BC.[1] The Manu laws in India prohibited, around 500 BC, the use of poisoned and other inhumane weapons.[2] But elsewhere barbaric practices often accompanied a victory in war. The maxim *vae victis* implied that a vanquished nation could expect little mercy. There was, for example, a practice in Abyssinia of cutting off the right hand and the left foot to show who had lost a battle.[3] The influence of religion on the regulation of warfare is readily recognised in modern times.[4] Philosophers like St Augustine and Thomas Aquinas had considerable influence on the historical development of humane warfare, as did certain specific Papal Edicts like the prohibition of certain weapons by Innocentius II in 1139 during the Second Lateran Council and the prescription by Alexander III of humane treatment of prisoners of war in 1179 during the Third Lateran Council.[5] There were early secular attempts like the rules issued in the fourteenth century by Casimir the Great of Poland[6] and by Richard II of England.[7]

[1] A Swedish Working Group Study, *Conventional Weapons, their Deployment and Effects from Humanitarian Aspects, Recommendations for the Modernization of International Law*, Stockholm, 1973, 11.

[2] *Ibid.*

[3] But Europeans could usually avoid such a fate by special treaties which secured sums of money for the treatment of European prisoners of war. G. W. Gong, *The Standard of Civilization in International Society*, Oxford, 1984, 122–3.

[4] *Ibid.*

[5] Cf. below, n. 75, p. 242. M. A. Marin, 'The evolution and present status of the laws of war', 92 *RCADI* 1957, ii, 656; H. Coursier, 'L'évolution du droit internationale humanitaire', 99 *RCADI* 1960, i, 380.

[6] A. Gorbiel, 'The protection of war victims under Polish legislation, up to the end of the eighteenth century', *IRRC*, 1975, 273.

[7] J. F. C. Fuller, *Armament and History: a Study of the Influence of Armaments on History from the Dawn of Classical Warfare to the Second World War*, London, 1946, 62; Marin, 'Evolution', 656.

The rules of chivalry[8] governed armed conflicts between knights but probably only because they considered themselves as equals.[9] If taken prisoner they were often released for ransom; the ordinary foot soldier had, on the other hand, no such treatment.[10]

The captor could initially keep the ransom for himself but, slowly, a new system developed which implied that if the captive was a person of some consequence the State, the king or the prince would consider him his own 'property'.[11] Later officers, but not privates, received privileged treatment by being released against ransom whereas the ordinary soldier did not.[12] The discrimination in treatment between officers and men could, however, be inverted as it was during the French Revolution. Thus, a French Decree of 1792 allowed reprisals only against enemy officers as these would be 'class enemies' but not against common soldiers who may defect to join the revolutionary cause.[13]

Some treaties during the seventeenth century showed some concern for non-combatants and provided that, for example, women and children, including boys under 12, would be released without ransom.[14] Unilateral regulations for armed forces also contributed to increased humanity in war.[15] Developments in philosophy during the

[8] See A. Nussbaum, *A Concise History of the Law of Nations*, New York, 1961, 18; J. F. Thomson, *Economic and Social History of Europe in the Later Middle Ages*, New York, 1960, 3; Fuller, *Armament*, 60; some claim that chivalry reappeared in the First World War, 'at least in air combat', J. M. Spaight, *Air Power and War Rights*, London, 1933, 107.

[9] For example, when Richard Lionheart's horse had been killed, Sultan Saladin is said to have provided him with another one before they resumed fighting, cf. statement by France, CDDH, III/SR.33–36, Annex V, vol. 14, 537.

[10] A. Gardot, 'Le droit de la guerre dans l'oeuvre des capitaines français du XVIe siècle', 72 *RCADI* 1948, i, 493. See, in general, Marin, 'Evolution', 655; Coursier, 'L'évolution', 380; A. Vagts, *A History of Militarism*, London, 1959; M. Locker, 'Das Kriegsgefangenrecht inbesonderes nach römischen und heutigen Recht', diss., Breslau, 1913.

[11] J. M. Spaight, *War Rights on Land*, London, 1911, 264.

[12] E.g. W. E. S. Flory, *Prisoners of War, a Study in the Development of International Law*, Washington, DC, 1942, 55. There was a price list of various grades of officers: C. Parry, 19 *The Consolidated Treaty Series*, New York, 1969, 79–93; see further H. P. Tuscher, *Die völkerrechtliche Regelung des Loses des Kriegsopfer vor dem Abschluss der Genfer Konvention von 1964*, Zurich, 1969, 77. The system of ransom survived until well into the nineteenth century, G. F. Martens, *Précis du droit des gens*, Paris, 1864, 241; H. Wheaton, *Elements of International Law*, London, 1866 (ed. 1936), 361; R. J. Phillimore, *Commentaries on International Law*, London, 1885, 164.

[13] 1 NRGT 363; cf. J. Basdevant, *La révolution française et droit de guerre continentale*, Paris, 1901.

[14] See the Treaties between France and the Netherlands 1673, Parry, 12 *The Consolidated Treaty Series*, 457–61, and of 1675, *ibid.*, 13, 379. Cf. articles 23–24 of the Treaty between the United States and Prussia of 1785, Parry, *ibid.*, 49, 349–52.

[15] For example, article 7 of the instructions issued by Catherine the Great in 1778

Age of the Enlightenment also had a mitigating effect on cruel practices in war. Montesquieu wrote, for example, that international law rests on the principle that nations 'doivent se faire dans la paix le plus grand bien et dans la guerre le moins de mal qu'il est possible sans nuire à leurs véritables intérêts'.[16]

Later theorists on war argued that since war is only the means to obtain an objective, that of forcing the enemy to submission, any unnecessary or revengeful destruction of life is not lawful. Plundering and devastation were thus condemned as barbarous and uncivilised, especially since such practices inflict little harm on the government but merely on the citizens.[17] States began, around the middle of the last century, to issue codes for conduct in war reflecting more humanitarian ideas.[18] The United States provided in its instruction for the Army that 'unnecessary or revengeful destruction of life is not lawful'[19] and France issued similar rules.[20] The St Petersburg Declaration was concluded as a treaty in 1868[21] and in 1899 dum-dum bullets were prohibited by another Convention.[22] In 1907 the comprehensive Hague Conventions were concluded on various aspects of warfare.[23] Later developments have included numerous treaties on the prohibitions of specific weapons.[24] All these rules are supplemented by special rules protecting human beings, both by exempting them from being targets of attack[25] an by being assured relief and assistance when in need.

The International Red Cross was created in 1870 to alleviate suffering in war.[26] A forerunner of the Red Cross had existed in Spain since 2 May 1808, the date of the insurrection of the Spaniards against the French, and bore the name Society of the Holy Cross of 2 May. This organisation was still effective during the Second Carlist War in Spain in 1872–6 and lent its support to the official sections of

stipulating that Turkish prisoners of war must be treated with humanity, see G. Butler and S. Maccoby, *The Development of International Law*, London, 1929.

[16] *L'esprit des lois*, i, ch. 3. Numerous writers who refer to this quotation leave out the last words, which introduce an important qualification to the statement.

[17] C. von Clausewitz, *Vom Kriege*, 1834, Bk. 1, ch. 1, 3; Bk. V, ch. 3, 13.

[18] Cf. Q. Wright, *A Study of War*, 2nd edn, Chicago, 1965, 332.

[19] Article 68 of the so-called 'Lieber' Code for Armies in the Field, 1863, named after the stateman and thinker Lieber. A similar code for naval warfare was adopted in 1899.

[20] Règlement 6.5.1859, Journal militaire officiel, no. 17, 243. On similar regulations issued by Russia, see Romberg, *Les belligérants et des prisonniers de guerre*, Paris, 1894, 288.

[21] 18 NRGT 474; below, p. 135.

[22] Hague Declaration 1899, 26 NRGT 2 série 1002, and below, p. 177.

[23] 26 NRGT 2 série 920; 3 NRGT 3 série 360–1002   [24] Below, p. 180.

[25] Below, p. 232.   [26] Boissier, *Histoire du Comité International de la Croix-Rouge*.

the Spanish Red Cross which had been created in various parts of the country since 1870.[27]

The ICRC has become a highly important organisation in contemporary warfare,[28] assisting and alleviating human suffering and contributing, by strict observance of confidentiality,[29] to the development of humanitarian law. It has also become an important catalyst in observing the Law of War.

B. THE FUNCTION OF THE LAWS OF WAR

i. *Force supplements unsatisfactory law*

When Machiavelli advocates force in the international community it is, *inter alia*, because the laws are not sufficient or satisfactory.[30] The 'laws', in this context, are those laws which fail to provide justice, or to provide what is required by one State, above what may be just. We may assume that it signifies 'laws' in general, as Machiavelli explains the behaviour of States by analogy to the behaviour of individuals when the 'laws' fail to satisfy their interests.

What Machiavelli says illustrates that if laws are sufficient for the interests which they serve, the risk of resorting to war will be lessened.[31] By analogy, one may also infer that if the laws of war are adequate for legitimate interests to be protected, then the risk of excessive force and cruelty may be avoided.

There may be occasions when humanitarian rules are prescribed by instinct. Certain African tribes have, it is said, respected occasional rules on non-combatants with respect to those who are wounded or to women and children.[32] But then in other situations they have not. For it is often cruelty, rather than restraint, that comes naturally to man. It is therefore desirable that behaviour is governed

[27] ICRC Bulletin, no. 4, July 1970, 173; see further J. Moreillon, *Le comité international de la Croix-Rouge et la protection des détenus politiques*, Lausanne, 1973, 14.

[28] A. Durand, *Histoire du Comité International de la Croix Rouge, de Sarajevo à Hiroshima*, Geneva, 1978; M. Huber, *The Red Cross, Principles and Problems*, Geneva, n.d.; cf. H. Haug, *Rotes Kreuz*, Stuttgart, 1966; and on specific activities, e.g., Moreillon, *Le comité*.

[29] Below, p. 326.

[30] Machiavelli, *Il Principe*, XVIII, ed. Vertelli, Milan, 1960, 72: 'Dovete adunque sapere como sono due generazioni di combattere: l'uno con le leggi, l'altro con la forza: quel primo é proprio dello uomo, quel secondo delle bestie: ma perché el primo molte volte non basta, conviene recorrere al secondo.'

[31] Although, as illustrated in *Il Principe*, some may wish for more than is justified.

[32] E. G. Bello, *African Customary Humanitarian Law*, Geneva, 1980, 34ff.

by reason rather than by impulse. As Clausewitz remarked, it may well be a fallacy to think that one can defeat an enemy without much bloodshed but then, as he added, 'war is such a dangerous business that the mistakes that come from kindness are the very worst'.[33] But, he continues, wars between 'civilized' nations are governed by the mind, not like the wars between savages which are ruled by passion. If, then, prisoners of war are not put to death, 'it is because intelligence plays a larger part in [the] method of warfare [of civilised nations] and has taught them more effective ways of using force than the crude expression of instinct'.[34] The Law of War must thus be adequate to safeguard the interests of its subjects; and it must be the expression of reason rather than of impulse.

ii. The international element

The Law of War is even more international than the law of peace. In the case of the Law of War, as, for example, case law on prize shows, there is no doubt that even when they appear before municipal courts issues must be dealt with by 'the law of nations' and not by the municipal law of any particular country.[35] Occasionally the Law of War is adapted to local customs,[36] but for the most part rules are of universal application.

On the other hand, each set of rules need not be applicable *in toto* for all interested parties. Treaties may often claim that there is no such right of 'separability'. For example, the Declaration of London of 1909[37] prescribed that its provisions must be treated as a 'whole' and could not be separated. Such a provision is usually inserted in view of the fact that parties have made concessions in consideration of others[38] and it would therefore not be satisfactory if one State could make a reservation[39] concerning a provision to which another con-

[33] Clausewitz, *On War*, 75.   [34] *Ibid.*, 76.

[35] *Le Laux* v. *Eden*, (1781) 2 Dougl. 594, 610, per Buller J. For application of international law in prize cases see *The Elsebe*, (1804) 5 C. Rob, 174, 180; *The Recovery*, (1897) 6 *ibid.*, 341, 348; *The Odessa*, (1915) P. 52, 61; *The Hakan*, (1916) P. 266; *The Zamora*, (1916) AC 77, 91 (PC); cf. *The Consul Corfitzon*, (1917) AC 550; cf. *The Sudenmark*, (1917) AC 620.

[36] Cf. reference above, p. 124, note 32, and M. Khadduri, *War and Peace in the Law of Islam*, Baltimore, 1955; S. V. Viswanatha, *International Law in Ancient India*, Bombay, 1925.

[37] See further below, p. 265, on the substance of the agreement.

[38] Like the modern 'package deal' technique used, *inter alia*, with regard to the 1982 Law of the Sea Convention.

[39] On the problems of fragmentation caused by reservations, a particularly unsatisfactory effect for law-making treaties, see my *Concept*, 104, and my *Essays*, 117.

tracting power attached considerable significance. However, in spite of such provisions, practice shows that a treaty may be applied with regard to certain rules only. This is often the case when a treaty has not come into force, either because of a time element or because it has not received the necessary support. Then certain rules may be selected and applied by States; one example, again, is the 1909 Declaration.[40] But one might suggest that it is not really the rules of a treaty that are applied: it may be that those rules merely reflect other rules which are binding anyway.[41]

iii. *The elements of complexity*

Even if the Law of War is thus 'international' and not fragmented by various national systems, it has become increasingly complex. It contains rules, some of which are highly technical, susceptible to different legal interpretations, embodied in a complicated interwoven network of conventions as well as entrenched in general international law. It has now even been suggested that 'adviser positions' should be established for all armed forces to ensure that the military commander is able to avail himself of the necessary expertise to secure compliance with the law.[42]

C. THE CONTENTS OF THE LAWS OF WAR

i. *Jus ad bellum* and *jus in bello*

A distinction has traditionally been made between the right to wage war and the rights and duties which operate once a war has started. The unlimited right to start war, the *jus ad bellum*, has gradually been restricted in State practice. Only certain wars would be allowed: if the war was 'just' it could be waged, but otherwise a State could not resort to war under international law. Theories soon flourished as to what precisely *bellum justum* implied. The various just war theories had considerable flaws, above all concerning who was to assess

---

[40] Cf. the application of the 1982 Law of the Sea Convention, which has not entered into force, by the International Court of Justice, in the *Tunisia* v. *Libya Case*, ICJ *Reports*, 1984, 18, and the *Libya* v. *Malta Case*, ICJ *Reports*, 1985, 13.

[41] On the underlying basis of obligation in such cases, see my *Essays*, 116–17.

[42] Obligations to ensure the presence of such advisers are assumed by the contracting parties under article 82 of Protocol I to the Geneva Conventions; for reference, above, p. 12.

whether a war was just. Since there could be few objective criteria it appeared that the test, in the final analysis, must be a subjective one. The just war theories, largely based on the teachings of St Augustine[43] and Thomas Aquinas,[44] certainly had the beneficial effect of restricting unlimited rights of war, especially after the rise of the nation States in Europe. But the theories also led to difficulties insofar as two enemy States sometimes both argued that they were fighting a just war.[45] Some were more concerned with the morale of the soldiers: they would fight better if they were engaged in a just war for they would not be afraid of anything, knowing they had justice on their side.[46]

The right to aggressive war has now been abolished, largely by the Briand–Kellogg Pact of 1928[47] and by the United Nations Charter.[48] No aggressive war can thus be justified under modern international law, but the right to self-defensive war remains, for example under article 51 of the Charter of the United Nations. Now that aggressive war has been outlawed one would expect the 'just war' theories to be of mere historical interest. Yet some Third World countries now claim that certain liberation wars are 'just wars'[49] and Ayatollah Khomeni claims that *jihad*, the Islamic concept of just war,[50] entitles him to authorise certain acts of violence.

The fact that a war is not a just war or that it is in violation of a treaty has been invoked as a reason for suspension of any duty to be called up to take part in such a war.[51] But in this respect States preserve their competence to recruit members of their armed forces.

Distinguishable from the thus largely obsolete *jus ad bellum*[52] are the rules on warfare and the humanitarian rules that apply within a war, the *jus in bello*. It may appear that since the right *to* war, or indeed the right to recourse to armed force, has been abolished, there would not be any need for rules *in* war. However, it is clear that given the number of and intensity of present-day conflicts, both international

---

[43] E.g. *Quaestiones in Heptateuchum*, vi, 10b. [44] *Summa Theologica*, II, ii, 40.
[45] Suarez, *De Caritate*, disp. xiii, vi, 1–4.
[46] Jean de Bueil, *Le Jouvencel*, 1466, ii c (ed. Favre and Lecestres, Paris, 1887), 20.
[47] 94 LNTS 57, and above, p. 56. [48] Above, p. 56. [49] See further above, p. 81.
[50] On this concept, see *inter alia*, A. Rechid, 'L'Islam et le droit des gens', 60 *RCADI* 1937, ii, 375; Khadduri, *War and Peace in the Law of Islam*, 51.
[51] *US* v. *Mitchell*, (1967) 386 US 972, concerning the Vietnam War.
[52] Unless restrictively understood as meaning only the right to wage aggressive war, *jus ad bellum* can be conveniently used as the right to resort to force under contemporary international law: Rousseau, *Conflits armés* 25; G. Scelle, '*Jus ad bellum*', 6 *NedTIR* 1959, 292; Bretton, *Le droit de la guerre*, 8.

and internal, there is a great need for the regulation of humanitarian issues.

The laws of war lessen the threat to survival of our civilisation and may ensure the survival of mankind.[53] Some visualise the humanitarian law applied in internal wars as a third type[54] but, as we shall see,[55] similar humanitarian rules may now, certainly *de lege ferenda*, apply in both international and internal wars. To the extent that they do not, *de lege lata*, they should at least be conceptually understood as part of the same complex of rules.

ii. The law of the Hague and the law of Geneva

The treatment of individuals in times of armed conflict is closely related to the field of human rights. Considerable attempts have, however, been made, both earlier and in recent times, to distinguish the 'law of Geneva' and 'the law of the Hague'. The latter 'law' concerns the behaviour of belligerents in war and neutrality and, in terms of traditionalists in international law, regulates primarily the behaviour of States, whereas the 'law of Geneva' concerns the protection of the person.[56]

However, it would seem indisputable that any regulation of the behaviour of belligerents in armed conflict will have inevitable effects on the individuals affected by a dispute: restrictions of certain types of arms, for example, the St Petersburg Declaration of 1868,[57] commonly held to form part of 'the law of the Hague',[58] forbidding certain types of bullets seem to have an immediate beneficiary effect on individuals. The rules of this Declaration are conceptually in a similar category to rules alleviating suffering of the wounded as by the Convention of 1864 on the Treatment of Wounded Persons in War.[59]

Yet it was thought necessary by many to distinguish between rules applying to belligerents in armed conflict and rules concerning the victims of that conflict. The coincidental fact that the major conven-

[53] B. V. A. Röling, 'The significance of the laws of war', in A. Cassese (ed.), *Current Problems of International Law*, Milan, 1975, 155. Cf. Gong, *Standard of Civilization*, 74.
[54] R. R. Baxter, '*Jus in bello interno*, the present and future law', in J. N. Moore (ed.), *Law and Civil War in the Modern World*, Baltimore, 1974.
[55] Below, p. 271.
[56] E.g. S. Nahlik, 'Droit dit "de Genève" et droit dit "de la Haye": unité ou dualité', *AFDI*, 1978, 9–10.
[57] 18 NRGT, 1 série, 474; 1 *AJIL* 1907, Suppl., 95.
[58] E.g. Nahlik, 'Unité ou dualité', 9–10.   [59] NRGT, 1 série, 612.

tions on methods of warfare were concluded at the Hague and the major conventions on protection of victims of warfare were concluded in Geneva contributed to entrenching the division between the two sets of rules.

Rules on victims cannot be separated from rules on warfare, as is shown by Protocol I of 1977.[60] Nor can rules on disarmament, to the extent that they exist, be completely separated from laws of warfare and weaponry. Some claim that disarmament questions are basically distinct from the laws of war, as disarmament *eliminates* certain weapons. But occasionally treaties on disarmament only forbid *certain uses* of a specific weapon and, to the extent that this is the case, the regulation is, of course, highly relevant to the application of the laws of war: the parties to a conflict are then in very much the same position as when they are bound by any other treaty on weaponry. Besides, the line between disarmament and arms control is, on close analysis, arbitrary and subjective. The complex interaction between disarmament and weaponry issues is illustrated, for example, by the operation of the Conventional Weapons Convention,[61] the En-mod Convention,[62] or the Biological Weapons Convention.[63]

iii. Identification of the laws of war

As indicated earlier in this work, the 'Law of War' signifies the body of rules which governs relationships in war.[64] This body of law consists of different sets of rules which are, albeit interlinked, of different substance.

The laws applicable to war as understood in this work thus comprise (1) laws on weapons; (2) laws on warfare, including rules on permissible tactics and strategies and on illegitimate targets; and (3) humanitarian rules.

a. Rules on weapons

Rules on weapons are those which abolish, restrict or regulate specific weapons or their use in war. Some of these rules have been discussed in connection with disarmament and with demilitarised zones.[65] So has the question of legality of certain weapons, particularly of nuclear weapons. Other questions to be analysed are questions of legality and restrictions of conventional weapons and of biological and chemical weapons.

[60] Cf. comments in the *Lugano Report*, 28; cf. below, p. 271.   [61] Below, p. 180.
[62] Below, p. 227.   [63] Below, p. 211.   [64] Above, p. xx.   [65] Above, pp. 88 and 89.

b. Rules on methods

Rules on methods concern primarily the question of what may be the target of combatants in war. Rules on legitimate and illegitimate targets are supplemented by provisions on certain permissible or forbidden strategies, tactics and practices of war.

c. Humanitarian rules

(1) *'Humanitarian law' and 'human rights'* 'Humanitarian law' is a branch of law which has been 'contaminated' by ethics and idealism[66] and constitutes 'that considerable portion of international public law which owes its inspiration to a feeling for humanity and which is centered on the protection of the individual [which] appears to combine two ideas of a different character, the one legal, the other moral'.[67] Humanitarian law concerns primarily the protection of individuals in war or in armed conflict and probably also some rules of refugee law.[68] However, in this work we have adopted a more narrow definition of humanitarian law by insisting[69] that rules protecting individuals from being attacked are conceptually part of the rules of methods of warfare. Yet, it is important to clarify whether there is any overlap between rules protecting individuals under the Law of War and in other instruments dealing with human rights.

The Secretary General of the United Nations was asked to submit reports to the General Assembly from 1969 onwards on 'Human Rights in Armed Conflicts', which made some writers question whether the right terms were being used. 'Human rights' concern, some say,[70] a different 'regime'[71] and the two areas should not be confused. The two sets of rules certainly have a different history and often a different field of application, both *ratione personae* and *ratione temporis*. Human rights thus apply to *all* people and humanitarian law applies to *certain* groups of persons (for example, to the wounded, to prisoners of war, to civilians) and, furthermore, humanitarian law

[66] J. Pictet, *International Humanitarian Law*, Geneva, 1985, 3.
[67] J. Pictet, *Humanitarian Law and the Protection of War Victims*, Leiden, 1975, 11. Cf. Pictet, *Développements et principes du droit international humanitaire*, Geneva, 1983, 4.
[68] Cf. O. Kimminich, *Humanitäres Völkerrecht – Humanitäre Aktion*, Munich, 1972, 77ff.
[69] Below, p. 271.
[70] E.g. G. I. A. D. Draper, 'The relationship between the human rights regime and the law of armed conflict', 1 *YHR* 1971, 193; cf. K. D. Suter, 'An inquiry into the meaning of the phrase "Human Rights in Armed Conflicts"', 15 *RDPMDG* 1976, 393.
[71] On the usefulness of the term, see my *Concept*, 38.

applies only in times of armed conflict.[72] On the other hand, 'human rights' and 'humanitarian law' regulate, *ratione materiae*, similar rights, at least insofar as they all intend to increase the protection of individuals, alleviate pain and suffering and secure the minimum standard[73] for persons in various situations.

One may perhaps say that 'human rights' is the genus of which 'humanitarian law' is a species,[74] but it seems desirable to retain a horizontal distinction, rather than to introduce a new, hierarchical one, as 'human rights' really concern rights enjoyed by all at all times,[75] but essentially in peacetime, whereas 'humanitarian rules' concern rights protecting individuals in armed conflicts. It would appear appropriate, therefore, to view 'human rights' and 'humanitarian law' as *ratione materiae* interrelated fields, both raising the level of behaviour towards individuals and both concerned with the rights and protection of individuals.

(2) Operation of human rights in war Most human rights documents have safeguards which permit the exclusion, or at least the partial exclusion, of certain provisions in times of war and armed conflict.[76] Thus, the United Nations Covenant on Civil and Political Rights of 1966[77] provides that States bound by the Covenant may derogate from it during times of emergency if such emergency is on such a scale that it 'threatens the life of the nation'. The measures taken must correspond to the demands of the emergency which appears to express a condition of proportionality. Furthermore, the measures must not, in any event, be taken with any discriminatory distinctions.

Equally, the European Convention on Human Rights provides[78]

---

[72] See below, p. 172 on the problem of establishing whether armed conflict exists.

[73] On the point concerning minimum standard, cf. A. S. Calogerospoulos-Stratis, *Droit humanitaire de droits de l'homme, la protection de la personne en période de conflit armé*, Geneva, 1980, 139.

[74] A. H. Robertson, 'Human rights as the basis of international humanitarian law', *Acte du congrès international de droit humanitaire*, San Remo, 1970, 174. Naturally one can perceive various subsections of humanitarian law according to different cultural conceptions, see J. Pictet, 'Les idées humanitaires à travers les divers courants de la pensée et des traditions culturelles' in Institut Henri Dunant (ed.), *Les dimensions internationales du droit humanitaire*, Geneva, 1986, 19ff.

[75] On suspension of instruments on human rights in times of armed conflict, see below, p. 132.

[76] On suspension or reduction of human rights in times of state of emergency, see E/C.N.4/Sub.2/NGO/93, 1981.

[77] Article 4.

[78] Article 15.

that in time of war or other public emergency, again 'threatening the life of the nation', contracting parties may derogate from the provisions, on the condition of similar rules of proportionality as enounced in the UN Covenant.

The American Convention on Human Rights also allows[79] such derogations 'in time of war, public danger or other emergency which threatens the independence or security of a party'. There is a condition on proportionality similar to that in the Covenant.

The latitude of action is certainly greater with regard to the American Convention, which introduces rather more flexible criteria concerning the threatened security and independence of the State.

But the derogation rules cannot be read in isolation. All three documents also refer to provisions from which States must not derogate under any circumstances. These are the provisions on the right to life,[80] the duty to refrain from torture, inhuman and degrading treatment,[81] and slavery.[82] There are numerous other provisions in the three documents from which no derogation must be made, for example on retroactive criminal legislation,[83] but in the finer details the three Conventions then diverge along slightly different paths.[84]

The question arises as to how these conventions, and the Universal Declaration on Human Rights,[85] can be implemented, with regard to the protection of the right to life, in case of armed conflict. When the Universal Declaration was drafted the French representative, René Cassin, emphasised that, had there been a similar document during the Second World War proclaiming the right to life, States might have taken some action to intervene instead of asking themselves whether they had any right to do so.[86]

It would therefore seem that the right to life, which is not suspended during armed conflict, implies that attempts must be made, even in times of such conflicts, to save life. Armed conflicts which are defensive and compatible with the provisions of the Charter may

---

[79] Article 27(1).

[80] Covenant, article 6; European Convention, article 2; American Convention, article 4.

[81] Covenant, article 7; European Convention, article 3; American Convention, article 5.

[82] Covenant, article 8; European Convention, article 4(1); American Convention, article 6.

[83] Covenant, article 15; European Convention, article 7; American Convention, article 9.

[84] Compelling provisions are, apart from those referred to in the Covenant, articles 11, 16 and 18; in the European Convention, there are no further such articles; in the American Convention, articles 3, 12, 17, 18, 19 and 20.

[85] Article 3 proclaims the right to life.   [86] E/CN.4/SR.13.

cause loss of life but, it has been claimed, this would not be done 'illegally'.[87] Within the rights enjoyed under the Law of War, there is internal hierarchy: some such rights are more important than others and may not be suspended in emergencies, whereas there may, in specific circumstances, be derogation from others. Article 75 of Protocol I and article 4 of Protocol II provide 'absolute' protection which must not be suspended even in times of emergency.[88]

It is important to emphasise that the provisions securing the right to life in the three mentioned documents on human rights, and in the Universal Declaration, protect all persons whether or not they are nationals of a party. In this sense these Conventions go further than, for example, Geneva Convention IV on Civilians, which does not protect the nationals of a State which has not ratified it.[89]

The Geneva Conventions and Protocols are not capable of safeguarding the right to life to the same extent as the Conventions on Human Rights, as the former are all instruments of the Law of War, designed to apply in times of armed conflict when, by definition, the right to life is diminished. On the other hand, the protection afforded by the Human Rights Conventions may be more detailed in certain aspects of life which are important in everyday life, such as freedom of religion, freedom of expression and freedom of assembly. But the Geneva Conventions and Protocols regulate, in greater detail, the specific situations occurring in armed conflicts and attempt to secure further protection for numerous individuals affected by such conflicts.

To the extent that the provisions of the Human Rights Conventions are not suspended during armed conflict, individuals seem to be entitled to cumulative treatment. But the adherence of certain States to the Human Rights Conventions could not dispense further adherence to the Law of War conventions, for example the Geneva Conventions and Protocols cover ground which sometimes overlaps but generally is distinct from that regulated by the Human Rights Conventions.

iv. Bodies participating in the elaboration of the laws of war

Present-day rules on warfare and humanitarian law are formed by constant feedback between various bodies. In particular, various or-

---

[87] See discussion in the General Assembly, A/C.3/SR/810, paras. 18ff.
[88] Cf. G. Herczegh, 'State of emergency and humanitarian law, on article 75 of Additional Protocol I', *IRRC*, 1984, 272. See further below, p. 170.
[89] On the development of the Convention into declaratory law, however, see below, p. 349.

gans of the United Nations and the International Committee of the Red Cross (ICRC) have been involved, as well as specialist *ad hoc* groups of experts.

Numerous resolutions of the General Assembly have thus 'endorsed' resolutions by the ICRC. For example, General Assembly Resolution 2444 (XXIII) of 1968 specifically approved of Resolution XXVIII of the XXth International Conference of the Red Cross in Vienna in 1965 which had re-emphasised that the right to adopt means of injuring the enemy is not unlimited;[90] that no attacks must be launched on the civilian population;[91] and that at all times distinction[92] must be made between those taking part in hostilities and the civilian population in order to spare the latter 'as much as possible'. General Assembly Resolution 2597 (XXIV) of 1969 furthermore endorsed the Resolution of the XXIst Conference of the Red Cross in Tehran in 1966 on the protection of civilians and combatants in conflicts arising from struggles for liberation.[93] General Assembly Resolution 2676 (XXV) of 1970 similarly endorsed the ICRC preceding resolution on prisoners of war.[94]

The ICRC was also involved with the preparatory phase of the Conventional Weapons Conventions, later transferred to the aegis of the United Nations.[95]

Other important links have been established between various bodies concerned with the Law of War. The co-operation between the Disarmament Conference (CD), still technically an intergovernmental State Conference, and the United Nations has developed into semi-organic contacts, whereby there is a constant cross-feed between the discussions in the General Assembly and other UN organs and CD. National delegations to CD also transfer their work from Geneva to New York during the sessions of the General Assembly to facilitate such contacts.

v. General principles of ethics of warfare

It may seem that war, as the ultimate type of violence, could not be restrained by specific rules. Yet, there is a body of *jus in bello* which operates during warfare. The substratum of these rules consists of rules on 'ethics' or 'humanity', forbidding in particular certain weapons and attacks against certain targets.[96] It has long been ac-

---

[90] Below, p. 135.   [91] Below, p. 232.   [92] Below, p. 236.
[93] Cf. above, p. 43.   [94] Below, p. 281.   [95] Below, p. 180.
[96] On the historical background see C. Calvo, 4 *Le droit international, théorie et pratique*, Paris, 1888, for example on early prohibition of poisoned weapons or, later, of guns

cepted that there are certain basic rules which must be respected. Perhaps helped by mechanisms like reciprocity,[97] certain rules have emerged.

The St Petersburg Declaration[98] indicated that since 'it is sufficient to disable the greatest possible number of men' to defeat the enemy it is not allowed to use 'arms which uselessly aggravate the sufferings of disabled men, or render their death inevitable'.

Article 22 of the Hague Regulations[99] emphasised that 'the right of belligerents to adopt means of injuring the enemy is not unlimited.[100] Article 23(e) of the Regulations introduced a complete prohibition of 'arms, projectiles or material calculated to cause unnecessary suffering'.

The English version of the Regulations speaks of prohibition of arms, projectiles and material which cause 'unnecessary suffering', whereas the French text refers to 'maux superflus', which in English would have been better translated as 'superfluous injuries'. 'Unnecessary suffering', which was adopted for the official English translation, introduces a different subjective element, not present in the French text. The clause came up for discussion during the 1973 Lucerne Conference on Conventional Weapons[101] and it was then deemed 'unthinkable' by the Conference to 'remove this subjective element ... from the body of international law' simply by preferring another translation of the original French text.[102] The incompatibility of the two versions was also questioned by delegates to the Conference on the Additional Protocols of 1977 to the Geneva Conventions.[103] On the other hand, the other qualification, which in English was rendered 'calculated to cause' as opposed to the French version, 'propres à causer', implied in the English version a more subjective assessment than the rather more objective French expression. The French qualification might, in this respect, be wider and cover situations even when there is no *intention* of causing 'unnecessary suffering' or 'maux superflus', but this is the inevitable effect of the type of weapon. In such cases, the French, less restrictive, notion should prevail in case of any doubt.[104]

firing two bullets (at pp. 171–2) or on the medieval restriction of the use of cannons against city walls but prohibited in field battle (at pp. 148–9).
[97] Below, p. 339.   [98] For reference, above, p. 123, note 21.
[99] For reference, above, p. 107, note 39.
[100] Cf GA Res. 2444 (XXIII), 1968. affirming 'that the right of the parties to a conflict to adopt means of injuring the enemy is not unlimited'.
[101] Below, p. 181.   [102] *Lucerne Report*, 1974, 8.
[103] E.g. Australia, CDDH/IV/SR.1., vol. 16, 16.   [104] *Lucerne Report*, 8.

Protocol I of 1977 uses a juxtaposition of the two expressions in its prohibition of use of any weapons which are of 'a nature to cause superfluous injury or unnecessary suffering'.[105]

'Suffering' may be something which is difficult to measure and quantify as different people experience pain differently. There was discussion at the Lucerne Conference whether psychological damage should be taken into account.[106] Such suffering would be even more difficult to quantify. But there is, *grosso modo*, some agreement of what type of suffering is envisaged by the relevant prohibitions.

The general rules mentioned above limit the right of belligerents in two ways. First, parties to a conflict must not choose weapons which have the effect of causing unnecessary suffering. Secondly, they must not use other permissible weapons in a *way* which causes such suffering, or employ tactics or practices which have such effect. Furthermore, the use of weapons is always subjected to the rules of necessity and proportionality.[107]

With regard to weapons it may then first be said that weapons which *inevitably* cause unnecessary suffering are prohibited.[108] All experts at Lucerne furthermore agreed that 'indiscriminate attacks' are forbidden,[109] from which it can be deduced that 'indiscriminate weapons' – which inevitably cause 'indiscriminate attacks' – must also be forbidden.[110] Furthermore, 'treacherous' weapons, already forbidden by the Hague Regulations,[111] or any weapons used 'with perfidy'[112] should also be forbidden.[113] Here, however, the Lucerne Conference crossed the area from weaponry to methods, as it is perfidy, or the *way* the weapon is *used* in the event, which warranted the prohibition.

---

[105] Article 35(2).
[106] *Lucerne Report*, 8. During the Conference it was suggested that 'inadequate' concepts like 'superfluous injury', 'unnecessary suffering', 'proportionality' and 'military necessity', should be discarded, *ibid.*, 13.
[107] Below, p. 179.   [108] Cf. British Report at Lucerne, *Lucerne Report*, 9.
[109] *Lucerne Report*, 10. The fact that specific weapons are prohibited may not warrant a conclusion that they would cause 'unnecessary suffering' if used or that they are necessarily indiscriminate, cf. *Lugano Report*, 1976, 29.
[110] Not all agreed at the Lucerne Conference that 'indiscriminate weapons' were prohibited, see *Lucerne Report*, 10, although this seems a logical conclusion from the first agreement on 'indiscriminate attacks'. On prohibition of attacks on the civilian population and the importance of discrimination, see GA Res. 2444 (XXIII) 1968, and 106ff., 232ff.
[111] Article 23(b). Cf. below, p. 183, on treacherous weapons regulated in Protocol II to the Weaponry Convention of 1981.
[112] Cf. 1977 Protocol I, article 37.   [113] *Lucerne Report*, 11.

We shall examine which types of weapons and methods of warfare are outlawed in contemporary international society, retaining the basic limitations introduced by the universally accepted basic rules of ethics of warfare as set out above.

6 SPATIAL APPLICATION OF THE LAWS OF WAR

A. TRADITIONAL SPATIAL APPLICATION

i. Delimitation of territory

Spatial notions are relevant in several ways to the application of the laws of war. It is often by examining whether an incursion has been made into the territory of a State that it can be established that the territorial rights of a State have been violated, activating the laws of war. It is thus important to ascertain the actual territory of a State and be clear about its land, water and air boundaries. Numerous disputes have been caused by disagreements over borders,[1] alleged incursions into a State's territory, violations of the water margin or the national air space.[2] Disputes over territorial limits can lead to conflict and even war.

Obvious geographical criteria that apply in peacetime establish the spatial limits of the belligerents themselves in war. Geographical delimitation of third States becomes of primary importance: incursions into neutral States are particularly serious violations of the laws of war.[3]

Apart from notions bearing on the geographical limitations of States, there is, in war, a need to establish the geographical region affected. It has often been thought important to distinguish certain areas where war itself would be enacted, and such areas have usually been referred to as 'theatres' and 'regions' of war.

---

[1] Above, p. 86.
[2] See, on various incidents, see my 'Foreign warships', 56. On right of passage see my *International Law and the Independent State*, 29–90.
[3] E.g. E. Castrén, 'La neutralité aérienne', *ZaöRVR*, 1951, 120.

ii. Region of war and theatre of war

A distinction has traditionally been made between the region of war and the theatre of war: the region is the larger notion within which the theatre is contained; the theatre is where hostilities actually take place[4] It is not altogether clear what purpose this distinction serves, apart from stating the obvious in that certain geographical areas are affected or involved in the war as forming part of the territories of the belligerents, whereas hostilities are limited to smaller areas where the fighting takes place.

First, the laws of war apply with equal force and to equal extent within both areas, a region or a theatre of war, although humanitarian law, for example, will be more likely to become more intensely relevant in the theatre of war.

Secondly, the distinction is no longer warranted in view of the nature of modern war. The distinction may have been valid once, when wars were primarily fought between armies, or navies, lined up with some symmetry against each other. However, the distinction has now lost its importance as modern warfare makes no distinction between regions included in the war and the actual theatres of war. The enemy can strike anywhere within the region of war; thus the territory of belligerents, with the exception listed below, forms part of the theatre of war. Modern weapons have made the distinction superfluous. It is naturally true that a war may be geographically limited: but in law there is no distinction between the region and the theatre of war. Aerial warfare is thus not confined to any location but comprises the whole of the sky.[5]

iii. Neutrals and neutralised areas

Some claim that neutrality presupposes the existence of 'war'.[6] But neutrality in modern times is often used to signify an alliance-free policy in peace as well. When there is a war, however, duties and rights of neutral States intensify. In particular, belligerents must respect the land and sea territory of neutral States where acts of war must not take place.[7]

[4] 2 Oppenheim, ed. H. Lauterpacht, London, 1952, para. 70ff, 237.
[5] Cour d'appel Montpellier, 20.6.1945, Gaz. Palais 18.9.1945: 'la zone de combat ... embrasse la totalité du ciel'.
[6] F. Castberg, *Noitralitet*, n.p., n.d., 275.
[7] T. Gihl, 'Svensk neutralitetsrättslig praxis under de båda världskrigen', *Jus Gentium*, 1949, 1.

Rules on rights and duties of neutrals are laid down in Hague Convention V of 1907.[8] But the provisions of the Convention are the result of the 'United States view'. Scandinavian views on armed neutrality are considerably stricter.[9]

Belligerents may have access to courts under 'neutrality legislation' of neutral States,[10] and innocent passage may be enjoyed through the territorial waters of a neutral State. But restrictions to any such rights may be imposed by special regulation of neutral States.[11] And further restrictions may follow upon violations by belligerents.[12]

Certain areas are exempt from being brought into hostilities in war. First, in peacetime certain areas or countries may be designated as 'neutral' and are consequently exempt from attack or involvement in future war. Such protection is sometimes afforded by a State's neutrality being entrenched in a treaty[13] or by a specific declaration.[14] A whole State can be excluded from normal war regions by its entrenched neutrality: thus Switzerland is permanently[15] neutral.[16]

Secondly, other areas may obtain similar protection by specific treaties which withdraw a certain territory from wars and their effect, by declared neutralisation.[17] A whole State may be neutralised in this way, as Austria was by the 1955 State Treaty.[18] Under the Lateran Treaty also the Vatican State is neutralised.[19] Neutralisation

---

[8] Cf. above, p. 19, and below, p. 309, on trade.

[9] E.g. T. Gihl, 'Om krigets natur och det ekonomiska kriget', *Svensk Tidskrift*, 1930, 454–5; cf. E. Hambro, 'Das Neutralitätsrecht der nordischen Staaten'. *ZaöRVR*, 1938, 32.

[10] Sweden promulgated such legislation in 1912, SFS 1912: 346 and in 1938, SFS 1938: 187.

[11] E.g. Swedish regulations during the First World War, KK 29 November 1915 and 19 July 1916, on the inner territorial waters, followed by protests by the Entente powers that the regulations violated the 'exhortation' in the Preamble in Hague Convention XIII of 1907 not to alter neutrality legislation during the course of a war.

[12] Cf. further Swedish restrictions under the 1938 restrictions by KK 12 April 1940 after the German invasion of Denmark and Norway; cf. also KK 28 June 1941 on outer territorial waters.

[13] As in the case of Austria under the State treaty of 1955, *AJIL*, 1955, Suppl., 162.

[14] As in the case of Sweden during the Second World War, see above notes 11 and 12.

[15] On the notion of permanent neutrality, see S. Verosta, *Die dauernde Neutralität*, Vienna, 1967.

[16] See R. Bindschedler, 'Die Neutralität im modernen Völkerrecht', 17 *ZaöRVR* 1956–7, 1.

[17] L. Delbez, 'Le concept d'internationalisation', *RGDIP*, 1967, 13: 'La neutralisation consiste à soustraire par traité d'une façon durable et juridiquement obligatoire un territoire déterminé à la guerre et à ses effets.'

[18] Staatsvertrag 1955, 217 UNTS 223. Cf. Bindschedler, 'Die Neutralität im modernen Völkerrecht', 29, 30. E.g. M. Rotter, *Die dauernde Neutralität*, Berlin, 1981.

[19] 1 Oppenheim, para. 106, and H. Wright, 'The status of the "Vatican City"', *AJIL*, 1944, 452.

can also apply to a part of a country, for example borderline territory[20] may be neutralised.

Other neutralised areas are the Åland Islands,[21] the Spitsbergen,[22]
the Magellan Straits[23] and the islands of Corfu and Paxo.[24] Important waterways are often neutralised, such as the Suez Canal under
the 1888 Convention as well as the Panama Canal.[25] Outer space has
been neutralised under the 1967 Treaty,[26] although there is increasing doubt about the effectiveness of regulation in face of the 'Star
Wars' plan.[27]

Neutralised zones may be used to denote areas designed to treat
the wounded or civilians. Such zones may be established by special
agreement, for example under Geneva Convention IV[28] or by unilateral declarations under Protocol II of 1977.[29] These areas are
specifically treated as 'undefended' and, as such, illegitimate targets
for attack.[30]

Neutralisation and neutral status entail by tradition numerous
legal effects with regard to rights and duties.[31] The rights of neutrals
to avoid the immediate effects of war are balanced by their duties to
remain passive in a conflict. Disrespect for the duties of neutrals will
suspend their rights. Thus, only 'effective' neutrality must be
respected by third States, i.e. the type of neutrality which actually
abides by the rule of passivity.[32]

It appears logical to assume that similar rights and duties devolve

[20] E.g. the Convention between Sweden and Norway on Demilitarisation, 1905,
demilitarising all land in the southern part of the border, *SÖFM*, 1905.
[21] Convention 1921 between Sweden, Finland, Estonia, Germany, Denmark, United
Kingdom, France, Italy, Latvia and Poland, 23 UKTS 1924, Cmd. 2203. See, further,
my *Independent State*.
[22] Convention 1920 between Norway, the United States, Denmark, Sweden, France,
Italy, Japan, Netherlands and the United Kingdom, 23 UKTS 1924, Cmd. 2092.
[23] Treaty between Chile and Argentina of 1881, 12 NRGT, 2ème série, 491.
[24] Treaty of London 1863 on neutralisation of the Ionian Islands, 18 NRGT 52;
Treaty revision 1864, 18 NRGT 65. Cf. H. Rettich, *Zur Theorie und Geschichte des Rechts
zum Kriege: völkerrechtliche Untersuchungen*, Stuttgart, 1888.
[25] On the regime in general cf. my *Independent State*, 43, 165–6, 182–3, 214–17.
[26] Below, pp. 143 and 144.   [27] See below, p. 146.
[28] Article 15. Cf. Geneva Convention I, article 23.   [29] Article 59.
[30] Below, p. 232.
[31] E.g. no act of hostility must take place in neutral States, Hague V, article 1; no
troops or convoys of either munitions of war or supplies must be moved through
neutral territories, *ibid.*, article 2; all hostilities in territorial waters of neutral States are
forbidden, Hague XIII, article 2.
[32] *The Tinos Case*, (1917) before the French Conseil des prises, *RGDIP*, 1918, jurisprudence, 3, shows that ships captured in Greek neutral waters had been validly taken,
as Greece had allowed numerous hostile acts. See further Rousseau, *Conflits armés*, 218.

on States which have sovereignty and control over neutralised territories. Furthermore, the duty of passivity is also activated in the
case where neutrality has not yet been declared in the event of war
between other parties. Until States have taken a position in a dispute they will be assumed to be neutral with ensuing rights and
duties.

This duty of passivity also covers, as has been discussed above,[33]
situations where there is internal war in another country.

On the other hand, although neutralisation means that an area is
exempt from being a target of belligerents, it does not limit the application of the laws of war. Thus, in the event of war (or civil war) in a
neutralised State, the laws of war apply with equal force as in any
other war situation.

iv. Demilitarised areas

No fixed military installations may be placed in demilitarised areas;
but within these areas there may, contrary to neutralised zones, be
war action. Demilitarisation, however, does not preclude defensive
measures.[34]

There are numerous examples of demilitarised areas in State practice.[35] The Rush–Bagot Treaty of 1817 on naval forces on the North
American lakes demilitarised the frontier between the United States
and Canada.[36] The Paris Peace Conference of 1856 demilitarised the
Black Sea and closed the Bosphorus and the Dardanelles to warships;
this regime was abrogated by the London Treaty of 1871[37] but
reaffirmed in the Lausanne Treaty of 1923,[38] in turn replaced by the
Montreux Convention in 1936, which provided for discriminatory
treatment of Black Sea States.[39] The Washington Treaty of 1922[40]
prohibits new fortifications of naval bases on islands in the Pacific,
except as specified. The Antarctic Treaty of 1959[41] introduced complete demilitarisation of a whole region. The sea bed is also demilitar-

---

[33] Above, p. 66.
[34] See on the revision of the 1921 Åland Convention A. Croneburg, 'Utrikesutskottet
vid 1939 års riksdag', *Statsvetenskaplig Tidskrift*, 1939, 262. Cf. my *Independence*, 183.
[35] For Danzig see 'Constitution of the Free City', *LNOJ*, 1922, Spec. Suppl. no. 7; for
Trieste see Permament Statute of the Free Territory, article 3 of Annex VI to Italian
Peace Treaty 1947, *AJIL*, 1947, Suppl., 40; cf. R. Erich, 'La question des zones
démilitarisés', *RCADI*, 1929, i, 591.
[36] UN, *Study on the Naval Arms Race*, 8.   [37] *AJIL*, 1907, Suppl., 89.
[38] *AJIL*, 1924, Suppl., 53.   [39] *AJIL*, 1937, Suppl., 1, article 11.
[40] *AJIL*, 1922, Suppl., 40.   [41] 402 UNTS 71.

ised as far as regards certain weapons.[42] Outer space is neutralised[43] and partially demilitarised.[44]

The Moon is demilitarised by the Outer Space Treaty of 1967, but there is only partial demilitarisation of outer space in general. A USSR Draft of 1983 suggested a widening of the prohibitions of space objects in orbit,[45] but, as often in similar contexts, verification presented insurmountable problems.[46]

The Partial Test Ban Treaty of 1963[47] and the Outer Space Treaty[48] forbid the testing and use of nuclear weapons in space, but both are silent on the legality of *other weapons* in outer space. There is also a differentiated regime for celestial bodies and for space in the 1979 Moon Treaty:[49] celestial bodies are thus completely demilitarised. Furthermore, in space in general it is prohibited only to place nuclear weapons, or other weapons of mass destruction, in orbit or in location in space,[50] but nuclear weapons could conceivably be used in other ways. Thus, the treaty does not prohibit *all* use of nuclear weapons or other weapons of mass destruction, nor does it prohibit the use of weapons which are not weapons of such mass destruction. In this respect it is important to underline that neither laser weapons nor particle beam weapons are forbidden by the Outer Space Treaty, as they are not weapons of mass destruction. On the contrary, they are usually devised to eliminate identifiable specific and limited targets.

Space should, according to numerous provisions in relevant treaties, be used for 'peaceful purposes'.[51] But it has seriously been argued by the United States that 'peaceful' merely means 'non-aggressive' and that therefore other military activities are allowed in outer space. The USSR claims[52] that 'peaceful' means non-military and is, in this respect, supported by many writers.[53]

---

[42] Treaty for the Prohibition of Emplacement of Nuclear Weapons and Weapons of Mass Destruction on the Sea-bed and the Ocean Floor and in the Subsoil thereof, 1971, *ILM*, 1971, 145, UKTS 1973 13; TIAS 7337; cf. above, p. 91, and below, p. 209.
[43] Above, p. 199.   [44] 610 UNTS 205; below, p. 199.
[45] B. Jasani and C. Lee, *Countdown to Space War*, London, 1984, 89.
[46] France suggested in 1978 that a special Intersatellite Moon Agency (ISMA) should be established; other suggestions have been to make use of already existing regional agencies, for example the European Space Agency in Paris, *ibid.*, 91.
[47] 480 UNTS 43.   [48] See note 44 above.   [49] UNTS, article III.
[50] Article 4(1) of the 1967 Space Treaty, above, note 44.
[51] Article 1 of the Outer Space Treaty; article III of the Moon Treaty.
[52] E.g. G. P. Zhukov, 'Practical problems of space law', 9 *International Affairs*, Moscow, 1963, 27.
[53] E.g. C. Gutierres Espada, 'What's the law on the military use of Outer Space?' in *Proceedings of the 28th Colloquium on the Law of Outer Space*, Stockholm, 1985, 32.

Special problems are caused by the placing of weapons in space, for example under the Strategic Defense Initiative of the United States, the so-called Star Wars plan.[54] The system would use space weapons, positioned above the United States as a 'shield', using various combinations of non-nuclear weapons such as laser, particle beam and kinetic energy weapons. Direct energy weapons depend on a stream of charged particles (protons, electrons and ions) accelerated to high energy and projected towards a target. The weapons can destroy targets at great distance but may have problems transmitting through the atmosphere and are therefore more designed to attack objects in space, such as missiles or satellites. The Star Wars system would, at a cost of some $1,000 billion 'or more', use different 'phases' for destroying enemy missiles, rising from silos, mid-flight or in their terminal approach.[55] Satellites perform essential functions under SDI. Passive satellites may be activated to function as battle stations using particularly laser and particle beam weapons. It is the use of satellites especially which will enable Star Wars to turn into an offensive, rather than a defensive, system.[56] Outer space is, as mentioned, only partially demilitarised and there is intense negotiation on whether a 'demilitarised sanctuary' in space could be established to prevent space turning into a battlefield between space-based systems.[57]

The En-Mod Convention of 1977[58] prohibits hostile use of environmental modification techniques to alter the dynamics, composition or structure of Earth or outer space. But it is not such techniques which are of primary interest for Star Wars. It is, first of all, whether the Star War plan is compatible with the ABM Treaty.

One pertinent question concerns whether the ABM Treaty of 1972 forbids the establishment of a weapon system like 'Star Wars'. The Treaty provides[59] that the 'Parties undertake not to develop, test or deploy ABM systems or components which are sea-based, air-based, space-based or mobile land-based'. An 'Agreed Statement' D, appended to the Treaty, stipulates further that the 'Parties agree that in the event ABM systems based on *other physical principles* and including components capable of substituting for ABM interceptor missiles, ABM launchers, or ABM radars are *created in the future*, specific limita-

[54] *Weekly Compilation of Presidential Documents*, 23 March 1983, 447.

[55] E. P. Thompson, *Star Wars*, Harmondsworth, 1985, 72.

[56] L. F. Martinez, 'Telecommunication as space activity for weapons of mass destruction', *Proceedings of the 28th Colloquium on the Law of Outer Space*, Stockholm, 1985, 94.

[57] See, for example, Statement by France in CD 1983 to this effect, CD/375, 1.

[58] See below, p. 227.   [59] Article V.

tion on such systems and other components would be subject to discussion in accordance with Article XIII or Article XIV of the Treaty' (emphasis added). The two articles referred to deal with implementation of rules and with revision; it is clear that in any event agreement by the other party is necessary for any new space weapons using 'new principles', as does the Star War system. Furthermore, under the ABM Treaty even land- or sea-based systems, prohibited under the Convention, would make 'military use' of outer space during trajectory flights.[60]

The United States initially accepted that no new weapons should be developed in space. But by 1985 the position had changed. One statement underlines that although deterrence 'based on threat of offensive nuclear retaliation' had formed the basis of United States security policy for the then 'foreseeable future', the United States 'should not be content to confine [itself] to that in perpetuity'.[61]

The problem concerns basically whether any 'development' – by itself forbidden by the ABM Treaty – could be allowed if forming part of 'research'. There is an argument that 'research' would allow some 'testing' and that certain 'testing' would not be confined to laboratories. The current position of the United States is that the Treaty is at least 'ambiguous' and allows for development of and experiments with new space weapons.[62]

One may question why the United States does not prefer to denounce the ABM Treaty rather than stretching an interpretation of the agreement which must deviate considerably from its wording.[63] But although the ABM Treaty does allow for denunciation,[64] there have to be 'extraordinary events' relating to the subject matter of the Treaty which have 'jeopardized the supreme interests' of the Party wishing to denounce the agreement. Any notification of withdrawal must be accompanied by a statement of such alleged 'extraordinary events'. It is understandable that it may be difficult, for political reasons, to phrase such a statement of denunciation.

[60] Other relevant Conventions regulating the use of outer space are the 1968 Agreement for Rescue of Astronauts; the 1972 Convention on International Liability for Damage Caused by Space Objects; and the 1975 Convention on Registration of Objects Launched in Space.
[61] P. H. Nitze, 'The ADI and the ABM Treaty', United States, Department of State, Bureau of Public Affairs, *Current Policy*, no. 711, 2, 30 May 1985.
[62] Statement by A. D. Sofaer, *ibid.*, no. 755, 22 October 1985.
[63] E.g. H. Thierry in Anglo-French Colloquium on Outer Space, University College London, 2 December 1986.
[64] Article XV requiring six months' notice.

However, even apart from possible contingent use of satellites and space weapons under the Star Wars programme, outer space is already heavily 'militarised' by satellites. The number of satellites in orbit is ever increasing and although they are for alleged 'peaceful' information purposes, such as telecommunications or maritime information, they all have possible 'military' uses. It may be impossible to distinguish peaceful, military and aggressive activities in space: all activities are inevitably of military importance.[65]

Certain areas which are neutralised under a treaty are also demilitarised. This is the case of Spitsbergen,[66] the Magellan Straits,[67] the Åland Islands,[68] and the southern border area between Sweden and Norway.[69] Similar regimes apply to Rhodes and other Greek islands[70] as well as to certain islands off the Tunisian coast,[71] and to Sicily and Sardinia.[72] In more recent practice, there has been demilitarisation of the Kuwait–Saudi Neutral Sector.[73]

Any territory can, *ad hoc*, be demilitarised by parties to a conflict.[74] 'Safety zones', an old Red Cross idea,[75] can also be used for such exemption purposes.[76] The doctrine of 'non-defended localities', e.g. 'open towns', can also be conceived as a system of demilitarisation. This doctrine was codified in the Hague Regulations of 1907;[77] Protocol I of 1977[78] developed the Hague regime by allowing for agree-

[65] S. H. Lay and H. J. Taubenfeld, *The Law Relating to Activities of Man in Space*, Chicago, 1970, 100.
[66] See Treaty of Paris, 9 February 1920, article 9; cf. C. Piccioni, 'Les Spitzberg et la Convention du 9.2.1920', *RGDIP*, 1923, 104ff.
[67] See Convention, 23 July 1881, 12 NRGT, 2ème série, 491.
[68] Geneva Convention, 20 October 1921; 12 NRGT, 3ème série, 65; Finlands Överenskommelser med Främmande Makter, 1922, no. 1; cf. the Treaty of Paris 1856, and the Finland Peace Treaty 1947, article 5; cf. my *Independent State*, 183ff; F. DeVisscher, 'La Convention relative à la non-fortification et à la neutralité des Iles d'Åland', *RDILC*, 1921, 568ff.
[69] Sweden, *Folkrätten i krig*.
[70] Italian Peace Treaty, 1947, article 14. See L. Leontiades, 'Die Neutralität Griechenlands während des Weltkrieges', *ZaöRVR*, 1930, 130.
[71] *Ibid.*, article 49 on Lampedusa, Lampione and Linosa.   [72] *Ibid.*, article 50.
[73] See the Convention of Uquair, 133 *BFSP*, ii, 726, and Treaty, 7 July 1965, 60 *AJIL* 1966, 744; M. El Ghoneimy, 'The legal status of Saadi–Arabia–Kuwait Neutral Zone', *ICLQ*, 1966, 690. There is some uncertainty whether 'neutral' has any meaning under this treaty in 'military' terms or refers only to 'common territory': M. Hosni, 'The partition of the Neutral Zone', *AJIL*, 1966, 635.
[74] Cf. article 60 of Protocol I of 1977.
[75] Spaight, *War Rights on Land*, 178; G. Debeyre, 'Localités et zones sanitaires en temps de guerre', *RGDIP*, 1939, 600.
[76] Cf. articles 14–15 of Geneva Convention IV.
[77] Article 25 of the Hague Regulations of 1907.   [78] Article 59.

ment on further localities. Such agreement is in any event possible but the protocol offers a convenient framework for further extending areas.

There are obligations under the 1982 Law of the Sea Convention to use the high seas only for 'peaceful purposes'.[79] This statement may be seen in relation to General Assembly resolutions to use the 'common heritage of mankind' for peaceful purposes only.[80] But it is questionable as to what 'peaceful purposes' imply. It may be an exhortation to refrain from force[81] but it is doubtful that the rules, which probably reflect general international law, establish any form of demilitarisation.[82] On the other hand, the provisions dealing with innocent passage in the 1982 Law of the Sea Convention[83] enumerate military or quasi-military activities which are to be regarded as 'non-innocent'.[84]

v. Denuclearised zones

Nuclear disarmament will, to the extent that it is successful, eliminate certain nuclear weapons or certain use of such weapons.[85] At the present stage of development, however, there are few such treaties. Even space is only partially denuclearised under the Outer Space Treaty.[86] And, in spite of the provisions of the Sea Bed Treaty,[87] certain nuclear mines are conceivably 'legal'.[88] On the other hand, there is a trend to limiting the geographical area within which nuclear weapons, or their testing, is allowed. Such objectives are carried out by the establishment of nuclear-free zones.

A new type of zone in which a specific type of weapon is prohibited has appeared. This is the denuclearised zone where nuclear weapons[89] are prohibited. One of the first zones of this type was

---

[78] Article 59.
[79] 21 *ILM* 1261. See article 301 for the general rule and articles 88 on the high seas; 58 on economic exclusive zone (EEZ); 131 and 155 on the 'area'; 141 on the sea bed; 147 on installations; 143(1), 240(a), 242(1) and 246(3) on marine research.
[80] See General Assembly Res. 2749 (XXV) 1970.
[81] See article 301.
[82] The Sea Bed Treaty, on the other hand, introduced a denuclearised regime, below, text to note 87.
[83] 21 *ILM* 1261.   [84] Article 19; cf. 35(c), 311(3), 53(3).   [85] Above, p. 90.
[86] Above, p. 143 and B. Cheng, 'Le Traité de 1967 sur l'Espace', *Journal de droit international*, 1968, 598.
[87] Above, p. 91.   [88] See below, p. 193.
[89] But see the Treaty of Rarotonga, 1985, below, p. 149, on a regime *sui generis*.

established by the Treaty of Tlatelolco of 1967[90] and provided for the 'military denuclearization of Latin America'. This Treaty was based on an earlier declaration, in the form of a *pactum de contrahendo* of 14 February 1963. Such statements are an important step towards possible future regulation forbidding nuclear weapons or tests in a specified area.

An individual State may also be denuclearised by treaty: this is the case of Austria under the State Treaty of 1955[91] which forbids the emplacement of nuclear weapons in Austria. Other States may be bound[92] not to possess, manufacture or develop nuclear weapons,[93] but such provisions do not prevent the stationing of nuclear weapons in the area if such weapons were manufactured elsewhere.[94]

Numerous declarations of intent have been made by regional bodies to establish similar zones, for example by the Conference for Security and Co-operation in Europe (CSCE),[95] which made a declaration in 1973 and 1975 on the denuclearisation of the Mediterranean.[96] Other such declarations are the 1964 Cairo Declaration by the Organization of African Unity on the denuclearisation of Africa,[97] the Lusaka Declaration on Non-Aligned Countries 1970 on

[90] 634 UNTS 326. The Treaty enables States of two types outside the region to adhere to its provisions, first, States which have responsibility for territories in the area, and, secondly, States possessing nuclear weapons. The United Kingdom (1969), for Belize, the Falklands and certain islands in the Caribbean, and the United States (1983) for Guantanamo Bay, Puerto Rico and the Virgin Islands have signed the Protocol, whereas France considers itself to have constitutional difficulties in signing this Protocol: see H. Gros Espiel, 'La signature du Traité de Tlatelolco par la Chine et la France', *AFDI*, 1973, 13; Gros Espiel, 'La signature par la France du Protocol I du Traité du Tlatelolco', *AFDI*, 1979, 806ff; United Kingdom (1969), United States (1971), France (1974), China (1974) and the USSR (1978) have all signed Protocol II.
[91] 217 UNTS 223, article 13.
[92] E.g. Peace Treaty on Germany, 23 October 1954, Dept. of State Publ. 5659, *International Organization and Conference Series*, II, 5; Peace Treaties with Finland, article 17, 42 *AJIL*, Suppl., 204; Bulgaria, article 13, *ibid.*, 190; Romania, article 14, *ibid.*, 262; Hungary, article 15, *ibid.*, 239.
[93] Furthermore, the prohibition concerns only the manufacture of weapons; Germany is a major exporter of nuclear reactors. One reactor was sold to Brazil in 1984 and one to Argentina in 1985: *New Scientist*, 3 October 1985.
[94] Cf. J. Quenéudec, 'Les zones denucléarisées', in Colloque de Montpellier (ed.), *Le droit international et les armes*, Paris, 1982.
[95] Above, p. 93.
[96] UN, *Study on the Naval Arms Race*, 121. Cf. GA Resolutions 36/102, 1981, 37/118, 1982, 38/189, 1983, and 39/153, 1984.
[97] The declaration was endorsed by GA Res. 2033 (XX) 1965; cf. GA Res. 1652 (XVI) 1961, and 1911 (XVIII) 1963.

the Indian Ocean as a 'Zone of Peace',[98] the ASEAN Declaration of 1971 on South-East Asia as a 'Zone of Peace, Freedom and Neutrality' (ZOPFAN),[99] and the Tuvalu Declaration of 1984 of the South Pacific forum on the South Pacific nuclear-free zone.[100]

This last declaration of intent did come to fruition in the Rarotonga Treaty concluded on 7 August 1985.[101] This treaty provides a regime *sui generis* where the banning of nuclear tests and weapons in a specific area, in a somewhat contradictory way, is combined with a provision which allows for specially authorised passage of nuclear ships.[102]

Other efforts[103] have been delayed by unwillingness even to adopt declarations of intent. This has, for example, happened in the Middle East. The General Assembly had encouraged projects in this important area,[104] but attempts at an agreement were foiled by the Israeli attack on Iraqi nuclear installations in 1981.[105]

Unilateral efforts to proclaim individual States nuclear-free have also been made, for example, by Romania for a Balkan Nuclear Free Zone.[106] Other efforts include Sweden in the Unden Plan of 1961[107] and Finland in the Kekkonen Plan in 1963.[108] These two efforts were clearly mere proposals. Discussions on a Nordic Nuclear Free Zone,[109] or a 'mini zone' comprising at least Sweden and Finland,[110] have been going on for some time and are clearly of paramount interest to the Nordic States.[111] On the other hand, the declaration by France on refraining from testing nuclear weapons in the Pacific during the nuclear test cases before the International Court of Justice[112] was a binding unilateral declaration.[113] Negative security assurances, that is pledges by States that they will not use nuclear

[98] *Ibid.*, 119. Cf. GA Resolutions encouraging negotiations for a nuclear-free zone comprising the Indian sub-continent, e.g. 3265 (XXIX) 1974; 36/88 1981; 36/88 1981.
[99] *Ibid.*, 120.
[100] Declaration by Australia, New Zealand, Cook Islands, Fiji, Niue, Papua New Guinea, Solomon Islands, Tonga, Tuvalu, Vanuatu and Western Samoa; *ibid.*, 122.
[101] *ILM* 1442.   [102] Article 5(2).
[103] Cf. *United Nations Study of Nuclear Weapons Free Zones*, revised edn, New York, 1984.
[104] See GA Res. 3263 (XXIX) 1974; Res. 36/82 A–B 1981.
[105] Cf. GA Res. 38/98 1981.
[106] R. Rydell, 'The Balkans, a nuclear weapons free zone?' *Bulletin of Atomic Scientists*, May 1982.
[107] ENDC/C.1.246.   [108] *Ibid.*   [109] Cf. *Svenska Dagbladet*, 25 July 1983.
[110] Cf. *Hufvudstadsbladet*, 19 May 1983; 9 August 1983; such a zone would be less favoured by the Soviet Union.
[111] R. Ekeus, *Nuclear Disengagement in Europe*, SIPRI, Stockholm, 1983.
[112] ICJ *Reports*, 1974, 253, 267.
[113] On the legal effects of unilateral undertakings, see my *Concept*, 105, and my *Law Making*, 216, 322ff.

weapons against States that do not have such weapons themselves, have been made within the Disarmament Conference in Geneva by all the nuclear powers.[114]

vi. *Areas under occupation*

The Law of War applies fully in occupied areas and specific rules have been designed to regulate precisely the relationship between occupying forces and the captured territory.[115]

Most of these rules concern the rights and duties of the occupying party with regard to movable and immovable property in the area and will be discussed in conjunction with other relevant rules bearing on property.[116]

A basic rule for wartime occupations stipulates that title or sovereignty of the territory does not pass to the occupying power.[117] But certain quasi-sovereign powers will be exercised in the occupied territory, for example legislative[118] and administrative[119] powers will be carried out. On the other hand, it is more uncertain whether an occupying power can exercise jurisdictional powers in the captured territory.[120] Nowadays arguments cannot be put forward that a territory has been 'annexed'[121] by force as conquest and annexation no longer afford legitimate title in international law.

[114] Declarations by France, China, the USSR, the United Kingdom and the United States, Arms Control Reporter 860–4, 1 September 1983.

[115] G. v. Glahn, *The Occupation of Enemy Territory: a Commentary on the Law and Practice of Belligerent Occupation*, London, 1957; on the historical background, see D. A. Graber, *The Development of Belligerent Occupation 1863–1914: a historical survey*, New York, 1949.

[116] Below, p. 303.

[117] Hague Regulations, article 43; *Affaire de la Dette Ottomane*, RIAA, 1925, 525; *Great War Criminals Case*, IMT Nuremberg, 13 *AD* 1946, 202; Cmnd. 6964, 1946; for France see the *Naoum Case*, Gaz. Palais, 1970, 1.62; and see Rousseau, *Conflits armés*, 137, for further examples in French and continental practice.

[118] E.g. *Reidar Haaland Case*, (1945) Norway, Hoyesterett, *AD*, 1943–5, 444. But, in principle, the occupied State retains power to legislate on matters which do not concern occupation: Belgium, *AD*, 1919–22, no. 311; *ibid.*, no. 310; Latvia, *ibid.*, no. 321; Poland, *ibid.*, 1927–28, no. 380; but *contra*, Greece, *ibid.*, 1929–30, no. 292. On Allied occupation of Germany exceeding powers of belligerent occupation see W. Friedmann, *The Allied Military Government of Germany*, London, 1947; cf. A. Roberts, 'What is military occupation?' *BYIL*, 1984, 268–71.

[119] *The Lighthouses Arbitration*, (1956) PCA, 23 *ILR* 659.

[120] E.g. Cass. belge, 4.12.1919, Pasicrisie 1920.1 and Rousseau, *Conflits armés*, 139. But see Geneva IV, articles 68, 70–73.

[121] See K. Marek, *Identity and Continuity of States in Public International Law*, Geneva, 1954; U. Scheuner, 'Die Annexion im modernen Völkerrecht', 49 *Friedenswarte* 1949, 81; W. Schätzel, 'Die Annexion im Völkerrecht' 2 *AVR* 1950, 1; G. Zimmer, *Gewaltsame territorielle Veränderungen und ihre völkerrechtliche Legitimation*, Berlin, 1971.

Specific duties of the occupying power are laid down in Geneva Convention IV of 1949 which regulates in great detail the treatment that must be afforded to the population in the territory.

There is an obligation to keep economic and social conditions as they are in occupied territories. But such rules may be suspended by alleged legitimising factors,[122] for example that the territories are not occupied but 'retaken', thus forming an integral part of another State. This is the argument put forward by Israel with regard to any part of Palestine to explain that the Geneva Convention on Civilians does not apply in this area.[123] On the other hand, this argument cannot be valid for other occupied territories, for example with regard to the Golan Heights, where the Convention at any rate must apply.[124]

The essential protection afforded to persons in occupied territories is designed to ensure respect for their lives.[125] No methods of coercion must be used[126] and, in particular, persons must not be subjected to murder, torture, corporal punishment, mutilation or medical experiments.[127] Nor must they be subjected to forced labour.[128] Power to order administrative detentions is limited.[129]

Persons in occupied territories must not be deported[130] but may, if necessary, be evacuated to another region.[131]

A particular question during occupation concerns the controversial right to resistance, which some see as a *jus insurrectionis*;[132] others deny that it exists.[133] The duty of 'obedience' to an established 'effective' occupier[134] would at least cease in the case of an occupier who has himself committed substantial violations of international law.[135]

---

[122] Cf. above, p. 71.
[123] M. Shamgar, 'The observance of international law in the administered territories', 1 *IYHR* 1971, 263.
[124] A. Boyd, 'The applicability of international law to the occupied territories', 1 *IYHR* 1971, 260; Y. Dinstein, 'Belligerent occupation and human rights', 8 *IYHR* 1971, 107. Similar claims were previously made with respect to Sinai. In Lebanon Israel claims that it has set up special units only for civilian assistance; *Report of the International Commission to Enquire into Reported Violations of International Law by Israel during its Invasion of the Lebanon*, Geneva, 1983, 114.
[125] Hague Regulation, article 46; Geneva IV, article 27.
[126] Geneva IV, article 31.   [127] Article 32.
[128] Hague Regulations, article 52; Geneva IV, article 51.   [129] Geneva IV, article 78.
[130] Geneva IV, article 49. See A. de Zayas, 'International law and mass population transfers', 16 *Harvard ILJ* 1975, 207.
[131] *Ibid.*   [132] Above, pp. 48 and 50 in relation to resistance and guerilla wars.
[133] Above, p. 84.   [134] Above, p. 84.
[135] *Flesch Case, Gestapo Chief in Norway*, (1948) *Retstidende*, 1948, 80.

vii. Positive and negative zones

The areas described above which are neutralised, demilitarised or denuclearised are all exempt from some effects of war by being enclosed in zones into which war activities, perhaps of a certain kind, are not to extend. Such zones are therefore negative in the sense that they prohibit war activity within a certain area.

Other zones may be positive in character in that they establish areas inside which war activities are to take place and into which, for example, neutrals must not enter; or if they enter, they do so at their own peril, for there is a presumption that anyone and anything inside a positive zone will be attacked.

The distinction between positive and negative zones has perhaps not been made in the literature. But it is a convenient conceptual way to explain the existence of war zones in the context of spatial application of the Law of War.

viii. War zones

As has been shown, territories may be withdrawn from the potential effect of war by treaty or by declared status of neutrality. The effect of such regulation is that it limits the geographical effect of war. But it does not result in exemption from the Law of War: the territories in question are still subject to the Law of War with regard to neutral rights and duties and, by a different construction, it could be said that their very status of being neutral or neutralised is itself part of the Law of War.

It has been suggested that theatres and regions of war are obsolete concepts.[136] On the other hand, there are special zones proclaimed by a belligerent, especially at sea, which serve as a special warning to neutrals: if they enter such a specific zone they do so at their own peril. This was the practice in the Second World War when Germany proclaimed large areas where neutral ships had to stay in specified lanes to avoid emplaced minefields.[137]

War zones are allowed if they are defensive and if they do not extend more than 12 miles off shore; they must also be effectively supervised.[138] 'Offensive' zones, in which merchant ships are sunk, are illegal even if warnings are provided.[139]

---

[136] Above, p. 139.   [137] See, e.g., Stone, *Legal Controls*, 572.
[138] J. Schmitt, *Die Zulässigkeit von Sperrgebieten im Seekrieg*, Hamburg, 1966, 135.
[139] *Ibid.*, 122. Cf. GA Res. 2749 (XXV) 1970.

War zones were claimed in the Falklands War in 1982. The 'Maritime Exclusion Zone' of 200 miles operated initially as a war zone in which Argentine warships or naval auxiliaries would be 'treated as hostile'.[140]

From 30 April 1982 the zone was amplified to a 'Total Exclusion Zone' (TEZ), which covered 'all ships and aircraft, whether military or civilian, operating in support of the illegal occupation of the Falkland Islands'.[141] Argentina declared a counter-zone, a 'fire-free' zone, also comprising 200 miles around the islands.[142] The sinking of the *General Belgrano* took place some 36 miles outside the Total Exclusion Zone, on 2 May 1982. The British zone was not far off the territorial limits claimed by Argentina.[143] The TEZ was replaced by a 150 miles 'Protection Zone' after the end of the hostilities, 28 July 1982.

The nature of war zones entails the presumption that not only is the law of war fully applicable within such a zone, but also that actual hostilities will take place and that any neutral subject, ship or aircraft enters such a zone at its own risk. State practice allows for such zones, although some commentators question the legality of 'offensive' war zones in which ships are sunk after warning.[144]

ix. Distinction between application in zones and inside states

Attention on the application of war in geographical terms was earlier focused on the 'theatre' or 'region' of war.[145] The distinction between these two concepts has certainly been blurred by the development and use of modern weapons. But the only geographical rules of application, established by positive or negative zones, represent but a partial picture of the problem of spatial application.

Furthermore, as has been indicated,[146] the spatial connotations of various zones concern more the limitation, albeit by legal regulation, of the physical effects of war; however, the application of the Law of War itself in such zones is not restricted but applies in full, and even lends legitimacy to the very establishment and regulation of such zones.

Nowadays the main difficulty is to establish whether and to what

---

[140] HC, Hansard, 7 April 1982, col. 1045.   [141] *Ibid.*, 29 April 1982, col. 980.
[142] A. R. Coll and A. C. Arend, *The Falkland War*, Winchester, Massachusetts, 1985, 97.
[143] Under Law No. 17,094 of 29 December 1966, *Boletin oficial*, 10.1.1967, Argentina claims a 'nautical zone' with full sovereignty 200 miles off shore.
[144] Schmitt, *Die Zulässigkeit*, 122.   [145] Above, p. 139.   [146] Above, p. 152.

extent the Law of War is applicable to non-States and inside States as well as 'between' them.

B. EXTENDED APPLICATION IN ZONES AND INTERNAL CONFLICTS

i. Application in internationalised conflicts

a. Declarations of adherence

In the first section we will consider the question of application of the Law of War to liberation movements. This problem may initially seem not to concern a 'spatial' application. Yet, liberation movements will be present on some States' territories and we are therefore faced, in the final analysis, with a question of application in the internal sphere of States.

In the Spanish Civil War there were early declarations, by both sides, that they would respect the Geneva Convention of 1929.[147] It must be in the humanitarian interest to allow as extensive an application as possible of such Conventions. The Geneva Conventions now provide a much more comprehensive regulation than the earlier 1929 Convention, and it is even clearer that their application would enhance humanitarian interests.

However, it has long been considered that, because of their lack of statehood, numerous liberation movements could not adhere to these Conventions, nor could they enjoy protection thereunder. Liberation movements have sometimes sought to apply the Conventions *mutatis mutandis*. For example, in Algeria the Provisional Government in Exile in Cairo made a Declaration of Accession to the Geneva Conventions in June 1960 to Switzerland, the appointed depositary. However, Switzerland issued a declaration declining to regard the accession as effective as the provisional government had not been formally recognised.[148]

On the other hand, liberation movements can accede if and when they are successful, for then they have themselves attained statehood.[149]

But 'declarations' that the Conventions 'apply' can be made. Such

---

[147] Declaration by Madrid, 3 September 1936; by Burgos, 15 September 1936; ICRC, *General Report*, 1934–8, 131.
[148] M. Bedjaoui, *Law and the Algerian Revolution*, Brussels, 1961, 183, 189.
[149] Cf. accession by Guinea Bissau in 1974, Notification to the Swiss Federal Department, 26 February 1974.

declarations, however, are not directed to the depositary, who would probably not accept them in the absence of recognition, but directed to the ICRC. For example, Algeria made such a declaration when the instrument of accession had been rejected by the depositary.[150]

A considerable practice has evolved of notifying the ICRC that a group involved in war will 'apply' the Geneva Conventions. Thus, in Hungary, in 1956, the National Committee of Gyor was swift to make a declaration of adherence to the Conventions.[151] Numerous declarations have now been made by, for example, the African National Congress (ANC),[152] SWAPO,[153] the PLO,[154] the Eritrean People's Liberation Front (EPLF),[155] the Union National pour l'Indépendance Totale d'Angola (UNITA),[156] by the Afghan groups ANLF,[157] HESLI ISLAMI,[158] ISA,[159] and by the Moro National Front in the Phillipines (MNLF).[160]

Declarations were also made in major wars, in some of which the secessionist movement was unsuccessful, for example Biafra in Nigeria,[161] and in some where a new State did emerge after the originally 'internal' war, as in Bangladesh.[162] In the Congo crisis all parties agreed that the Geneva Conventions applied.[163] Other liberation movements have made statements that they would 'respect' the Geneva Conventions. For example, FRELIMO made such a declaration in 1968.[164]

In the Vietnam War all parties allegedly 'recognised' the Geneva Conventions.[165] In Vietnam the ICRC appealed to the belligerents to apply the Geneva Conventions.[166] The United States did not clarify whether it considered itself bound, but affirmed that the Conventions would be applied.[167] The Saigon Government declared itself willing to apply the 'Geneva Accords',[168] which leaves some doubt as

---

[150] Bedjaoui, *Law and the Algerian Revolution*, 215.
[151] ICRC, *Report on Relief Action in Hungary 1956–1957*.
[152] Declaration to the ICRC, 29 November 1980.
[153] *Ibid.*, 25 August 1981.
[154] On numerous occasions, for example, *ibid.*, 7 June 1982.
[155] *Ibid.*, 25 February 1977.   [156] *Ibid.*, 25 July 1980.   [157] *Ibid.*, 24 December 1981.
[158] *Ibid.*, 7 September 1980.   [159] *Ibid.*, 6 January 1982.   [160] *Ibid.*, 18 May 1981.
[161] Declarations by both sides, ICRC, *Report*, 1967, 37.
[162] Declaration by the Popular Republic of Bangladesh to ICRC, 4 April 1972. At the time Bangladesh was recognised only by India and Bhutan.
[163] CICR, *Rapport annuel d'activités*, 1961, 48.
[164] See Rosas, *The Legal Status of Prisoners of War*, Helsinki, 1976, 161. See further E. Mondlande, *The Struggle for Mocambique*, London, 1969.
[165] 5 *IRRC* 1965, 477, 636.   [166] *RICR*, 1965, 385.
[167] *Ibid.*, 1965, 441; 1966, 130, 360.   [168] *Ibid.*, 1965, 165, 442.

to which instruments they had in mind. The NLF stated that for its part they were not bound by the Conventions. As it had not succeeded to the Conventions formally,[169] the NLF held that it was not bound by the accession of the Bao Dai Government, although the ICRC claimed that it was.[170] However, the NLF declared that it would, in any event, 'follow a humane and charitable policy' towards prisoners of war.[171]

The ICRC insisted that the 1949 Conventions applied in Vietnam, at least after the escalation that had taken place by 1965.[172]

b. Express provisions on applicability to liberation movements

Article 1(4) of Protocol I of 1977 extends the application of the Protocol to

all armed conflicts in which peoples are fighting against colonial domination and alien occupation and against racist regimes in the exercise of their right of self-determination, as enshrined in the Charter of the United Nations and the declaration on Principles of International Law Concerning Friendly Relations and Co-operation among States in accordance with the Charter of the United Nations.

The Conference took a long time over discussions of this particular paragraph and it may well be the most important one of the whole First Protocol, as it extends the application to liberation movements.

The so-called Martens clause,[173] which had been included in the Preamble of the 1899 and 1907 Hague Conventions,[174] has been given a higher status in the 1977 Protocol I by being included in the main text of article 1.[175] The clause provides that in situations not covered by the Protocol or by other international agreements 'civilians and combatants remain under the protection and authority of the principles of international law derived from established custom, from the principles of humanity and from the dictates of public conscience'.

The Martens clause is of the greatest importance in modern international law, especially in rebutting any suggestions that States are

[169] The Democratic Republic of Vietnam had formally acceded to the Conventions in 1957. D. Schindler and J. Toman, *The Law of Armed Conflict, a Collection of Conventions, Resolutions and Other Documents*, Leiden, 1973, 2nd edn, 1983, 482.
[170] 5 *IRRC* 1965, 477, 636.   [171] *Ibid.*, 360.
[172] CIRC, *Rapport annuel d'activités*, 1965, 8; *RICR*, 1965, 385.
[173] Named after the Russian delegate at the first Hague Conferences. Cf. p. 327.
[174] For reference, see above, p. 97.
[175] Article 1(2); in Protocol II, however, the Martens clause is again moved to the Preamble.

free to behave as they wish within their own territory, a consequence of the extreme emphasis of sovereignty usually encountered in the Eastern bloc and even more in Scandinavia. Extreme positivist views may gradually be mitigated by the insistence that the 'public conscience' can, at times, be relied on to assess what is right or wrong.

At the Diplomatic Conference it was suggested that the term 'public conscience' should be replaced by the expression 'universal conscience',[176] but it may be that such a global reference may make it more difficult to ascertain its contents.

It is important to underline the implications of the Martens clause. It is really the conscience of individuals, or of a group of individuals, perhaps a large body of individuals, that, in the last resort, will be relevant since States themselves have no such conscience.

World opinion would, in this respect, play an important role. The condemnation by such opinion of certain practices of liberation movements and States alike will contribute to the development of humanitarian law.

By the inclusion of the Martens clause in article 1, Protocol I extends the application of the clause specifically to the armed conflicts referred to in 1(4), i.e. to all types of liberation wars. The implication of the Martens clause is thus that it fills a supplementary function in cases when there are no clear rules.

The discussions on article 1(4) took up the most part of the first session of the Diplomatic Conference. There were naturally many problems of definition. If the article included 'armed conflicts in which peoples are fighting against colonial domination and alien occupation and against racist regimes' it is obviously important to establish to what level the 'armed conflict' must have developed. The delegation of the United Kingdom made it clear that, in their view, 'armed conflict ... implies a certain level of intensity of military operations which must be present before the Conventions or the Protocol are to apply to any given situation, and that this level of intensity cannot be less than that required for the application of Protocol II, by virtue of Article 1 of that Protocol'.[177] By this cross-reference the United Kingdom indicated that 'armed conflict', for the purposes of Protocol I, must have reached the level where a faction of dissident forces was organised under responsible command and in

[176] CDDH/SR.36, vol. 6, 62.
[177] Declaration made upon signature by the United Kingdom.

control of a part of the territory to enable them to carry out sustained and concerted military operations.[178]

There were numerous objections at the Conference with regard to the terms of article 1(4) and many delegations claimed that concepts like 'colonial domination', 'alien occupation' and 'racist regimes' lend themselves to arbitrary, subjective and politically motivated interpretation.[179]

c. Informal adherence of liberation movements

The legal implications of declarations of adherence by, for example, liberation movements have not been analysed by international lawyers. Since liberation movements do not adhere formally, they do not become parties to the Conventions. Does their undertaking have no legal effect? It is submitted here that it is a valid unilateral undertaking binding on the group making it, provided that the group fulfils the condition of being a belligerent.[180] This is the only possible effect in law which is compatible with contemporary political realities. The reluctance to allow legal effect of unilateral rules and promises and the urge to construe undertakings as 'treaties' is still noticeable in international law.[181] But such strained constructions become even more untenable when, on the one hand, jurists maintain that groups cannot, in any event, conclude 'treaties'. The more flexible notion of a unilateral undertaking, which, after all, carries significance in most internal legal systems, must be accepted if it is clear that, for example, a group wishes to enter into a binding arrangement. To deny any legal obligation of such undertakings would eventually damage interests of States too – apart from limiting the effect of the instruments – as a lop-sided situation would result in which States, but not guerillas, are bound by the laws of war.[182]

d. Formal adherence of liberation movements

The idea that liberation movements are international brings them, for many purposes, near the ambit of the 1949 Geneva Conven-

[178] See article 1 of Protocol II and further below, p. 172.
[179] Federal Republic of Germany, CDDH/SR.36, vol. 6, 61; cf. New Zealand, *ibid.*, 63, and Spain, *ibid.*, 64; cf. the statement by the United Kingdom that the language of article 1(4) is 'political' rather than 'legal', *ibid.*, 46.
[180] Above, p. 103.
[181] For theories refuting such constructions, see my *Law Making*, *passim*, and my *Concept*, 100, 102, 105.
[182] See below, p. 339 on reciprocity.

tions.[183] But since these Conventions apply only in armed conflict between the high contracting parties and liberation movements are not able to accede to the instruments, a formalisation must take place to extend the application of rules of the Law of War beyond what was possible under common article 3.[184]

The formalisation process has been carried out by Protocol I of 1977 with regard to armed conflicts involving liberation movements fighting against colonial domination, alien occupation and racist regimes. By formal declaration under article 96 liberation movements can accede to Protocol I of 1977;[185] and by similar process to the Conventional Arms Convention.[186] Other conflicts are still considered as internal and therefore hitherto only regulated by common article 3. For such conflicts Protocol II of 1977 ensures additional safeguards for the respect of specific rules of war.

The Conferences elaborating the two Protocols between 1974 and 1977 made a considerable distinction between liberation wars and other internal conflicts, although it is clear that the factual situation in the two types of conflict may be extremely similar which, in turn, would warrant a uniform application of internal rules.[187] Arguments were put forward during the 1980 Conference on Conventional Weapons[188] that rules on weapons should bind not only States[189] but should also apply to wars of national liberation[190] and thus coincide with the ambit of the new 1977 Protocols to the 1949 Geneva Conventions.[191] It would be consistent with political realities if the Conventional Weapons Conventions also extended to apply to liberation movements. The latter view was eventually accepted at the Conference and it was agreed to provide special conditions for the application of the Convention to liberation wars.[192]

Consequently, the Convention provides[193] that, in cases where a party to the Convention is also bound by Protocol I of 1977, the provisions of the Conventional Arms Convention, and those of its annexed Protocols, will apply to a conflict with an 'authority' if that

---

[183] Common article 2.   [184] Below, p. 167.
[185] Above, p. 48, and below, p. 160.   [186] Below, p. 180.
[187] The Swiss Federal Department published in 1977 a 17-volume series on the Conferences and it is this publication which is quoted below in the context of statements made during the Conferences. For a commentary see Bothe, Partsch and Solf, *New Rules on Victims of War*, which, however, does not refer to the volumes.
[188] Below, p. 182.   [189] As the Western bloc claimed, A/CONF.95/WG.L.1.
[190] As argued by non-aligned and socialist States, *ibid.*   [191] Below, p. 171.
[192] A/CONF.95/15 and below, p. 182.   [193] Article 7(4)(a).

'authority' has made a declaration under Protocol I of 1977,[194] provided the 'authority' has undertaken to apply the Weaponry Convention. Even if a State is not a party to Protocol I of 1977, the
Conventional Arms Convention will apply[195] if an 'authority' declares it will apply the Geneva Conventions and the Weaponry Convention. It is interesting that in that case, for example, an insurgent
group would be bound by the Geneva Convention and by the
Weaponry Convention, with Protocols, but not necessarily by Protocol I of 1977 which is not mentioned by the article.

A much discussed question was whether 'any' liberation movement
could enhance its own standing to that worthy of protection under
article 1(4) by a mere notification under article 96(3). This article
provides that 'the authority' leading a liberation movement 'may
undertake to apply the Conventions and this Protocol in relation to
the conflict by means of a unilateral declaration addressed to the
depositary' and such a declaration will have the effect that the Conventions and the Protocols are brought immediately into force to
protect the members of the movement.

Some commentators objected strongly that to confer 'belligerent
status on all liberation movements despite the absence of recognition
and heedless of the actual dimension [of the conflict] is palpably
absurd'.[196]

However, article 96(3) seems to indicate that at least the liberation
movement must have an 'authority' to represent it and this, in itself,
would indicate a certain level of organisation. Furthermore, the article speaks of *the* authority, and not *an* authority, which appears to
exclude a plurality of liberation movements.[197]

On balance, however, it appears that most of the alleged problems
caused by the inclusion of liberation wars in article 1(4) were grossly
exaggerated. The wording may be rightly criticised for focusing on
short-term political problems and, for this reason, was perhaps not
suitable for inclusion in a legal instrument intended to be of long-
term value.[198] But, on the other hand, such formulation of the article
must also reduce any objections to the extended ambit of its application as such extension would, in practice, be a mere transitory phase:
there are, for example, few colonial regimes left. The Holy See expressed the view that article 1(4) 'clearly reflects a particular histori-

[194] Article 96(3) and below, p. 182.   [195] Under article 7(4)(b).
[196] Dinstein, 'The new Geneva Protocols' 267.   [197] Cf. Bretton, *Le droit de la guerre*, 134.
[198] E.g. statement by Germany, CDDH/SR.36, vol. 6, 61.

cal situation undergoing rapid development'.[199] On the other hand, if both Protocols were adopted the chances of achieving the application of a uniform humanitarian law in all conflicts would be greatly enhanced.[200]

Some commentators claim that the actual ambit of article 1(4) is extremely narrow: it is argued that it applies only to the peoples of South Africa and Palestine.[201] However, the article seems to have much wider scope in its general formulation. On the other hand, the extension of the application of humanitarian rules to liberation movements by article 1(4) is not as far-reaching as has been alleged. For those who wish to extend humanitarian rules to a uniform network applicable to all armed conflicts the article does not go far enough, but is, on the other hand, supplemented by Protocol II. Yet the article could not be held to be excessively demanding to those who question the rights and status of liberation movements as such movements could always claim, in law if not always in fact, a certain standard of humanitarian treatment.[202]

e. Recognition of statehood

It has been shown that recognition of belligerency in internal war does not amount to recognition of statehood.[203] Similarly, attendance at conferences,[204] adherence to the Geneva Conventions or declarations on adhering to their principles do not imply recognition of any statehood.

Nor does application of common article 3 of the Geneva Conventions imply the recognition of a party as a State, or as an 'emerging' State: article 3(4) provides specifically that its application will 'not affect the legal status of the parties to the conflict'.

Declarations under article 96 of Protocol I or under article 7 of the Weaponry Convention do not imply recognition of statehood, as has been indicated above.[205] On the other hand, this does not mean that all these situations and acts are devoid of all implications for statehood. For example, liberation movements may not be recognised as States, but they are, as far the application of the Law of

[199] CDDH/SR.36, vol. 6, 62, statement by the Holy See.   [200] *Ibid.*
[201] F. Kalshoven, 'The reaffirmation and development of international humanitarian law applicable in armed conflicts, the Diplomatic Conference in Geneva 1974–77', 8 *NedTIR* 1977, 122. Cf. the assessment by Bothe, Partsch and Solf, *New Rules on Victims of War*, 52.
[202] See below, p. 167, on common article 3 of the Geneva Conventions.
[203] Above, p. 35.   [204] Above, p. 48.   [205] Above, p. 48.

War is concerned, treated more and more as somewhat similar units.

The prohibition of force as laid down in the United Nations Charter can also be viewed as breaking through the national walls of a State: in numerous situations it has been clear that a State cannot, for example, escape the consequences of prohibition of force by refusing to recognise another 'territory' as a State.[206]

It has occasionally been suggested that recognition by the ICRC would be of significance for statehood. It may be useful to place such recognition too in its proper legal and factual context to clarify the political repercussions of recognition by the ICRC.

The ICRC certainly treats States as 'important' units[207] and, it must be emphasised, the treatment the ICRC may afford to non-States by no means indicates that these units, in the opinion of the ICRC, are approaching statehood: the ICRC, as a humanitarian agency, is not competent to pronounce on such issues. Nor does recognition by the ICRC of specific Red Cross societies in various territories indicate that there are any implications for statehood of such areas. On the contrary, in many cases the ICRC has acknowledged the existence and functioning of Red Cross societies in countries which were not commonly recognised as States at the time of the ICRC action. For example, it was the Red China Red Cross Society, not that of Taiwan, that was recognised *before* the People's Republic of China had been accepted as a State, for example, in the United Nations.[208]

The IRCR has furthermore sometimes refrained from recognising a Red Cross society which represents and supports the views of a government if such views appeared to be contrary to the spirit of humanitarian law. Thus the ICRC did not recognise a society in Burundi, as the ICRC did not wish to associate itself with an organisation with as pro-Tutsi and anti-Hutu views as the Government itself.[209] Similarly, in Bangladesh the ICRC did not wish to recognise a society furthering the Bengali majority views as this would not be in the interest of the Bihari minority.[210]

[206] Bowett, *Self-Defence*, 154.
[207] D. P. Forsythe, *Humanitarian Politics, the ICRC*, Baltimore, 1977, 45.
[208] G. I. A. D. Draper, 'The People's Republic of China and the Red Cross', in A. Cohen (ed.), *China's Practice of International Law: Some Case Studies*, Cambridge, Massachusetts, 1972, 344.
[209] Forsythe, *Humanitarian Politics*, 16–17.
[210] *Ibid.*

ii. *Direct application of the laws of war in the internal sphere of states*

a. *Variability of constitutional provisions*

The traditional attitude of international lawyers is that international law does not operate inside States unless the constitutional machinery allows for such direct application. In England general rules of international law – but not treaties – are immediately applicable,[211] and certain treaties concluded by the United States are 'self-executing'. In France every ratified and duly published treaty forms part of French law and in the Netherlands any published treaty even takes precedence over both previous and later national legislation.[212]

The position thus varies from country to country but it can be said, *grosso modo*, that general rules of international law and/or treaties are either automatically incorporated in the internal system of a State, or, which is more common, they have to be 'converted' or 'transformed' into internal law.[213]

Some commentators claim that completely different rules apply in international and internal conflicts (or other non-State disputes)[214] and, in view of the above position of the operation of rules of international law, one may understand such consequences of the entrenched State paradigm.[215] The traditional doctrine on transformation is by far the most common one to be applied by municipal Courts. Only rarely are there systems by which international law is wholly part of the land, as in the Netherlands since the 1952 Constitution, or partly, for example with regard to general rules as in England, or with regard to certain treaties as in the United States.

b. *The uncertain nature of case law*

The position of the relationship between international law and internal law is, say many writers, clear in case law. But a case before a

---

[211] Cf. *Trendtex Trading Corporation* v. *the Central Bank of Nigeria*, (1977) 1 QB 529 (CA).
[212] On these and other examples, see, my *Law Making*, 274–85.
[213] There are then numerous subsidiary questions, for example concerning the 'overriding' effect of later international rules or treaties or of subsequent internal legislation; see, for example, on *lex posterior de rogat* my *Law Making*, 274ff.
[214] Above, p. 37.
[215] But it is argued by some writers that the Geneva Conventions of 1949 and the Protocols of 1977 are 'self-executing' and need only be ratified in most States, F. de Mulinen, 'Law of War and armed forces', in Société International de Droit Pénal Militaire et Droit de la Guerre, *Forces armées et développement du droit de la guerre*, Brussels, 1982.

Court presupposes that someone brought it there. There are numerous disputes which are solved in other ways and never comes before
Courts. There are also many situations which do not even grow into
disputes. Therefore, pronouncements of Courts often give little guidance on what the law is, at least in the field of international law.

This radical statement is at strong variance with the unquestioning
attitudes of Anglo-Saxon lawyers, who have been taught to rely heavily on case law. But pronouncements of Courts can state the law only
with respect to types of cases which have come before such judicial
bodies, and since there is a wide area where Courts have no jurisdiction, especially in international situations, it may well be that the
general law is different from isolated case law, however 'settled' this
case law appears to some.

Thus, the fact that municipal Courts, under the particular constitutional rules of their own countries, have taken a specific line on the
applicability of international law in the internal sphere of States is no
firm guide to whether there is such applicability in general.

It appears that the system of international law as presented in most
textbooks has difficulties explaining why, for example, human rights
are applicable in the municipal sphere. Individuals are, say, nearly
all international lawyers, not 'subjects' of international law; but if
they are not subjects of the international order, no human rights that
have not been 'transformed' by national legislation can protect them.
A few States, like England, allow general principles of international
law to apply directly in the country. Other States, like the Netherlands, allow treaties to apply without transformation.[216] No one has,
it seems, commented on the application of the Law of War in the
municipal sphere, although similar issues exist with regard to this
body of law as well.

c. The rationale behind applicability and non-applicability

Is there then anything which the Law of War contains which is so
controversial that States would have reason to dispute its applicability in their internal spheres? As we have seen,[217] the Law of War
consists largely of rules on weapons, rules on methods and targets of
warfare and humanitarian rules. The first two sets are normally
phrased as a series of restraints, whereas the last set of rules, on

[216] See further my *Concept*; *Trendtex* v. *Central Bank of Nigeria*, (1977) 1 QB 529 (CA);
on Netherlands practice see the Constitution of 1952.
[217] Above, p. 126.

humanitarian issues, involves both restraints (to refrain for attacking or harming) and positive duties of action (to assist and help). Such rules seem to deserve the widest application, by all individuals and groups on a State's territory, especially if the State itself is bound by them after having acceded to a specific convention.

If we examine the sets of rules in turn we shall find that certain rules on weapons, in the first set, are most likely to apply to internal groups if a State has adhered to a weaponry convention, at least in cases where weapons have been abolished or destroyed, or otherwise been made unavailable in the particular State.[218] But the situation would be different in cases of certain types of conventional weapons, for example booby traps. Such weapons have been gradually forbidden by international agreements, under, for example, Protocol II to the Conventional Arms Convention of 1981,[219] as many cause unnecessary suffering or have indiscriminate effects.[220] But a liberation movement or dissident group would still find it easy to produce some such weapons.

It is stipulated that application of the Weaponry Convention will entail equal rights and duties for an authority, for example a liberation movement, as those assumed by State parties.[221] The adherence mechanism to the Weaponry Convention,[222] by which liberation movements can be formally bound by an instrument of the Law of War, is an important step on the way to allow for application, in a State's own interest, of prohibitive rules in the internal municipal sphere. But the wording covers only 'liberation movements', which is thought to be a narrow title applicable to only a few groups. It may be in a State's interest to allow prohibitive rules on weapons to apply to other guerilla units, as well as to citizens in general.

The second group of rules of the Law of War, concerning methods and targets of warfare, would, for example, if guerilla warfare is considered, imply more benefits than drawbacks for the State, if such rules were applied by insurgents, or by guerillas and freedom fighters; although on the other hand it must be admitted that there may be situations where a State would wish to apply forceful methods which are not allowed under the Law of War.

Therefore, by claiming that 'there is no war' or that the Law of War does not apply in the internal sphere in internal situations, a State can take coercive action 'to quell a rebellion' and apply

[218] Below, p. 183 on different conventions.   [219] Below, p. 183.
[220] Above, p. 135, and below, p. 198.   [221] Article 7(4)(b)(ii).   [222] Below, p. 183.

measures of a degree that would not be allowed under the Law of War.

On the other hand, a number of prohibitions of methods in warfare, restrictions which could only benefit the State, do not, according to many writers,[223] apply to non-State groups engaged in war. For example, the taking of hostages is a prohibition of Geneva Convention IV on Civilians[224] which applies only to States.[225]

With regard to the third group, it would, again, seem advantageous to a State if internal fighting groups were bound to respect such rules.

Yet, States have been extremely reluctant to allow any application of any part of the Law of War to entities other than States. Why? The answer is probably that there is one area, and one area alone, where the State will not let go of its prerogatives: that of treating detainees as they wish. The turning point in the development of the Law of War in recent years is precisely the hotly disputed question of whether detainees are entitled to prisoner of war status. In Northern Ireland other complications enter the field, by the United Kingdom being bound by the European Convention on Human Rights to afford prisoners of all kinds, even political prisoners, certain treatment.[226]

d. The attitude of the ICRC

The International Committee of the Red Cross does not make any distinction between internal and external strife, as there may be suffering in either case warranting assistance. This has been its attitude since the relief given to Argentina in 1890.[227]

The ICRC has assisted in numerous internal wars and has often applied the same rules in such disputes as for international wars. It offered assistance in 1872, largely through the national society, in the Second Carlist War in Spain between 1872 and 1876. In 1865 the ICRC gave direct relief help in Herzegovina during the revolt against the Turks and to the refugees from that country in Montenegro at the request of the sovereign. Later help followed to the victims in the internal wars in a number of States. Thus, during 1880, 1890, 1893 and 1895 the ICRC gave assistance in Argentina; 1882 in Bos-

---

[223] See, for example, H. Lauterpacht, *Recognition in International Law*, London, 1947, 246.
[224] Article 34.   [225] Greenspan, *Modern Law of Land Warfare*, 413.
[226] European Court of Human Rights, *Ireland* v. *United Kingdom*, Judgment, 1977.
[227] Moreillon, *Le Comité international de la Croix Rouge*, 31.

nia; 1885 in Peru; 1890 in Transvaal; 1894 in Brazil; 1895, 1897 and 1912 in Cuba; 1896 in Rhodesia; 1897, 1903 and 1904 in Uruguay; 1903 in Macedonia; 1909 in Armenia; 1909 again in Spain and 1911 in China.[228] The ICRC has also assisted in all later wars, international or internal.[229]

e. Article 4A of Geneva Convention III

Geneva Convention III on Prisoners of War contains a provision which suggests that the drafters of the Convention might have had in mind its application to combatants of non-States. Article 4A(3) thus provides that 'members of the regular armed forces who profess allegiance to a Government or an authority not recognised by the Detaining Power' will be given prisoner of war status.[230] Some commentators have deduced from this provision that the Convention II on Prisoners of War applies to internal wars.[231] However, the drafters of the article probably had the situation of Free France against Germany in mind,[232] and it is likely that the Convention was not to apply to internal situations in general under this article.

On the other hand, article 4A(2) may cover resistance movements under certain conditions.[233] The article may also extend, at least according to a literary interpretation construed regardless of the intention of the drafters, to two types of internal warfare, both to consolidated resistance movements and to guerillas.

f. Common article 3 of the Geneva Conventions

The broadening of the notion 'international conflict'[234] is obviously one way to achieve the application of *all* the provisions of the Geneva Convention; but as things stand, at least common article 3 covers internal conflicts.[235] Article 3, which is included in all four Geneva Conventions and therefore usually referred to as 'common article 3', provides that certain basic humanitarian rules must be respected in internal disputes. The article provides, *inter alia*, that those who have laid down their arms and others *hors de combat* must not be subjected to

[228] Moreillon, *Le Comité international de la Croix Rouge*, 24–39.
[229] Above, p. 123, and below, p. 324.
[230] On such status, see below, p. 281, and above, p. 119.
[231] R. Falk, *Legal Order in a Violent World*, Princeton, 1968, 123; Seyersted, *United Nations Forces in the Law of Peace and War*, 200; T. J. Farer, 'The humanitarian laws of war in civil strife', 29.
[232] Rosas, *The Legal Status of Prisoners of War*, 256. [233] See note 231.
[234] Cf. above, p. 40 on internationalised conflicts.
[235] Cf. Farer, 'Humanitarian laws of war in civil strife', 17.

(a) violence to life and person, in particular murder of all kinds, mutilations, cruel treatment and torture;
(b) taking of hostages;
(c) outrages upon personal dignity, in particular humiliating treatment;
(d) the passing of sentences and the carrying out of executions without previous judgment pronounced by a regularly constituted court, affording all the judicial guarantees which are recognized as indispensable by civilized peoples.

This article has proved a useful provision and has been applied and supplied authority for action by the International Committee of the Red Cross (ICRC) in, for example, Guatemala in 1954 and Algeria after 1954.[236] The article is not entirely dependent on merely the good will of States but affects, if violated, their international responsibility.[237]

The attitudes of delegations of various States at the Conference where the Geneva Conventions were negotiated illustrate the complex problems involved. On the one hand, it was argued forcefully by the United States that every State has the right to put down rebellion and punish insurgents according to the law. Furthermore, said the United States, it is well known that premature recognition of insurgents is a 'tortious act' against the lawful government and constitutes a breach of international law.[238] Nevertheless, the argument continued, the Conventions should be applied to internal conflicts which amount to war under international law, that is they are waged by organisations with the characteristics of a State; it has *de facto* authority over defined territory; it has forces under organised military authority, and subjected to the laws of war; and the insurgent civil authority agrees to be bound by the provisions of the Conventions.[239]

On the other hand, other delegates were more in favour of a compromise clause and this was adopted. This clause was plain and 'innocuous' and merely binds the parties to protect non-combatants.[240] Contracting parties merely undertook not to do 'certain things, none of which any civilized State would be expected to do anyway',[241] for example, murder, torture, mutilations of prisoners

[236] Cf. Siotis, *Le droit de la guerre*, 209–12.
[237] Cf. *ibid.*, 219; on responsibility see further below, pp. 352ff.
[238] Cf. above, p. 35.
[239] Joint Committee, Report to the Plenary Assembly, Final Record, ii, B.128.
[240] Cf. above, p. 103, on qualifications for combatants. Common article 3 was drafted at a time when the criteria for combatant status were more stringent and the expression 'non-combatant', possibly covering guerilla forces, must be interpreted in that light.
[241] R. T. Yingling and R. W. Ginnane, 'The Geneva Conventions of 1949', 46 *AJIL* 1952, 393.

and of non-combatants. As a result the basic and elementary safe-guards of common article 3 are applicable to internal conflict when such a conflict has reached certain proportions.[242]

In spite of the modest ambitions of common article 3 States have still attempted to evade application of this article, claiming that a conflict did not fall within its ambit but constituted a mere 'police action'. This was, for a time, the position with regard to Algeria,[243] although the ICRC held that, by allowing Red Cross missions to visit Algeria, France had agreed that article 3 was applicable.[244]

In situations where it has not been clear, at least not to all parties, as to whether there was an international situation in which the Geneva Conventions, as a whole, applied to a contracting party, article 3 has retained its importance. For example, Leopoldville made declarations of accession to the 1949 Geneva Conventions in February 1961,[245] but it regarded Katanga forces as rebels. Still, the central government was obliged to apply article 3. Katanga, on the other hand, did not apply to accede to the Geneva Conventions at that stage but declared itself willing to adhere to principles recog-nised by all countries, presumably covering similar ground to com-mon article 3.[246]

In many cases the General Assembly appealed for a certain stan-dard of treatment of those involved in liberation wars to ensure that they were given some protection above the rudimentary provisions of common article 3. The General Assembly thus asked France to give the status of 'political prisoners' to Algerian captives in France, as they were not entitled to prisoner of war status under the Geneva Conventions.[247] The concern of the United Nations for the victims of war was such that repeated calls on all parties to give prisoner of war status to freedom fighters have been made by the General Assem-bly.[248] Similar calls have been made on Israel, but this State still refuses to give prisoner of war status to captured PLO combatants.[249]

---

[242] Cf. *ibid.*, 395–6.
[243] T. J. Farer, 'The humanitarian laws of war in civil strife', 30.
[244] ICRC, *ICRC and the Algerian Conflict*, Geneva, 1962, 4.
[245] Schindler and Toman, *Documents*, 2nd edn, 479.
[246] 43 *RICR* 1961, 140.
[247] Res. 1650 (XVI) 1961. Cf. Resolutions 2395 (XXIII) 1968; 2547 A (XXIV) 1969; 2207 (XXV) 1970; 2795 (XXVI) 1971; 2918 (XXVII) 1972 and 3113 (XXVIII) of 1973.
[248] Resolutions 2395 (XXIII); 2547 (XXIV) 1969; 2270 (XXV) 1970, 2795 (XXVI) 1971; 2918 (XXVII) 1972 and 3113 (XXVIII) 1973.
[249] E.g. PLO-Observer, A/C.6/37/SR.195, para. 18.

g. Analysis of provisions of Protocol II of 1977

(1) General background At the conference for negotiation of the
1977 Protocols there was much discussion about which rules should
apply in internal conflict. An ambitious project to adopt an extensive,
detailed set of rules to govern internal conflicts which are not liberation wars covered by Protocol I of 1977 failed, mainly due to a
determined intervention by Pakistan.[250] Pakistan had been 'concerned' about a lengthy text which ventured into the reserved
domain of States. Other Third World States soon became convinced
that any such regulation of internal conflicts inside their national
territories would infringe their rights of sovereignty and self-determination.

The developing States were quite content to have liberation wars
subsumed under Protocol I, but any other internal conflicts should
not be regulated by any international documents, at least not in any
detail, for any such regime would be 'tantamount to interference with
sovereign rights'.[251] Some even claimed that it is a 'sovereign right' of
every State 'to deal with rebel movements within its territories in any
manner it deems fit'.[252]

Not all Third World States were hostile to Protocol II,[253] but they
were certainly in a great majority. Many of these States have un-
stable governments which need consolidation, and they appeared
worried that Protocol II, in spite of its reassurances that it does not
affect the rules on non-intervention,[254] would entitle other States to
interfere in their domestic affairs. They would, in this context, care
little about the treatment of individuals in their territories. On the
other hand, European States who had suffered the plight of civil wars
became the staunchest supporters of Protocol II.[255]

However, the discussion at the Conference shows that the developing countries, much under the pressure of Pakistan[256] and India,[257]
found that many humanitarian rules of the proposed Protocol II
were unacceptable to them as the implementation of such rules would

[250] CDDH/427 and Corr. 1; cf. CDDH/I/SR.23, 58, vol. 8, 225.
[251] India, CDDH/I/SR.23, 48, vol. 8, 224.
[252] Philippines, CDDH/SR.56, Annex ll, vol. 7, 243.
[253] See, e.g., Guatemala, *ibid.*, 241. Cf. Egypt, which spoke of 'selective humanitarianism', CDDH/I/SR.24, 26, vol. 234.
[254] Article 3. Cf. Egypt, CDDH/I/SR.24, vol. 8, 234.
[255] Cf. D. P. Forsythe, 'Legal management of internal war', 72 *AJIL* 1978, 294–5.
[256] See above, note 250.   [257] CDDH/SR.49, vol. 7, 80–1.

be in violent conflict with their right of self-determination, in the sense of a right to behave as they wish within their own territory.

Many States claimed that their legislation was so advanced that any protection under Protocol II would be 'unnecessary'. Thus, the Indian delegate claimed that 'the Indian delegation does not need any lessons or lectures in humanitarianism from anyone. In fact, all provisions of Protocol II are, in one form or the other, embodied in the national laws of [India].' The Protocol would be unacceptable also because it interfered with the reserved domain. Thus, 'the provisions of Protocol II will only militate against the sovereignty of States and will interfere in their domestic affairs. The internal law and order situations are the sole concern of sovereign States and these problems are to be dealt with according to the domestic laws of the country.'[258] India went on to explain that newly independent countries which are endeavouring to consolidate their sovereignty are 'jealous of their sovereignty and will guard against any action which might constitute an interference in their internal affairs under whatever form or guise', particularly as developing countries, to some extent, are vulnerable victims of pressure by the superpowers. Third World countries 'are aware of the powerful means of communication and propaganda which the powerful countries of the world possess. The developing countries cannot rule out the possible misuse of Protocol II in this ideologically divided world'.[259] Some delegates claimed that 'it is incongruous for the international community to play on internal dissensions of sovereign States' and that the Protocol would, in fact, provide 'opportunity for mis-interpretation in countries endeavouring to consolidate their political and territorial sovereignty and this would accentuate such dissensions'.[260] In this context it may be important to underline that attitudes to intervention have changed in recent years, at least with regard to humanitarian intervention. It may be that the 'illegal area' has become increasingly smaller and that now only interventions to assist unrepresentative rebels or unrepresentative governments, or just to preserve one territorial unit of a State, are prohibited.[261] Those categorically against unilateral intervention are now in a pronounced minority[262] and

[258] India, CDDH/SR.49, vol. 7, 78.   [259] *Ibid.*, 81.
[260] Ghana, CDDH/SR.49, vol. 7, 80.
[261] R. Higgins, 'International law and civil conflict', in E. Luard (ed.), *International Regulation of Civil Wars*, London, 1972, and in C. Black and R. Falk (eds.), *The Future of the International Legal Order*, Princeton, 1971, 81.
[262] I. Brownlie, 'Humanitarian Intervention', 217.

others claim that the international legal system, in this respect, has changed.[263]

It has been demonstrated[264] that intervention often furnishes rebel forces with aid.[265] For these reasons, one must be wary of any misuse of such intervention.

However, it is quite possible to support the uniform humanitarian regulation of internal armed conflicts without condoning any such intervention efforts by third States.

There are obvious and compelling reasons for affording similar protection to victims of both international armed conflicts, liberation wars and internal conflicts, such as civil wars. There is certainly no logical reason for the introduction of a differentiated humanitarian regime for the two types of conflict covered by the Protocols, for liberation wars (and international armed conflicts) covered by Protocol I and for armed conflict and civil wars covered by Protocol II.[266] How could humanitarian rules be denied to one type of conflict? Some thought that 'Public opinion would be astonished at such discrimination.'[267]

(2) The ambit of article 1   According to article 1(1) of Protocol II the few humanitarian rules that remain in the final version will apply to conflicts in the territories of the contracting parties between the armed forces of such parties and 'dissident armed forces or other organised armed groups which, under responsible command, exercise such control over a part of its territory as to enable them to carry out sustained and concerted military operations and to implement this Protocol'. Such a text naturally evokes many problems of interpretation, as does Protocol I with its references to liberation wars.[268] One problem is how to distinguish internal conflicts covered by Protocol II from those covered by Protocol I. One would at least have expected an exclusion clause in the second Protocol, referring to the conflicts covered by Protocol I, to avoid duplication of rules for liberation movements.[269] The distinction is important as substantially higher protection is enjoyed under Protocol I.

A further problem in Protocol II is to determine, more particularly, when riots, tensions and 'sporadic acts of violence' exempted

---

[263] R. B. Lillich, 'A reply to Ian Brownlie and a plea for constructive alternatives', in J. N. Moore (ed.), *Civil War in the Modern World*, Baltimore, 1974, 229.
[264] Above, p. 67.   [265] See above, p. 69.
[266] Cf. Austria, CDDH/I/SR.23, vol. 8, 216.
[267] *Ibid.* [268] See above, p. 161.   [269] Australia, CDDH/I/SR.23, vol. 8, 219.

from the field of application of the second part of article 1 have developed so as to constitute armed conflicts under the first part of the article.

Third World States, supported by the socialist bloc, were responsible for raising the threshold of application of the Protocol. The Protocol is thus not activated until dissident forces control a part of the territory. But such a notion is relative[270] and it is therefore not clear when the Protocol will enter into force in a particular conflict. Some even understood the requirement of territorial control to imply an encouragement to further fighting: such a requirement would be 'dangerous' as such determination is likely to heighten the risks and suffering of the population.[271]

Other concepts are also hazy: who will determine whether forces are 'under responsible command' or what constitutes 'sustained' military operations?[272] Some suggested that the government side should expressly re-accept the Protocol in any concrete situation.[273] Numerous States claimed that only the State in whose territory the conflict takes place can decide on whether the conditions mentioned in article 1(1) are fulfilled.[274]

Many States were thus concerned that the actual application of Protocol II would not be entirely in their hands but automatically enter into application; such automatic activation of the Protocol could not be tolerated in the opinion of these States. For example, Argentina sponsored article 1(4) of Protocol I[275] which, it stated, recognised the 'final liquidation' of the colonial era, emphasising that the international society has a 'duty' to protect those who take part in liberation struggles by applying humanitarian rules of the 1949 Conventions and the Protocol.[276] However, when it came to Protocol II Argentina could not support the regulation as the Protocol provided no safeguard clause providing for, in each case, whether the conditions for application have been met.[277] Others were worried about whether conditions would be assessed not by government or dissident forces, but by third States and in this way violate the principle of non-intervention.[278]

[270] Cf. Forsythe, 'Legal management of internal war', 286.
[271] United Republic of Cameroon, CDDH/SR.49, vol. 7, 84.
[272] Colombia, CDDH/SR.49, vol. 7, 78.   [273] See Brazil, CDDH/I/SR.29, vol. 8, 286.
[274] E.g. Chile, CDDH/SR.47, vol. 7, 232; Colombia, *ibid.*, 77–8; Ecuador, *ibid.*, 79; Philippines, *ibid.*, 83; Tanzania, *ibid.*, 84.
[275] See above, p. 161.   [276] CDDH/SR.36, vol. 6, 50.   [277] CDDH/SR.49, vol. 7, 75.
[278] Brazil, CDDH/SR.49, vol. 7, 76.

Some delegates considered that the level at which the Protocol would enter into effect would be related to the level of organisation at which the dissident forces were able to implement the Protocol on their part.[279] However, such a reference would seem only to complicate matters further: the Protocol would appear apt to be implemented by anyone at any time, provided the factual situation had arisen which warranted a decision on how to treat individuals covered by the Protocol.

The threshold of application, especially with regard to the control of territory, may well be unrealistic in view of the tactics of modern guerilla warfare, which involve great mobility, so that there is continuous change of territorial control.[280] Some delegates found that the way the text was phrased, Protocol II would really apply only to full-scale civil war.[281] However, many lower levels of violence would be excluded, although terrorist attacks and kidnapping, which often form part of the pattern of certain types of warfare,[282] are specifically prohibited by the Protocol.[283] Such prohibitions are of importance as they often save civilians who are not taking part in hostilities[284] and they also constitute an important limit to a special type of warfare. But it is not only the acts which should not be perpetrated by insurgents that are relevant for the application of Protocol II but also, and perhaps more so, the treatment of individuals once they are taken by the other side.[285]

The ambit of article 1 thus raises numerous questions, many of which are impossible to answer in objective terms, but which, on the other hand, may be fairly self-evident in practical terms in each individual case.

[279] Canada, CDDH/SR.49, vol. 7, 77.   [280] Cf. Egypt, CDDH/I/SR.24, vol. 8, 235.
[281] Australia, CDDH/I/SR.23, 22, vol. 8, 219.
[282] Cf. Forsythe, 'Legal management of internal war', 293.
[283] Article 4.   [284] See below, p. 355.   [285] See further below on detainees, p. 290.

II

RULES ON BELLIGERENCE

i. The ambit of relevant rules

Suffering in war can be reduced by prohibiting certain weapons or regulating their use and, secondly, by forbidding certain modes of weapon use and prohibiting specific methods of warfare. In this section we shall deal with prohibitions with regard to weapons.

ii. The historical background

Treaties on weapons have developed in the light of the basic ethical principles of warfare.[1] Thus, the St Petersburg Declaration of 1868,[2] which forbade certain types of ammunition, was primarily designed to avoid unnecessary suffering. It was followed by other instruments recognising similar principles, such as the Declaration of 1874.[3] This Declaration states[4] that 'the laws of war do not recognize to belligerents an unlimited power in the adopting of means of injuring the enemy'.

The 1899 Hague Conventions further emphasised this principle. The first of the 1899 Conventions sought to encourage States not to resort to war,[5] but Hague Convention II regulates the very conduct of war.[6] A 'Declaration', fulfilling all the characteristics of a treaty, was also enacted at the 1899 Conference. By this document contracting parties undertook, on the understanding that the provisions would apply only in wars in which all the participants were

---

[1] Above, pp. 121 and 134.   [2] 18 NRGT 474.
[3] 4 NRGT 2, série 219; *BFSP*, 1873–4, 4, 1005; cf. 'The laws of war on land', Institut de Droit International, *Annuaire*, 1881–2, 156 (the Oxford Manual), below, p. 275.
[4] Article 12.
[5] International Convention I for the Pacific Settlement of International Disputes, 26 NRGT, 2 série, 920.
[6] International Convention II with Respect to the Laws and Conduct of War by Land, 26 NRGT, 2 série, 949.

contracting parties, to refrain from the use of certain gases[7] and certain ammunition, so-called 'dum-dum' bullets.[8]

The Hague Conventions of 1907[9] were also inspired by the thought that it was important to prevent unnecessary suffering in war. Most of the 1907 Conventions regulate methods of warfare[10] and have been, and will be, discussed in other contexts. But at least two Conventions of 1907 have primarily weapons in mind. Thus, Convention VIII Relative to the Laying of Contact Mines[11] does regulate the use of naval mines. Furthermore, Hague XIV Prohibiting the Discharge of Projectiles and Explosives from Balloons[12] at least attempted to regulate the use of bombs discharged from the air.[13] The rules laid down in Convention VIII on Naval Mines are still applicable today and probably enounce general rules of international Law.[14] Rules on bombardment, on the other hand, are more akin to other rules on methods and will be discussed in that context.[15] Conventional types of bombs are not forbidden as weapons by international law, but they can still be used in a prohibited manner, for example by area bombing.[16]

The Washington Conference of 1922 on Limitation of Armaments drafted rules for a Treaty Relating to the Use of Submarine and Noxious Gases in Warfare,[17] but the Treaty never entered into force.

However, important new rules on the use of noxious gases were included in the 1925 Geneva Gas Protocol.[18] This Protocol, caused by the practices of the First World War, is an effort to prohibit certain types of warfare and has recently been invoked in the Iran–Iraq War, as both States are bound by the Protocol.[19]

---

[7] Declaration I Prohibiting the Use of Asphyxiating Gases, 26 NRGT, 2 série, 998.

[8] Declaration II Prohibiting the Use of Expanding Bullets, *ibid.*, 1002. The name 'dum-dum' came from the location in India where the British manufactured these bullets. Cf. A. Ogston, 'The Peace Conference and the dum-dum bullets', *British Medical Journal*, 1899, 278; P. Bruns, *Über die Wirkung der Bleispitzengeschosse 'Dum Dum'*, Tübingen, 1898; E. M. Spiers, 'The ruse of dum-dum bullets in colonial warfare', *Journal of Imperial and Commonwealth History*, 1975, 4, 1.

[9] Above, p. 123.   [10] Below, p. 232.   [11] NRGT, 3 série, 580.   [12] *Ibid.*, 745.

[13] See also Hague IX Respecting Bombardments by Naval Forces in Time of War, *ibid.*, 604.

[14] Below, p. 349.   [15] Below, p. 132.

[16] Below, p. 239. On prohibited unconventional bombs, see below, p. 216.

[17] 25 LNTS 202, see further below, under biological weapons.

[18] Protocol for the Prohibition of the Use in War of Asphyxiating Poisonous and Other Gases and of Bacteriological Weapons of Warfare, 94 LNTS 65; it entered into force on 8 February 1928. See further below, p. 214.

[19] Iran acceded on 5 November 1929 and Iraq on 8 September 1931.

A series of studies was made in the United Nations, and two special Conferences on Conventional Weapons were held in Lucerne and Lugano in 1974 and 1976, a further Convention on Excessively Injurious Conventional Weapons being concluded in 1981.[20] There have been attempts to draw up further treaties prohibiting certain chemical and bacteriological weapons,[21] and numerous declarations in the General Assembly showing concern for 'biological' weapons[22] and for weapons of 'mass destruction'.[23] Some attempts have resulted in the 1977 Convention on the Prohibition of Environmental Techniques.[24] The basic principle of the Law of War, which provides that the choice of methods or weapons of warfare is not unlimited, is a rule which has been reinforced by Protocol I of 1977,[25] as has the rule which forbids weapons which are of a nature to cause superfluous injury or unnecessary suffering.[26] The Protocol also prohibits weapons which may cause 'widespread, long-term and severe damage' to the natural environment.[27]

Apart from obligations arising from specific treaties reducing or controlling the use of certain weapons, parties to Protocol I of 1977 are bound by a general undertaking to verify whether *any* new weapon and its use will be compatible with the provisions of the 1949 Geneva Conventions and with the Protocol.[28] Some writers have commented that this is a surprising provision in the Protocol in the context of its other articles, as the obligation to consider the use of certain weapons is more to be expected in a disarmament treaty.[29] But surely rules on weapons cannot be separated from what many

---

[20] Convention on Prohibitions on Restrictions on the Use of Certain Conventional Weapons Which may be Deemed to be Excessively Injurious or to Have Indiscriminate Effects, 19 *ILM* 1980, 1523; the Convention, and its Protocols, prohibit certain weapons which cause non-detectable fragments (Protocol II) or which are incendiary (Protocol III). Another Protocol deals with certain prohibited mines and booby-traps (Protocol III). See *in extenso* below, pp. 180ff.

[21] See report by the Secretary General, 1969, A/7575 Rev. 1, S/9292 Rev. 1, and the Conferences in Lucerne and Lugano, see below, p. 181.

[22] E.g. Res. 3465 (XXX) and 2936 (XXVII). Cf. Report by the Secretary General, A/7575 Rev. 1, S/9292, Rev. 1, 1969.

[23] E.g. Res. 3479 (XXX). See further below, p. 195.

[24] Convention on the Prohibition of Military and Any Other Hostile Use of Environmental Modification Techniques, *ILM*, 1977, 88.

[25] Article 35(1).   [26] Article 35(2). Cf. above, p. 135.

[27] Article 35(3) and cf. above, p. 89.

[28] Article 36. See further below, p. 180.

[29] P. Bretton, 'Le problème des "méthodes et moyens de guerre ou de combat" dans les Protocols additionnels aux Conventions de Genève du 12 août 1949', RGDIP, 1978, 61.

call 'humanitarian'[30] rules; both sets of rules are designed to improve
the conditions of individuals in war. At all times the use of weapons is
subjected to the compelling principle of ethics in warfare.[31]

A. CONVENTIONAL WEAPONS

i. *The meaning of conventional weapons*

'Conventional'[32] weapons have been said to be all weapons which are
not 'dealt' with in 'other contexts', i.e. they do not include nuclear,
chemical and biological weapons, radiological weapons and other
weapons of mass destruction.[33] The Resolution of the United Commission for Conventional Disarmament stated to the Security Council that the Commission would cover 'all armaments and armed
forces, except atomic weapons and weapons of mass destruction'.[34]

Such definitions are obviously unsatisfactory, relying as they do on
non-areas which are unclear in turn. For the Aristotelian method of
defining A by reference to non-A obviously works only if non-A is
fairly clear. Yet, there is a hazy area of weapons of 'mass destruction'[35] against which conventional weapons can be set, at least as a
working hypothesis. 'New' weapons need not necessarily be weapons
of 'mass destruction'. For example, laser-guided, particle beam or
other directed energy weapons are considered, by relevant expert
bodies, as 'conventional weapons'.[36]

ii. *The 1981 Weaponry Convention*

a. *The Lucerne and Lugano Conferences*
The General Assembly of the United Nations requested the Secretary
General in 1972 by Resolution 3032 (XXVII) to make a specific
survey of existing rules on the restrictions of specific weapons. The
Report[37] formed some basis for further discussion among experts.[38]

Following the International Conference on Reaffirmation and Development of International Humanitarian Law in Armed Conflict in

---

[30] See below, p. 271 on the meaning of the term and above, p. 88 on the questionable
distinction between arms control, disarmament and the Law of War.
[31] Above, p. 134.   [32] Cf. note 20 above, p. 179.
[33] United Nations, Group of Experts, A/39/349, 1985, 6.   [34] S/C.3/32/Rev. 1, 1948.
[35] Below, p. 195.   [36] United Nations, Group of Experts, A/39/349, 1985, 7.
[37] A/9215, vols. 1 and 2.   [38] Cf. GA Res. 3319 (XXIX) 1974.

1972, two important specialist Conferences were held to consider the use of certain conventional weapons. At the request of Resolution XIV of the XXnd International Conference of the ICRC in Tehran in 1976, a Conference of Government Experts was held in Lucerne in 1974, on Weapons that May Cause Unnecessary Suffering or Have Indiscriminate Effects. A second Conference of Government Experts was convened by the ICRC under the decision on follow-up of the Lucerne Conference[39] and was specifically endorsed by the *ad hoc* Committee of the Second Session of the Diplomatic Conference on the Reaffirmation and Development of International Humanitarian Law in Armed Conflict in 1975.[40] The second Conference of Government Experts was held in Lugano in 1976.

The General Assembly of the United Nations decided on a follow-up of the Diplomatic Conference of 1977 and decided by Resolution 32/152 to convene a Conference in 1979 on Conventional Weapons and, in advance of the delegates' meeting, a Preparatory Conference.

After the main Conference produced the 1981 Conventional Weapons Conventions, there had been great interest on the part of the General Assembly in promoting further research in the conventional arms area.[41]

b. The structure of the Convention

A Convention on Prohibition and Restriction of the Use of Certain Conventional Weapons that Cause Unnecessary Suffering or Have Indiscriminate Effects, together with three Protocols, was eventually concluded in 1981.[42] The Convention itself is of a formal character and contains only provisions on entry into force, dissolution and review conferences, whereas substantive provisions are relegated to the three separate Protocols. The Conventional Weapons Convention, normally called the Weaponry Convention, provides for an interesting mechanism of indirect obligation.

[39] Lucerne Report 1975, para. 282, 79.
[40] CDDH, 2nd sess./220 Rev. 1, paras. 56ff.
[41] See Res. 36/97 A 1981 on the establishment of a special Group of Experts on Conventional Weapons; cf. Res. 35/156 1980; see also Res. 38/188 A 1983 whereby the General Assembly requested the Group to continue its study; cf. United Nations, *Guidelines for the Study of Conventional Disarmament*, GAOR, 12th spec. sess., Suppl. no. 3, A/S–12/3. Annex III, 1982; Group of Experts on All Aspects of the Conventional Arms Race and on Disarmament Relating to Conventional Weapons and Armed Forces, A/39/348, 1985.
[42] 19 *ILM* 1523. There are 24 parties (1985), but most States of military significance have not acceded except for the USSR and the Nordic countries.

c. The mechanism of indirect obligation

The commentary to the Convention suggests that the principle of reciprocity has been adopted in the provisions. Thus, a State is only bound *vis-à-vis* another party which accepts and applies the Convention.[43] But the wording adopted does not provide for such reciprocity.[44] The question of factual application will add some vagueness to the obligations as it is difficult to ascertain implementation *in casu* of such rules. It would even seem that if a third party enters the conflict the original disputing parties will be bound between themselves even if the third party is not bound.[45] In this area the Convention itself is of vital importance and presents a great landmark in international law. The mechanism by which a party is bound is not only the traditional signature and/or ratification procedure,[46] but by what we in this work call 'indirect obligation': if a State is not a party to Protocol I of 1977 and an 'authority', for example a liberation movement,[47] 'accepts' and 'applies' the obligations of the Geneva Conventions and the Weaponry Convention, then the Geneva Convention and the Weaponry Convention, together with the 'relevant' Protocols, are brought into force at once.[48] There is not even a provision that the relevant State itself is a party to the Geneva Conventions.

Nor is there any provision that *all* Protocols have been adhered to by that State: by the wording *any* relevant Protocol will come into effect by the declaration of the liberation movement or other 'authority'. Furthermore, according to the literal wording of the Convention,[49] the Geneva Conventions and the Weaponry Convention (with 'relevant' Protocols) come into force for *all* parties to a dispute, which means that even third States will be bound in this indirect way.

d. Protocol I on Fragmentation Weapons

Fragmentation weapons usually produce a symmetrical pattern of fragments, with high-velocity impact, around the bursting munition or, sometimes, along a linear trajectory, especially in the case of anti-personnel mines.[50] Some of these fragments are not detectable by X-ray, making medical assistance difficult, and some fragments contain toxic substances such as uranium or zinc.

[43] A/AC.206/10, 22; cf. article 7(2) and 7(4).   [44] See further below, p. 339.
[45] Article 7(1).   [46] See further my *Essays*, 15ff.
[47] As under Protocol I of 1977, article 96(3).
[48] Article 7(4)(b)(i) and above, p. 158; cf. below on reciprocity, p. 339.
[49] Article 7(4)(b)(iii).
[50] SIPRI, *The Law of War and Dubious Weapons*, Stockholm, 1976, 70–1.

Flechettes, small arrows or needles, also hit their target with high velocity. Often they do not kill, but cause multiple injuries and a very high degree of pain. Some of these weapons are constructed with cluster warheads or other devices with many bomblets.[51] Such weapons tend to be indiscriminate in their effect over a large area and they also tend to cause much unnecessary suffering by dispersal of tiny fragments.[52] 'Flechettes' can be used in ammunition for rifles but are more common in warheads.

It is questionable whether military necessity[53] is ever great enough to outweigh the suffering caused by fragmentation weapons. Many military manuals prohibit some of these weapons, for example projectiles filled with glass.[54]

A proposal at the Diplomatic Conference was remitted to the Second Conference of Government Experts in Lugano in 1976. Following further negotiations leading up to the Weaponry Convention in 1981, it was agreed to include a comprehensive prohibition. It was decided to adopt Protocol I, annexed to the Convention, forbidding all weapons whose 'primary' effect is to injure by fragments which cannot be detected in the human body.

It may be noted that the prohibition in Protocol I to the 1981 Convention covers only fragmentation weapons 'designed' to injure by undetectable fragments but not those which contain fragments, and which, on an incidental basis, may contribute to such fragments entering the human body. It is, for example, not uncommon for mines to have plastic casings in order to evade being found by mine detectors.[55] Although mines are often made nowadays with plastic components or casings, they are not caught by the Protocol.[56]

Nor does the Protocol cover fragmentation weapons whose fragments are detectable, such as steel flechette weapons.[57]

e. *Protocol II on Treacherous Weapons*
Land mines are permissible under the Law of War as a defensive weapon. As an offensive weapon they become indiscriminate, liable

---

[51] On cluster bombs with numerous bomblets, BLU (bomb live units), see M. Krepon, 'Weapons potentially inhuman: the case of cluster bombs', in R. Falk (ed.) 4 *The Vietnam War and International Law*, Princeton, 1976, 266.
[52] *Lugano Report*, 204; cf. *Lucerne Report*, 49–61.
[53] Cf. below, p. 332.   [54] *Lugano Report*, 204.
[55] A/AC.206/10, 1981, 4.
[56] *Report of the Diplomatic Conference*, vol. 16, 526.
[57] Cf. GAOR, 33rd sess., Suppl. no. 44, A/33/44, Annex, ss. F and G (Mexico).

to kill civilians and other protected persons, and might therefore be prohibited as weapons used for advancing forces.

The main reason for condemning certain mines is that they are indiscriminate by nature. If a house is booby-trapped by a retiring army, the victims may not necessarily be enemy forces but the returning inhabitants.[58] Thus, the basic criterion for legality of mines is that of discrimination. If mines can be designed to be aimed at the enemy, distinguishing between members of the armed forces and civilians, between enemy warships and merchantmen, then there is no reason why mines should not be allowed, as much as ordinary weapons which are aimed at their target by soldiers.

New rules for land mines had been proposed as early as in the ICRC Draft Rules of 1956.[59] There had been further interest on the part of the ICRC.[60] The increased interest in land mines in recent years is partly due to the fact that booby-traps and similar contraptions are a favourite weapon of terrorists.[61] There is no doubt that these practices explain why Protocol II to the 1981 Convention was adopted.[62] The Mines Protocol to the 1981 Convention covers only land mines but not mines at sea.[63]

(1) General provisions Protocol II to the 1981 Weaponry Convention defines mines as 'munitions placed under, on or near the ground or other surface area and designed to be detonated or exploded by the presence, proximity or contact of a person or vehicle, and "remotely delivered mine" means any mine so delivered by artillery, rocket, mortar or similar means or dropped from an aircraft'.[64] This definition covers only land mines; the Protocol excludes specifically anti-ship mines at sea or in inland waterways.[65]

The Mine Protocol attempts to protect 'civilians', including UN mission and peace-keeping forces,[66] but does not define this term. Some commentators[67] assume an automatic reference to Protocol I of

---

[58] Greenspan, *Modern Law of Land Warfare*, 367.

[59] Articles 14–15. Draft Rules for the Limitation of the Dangers Incurred by the Civilian Population in Time of War, Schindler and Toman, *Documents*, 2nd edn, 187.

[60] See Res. XIII at the Istanbul Conference of 1969; cf. Res. XIV at the Tehran Conference in 1973.

[61] Cf. above, p. 19 on terrorism, and p. 50 on terrorist warfare.

[62] B. M. Carnahan, 'The law of land mine warfare, Protocol II to the UN Convention', 105 *MilLR* 1984, 73 at 75.

[63] See below p. 191, for rules on mines at sea.

[64] Article 2.   [65] Article 1.   [66] Cf. above, p. 104.

[67] Carnahan, 'Land mine warfare', 76.

1977 where 'civilians' are defined[68] as anyone who is not a member of the armed forces. But in view of the considerable difficulties of defining precisely the term 'member of the armed forces' we are no wiser even if such cross-reference is allowed by implication. The notion of 'combatants' is, as has been demonstrated,[69] a highly controversial and fluctuating term, and, conversely, so is the concept of 'civilians'.

Bearing in mind the recurring problems of the notions 'combatants' and 'civilians', the ambit of Protocol II to the Weaponry Convention provides certain restrictions on land mine warfare.

As has been mentioned, anti-personnel mines are a common way of impeding advances of the enemy in specific territory. The Protocol stipulates that no mines or booby traps may be used against civilians.[70] The Protocol also prohibits the indiscriminate use of mines and defines 'indiscriminate use' as any placing of weapons which is not directed against a military objective; or which uses a method of delivery which cannot be directed against a specific military target; or which may be effected to cause incidental loss of life of civilians, or injury to civilians,[71] or damage of civilian property or a combination thereof, provided finally that such injury (or damage) is excessive in relation to the direct military advantage anticipated.[72]

The article thus introduces several, conjunctive or successive, subjective tests. Who is to decide whether there is 'direct' military advantage? Views on such a matter in the opinion of the attacker and of the attacked may not necessarily coincide. Secondly, it is not even the imminent military advantage which is weighed up but the 'anticipated' military advantage. Are there any time limits or any organic connection of any other form linking the subjective assessment of 'military advantage' to a point in time near to action or can it also cover advantage which will accrue later? These questions appear to be pertinent but do not seem to have attracted much attention at the Conference or by writers.

(2) Remotely delivered mines At the Lucerne Conference it had been suggested that what were then called 'scatterable' mines would be covered by a future Convention. Such mines were later renamed 'remotely delivered mines', i.e. they are those which are delivered at long range by aircraft, guns, rockets or mortar.[73] Indiscriminate in-

---

[68] See Protocol I of 1977, article 50.   [69] Above, pp. 103ff.   [70] Article 3(2).
[71] Note that UN Forces are specially protected under the Protocol, see article 8.
[72] Article 3(4).   [73] *Lugano Report*, 50.

juries to civilians may follow on remotely delivered mines, which are often laid in very large numbers by aircraft. There are several hazards connected with such practices: the limits of the minefield will be uncertain, for no actual soldiers will have been there to demarcate any lines. Furthermore, there will inevitably be indiscriminate injuries to civilians and combatants alike, if the mines are not equipped with self-destruction devices and remain after the end of hostilities. At Lugano it was suggested[74] that all mine fields with more than twenty mines should be recorded, as was already the case in most armies with regard to manually delivered mines.

The final compromise understanding at the Weaponry Conference between those who wanted to forbid remotely delivered mines and those who advocated their permissibility was that general restrictions on warfare would apply to such mines.[75] This meant that the provisions of Protocol I of 1977 would, *mutatis mutandis*, apply, for example with respect to advance warning of attacks that might affect civilians.[76] It is indicated that by 'long range' is meant a distance greater than 2,000 metres; mines within that distance are equated with 'manually' delivered mines.[77]

The conditions which make such mines permissible are that they are fitted with neutralising devices or they are delivered within a distinctly marked field.[78]

But the provisions in Protocol II to the Weaponry Convention[79] that remotely delivered mines may not be used in towns or other places of civilian population are limited by the clause providing for an exception concerning imminent ground combat. Another exception which also hollows out the legal contents of the Protocol concerns authorised use of mines if a party finds itself in 'close vicinity' to a military objective of the other party. Finally, a third exception is designed to cover the case where civilians have been adequately 'warned'.[80]

(3) Booby-traps

Booby-traps are defined as 'any device or material, which is designed, constructed or adapted to kill or injure and

---

[74] *Lugano Report*, 50.
[75] Report of the Committee of the Whole, A/CONF/95/11, 1980/2; cf. *Lugano Report*, 20.
[76] See article 37(2) of Protocol I of 1977 and below, p. 241.
[77] Protocol II, article 2(1), 3, 5.
[78] *Lugano Report*, 50-1; see COLU/203 on distinction between anti-tank and anti-personnel mine fields.
[79] Article 4.   [80] Article 4(2)(b).

which functions unexpectedly when a person distributes or approaches an apparently harmless object or performs an apparently safe act'.[81] It may not always be easy to distinguish between booby-traps and other mines but the Protocol provides for special and 'unconditional' prohibition of certain so-called 'perfidious' booby-traps. By such booby-traps one usually understands explosive devices concealed in innocuous objects like children's toys, or in connection with protective emblems.[82] Many such devices may already be forbidden under the Hague Regulations.[83]

Protocol II distinguishes between booby-traps which are specifically treacherous or perfidious[84] and those which are designed to cause superfluous injury or unnecessary suffering.[85] The first group is subdivided into devices which are 'prefabricated' and encased in harmless objects and those which are attached or associated with protective emblems, signs or signals.[86] Other types of booby-traps are allowed only if 'due precautions are taken to protect civilians', as such devices expose civilians to particular risks.[87]

(4) Delayed action devices Other devices which are remotely or automatically detonated by delayed action pose special dangers to civilians and are prohibited by the Protocol unless special provisions are made to safeguard civilians from their effects.[88]

(5) Recording of minefields The Protocol provides that all 'preplanned' minefields are to be recorded[89] and parties must 'attempt' to record other minefields as well. But the term 'preplanned' is not defined.[90]

(6) Remnants of mines General Assembly Resolution 36/71 emphasised the hazards posed by 'material remnants' of war, especially

---

[81] Article 2.
[82] See list of examples in Protocol II to 1981 Weaponry Convention, article 6(1)(b); cf. Annex I of Protocol I of 1977, for list of protective signs and signals.
[83] Article 23(e); cf. below on ruses.   [84] Article 6(1).   [85] Article 6(2).
[86] Cf. article 35(2) of Protocol I of 1977 and below; cf. above, note 82.
[87] Article 6, 3 and 4. See *Lugano Report*, 51, and COLU/203, 214–5, 219; cf. COLU/206 on a proposal to forbid camouflage of devices among the civilian population.
[88] Article 4. Cf. *Lugano Report*, 51. Cf. COLU/213. Cf. CDDH/IV/201 proposing a total ban.
[89] Article 7(1).
[90] It is uncertain whether the term 'preplanned' implies any more planning than the word 'planned': T. Glynn, 'Land mine warfare', Lecture at British Institute of International Law, 27 July 1985.

by mines. Libya proposed this Resolution in the Assembly as that country had had the experience of numerous casualties caused by mines left after the Second World War.[91] Protocol II of 1981 consequently incorporates a provision for such cases. The Protocol provides for agreements after hostilities with other States and with organisations for information and technical assistance to remove or neutralise mines and booby-traps emplaced during a conflict. This is already common practice and there have been numerous agreements to dispose or reduce the risks of mines.[92] But the Protocol provides for information to be pooled to the Secretary General of the United Nations[93] and this may be a useful coordinating system to safeguard all persons after the end of hostilities. The obligation to supply information is the only substantive provision in the part of the Protocol for agreements 'to be made' are naturally not more than *pacta de contrahendo* and the Protocol does nothing more in that respect than encouraging, and perhaps providing a framework, for such agreements.

But the provision on information gave rise to ample discussion as the Protocol, in that part, entailed a legal duty. Under the original proposal[94] an occupied, but not an occupying, force would be required to supply information, although minefields laid by the occupied party might have constituted the only defensive means of 'counterbalancing' the occupation. The final text provides that disclosure of information is mandatory only in cases where the forces of neither party are in the territory of the adverse party.[95]

There is a technical Annex to Protocol II on Treacherous Weapons with guidelines. However, this Annex is merely explanatory and non-binding and entails no legal obligations.

f. Protocol III on Incendiary Weapons
There were some early attempts to outlaw certain incendiary weapons. Flame throwers were forbidden in several peace treaties after the First World War.[96]

The Geneva Disarmament Conference in 1932–3 provided for the

---

[91] Working Group, 1980, 6.
[92] E.g. Korea Armistice Treaty, 1953, 4 UNTS 234, article 2; Vietnam Treaty, 1973, 24 UNTS 148, article 5; Egypt–Israel Treaty, 1979, 18 *ILM* 362, article VI(4) of Appendix to Annex I.
[93] Article 7(3)(a).   [94] A/ASC.206/10, 1981, 6.
[95] Article 7(3)(a).
[96] See, Treaty of St Germain, article 135; Neuilly, article 82; Trianon, article 119 and Sèvres, article 176.

prohibition of incendiary projectiles in the Draft Convention[97] and included incendiary weapons along with chemical and biological weapons[98] in plans for qualitative disarmament.[99]

In more recent times, especially in connection with the Vietnam War, there has been further evidence that massive spread of fire by incendiary weapons is indiscriminte in its effects. Furthermore, injuries resulting from either direct use of the weapons or from fire caused by them are intensely painful, requiring assistance by medical resources far beyond the means of most countries.[100] The use of napalm in particular has been repeatedly condemned.[101] Another new type of incendiary weapons relies on the release of a thickened pyrophoric agent.

The ICRC included prohibition in the Draft Rules of 1956 for the Limitation of the Dangers Incurred by Civilian Population in Time of War.[102] The ICRC gave the question of incendiary weapons further attention at several of its conferences.[103] The International Human Rights Conference in Tehran in 1968 also gave the matter attention.[104]

Incendiary weapons have been defined as those which depend for their effects on the action of incendiary agents; such agents are substances which act through flame and/or heat derived from exothermic chemical reactions, *inter alia* normally combustion reactions.[105] There are four broad categories: metal incendiaries (e.g. magnesium); pyrotechnic (e.g. those igniting when exposed to air); pyrophoric (e.g. those which ignite spontaneously when exposed to air); and the oil-based types (e.g. napalm). All weapons based on these

[97] Part IV, article 48 of the British Draft Convention of 16 March 1933.
[98] Cf. below, p. oo.
[99] SIPRI, *Law of War*, 65.
[100] United Nations, *Report by the Secretary General on Napalm and Other Incendiary Weapons and All Aspects of their Possible Use*, 1972, A/8803 and E.73.1.3; cf. Replies from Governments, 1972, A/9207.
[101] E.g. A/9215; A/9207 Corr. 1 and Add. 1; cf. A/8803/Rev. 1, *Report of the Secretary General*; see also United Nations Secretariat, *Report on Existing Rules of International Law Concerning the Prohibition or Restriction of Specific Weapons*, A/9215, vols. 1 and 2, Cf. GA Resolutions on incendiary weapons, Resolutions 2444 (XXIII) 1968; 2852 (XXVI) 1971; 2932 A (XXVII) 1972; 3076 (XXVIII) 1973 urging the Diplomatic Conference to reach agreement to forbid napalm; 3255 A-B (XXIX) 1974; 3464 (XXX) 1975; 31/64 1976; 33/70 1977; 34/82 1978; 35/153 1979.
[102] ICRC, Draft Rules, Geneva, 1956, article 14.
[103] See, e.g., Resolution XVII at XXth Conference 1965.
[104] See Resolution XXIII of the Conference.
[105] United Nations, *Report by the Secretary General on Napalm and Other Incendiary Weapons and All Aspects of their Possible Use*, 1972.

types are indiscriminate in their effects and cause injuries which require exceptional medical resources for treatment.[106]

At the first session of the Diplomatic Conference in Geneva in 1974 the question of incendiary weapons was discussed in an *ad hoc* Committee. A proposal by one group of States[107] was expanded and supported by others.[108] These efforts[109] were later supplemented by detailed analysis by the two Conferences of Government Experts on the use of Certain Conventional Weapons.

The Expert Conferences at both Lucerne[110] and Lugano[111] suggested prohibitions of incendiary weapons.

(1) General provisions The definition, as suggested by the Lugano Conference and adopted by the Protocol, excludes munitions, which have secondary, or incidental, incendiary effects, for example illuminants, tracers, smoke or signalling systems.[112] Prohibitions include, on the other hand, those which combine incendiary effects with other destructive effects, *inter alia* shaped charge effect, designed, for example, to pierce armour or as defence against aircraft.[113] The Protocol thus affects most incendiary weapons in most circumstances.[114]

The Protocol states that it is forbidden, in all circumstances, to make the civilian population *per se* an object of attacks by incendiary weapons[115] or to attack any military objective located within a concentration of civilians.[116] Such attacks may already be forbidden under international law[117] but the Protocol usefully goes on to define what 'concentration of civilians' signifies. Such a concept is said to be the permanent or temporary concentration in inhabited parts or cities, towns or villages, camps or columns of refugees or evacuees or groups of nomads. The wording was chosen to convey a 'word picture' rather than exact mathematical criteria.[118] The definition as phrased seems to cover a wider sphere than normally subsumed under 'civilian population', for other references to concentration of civilians usually rely on its more static nature, whereas Protocol III especially mentions those who are on the move, either as refugees, evacuees or nomads.

'Military' and civilian objectives are, on the other hand, defined by

[106] SIPRI, *Law of War*, 64–5.
[107] Austria, Egypt, Mexico, Norway, Sudan, Sweden, Switzerland and Yugoslavia.
[108] Algeria, Iran, Ivory Coast, Lebanon, Lesotho, Mali, Mauritania, New Zealand, Tunisia, Tanzania, Venezuela and Zaire.
[109] CDDH–DT, 1975.   [110] *Lucerne Report*, 15–35.
[111] *Lugano Report*, 44–9, 128–9, 176, 183–8, 192–4 and 202.   [112] *Ibid.*, 203.   [113] *Ibid.*
[114] *Ibid.*   [115] Article 2(1) of Protocol III to the 1981 Convention.   [116] Article 2(3).
[117] Below, p. 232 on targets.   [118] 5 *United Nations Disarmament Yearbook* 1980, 320.

traditional provisions in the 1949 Geneva Conventions and in the 1977 Protocols.[119] The Protocol forbids attacks not only on civilian populations by incendiary weapons[120] but also on military targets within a concentration of civilians, as defined above, by all air-delivered incendiary weapons.[121] Furthermore, other than air-delivered incendiary weapons may be used only against military objectives within any concentration of civilians if military targets are separable from civilian objectives and all precautions have been taken to save civilians from attack.[122]

(2) *The jungle exception* By article 2(4) Protocol III to the Weaponry Convention it is forbidden to attack forests or 'other kind of plant cover' except if such 'natural elements' are used to cover, conceal or camouflage combatants or other military objectives, or are themselves military objectives.

It means that a State naturally covered by jungle vegetation will not have any protection under the Protocol against attacks by, for example, napalm weapons. Nor will any civilian target be protected, for an attacker cannot know whether or not the jungle conceals a 'military' or 'civilian' objective.

This surprising clause, which we may call the 'jungle exception', as this expression conveys the type of territory the negotiators had primarily in mind, is designed to undermine the functioning of Protocol III in a number of countries with dense tropical vegetation.

iii. Naval mines
The 1907 Hague Convention VIII on the Laying of Automatic Submarine Contact Mines[123] forbids unanchored mines unless they are made harmless one hour after control over them has been relinquished.[124] It is furthermore prohibited to anchor mines unless they are neutralised if they break loose from their mooring.[125] The same guidelines as apply for legality of land mines are relevant to mines at sea: it is the security of non-combatants and of civilians that is at the core of prohibitions.[126]

---

[119] Cf. below, p. 242.   [120] Article 3(1).
[121] Article 3(2). There was a last-minute compromise on this point by the United States and the other parties, A/AC.206/10, 16.
[122] *Ibid.*   [123] For reference, see NRGT, 3 série, 580; 2 *AJIL* 1908, 138.
[124] Article 1.   [125] *Ibid.*
[126] Cf. I. Bock, *Die Entwicklung des Minenrechts von 1900–1960*, Hamburg, 1963, *passim*; H. S. Levie, *Mine Warfare and International Law*, US Naval War College, Newport, 1980, 271.

But different problems are raised by naval mines than by land mines: at sea mines often pose enhanced risks to neutrals, both if they interfere with the freedom of the high seas and if they move, by currents or wind, to a place away from where they were emplaced.[127] Therefore, Hague Convention VIII provides that security of 'peaceful shipping' must always be safeguarded whenever automatic contact mines are emplaced.[128] On the other hand, Hague Convention VIII reflects the view that naval mines are not, *per se*, illegal, but their use has to be regulated. Yet the Regulation of Hague Convention VIII was, in the opinion of a number of States, so unsatisfactory that the United Kingdom made a specific reservation[129] to the effect that it reserved the view of the legitimacy of practice *not* prohibited by the Convention.[130] The United Kingdom thus sought to restrict mines to the territorial sea and to prohibit mines on the high seas altogether.[131]

The problem of discrimination is, as stated above, of primary importance to naval mines. The reason for regulating the use of contact mines in Hague Convention VIII was precisely that such mines do not, by definition, distinguish between ships and would pose particular hazards to neutral shipping. But other types of mines known at the time of the Hague Convention, for example command mines, were not forbidden by the Convention in 1907. Nowadays highly sophisticated mines have been developed, sometimes with discriminatory sensors, which can distinguish between different types of ships. Some mines are magnetic, acoustic or rely on a pressure effect or a combination thereof. They can usually be operated at a distance with great accuracy and have a high reliability factor. However, the provisions of Hague Convention VIII of 1907 on neutralising mechanisms[132] and information on danger zones[133] could form a foundation of useful concepts for further regulation of mine warfare at sea.[134]

But the compatibility of some modern mines with treaties other than the Hague Conventions may be questioned. For example, the tethered Continental Shelf Mine with a nuclear rocket-propelled warhead has such sensors for anti-submarine warfare.[135]

---

[127] Cf. Institut de Droit International, *Annuaire*, 1910.   [128] Article 3.
[129] Schindler and Toman, *Documents*, 2nd edn, 720; *Parliamentary Papers*, Misc. no. 5, 1909.
[130] Such a measure is not a reservation properly so-called as it does not restrict, but possibly extends, obligations assumed under a treaty: see my *Essays*, 50.
[131] A. G. Y. Thorpe, 'Mine warfare at sea, some legal aspects for the future', Lecture at the British Institute of International Law, 17 July 1985, MS, 5.
[132] Article 1.   [133] Article 3.   [134] UN, *Study on the Naval Arms Race*, 63.
[135] Thorpe, 'Mine warfare', 20.

If new discriminatory mines are designed, their legality may be judged differently from the old contact type of mine. It would be highly questionable to consider the tethered nuclear Continental Shelf Mine compatible with the provisions of the Sea Bed Treaty,[136] but writers have suggested that, since it is not anchored or emplaced but 'suspended', it might escape the prohibition of the Sea Bed Treaty. Authors who take this line are usually also influenced by the factor that the Continental Shelf mine is not a weapon of 'mass destruction' but designed only for anti-submarine warfare and that, for this additional reason, it is not prohibited under the Sea Bed Treaty.[137]

The importance of any obligation to notify neutral shipping of any mine field was made obvious in the *Corfu Channel Case*.[138] A duty to warn neutral ships today derives both from Hague Convention VIII and from Geneva Convention 1958 on the High Seas[139] and the 1982 Law of the Sea Convention,[140] all of which lay down already existing rules of international law.[141]

But even if shipping of third parties must be safeguarded in a dispute, there remains a possibility for using mines on the high seas for defensive purposes.[142]

Mines at sea are not made illegal by the Conventional Weapons Convention of 1981.[143] However, certain principles in the Mine Protocol to that Convention lay down certain general rules which, *mutatis mutandis*, also apply at sea.[144]

iv. Small calibre weapons

Weapons research has developed lighter weapons, with lighter ammunition of high velocity. Some of these high-velocity projectiles disintegrate on impact. Due to their high velocity small calibre bullets also tumble on impact in the human body and therefore present a broad face to tissues. The passage of such bullets also creates intense hydro-dynamic shock waves, which cause severe injury and mutila-

---

[136] Below, p. 210.
[137] O'Connell, *Influence of Law on Sea-Power*, 157. The Treaty does not apply to the sea bed beneath territorial waters.
[138] ICJ *Reports*, 1949, 71.   [139] Article 15.   [140] Article 24.
[141] See above, p. 147 on provisions of these instruments on the use of the high seas for peaceful purposes.
[142] Cf. C. Q. Christol and C. R. Davies, 'Maritime quarantine: the naval interdiction of offensive weapons and associated material to Cuba, 1962', 57 *AJIL* 1963, 525.
[143] Above, p. 180.   [144] Below, p. 264.

tion of tissue outside the actual trajectories.[145] The only regulation in
treaty law so far of munitions because of their shape and function is
the prohibition of munitions weighing less than 468 grams in the St
Petersburg Declaration of 1868[146] and of dum-dum bullets in the
Hague Declaration of 1899.[147]

Field manuals of some major countries go further than the Hague
Declaration and forbid 'irregular shaped bullets'.[148] Effective prohibition should, said the Lugano Conference, aim at all small calibre
projectiles which cause injuries beyond those necessary to disable the
enemy, whether such excessive injuries are due to the bullets' flatten-
ing, expansion, velocity or tumbling.[149]

The regulation of small calibre weapons did not form part of the
1981 Weaponry Convention or its Protocols. The Conference produced, however, a special Declaration, 'appealing' to States to exercise 'care' in developing such systems and encouraged further research in this area.[150] However, the Weaponry Convention of 1981
provides a useful framework wherein a further Protocol on small
calibre weapons can be included.

v. Other questionable weapons

Parties to Protocol I of 1977 are under obligation to consider whether
the use of 'new' weapons is compatible with the Protocol and with
general international law.[151] Naturally, even non-parties are obliged
to consider whether employment, or even possession, of any new
weapon is prohibited by any rule of general international law, although the wording of the relevant article in the Protocol indicates
that rules may not bind all States but that certain prohibitive rules
might affect only a certain party.

Certain new weapons, for example fuel explosive weapons, kill by
air shock waves. Fuel air explosives cause extensive damage and
painful injury by detonation of gaseous hydrocarbons.[152] But the
Conference which elaborated the 1981 Convention was not able even
to take a resolution with respect to fuel air explosives, in spite of
insistence by Sweden, Switzerland and Mexico.[153]

[145] *Lucerne Report*, 37–47; *Lugano Report*, 61–9, 116–19, 194–5, 205–6.
[146] Above, p. 177.   [147] Above, p. 178.   [148] *Lugano Report, 205.*   [149] Ibid.
[150] Resolution adopted by the Conference, 7th Plenary meeting, 23 September 1979,
Appendix E to Convention 1980, A/CONF.95/8, Annex 3.
[151] Article 36.
[152] Cf. B. Blomqvist, 'Fuel air explosives', *Armenytt*, 1976, 20.
[153] GAOR, 33rd sess., Suppl. no. 44, A/33, Annex E.

Some weapons, known as 'flame blast' munitions, combine the fuel–air explosive effect with radiation in chemical fireball munitions.[154] Other chemical fireball munitions produce thermic radiation.[155]

Laser weapons cause burns and blindness,[156] as do light flash devices.[157] Directed-energy weapons rely on laser systems.[158] High-intensity microwave radiation causes internal burns.[159] Infrasound devices, alone or in combination with stroboscopic light flashes, cause damage to the central nervous system.[160]

The use of any of these weapons would appear incompatible with the basic principles of ethics of warfare.[161]

B. WEAPONS OF MASS DESTRUCTION

i. General rules

One of the first institutional decisions taken by the General Assembly was to establish a Commission for, *inter alia*, the 'elimination of major weapons adaptable to mass destruction'.[162] Interest in prohibiting these weapons has been maintained, and has considerably intensified over the years. In 1980 the Disarmament Commission considered the question of weapons of mass destruction and recommended the negotiation of agreements for their prohibition as a priority for the Second Disarmament Decade.[163] There have been discussions also in the Committee on Disarmament,[164] in the Conference for Disarmament,[165] and in the General Assembly.[166]

a. Definition of weapons of mass destruction
The Commission for Conventional Armaments in 1948, in considering its own mandate, defines weapons of mass destruction to include

---

[154] *Lugano Report*, 82.   [155] *Ibid.*   [156] *Lucerne Report*, 73; *Lugano Report*, 1980–1.
[157] Some milder stroboscopic types are already used for riot control, see *Lucerne Report*, 75.
[158] E. A. Fessler, *Directed-Energy Weapons, a Juridical Analysis*, New York, 1979. 'Laser' stands for 'light amplification by simulated emissions of radiation'.
[159] *Lucerne Report*, 75.   [160] *Ibid.*, 74.   [161] Below, p. 195.
[162] GA Res. 1(1) of 24 January 1946.
[163] A/CN.10/PV.25–40; GAOR, 35th sess., Suppl. no. 42, A/35/42, para. 19, sect. C, para. 14.
[164] GAOR, *ibid.*, Suppl. no. 27, A/35/27, paras. 57ff.   [165] CD/732 1986, iiiff.
[166] GAOR, 35th sess., plenary mtgs, 4–33rd mtg, 94th mtg and First Committee 4–38th mtg.

atomic explosive weapons, radioactive material weapons, as well as certain 'lethal' chemical and biological weapons, and weapons developed in the future with similar destructive effects.[167] The General Assembly reiterated this expanded notion of weapons of mass destruction, defining such weapons as 'atomic explosive weapons, radioactive material weapons, lethal chemical and biological weapons, any weapons developed in the future which have characteristics comparable in destructive effect to those of the atomic bomb or weapons mentioned above'.[168]

The General Assembly expressed repeated concern about the use of these weapons.[169]

The ICRC considered weapons with uncontrollable effects in connection with their 1956 Draft Rules for Limitation of Dangers Incurred by the Civilian Population in Time of War.[170] Nuclear weapons are the main weapons of mass destruction. The Sea Bed Treaty clearly implies that nuclear weapons are weapons of mass destruction by referring to and prohibiting the emplacement of 'any nuclear weapons or any other types of weapons of mass destruction'.[171]

There are thus also other weapons of mass destruction which are not nuclear weapons. Which are they and what are their hallmarks?

The United Nations Commission for Conventional Disarmament characterised weapons of mass destruction both in terms of certain physical characteristics on which such weapons are based and in terms of the scale of the destructive effect of the weapons.[172] But this does not mean that new weapons of mass destruction, based on other physical principles, could not be invented, nor that any weapons of mass destruction hitherto classified as weapons of mass destruction could not become 'conventional', e.g. by being made smaller. The fact that some new conventional area weapons, such as cluster

---

[167] UN, S/C.3/32/Rev. 1; cf. *UN Study on Conventional Disarmament*, New York, 1985, 6–7.
[168] Res. 32/84 B 1977.
[169] See, for example, GA Resolutions 3479 (XXX) 1975, 31/74 1976; 32/84A 1977, 33/66B 1978, 34/79 1979; 35/149 1980; 36/89 1981; 37/77 1982, requesting CCD and CD respectively to intensify negotiations for an agreement to stop development and manufacturing of such weapons. Cf, GA Res. 32/84 B 1977 urging States to cease developing new weapons of mass destruction.
[170] Below, p. 207.
[171] Article 1, (emphasis added). See further above, p. 193, and below, p. 209.
[172] S/C.3/32/Rev. 1, 1948.

bombs,[173] fuel–air explosives[174] and incendiaries[175] might cause greater damage than 'small' nuclear weapons 'should not be permitted to blur the fundamental qualitative distinction between weapons of mass destruction and other types of weapons'.[176]

With such a static view one is compelled to ask why weapons should be grouped in a way that *a priori* excludes any future reclassification. Surely, criteria must be identified for a group called 'weapons of mass destruction' and when weapons no longer fulfil such criteria, they must either be declassified from this group, or we must redefine the essential criteria.

What then are the relevant intrinsic features of weapons of mass destruction? It may be desirable to interpret a text as it stands using the words in their normal context.[177] 'Mass' might just mean 'mass' even though the Sea Bed Treaty has introduced the curious use of the participle 'massed',[178] but most other texts, for example the Outer Space Treaty,[179] use the word 'mass destruction'. And 'weapons of mass destruction' might just mean 'weapons designed to destroy masses'.[180] Is it not precisely that such weapons are designed not to destroy one combatant at a time, not even groups of them, but a great part of (or the entire) population in an area that make such weapons 'weapons of mass destruction'? Any more complicated formula does not seem to serve much purpose for the reason for the patent illegality of these weapons is the absence of discrimination, the lack of use of the basic rule of distinction.[181] It must be these considerations that render weapons of mass destruction 'different' from other weapons which are aimed at the enemy, perhaps at individual soldiers or battalions, but not aimed at and able to wipe out entire towns,[182] provinces or countries. On the other hand, the physical criteria of such weapons adopted by the above definition[183] are not necessarily helpful. If nuclear weapons could be reduced to have an

---

[173] Above, p. 194.   [174] Above, p. 195.   [175] Above, p. 188.
[176] United Nations, Group of Experts, A/39/349, 1985, 6.
[177] Cf. Vienna Convention on the Law of Treaties, article 31 on interpretation.
[178] 'Massed' thus refers to 'destruction', perhaps implying 'intense destruction' rather than being the object of destruction.
[179] Above, p. 147.
[180] A. W. Thomas and A. J. Thomas, *Legal Limits on the Use of Chemical and Biological Weapons*, Dallas, 1970, 118, suggest that if 'mass' means 'people', weapons of mass destruction cannot include chemical weapons. The basis for this reasoning seems ill founded.
[181] On this, above, p. 106.   [182] On bombardment, see below, p. 239.
[183] Above, p. 196.

impact which could be directed at a combatant alone, there is legally no reason why such a weapon should be prohibited, unless it causes any unnecessary suffering. But it is, at present, unthinkable that nuclear weapons could have such limited effect and it is their indiscriminate effects rather than the physical principles on which they are founded that must form the guidelines for their illegality.

If indiscriminate attacks are forbidden under international law it could readily be deduced that indiscriminate weapons, which cause precisely such attacks, must be forbidden too. But such a conclusion, however justified to the student of logic, has not, in general, been accepted.[184] The British view at the Lucerne Conference in 1974 was that indiscriminate weapons should mean those which 'cannot' be accurately directed against military targets but not necessarily those which, in the past, had been used indiscriminately.

However, the ICRC experts held that both weapons which 'by nature' are indiscriminate and those whose normal and typical use had indiscriminate effects should be forbidden.[185]

Others argued that 'area weapons' may not necessarily be indiscriminate and that conventional weapons could be designed to be indiscriminate unless following a random course but, on the other hand, all weapons could be used, to some extent, indiscriminately.[186]

b. Identification of weapons of mass destruction

The decision whether or not a specific weapon is to be included in the group of weapons of mass destruction depends entirely upon how that group is defined. But if the above suggestions are accepted, that such weapons are designed or capable of destroying parts of whole populations, or other large groups in certain areas, the following weapons must be included. First, nuclear weapons must be in this group for they are all, at this stage of development, capable of such damage, even the Continental Shelf Mine[187] and nuclear 'hand' weapons. Furthermore, 'lethal'[188] chemical and biological weapons are included.[189] Geophysical and environmental warfare is indiscriminate

[184] On indiscriminate weapons, cf. Institut de Droit International, 52 *Annuaire* 1967, Report by F. A. v. d. Heydte. Cf. also *Lucerne Report*, 1974, 10: all experts agreed on prohibition of indiscriminate attacks but not on prohibition of indiscriminate weapons.
[185] ICRC, *Weapons That may Cause Unnecessary Suffering or Have Indiscriminate Effects*, Geneva, 1973, para. 27, 244.
[186] *Lucerne Report*, 10–11.   [187] Above, p. 191, and below, p. 209.
[188] On the relevant degree, see below, p. 224.
[189] The United Nations Commission for Conventional Armaments suggested this in 1948, see *United Nations and Disarmament 1945–1970*, no. 70, ix.1, ch. 1.

by implication.[190] Radiological weapons, as akin to nuclear weapons, are also included and, probably, infra-sound weapons.

The 1977 CCD session considered a USSR Draft Convention[191] which provided for an umbrella arrangement whereby a general prohibition of weapons of mass destruction could be supplemented by special agreements on prohibition of specific weapons. The Draft contained a list of weapons to be prohibited and there are special provisions for amendment of the list.

But the United States has traditionally preferred specific, rather than general, prohibitions. The United Kingdom has also emphasised that general treaties dealing with hypothetical weapons cannot provide for verification.[192] On the other hand, in the past arms control treaties have often dealt with areas of future concern, as did the Outer Space Treaty.[193]

The East European State members of CCD submitted a Draft Convention on nuclear neutron weapons in 1978 as a particularly inhumane weapon of mass destruction[194] and Poland suggested in the First Committee that such weapons should be prohibited, if not generally, at least on a 'contractual basis'.[195] But the United States considered neutron weapons or others involving enhanced radiation as nuclear weapons which should be dealt with separately in the context of nuclear disarmament.[196]

ii. *Nuclear weapons*

a. *The special case of nuclear weapons*
There is no shortage of evidence of the disastrous effect of nuclear weapons on health[197] and on the environment.[198] The destructive

---

[190] *Lucerne Report*, 75–6; cf. below, p. 226.
[191] CCD/511, Rev. 1, and GAOR, 32nd sess., Suppl. no. 27, A/32/27, vol. ii.
[192] CCD, 1980, GAOR, 35th sess., Suppl. no. 27, A/35/27.63.
[193] Above, p. 147, and GA Res. 2222 (XXI) 1966.
[194] CCD/559, and GAOR, 33rd sess., Suppl. no. 4, A–S–10/4, 111, para. 77.
[195] GAOR, 35th sess., 1980, First Committee, 4–38 mtg.
[196] See GA Res. 33/66 A & B 1978.
[197] For example, WHO, *Effect of Nuclear War on Health and Health Services*, Geneva, 1984; E. Chiviam (ed.), *Last Aid: the Medical Dimensions of Nuclear War; International Physicians for the Prevention of Nuclear War*, San Francisco and Washington, DC, 1981; S. Glasstone and P. J. Doland (eds.), *The Effects of Nuclear Weapons*, 3rd edn, Washington, DC, 1977.
[198] For example, SIPRI, *Weapons of Mass Destruction and the Environment*, Stockholm and London, 1977, with extensive bibliography; J. London and G. White (eds.), *The Environmental Effects of Nuclear War*, Washington, DC 1984.

power of nuclear armouries, even as early as 1967, far exceeded all the conventional explosives used since the discovery of gunpowder.[199]

b. Reduction of hazards?

Actual use presupposes possession of such weapons and, therefore, the network of treaties prohibiting production and possession of nuclear weapons[200] reduces the number of parties who can develop such weapons.

Other treaties, like the Non-Proliferation Treaty,[201] restrict the number of States which can obtain nuclear weapons. Other agreements, such as the Test Ban Treaty,[202] the Outer Space Treaty of 1967[203] and the Antarctic Treaty,[204] restrict the use of nuclear weapons in certain geographical areas.

According to the introduction to the Draft Protocol to the Geneva Conventions,[205] what became Protocol I of 1977, the Protocol was never intended to deal with nuclear, bacteriological or chemical warfare. In spite of this clarification, certain States felt obliged to make specific statements during the negotiations to emphasise that, with regard to nuclear weapons, the Protocol must not impair their right of 'sovereignty'. France, for example, argued that Protocol I merges humanitarian law[206] with the Law of War in a way which is 'not without dangers'. Any instrument which sets out to govern the conduct of warfare must, said France, take scrupulous care to respect the sovereignty of States and their inalienable right to self-defence in case of aggression. Some provisions of Protocol I might well, insisted France, impair that right.[207] One such provision concerned the pro-

[199] United Nations, *Effects of the Possible Use of Nuclear Weapons and the Security and Economic Implications for States of the Acquisition and Further Development of these Weapons*, Report by the Secretary General, 1967, republished in United Nations, *Basic Problems of Disarmament*, 1970, 70.I.14, 79.

[200] Such as the Peace Treaties with Finland, Hungary, Bulgaria and Romania and Italy in 1947 (the obligation on Italy in this respect was annulled by the Allies in 1951); the Paris Agreement with Germany of 1954; the Austrian State Treaty of 1955; see above, p. 148; and the Treaty of Tlatelolco, above, p. 148.

[201] 729 UNTS 161 and above, p. 91. Cf. SIPRI (ed.), *Internationalization to Prevent the Spread of Nuclear Weapons*, London, 1980.

[202] Treaty Banning Nuclear Weapon Tests in the Atmosphere, in Outer Space and Under Water, 1963, 480 UNTS 43, and above, p. 91.

[203] 610 UNTS 205, and above, p. 148. Cf. GA Res. 2222 (XXI) 1966 endorsing the Draft Treaty; cf. GA Res. 1962 (XVIII) on nuclear activities in outer space.

[204] Above, p. 142.   [205] ICRC, 1973, 2.

[206] For meaning of 'humanitarian law' see below, p. 271.

[207] A/C.6/37/SR.18.3; France CDDH/SR.41, vol. 6, 186.

tection of civilians against hostilities;[208] another was related to the principle of distinction between military targets and civilian objectives.[209] Both such provisions would be prejudicial to the exercise of France's national right of legitimate defence and, as a result, France made a specific declaration when acceding to Protocol II that it had found itself unable to ratify Protocol I as this instrument ostensibly impaired France's right to use nuclear weapons whether in defence or as a deterrent.

However, Protocol I of 1977 does not explicitly forbid the use of nuclear weapons. But since such weapons are by nature indiscriminate and have effects which cannot be isolated from the civilian population in an attacked territory, nuclear weapons are indirectly prohibited by the Protocol's provisions of indiscriminate or area attacks.[210]

Other States also made statements to similar effect, considering that ratification of Protocol I of 1977 would not be possible if it in any way restricted the right to use nuclear weapons.[211]

There may be a network of treaties and conventions today which all further reduce the field of who may use nuclear weapons and where nuclear weapons might be used. But these agreements do not necessarily reduce the likelihood of such weapons being used, especially in the light of the pronouncements by States of their 'sovereign' right to nuclear weapons. It may well be that the risk of nuclear conflict actually escalates in proportion to the reduction of the nuclear arsenal of the now few nuclear States, by consolidation of such arsenals coupled with the polarisation of the two superpowers.

c. Criteria for legality

It has been shown earlier[212] that the question of nuclear arms and war is normally discussed in the context of disarmament negotiations. There have been several treaties restricting the actual use of nuclear weapons and such prohibitions will, especially if combined with actual reduction of the arms supplies, affect the war-waging material of a State.[213] There is a further question of great importance going to

[208] Cf. Article 43 of the Draft and article 48 of the Final Protocol.
[209] Draft article 47, adopted as article 52 of Protocol I.   [210] Below, p. 209.
[211] For text of United States declaration on signature see Schindler and Toman, *Documents*, 2nd edn, 636; for a declaration by the United Kingdom see *ibid.*, 634. On the nature of such declarations, which do not constitute 'reservations', see my *Essays*.
[212] Above, p. 90.
[213] Above, p. 102. On decisions to acquire nuclear weapons, see S. McLean (ed.), *How Nuclear Weapons Decisions are Made*, London, 1986.

the core of the use of nuclear arms: that is the question of their alleged inherent illegality under international law. The test for legality of weapons could be said to be that they must not cause destruction which is disproportionate to the military advantage.[214]

(1) Basic restrictions. The use of nuclear weapons – and all other weapons – is subject to three basic principles: the necessity to use them; the proportionality of their use; and the obligation not to cause unnecessary suffering.[215] But it has been suggested that these principles regulate only the use of conventional weapons and that nuclear weapons are legal in the absence of any customary rule of international law or by any international convention restricting their employment.[216] But any reference to 'customary law' in this context invariably leads to difficulty: one would have to rely on an unacceptable fiction of 'negative' custom.[217] The first time an atom bomb was used in war all these principles were violated, as shown in the *Shimoda Case*.[218] The District Court of Tokyo in that case also emphasised that if the use of a weapon is contrary to the customs of civilised countries and the principles of international law, its use must be prohibited even if there is no express provision to this effect.[219]

But then some claim that the aforementioned principles cannot be applied 'strictly' in view of political 'realities'.[220] Others have been worried that any condemnation of nuclear weapons[221] may lead to a

[214] Cf. below, p. 332 on military necessity. Legality cannot depend only on the wording of treaties, cf. R. Falk, L. Meyrowitz and J. Sanderson, *Nuclear Weapons and International Law*, Princeton, 1981, 22.

[215] Cf. United States Field Manual 27–10, *The Law of Land Warfare*, 1956, para. 3(a), 41, 35.

[216] *Ibid.*, para. 35. On the distinction between tactical and strategic nuclear weapons see SIPRI (ed.), *Tactical Nuclear Weapons, European Perspective*, London, 1978, 344–89. On the MC14/3 chemical warfare policy of NATO adopted in 1967 and reaffirmed in 1986 to include binary nerve gas munitions, see J. P. P. Robinson, 'Disarmament and other options for Western policy making on chemical warfare', *International Affairs*, 1986–7, 69.

[217] For a rejection of the notion of customary law in its traditional form, see my *Concept*, 112.

[218] See the *Case of Shimoda* v. *Japan*, 1963, 8 *Japanese Annual of International Law*, 1964–5, 212.

[219] *Ibid.*

[220] M. E. E. McGrath, 'Nuclear weapons, a crisis of conscience', 107 *MilLR* 1985, 205.

[221] Like the one by American Roman Catholic Bishops in a Pastoral Letter of 1983, *Challenge to Peace: God's Promise and Our Response*, 19 May 1985. The letter states that States have a right to defend their territory but not by nuclear weapons: 1.C.1, 9; deterrence based on balance of forces of nuclear stocks can be morally acceptable only if it remains a step in progressive disarmament, II, A, 14; 11, D, 2, 17–18; III, A, 3, 21.

new tradition of 'nuclear pacifism' which could present a serious challenge to, for example, the United States armed forces by making recruitment less attractive.[222]

(2) Narrowing down the criteria Because of the moral implications of any use of nuclear weapons there is a danger that one may confuse what appears to be desirable in the international society *de lege ferenda* with what is actually prohibited or outlawed, that is to say with what exists *de lege lata*.

Nuclear weapons cause, as General Assembly Resolution 1653 (XVI)[223] reminds us, indiscriminate suffering and destruction and, as such, their use is 'contrary to the rules of International Law and to the laws of humanity'. Such weapons cannot be directed only against the enemy but are aimed at mankind in general. Third parties not involved in a war would be subjected to all the consequences by the use of nuclear weapons.

Writers, too, have deduced that nuclear weapons are of questionable legality as they are 'different' from conventional weapons.[224] But it has not been adequately established exactly what criteria lead to such illegality.

Nuclear radiation may, according to some, come under the prohibition of the Hague Regulations[225] which forbid poisonous weapons, or of the Geneva Protocol[226] under the additional phrase forbidding 'all analogous liquids, materials and devices'.[227] Even if the output of nuclear weapons is technically not a gas, radioactivity should 'as a poisonous weapon' be prohibited by inference or analogy on the basis of the principles contained in the Geneva Protocol.[228] Another ground for illegality has been found under the Genocide Convention,[229] as nuclear weapons are inevitably directed against large groups of the population.

One element relevant for the assessment of illegality is obviously

[222] McGrath, 'Nuclear weapons', 231.   [223] Above, p. 196.
[224] B. H. Weston, 'Nuclear weapons v. international law', 78 *McGill L. J.* 3, 1983; E. L. Meyrowitz, 'The laws of war and nuclear weapons', 9 *Brooklyn Journal of International Law* 2, 1983, both reprinted in A. S. Miller and M. Feinrider (eds.), *Nuclear Weapons and Law*, Westport, Connecticut, 1984; I. Brownlie, 'Some legal aspects of nuclear weapons', *ICLQ* 1965, 437.
[225] Article 23(a) on poisonous weapons, see above, p. 123; N. Singh, *Nuclear Weapons and International Law*, London, 1959.
[226] Above, p. 178. Cf. Brownlie, 'Legal aspects', 442.
[227] Greenspan, *Modern Law of Land Warfare*, 372–3.
[228] *Ibid.*, 373.   [229] Brownlie, 'Legal aspects', 443.

the lack of discrimination of nuclear weapons,[230] akin to all weapons of mass destruction.[231] Weapons of such range and intensity cannot, and are not designed to, distinguish between military and civilian objectives. This is a major argument in the assessment of illegality of nuclear weapons. But, on the other hand, it may entail the lessened validity of some other arguments, for example the alleged illegality under the Genocide Convention.[232] For violation of that Convention entails the singling out of groups, whereas the employment of nuclear weapons does not intrinsically distinguish between anyone or anything within, and outside, the impact area.

(3) Criteria applied to nuclear weapons To assess illegality it must first be asserted what precisely is alleged to be illegal: is it the possession, the placing, the first use or any use of nuclear weapons? The answer as to what is illegal would seem to differ according to the relevant category.

There has, in recent years, been an intense discussion of the legality of nuclear weapons in the doctrine.[233] After the war some claimed that, in legal and moral terms, the atom bomb had been a 'good thing' and, had, in a way, saved countless lives by ending the war quickly.[234] But in later years most writers would question the legality of nuclear weapons for offensive purposes[235] and claim that even for defensive purposes[236] the use of such weapons is not compatible with international law.

Drastic statements by politicians sometimes distort the contents of

---

[230] Cf. Institut de Droit International, *Annuaire*, 1969, 48ff, 358ff; 2 *ibid.* 1967, 1ff and 527ff.
[231] Cf. below, p. 241.   [232] Above, note 229.
[233] A. Miatello, *La responsabilité internationale encourue en raison des activités liées à l'utilisation de l'énergie nucléaire*, Geneva, 1985; R. Falk, 'Toward a legal regime for nuclear weapons', in Miller and Feinrider, *Nuclear Weapons and Law*, 107ff; H. H. Almond, 'Deterrence and a policy oriented perspective on the legality of nuclear weapons', in *ibid.*, 57ff; C. A. Dunshee de Abranches, *Prosericao das armas nucleares*, Rio de Janeiro, 1964; F. Menzel, *Legalität oder Illegalität der Anwendung von Atomwaffen*, Tübingen, 1960; M. Setalvad, 'Nuclear weapons and international law', *Indian Journal of International Law*, 1963, 383. On the problems of neutron weapons see H. Meyrowitz, 'Problèmes juridiques relatifs à l'arme à neutron', *AFDI*, 1981, 87.
[234] E. C. Stowell, 'The laws of war and the atomic bomb', 39 *AJIL* 1945, 784, 786.
[235] See G. I. A. D. Draper, *The Red Cross Conventions*, London, 1958, 99, for a view that the use of nuclear weapons is not legal against an aggressor who has not himself used them.
[236] Cf. Weston, 'Nuclear weapons and international law'; Meyrowitz, 'The laws of war and nuclear weapons'; but see G. Schwarzenberger, *The Legality of Nuclear Weapons*, London, 1958, who considers defensive use 'legal'.

international law. Thus, a Minister of State in the West German Foreign Ministry claimed in 1983 that not even first use of nuclear weapons is banned by international law.[237] But there is overwhelming agreement that prohibitions exist in the international legal system against first use.[238] Legality of use in self-defence, however, is more problematic. On the one hand, there is considerable support for the view that such use is 'different' from first use and that it may be justified to preclude further attacks. But the scale and effect of use of nuclear weapons are such that it is questionable whether the international system can allow even defensive use, which may entail devastating effects, augmenting those caused by the first user, and perhaps, precisely in juxtaposition with the first attack, cause the feared climatic changes of 'nuclear winter'. Legality of counter-attack must then, considering duties to neutrals and other uninvolved countries, depend on the scale and nature of nuclear force used.

If we further consider the alleged illegality of the use of nuclear weapons, there is considerable agreement that the use of such weapons against an aggressor who has not himself used them, i.e. first use of nuclear weapons, is illegal.[239] There is furthermore a growing body of opinion suggesting that also the second use, i.e. use in self-defence against a nuclear attack, is illegal. One reason for such a standpoint is that it can never be a rational war aim to use nuclear weapons.[240] The General Assembly has also warned against the dangers of 'catastrophe' caused by any new such doctrine of limited or partial, use of nuclear warfare.[241]

There is ostensibly no rational war aim[242] and the use of nuclear weapons would prevent obedience to further rules concerning the conduct of hostilities[243] and undermine respect for neutrals.[244] Above all, any use violates the dictates of public conscience.[245] The General Assembly has emphasised that any use of nuclear weapons would amount to a violation of the Charter as against 'laws of humanity and constituting a crime against mankind and civilization'.[246] This im-

[237] Institute of Defence and Disarmament Studies, *The Arms Control Reporter*, 403 B 189, statement by Mr Alois Mertes, 14 October 1983.
[238] E.g. F. Blackaby, J. Goldblat and S. Lodgaard, *No-First-Use*, London (SIPRI), 1984, and above, p. 203.
[239] So Draper, *The Red Cross Conventions*, 99.
[240] H. E. Fried, 'International law prohibits the first use of nuclear weapons', *RBDI*, 1981–2, 35.
[241] GA Res. 35/152 B 1980.
[242] Fried, 'International law prohibits the first use of nuclear weapons', 33.
[243] *Ibid.*, 37.   [244] *Ibid.*, 42.   [245] *Ibid.*, 33.   [246] Res. 1653 (XVI) 1961.

portant Resolution, the Declaration on the Prohibition of the Use of Nuclear and Thermonuclear Weapons, states that the use of such weapons is contrary to the United Nations 'spirit, letter and aims' and their use would 'exceed even the scope of war'.

Later, the General Assembly referred to the use of nuclear weapons as being under a 'permanent prohibition', indicating that such weapons are forbidden in any circumstances, including self-defence.[247] In this Resolution the use of nuclear weapons was related to the use of force as outlawed by the Charter. Numerous subsequent Resolutions refer to the need for further safeguards.[248]

The illegality of first use of nuclear weapons does not, according to some,[249] make deterrence unlawful. Possession of such weapons may constitute a lawful deterrent as weapons are possessed only to be *potentially* used.[250] But since use is an inevitable and non-excluded contingency it could be argued that even 'passive' possession is of questionable legality. Yet the present trend is probably to view possession in terms of security and allow possession of a negotiated number of nuclear weapons for deterrence purposes.

The placing of nuclear weapons has evoked considerable discussion. Much is couched in political terms. Tunkin, for example, asserts that the placing of American missiles in Europe is contrary to international law; but he does not specify which rules of international law such action would violate, apart from indicating that there would be a breach of good faith: the positioning of the United States missiles would, says Tunkin, be contrary to the good faith of the arms talks negotiations.[251] By implication he claims that there is a lack of symmetry: the United States can place missiles near USSR

---

[247] Res. 2936 (XXVII) 1972. Cf. Res. 1909 (XVIII) 1963. See Nagendra Singh, *Nuclear Weapons and International Law*, London, 1959; R. E. Charlier, 'Questions soulévées pour l'évolution de la science atomique', 91 *RCADI*, 1957, i, 213, 350; Brownlie, 'Legal aspects', 437.

[248] E.g. Resolutions 34/83 J 1979; 34/85 1979.

[249] Brownlie, 'Legal aspects', 444, who states that it is at least 'not clear if use only or also deterrence [is] illegal'. Brownlie also states that 'the provisions [on genocide] must create a presumption of the illegality of resort to nuclear weapons as part of a policy of deterrence', 'Legal aspects', 444. Presumably the 'illegality' refers to 'use' rather than (also) to 'policy of deterrence'.

[250] See, on deterrence, e.g. S. E. Miller, *Strategy and Nuclear Deterrence*, Princeton, 1984; D. M. Snow, *Nuclear Strategy in a Dynamic World*, University of Alabama, 1981; cf. R. Jervis, *The Illogic of American Nuclear Strategy*, Ithaca, 1984.

[251] G. Tounkine (Tunkin), 'L'installation des missiles américains en Europe viole le droit international', in *Les conséquences juridiques de l'installation éventuelle de missiles cruises et pershing en Europe, Acte du Colloque*, Bruxelles, 1–2 octobre 1982, Brussels, 1984, 107.

frontiers whereas the USSR cannot do the same near the United States.[252]

With regard to the placing of missiles in the territory of other States one may discern the following legal criteria. There must be full consent by the territorial State.[253] Such agreement should, if one applies the rules insisted upon by both superpowers, not only have the approval of the government but also the democratic consent of the people in that territory.[254] It may be noted that in the United Kingdom there is little evidence of debate in Parliament of agreements concerning the placing of United States missiles in the United Kingdom.[255]

Agreements on the stationing of foreign missiles, belonging to the group of treaties which restrict the exercise of the sovereignty of a State *in its own territory*, are probably valid only as long as the territorial State so wishes under the doctrine we have called 'continuous consent'.[256] It could be argued that such consent must be of the 'people', i.e. constitute genuine democratic consent, rather than the mere formal consent of the acting government.

d. Nuclear weapons and recent developments in the Law of War

There is no doubt that the Law of War applies to nuclear weapons.[257] The use of such weapons is subject to specific agreement on arms control and disarmament[258] and there have been further attempts to 'regulate' the use of such weapons. The ICRC suggested a special prohibition of nuclear weapons in the 1956 Draft Rules[259] and the 1973 Draft Protocols[260] referred to such weapons as being 'subject to international agreement or negotiations', circumstances which would make it impossible to regulate the use of nuclear weapons in the planned Additional Protocols[261] to the 1949 Geneva Conventions.

---

[252] Cf. above, p. 80, on spheres of influence.
[253] See my *Independent State*, pp. 197ff.
[254] *Ibid.*, p. 166, and above, p. 24 on democratisation of international society.
[255] The only published treaties concern the stationing of visiting United States forces; on such agreements see my 'Foreign warships', 54.
[256] Such treaties imply the reduction of a State's power in its own territory and thus belong to a special category subjected to special rules on consent, see further for this theory my *Independent State*, 197ff.
[257] Res. XXVIII of the 20th Red Cross Conference in Vienna in 1965.
[258] Above, p. 90.   [259] Article 14, cf. above, p. 184.   [260] Below, p. 208.
[261] For reference, above, p. 108.

During the Diplomatic Conference for the negotiation of the Additional Protocols the United States,[262] the United Kingdom[263] and France[264] all made statements, repeated, with the exception of France, at the time of signature,[265] to the effect that they assumed the Protocols regulated only conventional warfare, as special agreements were needed on nuclear weapons.

According to the Introduction to the Draft Protocol,[266] the Protocol of 1977 to the 1949 Geneva Conventions[267] was never intended to deal with nuclear, bacteriological or chemical warfare. In spite of such clarification certain States felt its provisions would impair their right of national policy with regard to the use of nuclear weapons. France, for example, argued that Protocol I merges humanitarian law with the laws of war in a way that is not without dangers. Any instrument which sets out to govern the conduct of warfare must, said France, take scrupulous care to respect the sovereignty of States and their inalienable right of self-determination in case of aggression. Some provisions in Protocol I may well, in the opinion of France, impair that right.[268]

The question of the Protocol's application to nuclear arms was raised during the Conference in the context of provisions concerning protection of the civilian population. France claimed that a provision[269] which is concerned with the general protection of the civilian population against the effect of hostilities went beyond the specific context of humanitarian law for regulating the laws of war. Although the provision might have been drafted with a humanitarian purpose in view, it had, claimed France, direct implications as regards a State's organisation and conduct and defence against an invader.[270] The French delegation, though not having opposed the adoption of such rules, made it clear that if it had been put to the vote, France would have abstained.[271]

Furthermore, France stated in relation to the provisions dealing with distinction between military and civilian targets[272] that it is difficult in many situations of armed conflict, if not impossible, to

---

[262] CDDH/SR.56, para. 82.   [263] *Ibid.*, para. 114.   [264] *Ibid.*, para. 3.
[265] See below, p. 209. The statements made at the time of signature were not in the form of reservations, see my *Essays*, 47ff.
[266] See ICRC, Draft Additional Protocol to the Geneva Conventions of 1949, 1973, 2.
[267] Above, p. 156.   [268] A/C.6/37/SR.18.3.
[269] Article 43 of the Draft, now article 48 in the final version of the Protocol.
[270] France, CDDH/SR.41, vol. 6, 186.   [271] *Ibid.*
[272] Draft article 47, adopted as article 52.

determine precisely what constitutes a military objective, especially in large towns and in wooded areas, either of which might harbour enemy military forces and groups of civilians more or less closely mixed together. France, therefore, could not 'accept' such a prohibition as included in the Protocol. Although it was intended to benefit the civilian population, the prohibition was too categorical and likely to be prejudicial to the exercise of France's national right of legitimate defence.[273] For the said reasons, France made a declaration when acceding to Protocol II[274] (which in a sense went further than Protocol I by regulating internal strife) that it found itself unable to ratify Protocol I as it ostensibly impaired France's right to use nuclear weapons in defence or as a deterrent.[275]

It may be commented that Protocol I does not explicitly forbid the use of nuclear weapons or any particular types of conventional weapons. Some such weapons are, however, by nature indiscriminate and have effects which cannot be isolated from civilian populations in an attacked territory, and are in this respect forbidden by Protocol I's provisions on indiscriminate or area attacks.[276] On the other hand, it is indisputable that restrictions on the use of indiscriminate weapons by the Protocol will promote humanitarian interests that must prevail over the right States may claim to have to defend themselves with 'any' means.

The effect in law of the statements of France and other States at the Conference for the 1977 Protocols regarding national liberty to nuclear weapons[277] is doubtful. None of these States has ratified the Protocol. However, the Protocol will remain in force even in nuclear armed conflict and the contracting parties are bound by assumed obligations. But also here there might be obligations which are binding on third parties: the obligations under the Protocol support further the argument that the use of nuclear weapons is not compatible with international law. The clarification on this point by the Protocol may indicate rules that exist outside this instrument in general international law.[278] Similar arguments may be advanced to show that first use of nuclear weapons not banned by treaties is still illegal.

Illegality of nuclear mines under the Sea Bed Treaty is not clear.

---

[273] *Ibid.*   [274] See above p. 170.
[275] See declaration on ratification of Protocol II by France to the depositary, 24 February 1984 (unpublished).
[276] See below, p. 239.   [277] Above, p. 200.
[278] On the overlap of underlying obligations, see above, and my *Essays*, 116ff.

The Treaty refers to 'emplantation' or 'emplacement' on the sea bed which leaves it open whether mobile or suspended mines are permissible. The new tethered shelf mine which has a rocket-propelled nuclear warhead is one such type of mine which is not clearly illegal.

It has also been suggested that the Treaty is designed to prohibit the use of weapons of mass destruction and therefore mines for antisubmarine warfare (ASW) might be permissible.[279]

C. RADIOLOGICAL WEAPONS

The United Nations and the disarmament bodies[280] have for some time taken an interest in limiting or prohibiting the use of radiological weapons. By General Assembly Resolution 2602 C (XXIV) in 1969[281] the General Assembly invited CCD to consider radiological weapons. But the CCD had, at that time, other priorities and did not proceed with any study. The General Assembly requested the CCD further[282] and later also CD[283] to proceed to work on an agreement to prohibit new weapons of mass destruction, *inter alia* radiological weapons. CD has now placed the item on the agenda for future negotiation.[284]

Radiological warfare may be conducted basically by two methods. First, such warfare may imply the use of 'dirty' nuclear weapons which maximise radioactive effects by increasing the radioactive fallout. Secondly, separate radioactive agents independent of nuclear explosions can be used as special weapons.[285]

It is the second type of warfare or weapons that the General Assembly has invited CCD/CD to consider so that work could be initiated for the purpose of a 'prohibitive regime'.[286] Sweden insisted that prohibition of 'dirty' nuclear weapons was also included in the mandate, as well as particle beam weapons which have not always come within the ambit of the term 'nuclear explosive device' as used in CCD/CD Working Groups,[287] but a decision limiting the scope of interest as indicated was preferred.

[279] O'Connell, *Influence of Law on Sea-Power*, 157.   [280] Above, p. 88.
[281] Cf. GA Resolutions 3479 (XXX) 1975; 34/87A 1979; 35/156 G 1980.
[282] Resolutions 31/74 1976; 32/84 A 1977; 33/66B 1978; 34/79 1979.
[283] Res. 35/149 1980.   [284] See CD/732, 111 and CD/722, 1986.
[285] CD/RW/WP.6 (Sweden).
[286] Cf. Netherlands, WP, CCD/291; Joint US–USSR Proposal, 1979, GAOR, 34th sess., Suppl. no. 27, A/34/27 and Corr. 1, Appendix III; CD/53 and Corr. 1, vol. II; CD/31 and CD/32; Joint US–USSR Draft Resolution 1979; and GA Res. 34/87 A 1979.
[287] See, e.g., Report of Working Group, GAOR, 35th sess., Suppl. no. 27, A/35/27, para. 61.

D. BIOLOGICAL AND CHEMICAL WEAPONS

i. *CBWs: the common background*

Biological and chemical weapons are usually referred to in the reverse order as CBWs, an abbreviation from the time before it was known that agreement would be reached on biological weapons long before there was any *ad idem* on chemical weapons. Initially the two types of weapon had a similar history and evolution towards prohibition and were treated together in negotiations. CBWs are 'different' from other weapons and perhaps 'stand in a class of their own as armaments which exercise their effect solely on living matter'.[288] They are 'aimed' at large groups and not at any individual soldier(s).[289] The two types of weapon have formed the subject of numerous lengthy negotiations in recent years. The main reason that it has become important to reach agreement on the limitation of these weapons is that they have been developed and used extensively to combat guerillas in modern conflicts by 'scientific' warfare;[290] such weapons have also been increasingly used in the Iran–Iraq War.

a. *The historical background*

It is not new to use poisoned arms or to poison the enemy's water supply. There are known instances of, for example, water poisoning around 600 BC, when Solon of Athens poisoned water in Pleistos. And Frederick Barbarossa took Tortona by a similar strategy in 1155. Akin practices include throwing plague victims over city walls to spread disease, as the Tartars did in Caffa in 1343.[291] Europeans gave or sold infected utensils to poison the indigenous population of America[292] and many States resorted to such weapons in their colonialisation processes.[293]

---

[288] United Nations, *Chemical, Bacteriological (Biological) Weapons and the Effects of their Possible Use*, 1969, S.69.1.24.
[289] Cf. above on mass destruction.
[290] A. Beaufré, *La guerre révolutionnaire*, Paris, 1972, 237.
[291] It has been claimed the Great Plague started in this way. For lists of early uses of CBW see D. Riche, *La guerre chimique et biologique*, Paris, 1982, 305. See also background examples in SIPRI, *The Problem of Chemical and Biological Warfare, a Study on the Historical, Technical, Military, Legal and Political Aspects of CBW and Possible Disarmament Measures*, Stockholm, 1971–8, 6 vols.
[292] S. Rose (ed.), *Chemical and Biological Warfare*, Boston, 1969, 49.
[293] Cf. J. A. Farrer, *Military Manners and Customs*, London, 1885, 173.

After the establishment of colonies it became common to use CBWs against insurgents, for example to drive them out of caves or hiding places, like the French in Algeria in the middle of last century.[294] There is no doubt that the British used gas in the Boer War.[295]

b. Modern times

The Hague Regulations of 1899 and 1907 prohibit[296] 'poison or poisoned weapons'. This is the first clear prohibition of CBWs and it is clear that it covers weapons deliberately contaminated with germs or poisonous agents. But it is unclear whether this prohibition covers gas. Some writers have interpreted the prohibition to mean only the actual use of poisonous agents, alone or applied to weapons,[297] whereas others have held that the prohibition, by implication, also covers gas.[298]

c. The question of gas

(1) The application of early rules The question of whether or not gas was prohibited under various regulations became, over the years, the most discussed and controversial question. Even in recent years, for example in the Vietnam War, the question of prohibition of gas and other similar chemical and biological weapons was at the core of legal discussions on CBW.

There was alleged use of CBW in both world wars; in Abyssinia;[299] in the Chinese–Japanese War;[300] in Vietnam;[301] and in the Iran–Iraq War.[302]

There was some doubt whether the Gas Declaration of 1899 im-

---

[294] P. J. Proudhon, *La guerre et la paix. Recherches sur le principe et la constitution du droit des gens*, Paris, 1927, 241.

[295] J. B. Kelly, 'Gas warfare in international law', *MilLR*, 1960, 5.

[296] By article 23(e).

[297] M. S. McDougal and F. P. Feliciano, *Law and Minimum World Public Order*, New Haven, 1961, 663.

[298] H. Kelsen, *Principles of International Law*, 2nd edn, 1966, 97.

[299] Ch. Rousseau, 'Le conflit italo-éthiopien', *RGDIP*, 1937, 692.

[300] See *LNOJ*, 19th session, 1938, Plenary Meeting, Spec. Suppl., 136, 307; for League Resolution see 378.

[301] W. D. Verwey, *Riot Control Agents and Herbicides in War*, Leiden, 1977.

[302] E.g. UN, CD/PV 130, 1981, 29; the Security Council condemned the use of CBW and urged belligerents to abstain from resorting to such weapons without alleging that such use had occurred. Note that both belligerents are bound by the Geneva Protocol: Iran acceded on 5 November 1929 and Iraq on 8 September 1931. For allegations on the use of mustard gas and tabun by Iraq, see CD 1315, 16 April 1985.

plied only actually 'lethal' gas or other 'control agents' like tear gas and herbicides as well.[303] The Hague Regulations of 1899[304] and 1907[305] do not cover chemical warfare in the opinion of many.[306] But others have looked more to the spirit of the Regulations than to the letter and held that chemical weapons are covered by the provisions.[307]

Different interpretations depend largely on whether or not a 'policy' prohibition was intended by the Hague Regulations, i.e. an attempt seeking to prohibit chemical and biological warfare as envisaged as practically feasible at the time.[308] Another line would be to inquire whether one could rely on the analogy between, for example, contaminated water supply and the use of gas.[309] A third position would be to hold that only specific weapons, as indicated by the wording, were prohibited.[310]

In connection with the prohibition of dum-dum bullets by the Hague Declaration in 1899[311] there was another Declaration to 'abstain from the use of projectiles the sole object of which is the diffusion of asphyxiating or deleterious gases'.[312] The question of 'sole object' would be assessed by comparing the proportion of gas and splinter effects of a projectile; but the Declaration left open as to what 'gas' the Declaration applied.[313]

Certain States interpreted the Declaration literally and, since it prohibited dispersion of gas by projectiles, they saw themselves legally entitled to do so from stationary cylinders. For example, Germany resorted to this practice, relying on the actual wording rather than the spirit of the Declaration.[314]

On the other hand, it was claimed that there was already a prohi-

---

[303] Verwey, *Riot*, 224–5.   [304] Article 23(a), Convention II.
[305] Article 23(a), Convention IV.
[306] E.g. McDougal and Feliciano, *Law and Minimum World Public Order*, 663.
[307] Greenspan, *Modern Law of Land Warfare*, 359. M. Bothe, *Das völkerrechtliche Verbot des Einsatzes chemischer und bakteriologischer Waffen*, Cologne, 1973; Kelsen, *Principles*, 117; W. G. M. van Eysinga, 'La guerre chimique et le movement pour sa repression', 16 *RCADI* 1927, i, 347.
[308] Greenspan, *Modern Law of Land Warfare*, 359, Cf. W. H. Neinast, 'United States use of biological warfare', 24 *Military Law Journal*, 1964, 27.
[309] Stone, *Legal Controls*, 557.
[310] J. L. Kunz, *Gaskrieg und Völkerrecht*, Vienna, 1927, 26.   [311] Above, p. 177.
[312] Declaration IV(2) 1899. Concerning Asphyxiating Gases, 26 *NRGT*, 2 série, 1002; 1, *AJIL* 1907, Suppl., 155. Like the other Hague Declaration, above, p. 177, there were clear undertakings in the form of a treaty. Most military powers were bound by this treaty: the United Kingdom ratified it in 1907.
[313] Kunz, *Gaskrieg*, 81.   [314] Cf. Stone, *Legal Controls*, 556.

bition, by analogy with the 1868 St Petersburg Declaration,[315] for all chemical and biological weapons.[316] It may be questioned whether one could stretch the wording of the St Petersburg Declaration that far[317] but it could be argued, on the other hand, that such an analogy could be drawn with the prohibitions in the Hague Regulations.[318]

The Versailles Treaty after the First World War stated that 'the use of asphyxiating, poisonous or other gases and all analogous liquids, materials or devices being prohibited, their manufacture and importation are strictly forbidden in Germany'.[319] The wording suggests that the 'use' of gas and 'analogous' substances had been prohibited previously everywhere for military purposes. The language chosen by the Draft Treaty of Washington of 1922[320] suggests a similar attitude of mind in its provisions on this point. The Treaty provides that

The use of asphyxiating, poisonous or other gases and all analogous liquids, material and devices, *having been justly condemned* by the general opinion of the civilised world and a prohibition of such use having been declared in *Treaties* to which a majority of the civilised Powers are parties, the Signatory Powers, *to the end* that this prohibition shall be accepted as a part of International Law binding alike on the conscience and practice of nations, declare their assent to such prohibition, and agree to be bound thereby as between themselves and *invite* all other civilised nations to adhere thereto. (emphasis added)[321]

On the one hand, the statement seems to indicate that the drafters refer to a previous condemnation of the use of gas (and analogous substances). Some find it questionable whether general international law had, at that time, condemned the use of gas.[322] But the statement also refers to 'Treaties': but which are they? The Peace Treaties, which had used a similar wording? Or the 1899–1907 Regulations? The reference to the intention to 'invite' others to 'accept' the prohibition also probably contradicts the earlier half of the statement. This pronouncement, however, even if only in the form of a Draft Treaty, is possibly indicative of attitudes, and appears to have some legal signification in that respect, especially as the wording is reiterated by the subsequent Geneva Protocol.

[315] Above, pp. 89 and 135.   [316] Greenspan, *Modern Law of Land Warfare*, 360.
[317] Cf. Castrén, *The Present Law of War and Neutrality*, 190.
[318] Above, p. 107 and article 23(e).
[319] Article 171; cf. the Treaties of St German, article 135; Neuilly, article 82; Trianon, article 119.
[320] 16 *AJIL* 1922, Suppl., 57.   [321] Article 5.
[322] Thomas and Thomas, *Legal Limits*, 66.

(2) The Geneva Gas Protocol By the Geneva Gas Protocol of 1925[323] the parties refer to a similar, chronologically earlier condemnation of the use of gas and similar agents. The Protocol provides that 'Whereas the use of asphyxiating, poisonous or other gases and of all analogous liquids, material or devices, has been justly condemned by the general opinion of the civilised world; and Whereas the prohibition of such use has been declared in Treaties to which the majority of the Powers of the World are Parties'.[324] The reference to a condemnation from sources outside the ambit of the Protocol[325] as to 'treaties' is, especially in conjunction with earlier statements,[326] a most important relevant element when assessing the ambit of the prohibition and/or when interpreting what the underlying 'treaties', presumably the Hague Regulations, implied in the opinion of the contracting parties to the Geneva Protocol.

The text is very short and consists in a Declaration to the effect that the parties 'accept' insofar as they are not already bound to do so the (already existing) 'prohibition' (of the use of gas, etc.) and agree to extend this prohibition to 'the use of bacteriological methods of warfare'.

The text thus indicates, first, that the clause outlawing certain weapons in the Hague Regulations is to be interpreted, in the opinion of contracting parties, as covering gas and associated substances as well. The contracting parties to the Geneva Protocol include all the major military powers who were bound by Hague Convention 1907 together with the Hague Regulations.

Secondly, the wording indicates that, since the prohibition is reiterated and strengthened, abuses such as using stationary gas dispensers, or other use of gas, as in the First World War, will discontinue.[327]

The Protocol regime is riddled with a network of reservations.[328] Most of the reservations are modelled on the one made by France to the effect that application of the prohibitions will be on the basis of

---

[323] 94 LNTS (1929) 65. There are 105 parties (1985), including all States of military significance.
[324] Preamble of the Protocol.   [325] Cf. comments above, p. 135.
[326] Cf. Draft Treaty of Washington, 1922, above, p. 89.
[327] But the Red Cross was less convinced that use of gas would cease. The ICRC reminded States signatories of the Geneva Convention of 1864 as revised 1906 that protection of civilians against 'chemical war' was a 'national matter'. National commissions should consider suitable protective equipment against gas attacks, *RICR*, 1930, 15.
[328] For a fragmentation of obligations, see my *Essays*, 117.

strict reciprocity[329] – such reciprocity implies that a party is released from obligations under the Protocol the moment another party to a conflict ceases to respect its obligations.

There are different interpretations of the Geneva Protocol, especially as to whether it covers herbicides and tear gas, i.e. agents which are not lethal to man. A semantic element has been of importance when assessing whether the Protocol covers tear gas and other riot agents. The English version of the Protocol indicates that the Protocol prohibits 'asphyxiating, poisonous and other gases', whereas the French text forbids 'gaz asphyxiants, toxiques ou similaires'. The 'other' in the English version is probably wider than the 'ou similaires' in the French text.[330]

But even the French text could be interpreted as extending the application of the Protocol to, for example, chemical agents which are not normally lethal to man: if 'similaires' had no such extending function it would be a superfluous word.[331]

The usefulness of the Geneva Protocol[332] was greatly undermined by the absence of the United States from the ratifying parties. The United States did not adhere to the Protocol until 1975; even then, its adherence was marred by a reservation which exempts tear gas and herbicides from the application of the Protocol.[333]

Both the British and the French governments agreed at the 1930 Disarmament Conference[334] that the Protocol covered, for example, tear gas.[335] However, the United States disagreed, stating that, since tear gas is legal in peacetime for riot control, it must also be legal in war.[336]

The United States has held that the use of chemical and biological weapons is a matter of 'national policy'.[337] Throughout the Vietnam War the United States emphasised that it is not a party to any treaty

---

[329] See below, p. 339.

[330] J. Miramanoff, *La Croix Rouge et les armes biologiques et chimiques*, Geneva, 1970, 344.

[331] Cf. H. Meyrowitz 'Les armes psychochimiques et le droit international', *AFDI*, 1964, 94.

[332] Cf. R. R. Baxter and T. Buergenthal, 'Legal aspects of the Geneva Protocol of 1925', *AJIL*, 1970, 853.

[333] 14 *ILM* 1975, 49. Cf. J. N. Moore 'Ratification of the Geneva Protocol on Gas and Bacteriological Warfare, a legal and political analysis', 3 *Virginia LR* 1972, 419.

[334] On the Conference, above, p. 89.

[335] League of Nations, Preparatory Commission, Disarmament Conference, 1931, X, 6th sess., 311.

[336] *Ibid.*, 312.

[337] US, Dept. of the Army, FM 3–10, *Employment of Chemical and Biological Agents*, 1966, 4.

which prohibits the use of toxic or non-toxic gases or the destruction of crops by chemicals 'harmless to man'.[338] But the United States also undoubtedly resorted to the use of anti-personnel gas in Vietnam.[339]

The United Kingdom, although more interested in having tear gas allowed than herbicides, took a similar position long after its adherence to the Protocol. Although no formal reservation had been made to this effect, it was claimed by the United Kingdom that it was not bound by any prohibitions of tear gas. This was a change of attitude by the United Kingdom due to the need for tear gas to control internal unrest in its own country, mainly in Northern Ireland. The reason for the alleged legality is, it was claimed, that 'modern' tear gas is so 'mild' that there is no reason why it should be prohibited. It does not, for example, come under any prohibition in the Geneva Protocol which was drafted when tear gas implied something different from today.[340]

An extensive interpretation of the Geneva Protocol is founded, by some writers, on the alleged existence of rules outside the Protocol, prohibiting all biochemical weapons. The Geneva Protocol 'must be regarded as binding on the community independently of treaty obligations'.[341] This view appears reasonable.[342] Such wide interpretation has been endorsed by Resolutions of the UN General Assembly,[343] some of which have specifically referred to the ambit of the Geneva Protocol as covering gas which affects not only human beings but plants. For example the 21 Power Resolution 2601 A (XXIV) of 1969 emphasised that the Geneva Protocol embodies the generally recognised rules of international law prohibiting the use in international armed conflicts of all biological and chemical methods of warfare, regardless of any technical development. The Resolution thus prohibits

---

[338] US, Dept. of the Army, FM-27–0, *The Law of Land Warfare*, 1965, 18; United States Congress, Committee on Foreign Affairs, *Chemical and Biological Warfare: United States Policies and International Effects*, Washington, DC, 1970; US Congress, Committee on Foreign Relations, *The Geneva Protocol of 1925, Hearing Before 92nd Congress 1st sess.*, Washington, DC, 1972.

[339] For a list of types authorised to General Westmoreland in 1965 see H. Weiler, *Vietnam*, Montreux, 1869, 250–1.

[340] Statement by the Foreign Secretary, 795 *HC*, 1970, col. 18.

[341] Greenspan, *Modern Law of Land Warfare*, 354.

[342] Cf. Y. Sandoz, *Des armes interdites en droit de la guerre*, Geneva, 1975, 88; G. Fischer, 'Les armes chimiques et bactériologiques', *AFDI*, 1969, 127; cf. the view of the Secretary General.

[343] For example, Res. 2162 B (XXI) 1966; 2454 A (XXIII) 1968.

(a) any chemical agent of warfare – chemical substances, whether gaseous, liquid or solid – which might be employed because of their direct toxic effect on man, animals or plants;

(b) any biological agents of warfare – living organisms, whatever their nature, or infective material derived from them – which are *intended* to cause disease or death in man, animals or plants, and which depend for their effects on their ability to multiply in the person, animal or plant attacked. (emphasis added)

There were serious drafting ambiguities. Thus, 'intention' is required for biological weapons but not under (a) for chemical weapons. Furthermore, the threshold of injury appears to be higher for biological weapons than for chemical weapons: 'toxic effects' are surely less drastic than 'disease and death'?

In spite of drafting technicalities, the Resolution is an important expression for the attitude of a number of States on the ambit of the Geneva Protocol and must carry some weight in the interpretation of its provisions.

There was much interest in the United Nations in encouraging further research into the use of CBWs with a view to prohibiting such weapons by a Convention. The Secretary General carried out one study on the subject[344] and there were a great number of Resolutions on the theme by the General Assembly.[345] There have also been a number of relevant resolutions and comprehensive studies in the specialised agencies, such as the World Health Organization.[346]

(3) Efforts of disarmament bodies The Eighteen Power Disarmament Conference (ENCD)[347] considered prohibition of CBW. The USSR Draft Treaty on General and Complete Disarmament covered, *inter alia*, such weapons, and so did the more limited United States Draft Basic Provisions.[348] Later the Committee of the Confer-

---

[344] *Report by the Secretary General on Chemical and Bacteriological (Biological) Weapons and the Effects of their Potential Use*, 1969, E.69.1.24.

[345] GA Res. 2262 (XXV) 1970; 2827 A (XXVI) 1971; 2933 (XXVII) 1972; 3077 (XXVIII) 1973; 3256 (XXIX) 1974; 3465 (XXX) 1975; 31/65 1976; 32/77 1977; S-10/2, 33/71 A and 33/71 H 1978, 34/72 1979; 35/144 A, B, C 1980; 37/98 1982; 38/187 1983.

[346] WHA, *Resolutions*, World Health Assembly, 2054.1967; 22.58.1969; 23.53.1970; Exe. Res. EB45.R17, n.d.; see WHO, *Public Health and Chemical and Biological Weapons*, 1970.

[347] Above, p. 93.

[348] DCOR, Suppl., 1961, Docs. DC/203, Annex I, Sect. C; ENDC/2 and F; ENDC/30, DC 205, Annex 1, Sect. D; ENDC/2/Add. 1 and E and F; ENDC/30/Add. 1 and 2.

ence of Disarmament (CCD)[349] considered a United Kingdom Draft submitted in 1969[350] and an East European Draft Convention.[351] It soon became apparent that the treatment of the two types of weapons should be separated as there seemed to be reason to think that agreement could more easily be reached on biological than on chemical weapons.

ii. Biological weapons

a. Provisions of the 1972 Convention (BWC)

The Convention on Prohibition of the Development, Production and Stockpiling of Bacteriological (Biological) and Toxin Weapons and Their Destruction was concluded in 1972.[352] By this Convention States bind themselves not to develop, produce or stockpile certain weapons, i.e. (1) microbial or other biological agents or toxins, whatever their origin or method of production, of types or in quantities that have no justification for prophylactic, protective or other peaceful purposes; (2) weapons, equipment or means of delivery designed to use such agents or toxins for hostile purposes or in armed conflict. It is to be noted that toxins are included in the BWC together with biological agents although they are, strictly speaking, chemicals.[353] All parties undertake to destroy not later than nine months after the entry into force of the Convention all biological agents, toxins, weapons or equipment.

Some have called this Convention the 'first' disarmament Convention,[354] but it may be questioned whether such qualification adds much to its impact: since States are obliged only to destroy biological agents above a certain quantitative limit where stocks indicate non-peaceful purposes, the agents will still exist and hence constitute 'potential weapons'.

The Convention prohibits the transfer of specified biological agents to other States, groups of States or international organisations.[355] But

---

[349] Above, p. 93.   [350] CD, Official Record, Suppl., 1969, Doc. ENDC/225.
[351] GAOR, 24th sess., item 104, A/7655.
[352] Cf. GA Res. 2826 (XXVI) 1971. The Convention entered into force on 23 March 1975. Cf., for background, *Report by Secretary General*, 1969, A/7575, Rev. 1, S/9292, Rev. 1. There are 100 parties (1985), including most States of military significance except Israel.
[353] N. Sims, 'Biological and toxic weapons: issues in the 1986 Review Conference', *Faraday Discussion Paper No. 7*, London, 1986, 6.
[354] Rosas, *The Legal Status of Prisoners of War*, 32.   [355] Article III.

the Convention is silent on transfer to individuals, groups of individuals or, for example, liberation movements or guerilla groups. The Convention thus does not appear to prohibit export of any biological agents like, for example, herbicides in any quantities to any individual, group or body.

The States parties to the Convention undertake[356] to implement the provisions of the Convention in their respective territories according to their constitutional provisions,[357] but there is no obligation restraining States from transferring agents and toxins, weapons or equipment covered by the Convention to individuals or groups of individuals elsewhere if they buy from different sources. And what if they, in turn, transfer these agents to other States?

But 'use' of biological weapons is not prohibited, in spite of successive United Kingdom Drafts urging for such extension. Yet, if a biological weapon is 'used', prior violation of article (a) (on developing, possessing and stockpiling) can be deduced from such 'use'.[358] Similar comments may be made with respect to transfer for someone else to 'use'.

Parties are also under some duty to 'facilitate' technical information for peaceful purposes and they shall, under the Convention, also be given the right to participate in such information. A vague obligation on cooperation in this respect is laid down in the Convention,[359] but a more specific duty exists with regard to developing nations: the Convention shall be 'implemented' in a manner designed to 'avoid hampering' the economic or technological development of State parties to the Convention.

A considerable weakness of the Convention is the lack of verification methods. States bind themselves only to cooperate and consult to solve any arising 'problems'.[360] It has been questioned whether 'clarification' of Article V could ever be widened to include institutions to assess alleged violations or reciprocal on-site inspections.[361]

But here there are two distinct problems, which entail different solutions. By the theory of 'implied powers' and/or the theory of 'competence of competence' as understood and developed by some writers,[362] institutions can always be created to safeguard and imple-

---

[356] Article IV.   [357] On transformation, see above, p. 163.
[358] N. Sims, 'Reform of the 1972 Convention on Biological and Toxin Weapons, issues arising for the Second Review Conference', MS, 1985, 14.
[359] Article X(1).   [360] Article V.   [361] Sims, 'Reform', 19.
[362] See my *Law Making*, 29ff.

ment the objectives of a treaty. Powers to 'assess' violations would certainly come within that scope. But on-site inspections, implying territorial access to a State, widen the framework of powers granted under a treaty. Therefore, for such an enlargement of powers further consent by States is required.[363] If States do consent, such inspections can be allowed on a reciprocal or wider basis, and this would, from the point of theory of treaties, be construed as a *de facto revision*.[364]

But by an important additional agreement of 26 September 1986 the United States, the Soviet Union and 101 other States agreed to strengthen the implementation of the 1972 Treaty. Parties have now assumed obligations to call prompt meetings to examine alleged violations, to initiate action under the United Nations, or to request assistance by the specialised agencies.[365]

An inquiry into alleged violations, as the claim by Iran that Iraq has used BWs in the Jofeir area and on the Madjnoum Islands, may result in condemnation of BWs, without assertion of guilt of any of the belligerents.[366]

There is an interesting duty to uphold the rules of the Convention to assist another State party whose rights under the Convention have been violated, provided the violated State requests assistance and the Security Council has pronounced itself to the effect that there has been a violation.[367] In other words, it is for the Security Council to decide whether violations have taken place, at least if they are to engender what may be called 'solidarity assistance' by other parties.

Secondly, it is a rare provision in treaty law insofar as innocent parties are under a duty to assist another innocent party whose treaty rights have been violated. Such assistance increases the substantive obligations of other parties, although it must be queried as to how and in what form, and in what circumstances, such assistance would actually be given.

It is often wrongly assumed that the Convention prohibits research on toxins; but there is no provision in the Convention to this effect.[368] This is a general limitation of the Convention's impact as research and development are invariably interlinked. Even if verification is

[363] See my *Independent State*, 197.
[364] See my *Law Making*, 37ff, and my *Essays*, 71ff.   [365] BWC/CONF. II/11, 1986.
[366] *Report by a Delegation Sent by the Secretary General*, S/16433, 1984.   [367] Article VII.
[368] The United Kingdom Working Paper had proposed such prohibition. See Sims, 'Reform', 5–6.

difficult with regard to research, a ban would have enhanced the effectiveness of the Convention.

b. The Review Conference mechanism

The Convention provides for Review Conferences[369] to analyse the operation of the Convention, especially in the light of new scientific and technical development. The First Review Conference in 1980 thus considered Ebula, Lassa and Marburg viruses as well as the Legionella bacterium; all these had been identified by medical research since the conclusion of the 1972 Convention.[370] But there was no need to revise the Convention.

iii. Chemical weapons (CWs)

a. Separate treatment of biological and chemical weapons (CBWs)

The reason for separate treatment of biological and chemical weapons was mainly that some States were more optimistic about reaching an agreement on biological weapons. But a special article was inserted in the Biological Weapons Convention when that treaty was concluded to the effect that the Committee on Disarmament (as it then was[371]) was urged to continue negotiations for a Chemical Weapons Convention. Thirteen years later there has still not been any agreement on such weapons.

b. Regulation by special treaties

Some chemical weapons are forbidden in other treaties. Thus, the Hague Regulations[372] and the Geneva Gas Protocol[373] clearly cover some ground. Furthermore, toxins have been forbidden by the Biological Weapons Convention,[374] although they, technically speaking, are chemical, not biological, weapons.

c. Various drafts

In 1972 an East European Draft Convention on chemical weapons was submitted to CCD, proposing a comprehensive approach based on a 'purpose criterion' which would establish whether or not the

---

[369] Article XII.

[370] Sims, 'Reform', 30. On the rapidly changing potential for development of biological (BW) and toxic weapons (TW) since the Convention – which makes the Conventional framework unsatisfactory – see E. Geissler, *Biological and Toxin Weapons Today*, Stockholm (SIPRI), 1986.

[371] See above, p. 93 on the disarmament bodies.

[372] Above, p. 107.   [373] Above, p. 214.   [374] Above, p. 219.

production of chemicals of certain types or in certain quantities had any peaceful justification.[375] Another proposal by ten non-aligned States was put forward the following year elaborating proposals for verification, for example (as suggested by Sweden) involving simultaneous application of different verification methods to enhance compliance with the substantive obligations.[376]

Another Draft Convention was presented by Japan in 1974 based on the 'purpose criterion' and providing for a gradual elimination of chemical weapons;[377] and there were numerous Working Papers.[378]

A Draft Convention was produced by the United Kingdom in 1976 as an attempt to combine constructive elements of earlier drafts together with new suggestions for the initial stages of implementation. The Draft prohibits all lethal chemical agents and toxic chemical agents that might cause long-term physical effects. Proposals for on-site verification would, as the United Kingdom delegation suggested, be subject to separate negotiations.[379]

A Joint Report by the USSR and the United States was elaborated in 1979,[380] on the basis of an earlier understanding between the two powers in 1974[381] that the most dangerous lethal chemical weapons must be outlawed by a convention. A further Joint Report was elaborated in 1980.[382] A further Draft Convention was submitted to CD by the United States in 1984.[383] The United States Draft includes verification procedures which envisage inspection of all military or government-owned 'localities and facilities'. Such a formula may appear both too broad, by including government-owned establishments which have no connection with chemical weapons, and too narrow, by excluding the private sector of the chemical industry.[384]

There is now a document under negotiation in CD. This 'Draft', elaborated in 1985, is not even termed 'Draft Convention', but it is emphasised that there are still ongoing negotiations.[385] But the paper

---

[375] CD, Official Record, 1972, CCD/361.
[376] CCD/400, 1973 and GAOR, 28th sess., Suppl. no. 31, A/9141.
[377] CCD/420 1974, and GAOR, 29th sess., Suppl. no. 27, A/9627. See modifications proposed by Japan, CCD/483, 1976, and GAOR, 31st sess., Suppl. no. 27, A/31/27, Annex III.
[378] See Working Papers by Canada, Finland, Federal Republic of Germany and Sweden, GAOR, 29th sess., Suppl. no. 27, A/10027, Annex II.
[379] CCD/512, 1976. [380] CD 53 and Corr. 1 and CD/48, 1979.
[381] CCD/431, GAOR, 29th sess., Suppl. no. 27, A. 9627, Annex II.
[382] CD/112, 1980. [383] CD/500, 1984.
[384] Sims, 'Chemical weapons', 8. See further, in detail, J. P. P. Robinson, *Disarmament and other Options for Western Policy Making on Chemical Warfare* (NATO).
[385] CD/636, 1985.

is expressed in a form of a partial Draft Convention. It is based, as numerous earlier proposals, on a distinction between the level of toxicity of certain chemicals. It also introduces some new categories in this respect. There is thus a distinction between 'super-toxic', 'other lethal chemicals', and 'other harmful' chemicals.[386]

It will be easier to reach an agreement on the super-toxic chemicals,[387] which will be prohibited outright, whereas those of a lower toxicity may be allowed for 'non-hostile' purposes, such as industrial or agricultural research or medical purposes as well as 'domestic law enforcement purposes'.[388]

The Draft also considers 'binary weapons', which have attracted much attention in recent years.[389] Such weapons rely on substances which *per se* are not of any toxic significance but together generate an extremely toxic substance when combined, during delivery or upon impact.[390]

The Draft uses the term 'precursors' to mean chemical reagents which take part in the production of a toxic chemical and 'key precursors' to mean those precursors which pose a significant risk to the objectives of the Convention by virtue of their importance in the production of a toxic chemical.[391] The notion of 'precursors' can conveniently be used to describe both general CWs and certain binary weapons which will be prohibited.

There is thus some ground prepared for a future Chemical Weapons Convention. But as negotiations stand there will still be a problem with regard to non-lethal chemical weapons.

There are several types of non-lethal chemicals which are used in war: in the case of tear gas,[392] to control the movements of the enemy; in the case of smoke and incendiary devices, for other strategic reasons;[393] in the case of LSD, to reduce the enemy's capabili-

[386] CD/636, 1985, Draft, Article 2(a), (b) and (c).
[387] See suggestion in the Draft Convention submitted by Japan in 1974, above, note 377.
[388] Cf. *ibid.*, article 3, which defines 'permitted purposes' or 'non-hostile purposes'.
[389] See, for example, discussions in the Committee on Disarmament in 1980, GAOR, 35th sess., Suppl. no. 27, A/35/27, comments by Belgium. On United States funds to improve effectiveness of binary CWs, see R. G. Lauren, 'War, peace and the environment', in R. N. Barrett (ed.), *International Dimensions of the Environmental Crisis*, Boulder, Colorado, 1982, 81.
[390] *Ibid.*, article II(1).   [391] CD, Draft Convention 1985, Article II 4 (a), CD/636.
[392] Above, p. 217.
[393] Thomas and Thomas, *Legal Limits*, 3. On policies advocating first use of CWs as 'legal', see J. P. Robinson, 'Disarmament and other options' *International Affairs* 1986/7, 69; see further Robinson, *Chemical Warfare Arms Control*.

ties;[394] and, in the case of herbicides, to attack vegetation rather than enemy forces.[395].

In recent negotiations great attention has been attached to the degree of lethal effect of chemical weapons. There has been little agreement on the above-mentioned types of non-lethal chemical weapons which many States consider essential to warfare. Another problem is that States often consider some of these weapons useful for riot control in peacetime and therefore insist on having them available for 'peaceful purposes'.

Secondly, chemicals, like herbicides, are necessary for agricultural purposes and it is going to be difficult for any future Convention to regulate or restrict the use of herbicides as a means of warfare. The last comment may illustrate the particular difficulties of verification in this area. Yet there has been a recent proposal to the effect that 'each State Party undertakes not to use herbicides as a method of warfare' and that 'such a prohibition should not preclude other use of herbicides'.[396]

A Tass notice of a statement by Mr Gorbachev indicates there may be some hope for further negotiations on CWs. The statement said that

The Soviet Union is in favour of an early and complete elimination of these weapons and of the industrial base for their production. We are prepared for a timely declaration of the location of enterprises producing chemical weapons and for the cessation of their production and ready to start developing procedures for destroying the relevant industrial base and to proceed, soon after the Convention enters into force, to eliminating the stockpiles of chemical weapons. All these measures would be carried out under strict control including international on-site inspections.[397]

The reference to a duty to indicate the location of production is an innovation, as previously only questions of possession were raised. The adjective 'timely' may indicate a willingness to make a declaration to sign; the other chronological reference to 'soon' leads to speculation whether this would mean less than the 8–9 years often found acceptable in disarmament negotiations. The reference to on-site inspections, on the other hand, is ambiguous: if complete destruction of

---

[394] Meyrowitz, 'Les armes psychochimiques', 81.   [395] Above, p. 217.
[396] Proposal by the Chairman of the 'Open-Ended Consultation', CD/836, 1985, Appendix I, 2, note. On herbicides, see A. H. Westing (ed.), *Herbicides in War*, London (SIPRI), 1984; Westing, *Ecological Consequences of the Second Indochina War*, Stockholm (SIPRI), 1976.
[397] Tass statement, 15 January 1986.

the industrial base has taken place, there is no longer any 'site' to inspect.

E. ENVIRONMENTAL WEAPONS[398]

i. Specific prohibition by general treaties

There has been a marked trend in recent years to consider the importance of the human environment.[399] For example, 'material remnants' of war pose a threat to the environment[400] and formed the subject of special regulation in the 1981 Weaponry Convention.[401] Other harmful acts to the environment were prohibited by Protocol I of 1977 to the 1949 Geneva Conventions. The Protocol stipulates that it is prohibited 'to employ methods or means of warfare which are intended, or may be expected, to cause widespread, long-term and severe damage to the natural environment'.[402] This provision is slightly duplicated by a later article which provides that

1. Care shall be taken in warfare to protect the natural environment against wide-spread, long-term and severe damage. This protection includes a prohibition of the use of methods or means of warfare which are intended or may be expected to cause such damage to the natural environment and thereby to prejudice the health or survival of the population.
2. Attacks against the natural environment by way of reprisals are prohibited.[403]

A further relevant provision in Protocol I of 1977,[404] repeated in Protocol II,[405] is the prohibition against attacks on 'dangerous instal-

---

[398] See below, p. 232, on the relationship between weapons and methods.
[399] See e.g. the UN General Assembly Resolution on Environment 2849 (XXVI) 1971 on the importance of the environment to mankind; the Declaration of the Stockholm Conference on the Human Environment in 1972: on this see my article on 'The UN Special Conference on the Environment', in P. Taylor and J. Groom (eds.), *UN Special Conferences*, London, 1987; later resolutions of the General Assembly, e.g. 3154 (XXVIII) 1973 on the responsibility of the international community to preserve and enhance the natural environment; 3264 (XXIX) 1974, deploring pollution by ionising radiation from testing nuclear weapons.
[400] Study by United Nations Environmental Programme (UNEP), UNEP/G.C./ INF./5; and GA Res. 3435 (XXX) 1975 and Resolution IV of the Lima Conference of Ministers of Foreign Affairs of Non-Aligned Countries, 1975, on Hazards of Material Remnants of War and Aggression; cf. G. Herezegh, 'La protection de l'environnement et le droit humanitaire', in *Etudes et essais sur le droit international humanitaire et sur les principes de la Croix Rouge, en honneur de Jean Pictet*, Geneva, 1984, 725.
[401] Above, p. 180.   [402] Article 35(3).
[403] Article 55 on 'Protection of the Natural Environment'.   [404] Article 56.
[405] Article 15.

lations'.[406] These are, for example, dams and dykes, which when attacked can release dangerous forces to the detriment of the environment and to the civilian population. Of particular significance are attacks against nuclear installations which can cause considerable environmental damage. Attacks against such targets are prohibited by the 1977 Protocols[407] and had recently been considered at the Conference for Disarmament for further regulation.[408]

The 1982 Convention on the Law of the Sea is also relevant to environmental warfare: even if there are no explicit provisions in the Law of the Sea Convention on protection of the marine environment against consequences of armed attacks, it is necessary to assume such protection[409] in the context of the provisions of the Convention with regard to pollution.[410] Recent events in the Gulf amply illustrate hazards to the marine environment.[411]

But it is above all warfare on land that has contributed to the urgent need for a comprehensive Convention on environmental techniques. Defoliant action in Vietnam,[412] although intended to have an impact on vegatation, also harmed combatants by chemicals, and, above all, had detrimental effects on the civilian population, both by exposing them to health hazards and by depriving them of crops and other means of survival.

ii. *The En-Mod Convention of 1977*

There has been special concern about influencing the environment, for example, by artificial rainfall or droughts, possibly leading to the disruption of water and heat balance in a region and to the destruction of the ozone layer which protects the earth from the sun's ultra-violet rays.

During discussions in the Conference of the Committee on Disarmament, CCD, in 1974[413] Sweden emphasised the importance of preventing meteorological warfare.[414] The United States and the USSR urged, in a Joint Statement,[415] that effective measures be taken to prevent environmental modification for military or 'other' hostile use.

The United Nations General Assembly took Resolution 3664

---

[406] Cf. below, p. 249.   [407] *Ibid.*
[408] See CD, *Report*, 1985. Cf. SIPRI, *Law of War*, 63.
[409] UN, *Study on the Naval Arms Race*, 153.   [410] Part XII.   [411] *Ibid.*
[412] Above, p. 217.   [413] GAOR, 29th sess., Suppl. no. 27, A/9627, paras. 157ff.
[414] A/9698, Annex 4.   [415] A/9627, paras. 158ff.

(XXIX) in 1974[416] requesting CCD to adopt a Convention on the matter. New draft conventions, separate but identical, were submitted by the United States and by the USSR in 1975.[417] The text was discussed and revised[418] both after discussion in CCD and in the First Committee of the General Assembly.[419]

In 1976 Mexico had emphasised, in the form of a draft resolution[420] in the First Committee of the General Assembly, that article 1 in the Draft Convention prohibited only en-mod techniques which had widespread, long-lasting or severe effects; by such limitation there was an inference that techniques of lesser ambit would be permissible.

The final Convention on the Prohibition of Military or Any Other Hostile Use of Environmental Modification Techniques, normally referred to as the En-Mod Convention, was adopted in 1977.[421] The Convention was, when opened for signature,[422] signed by 34 States, including all the major military powers except France. The Convention consists of a preamble and six substantive articles and another four formal ones on temporal application of unlimited duration, on review conferences, ratification procedures, depositories and authenticity of texts.

Article I deals with the area where most problems have been encountered and which goes to the root of the whole Convention; for article I controls its ambit of application. The final Convention adopted the unsatisfactory article I and prohibits only environmental warfare which has 'widespread, long-lasting or severe' effects. The threshold of the application of article I of the Convention is now at the centre of attention of further discussions. The main problem concerns further prohibition of environmental techniques which do *not*

[416] On the basis of a revised USSR Draft Resolution and Convention, endorsed by 23 States; cf. A/C.1/1,675 and Rev. 1.
[417] CCD/471 and CCD/472; GAOR, 30th sess., Suppl. no. 27, A/10027, para. 45.
[418] See, e.g., Working Paper by Canada, CCD/463, GAOR, 30th sess., Suppl. no. 27, A/10027, Annex II; by Sweden, CCD/465 and GAOR, 31st sess., Suppl. no. 27, A/31/27, para. 277 for revisions, and paras. 91–370 on text.
[419] Cf. GA Res. 3475 (XXX) requesting CCD to agree on a text.
[420] The Resolution was sponsored by eleven Latin American States and by Haiti and Cyprus, A/C.1/31/L.4, and, for comments, GAOR, 31st sess., A/31/27, paras. 297–333; GAOR, 37th sess., First Committee, 45th mtg (Mexico and Argentina) reiterating the need for a resolution.
[421] The Convention entered into force on 5 October 1978. There are 47 parties (1985), including most States of military significance except China, France, South Africa and Israel.
[422] See GA Res. 31/72 1977.

have widespread, long-lasting or severe effects. For there is clearly a large category of permissible environmental weapons subsumed under the wide formula of article I as it stands. Secondly, as is always the case with concepts involving latitudes, there is a further problem as to *who* is to assess whether the relevant threshold has been crossed, i.e. whether environmental damage, in a specific case, is 'widespread', 'long-lasting' or 'severe'.[423] An interesting technique for interpretative 'understandings', separated from the main text, has been adopted. Thus, CCD reached an 'understanding' that, for the purposes of the Convention, 'widespread' would mean encompassing an area on the scale of several hundred square kilometres; 'long-lasting' would imply a period of months or approximately a season; and 'severe' would mean serious or significant disruption or harm to human life, natural and economic resources or other assets.[424] Such 'understandings' are clearly relevant to the interpretation of the treaty, especially as they form part, in this particular case, of the *travaux préparatoires* which always guide the interpretation of a text in the absence of clear wording.[425] But if, on the one hand, such 'understandings' indicate the ambit of article I of the En-Mod Convention in a fairly conclusive way, they hollow out, on the other hand, the actual scope of the Convention.

Article II defines en-mod techniques as 'any technique for changing – through the deliberate manipulation of natural processes – the dynamics, composition or structure of the earth, including its biota, lithosphere, phydrosphere and atmosphere, or of outer space'. A list of examples that had figured in earlier drafts was deleted, but there was another 'understanding'[426] that the following examples were illustrative of phenomena that could be caused by en-mod techniques: earthquakes, tsunamis (the Japanese word for tidal waves), upsets in ecological balance, changes in weather or climate pattern, of ocean currents or of the ozone layer or of the ionosphere. There was also a presumption that such phenomena would be, as required by article I, for the application of the Convention, of 'widespread, long-lasting or severe' effect.[427]

In accordance with the original mandate of the General Assembly

---

[423] On similar subjectives tests, see above, p. 135.
[424] GAOR, 31st sess., 1976 Suppl. no. 27, A/31/27, paras. 297–333.
[425] Vienna Convention on the Law of Treaties, 1961, article 32.
[426] Cf. comments above.
[427] GAOR, 37th sess., Suppl. no. 27, A/31/27, paras. 334–43.

to the Committee on Disarmament[428] to keep further development of en-mod techniques under review, in conjunction with the provisions of the Convention itself[429] it is now subjected to periodic Review Conferences. The First Review Conference was held in 1984 and dealt, above all, with the recurrent problems caused by the very limited scope of article I.[430] Article III provides, by an additional clause inserted late in the negotiations, that the Convention will be without prejudice to generally recognised rules of international law concerning en-mod techniques. There is a stipulation, in connection with this provision, that the Convention shall not hinder en-mod techniques for peaceful purposes. The article also provides, in a second paragraph, for the fullest possible exchange of information on en-mod techniques for peaceful purposes, although there was strong pressure at the Conference by the USSR to delete such alleged duty of cooperation in a field which was not germane to the Convention.[431]

By article V States undertake to cooperate in areas relevant to the Convention either directly or – as was added by a late revision of the draft Convention – through the United Nations. But there are only vague provisions on verification. A procedure is set out in the article for convening a Consultative Committee of Experts to which information can be transmitted by States. In practice, this provision has been supplemented by other methods; for the Review Conference in 1984 information was also transmitted[432] to the Preparatory Committee for the Conference, established but not named under article VIII of the Convention.[433] In the case of suspected breach of the Convention a State may lodge a complaint with the Security Council; contracting States undertake to 'cooperate' in any investigation by the Security Council.[434] This is thus another type of what we have called 'solidarity assistance'.[435]

Article IV provides for the transformation into national law[436] of the provisions of the Convention and provides that national rules shall incorporate necessary prohibitions and preventions.

[428] GAOR, 10th spec. sess., Suppl. no. 4, A/S-10/4, 1978.
[429] Article VIII. See A. H. Westing (ed.), *Environmental Warfare: a Technical, Legal and Policy Appraisal*, London (SIPRI), 1984. On 'weather war' see also R. G. Lauren, 'War, peace and the environment', in R. N. Barrett (ed.), *International Dimensions of the Environmental Crisis*, Boulder, Colorado, 1982, 83.
[430] See above.   [431] GAOR, 31st sess., Suppl. no. 27, A/31/27, paras. 344ff.
[432] For such information see En-Mod/CONF.1/4, 1984.
[433] Cf. above, p. 220 on implied powers.   [434] Article VIII(3)(4).
[435] Cf. my work on the *Concept of International Law*, p. 124.
[436] On such techniques, see above, p. 163.

A Review Conference was convened in 1984 under article VIII of the Convention.[437] The Conference made a Final Declaration whereby States reaffirmed their interest in preventing en-mod techniques for military or any other hostile use. The Conference noted that article I had been 'faithfully observed' by the State parties.[438] There had not been any complaints under article VIII.[439]

Although there had been considerable discussion on the threshold of application of the Convention under article I there was no amendment of this article. The Declaration affirmed each and every one of the articles of the Convention and declared that another Review Conference would be convened in 1989.

The main concern of the Review Conference was with the defects of article I. By its wording it provides that environmental modifications on a smaller scale are not covered by the Convention.[440] Proposals were made, again by Mexico, to widen the scope of the Convention; but, after much discussion, the Review Conference refrained from taking any decision.

---

[437] GA Res. 37/99 I 1982.   [438] En-Mod/CONF.1.1/11, 6.   [439] *Ibid.*, 6–7.
[440] En-Mod/CONF.1/4.1984, 4.

A. GENERAL RULES FOR ALL WARFARE

So far, certain general rules and rules pertaining to weapons in warfare have been discussed. Weapons have been thought to be the primary 'means' of warfare and rules relating to their prohibition or regulated use are at the core of the Law of War; for without weapons few wars would be fought.

We shall now seek to discern relevant rules for the methods of warfare as opposed to the means. The difference between means and methods in warfare is relative and not easy to maintain. Often weapons are used in a specific way which is in violation of the Law of War. Is it then a question of an illegitimate method or an illegitimate use of a weapon? This preliminary provocative question is only raised in this context so that the reader can bear in mind the interwoven character of the rules of the Law of War on means and methods. On the whole, one can often distinguish whole sets of problems that pertain more to 'method' than to 'means' and often it is fairly clear what is a practice rather than use resulting from the intrinsic characteristics of a weapon. Methods, as well as the use of weapons, are subjected to the general ethics of warfare.[1] Belligerents and combatants must all follow the basic rules.

However, one question of method is more fundamental than others: that is the question of targets, i.e. targets against which permissible weapons may be directed.

i. The doctrine of illegitimate objectives

The question of targets goes to the root of the Law of War, just as much as the distinction between combatant and civilian.[2] In fact and

---

[1] Above, p. 134.   [2] Above, p 106.

in law, the two questions are two sides of the same problem: the problem of distinction. A combatant must distinguish himself from the civilian population[3] so that the war is kept between combatants themselves. The combatant will, if he is captured, be treated as a prisoner of war[4] provided he has complied with the rudimentary rules of distinction. The civilian, in turn, will not be attacked by the enemy combatant. He is, as it were, immune from attack; and that is precisely the link between the question of distinction between combatant and civilians and the question of targets. For the rule of distinction applies here too. It is military targets that may be attacked in war whereas civilian objectives are, so to speak, immune[5] from attack.

These are the principles. In actual warfare things may be different. But in all recent wars belligerents have been aware of the limits and rules in this respect and have been eager to explain that damage or injury in the immune sector was 'inevitable' or justified by military necessity.[6]

ii. Identification of exempt objectives

It is important to clarify which objectives are immune under the modern Law of War. The places and areas which are immune from attack should possibly be called immune 'objectives' and not immune 'targets', as the very notion 'target' implies something which is aimed at and it is this action, this 'aiming', which is prohibited.

a. Zones

First, one may refer to the demilitarised and neutralised areas, and, if relevant, the denuclearised zones discussed earlier in connection with spatial notions.[7] Additional Protocol I of 1977 specifically recognises that such zones are exempt from attack.[8] Other areas which are placed on the same footing as such zones, as indicated above,[9] are neutral countries, which, by presumption, include all third States, until they join hostilities.[10]

b. Open towns

A second category is that of so-called 'undefended towns' or 'open towns'. This term has not been defined in treaties, but there is much

---

[3] On criteria, above, p. 103.   [4] Below, p. 281.
[5] The word 'immune' is naturally not used here in its accepted legal sense which means 'exempt from jurisdiction', see my 'Foreign warships', 55.
[6] Below, p. 332.   [7] Above, p. 138.   [8] Article 60 of Protocol I.
[9] Above, p. 152.   [10] Cf. above, on irrelevance of declarations of war.

guidance in the doctrine on the requirements for an undefended town.[11]

The rules on open towns were laid down[12] in the Brussels Declaration of 1874[13] and re-adopted in the Hague Regulations.[14] A similar rule was also included in Hague Convention IX of 1907 on Naval Bombardment.[15] There are detailed contingency rules. Protection by, for example, submarine contact mines does not alter a port's state of being undefended; but military or naval installations, weapons or ammunition, are military targets and may be attacked even if inside an open town. If required, the undefended part has a duty to provide supplies, proportionate to local resources, against payment, to the naval forces in its proximity,[16] and, should it refuse to do so, the naval forces may bombard the town. Obviously such rules lead to problems: who is going to assess whether the port has supplies?[17]

But the Draft Hague Rules on Aerial Warfare abandoned the notion of 'open towns' and distinguished instead in more general terms between military and civilian objectives.

The reason why the Hague Draft Rules on Aerial Warfare abandoned the notion of 'open towns' explains the difficulty of the concept in relation to the question of bombardment. The idea of undefended open towns was designed for conditions of land or possibly naval warfare, but totally remote from the context of aerial warfare where attack will necessarily have a much lesser degree of distinction. Furthermore, there had been numerous attacks on open towns, in the Italian Ethiopian War, the Spanish Civil War,[18] the Sino-Japanese War and the Second World War.[19] In the Korean War in 1952, and even more in Vietnam from 1965 to 1972, the protection that open

---

[11] See, above all, R. Y. Jennings, 'Open towns', 22 *BYIL* 1945, 258; cf. W. R. Born, *Die offene Stadt, Schützzonen und Guerillakämpfer, Regelungen zum Schütze der Zivilbevölkerung in Kriegszeiten*, Berlin, 1978; A. M. Zayas, 'Open towns', in 4 *Encyclopedia of Public International Law*, 69; J. Tromm, 'Open Steden', 59 *Militair-rechtelijk tijdschrift* 1966, 321: E. Schmitz, 'Die offene Stadt im geltenden Kriegsrecht', 10 *ZaöRVR*, 1940–1, 618.

[12] See, on details of history, Rousseau, *Conflits armés*, 128–9.

[13] Declaration, 27 August 1974, article 15.   [14] Article 25.

[15] Article 1. For reference, see above p. 178. See H. Hartig, *Die Beschiessung durch Seestreitkräfte im Kriegszeiten*, Berlin, 1911.

[16] *Ibid.*, article 3.   [17] Cf. above, p. 135, and below, p. 236, on subjective criteria.

[18] It was the horror of the attack on an undefended town on 27 April 1937 that Picasso depicted in his painting *Guernica*.

[19] For example, the raids on London from 7 September to 3 December 1940; the attacks on Rotterdam, 14 May 1940, and Warsaw, from 1 September 1939. Paris and Rome were both treated as open towns in 1940 and 1943 respectively and the rules on hostile acts by inhabitants were largely respected; this was not the case in Manila in 1941. Wulff, *Handbok i folkrätt under krig*, 95.

towns should have had under the Law of War was largely disregarded.[20] Violations of the rules on protection of open towns from naval bombardment had also been violated, for example by the bombing of Barcelona during the Spanish Civil War, and by the attack on Haiphong by the French Navy in 1946 and of Inchon and Chongjin in Korea by British and American ships.[21] But the prohibition on attacking an open town still applies and, for example, the British manual of military law[22] emphasises that the distinction between defended and undefended localities is not obliterated by the 'great destructive power of modern artillery and guided missiles'.

The attempts[23] to prohibit all bombardment from the air have long since been abandoned as unrealistic. Even the duty to warn civilians of an imminent attack[24] was thought not to apply to air attacks,[25] although there may be some indications to the contrary in case law.[26]

Protocol I of 1977 uses the new term 'non-defended locality' to describe an open town. To be exempt from attack such a place must be free of combatants, mobile weapons and its fixed military installations must not be used for any hostile purpose; nor must any other type of hostile act, or act to assist military operations, be committed by the authorities or by the population.[27] Under the Protocol a place may be declared a non-defended locality provided no hostile acts will be committed against the enemy by fixed military installations, or by the authorities or population, and provided there are no acts supporting military operations.[28]

Although the notion of 'open town' is still accepted as forming part of binding rules of warfare today, as is indicated by the reaffirmation of the principle in Protocol I of 1977,[29] it is now used only as a supplementary concept to the one concerning military objectives. There is a requirement of reasonable proportionality between damage and military gain.[30] Any 'strategy of devastation' is in violation of this rule.[31]

---

[20] Rousseau, *Conflits armés*, 365–7.   [21] *Ibid.*, 238–9.
[22] 1958 article 290; cf. article 284.
[23] 26 NRGT, 2 série, 994; 1 *AJIL* 1907, Suppl., 153.
[24] Hague Regulations, article 26.
[25] D. Fleck, 'Die rechtliche Garantien des Verbots von unmittelbaren Kampfhandlungen gegen Zivilpersonen', *RDPMDG*, 1966, 97–8.
[26] E.g. Greek–German Mixed Commission, in *Coenca* v. *Germany*, (1927) 7 *RIAA* 183; *Kiriadolou* v. *Germany*, 1930, 10 *ibid.* 100.
[27] Article 59. For reference, above, p. 108.   [28] *Ibid.*   [29] Article 59.
[30] H. Meyrowitz, 'The Law of War in the Vietnamese conflict' in Falk, 2 *The Vietnam War*, 567.   [31] *Ibid.*

c. Military and civilian objectives distinguished

(1) The notion of military targets It is vital to establish what a belligerent and its combatants must not use as a target for its military action. The concept of 'military target' is used to indicate that it is legitimate to attack. Thus, what is not such a target is a civilian objective, exempt from attack.

(2) The enumerative approach The Hague Draft Rules of 1923[32] prescribed that attacks from the air would be permitted only if directed against a military objective, the total or partial destruction of which presented a 'distinct military advantage' to the attacker. The level of the operative words may have been slightly less demanding in the French version which refers to 'un avantage militaire net'.[33] The Rules go on to enumerate such military objectives as 'military forces; military works; military establishments or depots; factories constituting important and well known centres engaged in the manufacturing of arms, ammunition or distinctively military supplies; lines of communication or transport used for military purposes'.[34] The German version omits the equivalent to the word 'distinctively' in relation to military supplies.[35] The French text speaks of 'fournitures militaires caractérisés' which possibly conveys the impression that, to be of a military nature, the supplies must have been characterised as such by some authority. If this is so, it raises the question whether such subjective[36] classification overrides the objective nature of such supplies. In other words, could one, under the French text, classify *anything* as military supplies? Secondly, if this is so, how would information of such classification reach the enemy?

Furthermore, the German text covers more clearly than the English text radio stations and other news media, which are not too obviously included in the English expression 'lines of communication'[37]

The enumeration in article 24(2) has been held to be an 'exhaustive' list which, even though the Draft Rules never entered into force, provides a guide to the position of international law on the subject, especially, it is claimed, since there is little disagreement in the doc-

---

[32] *AJIL*, 1923, Suppl., 245; Schindler and Toman, *Documents*, 2nd edn, 147.
[33] Article 24(2).   [34] Article 24(2).
[35] The German version simply refers to 'militärische Ausrüstungsgegenstände';
[36] Cf. above, pp. 135 and 234.
[37] The German text uses the words 'Nachrichten und Verkehrsmittel'.

trine on the subject.[38] But, as has been shown above, merely the discrepancies between the various texts in different languages would seem to indicate some uncertainty on the subject.

Some have claimed that it would follow from the Hague Rules of 1923 that 'military persons' do not include those who, for example, contribute to the war effort, or the so-called quasi-combatants; that industries, even those of the extracting type, like coal mines, or the refining type, are not included as military works as they are not 'purely military'; nor are those involved in transportation or storage of such material; and, finally, that government buildings are not included among military targets.[39] But others emphasise that it is more important to examine whether installations are put to predominantly civilian or military use.[40]

The International Law Association (ILA) devoted some attention to the subject during its Conference in Stockholm in 1924. The Conference adopted the definition of military targets in the Hague Rules of 1923.[41] In 1938 the Association elaborated the definition of 'belligerent establishments' to include 'military, naval or air establishments, or barracks, arsenals, munition stores or factories, aerodromes or aeroplane workshops, or ships of war, naval dockyards, forts or fortifications for defensive or offensive purposes or entrenchments'.[42] A further illustrating list was included in the Hague Convention for the Protection of Cultural Property of 1954 which indicates that property will only be protected under the Convention[43] provided it is situated away from military objectives like 'any large industrial centre or from any important military objective, constituting a vulnerable point, such as, for example, an aerodrome, broadcasting station, establishment engaged upon work of national defence, a port or a railway station of relative importance or a main line of communication'.[44]

With regard to some of these examples, for example a broadcasting

---

[38] A. Euler, *Die Atomwaffe im Luftkriegsrecht*, Cologne, 1940, 47.

[39] A. Meyer, *Völkerrechtliche Schutz friedlicher Personen und Sachen gegen Luftangriffe*, Königsberg, 1935, 99.

[40] J. M. Spaight, *Air Power and the Cities*, London, 1930, 208. Note that towards the end of the last century postal services were thought to be an exempt target, in spite of their use to belligerents, whereas the telegraph services were 'par excellence un moyen de guerre' which could be occupied or even ('même') intercepted; yet the installations themselves constituted proprietary rights, see C. Calvo, 4 *Le droit international, théorie et pratique*, Paris, 1888, 262; on property rights, cf. below, p. 303.

[41] 33 *Report* ILA, Stockholm, 1924.   [42] 40 *Report* ILA, Amsterdam, 1938.

[43] See further below, p. 249.

[44] Hague Convention 1954, 249 UNTS 240, Article 8(1)(a).

station, it may be remarked that such an objective would not, unless there were clear intelligence reports, be identifiable from the air as such. The reference to 'ports' of at least some 'importance' seems to exclude the protection some ports would enjoy under the open town doctrine.[45]

The insistence that only military targets may be attacked in war is again found in the Mine Protocol of 1980 which expressly provides that mines (and other devices) may be used only against military areas which are themselves military objectives or which contain military objectives.[46]

(3) Relevant criteria Some writers insist that military objectives cannot be defined *in vacuo* but must relate to a purpose to which they can be employed.[47] Others have elaborated theories of 'adequate causation' and suggest that only objectives which stand in such relation to the war effort qualify as military objectives.[48]

But such suggestions offend against the basic principle of foreseeability and knowledge of the enemy: how is he expected to know the planned use of any particular installation? Surely objective criteria must be preferred rather than those which presuppose a detailed knowledge of enemy strategies.[49] It is almost better to resort to large presumption of use and thus classify all industrial centres as military objectives.[50]

Protocol I provides rules on military and non-military objectives, but does not clearly define military targets. Although the Protocol refers to civilian and military targets in numerous articles,[51] it is not clear where to draw the line between military and civilian targets. Earlier attempts to regulate air warfare often relied on a list of 'legitimate' military objectives, for example as enumerated in the Hague Rules of 1923[52] against which bombardment had to be exclusively directed.

Protocol I refrains from providing such an enumerating list, but it is questionable whether much is lost by a loose and abstract reference to 'military' targets, in view of the largely accepted criteria such targets must fulfil.

[45] Above, p. 233.   [46] Article 5.   [47] Spaight, *Air Power*, 215.
[48] Meyer, *Völkerrechtlicher Schutz*, 83.
[49] Cf. on subjective assessment above, p. 236.
[50] Ming-Min-Peng, 'Le bombardement aérien et la population civile depuis la seconde guerre mondiale', *Revue général de l'air*, 1952, 302ff.
[51] E.g. articles 48, 51, 52 and 56.   [52] Above, p. 234.

Certain civilian objects have enhanced protection under the Protocol beyond that already granted by the 1954 Hague Convention,[53] which, in turn, expanded the rudimentary protection given by the Hague Regulations of 1907.[54] Protocol I of 1977 defines military objectives as those objects which by their nature, location, purpose or use make effective contribution to military action as well as those 'whose total or partial destruction, capture or neutralisation, in the circumstances at the time, offers a definite military advantage'.[55] The second part of the provision thus brings back the unfortunate subjective criteria[56] which are so likely to cause problems in practice.

The Protocol defines 'military' and 'non-military' objectives, as distinct from civilian objectives, in abstract terms, without the traditional reference to typical examples.[57]

iii. Consequential protection

From the distinction made above between military and civilian objectives certain rules follow exempting certain objectives from attack. Many of these rules are codified in Protocol I of 1977. It must be noted that the scope of the Protocol covers inter-State wars as well as liberation wars, which are equated to 'international' wars.[58] Protocol II of 1977 covers many facets of internal wars which do not constitute liberation wars.[59]

a. Prohibition of area bombing

Rules on bombardment are often discussed by writers under a separate heading on aerial warfare; but the prohibition rules in this respect apply to bombardment from air, sea or land. In view of modern reliance on, for example, land-based missiles, or on those launched from submarines, it appears more appropriate to deal with bombardment in connection with rules applicable to all warfare.

It is universally accepted that bombardment exclusively directed against the civilian population is prohibited. Such rules form the basis of the Hague Draft Rules of 1923 and have been regarded in both doctrine and practice as a binding rule. In *Coenca frères* v.

[53] 249 UNTS 240.
[54] Hague Regulations to Convention II 1899, 26 NRGT, 2 série, 949; 1 *AJIL* 1907, Suppl., 129, and Hague Regulations to Convention IV of 1907, 3 NRGT, 2 série, 949; 1 *AJIL* 1907, Suppl., 129.
[55] Article 52.　[56] Above, p. 236.　[58] Above, p. 73.　[59] Above, p. 170.

Germany[60] the Tribunal held that warnings to civilians, a rule which has long been compulsory in land warfare, also applied to bombardment. Lack of such warning may entitle civilians to a right to compensation for damage to property. Another case, *Kiriadolou* v. *Germany*,[61] emphasised the need for giving warning of aerial bombardment to civilians and added that chemical warfare by aeroplane is particularly forbidden.

One indication of the binding nature of this obligation is also the efforts States have made to 'justify', in terms of military necessity,[62] any attacks which have affected the civilian population.[63] The obligation has been reaffirmed in many General Assembly resolutions[64] and is reaffirmed in Protocol I of 1977.

Area bombing was extensively used by the United Kingdom and later by the United States in the Second World War.[65] The theory of 'strategic bombing' was elaborated and adopted as a method of warfare by the United States and United Kingdom High Command in Casablanca on 21 January 1943. The plan to use this method was mainly implemented by zone bombardment or target area bombing by which numerous aeroplanes attacked several military targets between which there were pockets of civilian population. As a result of this strategy some 593,000 German civilians were killed as against 60,500 in the United Kingdom and some 60,000 in France.[66] Yet area bombing was in sharp contradiction to the Declaration on 1 September 1939 by Cordell-Hull stating that any general bombing of areas where there were large civilian populations was contrary to the principles of international law and of humanity.[67] And on 2 December 1939 the United States stated that the American Government wholeheartedly condemned 'unprovoked' bombing of civilian population from the air.[68] But the strategy or area bombing was later expanded and applied systematically in Vietnam.[69]

Protocol I of 1977 is the first agreement in treaty form to prohibit area bombing. The Protocol prohibits indiscriminate attacks and area bombing is one of the prime forms of such attacks.

[60] 7 *RIAA* 683.   [61] 10 *RIAA* 100.   [62] Below, p. 332.
[63] Above, p. 233.   [64] For example, Resolution 2444 (XXIII) 1968.
[65] E. Castrén, 'La protection juridique de la population civile dans la guerre moderne', *RGDIP*, 1955, 13.
[66] Rousseau, *Conflits armés*, 131.
[67] 6 Hackworth 267; cf. statements by United States to Japan, 22 September 1937 and 14 June 1940, *ibid.*, 266, and by the United States to Italy, 23 October 1940, *ibid.*, 268.
[68] *Ibid.*, 267.
[69] Ch. Rousseau, 'Chronique des faits internationaux', *RGDIP*, 1973, 826.

According to the Protocol there must be no indiscriminate attacks of any form. Such attacks are, for example, bombardment which is not directed against a specific military objective or one which employs methods which cannot be directed against such a target or other means which cannot be limited as to their effect.[70] The prohibition is not limited to air warfare but such bombardment from planes is the obvious method for such attacks. One specific form of such 'indiscriminate' bombardment, so-called 'area bombing', has now been specifically prohibited by Protocol I by a further provision forbidding bombardment 'by any methods or means', or treating as a single military objective, several military targets located for example in a city where there is 'similar' concentration of civilian population. Furthermore, any attack which may be expected to cause incidental loss among civilians, or civilian objects, is prohibited unless outweighed by concrete and direct military advantage.[71]

b. Specific exemptions from attack

(1) Civilians and persons hors de combat If the distinction between military and civilian objectives is difficult to draw in practice, it is still clear that the civilian population as such is the primary group on which attacks must not be launched. This obvious statement has not, in general terms, been entrenched in treaty law until recently.

From the prohibition of attacks on civilian objectives it follows that civilians, as groups or as individuals, may be attacked. Alternatively, one could deduce the prohibition of attacks on civilian targets precisely from the protection that individual civilians enjoy as noncombatants[72] and, as such, being exempt from the war.

But history shows that civilians, in spite of this protective regime, are increasingly at risk in war. In the First World War some 5 per cent of the victims were civilians; in the Second World War this figure had risen to 48, to escalate in the Korean war to 84 and in the Vietnam War to 90 per cent.[73] Not all the increase in this proportion can be explained by difficulties of distinction between combatants and civilians.[74]

The protection of civilians is, from the humanitarian point of view, the most important task of any legislative effort on warfare, as such

---

[70] Article 51(1).
[71] Article 51(5)(g). See further on military necessity below, pp. 332ff.
[72] Above, p. 103.   [73] Wulff, *Handbok i folkrätt under krig*, 102.   [74] Above, p. 106.

persons include the weakest members of the community, most in need of protection, such as women, children and the aged. Another reason for their specific protection is that civilians must normally be assumed to have wished to abstain from any involvement in the conflict. Even if numeric reasons are not always relevant, it is furthermore important to consider that the civilian population normally represents a much larger number of people than the combatants.

Before the time of Grotius, civilians enjoyed little or no protection and women and children were in no way immune from attack,[75] although there were isolated regulations, such as that of Henry V of England in 1515, or of the Holy Roman Empire in 1442 and 1570, whereby women, children, priests, monks and nuns were immune from attack.[76]

Civilians, who had received some rudimentary protection under the Hague Conventions of 1899 and 1907,[77] benefited from a general clause on prohibition of attacks on undefended localities under the Hague Regulations,[78] and also, in a much more comprehensive way, under the Fourth Geneva Convention of 1949,[79] which did not seek to abrogate the earlier Hague Conventions but expressly attempted to supplement them. The Fourth Convention, for example, extends rules relating to the treatment of alien enemies 'in the light of recent practices of civilized nations'.[80]

The Fourth Geneva Convention also introduced, for the first time, criteria of distinction between civilians and combatants.[81] But if 'civilian' means someone who is not a combatant,[82] this also means

[75] E. Nys, *Les origines du droit international*, Brussels, 1894, 205; Nys, *Le droit de la guerre et les précurseurs de Grotius*, 118. But, for statements that civilians did enjoy certain protection and that it is 'wrong' to imprison old men, blind men, women and children who took no part in the war, see H. Bonet, *L'arbre des batailles*, Paris or Avignon, 1387, ed. and trans. G. W. Coopland as *The Tree of Battles*, Liverpool, 1949, chs. 94–95, pp. 184–5; cf. ch. 48.

[76] Nys, *Les origines*, 125. Cf. further M. Keen, *The Laws of War in the Later Middle Ages*, Oxford, 1965, 190–1, 196. For the decree of Sigismund the Elder in Poland in 1530, see A. Gorbiel, 'The protection of war victims under Polish legislation up to the end of the eighteenth century', *IRRC*, 1975, 274.

[77] For references, see above, note 123.   [78] Article 25. Cf. article 27.

[79] For example in time of occupation, see articles 42–56 of the Hague Regulations of 1899 and 1907.

[80] Yingling and Ginnane, 'The Geneva Conventions of 1949', 411.

[81] A Diplomatic Conference of 1929 had recommended a further Convention for the Protection of Civilians. The ICRC prepared Draft Rules at the Tokyo Conference in 1934 but these Rules were never considered by the Diplomatic Conference because of the outbreak of the Second World War. On the principle of distinction, see further p. 106.

[82] Above, p. 103.

that problems connected with the identification of 'combatants' are carried over to the field of protection of 'civilians'. A further question is that the distinction is eroded by actual or threatened use of weapons of mass destruction.[83]

Protocol I of 1977 expands protection of civilians considerably, especially by a paramount presumption that anyone who is not proved to be a combatant has civilian status.[84] The Protocol extends the protection of the Fourth Geneva Convention by prohibiting any attacks on the civilian populations either to gain military advantage or to take reprisals.[85] Civilians comprise two distinct groups, those who never took part in the hostilities and who form part of the normal civilian population and those who were combatants but are *hors de combat* and no longer take part in the hostilities, perhaps because they are wounded or because they have, for other reasons, permanently rejoined the civilian population.[86] The protection of the civilian population may even be the main aim of Protocol I of 1977[87] and is achieved by the prohibition of certain methods of warfare as well as by some mandatory provisions on the treatment of victims of war. The rules on belligerency obviously concern the combatants in the first place,[88] but will have as their objective and inevitable result an improved protection of civilians. Other rules envisage more directly the treatment of civilians or combatants *hors de combat* such as the wounded and prisoners of war. The fusion of rules previously found in the instruments on the law of the Hague with those in documents on the law of Geneva has, as some commentators point out,[89] upset the traditional division between the two sets of rules, a division which was perhaps never well founded.[90]

Protocol I codifies, for the first time, the established rule that civilians must not form the object of attack.[91] Furthermore, acts which are intended to spread terror among the civilian population

[83] Cf. Rousseau, *Conflits armés*, 81.
[84] Article 50. Such status is refused only if the 'civilian' takes direct part in the hostilities, see article 51.
[85] Article 51(2) of Protocol I; cf. article 13(2) of Protocol II.
[86] Cf. P. Bretton, 'Le problème des "méthodes et moyens de guerre ou de combat"', 43.
[87] E.g. CDDH/SR.5, 81, vol. 7, 136.
[88] On alleged difficulties caused by 'vagueness' of the law, making interpretation by members of the armed forces difficult, see R. Lapidoth, 'Qui a droit au statut de prisonnier de guerre?' *RGDIP*, 1978, 210.
[89] Siotis, *Le droit de la guerre*, 226.
[90] Cf. above, p. 128.
[91] The 1922 Draft Rules on Air Warfare were never ratified.

are prohibited.[92] Such acts may, for example, be area bombardment, like the Blitz of London.[93]

Civilians are also specifically protected in Protocol II of 1977. Protocol II is very short in its final truncated form,[94] but it contains some important provisions which represent innovation in the rules of warfare.

One such new provision is the prohibition of attacks on civilians. Although common article 3 had secured a certain level of treatment of non-combatants, it had not clearly precluded military operations directed against civilians or against civilian targets. Protocol II of 1977 now includes such clear prohibition of attacks of non-military targets.[95]

In the Iran–Iraq War the Iraqi Air Force carried out indiscriminate bombing attacks on Iranian built-up areas, causing considerable destruction of purely civilian property with ensuing loss of life and personal injuries to civilians.[96] But severe criticism by the United Nations Secretary General on 9 June 1984 resulted in a special undertaking by both Iran and Iraq to cease military attacks on purely civilian population centres in either country from 0001 GMT, 12 June 1984.[97] Swift condemnation by leaders and organs of world society may indicate that, even if the special rule is violated, it is nevertheless a fundamental rule of the Law of War.

(2) Parachutists Parachutists are equated to persons *hors de combat* under Protocol I of 1977. Aeroplanes of the enemy are, of course, an obvious target for a belligerent, both for defensive and offensive purposes. However, it has been argued that parachutists jumping from aeroplanes would not be legitimate targets as they are, as it were, not combatants in action until they reach the ground. Whether or not this is a proved fact may be disputed.

However, Protocol I of 1977 has introduced certain specific rules on this topic prescribing, *inter alia*, that parachutists jumping from an aircraft in distress must not be attacked and, if they land in enemy territory, they must be given an opportunity to surrender.[98] This regulation may codify earlier law.[99] Parachutists in such situations

---

[92] Article 51(2).   [93] Below, p. 241.   [94] Above, p. 170.   [95] Article 13.
[96] ICRC, *2nd Memorandum to Governments Participating in the Geneva Conventions of 1949 on the Conflict between the Islamic Republic of Iran and the Republic of Iraq*, 10 February 1984.
[97] *United Nations Weekly News Summary*, 13 June 1984.
[98] Article 42(1)(2).   [99] Cf. Spaight, *Air Power*, 152ff.

can be compared with the shipwrecked[100] for they are, as it were, 'shipwrecked in the air'.[101] The question was raised whether parachutists should enjoy protection only if they descend into enemy-controlled territory where they could easily be rendered *hors de combat*, or whether their protection is unqualified.[102] Naturally, humanitarian considerations do not present themselves with the same intensity if a parachutist lands in friendly territory. The Arab group at the Conference argued that in such situations airmen should not be protected.[103] After ICRC Vice-President Pictet had indicated his reservations about adoption of a text authorising killing of any parachutists descending from aircrafts in distress, the Conference adopted an article affording protection without any qualification.[104] The provisions of the Protocol are important because of their practical applications in modern-day armed conflict. The Israeli air raid against Arab territory in 1967 and 1973 and the American actions in Vietnam induced the Conference drafting the 1977 Protocols to adopt a proviso exempting from protection any 'airborne troops'.[105]

(3) Parlamentaires Parlamentaires and other messengers authorised to negotiate with the enemy must not be attacked.[106] The root of this inviolability is the same as the one for diplomats and envoys. It forms part of the oldest part of international law and is reinforced by tradition and reciprocity.

(4) Food supplies and crops Objects necessary for the survival of the civilian population, for example foodstuffs, livestock and drinking-water installations, are protected from attack.[107] It has been shown above that such supplies must not be attacked by chemical,[108] biological[109] or environmental warfare.[110]

Protocol I of 1977 enlarges this protection by specifying that such objects are illegitimate targets, either as a strategy to starve the civilian population[111] or as a means to force civilians to move from an area.[112] But a belligerent may, on the other hand, destroy its *own* food supply in certain circumstances.[113]

[100] CDDH/III/SR. 47, 51, 79.   [101] ICRC, M. Pictet, CDDH/SR.39, 88.
[102] CDDH/IIISR.47 at 51, 79.   [103] CDDH/414.   [104] CDDH/SR.39, 110.
[105] Article 43(3).
[106] Hague Regulations, article 32; a parlamentaire would normally display a white flag, cf. above, p. 107; immunity extends to interpreters who accompany him.
[107] See also below, p. 252 on starvation.   [108] Above, p. 210.   [109] Above, p. 211.
[110] Above, p. 226.   [111] See below, p. 252 on starvation and siege.
[112] Article 54.   [113] See below, p. 261 on 'scorched earth policy'.

(5) Civilian ships Civilian ships may be an unusual expression, but it seems to cover the ships that may not be attacked in warfare, including, for example, both merchantmen and other non-warships. There are certain accepted guidelines on the criteria necessary for a ship to qualify as a warship: it must be commanded by a naval officer, have a crew subject to his authority, and it must normally be entered in the list of warships in the flag State.[114]

It has long been accepted that, for example, merchant ships are not legitimate targets. Their cargo may assist the enemy and it is often important to intercept merchantmen carrying valuable supplies to the enemy. But this must be done by capturing such vessels as prize[115] and not by attacking or sinking the ships.

Ships that are not subject to the law of prize always constitute illegal targets, for example hospital ships,[116] ships used for the transport of medical supplies or of wounded,[117] cartel ships used to carry prisoners of war,[118] and postal ships.[119]

There is thus a certain relationship between the law of prize and the position of certain ships with regard to targets. However, the ambit of the law of prize is wider than that of illegal targets insofar as enemy merchantmen may be taken as prize but they may not be attacked.[120] But, as has just been pointed out, from the other point of view the scope of the law of prize is narrower in the sense that ships that are immune from military attack may also be immune to capture as prize.

It was sometimes argued that the privilege of merchantmen, of being exempt from attack, would be forfeited if merchant ships accompanied warships in a convoy.[121]

Special rules regulate protection from attack by submarines. How-

---

[114] See my 'Foreign warships', 66. On the right of visit and search to verify civilian character see *The Mariana Flory* (1826), 11 Wheaton 1; and on such measures against a British vessel in a French 'security zone' during the Algerian War, see *The West Breeze* incident, discussed by A. Zwanenberg, in 'Interference with ships on the high seas', 10 *ICLQ* 785.

[115] Below, p. 305.

[116] Hague 1907 XI, article 3; Geneva II, articles 22, 24, 26, 27, 29, 30, 43; cf. articles 34–5.

[117] Geneva IV, article 21; Protocol I of 1977, article 23.

[118] Below, p. 281.   [119] Below, p. 299.

[120] See below, on the sinking of merchantmen from which passengers and crew are evacuated; but prize proceedings must still follow, cf. below, p. 306, and cf. Pearce Higgins, 'Submarine warfare', 1 *BYIL* 1920, 149, 152ff. Cf. the Washington Draft Treaty of 1922, article 22, and below p. 267.

[121] E.g. *The Donitz and Raeder Cases* before the International Military Tribunal at Nuremberg, 1 Nuremberg 1947, 331; 41 *AJIL 1947, 172, 303. Cf.* D. P. O'Connell,

ever, since submarine warfare is specific to warfare at sea, some relevant questions will be discussed in connection with naval war.[122] Submarines are highly vulnerable to even lightly armed merchant vessels. There has been some uncertainty with regard to the question whether submarines which are threatened by armed merchantmen have any right to attack.[123] But it must be emphasised that the unequal strength is such that no 'threat' by merchantmen can entitle submarines to attack them.[124]

There are some early basic rules that civilians at sea must not be attacked. However, such rules are often undermined by other rules on naval warfare. The Treaty for the Limitation and Reduction of Naval Armaments of 1930[125] together with the Protocol of 1936[126] allowed warships to sink merchant vessels provided passengers and crew were removed to a place of safety. If a merchant vessel refused to stop or to be subjected to visit and search, the vessel could be sunk without such precautionary measures.

The new protection of Protocol I of 1977 concerning presumption of civilian status also extends to naval warfare and increases the protection of civilians on board merchant vessels.[127]

(6) Hospitals, hospital ships and medical units   Hospitals must not be attacked,[128] nor must medical units, whether military or civilian, be subjected to any military offensive operations.[129] The right of hospitals to exemption from attack has been entrenched as a higher duty: 'in no circumstances' may they be the object of attack.[130] Hospital ships[131] are protected and must not be attacked; and sick bays on board warships must not form part of attacks but be 'spared as much as possible'.[132] Hospital trains[133] are furthermore specially protected and protection also applies to mobile medical units.[134]

This protection is clearly accepted as a binding rule of interna-

---

'International law and contemporary naval operations', *44 BYIL* 1970, 19, 51, on the right of submarines to attack merchant ships if there is an imminent *air* attack.
[122] Below, p. 263.   [123] O'Connell, *Influence of Law on Sea-Power*, 46.
[124] Below, p. 267.   [125] Cmnd. 3548.   [126] UKTS 29 1936; *AJIL*, 1937, Suppl., 137.
[127] Cf. United Kingdom, CDDH/III/SR.3, vol. 14, 21.
[128] Hague Regulations, article 27. Geneva Convention IV, article 19; article 18 of Geneva IV and article 12 of Protocol I of 1977 extend protection to all civilian hospitals.
[129] Protocol I, 1977, article 12.   [130] Geneva IV, article 18.
[131] Geneva I, article 20, and below. p. 279.
[132] Geneva II, article 28; cf. articles 34–5.   [133] Geneva I, article 21.
[134] For a wide definition of 'medical unit' see Protocol I of 1977, article 8.

tional law in doctrine and in practice.[135] Since such protection exists there arises on the part of the authorities in charge of medical hospitals and units a twofold duty.

On the one hand there is a duty on the part of a belligerent to keep medical units away from military targets,[136] implying, for example, that medical units must not be used to conceal or shield military objectives; such methods would amount to prohibited ruses of war.[137]

Secondly, the authorities, and/or the medical units themselves, must ensure that there is a clear marking of the units by a sign notified to the enemy[138] or by a Red Cross mark.[139] Ever since the establishment of the Red Cross organisation[140] the emblem of the Red Cross has been universally recognised and respected, its coverage extending to non-Christian countries like Japan,[141] Siam[142] or the Moslem countries.[143] During the 1907 Hague Conferences there was discussion on whether other signs should also be allowed, like the Red Lion for Persia and the Red Crescent for Turkey. But since neither of these two countries ratified the Hague Conventions, the question lapsed. Renewed discussions were instigated during the negotiations for the 1929 Convention on the Wounded,[144] when it was agreed that the alternatives Red Crescent and Red Lion would be allowed, mainly to satisfy demands by Turkey and Persia, as well as the special sign of the Red Sun for Japan. Some commentators were unhappy not to have the unity of one sign and regarded the novel signs as regrettable deviations.[145] Efforts to obtain the right to use other signs have been rejected, for example the proposals by Israel for the Red Star of David[146] as well as demands for signs without religious significance, such as the Red Heart for Ethiopia[147] or a reverse red swastika for Sri Lanka.[148]

[135] E.g. Rousseau, *Conflits armés*, 109.
[136] Hague Regulations, article 27; Geneva I, article 19; Geneva IV, article 18; Protocol I of 1977, article 12.
[137] See further below, p. 263.   [138] Hague Regulations, article 27.
[139] Geneva I, articles 38 and 42; Geneva IV, articles 18 and 21; Protocol I of 1977, article 18, and Annex, articles 3–4.
[140] Above, p. 123.
[141] F. Buignon, *The Emblem of the Red Cross*, Geneva, 1977, 22. But Israel made an explicit reservation to article 38 of Geneva I that the sign of the Red Star of David would be used in Israel. See *IRRC*, 1976, 121.
[142] *Ibid.* [143] *Ibid.* [144] UKTS 36 1931; Cmnd. 3793.
[145] De Gouttes, 'La Convention de Genève pour l'Amélioration du Sort des Blessés et Malades dans les Armées en Campagne, du 27 juillet 1929', in CICR, *Commentaire*, 1930, 44 and 35.
[146] Buignon, *The Emblem*, 41, 56.   [147] *Ibid.*, 55.   [148] *Ibid.*, 70.

It is probably desirable to avoid confusion by too many unrecognised signs. Apart from being universally recognised and immediately connected with a certain protected status, the emblem of the Red Cross has also, because of its colour and simplicity, the obvious advantage of being more readily recognised from the air than most other signs.

(7) Attacks on dangerous installations Methods of warfare which will endanger certain installations containing dangerous forces, such as dams, dykes and nuclear electrical generating stations, are furthermore prohibited.[149]

Protocol II of 1977 also contains a prohibition of attacks on installations containing dangerous forces, such as dams, dykes or nuclear electrical generating stations.[150]

Attacks against such installations pose particular threats to the safety of civilians by releasing dangerous forces. The protection of these installations from attack has recently been at the focus of attention of the Disarmament Conference because of the considerable danger posed by attacks on, for example, nuclear installations when considerable radiation could be released affecting whole regions.

(8) Government buildings Government administration buildings are not, it is often claimed, permissible targets in warfare.[151] But in many conflicts, for example in the Vietnam War, there is a problem whether a target constitutes a 'government' building if the authority using that building is not recognised as a 'government'. Furthermore, political realities indicate that the heart of government constitutes not an exempt but a prime target for attack. It is questionable whether government buildings are excluded under any clear rule of law from enemy attack.

(9) Cultural property

(i) Provisions for international wars and for liberation wars As has been shown,[152] liberation wars are equated with international wars for the purpose of the Law of War. Rules on the protection of property follow this pattern and grant, therefore, protection which is different in such wars from other 'internal' wars.

---

[149] Article 56.   [150] Article 15.
[151] J. W. Garner, 'La réglementation de la guerre aérienne', *RGDIP*, 1923, 386.
[152] Above, p. 43.

The Hague Convention of 1954[153] affords special protection to 'cultural property' which is stated to be property of 'great importance to the cultural heritage', for example monuments, architectural sites, works of art, museums, manuscripts and books of artistic, historical or archaeological interest, libraries and archives, provided such property is clearly marked by a blue and white sign. Special protection can be afforded to certain property provided it is located away from military targets.[154] Furthermore, in order to enjoy such enhanced protection, the relevant type of property must be registered with UNESCO in peacetime.[155] But there are wide escape clauses for military necessity undermining protection granted by the Convention.[156]

The Hague Convention of 1954 was primarily intended to protect cultural buildings and monuments, and numerous places of worship would doubtless come into this category. Protocol I widens this protection to all places of worship and other civilian objects and buildings whether or not they are of the quality demanded by the Hague Convention. However, there were some objections against such protection of, for example, churches at the Diplomatic Conference, since 'church steeples make excellent observation posts'.[157] At the Conference it was thus questioned whether *all* churches were protected or merely those which form part of the 'cultural heritage'.[158] The way the article was finally drafted it could, albeit against the spirit of both the 1954 Hague Convention and the 1977 Protocol, be read to imply the more limited protection.[159]

In the context of civilian objects the Protocol adopts the same system of presumption as that regarding civilians: if there is any doubt as to whether an object is civilian or not, it must be presumed to be civilian and thus protected under the Protocol. Furthermore, foodstuffs and objects indispensable for the survival of the civilian population are immune from attack.[160]

(ii) Provisions for internal warfare   Protocol II of 1977 adds certain protection of civilian objects, such as cultural objects and places of worship.[161] An article further strengthening the protection and inviolability of civilian property was deleted. Some Islamic states sup-

[153] 249 UNTS 240.   [154] Article 8.   [155] Regulations to the Convention, article 12.
[156] Below, p. 332.   [157] Cf. Bothe, Partsch and Solf, *New Rules on Victims of War*, 331.
[158] CDDH/III/17, Rev. 1, XV OR 213.
[159] Cf. Bothe, Partsch and Solf, *New Rules on Victims of War*, 332.
[160] ICRC, Mme Bindschedler-Robert, CDDH III/SR.14, vol. 4, 109.
[161] Article 16.

ported the deletion as 'obviously a *de jure* State would never try to exterminate its nationals or damage the environment'.[162]

In any event, national legislation is often sufficient to protect such interests. Islamic legislation, claimed the Saudi Arabian delegate, was 'generally opposed to war as such ... In Islamic society war is always defensive, merciful and humanitarian, and its sole aim is is repel aggressors, without exposing either civilians, cultural objects or the environment to danger.'[163] As superfluous and repetitious, the proposed provisions had no place in Protocol II. Not only the Islamic States supported such notions. The United Kingdom also voted against the adoption of the expanded article,[164] arguing that it would be wrong to preserve protection for objects when so many articles on individuals had been deleted. Finland, too, found that any extended protection of property would 'unbalance' the Protocol.[165]

It is difficult to see why the protection of such property had to be sacrificed to satisfy any artificial symmetrical balance of interests. Surely it would not help individuals if protection of their property was reduced. One representative pointed out that even if human life is obviously more precious than buildings, certain such property may be 'repositories of culture and spiritual life' and, as such, worthy of protection against the vandalism of war.[166]

(10) Places for religious worship There is special protection for buildings for religious worship and any attacks on such places are held to be illegitimate.[167] But protection is afforded only if such buildings are clearly indicated to be places of religious worship and provided they are not used for military purposes.[168] Some such buildings may also be specifically protected under the Hague Convention for Cultural Property of 1954 and possibly enjoy widened protection under Protocol I of 1977.[169]

(11) Civil defence Civil defence activities can be defined as certain humanitarian assistance to the civilian population in armed conflict, such as the establishment and operation of warning systems, and arrangements for fire-fighting, evacuation and shelters.[170]

Permanent civil defence personnel, including military persons on

---

[162] Saudi Arabia, CDDH/SR.51, vol. 7, 123.   [163] *Ibid.*
[164] Draft article 20. For the UK see *ibid.*, 163.   [165] *Ibid.*, 157.   [166] *Ibid.*
[167] Hague Regulations, article 27; Protocol I of 1977, article 53.
[168] Cf. below, p. 352. on ruses.   [169] See above, p. 250 and text to notes 157-9.
[170] Cf. Protocol I of 1977, article 61.

special, exclusive and permanent assignment,[171] come under the ambit of new protection under Protocol I of 1977. But others connected with civil defence activities are also protected, for example those who perform by responding to calls by the authorities for civil defence action.[172]

Civil defence personnel, buildings and assets, clearly indicated as such by a distinctive sign, are immune from attack under Protocol I of 1977.[173] A blue triangle on an orange background has been adopted as a 'distinctive sign', and for further identification purposes all civil defence personnel are to be equipped with a special identity card which must be carried if such personnel are in the combat zone.[174]

iv. Specifically prohibited methods

a. 'No quarter'

It has long been held that any order of 'no quarter' is inhumane and should not be allowed as a permissible method of warfare. Such an order implies that no survivors must be left after an attack, for example when a city is stormed.

Protocol I of 1977 provides a specific prohibition of orders concerning 'no quarter'.[175] But there is some uncertainty whether the prohibition extends to combatants or merely to civilians, as the provision is included in a section concerning non-combatants.[176] However, considering the often illogical arrangement[177] of provisions and sections in the Protocol, one may assume that the drafters intended to protect both groups.

b. Starvation

Siege is one example of 'attacks' on civilians, by exposing them to starvation and hardship, by which a belligerent could seek to conquer his enemy.[178] The rules on 'open towns'[179] did not always suffice to protect the civilian population when the town did not qualify

---

[171] Assigned military personnel may perform civil defence duties only in their own country but not in occupied territory, see article 67.
[172] Articles 62–7.   [173] Article 62.   [174] *Ibid.*, article 66 and Annex I, articles 14–15.
[175] Article 40.
[176] Cf. Bretton, 'Le problème des "méthodes et moyens de guerre ou de combat"', 41.
[177] Cf. below, p. 338.
[178] Cf. Nurick, 'The distinction between combatant and non-combatant', 686.
[179] Above, p. 233.

as being undefended. In the case of a defended town, all the attacker had to do once he had encircled the area and cut off further supplies of ammunition and food was to wait.

The method by which civilian populations are subjected to starvation as a strategic way of defeating the enemy had been somewhat restrained by the Hague Regulations of 1907,[180] at least insofar as foodstuffs and necessities for survival were considered as 'the enemy's property' which could not be destroyed unless demanded by the 'necessities of war'.[181] There were also some other rudimentary rules to the effect that medical stores were allowed through a besieged area.[182] These vague rules of protection for the benefit of the civilian population have been greatly improved by Protocol I of 1977. This recent attempt is intended to prohibit starvation being used as a method of warfare[183] and such regulation thus prohibits siege in the old meaning and function of the term.[184]

The International Committee of the Red Cross had, in its initial draft,[185] visualised only an indirect prohibition of starvation as a method of warfare.[186] However, an amendment proposed by the United Kingdom and Belgium provoked a more detailed treatment which resulted in the more definite prohibition in the text of Protocol I.[187] The prohibition is not intended to alter the rules on naval blockade,[188] but even if they do not have this effect, the new rules will be of great benefit to the civilian population.

Protocol I of 1977 further grants special protection to relief actions and to persons involved in such activities.[189] The Protocol expands the fairly limited protection previously enjoyed by certain relief personnel under the Fourth Geneva Convention of 1949.[190]

Starvation is specifically prohibited also as a means of internal

---

[180] Article 23(g). For reference see above, note 54.
[181] On military necessity, see further below, pp. 332ff.
[182] Geneva IV, article 23.   [183] Protocol I of 1977, article 54(1).
[184] Article 54(1).   [185] See above.
[186] CDDH/III/SR.15, vol. 14, 119 and 139. Cf. Bretton, 'Le problème des "méthodes et moyens de guerre ou de combat"', 45.
[187] Article 54. See below, p. 254 on Protocol II.
[188] Article 49(3) and CDDH/215, Rev. 1, 73, vol. 15, 322 Cf. Bretton, 'Le problème des "méthodes et moyens de guerre et de combat"', 45.
[189] Articles 68–70.
[190] Under articles 23, 55 and 59ff. See further O. Kimminich, *Schutz der Menschen in bewaffneten Konflikten: Zur Fortentwicklung des humanitären Völkerrechts*, Munich, 1979, 186ff; *et seq*; cf. M. Bothe, 'Rechtsprobleme humanitärischer Hilfsaktionen zugunsten der Zivilbevölkerung bei bewaffneten Konflikten', in P. Fleck (ed.), *Beiträge zur Weiterentwicklung des humanitären Völkerrechts für bewaffnete Konflikte*, Hamburg, 1973, 45ff.

warfare.[191] The article on starvation only 'survived' due to what some have termed an 'energetic'[192] and others an 'eloquent'[193] intervention of the representative of the Holy See at the Conference. The article had been due for deletion, together with numerous others cut from the initial text, when it was decided, after the forceful intervention which created considerable debate, to retain it. In the final discussion even the Soviet Union had rallied to the support of the Holy See to retain the article.[194]

c. Reprisals

There has for some time been confusion in the doctrine concerning the nature and the right of reprisals. Most writers have somehow sought to reconcile belligerent reprisals with the traditional notion of general reprisals in international law. The traditional concept implies the right of a State, in response to a violation of international law by another State, to resort to force against that State, or to take other counter-measures; the degree of force and the nature of other acts may be such that the acts would themselves have amounted to violations of international law unless they were 'legitimised' as justified response to the initial violation.[195]

Such reprisals against a State are legitimate provided they are proportionate to the violation, and, above all, provided there actually was a violation in the first place by the other State.[196] There are clear limits to the right of reprisals[197] and the law is fairly settled since the leading *Naulilaa Case* in 1922.[198]

But belligerent reprisals are of a completely different type: they are

---

[191] Protocol II of 1977, article 14. Cf. comments to article 54 of Protocol I, above, text to notes 183–4.

[192] Bretton, 'Le problème des "méthodes et moyens de guerre et de combat"', 45.

[193] Bothe, Partsch and Solf, *New Rules on Victims of War*, 681.

[194] CDDH/SR.52, vol. 7, 136. The delegate of the Soviet Union said he 'wholeheartedly supported the Holy See's position on [the article on starvation] for it was one of the most humane provisions in the entire field of humanitarian law'.

[195] Cf. above, p. 74 on legitimising elements for the use of force.

[196] On a chain of 'reprisals', when it became difficult to discern where the line had started, see, on economic reprisals, my *Finance and Investment in Developing Countries*, 2nd edn, London, 1986, 76–8.

[197] See, e.g., C. Dominicé, 'Observations sur les droits de l'Etat victime d'un fait internationalement illicite', in Institut de Hautes Etudes Internationales (Geneva) (ed.), 2 *Droit international*, Paris, 1981–2.

[198] 2 *RIAA* 1073. On proportionality, cf. *The I'm Alone*, (1929) 3 *RIAA* 1609 and the *Case Concerning the Air Services Agreement of 27 March 1946*, Arbitral Award, 9 December 1978, 54 *ILM* 304.

not used to retaliate against a State for what that State has done in violation of international law. In a large majority of cases it is individuals who have committed an act of hostility, perhaps in violation of the laws of war by using civilian status,[199] or by abusing the protective status of an open town,[200] and the reprisals are taken against other innocent individuals, usually against civilians.

Such action, lying as it does on the plane between individuals, or at least between individuals, as civilians, on the one side and the belligerent forces on the other, is, in nature and function quite different from traditional State reprisals. Belligerent reprisals can thus not be defined in the same way as State reprisals, although some insist that they are acts against an occupied 'State'.[201] But belligerent reprisals could perhaps be better defined as

acts of victimisation or vengeance by a belligerent directed against groups of civilians, prisoners-of-war or other persons hors de combat, *in response to an attack by persons of unprivileged status or by persons not immediately connected with the regular forces of the enemy.*

For example, when a lorry carrying German military was attacked in Rome in Via Rasella in March 1944, orders were given by Hitler that ten Italian soldiers were to be shot for every German soldier killed in the attack. Consequently, 335 prisoners were taken from prisons in Rome and shot in the Catacombs.[202] An Italian decision of the Supreme Military Tribunal in 1952[203] also emphasises that the initial action, the attack on the Germans, could not have been imputed to the Italian State: hence reprisals were illegitimate.[204]

Another example, which will also illustrate the definition we have adopted above of belligerent reprisals, was when some German soldiers were shot by Greek guerillas outside the village of Klissura in Greece in 1944. Under the commander, General Felmy, 215 men, women and children in the village were shot.[205] It is this type of reprisal that is typical of inhumane warfare and which is undesirable.

---

[199] Above, p. 103.   [200] Above, p. 233.
[201] F. Kalshoven, *Belligerent Reprisals*, Leiden, 1971, 37, who defines belligerent reprisals as 'coercive measures taken by one State against another and motivated by an international wrong committed by the latter to the prejudice of the former State', at 22; cf. 33.
[202] Wulff, *Handbok i folkrätt under krig*, 65.
[203] Tribunale supremo militare, 25 October 1952, *Rivista* 1953, 193, and note by Ago, 200.
[204] *Ibid.*, 198 and note by Ago at 206.   [205] *Ibid.*

It is reprisals against persons protected by the Geneva Conventions which are prohibited, not reprisals in general.[206]

State reprisals, on the other hand, like the reprisals by Germany in attacking London by bombardment in response to similar attacks on German cities, lie on another plane and merit different considerations.[207] They too may be unlawful under the Law of War, not because they involve reprisals, but because they imply indiscriminate attacks, inevitably affecting civilian objectives.

The regulation of reprisals in war by international conventions also seem to correspond to the definition adopted above and concern primarily the protection of civilians and of prisoners of war from acts of reprisal.

The Hague Conventions prohibited the use of reprisals against the 'population' and granted some basic protection to prisoners of war as well.[208] Other instruments regulating warfare had largely been silent on this question. The Geneva Convention of 1929 restricted further the right of reprisals.[209] Still, during the Second World War reprisals against protected persons were used as a means of warfare.[210] But, as was shown in the Nuremberg trials, such practices were forbidden by the Law of War and the belligerents were bound by duties not to resort to reprisals by maltreatment or by the taking of hostages.[211]

The right of reprisals against civilians was restricted by rules laid down in the Judgments of the Military Tribunal at Nuremberg. The Tribunal emphasised that reprisals must at least be limited geographically to one area, mainly as actions against persons in one area could have little deterrent effect on people in other areas. If there was not such geographical connection a 'functional' link might be acceptable as limiting the right of reprisals: there had thus to be some connection between the reprisals and the civilians against whom action was taken.[212] The Tribunal furthermore rules out reprisals for

---

[206] Cf. H. Meyrowitz, 'The Law of War in the Vietnamese conflict', 567, n. 120. But, for a different view, defining reprisals as including State reprisals, see Kalshoven, *Belligerent Reprisals*, 22.

[207] For example, see above, p. 239 on area bombing.

[208] Hague Regulations, article 4ff; cf. below, p. 281.

[209] Article 2(3).

[210] ICRC, 1 *Report on Activities during the Second World War*, Geneva, 1949 and 1977, 365, 522; J. Hinz, *Das Kriegsgefangenenrecht*, Berlin, 1955, 58; Kalshoven, *Belligerent Reprisals*, 193.

[211] Cf. *The Great War Criminal Cases*, AD, 1946, 26; *The List Case*, AD, 1948, 632.

[212] For example, *Re Kappler*, AD, 1948, 480; such 'functional connection' could be that of office or works.

which certain ethnic, religious or political groups had been selected.[213]

Reprisals as a means of warfare were forbidden by the Four
Geneva Conventions,[214] but not in any particular detail.

Protocol I of 1977 widens the protection enjoyed previously.[215] In
this part the new rules have been criticised by commentators as,
indeed, the Geneva rules had been as well. The original protection in,
for example, the Fourth Geneva Convention had been questioned, as
some writers claimed it would lead to fragmentation and resistance,[216] since such rules protecting persons against reprisals cannot
easily be reconciled with the idea of war. Some claimed that the rules
would favour resistance and, 'as no belligerent will keep the rules if
his very existence is threatened', the new rules (of the Geneva Conventions) would 'only contribute to more anger, more accusation,
more reprisals, more deviation from valid law'.[217]

The protection granted by Geneva Convention IV with respect to
civilians has been supplemented by further protection under the 1954
Hague Convention with regard to property which must not form the
object of reprisals under the Convention.[218] Protocol I improves protection against reprisals and the regulation of the matter forbids any
reprisals against the civilian population[219] and against civilian objects.[220]

During the Conference some delegations argued that reprisals have
a function to fill in war as 'a reprisal is a sanction to deter further
violations of the law. It is not an act of vengeance. The availability of
this sanction may persuade an adversary not to commit violations of
the law in the first place.'[221] Others claimed that the protection given
by Protocol I of 1977 with regard to reprisals was so extended that
the rules risk becoming a dead letter.[222]

Yet, in the light of experiences in the Second World War and of

---

[213] See the *von Mackesen Case*, 8 *War Crimes Report* 1945, 2.
[214] Convention I, article 46; Convention II, article 47; Convention II, article 13; and
Convention IV, article 33.
[215] Cf. S. Nahlik, 'Le problème des répresailles à la lumière des travaux de la Conférence diplomatique sur le droit humanitaire', *RGDIP*, 1978, 130ff.
[216] See A. Krafft, 'The present position of the Red Cross Geneva Conventions', 37
TransGrotSoc 1951, 146.
[217] R. V. A. Röling 'The Law of War and the national jurisdiction since 1945', 100
RCADI 1960, ii, 428.
[218] 249 UNTS 240.   [219] Articles 51(6) and 75.   [220] Article 53.
[221] Australia, CDDH/SR.41, vol. 6, 176.
[222] Dinstein, 'Another step in codifying the laws of war', 288.

numerous recent armed conflicts, it cannot be denied that a general prohibition of reprisals as that afforded by Protocol I can only further the level of treatment in times of armed conflict. Such regulation would also prevent the 'chain reaction', when reprisals against civilians, prisoners of war or detainees by one belligerent lead to subsequent further reprisals by another. Attacks by the French Resistance on German soldiers in 1944 led Germany to execute 80 of its French 'political' prisoners in Lyon, whereupon the French authorities in the Annecy district decided to shoot 80 German prisoners. The ICRC appealed to the French in Annecy to delay the execution for six days pending negotiations with Berlin to obtain an agreement by which the Germans would bind themselves to execute French civilians no longer and to allow French partisans to enjoy prisoner of war status. The time elapsed without an agreement, however, and the German prisoners were executed.[223]

But what about reprisals in internal war? Are those not equally contrary to the basic tenets of the Law of War? There were attempts during the negotiation of Protocol II of 1977 to include an article on reprisals.[224] But Nigeria made a forceful protest against the inclusion of any such article in the final Convention and said that such an article dealt with reprisals and, as such, it had no place in an instrument on internal conflict. Reprisals, said Nigeria, belong to inter-State relations[225] and stated further that

it is not inconceivable that in the course of an internal conflict, rebels ... deliberately commit acts to which the normal reaction would be in the nature of reprisal, but because of a prohibition act such as this, governments would feel bound to fold their arms while dissident groups go on a rampage killing and maiming innocent civilians and burning dwellings and food crops.[226]

But it is not against such acts that the provisions were designed to function, but to protect civilians. Again, it may have been the confused notion of belligerent reprisals as being undefined and mistaken for having similar characterics and legal effects as State reprisals[227] which was responsible for the failure to incorporate reprisals in Protocol II on internal war.

---

[223] *Report on Activities during the Second World War*, 542.
[224] Article 10(2) of the Draft.
[225] CDDG/SR.51, vol. 7, 122. Cf. above, p. 74 on State reprisals.
[226] *Ibid.*
[227] Above p. 74.

d. Perfidy

(1) General rules Force and fraud may be cardinal virtues in war.[228] But although all warfare may be based on deception,[229] a strict distinction must be drawn between deception or ruses (*stratagems* or *Kriegslist*) and perfidy. Treachery, perfidy and impermissible ruses are practices 'within' a war. A whole war cannot be 'treacherous' although the prosecution sought to allege this in the Tokyo trials.[230]

Military necessity[231] is said to warrant the use of 'deception' for military ends but does not allow the use of perfidy. The Lieber Code had already acknowledged this basic tenet of the Law of War.[232] The Hague Regulations allow what is commonly called 'ruses'[233] and it is this term which is commonly used to denote deception as opposed to perfidy or treachery, which are prohibited under the Law of War.[234] The prohibition is reaffirmed in Protocol I of 1977[235] and there is ample evidence[236] that these rules form part of the Law of War whether or not a party has adhered to a treaty as these rules reflect what is binding on the basis of general international law.[237]

(2) Specific practices Permissible ruses include the use of camouflage, decoys and mock operations as well as ambush.[238] False signals are allowed,[239] including the jamming of communications.

Improper use of a white flag constitutes treachery[240] as well as feigning surrender in other ways or pretending to have wounded or civilian status.[241] Once capitulations have been agreed, they must also be observed, and it is treachery for soldiers who have surrendered to take up arms and attack the enemy.[242] It also constitutes perfidy to

---

[228] T. Hobbes, *Leviathan, or The Matter, Forme and Power of a Commonwealth, Ecclesiastical and Civil*, London, 1651, reprinted Oxford, 1929, 1, ch. 13.

[229] Sun Tse, *The Art of War*, ed. and trans. S. B. Griffiths, Oxford, 1963, 66; cf. H. D. Becker, *Die Dreizehn Gebote der Kriegskunst*, Munich, 1972, 50.

[230] See, for criticism of this standpoint, Judge Pal, in B. V. A. Röling and C. F. Ruter (eds), *The Tokyo Trials*, Amsterdam, 1971, 626.

[231] See below.   [232] Article 16. Cf. above, p. 123.   [233] Article 24.

[234] Hague Regulations, article 23(b).   [235] Article 37.

[236] E.g. D. Fleck, 'Ruses of war and prohibition of perfidy', *Revue du droit de la guerre*, 1974, 269; R. Bourdoncle, *De l'influence des ruses sur l'évolution du droit de la guerre*, Paris, 1958.

[237] On the underlying obligation, see my *Essays*, 117.

[238] Greenspan. *Modern Law of Land Warfare*, 319.   [239] *Ibid.*

[240] Hague Regulations, article 23(f); Protocol I of 1977, article 37.

[241] Protocol I of 1977, article 37.   [242] Hague Regulations, article 35.

use the uniforms of the enemy[243] or of neutral States.[244] Similar abuse of the Red Cross sign or of equivalent emblems is also expressly forbidden.[245]

The law of land warfare has, for a long time, prohibited the use of the enemy's flag[246] but, contrary to these rules, it has been claimed that warships are entitled to fly false flag, and even the flag of the enemy, or be disguised as merchant ships of their enemy or of a neutral State.[247] At least such 'ruses' would be allowed, it is claimed, before the ship goes into action. It has certainly been common practice to hoist the ship's own flag before going into hostilities; but some ships have not disclosed their true identity, like the *Graf Spee*, which sailed under false flag even during action.[248] However, the rather curious practice of using false flag has not gone unchallenged. The Institute de Droit International questioned in 1913 whether this practice was compatible with the Law of War.[249] It could be argued that the swift nature of modern naval warfare has made the use of different rules from land warfare obsolete. In State practice there is also ample evidence that neutral powers whose flags were often abused during the Second World War certainly did not consider this practice to be lawful and made serious protests.

There have also been attempts to outlaw, at least partially, the practice of false flag at sea. Thus under article 2 of the Havana Convention on Rights and Duties of States in the Event of Civil Strife of 1928[250] any insurgent vessel, whether warship or merchantman, which flies the flag of a foreign country to shield its action may be captured and 'tried' by the State whose flag it has adopted. This provision raises several interesting points. First, the term 'tried' in relation to a ship must indicate that it can be taken, together with its

[243] Hague Regulations, article 23(f); Protocol I of 1977, article 39; cf. V. Jobst, 'Is the wearing of the enemy's uniform a violation of the Laws of War?' 35 *AJIL* 1941, 435; on the relevance of the wearing of uniform, see also my 'Foreign warships', 61ff. But the wearing of the enemy's uniform has not always led to condemnation or loss of POW status: see the *Skorzeny Case*, 9 Nuremberg 90 and 95, where the prohibition was held to concern only the time of 'actual fighting' but not any time before.

[244] Protocol I of 1977, articles 37 and 39.

[245] Geneva I, article 44; Geneva II, article 43–45; Protocol I of 1977, article 38. Cf. Hague Regulations, article 23(f).

[246] Hague Regulations, article 23(f); Protocol I of 1977, article 37.

[247] C. J. Colombos, *International Law of the Sea*, London, 1962, 496–8.

[248] Rousseau, *Conflits armés*, 237.

[249] Institut de Droit International, *Annuaire*, 1913; cf. *The Oxford Manual*, 5 *Annuaire* 1881–2, 156, 1913.

[250] 35 LNTS 1932, 187.

cargo, as prize.[251] Secondly, the jurisdiction granted to the 'abused' flag State is reminiscent of some recent hijacking treaties, giving jurisdiction to a State away from the territorial crime and separate from the actual nationality of the perpetrators.

It may be argued that the prohibition in the Havana Convention reflects the law in general as it stands today. One reason in support of considering this to be the case is that air warfare has adopted the same rule as applies on land and therefore prohibits the use of false external identification marks on aircraft.[252] A consequence of using false or no external marks on aeroplanes is that the plane will be considered as having been used for espionage and its pilot will not be entitled to prisoner of war status but will be tried as a common spy.[253] On the other hand it is lawful to use reconnaissance scouts in war[254] and espionage, or the 'gathering of information', by such scouts is not perfidious or in violation of the Law of War.[255]

It has been questioned whether warfare by submarines, by nature 'perfidious' vessels, amounts to treachery. There were attempts to outlaw such warfare or at least to restrict its use.[256] But modern warfare undoubtedly allows submarines which, however, like all warships, are under strict duty not to attack merchant vessels.[257]

The 'scorched earth' strategy is not a treacherous practice and is specifically allowed by Protocol I of 1977.[258] This provision allows the destruction of foodstuffs and crops in derogation of the general rule[259] if such action is indispensable for defence against invasion. This is thus a provision subjected to military necessity.[260]

It is a particularly serious violation of the Law of War to shield military targets from attack by placing or moving them to densely populated areas or to move civilians near military targets to protect such targets from attack.[261] Nor must medical units[262] or places for

[251] Below, p. 305.   [252] Hague Regulations, article 19.
[253] See my 'Foreign warships', 65–6 on the *Gary Powers Case* and other incidents; cf. above, p. 119 on spies, and below, p. 281 on prisoners of war.
[254] *The Flesche Case*, (1949), Dutch Court of Cassation, 16 *ILR* 266; and my 'Foreign warships', 67; and above, p. 119.
[255] But, again, the relevant criterion whether the scout is to be granted POW status or be executed as a common spy is the wearing of uniform, see above, note 253.
[256] Above, p. 266.   [257] See above.   [258] Article 54.
[259] Below, p. 00 on starvation.
[260] See United States Military Tribunal, *Hostages Trial*, (1948) 15 *ILR* 632 and below, p. 00.
[261] Geneva IV, article 28; Protocol I of 1977, article 51(7); cf. *ibid.*, article 58.
[262] Protocol I of 1977, article 12; cf. Geneva I, article 19; cf. also Hague Regulations, article 27.

religious worship[263] be used to shield military targets from attack. Such prohibition also extends to cultural property[264] and, by analogy, to civil defence property.[265]

It may be questioned whether hostile propaganda is permissible as a ruse of war or whether it amounts to treachery. The better view is probably that it is not unlawful under the Law of War. Such propaganda in time of war is normally dispersed by an enemy government and may contain disinformation and misleading facts. To the extent that propaganda is broadcast by individuals it may be noted that States are rarely under any obligation to suppress propaganda directed against another State even if such propaganda incites rebellion against the internal order.[266] The position in Western countries is usually a clear conflict, in such cases, between the propaganda and the freedom of free speech.[267] There is no duty of territorial States to prevent subversive propaganda,[268] although some have asserted that there is a duty to suppress revolutionary activities against another State.[269] Production and distribution of counterfeited enemy money, which in peacetime have been said to constitute veritable *delicta juris gentium*,[270] probably also constitute permissible ruses from which belligerents may abstain only by the knowledge of retaliation on the basis of reciprocity.[271]

The rules of Protocol I of 1977 extend the earlier provisions in the Hague Regulations which merely mentioned treachery[272] and forbid killing by perfidy and a more precise meaning is given to this term[273] in view of recent practices by guerillas.[274]

[263] Protocol I of 1977, article 53.   [264] Hague Convention 1954, articles 4 and 8.
[265] Protocol I of 1977, article 65.
[266] But see the Convention Concerning the Use of Broadcasting in the Cause of Peace, 1936, 5 Hudson 409; and the South American Convention on Radio Communications, 1935, 7 Hudson 47.
[267] See, for example, the notification of the United States Secretary of State to the Mexican Ambassador on 7 June 1911 to the effect that the United States could not interfere with hostile propaganda against Mexico because of the constitutional right of freedom of speech in the United States, 2 Hackworth 142; on the defamation of the Mexican Government by the Hearst newspaper group, see E. D. Dickinson, 'Defamation of foreign government', *AJIL*, 1928, 840.
[268] See L. Preuss, 'International responsibility for hostile propaganda against foreign states', *AJIL*, 1934, 649.
[269] Cf. above on intervention, p. 57, and cf. A. K. Kuhn, 'The complaint of Yugoslavia against Hungary with reference to the assassination of King Alexander', *AJIL*, 1935, 87.
[270] Harvard Draft Convention 1929, 23 *AJIL* 1929, 78.
[271] For regulation in peacetime, see, for example, the Convention for the Suppression of Counterfeiting Currency (1929), 4 Hudson 2692; cf. *United States* v. *Arjona*, (1887) 120 US 479; *Emperor of Austria* v. *Day and Kossuth*, (1961) 30 *LJ*, ch. 690.
[272] Article 23(1)(b).   [273] Protocol I of 1977, article 44(3).   [274] Above, p. 50.

(3) The legal effects of perfidy Exemption from the rules on targets[275] or protection under humanitarian rules[276] can be suspended by acts of perfidy. Even if there is no intention of deceiving the enemy, any link between protected objectives or persons and military activities may cause the disruption of the protective regime.

Thus, protection of, for example, medical units[277] is forfeited if acts harmful to the enemy are committed, in violation of the conditions for protection, by or through medical units. However, only quite considerable involvement with military efforts is to lead to this result. For example, the mere carrying of weapons for self-defence or for the defence of the sick and wounded is not such an act,[278] nor is the establishment of guards or escorts,[279] nor does the presence of military persons for medical reasons lead to protection being forfeited.[280] The presence of civilian sick and wounded in a military unit does not lay such civilians open to attack[281] and is not to be considered as a link of such intensity that protection is forfeited.

Similar rules apply to other objectives which are exempt from being targets and/or which are specially protected. For example, civil defence personnel and buildings will lose their immunity if they are used for military purposes. But acts that benefit those who are *hors de combat* do not lead to such results, nor does the fact that people are carrying light weapons for personal self-defence, or to 'maintain order'.[282] Even certain action under or in cooperation with military authorities is permissible without loss of *hors de combat* status.[283] By the application of similar rules, a parlamentaire loses his protection[284] if he abuses his position to commit an act of treachery.[285] However, with regard to this last example, it must be added that here the quantum of proof required possibly increases: the immunity of a parlamentaire or other envoy is a 'strong' rule and it must be proved beyond any doubt that he took undue advantage of the situation.

B. SPECIFIC RULES FOR NAVAL WARFARE

i. The special case of warfare at sea

Certain prohibited methods of warfare relating to all types of warfare have been discussed and described above. The regulation of naval

---

[275] Above, p. 232.   [276] Below, p. 271.   [277] Above, p. 247 and below, p. 352.
[278] Geneva I, article 22; Protocol I of 1977, article 13(2).   [279] *Ibid.*
[280] Geneva IV, article 19.   [281] Geneva I, article 22.
[282] But in the combat zone only hand guns are allowed. Protocol I of 1977, article 65.
[283] *Ibid.*   [284] Above, p. 245.   [285] Hague Regulations, article 34.

warfare differs insofar as there are a number of traditional practices which are pertinent only to warfare at sea. However, some of these practices, such as the law of prize, are better discussed in relation to other interference with property,[286] and so is the unusual practice of angary.[287] Furthermore, a few questions relating to submarine warfare have been dealt with in connection with perfidy.[288] There remains, however, in this section, a need to comment on submarine warfare and on blockade as methods of naval warfare.

First, some general comments may be made. The Law of War has, by tradition, included certain practices which are special to war on the seas and has recognised and regulated these practices, some of which are in decline. However, the general rules described earlier in this work also apply to naval warfare. For example, rules on the nature of the high seas imply, as has been shown,[289] that hostilities must not take place on the high seas,[290] which must be used only for peaceful purposes. Such general rules, as well as the establishment of positive and negative zones,[291] will have an impact on the location of naval warfare.

Next, it must be considered that naval warfare is different in nature to land warfare as land warfare has as its objective taking over and occupying the enemy's territory. At sea, war is often about 'maritime superiority', and naval warfare implies uses of the sea for its own purposes rather than occupying and annexing any specific areas. On the other hand, superiority at sea is not an aim in itself but a means to achieve 'national survival' or victory on land.[292]

Land warfare thus aims at victory over the enemy who, after his territory has been taken, cannot escape; war at sea implies also a war against the enemy's trade.[293] But the trend towards 'total war' in the Second World War has erased this sharp distinction; all types of war involve attacks on commerce.[294] In the Second World War special ministries for 'economic warfare' were created to plan strategies to strangle the enemy's trade. At sea this type of warfare is important. British ships, for example, adopted the practice of exercising their power of visit and search of neutral ships on the high seas and issued special navigation certificates if the examination of cargo and ship's

---

[286] Below, p. 303.   [287] Below, p. 314.   [288] Above, p. 259.   [289] Above, p. 147.
[290] D. P. O'Connell, 'Contemporary naval operations', 44 *BYIL* 1970, 27.
[291] Above, p. 152.   [292] UN *Study on the Naval Arms Race*, 30.
[293] H. Wehberg, *Seekriegsrecht*, Stuttgart, 1915, 3–4; Schmitt, *Die Zulässigkeit von Sperrgebieten im Seekrieg*, Hamburg, 1966, 48.
[294] Stone, *Legal Controls*, 457.

papers warranted such 'approval'. This method, the so called Navi-cert System, became an important method of economic warfare.[295]

The system of intercepting merchant vessels carrying goods that might be destined for enemy use[296] is still used, for example in the Iran–Iraq War, where this method of warfare has been thought essential to undermine the enemy's economy in general as well as to stem the flow of war supplies.

The nature of naval warfare has changed considerably over the last fifty years.[297] Now, the blue-water navies and coastal navies are all highly specialised and technically alien to earlier navies: after the 'nuclear revolution' commencing with the *USS Nautilus* being commissioned as a nuclear powered ship in 1952[298] and the 'electronic revolution' leading to drastic changes in the weapons systems, there is little in modern navies that resembles traditional equipment. For example, traditional guns would be used today only for minor or undefended targets. For other targets 'fire-and-forget' missiles, whose trajectory cannot be corrected, might be used.[299] Other technical developments, like the closed cycle combustion system, allow submarines to be submerged for weeks rather than days.[300]

The relevant treaties regulating naval warfare fall into two broad groups. The first group includes a number of treaties which restrict the use of force at sea and provide rules on self-defence or collective security at sea; this group has been largely discussed in relation to the use of force.[301] The second group of relevant treaties includes those which regulate typical naval strategies, such as blockade or submarine warfare. Among these treaties we find the Declaration of Paris of 1856,[302] seven of the 1907 Hague Conventions,[303] the Declaration of London of 1909,[304] the Treaty of London of 1930[305] and the Protocol of London of 1936,[306] both on, *inter alia* submarine warfare, and, finally, Geneva Convention II[307] on the shipwrecked.

The rules in these Conventions are well accepted by all the mari-

---

[295] See D. Steinecke, *Das Navicertsystem*, 2 vols., Hamburg, 1966.
[296] Cf. below, p. 305. on contraband.
[297] On earlier developments, see P. Reuter, 'Le droit de la guerre maritime et les jurisdictions internationales temporaires issues des Traités de paix de la grande guerre', *RDI*, 1934, 375.
[298] UN *Study on the Naval Arms Race*, 33–4, 41–2.   [299] *Ibid.*, 47–8.   [300] *Ibid.*, 49.
[301] Above, p. 54.   [302] 1 *AJIL* 1907, Suppl., 89.   [303] For a list see above p. 123.
[304] 104 *BFSP* 1911, 242; 3 *AJIL* 1909, 179, and above.
[305] 25 *AJIL* 1931, Suppl., 63, and above.
[306] 31 *AJIL* 1937, 137.
[307] 75 UNTS 85; cf. above, p. 107; and below p. 276.

time nations but these have often justified deviations from the rules by arguments on military necessity,[308] accepting that the rules, *per se*, were binding but inapplicable in the specific event because of over-riding factors.[309]

ii. *Submarine warfare*

When submarines were first used the British attitude was that submarines, 'perfidious' by nature, were designed precisely to attack merchantmen and of less importance in fighting warships: submarines should therefore be prohibited. Furthermore, submarines could not treat merchantmen as conventional warships, by subjecting such merchant vessels to visit and search and taking cargo as prize. Such views were strongly opposed by the German attitude that 'military necessity'[310] demanded attacks by submarines on merchant vessels. The French intermediate position advocated 'regulated' use of submarines, dismissing both the British and the German extreme positions. The German view was not compatible with the Law of War and the British view, said the French, confused perfidy and ruses, ignoring the effect of submarine attacks on warships as well as extensive French case law on prize taken by submarines.[311]

The Declaration of London of 1909 was not ratified by, for example, the United Kingdom and never entered into force. Yet, since it codified existing rules its substantive regulation was still effective in terms of binding obligations[312] arising and the United Kingdom itself applied the Convention in the First World War.[313] The Declaration of London, however, was an attempt to codify 'acknowledged principles of International Law'.[314] Courts also applied it as it, in their opinion, embodied general international law[315] even though a Maritime Rights Order-in-Council[316] had expressly revoked the Declaration.

Germany's unlimited submarine warfare, proclaimed in 1917, also involved attacks on neutral ships in certain zones[317] and, in spite of dubious legality, such strategies were repeated during the Second World War.

---

[308] Below, p. 332.   [309] Below, p. 334.   [310] Below, p. 332.
[311] Rousseau, *Conflits armés*, 245–7.
[312] On underlying obligations, see my *Essays*.
[313] Rousseau, *Conflits armés*, 214.   [314] C. J. Colombos, *Prize Law*, London, 1926, 342.
[315] *The Hakan*, (1918) AC 148, 152.   [316] Order-in-Council, 7 July 1916.
[317] Above, p. 233.

The Washington Treaty on the Use of Submarines, the so called 'Root Resolution',[318] prohibited surprise attacks on merchant vessels and provided 'standards' for submarine warfare as 'established part of International Law'. But the Treaty never entered into force.[319] The Draft Treaty had sought to prohibit submarine warfare against merchantmen. At the Conference there had even been suggestions, *inter alios* by the United Kingdom, that submarines should be forbidden altogether.[320] But the French did not go that far and did not prohibit submarines in general. Although the Treaty of Washington never entered into force it was, by article 22 of the London Treaty of 22 April 1930, incorporated as 'declaratory' of international law. When the 1930 Treaty expired in 1936, this article 22 was, in turn, incorporated into the London Protocol of 6 November 1936.[321] Up to this point the 1922 rules on submarine warfare had been regarded, by the large maritime nations, as declaratory of international law. The explicit 1936 Protocol was prompted merely by the fact that the last paragraph of article 22 'invited' all other powers to express their assent to the rules on, for example, surprise attack;[322] but it was thought to add little to already existing rules on submarine warfare.

The Treaty of London imposed a duty on submarines not to attack merchantmen, unless such ships had refused visit and search. But there are doubts as to whether the term 'merchant ships' covers those which are armed.[323]

It has been suggested lately that submarines are vulnerable to attacks by lightly armed merchant vessels.[324] But even if this is so, submarines undoubtedly pose a greater threat to merchantmen than that to which they are exposed themselves and must strictly adhere to rules on exempt targets.[325]

iii. Blockade

One of the earliest treaties on the Law of War in modern times, the Declaration of Paris of 1856,[326] deals with the regulation of blockade. But the treaty contains no definition of the term. Blockade implies the cutting off of the enemy's coastline by forceful measures so that supplies to and from the enemy are restricted. Blockade must thus not be

[318] 16 *AJIL* 1922, Suppl., 57. [319] Above, p. 247.
[320] Rousseau, *Conflits armés*, 245. [321] 31 *AJIL* 1937, 137.
[322] UN, *Study on the Naval Arms Race*, 11. [323] Rousseau, *Conflits armés*, 253.
[324] O'Connell, *Influence of Law on Sea-Power*, 46. [325] Above, p. 232.
[326] 1 *AJIL* 1907, Suppl., 89.

confused with the mere policing of a coastline for limited purposes, for example to prevent rebels from reaching a specific port.[327] Nor must it be confused with the closure of ports.[328]

A blockade, in order to be recognised as such by third parties, for example by neutral States, must be effective.[329] This rule was probably accepted by international society long before the Declaration.[330] A blockade cannot be effectively maintained only by mining,[331] and probably not only by submarines.[332] On the other hand, with modern weapons even long-distance blockades can probably be made effective.

There are other conditions for the legality of a naval blockade in war, such as that it must be limited to the coast of the enemy.[333] The blockade must also be declared and notified in order to be recognised. Knowledge is not necessary on the part of the ship's master, unless it is clear that he did not, and could not have had, actual or presumptive knowledge of the blockade.[334]

Certain rules thus limit geographical application to the enemy's coastline.[335] This area is further restricted to exclude straits or part of straits which must not be subjected to blockades.[336] Similar prohibitions are inserted in treaties regulating international canals, for example in the Constantinople Convention of 1888 on the Suez Canal.[337]

There has been an increasing decline in the use of blockades as a method of naval warfare. In the First World War some ten blockades

[327] Rousseau, *Conflits armés*, 259–60.
[328] *Ibid.*, 259–60, and *e.g.*, the *Portendinck Affair*, 1 *RIAA* 512.
[329] Declaration of Paris, 15 NRGT, 1 série, 791; 1 *AJIL* 1907, Suppl., 89. Declaration of London on the Laws of Naval War, 1909, 3 *AJIL* 1909, Suppl., 179.
[330] *The Betsey*, (1798) 1 C. Rob. 93.
[331] *Ibid.*, cf. Hague Convention VIII 1907, article VIII.   [332] 2 Oppenheim 780.
[333] Declaration of London 1909, article 1; cf. articles 18–19 forbidding blockades of neutral ports.
[334] *The Franziska*, (1855) Spinks 287, 298. Cf. Declaration of London of 1909, articles 8–11. Knowledge is presumed if a neutral vessel left port subsequent to the notification of the blockade to the port authorities at that port, *ibid.*, article 12. On French and other continental views on requirements of knowledge, see Rousseau, *Conflits armés*, 270–1.
[335] Above, p. 138.   [336] 2 Oppenheim 773.
[337] 3 *AJIL* 1909, Suppl., 123. But interception of contraband has been carried out: T. D. Brown, 'World War prize law applied in a limited war situation: Egyptian restrictions on neutral shipping with Israel', 50 *Minnesota LR* 1965, 849 L. Gross, 'Passage through the Suez Canal of Israeli bound cargo and Israeli ships', 51 *AJIL* 1957, 530; R. Lapidoth, 'The reopened Suez Canal in international law', 4 *Syracuse Law Journal of International Law and Commerce* 1976, 37.

were imposed. In the Second World War they became even rarer, and one can perhaps point out only the Soviet blockade of Finland during the Winter War in 1939, and the Japanese blockades of Hong Kong in 1941 and Java in 1942.[338] In recent years blockade has fallen into even greater disuse. The measures applied by the United States to stifle any supply of arms to Cuba probably constituted a 'peaceful blockade', although the United States insisted on calling it a 'Quarantine' to avoid the connotations of a blockade.[339] But in the Cuban crisis there was no armed conflict and therefore the rules on naval blockade in war would still not be relevant. Nor was there any war in which the United Nations and Rhodesia, or the United Kingdom and Rhodesia,[340] were involved when the Security Council authorised the United Kingdom to impose a blockade on Rhodesia to prevent oil tankers from reaching the port of Umtali.[341]

One of the few blockades imposed in wartime in recent years was the United States blockade of Haiphong in Vietnam in 1972.[342] A blockade might also have been briefly applied in the India–Pakistan War in 1971.[343]

There is a school of thought that no blockade can be declared unless there exists a state of war; at least a blockade imposed in other situations may not be 'recognised' by third parties as 'effective'. Since the United States insisted, in 1967, that there was no war with Vietnam, the United States was inhibited from declaring any blockade of any part of that country. Any blockade in that situation would, it was said, be of 'doubtful legality'.[344] But by 1972 the attitude had changed and the United States imposed a blockade to stem the flow

[338] See further J. F. McNulty, 'Blockade, evolution and expectation', in US Naval War College (ed.), *International Law Situations*, Newport, 1980, 172.
[339] Wright, 'The Cuban Quarantine', 546; McDougal, 'The Soviet Cuban Quarantine and self-defence', 597; A. L. Kolodkin, 'Morskaya blokada i sovremennoe mezhdunarodnoe pravo', *Sovetskoe gosudarstvo i pravo*, Moscow, 1963, no. 4, 92; M. A. D'Estefano, 'La Curantena y el derecho internacional', *Politica Internacional*, no. 4, Havana, 1963; Christol and Davies, 'Maritime quarantine', 525; L. Meeker, 'Defensive quarantine and the law', 57 *AJIL* 1963, 515; C. G. Fenwick, 'The Quarantine against Cuba, legal or illegal?', *ibid.*, 588.
[340] See above, p. 41 on internationalised conflicts.
[341] SC 221 1966. Cf. McNair and Watts, *Legal Effects*, 20ff on formal measures short of war, e.g. – apart from blockade – embargo; this concept initially implied the taking of ships, usually in territorial waters, coupled with later restitution without compensation; later, it came to mean prohibition of exports without any necessary maritime connection, see *ibid.*
[342] O'Connell, *Influence of Law on Sea-Power*, 129–30.
[343] *Ibid.*   [344] Carlisle, 'The interrelationship', 23.

of arms into Haiphong in Vietnam.[345] The Haiphong blockade consisted of time-delayed mines that would become active after three days[346] to enable warning to be given to neutral ships to depart. But even these measures may not have amounted to a traditional naval blockade, as the system mainly relied on mines and one of the basic rules of blockades is that they cannot be imposed by mines alone.[347]

Protocol I of 1977 explicitly exempts blockade from regulation.[348] However, it is difficult to reconcile this exemption with the Protocol's own prohibition of starvation as a method of warfare,[349] a prohibition which has led to the outlawing of sieges in land war.[350]

---

[345] O'Connell, *Influence of Law on Sea-Power*, 95.
[346] Not three hours as indicated in D. P. O'Connell, 2 *The International Law of the Sea*, Oxford, 1984, 1139.
[347] Above, p. 191.   [348] See the preamble of the Protocol.
[349] Article 54(1).   [350] Above, p. 252.

9 HUMANITARIAN RULES

A. THE REALISTIC MEANING

The nature and function of humanitarian rules have already been explored in this work.[1] In this context the substance of the basic rules will be described. However, at all times it must be borne in mind that the humanitarian rules supplement other rules analysed above, which deal with restriction of weapons[2] and regulation of methods of warfare.[3] Furthermore, humanitarian rules must be seen and interpreted against the background of general ethics in war,[4] especially the rules which relate to unnecessary suffering which go to the root of the Law of War.

Many writers subsume under humanitarian law also rules which exempt civilians or other non-combatants from being targets of warfare. However, such rules are very similar in character to those which exempt non-military targets in general; the difference is one of quantity rather than quality. In other words, the rules which stipulate that a village inhabited by 5,000 civilians, without military installations, must not be stormed or bombed is akin to the rule saying that one unarmed civilian must not be attacked.

Therefore, in this work the term 'humanitarian law' has been reserved mainly for those rules that protect the human person, but go beyond rules concerning attack or exempting persons from constituting targets.[5] Rules on weapons and methods in war inevitably present a negative element, insofar as they restrain the way force is used.[6] Some humanitarian rules, especially concerning prisoners of war, involve both negative restraint provisions as well as rules for positive measures. However, most humanitarian rules are basically

---

[1] Above, p. 130.   2 Above, p. 176.   [3] Above, p. 232.   [4] Above, p. 134.
[5] Protection of property and equipment may be ancillary to the protection of individuals.
[6] Cf. above, p. 232.

positive, demanding specific action on the part of belligerents and combatants. This restriced notion of humanitarian rules will be more realistic and, by being less hazy, perhaps more easily subsumed under a viable Law of War.

It is not in the interest of consolidation of the Law of War for humanitarian rules to include heterogeneous rules, like rules on targets for attack, as they are more akin to other rules on methods of warfare. To shelve these rules on targets, when they involve, for example, civilians, from the Law of War and insert them in a conglomeration of rules on the specific protection of children, or care of the wounded, or treatment of prisoners of war, will not enhance their value in practical terms: such rules risk floating away in an undefined mass of vague human rights. On the contrary, it is only by a stringent division of rules on methods of warfare, including strict prohibitions of attacks on, for example, civilians that humanitarian values will be enhanced, not by separating rules concerning individuals, regardless of the contents of the rules, to form part of an anomalous 'humanitarian law' marked only by its vagueness. Thus, by restricting the very meaning of humanitarian law by a narrower definition and by dealing with other rules on individuals, for example concerning targets, in their organic context, the interests of individuals may, by a clearer synthesis of rules, be enhanced.

B. SPECIFIC RULES

i. Treatment of civilians

Like all rules in warfare, humanitarian rules turn on the question of distinction[7] and, in the field of humanitarian law, the impact of the application of this principle is perhaps most acute.

On the other hand, it is really only in peacetime that a clear distinction exists between civilians and military forces.[8] But the network of conventions and treaties which seeks to improve the situation of non-combatants in war is naturally limited to basing the increased protection that they grant upon the status of persons, as determined by the principle of distinction. This, however, will occasionally lead to some undeserving groups being treated better in practice than they should under the laws of war and some deserving persons being

---

[7] Above, p. 106.   [8] Cf. CDDH/SR.41, vol. 6, 180.

denied protection, because of the hazy distinction between new forms of combatants and civilians.[9]

Civilians comprise both those who never took part in hostilities and combatants who are *hors de combat*.[10]

It may be difficult to ensure that civilians are adequately protected in the case of total war,[11] but a belligerent cannot escape liability for serious violations of these rights. Most protection that civilians enjoy is based on the system laid down in Geneva Convention IV of 1949 on Civilians. This Convention ensures rights that are so firm they cannot be denounced by individual civilians or a group of them.[12] The rights laid down in Geneva Convention IV are now extensively supplemented by the provisions of Protocols I and II of 1977.[13] The protection granted to civilians is also factually extended by a far-reaching presumption in the 1977 Protocols that anyone who is not a combatant is presumed to be a civilian.[14] Another valuable contribution of the Protocols is that they include a catalogue of forbidden practices to which civilians and persons *hors de combat* must not be subjected. These forbidden practices include under Protocol I:

(a) violence to the life, health, or physical or mental well-being of persons, in particular:
   (i) murder;
   (ii) torture of all kinds, whether physical or mental;
   (iii) corporal punishment; and
   (iv) mutilation;
(b) outrages upon personal dignity, in particular humiliating and degrading treatment, enforced prostitution and any form of indecent assault;
(c) the taking of hostages;
(d) collective punishments; and
(e) threats to commit any of the foregoing acts.[15]

Protocol II contains a similar catalogue of prohibited practices:

(a) violence to life, health and physical or mental well-being of persons, in particular murder as well as cruel treatment such as torture, mutilation or any form of corporal punishment;
(b) collective punishments;
(c) taking of hostages;
(d) acts of terrorism;
(e) outrages upon personal dignity, in particular humiliating and degrading treatment, rape, enforced prostitution and any form of indecent assault;

---

[9] Above, p. 103.   [10] Above, p. 273.
[11] *Cie. d'assurance le Soleil* v. *Français*, *RGDIP*, 1947, 259.
[12] Geneva IV, article 8.   [13] Protocol I, article 51(1); Protocol II, article 13.
[14] Above, p. 273.   [15] Protocol I, article 75.

(f) slavery and the slave trade in all their forms;
(g) pillage;
(h) threats to commit any of the foregoing acts.[16]

Civilians must not be subjected to any action which causes physical suffering or their intimidation. Such acts are particularly prohibited if they are designed to obtain information.[17] There must be no collective penalties[18] and no hostages must be taken.[19] Civilians must not be transferred to protect a place from being a military target.[20] They must not be deprived of their food by requisitions from an occupying power.[21]

If civilians are interned they must be given adequate clothes, light and heating.[22] They must not be subjected to forced mass transfers.[23]

Relief to civilian populations must be allowed through,[24] and those who accompany such consignment of relief goods must also enjoy protection.

ii. *Treatment of wounded, sick and shipwrecked*

Some victims of war, for example prisoners of war, received rudimentary protection under the 1864 Geneva Convention on the Treatment of Wounded.[25] Ratifications of the Convention did not come forth but, with some success, the newly founded International Committee of the Red Cross sought to prompt governments to accede to the Convention. In 1866 Prussia began hostilities against Austria and the Convention received its first test. Austria had, when the hostilities opened, not yet ratified the Convention, but Prussia notified the Committee of the Red Cross that it would apply the Convention regardless of Austria's non-ratification.[26]

---

[16] Protocol II, article 15.
[17] Hague Regulations, article 44; Geneva IV, articles 31, 33.
[18] Geneva IV, article 33.   [19] *Ibid*., article 34.
[20] *Ibid*., article 28; above, p. 259.
[21] Hague Regulations, article 52(1); Geneva IV, articles 36, 55; Protocol I of 1977, article 54(1); Protocol II of 1977, article 14; cf. below, p. 312 on requisitions; and above, p. 252 on starvation as a prohibited method of warfare.
[22] Geneva IV, articles 90 and 85.   [23] Zayas, 'Population transfers', 207.
[24] Protocol I of 1977, articles 68–71, supplementing Geneva IV, article 23, 55 and 59; Kimminich, *Schutz der Menschen in bewaffneten Konflikten*, 186ff; cf. M. Bothe, 'Rechtsprobleme humanitärischer Hilfsaktionen', 45ff.
[25] 19 NRGT, 1 série, 607. The Additional Articles of 1868 were never ratified, but the 1864 Convention remained an important instrument until it was replaced, between certain parties, by the 1929 Convention (see below, p. 282) and finally completely replaced by the 1949 Conventions (see below, p. 282).
[26] P. Boissier, *Histoire du Comité International de la Croix-Rouge*, 236.

This Convention was extended to cover the wounded and shipwrecked at sea, including protection for hospital ships, by the Third Hague Convention 1899.[27] The 1906 Geneva Convention on the Wounded and Sick[28] expanded the Third Hague Convention of 1899. Prisoners of war were the subject of declaratory rules laid down by the Institut de Droit International in the so-called *Oxford Manual* of 1888,[29] of which some rules were adopted in the 1899[30] and the 1907 Hague Conventions.[31] Prisoners of war also received some protection under the Hague Regulations,[32] which gave some additional basic protection to civilians by laying down certain criteria to distinguish them from combatants.[33]

The situation of such prisoners of war was greatly improved by the conclusion, in 1929, of a new Convention on Prisoners of War.[34] The Convention was the result of certain draft rules drawn up by the International Committee of the Red Cross (ICRC) and contained certain innovations with regard to restriction of the right to reprisals[35] and with regard to functions of protective powers.[36]

Another Convention of 1929 improved the conditions of the wounded and the sick in armed conflict.[37] This Convention, together with the 1929 Convention on Prisoners of War,[38] replaced, as between contracting parties, the 1864 Geneva Convention and supplemented the rudimentary protection afforded by the 1907 Hague Regulations. They were themselves replaced, again as between contracting parties, by the First and Third 1949 Geneva Conventions.

The major advance, in modern times, with regard to the condition of wounded, sick and shipwrecked, of prisoners of war, and by civilians, was made by the 1949 Conventions, the four so-called Red Cross Conventions.[39] The First Red Cross Convention expanded the

[27]   International Convention III for Adapting to Maritime Warfare the Principles of the Geneva Convention of 22 August 1864, 26 NRGT 979.
[28]   1 *AJIL* 1907, Suppl., 201.   [29]   5 *Annuaire* 1881–2, 156.
[30]   26 NRGT, 2 série, 976.   [31]   3 NRGT, 3 série, 630.
[32]   Articles 4–21 of the Regulations Respecting the Laws and Customs of War on Land, Annex to Convention IV, see above, note 31.
[33]   Chapter I of the Regulations. See further on the relevant criteria p. 103.
[34]   108 LNTS 343.
[35]   Article 2(3).   [36]   Articles 86–7.   [37]   108 LNTS 303.   [38]   108 LNTS 343.
[39]   Convention I For the Protection of War Victims Concerning the Amelioration of the Condition of Wounded and Sick in Armed Forces in the Field, 75 UNTS 31; Convention II for the Amelioration of the Condition of Wounded, Sick and Shipwrecked Members of Armed Forces at Sea; *ibid.*, 85; Convention III Relative to the Treatment of Prisoners of War, *ibid.*, 135; Convention IV Relative to the Protection of Civilian Persons in Time of War, *ibid.*, 287.

protection of the wounded and sick in the field and the Second Convention increased protection of the wounded, sick and shipwrecked at sea.

It is a great advance of Protocol I 1977 that it supplies a definition of the terms 'wounded', 'sick' and 'shipwrecked'.[40] The Geneva Conventions had a shortcoming insofar as they failed to specify relevant definitions of such categories of persons.

The wounded, sick and shipwrecked enjoy, like everyone involved in armed conflicts, the fundamental human rights enounced by the Protocol,[41] as well as specific protection due to their condition.[42] If they are taken prisoner, they enjoy the cumulative protection of such provisions relating to wounded, sick and shipwrecked as well as to prisoners of war.[43] The Protocol provides further that protected persons must not be subjected to mutilations, transplants or to any medical experiments.[44] The Protocol affords protection beyond that under the 1949 Conventions by including all wounded, sick and shipwrecked in its ambit and not merely those in the power of the adversary party.

Under the first two Geneva Conventions the category of wounded, sick and shipwrecked comprises members of a belligerent's forces that fulfil the requirement of combatant status.[45] This category is extended by Protocol I of 1977.[46] Protection of wounded, sick and shipwrecked extends to all who qualify as combatants[47] on the condition that they abstain from any hostile activity.[48] The protected persons shall be respected, treated humanely and there must be no attempts on their lives or violence to their persons. In particular, they must not be subjected to murder, torture, or any biological experiments.[49]

Positive obligations of the captor include the duty to search for and collect enemy wounded, sick and shipwrecked and to give them adequate care.[50] The military command has the right to 'appeal to the charity' of the civilian population in the relevant territory to voluntarily collect and care for the sick and wounded,[51] and of commanders of neutral merchant vessels, yachts or other craft to take on board and care for wounded, sick and shipwrecked persons.[52] In the

---

[40] Article 8.   [41] Article 75. Cf. below, p. 293.   [42] Article 8.
[43] See below, pp. 281ff.   [44] Article 11.   [45] Above, p. 103.   [46] Above, p. 108.
[47] Above, p. 106 on requirements.   [48] Cf. above, p. 259 on perfidy.
[49] Geneva I and II, article 12.   [50] Geneva I, article 15; Geneva II, article 18.
[51] Geneva I, article 18.   [52] Geneva II, article 21.

case of shipwreck, the military authorities may also ask for assistance to collect the dead.[53] On the other hand, civilians who respond to the calls for charitable assistance must not subsequently be held responsible for having aided the enemy or for other acts relating to their care; nor must they be molested for having lent assistance.[54] Commanders of other vessels who assist in a similar way must not be captured on account of their transporting protected persons, but remain liable to capture for other acts implying violations of neutrality.[55]

The identity of all sick, wounded and shipwrecked, as well as of the dead, must be ascertained and relevant information transmitted to the Information Bureau of the ICRC in Geneva.[56] They must also be protected against pillage and ill treatment.[57] Special agreements may be concluded by belligerents for the removal or exchange of sick, wounded and shipwrecked from a besieged or encircled area or to allow the passage of relief aid.[58] Protected persons who remain in the hands of the enemy shall qualify as prisoners of war and be guaranteed further protection as such.[59] Warships of belligerents have the right to demand the transfer of their sick, wounded and shipwrecked from other vessels, except neutral warships, who have lent assistance[60] provided the protected persons are in a fit state to be moved, and provided the warship can provide adequate care.[61] If the protected persons are on board a neutral warship the flag State must ensure that the protected persons take no further part in the hostilities and shall be 'guarded' to that effect.[62]

iii. *Specially protected groups*

Certain rules increase previous protection afforded to certain groups of persons, above that granted to all civilians.

a. *Women and children*

Women received some protection under Geneva Convention IV which prescribed that they must not be subjected to attacks on

---

[53] Geneva II, article 21(1).　　[54] Geneva I, article 18.
[55] Geneva II, article 21(3); cf. below, p. 281 on capture.
[56] Geneva I, article 16; Geneva II, article 19. An Information Bureau was to be established under article 122 of Geneva III to process information on dead, sick, wounded and shipwrecked, as well as of prisoners of war. The services of the ICRC have been used in practice for this purpose.
[57] Geneva I, article 15; Geneva II, article 18.　　[58] *Ibid.* and above, p. 281 on relief aid.
[59] Geneva I, article 14; Geneva II, article 16; cf. below, p. 253 on prisoner of war status.
[60] Above, p. 140.　　[61] Geneva II, article 14.　　[62] Geneva II, articles 15–17.

their honour, rape, enforced prostitution, or any form of indecent assault.[63] Special protection was also afforded to pregnant women and women with newborn babies.[64] Under the same Convention, particular duties were imposed on the parties to ensure the safety of children under 15 who are orphaned or separated from their families as a result of war, so that they are not left to their own resources.[65]

Protocol I of 1977 extends protection of women by specifying certain mandatory rules in their favour and granting enhanced protection to the most vulnerable group, that of pregnant women or mothers with dependent infants.[66] Children receive special protection by detailed provision dealing with both their safety[67] and their evacuation in case of need.[68]

b. *Journalists*
War correspondents received some protection under the 1949 Conventions insofar as they were to be given prisoner of war status if captured.[69] It may be surprising that one category singled out for further protection by Protocol I of 1977 was that of journalists. However, considering that journalists are extremely useful as part of the machinery which ensures the implementation of rules of war when most means of enforcement is lacking, such protection is most important.[70] It is often through journalists' reports that inhuman practices in wars are made known to the rest of the world and their function of transmitting news to those outside a particular conflict may often lead to world opinion condemning a certain method of warfare or a particular state of affairs.

c. *Civil defence personnel*
Under Geneva Convention IV there is a tentative regulation of protection of civil defence organisations during occupation.[71] Such entities are ensured the right to continue their work 'subject to temporary and exceptional measures imposed for urgent reasons of security'.[72]

---

[63] Geneva IV, article 27(2).
[64] Geneva IV, articles 16, 17; cf. 14, 21–3, 89, 91 and 132. On occupation see article 50.
[65] *Ibid.*, article 24; cf. 14, 51, 49, 89, 94, 132, 136. On occupation see article 50.
[66] Protocol I of 1977, article 76; cf. article 8. See further Y. Khushlana, *Dignity and Honour of Women and Basic Fundamental Human Rights*, The Hague, 1982, 63ff, 69–73.
[67] Article 77.   [68] Article 78.   [69] Convention III, article 4 A(4).
[70] Cf. Best, *Humanity in Warfare*, 329.   [71] Article 63.
[72] On military necessity, see below, p. 332.

The rationale of any protection of civil defence units is that they protect civilians from attack.[73]

Protocol I of 1977 recognises that civil defence personnel should be protected, as they do not form part of the ordinary armed forces. Ancillary protection should also be granted to certain equipment.[74] Such protection is entirely novel in international law.[75]

During the Conference some delegations expressed the opinion that civil defence personnel ought to have been given a status similar to that of medical personnel and thus protected from being taken as prisoners of war.[76] Yet, even if the final articles were a compromise of conflicting views as, indeed, many other articles of the Protocol were, the innovating protection of civil defence personnel and equipment is another step in the development of the laws of warfare.

d. Medical personnel

As has been described above,[77] medical units are protected from attacks. They are also ensured special treatment by the Geneva Conventions.[78] Medical personnel include hospital administrative personnel,[79] members of the armed forces assigned to medical units,[80] members of Red Cross organisations, other volunteers[81] and, by an extension of Protocol I of 1977, all civilian medical personnel.[82] If medical personnel are captured they must normally not be made prisoners of war but may be kept in POW camps to give medical assistance provided a number of prisoners require such help.[83] There are specific rules by which medical personnel will carry out their duties giving priority to their own sick and wounded, and they are guaranteed certain facilities to ensure this work.[84] Medical personnel at sea who fall into the enemy's hands shall be 'respected and protected' and they may continue to carry on their medical duties for as long as is necessary. They shall be sent 'back' when the Commander-in-Chief under whose authority they find themselves considers it practicable.[85]

---

[73] N. Gelsvik, 'Millitaert forsvar eller civilt vaern', *Syn og Segn*, Oslo, 1930.

[74] Articles 61–7.

[75] See B. Jakovljevic, *New International Status of Civil Defence as an Instrument for Strengthening the Protection of Human Rights*, The Hague, 1982, 32ff.

[76] E.g. Switzerland, CDDH/SR.43, vol. 6, 276.   [77] Above, p. 247.

[78] Geneva I, article 24; Geneva IV, article 20; on identification, see above, p. 248, and Geneva I, article 40; Protocol I of 1977, article 18(3) and its Annex.

[79] Geneva I, article 24.   [80] Geneva I, article 25 and above, p. 24.

[81] Geneva I, article 26.   [82] Protocol I, articles 8 and 15; cf. above, p. 24.

[83] Geneva I, article 28.   [84] Geneva I, articles 28, 30, 31.   [85] Geneva II, article 37.

Fixed medical installations and medical transport units are protected under the rules on methods of warfare exempting them from being targets.[86] The Protocol of 1977 extends protection previously granted to medical personnel under the Geneva Conventions to civilians who care for the sick and wounded.[87] Problems related to medical transport by air were not solved by the 1929 Convention[88] nor by the 1949 Red Cross Conventions. The Protocols,[89] on the other hand, 'ont un immense mérite: ils tiennent largement compte des exigences de la médecine et des réalités opérationelles et technique de l'aéronautique dans le temps ou nous vivons'.[90]

Protocol I adopts a varied system for overflight by medical transport, attempting to establish a balance between humanitarian demands and the legitimate fear of parties to armed conflicts that any overflights might have a military purpose. The Geneva Convention had required prior agreement for all medical flights.[91] Such authorisation in advance is not always compatible with speedy medical assistance. Protocol I still requires consent, however, for flights over enemy or neutral territory.[92] Under the new Protocol there are also extended possibilities for third parties to provide medical assistance.[93] The Protocol extends protection to certain small medical crafts at sea, even though no notification has been given[94] as previously required by the Geneva Convention on the Sick and Wounded and Shipwrecked.[95] The Protocol also remedies the deficiencies in this Geneva Convention by prescribing that protection applies at sea or in any other waters,[96] thereby including rivers and lakes under the ambit of the Protocol. The Protocol furthermore provides more detailed and specific rules for the identification of medical transport.[97]

e. Religious personnel

Military religious personnel, such as military priests, enjoy protection under the Geneva Conventions.[98] Protocol I extends this protection

---

[86] Above, p. 247.   [87] Articles 8 and 15.   [88] See above, note 34.

[89] For Protocol II, see below, p. 291.

[90] E. Evrard, 'Le nouveau statut protecteur des transports sanitaires par voie aérienne en temps de conflit armé', *RGDIP*, 1978, 234.

[91] Convention I, article 36, and Convention II, article 39.   [92] Articles 27 and 31.

[93] Articles 9(2) and 22(2); cf. comments by Bothe, Partsch and Solf, *New Rules on Victims of War*, 145.

[94] Article 22.   [95] Convention II, article 27.   [96] Article 23.

[97] Articles 8, 18, 24 and Annex I, Schindler and Toman, *Documents*, 2nd edn, 609.

[98] Articles 24 and 28 of Convention I.

also to civilian religious personnel.[99] Military[100] and civilian[101] priests must not be made prisoners of war but must be treated in a similar way to medical personnel and therefore be 'respected' and retained only to carry out their ordinary duties.

f. Prisoners of war

Some victims of war, for example prisoners of war, were afforded rudimentary protection under the 1864 Geneva Convention on the Treatment of Wounded.[102] There had been earlier privileges only for certain classes of prisoners of war.[103] Ratifications of the Convention did not come forth but, with some success, the newly founded International Committee of the Red Cross sought to prompt governments to accede to the Convention. As mentioned above, Austria had, when it was attacked by Prussia in 1866, not yet ratified the Convention. Yet Prussia notified the Committee of the Red Cross that it would apply the Convention regardless of Austria's non-ratification.[104] This Convention was extended to cover the wounded and shipwrecked at sea as well, including protection for hospital ships, by the Third Hague Convention.[105]

The 1906 Geneva Convention on the Wounded and Sick[106] expanded the Third Hague Convention of 1899. Prisoners of war were the subject of declaratory rules laid down by the Institut de Droit International in the so-called *Oxford Manual* of 1888,[107] of which some rules were adopted in the 1899[108] and the 1907 Hague Conventions.[109] Prisoners of war also received some protection under the Hague Regulations.[110] The Regulations also gave some basic protection to civilians by laying down certain criteria to distinguish them from combatants.[111]

---

[99] Article 15(5). [100] Geneva I, articles 24, 28. [101] Protocol I of 1977, article 15.
[102] 19 NRGT, 1 série, 607. The Additional Articles of 1868 were never ratified but the 1864 Convention remained an important instrument until it was replaced, between certain parties, by the 1929 Convention (see above, p. 154) and finally completely replaced by the 1949 Conventions (see below, p. 282).
[103] Above, on the historical background, p. 122.
[104] Boissier, *Histoire du Comité International de la Croix-Rouge*, 236.
[105] International Convention III for Adapting to Maritime Warfare the Principles of the Geneva Convention of 22 August 1864, 26 NRGT 979.
[106] 1 *AJIL* 1907, Suppl., 201. [107] 5 *Annuaire* 1881–2, 156.
[108] 26 NRGT, 2 série, 976; cf. above, note 30.
[109] 3 NRGT, 3 série, 630; cf. above, note 31.
[110] Articles 4–21 of the Regulations Respecting the Laws and Customs of War on Land, Annex to Convention IV, see above, note 32.
[111] Chapter I of the Regulations. See further on the relevant criteria p. 103.

The situation of such prisoners of war was greatly improved by the conclusion, in 1929, of a new Convention on Prisoners-of-War.[112] Another Convention of 1929 improved the conditions of the wounded and the sick in armed conflict.[113] This Convention replaced, as between contracting parties, the 1864 Geneva Convention and supplemented the rudimentary protection afforded by the 1907 Hague Regulations. They were themselves replaced, again as between contracting parties, by the First and Third 1949 Geneva Conventions.

The essence of treatment of prisoners of war is that it must not constitute a sanction, but a set of precautionary measures.[114] It is as a consequence of such considerations that it appears reasonable that prisoners of war are humanely treated.

The Hague Regulations of 1899 included provisions intended to prevent any harsh interrogation of prisoners of war.[115] The 1907 Hague Regulations provided a very much more detailed regulation of the required treatment of prisoners of war.[116] Geneva Convention III had improved on the treatment of prisoners of war under the 1929 Convention by specifying the categories of persons who would be entitled to protection. Convention III divides persons into broad categories, those who had fallen into the enemy's hands, including a new category of civilian crew members of military aircraft, and those in occupied or non-belligerent territories which should, especially in light of events in the Second World War, be treated as prisoners of war. Entitlement to prisoner of war status under the Geneva Conventions is restricted to those who can show that they fulfil the four conditions of 'combatants'.[117] The Geneva Convention extended privileged prisoner of war treatment to resistance movements operating in occupied territory.[118] Another new category, possibly not identical with the aforementioned group, qualifying for prisoner of war status, includes members of armed forces who profess allegiance to a government or an 'authority' not recognised by the detaining power. Such members would, in any event, fight 'on behalf' of a party to a conflict. There is some uncertainty as to what link is required be-

---

[112] 108 LNTS 343. The Convention was the result of certain draft rules drawn up by the International Committee of the Red Cross (ICRC) and contained certain innovations with regard to restriction of the right to reprisals (article 2(3)) and with regard to functions of protective powers (articles 86–7).

[113] *Ibid.*, 303.   [114] Cf. Rousseau, *Conflits armés*, 90.

[115] Below, p. 286.   [116] Articles 4–20.   [117] See above, p. 103.

[118] Article 4A(2).

tween independent forces, such as resistance movements, and parties to the Conventions.[119]

By changing the required conditions for combatants Protocol I of 1977 widens the protection of prisoners of war: since the conditions are reduced[120] a person may now qualify as a prisoner of war although he would not have enjoyed protection under Geneva Convention III. This extension will prove to be more useful than the presumption clause in the Geneva Convention that protection as a prisoner of war will be enjoyed until any questionable status is settled by a competent tribunal.[121]

In practice, even persons who do not fulfil the conditions of combatancy have been given prisoner of war status. To encourage the surrender of guerillas and spies commanders have sometimes asked the political organs of their home State for special permission to treat unprivileged combatants as prisoners of war. Such a practice developed, for example, in the Malaysian conflict to distinguish between 'captured enemy personnel' (CEP) and 'surrendered enemy personnel' (SEP), whereby the latter group would also be treated as prisoners of war.[122] At times the all-important question for prisoner of war status has been whether there is a 'war'. If a State can argue that there is no such conflict it may also attempt to evade all obligations incumbent on it for specific treatment of prisoners of war. It is clear that non-recognition of an entity as a State does not necessarily lead to non-combatant status of persons.[123] China refused to admit that there was a state of war in Korea and denied United States pilots, on that basis, the status of prisoners of war. They were instead treated as 'spies' captured overflying China's territory.[124] Such objections make the qualification of a conflict as 'war' according to objective rather than subjective criteria[125] even more pertinent.

Some claim that intelligence forces have no right to be treated as

---

[119] Cf. above, p. 103. Some writers claim that the 'authority' to which members of armed forces may profess allegiance may even be the United Nations, T. J. Farer, 'The humanitarian laws of war in civil strife: towards a definition of armed conflict', 7 *RBDI* 1971, 29; cf. G. I. A. D. Draper, 'The Geneva Conventions of 1949', 114 *RCADI* 1965, i, 114.
[120] See above, p. 108.   [121] Geneva III, article 5(2).
[122] Miller, *The Law of War*, 258ff.
[123] *The Fjeld*, (1950) Prize Court of Alexandria, 17 *ILR* 1950, 345; *Diab* v. *AG*, (1952) Supreme Court of Israel, 19 *ILR* 1952, 550.
[124] Cf. GA Res. 906 (IX) 1954 condemning the treatment as contrary to the Korean Armistice Agreement at Panmunjom on 25 September 1953.
[125] Above, p. 11.

prisoners of war,[126] but this is probably true only for spies who are not in uniform.[127] There is no evidence that reconnaissance soldiers would be deprived of protection as prisoners of war.[128]

Furthermore, the most severe acts, like torture, are forbidden even if applied to those who do not qualify for combatant status: these may be liable to execution but they must not be tortured.[129]

Defectors are said not to qualify for prisoner of war status as they have not 'fallen into the hands' of the enemy.[130] Consequently, there is legally no duty to hand defectors over. But the difference between defectors and deserters is not always easy to draw. It could perhaps be said that defectors wish to change allegiance and deserters wish only to avoid military service,[131] but it is not always easy to establish the subjective motives of a person.[132]

Protocol I of 1977 effectively extends the qualitative treatment of prisoners of war by subjecting them, along with other persons, to certain fundamental guarantees.[133] Although other persons are also protected under this provision, it is to prisoners of war that these guarantees will be particularly important as it is they who, by definition, find themselves in the hands of the enemy. The guarantees imply that, *inter alia*, a prisoner of war must not be subjected to any act included in the catalogues of prohibited practices.[134]

But the ambit of the protection of prisoners of war is still uncertain. There are specific provisions in Geneva Convention III to the effect that persons who have been prosecuted for acts prior to capture will retain the benefits of the Convention.[135] In other words, if a person is a war criminal[136] he still qualifies for prisoner of war status. The Eastern bloc made significant reservations to this article. The Soviet Union said in its reservation that it would not

consider itself bound by the obligation, which follows from article 85, to extend the application of the Convention to prisoners of war who have been convicted under the law of the Detaining Power, in accordance with the principles of the Nuremberg Trial, for war crimes and crimes against humanity, it being understood that persons convicted of such crimes must be subject to the conditions obtaining in the country in question for those who undergo their punishment.[137]

[126] Rosas, *The Legal Status of Prisoners of War*, 233; cf. 231.   [127] See above.
[128] Cf. my 'Foreign warships', 67.   [129] Norwegian Supreme Court, *AD*, 1946, 391.
[130] Draper, *The Red Cross Conventions*, 53.
[131] A. J. Esgain and W. A. Solf, 'The 1949 Geneva Conventions relative to the treatment of prisoners of war', 41 *North Carolina LR* 1963, 555.
[132] Cf. on mercenaries, see above.   [133] Article 75.   [134] See above.
[135] *Ibid.*, article 85.   [136] See below.   [137] For text see 3 *Commentaire* 449.

The other socialist States made similar reservations, although they did not all refer to 'convicted' but to 'prosecuted and convicted' persons, thus indicating that there would have had to be a 'trial'.[138] But the United Kingdom, Australia and New Zealand made protests against these reservations and declared that they would treat any application of the reservations as a breach of the Convention.[139] The Democratic Republic of Vietnam considered the United States raids on its territory as war crimes and stated therefore that captured pilots would be liable for judgment as war criminals and would not enjoy prisoner of war status.[140] Other incidents, for example in Kashmir in 1965, when Pakistani forces crossed the border, show that prisoner of war status may be denied persons who do not wear uniform and therefore become suspected of being infiltrators or 'freedom fighters'.[141]

Although Italy had made no reservation to article 85, Italian courts have held that article 85 of the Prisoner-of-War Convention of 1949 must be interpreted to 'exclude' benefits of the Convention to prisoners of war who have committed war crimes.[142] Even safeguards on court procedure in article 87 only concern civilians during captivity and are 'inoperative' with regard to war crimes committed previously.

Some assert that the rules concerning the required treatment of prisoners of war during captivity or repatriation are unchallenged by States, although the rules concerning, for example, reprisals[143] are less clear.[144] There have been numerous allegations of violations of the rights of prisoners of war, especially as regards torture.[145]

---

[138] Democratic Republic of Vietnam, *ibid.*

[139] Schindler and Toman, *Documents*, 2nd edn, 485.

[140] 5 *IRRC* 1965, 528. The Democratic Republic of Vietnam added that captured pilots were 'well treated'.

[141] 6 *IRRC* 1966, 19; UN, *Yearbook*, 1965, 161; below, p. 291.

[142] Tribunale Supremo Militare, 25 October 1952, *Rivista*, 1953, 193 and note by Ago. In the event the crime consisted in reprisals against the civilian population for attacks on German soldiers by Italian non-combatants. Cf. below, p. 351.

[143] Above, p. 254.   [144] Rosas, *Legal Status*, 101.

[145] Pakistani allegations of torture of prisoners of war by India, S/10560, 10579 and 10589, 1973; International Observer Team in Nigeria, 1968, *Report, Sverige och konflikten i Nigeria*, Stockholm, 1970, 212, 243; allegations of Israeli violations, S/9614; allegations of Syrian violations, S/9621; allegations of violations in the Iran–Iraq War, *Report by a Mission Dispatched by the Secretary General*, S/16962, 1985; on allegations considered by a court, see the *Weizacker Case*, AD, 1949, 351; the *Malzer Case*, AD, 1946, 289; on bad treatment by both camp authorities and civilians, see the *Heyer Case*, AD, 1946, 287; in Algeria torture was even defended, J. Massu, *La vraie bataille d'Algers*, Evreux, 1971, 165ff; cf. GA Resolutions 3059 (XXVIII) 1973; 3218 (XXIX) 1974; 3452 and 3453 (XXX) 1975.

The specific rights of prisoners of war imply that they must be humanely treated.[146] The rights to which prisoners of war are entitled are fairly well consolidated, but certain ancillary rights may be suspended or modified by local customs and traditions.[147]

Summary executions are strictly forbidden.[148] Prisoners of war must not be subjected to biological experiments[149] nor must they be subjected to torture.[150] Above all, prisoners of war must not be the object of reprisals.[151] The Soviet Union declared expressly in 1942 that reprisals would not be taken against German prisoners of war despite the flagrant violations of the Law of War that the prisoners had committed.[152] This statement affirms that prohibition of reprisals against prisoners of war is rooted in general international law: the Soviet Union was not bound by the Geneva Convention of 1929.[153]

Prisoners of war must not be subjected to interrogations. All 'illegal' methods of obtaining information are prohibited.[154] Prisoners of war are entitled not to disclose anything but their name, rank and serial number.[155] This limitation of the Law of War can operate to the disadvantage of other individuals who were victims of earlier acts by a captured person. An illustration of this was the Astiz affair during the Falklands War. Here, an Argentinian officer who had very likely committed atrocities in Argentina in the 1970s was released after the end of hostilities, having been asked merely to identify himself.[156]

There were numerous reservations to the clause in the 1899 Regulations protecting prisoners of war from interrogation.[157] The 1929 Convention[158] improved protection with regard to questioning but, since many states did not ratify either this Convention or the 1907

---

[146] Hague Regulations, article 4; Geneva Convention 1929, article 48; Geneva III, articles 13–14.
[147] Miller, *The Law of War*, 107ff.
[148] *The Wielen Case, AD*, 1946, 292; cf. Rousseau, *Conflits armés*, 100, on other case law.
[149] *The Brandt Case, AD*, 1947, 296.
[150] See above, p. 273; Geneva II, article 3(1)(a); Protocol I of 1977, article 75(2).
[151] Geneva Convention 1929, article 2(3); Geneva III, 1949, article 13(3); on reprisals cf. above, p. 168.
[152] USSR Academy (ed.), *International Law*, Moscow, 1960, 418.
[153] Below, p. 332 on breach and p. 339 on reciprocity.
[154] *Killinger Case, AD*, 1946, 290.
[155] Geneva III, article 17.
[156] Ch. Rousseau, 'Chronique des faits internationaux', *RGDIP*, 1982, no. 4, 763.
[157] See reservations to article 44 by Austria, Germany, Japan and Russia.
[158] Article 5; cf. article 31. See above, note 34 for reference.

Conventions,[159] there was no satisfactory regulation until the Geneva Conventions of 1949.[160] Protocol I of 1977 now extends such protection to all who qualify as combatants under the more generous conditions of the Protocol.[161]

Prisoners of war must be given sufficient food,[162] clothing[163] and health care.[164] There must be adequate standards of hygiene in prisoner of war camps.[165] Prisoners of war may be evacuated[166] or transferred to other areas, but only in such circumstances that are apt for their condition.[167] They must not be interned in areas where conditions are injurious to their health.[168] This provision is different from the earlier regulation in the 1929 Convention under which prisoners of war originating from temperate climates should be transferred from unhealthy localities where they had been captured.[169] Such obligations were often difficult to carry out and were not altogether justified in segregating treatment according to country of origin.

Prisoners of war must not be confined to quarters not lighted by daylight.[170] They must not be transferred to prisons or other places of close confinement.[171] If they try to escape they may be disciplined but not punished.[172] There have, however, been frequent violations of this rule.[173] There must be a fair trial if judicial action is taken for

[159] For example, certain Latin American States, such as Argentina, Chile, Colombia, Ecuador, Paraguay, Uruguay and Venezuela, as well as some European powers such as Italy, Greece and Spain. These countries were, for a considerable time, including the period of the First World War, bound only by the 1899 Conventions in this respect.

[160] See articles 17 and 50 of Geneva III. For an illustration of the problems involved in shifting the allegiance of prisoners of war by requesting them to carry out certain work, see *US* v. *Krupp*, 9 *Trial of War Criminals*, 1395: French prisoners of war could not be allowed to work in German armaments factories; even if there had been an agreement to this effect between Germany and the Vichy Government, such an agreement would be *contra bonos mores* and void under international law.

[161] Protocol I of 1977, article 44.

[162] Geneva III, article 26.

[163] *Ibid.*, article 27.   [164] *Ibid.*, articles 25–7.   [165] *Ibid.*, articles 29–32.

[166] *Ibid.*, article 20.   [167] *Ibid.*, articles 46–8.   [168] *Ibid.*, article 25(1).

[169] Geneva Convention 1929, article 9.   [170] *Ibid.*, article 25(3).

[171] Geneva Convention 1929, article 48; Geneva III, article 21.

[172] Hague Regulations, article 8(2); Geneva III, articles 92, 91, 89; cf. article 90; for a list of permissible types of disciplinary penalties, see Geneva III, article 89; on the difficult distinction between disciplinary and penal action, see the *Campbell Case* before the European Commission of Human Rights, (1985) 7 EURR 165; cf. the *Engel Case*, Reports of the European Court of Human Rights, 1976.

[173] For German Order of 1942 imposing the death penalty for escape attempts, see D. 1942 L.87; and Rousseau, *Conflits armés*, 97.

crimes.[174] The disciplinary power of the camp commander cannot be delegated to another prisoner of war.[175]

Prisoners of war had already been relieved under the 1899 Hague Conventions from any duty to take part in military service against their own country.[176] This exemption was reiterated in the 1907 Hague Convention[177] and then coupled with a rule that a prisoner of war should not be required to disclose any information about his own army or about the means of defence of his own country.[178]

A prisoner of war who is an officer must not be compelled to work; non-commissioned officers may be required only to supervise.[179] A prisoner of war is not obliged to carry out any work that could be detrimental to his home State.[180] The Geneva Convention of 1929 prohibits work which has direct connection with the home State,[181] but there have been frequent abuses.[182] Geneva Convention III of 1949 does not incorporate this provision, but specifies certain activities in which prisoners of war shall be allowed to work.[183] Such works include administration, installations and maintenance of the prisoner of war camp; activities in agriculture, raw material and manufacturing industries, except metallurgical, machinery or chemical industries; public works and building works without military character; transport and handling of non-military stores; commercial business; domestic service and public utility services having no military character or purpose.[184] Prisoners of war must not be asked to do dangerous work, such as removing mines, or unhealthy or degrading work.[185] Prisoners of war are to have a monthly allowance.[186]

There must be certain facilities for prisoners of war to contact the outside world. They shall, for example, be allowed to send out a 'capture card' to the Prisoner-of-War Agency[187] and they must be allowed to send two letters and four cards every month.[188] There are

---

[174] Geneva Convention 1929, articles 50ff; Geneva III, 1949, article 84.

[175] Geneva III, article 96(3).   [176] Article 44 of the Hague Regulations of 1899.

[177] Article 23(h) of the 1907 Hague Regulations.

[178] Article 44 of the Regulations.

[179] 1899 Hague Regulations, article 44, cf. 1907 Regulations, and Geneva III, article 49; ICRC, *Commentaire*, 259; Greenspan, *Modern Law of Land Warfare*, 118; H. S. Levie, 'Employment of prisoners-of-war', 57 *AJIL* 1963, 318; Esgain and Solf, 'Geneva Conventions', 571.

[180] Hague Regulations, article 6(1).   [181] Geneva Convention 1929, article 31.

[182] *The Leeb Case, AD*, 1948, 394; *The Lewinsky Case, AD*, 1949, 515; *The Student Case, AD*, 1946, 296; *The Milch Case*, 17/4/1947, Nuremberg.

[183] Geneva III, 1949, article 50.   [184] *Ibid.*

[185] Geneva III, article 52.   [186] Geneva III, articles 58–68.

[187] *Ibid.*, article 69.   [188] *Ibid.*, article 71.

also certain provisions to ensure that relief shipments are distributed.[189]

Prisoners of war must be repatriated at the end of hostilities[190] and sometimes such delivery of prisoners marks the end of war itself.[191] Seriously wounded persons have the right to be repatriated during hostilities.[192] Repatriation by force during hostilities, however, is forbidden, although it is questionable what constitutes 'force' against a seriously wounded person.

The ICRC assists in repatriation as a general rule unless there are serious reasons for fearing that prisoners of war will be subject to 'unjust measures', especially on grounds of race, class or political views, in which case repatriation may be 'contrary to general principles of international law for the protection of the human being'.[193] There is a general rule not to apply force[194] and the United Nations General Assembly stressed in Resolution 610 (VII) 1952 that force must not be used against prisoners of war to prevent or effect their return to their homeland. Provisions on choice relating to where a prisoner may wish to go were rejected by the Conference.[195] But a conflict arises if a prisoner of war does not wish to return to his State. Armistice in Korea was delayed until 1953, partly due to disagreement on repatriation.[196]

The rights of prisoners of war cannot be denounced and are thus 'inalienable'.[197] This provision has occasionally been interpreted to the detriment of prisoners of war, implying that they cannot refuse to be repatriated. After the Second World War, before the new 1949 Geneva Conventions came into effect, there were several problems relating to the repatriation of prisoners of war. The notable case

---

[189] *Ibid.*, articles 73–5.
[190] 'As soon as possible after the end of hostilities', Hague Regulations, article 20; 'as soon as possible', Geneva Convention 1929, article 75(1); 'without delay', Geneva III, 1949, article 118(1); for detailed rules see *ibid.*, articles 118–21 on release from belligerents; articles 109–10 on release from neutral parties.
[191] Below, p. 298.   [192] Geneva III, article 109(3).   [193] ICRC, *Commentaire*, 546.
[194] R. R. Baxter, 'Asylum to prisoners-of-war', 30 *BYIL* 1953, 489; J. Charmatz and H. M. Wit, 'Repatriation of prisoners of war and the Geneva Convention', 62 *Yale LJ* 1952–3, 391; J. Gutteridge, 'The repatriation of prisoners-of-war', 2 *ICLQ* 1953, 207; Esgain and Solf, 'Geneva Conventions', 592; M. R. Garcia-Mora, *International Law and Asylum as a Human Right*, Washington, DC, 1956, 112; M. Flory, 'Vers une nouvelle conception du prisonnier de guerre', 59 *RGDIP* 1954, 67; O. Kimminich, *Asylrecht*, Berlin, 1968, 39; J. Mayda, 'The Korean repatriation problem and international law', 47 *AJIL* 1953, 414.
[195] Rosas, *The Legal Status of Prisoners of War*, 480.   [196] *Ibid.*, 478–9.
[197] Geneva III, article 7.

became the one concerning repatriation to the Soviet Union of soldiers from the Baltic States who had served in the German Army. There was no support in international law for their repatriation to the Soviet Union: even their citizenship was in many cases questionable until international society at large had recognised the incorporation of the Baltic republics into the Soviet Union.[198] Finland was probably not required under the Peace Treaty to extradite the Baltic soldiers and Sweden had, in spite of a legally and morally questionable decision to hand over prisoners, even less reason to grant extradition.[199]

Similar incidents arose during the Korean conflict.[200] There is probably a right to refuse repatriation.[201] Considerable difficulties would arise if there were not such a right, especially considering the difficult line between defectors, deserters and those who might have changed their attitudes during captivity. The problem turns mainly on a concern that the prisoner of war himself is allowed to make his decision freely. The privileges of prisoners of war are coupled with important duties.

The right to protection as a prisoner of war can be forfeited if illegitimate acts are committed. One such act is to carry arms; formerly, this would have led to execution,[202] but would now normally be punished in other ways.[203] There is some practice to the effect that officers who ordered execution of prisoners of war may be liable for war crimes. Thus, German officers who executed United States Commando troops in the Second World War were themselves executed as war criminals.[204]

g. Detainees

In internal conflicts, rebels are still citizens and subject to the laws of the country. They are, therefore, under most municipal laws, liable

[198] H. Granfelt, 'Finland och baltflyktingarna', *Statsvetenskaplig Tidskrift*, 1948, 60.
[199] Cf. *ibid.*, 61.
[200] Draper, *The Red Cross Conventions*, 69; Mayda, 'The Korean repatriation problem', 414; Charmatz and Wit, 'Repatriation', 391; R. R. Baxter, 'Asylum to prisoners-of-war', 489; cf. 10 Whiteman 1968, 203, 257 and 503.
[201] Cf. Note, 'Right of non-repatriation of prisoners-of-war captured by the United States', *Yale LJ*, 1973, 358; cf. Versailles Treaty, article 220(2); Brest–Litovsk Treaty, 1918, article 17(1).
[202] See German note, through the Swiss legation in charge of German interests in the United States, September 1918, 6 Hackworth 271–2.
[203] Above, p. 259.
[204] *The Dostler Case, AD*, 1946, 280; cf. *The Falkenhorst Case, AD*, 1946, 282; *The Bauer Case, AD*, 1946, 305.

for treason for their acts if such acts are directed against the State. Modern internal warfare deviates from the civil war pattern and the traditional practice of recognising belligerency has fallen into disuse.[205] In the contemporary world there are, however, several full-scale internal wars, where the insurgents or freedom fighters have passed the threshold[206] of being rebellious subjects to being consolidated belligerents which the State must fight as it fights other States; it is as if, at a given stage, the State has lost its power of quelling a rebellion and trying the perpetrators for treason.

Once the insurgents have reached this stage they are very much like traditional recognised belligerents who may take prisoners of war, and whose own men may be captured by the other side.

Naturally, the State has a problem in deciding at what stage it is willing to treat its own subjects as anything equal to prisoners of war. Freedom fighters are, when captured, usually called 'detainees' to indicate that they have a status different from that of ordinary prisoners of war. But the treatment the captured persons are to be ensured under Protocol II of 1977 is not so drastic that it could not be easily compatible with any standards of a State respecting the rule of law, a *Rechtsstaat*.

The problem arises in internal armed conflict as to whether detainees have any right to special consideration. If the conflict had been an international or a liberation war such persons would have enjoyed prisoner of war status under Protocol I of 1977. But because internal conflicts are still treated differently, such persons, even in uniform and as members of organised forces, are merely 'detainees' under Protocol II and, as such, exempt from any favourable treatment under any other conventions concerning the laws of war.[207] On the other hand, the General Assembly called on parties to give prisoner of war status to all freedom fighters.[208]

Detained persons have the right under Protocol II of 1977 to food, drinking water and medical relief.[209] They are specifically assured of the right to take part in religious practices.[210] If they are wounded, sick or shipwrecked they have the same rights as civilians in these conditions.[211]

[205] Above, p. 135.   [206] Above, p. 18.
[207] But see above, p. 130 on human rights under certain treaties.
[208] E.g. Resolutions 2395 (XXIII) 1968; 2547 (XXIV) 1969; 2207 (XXV) 1970; 2795 (XXVI) 1971; 2918 (XXVII) 1972; 3113 (XXVIII) 1973.
[209] Article 5(1)(b) and (c).   [210] Article 5(1)(d).
[211] Article 5(1)(a) and article 7.

Three provisions that would have been important to the treatment of detainees were deleted. One provision concerned the prohibition of reprisals.[212] It was held that such rules did not have any place in an instrument on internal conflicts as reprisals, it was claimed, belong to the inter-State field.[213] Reprisals against rebels were defended, as

it is not inconceivable that in the course of internal conflict, rebels ... deliberately commit acts to which the normal reaction would be in the nature of reprisals, but because of a prohibiting article such as this, governments feel bound to fold their arms while dissident groups go on a rampage, killing and maiming innocent civilians and burning dwellings and foodcrops.[214]

But some voted in favour of the article precisely because it forbade reprisals and, as such, would increase humanitarian protection.[215]

It is difficult to conceive why offending rebels could not have been subjected to due process of law rather than remaining a legitimate target for reprisals. Such reprisals are often directed against persons who did not themselves perpetrate acts of violence and who perhaps are civilians. Reprisals, which no doubt have a deterrent effect, would appear to expose innocent persons to arbitrary actions.

A provision concerning preferential treatment of a prosecuted person who could show that he had abided by the rules of Protocol II was deleted. Nigeria had found such a rule an intrusion in internal affairs and, besides, ample guarantees were already in the Constitution and in national legislation.[216] By this deletion an important fundamental principle of humanitarian law was set aside, as remarked by some delegates.[217]

Another provision which would have afforded further protection, especially to detainees, concerned the deferment of the death penalty until the end of hostilities.[218] There had been a 'gentlemen's agreement' among some Third World States 'not to press' for the inclusion of this article.[219] All that was left were some judicial guarantees[220] to secure due process of law. Even these may not be implemented in practice since they are, in some countries, somewhat unrealistic when applied to detainees in civil armed conflict. However, it is important to retain at least some level of judicial protection, not only as a target,

---

[212] Draft article 10 (bis). Cf. above, p. 258 on reprisals in the context of Protocol II.
[213] Nigerian CDDH/SR.51, vol. 7, 122.   [214] *Ibid.*   [215] *Ibid.*, 120.
[216] CDDH/SR.50, 102.   [217] *Ibid.*, 99.   [218] Draft Article 10(5).
[219] E.g. Iraq, CDDH/SR.50, vol. 7, 108.
[220] Article 6(2).

but as actual binding legal obligations, even if States could not agree to defer death penalties until the end of hostilities.[221]

But detainees are still subject to certain 'fundamental guarantees' under Protocol II, similar to those that apply in the case of Protocol I.[222] Protocol II thus provides that anyone who does not take part in hostilities, or has ceased to do so, must not be subjected to the practices forbidden in the catalogue.[223] The standards imposed by these rules would not be too lofty for any State. But what is often not sufficiently emphasised is that the freedom fighters too are bound by these rules, and they must also refrain from such acts against persons in their power.[224]

---

[221] Cf. the present plans in the United Nations to adopt a Convention Forbidding the Death Penalty.
[222] Above, p. 273.   [223] Above, p. 273.   [224] Cf. below, p. 339 on reciprocity.

III

CONSEQUENTIAL ASPECTS OF THE LAW OF WAR

A. THE TIME SPAN OF WAR

i. Inception of war

This work has discussed in some detail the question of when war starts[1] and whether or not a declaration of war is necessary for war to exist.[2] It is fairly clear that objective elements now guide the question of whether war has started, although there will remain an area of doubt as to whether the relevant threshold of hostilities has been crossed and there is no longer a question of merely intermittent hostilities.[3] The time span of war thus stretches from the point when hostilities intensify into a sustained pattern of action.[4]

ii. The end of war

Hostilities may often end by the conclusion of an armistice agreement, in writing or orally, with general or local application. An armistice agreement implies only the provisional suspension of hostilities and constitutes, contrary to the final peace, only a brief cessation of fighting on the battlefield. It must be of a certain duration or it must concern a definitive and final ending of hostilities, which is historically often the case.[5] Sometimes there are formal peace treaties – but not always.[6]

The fervent objections to the existence of war without a declara-

---

[1] Above, pp. 16ff.   [2] Above, p. 8.   [3] Above, p. 18.
[4] Above, p. 24 on the definition of war.
[5] A. Klawkowski, 'Les formes de cessation de l'état de guerre en droit international', *RCADI*, 1976, i, 217. Cf. Rousseau, *Conflits armés*, 188–91.
[6] G. H. Hackworth, 6 *Digest of International Law*, Washington, DC, 1943. On historical examples, cf. C. Phillipson, *Termination of War and Treaties of Peace*, London, 1916, 55ff.

tion of war[7] are not coupled with similar concern for when war ends. For if it is denied that war existed initially, whatever the objective circumstances seemed to indicate, there is no need to acknowledge the end of something which allegedly never existed. If, on the other hand, the initiation of war without a declaration is allowed, as current practice and law seem to indicate,[8] such a concession to formlessness leads to a natural disposition to accept that war ends when actual hostilities have ceased.

Occasionally, treaties have not come into operation until a date after the actual end of hostilities, and a point such as the repatriation of prisoners of war, or the cessation of functions of UN forces, has been chosen.[9] But it may be assumed that such dates do not mark the end of war but follow upon the legal end of war.

Special national announcements often clarify when war will not longer affect private law transactions of individuals.[10] For example, it is usually specifically announced that, after a certain date, trade with the former enemy may resume.[11] Again, such announcements may follow later than the legal end of war in international law and are repercussions of the effect of such an end. For war must have ended when hostilities finally ceased for it is this definitive end of war that gives rise to numerous obligations on the part of belligerents, above all with respect to repatriation of prisoners of war.[12]

B. EFFECTS ON COMMUNICATIONS

Communications in war will, of course, have been disrupted by the physical effects of warfare which prevent mail being forwarded and railways being used. Apart from such factual effects there will also, by special national legislation, be further severance of communications.

Letters and other communications to the enemy may be more damaging to the war effort on one side than the supply of arms and ammunition.[13] By clear powers of the eminent domain[14] belligerents may, to secure their war effort, subject any agency of communication to immediate control when public safety so demands.[15] Common

---

[7] Above, p. 8.   [8] Above, p. 11.   [9] See below, p. 300.
[10] Above, p. 12.   [11] 6 Hackworth 330–1; 431.   [12] Above, p. 289.
[13] Cf. Pearce A. Higgins, 'The treatment of mails in time of war', *BYIL*, 1928, 31.
[14] On the concept, see my *Finance*, 61.
[15] E.g. United States, Trading with the Enemy Act, 1917, para. 3(d) on the powers of the President to 'cause to be censored' any communication by mail, cable or radio; cf. 3 Hyde 1719.

orders include prohibition of any kind of mail being transmitted to enemy States during hostilities as well as to other countries if any transit through enemy territory is required.[16] Other usual measures include censorship of varying degree.[17]

The Conventions of the Universal Postal Union (UPU)[18] are not terminated,[19] but belligerents may suspend their execution insofar as they themselves are concerned.[20] On the other hand, the UPU Conventions on closed mail probably apply in war.[21] Due to vigorous suggestions by some negotiators at the 1907 Hague Conference[22] it was held that international law, as it then stood, lacked effective guarantees for the transportation of postal correspondence in war, particularly at sea. It was therefore agreed that Hague Convention XI would include specific rules to guarantee the inviolability of the correspondence of both belligerents and neutrals.[23]

The mail found on board a captured ship, a neutral or even an enemy ship was to be forwarded without delay by the captor, except to a blockaded[24] port.[25] Furthermore, neutral merchant ships carrying mail were to be exempted from search[26] except if such a measure was 'absolutely necessary'.[27] During the First World War it was often clear that belligerents did consider the exercise of the power of search necessary.[28]

Other means of communications, for example by radio, remain regulated by the rules of the International Telecommunications Union (ITU),[29] although States will exercise far-going measures to restrict any transmissions of persons within their jurisdiction and also often proceed to jamming techniques.[30]

C. LEGAL EFFECTS

Some of the effects of war described above include certain 'legal' effects insofar as the situation of individuals, in law, may be affected.

[16] E.g. United States, Order by the Postmaster General, 1918, For. Rel. Suppl., 2, 412; 6 Hackworth 316.
[17] On British censorship in South Africa, see 10 *AJIL* 1966, Suppl., 413, 416.
[18] On relevant rules see my *Law Making*, 217ff.
[19] Cf. below, p. 300 on suspension of treaties.
[20] 2 Oppenheim 304.   [21] Pearce Higgins, 'Treatment', 38.
[22] E.g. by M. Henri Fromageot; see Pearce Higgins, 'Treatment', 31.
[23] Articles 1 and 2.   [24] Above, p. 267.   [25] Hague XI, article 1.
[26] Below, p. 309.   [27] See below, p. 332 on military necessity.
[28] Pearce Higgins, 'Treatment', 33–4, 38–9.
[29] On relevant rules, see my *Law Making*, 223ff.   [30] Above, p. 264.

But there are some more general effects of this type which should be mentioned.

i. *Entry into force of rules of war*

The most immediate effect of a state of war is that it activates the Law of War itself. This may be a simple way of expressing things; for from the point of view of logic, it is by the force of the Law of War itself that we can establish that a war has commenced. If we discard this correct, but practically unhelpful, argument it is clear that the network of the rules of warfare will apply only when and if there is a war. This, at least, is the traditional position and this attitude also explains why some writers still avoid speaking of 'war' and prefer the term 'armed conflict',[31] as if there were a block of rules which would complicate life for States and individuals if they entered into force prematurely or without a good foundation. A close scrutiny of the laws of war seems to indicate that the rules can conceptually be conceived as latently present, providing rights and duties, and there are few real complications, either to States or to individuals as to when the rules are activated. States will apply the rules of neutrality and respect blockades when there are objective demands to do so; individuals will be much guided in their approach to overseas trade or business by instructions flowing from their own government.

ii. *The effect of war on treaties*

There is considerable controversy over whether the state of war has any effect on treaties and, if so, which types of treaties are affected.[32] The Institut de Droit International has recently been considering the question of the effect of war on multilateral treaties.[33] Some of its members have provided examples of treaties to show that some had

[31] Above, p. 16.
[32] W. Schätzel, *Der Krieg als Endigungsgrund von Verträgen*, Berlin, 1911; D. Anzilotti, 'Effeti della guerra sui trattati internazionale', *Rivista*, 1918, 53; A. D. McNair, 'Les effets de la guerre sur les traités', 49 *RCADI* 1937, i, 527; G. Scelle, 'De l'influence de l'état de guerre sur le droit conventionnel', *JDI*, 1950, 26; R. Monaco, 'La sospensione delle norme giuridiche internazionale in tempo di guerra', *Jus*, 1941, 236; F. Capotorti, 'L'extinction et la suspension des traités', 134 *RCADI* 1971, iii, 554–5; F. Klein, 'Kriegsausbruch und Staatsverträgen', 3 *JIR* 1950–1, 30; C. J. B. Hurst, 'The effect of war on treaties', *BYIL*, 1921–2, 37ff; R. Ränk, *Einwirkung des Krieges auf die nicht-politischen Staatsverträge*, Uppsala, 1949, 24.
[33] 59 *Annuaire* 1981, i.

and others had not been affected by war.[34] A Draft Resolution was put forward in 1981 by which treaties between belligerents and third States would remain in force in their mutual relations, whereas multi-lateral treaties binding parties to an armed conflict would be 'suspended if there is such a fundamental change of circumstances that the performance of the treaty would be unduly hampered'.[35] Furthermore, the existence of an armed conflict between some of the parties to a treaty establishing an international organisation would not 'in itself affect the operation' of the treaty unless, again, performance were unduly 'hampered'.

But this Draft was not adopted and another revised Draft Resolution was put forward, entirely different from the first one, eliminating the references to criteria like 'unduly hampered'.[36] The Institut discussed the revised Draft in 1985 and produced a final Resolution. In this Resolution[37] the Institut dispenses with the unfortunate expression of 'unduly hampers' and declares, instead, that the outbreak of war does not *ipso facto* suspend any treaties (whether bilateral or multilateral) between the belligerents,[38] or bilateral treaties between a belligerent and a third party,[39] or multilateral treaties to which some belligerents are parties.[40] A treaty establishing an international organisation is not at all affected.[41] Treaties may be suspended only in the exercise of self-defence in accordance with the Charter[42] or to ensure compliance with a Security Council Resolution with respect to 'the peace, breaches of the peace or acts of aggression'.[43] The Resolution, as it stands, offers little guidance on the effect of war on treaties.

But there are presumptions and there are distinctions. For example, treaties relating to restrictions of territorial sovereignty of a belligerent in favour of another belligerent are invariably suspended in

---

[34] *Ibid.*, ii, 267 (Schindler); see further *Reports*, i, 201–93 and *Debates*, ii, 175–244.

[35] Cf. Report by B. Broms, 59 *Annuaire* I 1981, 201; 59 *Annuaire* II 1982, 175; 61 *Annuaire* I 1985, 1. Although not much discussed in the Institut, there is a close relationship between the effect of war on treaties and problems relating to State succession; for these see G. Sperduti, 'Dalla disfatta della Germania agli accordi contrattuali di Bonn', *Comunità internazionale*, 1952, 570; E. Plischke, 'Reactivation of pre-war German treaties', *AJIL*, 1954, 245; and, in general, D. P. O'Connell, *State Succession, the Municipal Law and International Law*, 2 vols., Cambridge, 1967, and the ILC discussions. Nor was there any mention of the relationship to termination of treaties in general, see A. D. McNair, *The Law of Treaties*, Oxford, 1962; cf. my *Essays*.

[36] 61 *Annuaire* 1985, i, 2.

[37] Resolution, 28 August 1985, 61 *Annuaire* 1985, ii.

[38] *Ibid.*, article 2.   [39] Article 5(1).   [40] Article 5(2).   [41] Article 6.
[42] Article 7.   [43] Article 8.

time of armed conflict.[44] For a belligerent could not allow restrictions of the exercise of its sovereignty *in its own territory* in case of war, in favour of another belligerent.[45] Other treaties that always cease to have effect are those which establish alliances with another belligerent, or ensure assistance, guarantees or subsidies to such a State.

Could one envisage the armed conflict between two powers of a defence alliance without such a treaty being suspended between the belligerents? At the very least, the treaty would be, if not temporarily suspended, of 'temporary irrelevance' as a situation developed at variance with the contingency provisions of the treaty.

For other treaties there are other fairly clear presumptions. Courts have emphasised that States have the power to suspend treaties which have a purpose incompatible with war. For example, treaties on the immunity of State-owned ships can thus be suspended.[46] Other treaties may grant nationality status to aliens, like the Treaty of 1795 between the United States and the United Kingdom, under which all United States citizens who held land in the United Kingdom on 28 November 1795, and their heirs and assigns, are considered as UK citizens. But such a treaty has a purpose which would be incompatible with war between the two parties and would be suspended by such an occurrence.[47] Other treaties, again, which would invariably be suspended are those which restrict territorial sovereignty in one State in favour of the enemy.[48] Furthermore, treaties under which individuals claim rights are usually not suspended by war. For example, the Madrid Convention on Registration of Trade Marks of 1891 was not suspended as it belonged, said a court, to 'that category' of treaties.[49]

It is not a question of rights acquired under a treaty,[50] but a question of a framework for claims of which a person would be deprived were the relevant treaty considered as suspended or terminated. Thus, a treaty, in the event of rights of claims for workmen's

[44] This may even be the case if a State changes its foreign policy, see my *Independent State*, 218.

[45] *Ibid.* and above, p. 76 on the doctrine of continuous consent.

[46] *The Christina*, (1937) 4 All ER 313.   [47] *Sutton* v. *Sutton*, (1830) 1 R & M 663.

[48] On military base agreements and the theory of continuous consent, see my *Independent State*, 141 ff.

[49] *The Trade Mark Registration Case*, German Federal Patent Court, 6 Fontes juris gentium 1966–1970, A II, 262; 59 ILR 480. Cf. *Society for the Propagation of the Gospel* v. *New Haven and Wheeler*, (1823) 8 Wheaton 464; *Bussi* v. *Menetti*, (1943) C. cass. *AD*, 1943–5, no. 103; *Techt* v. *Hughes*, (1920) 229 NY 222.

[50] For criticism of the theory of acquired rights, see my *Finance*, 105.

compensation of 1928, was held to be in force so that claims could be presented by individuals.[51]

The Brazilian Foreign Ministry went into great detail on this point in the context of the question of the Havana Convention of 1928, incorporated into the laws of Brazil in 1929.[52] The internal legislation of Brazil dealt with termination of treaties but did not specify rules for the contingency of war or armed conflict. The Brazilian Foreign Ministry stated that the 'absolute' theory of abrogation, depriving treaties in general of effect in war, cannot be accepted. On the other hand, certain treaties which do cease to have effect are political treaties with the other belligerents, particularly those assuring alliance, for such treaties have been abrogated by action. Another group of treaties suspended consists of those whose interpretation gave rise to the dispute.[53] Again, could one envisage an armed conflict about a border treaty where that treaty was not suspended between the belligerents?

It was fortunate that the Institut exempted treaties which establish international organisations from any suspension along the criterion of 'unduly hampered'; but the Institut should have added that there is a presumption that conventions and regulations incidental to the treaties establishing international organisations also retain their force in war.[54] These are often of real practical importance, for example implementing the rules of the Universal Postal Union (UPU) and the International Telecommunications Union (ITU).[55] But since these rules usually have a unilateral character,[56] they presumably fell outside the scope of the Resolution on treaties of the Institut.

iii. Private law effects

a. The effects of war on property

It has been shown above that certain State property, for example part of the cultural assets of a country, are specially protected under

---

[51] *The Miletich Case*, (1946) 12 *AD* 1943–5, 456, on a Convention on compensation between Argentina and Yugoslavia in 1928. For similar views that individual rights are in a special category, see A. C. Gialdino, *Gli effetti della guerra sui trattati*, Milan, 1959, 251; cf. A. de la Pradelle, 'The effect of war on private law treaties', *ICLQ*, 1948–9, 570.

[52] Decree 18.956 of 22 October 1929.

[53] Pareceros dos Consultores juridicos do Ministerio das Relacoes Exteriore, 1935–45, Dept. de Imprensa Nacional, 1961, 599, reproduced in Cancado Trindade, *Repertorio Pratica brasileria do direito internacional*, Brasilia, 1984, 338; cf. Lafayette, 2 *Principios de direito internacional*, para. 317; Clovis Bevilaqua, *Direito publico internacional*, vii, para. 179; H. Accioly, 2 *Tratado de direito internacional publico*, no. 1548.

[54] Above, p. 299.   [55] See my *Law Making*, 217ff.   [56] *Ibid., passim.*

the Law of War.[57] Other State property, as well as certain private property, may often be entitled to special protection as belonging to the civilian population and, as such, forming part of non-military objectives of bombardment.[58] Furthermore, the Hague Regulations had already prohibited destruction or seizure of public or private enemy property unless such acts were demanded by the necessities of war.[59]

On the other hand, there are numerous situations when public and private property will be subjected to the hazardous destruction of war and there are few remedies individuals have to obtain compensation. However, in one much overlooked case it was held that any party to a war who was unable to keep its destructive effects to military targets was liable for compensation to a private citizen who had suffered injury and damage due to the inability of a pilot to avoid destroying private property.[60] This case furnishes new dimensions to the problem of indiscriminate weapons[61] and also throws some light on the position of civilian property in a war situation.

Apart from the factual destruction caused by war, there are special situations when public or private property may be taken by the enemy. These areas are of decreasing size as the power to take enemy property is gradually diminished.

(1) Booty According to traditional rules of war, title to taken property on the battlefield or in the war area passes to the taking State without any court order.[62] All movable property could, in the past, be taken provided it is owned by the enemy State.

However, the Hague Regulations introduced new prohibitions to protect private property: such property could, for example, not be confiscated by an occupying Power,[63] nor would pillage be allowed.[64] Under the Hague Regulations cultural property of the State

---

[57] Above, p. 249.   [58] Above, p. 241.   [59] Below, p. 332.

[60] *The Zeppelin Case, Coenca Frères* v. *Germany*, 7 *RIAA* 683; cf. above, p. 239.

[61] Above, p. 136.

[62] See W. G. Downey, 'Captured enemy property, booty of war and seized enemy property', 44 *AJIL* 1950, 488; A. V. Freeman, 'General note on the law of war booty', *AJIL*, 1946, 795.

[63] Article 46. For application, see e.g. the Polish judgment, (1927) *AD*, 1927–8, no. 381.

[64] Article 47; cf. A. V. Freeman, 'Responsibility of states for unlawful acts of their armed forces', 88 *RCADI* 1955, ii, 325. According to a proposal of the Institut de Droit International of 1880, private property should be protected as the purpose of war is only to weaken the *military* strength of the enemy. On the principle that the least

or of municipalities would, however, be 'treated as private property'.[65] Under the later Hague Convention for the Protection of Cultural Property of 1954[66] all forms of taking or damaging cultural property by the enemy are categorically outlawed.[67]

Such regulation has, it appears, put a stop to the traditional wide rules on booty and restricts the former rights of a belligerent considerably. But an area of possible booty remains in the case of State property which is not subsumed under the category of cultural property.

Private property, on the other hand, is outside the ambit of booty. The taking of such property from civilians or from enemy soldiers constitutes pillage, expressly forbidden in numerous treaties.[68] Claims to treasure troves are not normally allowed in war. A claim to $150,000 found in a cave in Vietnam was thus refused and it was held that the money constituted public property of the home State of the soldier who had found it.[69]

(2) Prize and confiscation of contraband Enemy merchant ships may be taken by warships as 'prize'. The capture is confirmed by well settled rules in civil prize proceedings in special prize courts.[70]

When war has broken out[71] all enemy merchant vessels are liable to capture. Even aeroplanes have been held subjected to such law of prize,[72] and several States have promulgated national legislation to allow for the seizure of aircraft as prize.[73] Enemy warships,[74] the

possible damage to private property should be caused and for a commentary of discussions in the Institut, see N. Bentwich, *The Law of Private Property in War*, London, 1907, 27ff. On protection of private property at sea, see below, p. 307.

[65] Article 56.   [66] Above, p. 249.

[67] Article 4(3). But see below on military necessity.

[68] Hague Regulations, article 28 for assault situations; article 47 for occupation; Hague IX, article 5; Geneva I, article 15; Geneva II, article 18; Geneva III, article 33; Hague Convention on the Protection of Cultural Property 1954, article 4(3).

[69] *Morrison* v. *United States*, (1974) US Court of Claims, 422 F. 2nd 1219.

[70] See P. Reuter, *Etude de la règle 'toute prise doit être jugée'*, Nancy, 1933; L. Sico, *Toute prise doit être jugée, Il giudizio delle prede nel diritto internazionale*, Naples, 1971. But the idea that private property, for example merchant ships, may be taken as prize constitutes an exception to the rule that private property is 'inviolable'. See C. de Boeck, *De la propriété privée ennemie sous pavillon ennemi*, Paris, 1982, 493. Cf. *ibid.*, 493–513 on the work of the Institut de Droit International to bring about a new prize regime. Cf. B. Ranft, 'Restraint of war at sea before 1945', in M. Howard (ed.), *Restraints on War*, Oxford, 1979, 43ff.

[71] Above, p. 298.

[72] See UK Prize Act 1939, 2 & 3 Geo. 6 ch. 65, s. 1(1) and *The Yankee Clipper Case*, (1945) AC.

[73] Italian Decree, 8 July 1938, articles 239–40, 256; UK Prize Act 1939, s. 1; cf. Dutch Prize Regulations, Rousseau, *Conflits*, 361.

[74] For definition, above, p. 102.

natural target for attack at sea, are not, however, subject to the law of prize but may be taken outright by the enemy.[75]

Most countries have clear and detailed rules on prize proceedings.[76] Jurisdiction for prize has existed in England since at least the fourteenth century.[77] The details of a body of law developed over the centuries and became more or less uniformly settled by all major maritime States, usually through the special Prize Courts.[78] These courts and their jurisdiction present a wealth of interesting problems to international lawyers but have recently attracted little attention. One reason for this is undoubtedly that the practice of prize has dwindled as a type of maritime strategy, and it is this dislocation from naval warfare that makes it more suitable to include rules on prize in the section of this work which deals specifically with the effect of war on property. For it is as such that the law of prize must be conceived, implying as it does the right to interfere and take, without compensation, public and private property, contrary to other trends in international law to protect at least certain such property.

The law of prize is different from other parts of international law in its very 'international essence'. Other sections of international law are often deflected by national or regional preferences, applying their stamp on the very substance of rules. But prize courts use, unquestioningly, uniform international law.[79] Furthermore, they do so without any such rules having been converted into national rules.[80] The rules of prize therefore show the most immediate impact of international law in the internal law of States and on municipal courts. It is as if the writers who claim that there is a complete separation between international and internal law[81] had never studied the precedents of prize law.

The areas where prizes may be taken are the high seas or enemy

---

[75] See A. Pearce Higgins, 'Ships of war as prize', *BYIL*, 1925, 103.

[76] C. J. Colombos, *A Treatise on the Law of Prize*, London, 1926; J. Kunz, 'British Prize Law', *Law Quarterly Review*, 1945, 49; Kunz, *ibid.*, 1946, 237; P. Parfond, *Le droit de prise et son application dans la marine française*, Paris, 1955; A. Gervais, 'La jurisprudence italienne des prises maritimes durant la seconde guerre mondiale', *RGDIP*, 1950, 251ff, 433ff; Gervais, 'La jurisprudence allemande des prises maritimes durant la seconde guerre mondiale', *RGDIP*, 1951, 481ff; on the procedural burden of proof in various prize jurisdictions, see Colombos, *Law of Prize*, 184ff.

[77] Colombos, *Law of Prize*, 1.

[78] *Ibid.*, 38ff. For subsidiary rules on recapture see Rousseau, *Conflits armés*, 313.

[79] *The Zamora*, (1916) 2 AC 77, 91, 550.   [80] Above, p. 163.

[81] For example, H. Triepel, 'Les rapports entre le droit international et le droit interne', 23 *RCADI* 1923, i, 77.

waters. Prizes must not be taken in neutral territorial waters.[82] Such rules also indicate how important it is to have clear knowledge of the width of territorial waters[83] and of the methods by which these are measured.[84] Nor may prizes be taken in internal waters, in rivers, ports, river basins or lakes.[85]

The type of vessels that must not be taken include hospital ships[86] or those carrying wounded or medical supplies.[87]

Fishing vessels are not subject to prize[88] provided they are only engaged in coastal shipping[89] and provided they do not take part in hostilities.[90] Vessels engaged in small local trade are also exempt,[91] again on the condition that they do not join in hostilities.[92] Ships for religious purposes are also protected on analogy with hospital ships.[93] There are special rules for ships under construction.[94] Neutral vessels are not subject to prize as laid down in the Declaration of Paris of 1856.[95] In this respect the Declaration clarified and entrenched a controversial rule.[96] According to the same Declaration neutral property on board enemy ships is also immune from prize.[97] The Declaration of Paris was soon regarded as codifying the law of nations.[98]

Does the law of prize apply only to private ships? There is naturally a problem of imbalance in case the 'international'[99] law of prize

---

[82] E.g. *The Vrow Anna Catharina*, (1805), 6 C. Rob. 45.
[83] For the relevance to prize law, see Colombos, *Law of Prize*, 110.
[84] For the background see D. P. O'Connell, 'The juridical nature of the territorial sea', *BYIL*, 1971, 303.
[85] For cases, see Rousseau, *Conflits armés*, 284–5.
[86] Hague X, article 3; cf. Geneva II, articles 22 and 24; cf. articles 26, 27, 29, 30, 34, 35 and 48; Protocol I of 1977, article 22; *The Ophelia*, (1915) P. 129; Colombos, *Law of Prize*, 145ff; for violations see Rousseau, *Conflits armés*, 295.
[87] Geneva II, article 38; Geneva IV, article 21; Protocol I of 1977, article 23.
[88] *The Young Jacob and Johanna*, (1798) 1 C. Rob. 19.a.
[89] *The Stoer*, (1916) 5 LRPC 18; *The Paquete Habana*, *The Lola*.
[90] Hague XI, article 3(2).
[91] Hague XI, article 3(1). But tugs and lighters are not protected: *The Atlas*, (1916) 2 B & CPC 470.
[92] Hague XI, article 3(2).
[93] Hague XI, article 4; *The Paklat*, (1915) 1 B & CPC 515.
[94] *The Hermes, Schiffahrt Treuhand and Others* v. *HM Procurator General*, (1953) AC 232.
[95] Article 2. On the historical background, see C. G. Westman, *Folkrätten och den neutrala handeln*, Stockholm, 1924, 12ff.
[96] Colombos, *Law of Prize*, 164.   [97] Article 3.
[98] E.g. *The Marie Glaeser*, (1914) P. 218, 233; cf. *The Kronprinsessan Margareta*, (1921) 1 AC 486, 503; *The Schlesien*, (1914) 1 B & CPC 13; *The Miramichi*, (1915) P. 71; *The Batavier*, (1918) P. 66; *The Roumanian*, (1916) AC 124.
[99] Above, p. 306.

cannot be applied to all political systems equally. In the socialist States there are no 'private' ships so if the law of prize applies only to such vessels it would greatly undermine the uniformity of rules. Therefore, it is suggested that the law of prize applies to all merchant ships which are not warships, even those which are State-owned. Such rules would be consistent with new attitudes on loss of immunity of States for commercial activities.[100] But State practice is somewhat hesitant, as the interception of the Soviet ships *Selenga* and *Vladimir Mayakowski* in 1940 may show. These ships were transferred to French authorities for 'administrative reasons' and then released.[101]

Enemy character[102] is usually assessed in the Anglo-Saxon world by the domicile[103] and elsewhere by the nationality.[104] For companies, the registration[105] or enemy control[106] is usually decisive.

In the case of ships the normal rule of attaching enemy character is the flag,[107] but such rules are probably supplemented to cater for the case of flags of convenience.[108] The possible enemy nature of the cargo is assessed by the domicile of the owner[109] or by his nationality, supplemented by a rule of inherent enemy character of all produce of enemy soil.[110] There is also a presumption for enemy character of the cargo of an enemy merchant ship.[111]

There are temporal limitations to the right of capture. There are sometimes days of grace for neutral vessels in the port of a belligerent

[100] Cf. my 'Foreign warships', 57–60.   [101] Rousseau, *Conflits armés*, 289–90.
[102] See above, p. 102.   [103] *The Anglo-Mexican*, (1918), AC 422.
[104] The nationality principle is adopted and applied by all States of Western and Eastern Europe except for the United Kingdom. Only in case of 'formal' nationality will exceptions be made to this general rule: *Desiree* v. *Withold Szwabowics*, (1956) *Nytt Juridiskt Arkiv*, 337.
[105] *The Poona*, (1915) 1 B & CPC 275; cf. *The Tommi*, (1914) P. 251; for the United States, see *Fritz Schultz Co.* v. *Raimes & Co.*, (1917) 164 NYS 454, 458.
[106] *Continental Tyre & Rubber Co. Ltd* v. *Daimler Co. Ltd*, (1916) 2 AC 307.
[107] *The Vrow Elizabeth*, (1803) 5 C. Rob. 2; *The Unitas*, (1950) AC 536 (PC); *The Hamborn*, AD, 1919–22, 425.
[108] Rousseau, *Conflits armés*, 298–9 on other criteria. There are special rules for the effects of change of flag, see Declaration of London, 1909, articles 55–6, involving similar precautions as in bankruptcy and tax cases on presumptions and time limits: thus, transfers may be held valid if they take place more than 60 days before the opening of hostilities; later transfers are valid only if certain presumptions of illegality are not rebutted: Dacia, Conseil des prises français, *RGDIP*, 1915, 83; *ibid.*, 1917, 45.
[109] *The William Bagaley* (1866) 5 Wall. 377, 408; cf. Lewis, 'Domicile as a test of enemy character', 4 *BYIL* 1923–4, 60, 62.
[110] *The Phoenix*, (1803) 5 C. Rob. 20, 21; cf. Declaration of London 1903, article 58, 3 *AJIL* 1909, Suppl., 186.
[111] Cf. Declaration of London 1909, article 59; cf. below, p. 102.

at the time of commencement of war.[112] If a merchant ship is in enemy port at the outbreak of hostilities it will either be allowed to depart at once or after some interval, or, alternatively, ordered to remain in port until hostilities have ended, when it must be released. The port State retains a requisitioning power against adequate compensation, but has no right of capture.[113] According to most authorities, the right of capture is suspended during armistice. Yet German doctrine claims that the right still exists.[114]

A neutral vessel can lose its privilege of not being subjected to prize either by carrying contraband or by performing other 'unneutral services' of a direct or indirect nature. Among such services is the carrying of information or despatches or transmitting such information by telegraphy[115] or by carrying military personnel, however small the numbers.[116]

Neutral merchant vessels are subjected to a belligerent's right of visit and search so that the nature of their cargo can be established.[117] After inspection of the cargo and the ship's papers a neutral merchantman must be allowed to sail.

Enemy cargo may always be taken as prize together with the ship or independently of the ship. But cargo on a neutral ship may be captured only if it constitutes contraband.[118] This applies to cargo owned by the enemy, at least as far as private goods are concerned.[119] The right of prize is even extended to ancillary depots in port.[120] Types of contraband that will make neutral vessels and neutral cargo liable to seizure were initially classified in groups of 'absolute' and 'conditional' contraband. Types of absolute contraband are, accord-

[112] Colombos, *Law of Prize*, 121ff.   [113] Hague VI, articles 1–2.
[114] *The Goulfar*, II, Hamburg Prisengericht, 19.12.1940; *The Leontios Tergazos* and *The Paolina Perla*, *AD*, 1943–5, 141, 167, 466; 1969, 414. *RGDIP*, 1950, 301. E. Kappelhoff-Wulff, *Die Zulässigkeit der Ausübung des Prisenrechts während eines Waffenstillstandes*, Hamburg, 1973.
[115] *The Edna*, (1921) AC 735, 745.
[116] *The Orozembo*, (1807) 6 C. Rob. 430, 434; French Conseil des prises, *The Federico*, 10.5.1915, *JO*, 1915, 2995; *ibid.*, 17.8.1916, *JO*, 1916, 7505.
[117] *The Marianne Flora*, (1826) 11 Wheaton 3; Colombos, *Law of Prize*, 711; Pearce Higgins, 'Visit search and detention', *BYIL*, 1926, 43. See also *The West Breeze* incident involving a British ship during the Algerian War, A. van Zwanenberg, 'Interference with ships on the high seas', 10 *ICLQ* 785.
[118] Cf. Declaration of Paris of 1856, article 2, 1 *AJIL* 1907, Suppl., 89.
[119] On public goods, see H. A. Smith, 'The Declaration of Paris in modern war', 55 *Law Quarterly Review* 1939, 237.
[120] *Roumanian*, *AD*, 1939–42, 299; *Anichab*, *AD*, 1942, 483; *Salmonpool*, *AD*, 1943–5, 471; *Kanto Maru*, *ibid.*, 496.

ing to the London Declaration of 1909,[121] goods like weapons and ammunition, and other articles designed for war. Conditional contraband is what may be used either for war or for peaceful purposes.[122] According to the London Declaration[123] certain raw materials can never be considered as contraband.

However, in practice this sharp division between different types of contraband has been difficult to maintain[124] and often other criteria than adaptability for war use have been thought relevant. The condition that contraband must be susceptible to belligerent use has gradually been abandoned as any goods can be useful to the enemy. The identification of contraband was widened during the First World War by the operations of numerous presumptions of belligerent use, for example in the case of goods that were destined for use by an enemy government or its administration,[125] or if they were destined for an enemy port. Such considerations of belligerent use applied even in the case of foodstuffs,[126] reasoning being that food for the civilian population will indirectly raise the rations of food given to the armed forces.

It could be questioned whether such reasoning is compatible with the new prohibitions of starvation methods of war.[127] The prohibition may not affect blockade,[128] but capture by prize would have very much the same effect provided such capture concerned sufficient quantities of foodstuffs.

The theory of 'infection' – that innocent goods lose their quality of being innocent if they are shipped together with contraband – was first laid down in the Declaration of London of 1909 and widened considerably the right of capture by prize. The theory depended, in its practical application, on the relative proportion of contraband in relation to the whole cargo[129] and was widely applied,[130] although States were not technically bound by the London Declaration.[131]

The theory was usually applied by objective criteria and the per-

---

[121] Article 22; the list was elaborated by the Fourth Committee at the 1907 Hague Conference.
[122] *Ibid.*, article 24.   [123] *Ibid.*, articles 28–9.
[124] J. W. Garner, 'Violations of maritime law by the Allied powers during the World War', 25 *AJIL* 1931, 26, 33.
[125] *The Kim*, (1915) P. 215.   [126] *The Håkan*, (1918) AC 148, 151.
[127] Above, p. 252.   [128] Above, p. 267.
[129] *The Håkan*, (1916) P. 284.
[130] *The Frédéric*, French Conseil des prises, 19.5.1922, *JO*, 1922, 5277; *The Kyzicos*, Italian Corte di prede, 24.5.1916, Gazz. Uff., 1916.
[131] Above, p. 265.

sonal *culpa* or knowledge of the owner or master was irrelevant,[132] or knowledge would be 'inferred' from the quantity of carried contraband.[133] But in later decisions at least English Courts required a shipowner's knowledge of the nature of the cargo before a ship could be forfeited.[134] This applies even if the ship is under charter when knowledge of the charterers does not dispense with the shipowner's knowledge.[135] In conjunction with the criterion of susceptibility to belligerent use, the actual enemy destination has been decisive and the assessment of such destination includes transit and transhipment.

This area of law is still of topical importance, as is shown by numerous cases relating to goods bound for Israel. In recent years Egypt has intercepted contraband bound for Israel in the Suez Canal,[136] but the Security Council has held that this is an abuse of the right at sea of visit, search and seizure.[137]

The ultimate destination is objectively assessed independently of the intention of shipper or master,[138] and is subject to the doctrine of a construed 'continuous voyage'.[139] This doctrine has been applied to all types of contraband,[140] but does not apply to blockades.[141]

Any shipment by endorsable Bill of Lading creates a presumption of hostile destination.[142] The same applies in the case of blacklisted consignors and consignees[143] in what has been called 'statistical' cases[144] where the presumption of hostile destination is caused by a sudden and disproportionate increase in imports to a neutral country: by the sheer quantity criterion some goods are 'likely' to be re-

---

[132] *The Kronprinsessan Margareta*, (1921) 1 AC 486, 505; *The Lorenzo*, (1914) 1 B & CPC 226; but for earlier views on the relevance of subjective criteria see *The Ringende Jacob*, (1798) 1 C. Rob. 89.
[133] *The Hakan*, (1916) P. 266.
[134] *The Zamora*, (1921) 1 AC 810.
[135] *The Ran*, (1919) P. 317.
[136] On Suez traffic see Brown, 'World prize law applied in a limited war situation', 849; M. Cross, 'Passage through the Suez Canal of Israeli bound cargo and Israeli ships', 51 *AJIL* 1957, 530.
[137] E.g. SC, S/2322, 1951. Cf. R. Lapidoth, 'The reopened Suez Canal in international law', 4 *Syracuse Journal of International Law and Commerce* 1976, 37.
[138] *The Norden*, Hamburg Prisengericht, (1917) 1 *Grotius Annuaire International* 1917, 272; *The Pacific*, (1920) 5 Lloyd's 103, 106.
[139] *The Balto*, (1917) P. 79: there are stringent requirements for breaks in the chain; *The Kim*, (1915) P. 215, 249.
[140] *The Kyzicos*, Italian Corte di prede, (1916) Gaz. Uff., 24.5.1916, no. 122.
[141] Cf. article 19 of the Declaration of London 1909.
[142] *The Louisiana*, (1918) AC 261; *The Kim*, (1915) P. 215; French Conseil des prises, *The Fortuna*, 14.6.1915, *JO*, 1915, 3903; *ibid.*, 27.4.1917, *JO*, 1917, 3362.
[143] *The Stanton*, (1917) AC 380.   [144] Colombos, *Prize*, 195.

exported to the enemy.[145] There is even a constructive enemy destination if neutral territory is used by the enemy for supplies[146] or if a
State is under 'strong influence' by one of the belligerents.[147]

The rules on contraband, developed in detail for the law of prize,
have been analogously applied to justify confiscation of contraband
elsewhere than at sea. Here, too, criteria of likely belligerent use has
often been held to be decisive. Thus, in considering whether 'oil'
constitutes 'munitions of war', courts have attached importance to
the fact that it had to be refined before it could be put to military use
and that, therefore, if it had not undergone relevant refining processes, it did not constitute contraband.[148]

(3) Requisition There are provisions for the protection of private
property, and of certain State property, during assault and during
occupation.[149] However, an occupying power has a right to levy
taxes provided this is done, as far as possible, in accordance with the
rules of assessment in force.[150] An occupying power has also a far-
reaching power of requisition for the 'needs' of the army of occupation. Such requisitions must be in proportion to the resources of the
occupied country.[151] Furthermore, there must be a real military
necessity for the taking.[152] The power may take only what belongs to
the occupied State or its citizens. Ownership of property to be taken
should be verified before seizure.[153] There is a provision that the
occupying power shall pay for requisitions 'as far as possible in

[145] *The Baron Stjernblad*, (1918) AC 173.
[146] French Conseil des prises, 21.5.1918, *JO*, 1918, 4464.
[147] *The Blommersdijk*, (1917) Hamburg Prisengericht, 1 *Grotius Annuaire International*, 1917, 245.
[148] *NV de Bataafsche Petroleum Maatschappij and Others* v. *War Damage Commission*, (1956) Singapore Court of Appeal, 23 *ILR* 810.
[149] Above, p. 150.
[150] Hague Regulations, article 48; *The Lighthouse Case*, (1956), French–Greek Arbitration Tribunal, *RGDIP*, 1959, 282. But 'contributions' to an occupying force must not be used as reprisals, above, p. oo; cf. I. Seidl-Hohenveldern, Kontribution, in K. Strupp and H. J. Schlochauer, *Wörterbuch des Völkerrechts*, 2nd edn, Berlin, 1969, 300.
[151] Hague Regulations, article 52(1); W. M. Franklin, 'Municipal property under belligerent occupation', *AJIL*, 1944, 383; P. Jessup, 'A belligerent occupant's power over property', *AJIL*, 1944, 457; L. H. Woolsey, 'The forced transfer of property in enemy occupied territory', *AJIL*, 1943, 282.
[152] Cf. The Beth-El Case, (1978) Supreme Court of Israel, reported in M. Shamgar, *Military Government in the Territories Administered by Israel 1967–1980*, Jerusalem, 1982, 371; cf. *The Matityahu Case*, (1979), *ibid.*, 398.
[153] Cf. C. Dominicé, 'La notion de caractère ennemi des biens privés dans la guerre sur terre', diss., Geneva, 1961.

cash'.[154] If this is not possible, a receipt shall be given and 'the payment of the amount due shall be made as soon as possible'.[155]

The power in occupation may take possession of cash and all other movable State property as well as appliances for the transmission of news or other appliances adapted for transport and other 'munitions' of war, even if owned by private individuals.[156] This constitutes what might be called 'vital' property for the war effort and slightly different rules apply with regard to promptness of compensation. All taken property must be returned after the end of war when compensation must also be fixed if not already assessed and paid.[157] However, there have been cases where property was confiscated without compensation.[158] Requisitions of private property without compensation in violation of these rules are equivalent to theft.[159] Even heirs can sue for compensation if property has been wrongly taken.[160] If property is taken without compensation extraterritorial effect of the transfer may also be denied.[161]

But it may be difficult for persons to retrieve property or obtain compensation by suing in foreign courts as States are often granted immunity for requisitions.[162]

The right of requisition may also exist *vis-à-vis* neutrals, but full compensation must be paid.[163] However, the remedies under rules of *postliminium*[164] might assist a rightful owner after occupation has ceased to retrieve requisitioned goods which were taken from him.[165]

There is also a right over enemy property situated in the territory

---

[154] Hague Regulations, article 52(3); cf. Austria, BGH (1951), *ILR* 1951, 694.
[155] Hague Regulations, article 52(3).   [156] *Ibid.*, article 53(1) and (2).
[157] *Ibid.*, article 53(2).   [158] Cf. *The Interhandel Case, ICLQ*, 1961, 495.
[159] *Rosenberg* v. *Fischer*, (1948) Swiss BGH, *AD*, 1948, 467.
[160] See *The French Company Compensation Case*, (1966) Federal Supreme Court of Germany, *AD*, 1966, 454, where the German administration had taken property in 1940 and transferred it to a French–German partnership; compensation was due by the heirs of the German partner to the heirs of the French partner.
[161] E.g. *United Bank* v. *Cosmis International Incorporated*, (1976) 542 2nd 868, on nationalisation in Bangladesh without compensation; effects were denied in the United States as far as debts in that country were concerned; *Tran Qui Than* v. *Blumenthal*, (1979) US District Court, Northern District California, 469 F. Suppl., 1202.
[162] See *Ministry of Foreign Affairs* v. *Federici and Japanese State*, (1968) Trib. of Rome, 65 *ILR* 275, 279; cf. *NV Exploitatie Maatschappij Benkalis* v. *Bank of Indonesia*, (1963) 65 *ILR* 348; cf. also *The Oder-Neisse Expropriation Case*, (1975) Oberlandesgericht Munich, *Neue juristische Wochenschrift*, 1975, 2144; 65 *ILR* 127.
[163] *Norwegian Shipowners Claim*, (1922) 11 *RIAA* 237.
[164] F. Castberg, *Postliminium*, Uppsala, 1944, 28.
[165] E.g. Poland, *AD*, 1919–22, no. 342; Belgium, *ibid.*, no. 343; Italy, *ibid.*, 1927–8, no. 384.

of a belligerent.[166] Thus, private enemy assets in a country which is not occupied may be taken. Sometimes such assets are used to indemnify a State's own nationals for war damage. This was the case with regard to taken enemy assets in the United States after the Second World War under the War Claims Act of 1962.[167]

(4) Angary Angary implies the right to take *foreign* merchant ships for own use against compensation. The property at risk under such a right is thus the property of non-belligerents, and very often the property of neutrals.[168] Established rules of naval warfare stipulate that such seizure may take place only in territorial waters.[169] The right of angary is mainly designed for emergencies[170] and can be exercised only in cases of clear 'necessity'.[171] The existence of necessity comes near usual arguments on military necessity[172] and some have linked the two concepts.[173]

The nature of angary is different from requisitions. Angary leaves ownership unaltered and, therefore, there is a clear distinction between angary and requisitions or forms of expropriation.[174]

But the right of angary has often been abused and shows yet another instance where 'military necessity' distorts, rather than adapts, the Law of War.[175] The leading case is said to be the *Duclair Case*, when German troops sank six, possibly seven, British coal ships to block the passage of the Seine in 1871 during the German war with France. Bismarck suggested that this was permissible under the Law

[166] Cf. E. Turlington, 'Treatment of enemy property in the United States before the World War', *AJIL*, 1928, 270; Dominicé, 'La notion de caractère ennemi'; J. A. Gathings, *International Law and American Treatment of Alien Enemy Property*, Washington, DC, 1940.
[167] M. Domke, 'The War Claims Act of 1962', *AJIL*, 1963, 354.
[168] E. Albrecht, 'Requisitionen von neutralen Privateigentum inbesondere von Schiffen', 6 *ŻaöRVR*, Suppl., 1912.
[169] A. H. Schröder, *Das Angarienrecht, die Beschlagnahmne von Handelsschiffen im Kriege*, Kiel, 1965, 21ff; for a discussion of definitions, see R. Arnsberg, 'Das Angarienrecht', diss., Greifswald, 1922, 49.
[170] Arnsberg, 'Das Angarienrecht', 49; G. Balladore Pallieri, *3 Diritto internazionale pubblico, La guerra*, Padua, 1946, 403; G. Dahm, 1 *Völkerrecht*, Kiel, 1952, 638: angary is 'ein Notstandrecht'.
[171] 3 Phillimore 84 speaks of 'overriding necessity'; cf. 3 Calvo 138 on 'nécessité d'ordre supérieur'.
[172] Below, p. 332.
[173] J. C. Bluntschli, *Das moderne Völkerrecht*, Nördlingen, 1878, 795; J. C. den Beer Poortugael, *Het internationaal maritiem recht*, Breda, 1888, 413.
[174] J. S. Constantinides, *La requisition des navires étrangers*, Marseilles, 1942; cf. 4 Moore 3791.
[175] Cf. below, p. 332.

of War as the action was caused by necessity and the action taken formed part of *jus angariae*.[176] Bismarck even claimed that France should pay compensation for the neutral coal ships but, to avoid British intervention in the Franco–German war, Germany eventually offered to pay compensation. It is remarkable that there were no protests from the United Kingdom with regard to the legitimacy of the action and to the claims that such measures would form part of the right of angary.[177]

The right of angary is, if it is ever legitimate, explained as interference with property, against compensation, for the war effort. It is not, on the one hand, meant to deprive the owner of assets of his property, as in the case of requisition or expropriation, but, as ownership remains, to use property on some limited time basis. The property may, subjected as it will be to the hazards of war, be destroyed, but that is a contingency to be taken into account when compensation is assessed and does not form part of any original intention.

Some have defended the *Duclair Case* as actually illustrating the right of angary, rather than the illegitimate interference with neutral goods, as the incident rather seems to suggest. Such writers have argued that it is merely the time limit which is different in the case of typical angary and in the event of that case: if there had been a time gap between the taking and the destruction of the ships it would have constituted a normal case of angary; even though there was no such gap the taking comes under the same heading.[178]

The use of angary has sharply declined and few modern examples can be furnished.[179] There has also been a tendency to preclude the use of any such right by prohibition by treaty.[180]

(5) The uneven right of taking The right to capture ships as prize is a right of States. Any attempt by a resistance movement or guerilla group to take a ship of any kind[181] would, in peacetime, be classified as hijacking, terrorism or theft, or, in some cases, piracy. In war it would be legitimate only if it concerned enemy warships.

---

[176] 21 Staatsarchiv, Urkunden, 4498.
[177] See letter from Lord Granville, *ibid.*, 4505; cf. J. E. Hartley, 'The law of angary', 13 *AJIL* 1919, 290.
[178] J. Le Clere, *Les mesures coércitives sur les navires de commerce étrangers, Angarie-Embargo*, Paris, 1940.
[179] But see Greek–Bulgarian Arbitration Commission, (1926), *AD*, 1925–6, 456; *The Zamora*, (1915) (PC); Tribunal de Commerce de Marseille (1945), *AD*, 1946, 238.
[180] See Schröder, *Das Angarienrecht*, 40ff.
[181] E.g. the taking of the *Achille Lauro* in 1985.

But the right to requisition has been thought to be a right also of resistance forces who, in this respect, are put on an equal footing with a State. However, only resistance movements of considerable consolidation in emergency situations in wartime have been held entitled to requisition property.[182]

b. The effects of war on contracts

Contracts between citizens of a belligerent and alien enemies are normally not allowed and in the Anglo-Saxon world often regarded as *ipso facto* dissolved and terminated. Earlier contracts will be suspended if necessary.[183] The peace treaties after the First World War[184] and the Second World War[185] followed the Anglo-Saxon practice of holding private contracts concluded with the enemy void. Courts in France had similar attitudes even earlier[186] and will now normally consider contracts with the enemy null and void as being contrary to public policy.[187] Although national legislation often existed on the prohibition of payment, practice in Germany did not regard any contracts as *ipso facto* dissolved, but decided *in casu* whether there had been impossibility, as in any private contract situation.[188]

Contracts are regarded as frustrated[189] or affected by impossibility at least as far as regards certain executory contracts.[190] Such contracts are not even revived after peace.[191]

The rationale of this rule is that no contract must benefit the enemy. Consequently, contracts between enemy aliens, both resident in another State, may be upheld.[192] In a similar vein, specific performance may be obtained for a contract under which the plaintiff had taken possession of the relevant property when war broke out and there was no gain accruing to the enemy by the execution of a deed.[193]

---

[182] For France, *The Herzog Case*, Conseil d'Etat, 15.6.1951, *RGDIP/RDP*, 1953, 1131; Italy, Turin, 11.7.1947, *AD*, 1948, 428; Rousseau, *Conflits armés*, 77ff.
[183] *AD*, 1919–22, 394.   [184] Treaty of Versailles, e.g. article 299.
[185] E.g. Peace Treaty with Italy, 1947, Annex 16.
[186] M. Markovitch, *Des effets de la guerre sur les contracts entre particuliers*, Paris, 1912.
[187] Rousseau, *Conflits armés*, 52.   [188] 2 Berber 205.
[189] McNair, *Legal Effects*, 4th edn, 133.
[190] *2nd Russian Insurance Co.* v. *Miller, Alien Custodian*, (1924), 297 Fed. 407; (1925), aff'd 268 US 552; *Heidner* v. *St Paul & Tacoma Lumber Company of New York*, (1923) 124 Wash. 652.
[191] *Neumond* v. *Farmers Feed Co. of NY*, (1926) 244 Fed. 202.
[192] *Kannengiesser* v. *Israelowitz*, (1919) 107 Misc. 349, 176 NY Suppl., 535.
[193] *Hoshang and Others* v. *Eddie Barucha and Others*, (1966) High Court of Pakistan, PLD Karachi 752; 53 *ILR* 607.

Conversely, a contract with a 'loyal citizen' in enemy country will be prohibited if, as a result of his actions, resources will be furnished to the enemy.[194] It is not the war which prevents the performance of a contract but acts done in furtherance of actual war. A contract, in the event a charter party, was not automatically frustrated by the Iran–Iraq War.[195] A contract may come to an end because it amounts to 'trading with the enemy'.[196] But apart from that doctrine a court will consider whether a contract is affected by the war and, secondly, whether the duration of the war will cause the factual impossibility of performance.[197]

The projected length of war will be decisive to a court's attitude as to whether performance is realistically possible.[198] In contract, it is thus mainly a question of delay of performance, a delay which, if it is likely to be substantial, will lead to frustration of the contract. If the cause of the delay is 'coterminous' with the war itself, or with an act in the furtherance of war, such as, for example, blockade, a presumption arises that the contract is frustrated.[199]

An executory contract which is to be considered abrogated must either 'involve intercourse [with the enemy], or its continued existence must in some way [be] against public policy as that has been laid down in decided cases'.[200]

If a contract does not require execution by transactions with the enemy, it will normally not be terminated.[201] Furthermore, 'acquired rights'[202] are not affected according to some authorities, often by asserting that the transaction is of no benefit to the enemy.[203]

---

[194] *Sutherland (Alien Property Custodian)* v. *Mayer*, (1926) 271 US 272.
[195] *Finelvet AG* v. *Vinava Shipping Co. Ltd, The Chrysalis*, (1983) 2 Lloyds LR 658, *per* Mustill J.; cf. *Akties Nord-Osterso Rederiet* v. *E. A. Casper Edgar & Co. Ltd*, (1923) 14 Lloyds LR 203; see *Geipel* v. *Smith*, (1872) LR 7 QB 404 on difficulties on performing during the French–German War; *Horlock* v. *Beal*, (1916) 1 AC 486 on contract being affected by acts during the First World War.
[196] Above, p. 316.
[197] *Akties Nord-Osterso Rederiet* v. *E. A. Casper Edgar & Co.*, (1923) 14 Lloyds LR 203 at 207 *per* Lord Sumner.
[198] *Kodros Shipping Corp.* v. *Empresa Cubana de Fleta, The Evia*, (1982) 3 All ER 350. Cf. e.g. *Bank Line Ltd* v. *Arthur Capel*, (1919) AC 435; *Denny Mott & Dickson Ltd* v. *James B. Fraser & Co.*, (1944) 1 All ER 678 AC.
[199] R. G. McElroy and G. L. Williams, *Impossibility of Performance*, Cambridge, 1941, 176.
[200] *Ertel Bieber & Co.* v. *Rio Tinto Co. Ltd*, (1918) AC 260, 269.
[201] For a secondary 'viable' contract arising out of a previous terminated one, see *Ottoman* v. *Jebara*, (1928) AC 269 *per* Viscount Dunedin.
[202] But for a criticism of the doctrine of acquired rights see my *Finance*, 105ff.
[203] E.g. *Tingley* v. *Muller*, (1917) 2 Ch. 144.

Some executory contracts relating to rights of property, especially between landlord and tenant, are not avoided by war.[204] Interest may also be payable on a debt as 'incidental' to another transaction.[205]

Occasionally an alien may be refused to take inheritance under national laws,[206] but in other cases it has been held that such private rights, especially if entrenched by treaty, are unaffected by war,[207] even if a disposition was made to a resident in enemy country,[208] as such taking did not come within the Trading with the Enemy Act.[209]

An enemy alien is often deprived of the power to sue in local courts. The normal rule is that an enemy alien cannot sue,[210] but he has the right to defend himself.[271] Trading with the Enemy Acts often contain provisions to deprive enemy aliens of certain judicial remedies.[212] Such restrictions sometimes affect only those who owe allegiance to an enemy country.[213] In other cases courts have inferred enemy character from residence or from the 'likely gain' to the enemy if the suit is allowed.[214]

Identification of 'enemy alien' status in a Trading with the Enemy Act may depend solely on residence, so that aliens not so classified may continue their business unhampered and trade 'without the slightest governmental supervision'.[215] Other Courts have held that 'mere' residence does not lead to enemy character,[216] and may prefer criteria similar to those used to assess enemy character in prize law.[217]

There is a complicated question of when a company is to be of

---

[204] E.g. *Halsey* v. *Lowenfeld*, (1916) 2 KB 707, 716, where a contract on rent due to an enemy alien was not avoided by war; *Tingley* v. *Muller*, (1917) 2 Ch. 144 on a viable contract to buy a leasehold.

[205] *Hicks (Alien Property Custodian)* v. *Guiness*, (1925) 269 US 71.

[206] *Techt* v. *Hughes*, (1920) 229 NY 222.

[207] *Goos* v. *Brocks*, (1929) 117 Nebr. 750; *In Roeck's Estate*, (1922) 119 Misc. 190, 195 NY Suppl., 505.

[208] *Gregg's Estate*, (1920) 266 Pa. 189, 109 Atl. 777.   [209] Above, p. 00.

[210] *Ass. Cement Cos. Ltd* v. *Pakistan*, (1972) Pakistan PLD Lahore 201;*Guru Das Saha* v. *Deputy Custodian of Enemy Property*, (1969) PLD Dacca 841.

[211] *Province of East Pakistan* v. *Allahbad Bank Ltd*, (1968) PLD Dacca 1; *Haji Mohiuddin* v. *Sirajul Alam Chowdhury*, (1967) PLD Dacca 515.

[212] E.g. *Trading with the Enemy Act*, 1917, article 7(b), 40 Stat. 411, 417.

[213] *Ozbolt* v. *Lumbermen's Indemnity Exchange*, (1918) 204 SW 252.

[214] *Re Ref. No. 1 of 1965*, (1966) High Court of Pakistan, PLD Karachi 160; 53 ILR 613.

[215] *Tortoriello* v. *Seghorn*, (1918) 103 Atl. 393.

[216] *S. A. Latif* v. *J. B. Dubash*, (1970) Karachi PLD 220.

[217] Above, p. 308.

enemy character. Such character has been held to attach if the company was under 'enemy control'.[218]

Apart from the effect that war has on contract with the enemy there are also problems relating to contracts concluded between citizens in any one country, for example with regard to insurance of goods or transactions affected by a war. For instance, in the Iran–Iraq War a group of London underwriters decided, some six months before the outbreak of war, that rates for the area of the Gulf west and north of the Straits of Hormuz were to be increased. As for land, war risks have not been written since the Spanish Civil War, when, in 1937, it was decided by a consensus of underwriters that such insurance was no longer prudent.[219]

War risk now covers only marine insurance. Rates are increased from the normal war risk of 0.025 per cent in 1987 to about 0.05 in time of actual war. Underwriters are not concerned whether there is an inter-State or internal war and whether war has been declared or not: they will assess factual risks according to objective circumstances as reported to them.

In the Falklands War one substantial claim under war risk was made to Lloyds for a United States tanker hit in the area. This vessel had been well outside the zone.[220] Had it been inside the zone itself it would have entered at its own peril or possibly been guilty of nondisclosure of its planned course which must be reported to the insurance brokers for accurate assessment of the rate of premium.

---

[218] *Daimler Co. Ltd* v.*Continental Rubber Co. (GB) Ltd*, (1916) AC 307, 345. For detailed rules see McNair, *The Legal Effects of War*, 3rd edn, 1948, 44–69; for new rules that may be relevant in war situations as well, see *Barcelona Traction Case*, ICJ, *Report* (1970), 42.
[219] D. W. Gibb, *Lloyds of London*, London, 1957, 231.   [220] Above, p. 152.

Execution of an international convention implies the implementation of its provisions in practice. Without such execution the document's value in practical terms will be much reduced, even it if may still have important guiding functions for the behaviour of parties.

The shortage of rules on judicial settlement or arbitration in conventions is notorious. Often States can unilaterally denounce treaties and then mechanisms for execution become demoted even further; for if a State is allowed to rid itself of the obligations under a treaty it may prefer to do so rather than to subject itself to any apparently 'compulsory' procedure of settlement. On the other hand, there is a growing body of opinion in many States that certain treaties could not be denounced, especially those in the field of human rights or laws of war, as such treaties often lay down basic rights that are either valid already under international law[1] or under respective national constitutions.[2]

A. METHODS OF IMPLEMENTATION

i. The Weapons Conventions

The considerable problems of verification of compliance with the Weapons Conventions have been discussed earlier.[3] These problems, which have given rise to considerable literature on the subject,[4] have been more in focus than legal problems concerning breaches. For verification seeks to ensure compliance with a treaty, whereas provi-

---

[1] See above, p. 134 on the underlying obligation.
[2] See, for example, the French Constitution of 1958, embodying in its Preamble numerous human rights; it may even be that international law derived certain formulae on human rights from this Constitution.
[3] Above, pp. 92 and 230.
[4] See, for example, note 59, p. 92.

sions on breaches become relevant only once a breach has been verified. Verification has thus a twofold purpose: by various inspection methods and by the very existence of certain mechanisms, verification is intended to *preclude* that any breaches occur; and, secondly, by the same methods or mechanisms verification will furnish actual evidence and *prove* that there have been certain breaches of the obligations under a convention.

Apart from the verification procedures, which in themselves are weak and rudimentary in the Weapons Conventions, there are generally no specific provisions for breaches in these treaties and the rules on legal effects of breaches are left to general international law.[5] In one treaty, the En-Mod Convention, which stands half way between weapons agreements and treaties on warfare methods,[6] there is no clause on denunciation. On the contrary, the treaty is said to be for 'unlimited duration'.[7] However, such a stipulation would not normally preclude the denunciation of a treaty.[8] On the other hand, there are specific provisions on revision,[9] although such rights for amendment exist, without special authorisation, under the general law of treaties.[10] The En-Mod Convention also has a report system for breaches which implies that a party which has 'reason to believe' that there has been a breach may lodge a complaint with the Security Council. This provision is accompanied by a curious statement that a complaint must include 'all relevant information as well as all possible evidence to support its validity'.[11] Surely, any 'evidence' will come under 'relevant information' and it would therefore have been clearer if the provision had used the word 'including' instead of the misleading expression 'as well as'.

The State parties undertake to co-operate in any investigation which the Security Council may initiate in accordance with the Charter.[12] There are thus no sanctions for breaches incorporated in the Convention itself. On the other hand, when relevant information is brought to the notice of the Security Council it may proceed to other powers it has under the Charter and determine, *ex officio* that there is a threat to the peace warranting enforcement action. In this indirect way, therefore, one could possibly say that there are sanctions for certain breaches of this particular Convention.

---

[5] See, on the effect of breach in general, R. P. Mazzeschi, *Risoluzione e sospensione dei trattati per inadempimento*, Milan, 1984.
[6] Above, p. 227.   [7] Article VII.   [8] See my *Essays*, 89ff.   [9] Article VI.
[10] See my *Essays*, 71 ff.   [11] Article V(3).   [12] Article V(4).

ii. Treaties on methods and humanitarian rules

In the field of rules on warfare methods and humanitarian issues the position is different. Here, it is not the lack of provisions for implementation but the difficulty in applying these in practice that has given rise to problems. Thus, the Geneva Conventions have been difficult to implement although they had provisions dealing with execution.[13] There had been numerous armed conflicts when the Geneva Conventions had applied only through the mediation of the Red Cross.[14] Protocol I of 1977, but not Protocol II, includes provisions to ensure its execution. There is a stipulation that the high contracting parties *and* the parties to the conflict shall take all necessary measures to implement their obligations under the Protocol.[15] For its execution Protocol I thus relies on the assistance of groups which are not States.

The elaboration of new humanitarian obligations would be a hollow and futile exercise if there were no effective steps to bring about the compliance of assumed obligations.[16] However, when it came to ensure that the Protocols were coupled with adequate enforcement mechanisms, most States at the Conference refrained from action. Virtually all States present 'were responsible for the failure to include enforcement mechanism'.[17] Protocol I provides that all parties shall, without delay, take all necessary measures for the execution of their obligations under the Protocol.[18] Such measures are more comprehensive than the previous provisions in the Hague Regulations which referred only to orders to the land forces[19] or the Geneva Conventions.[20] Under article 84 all legislative and other measures must be communicated to the other parties of the Protocol.[21]

a. Protective power system

For the implementation of humanitarian rules the Geneva Conventions have adopted another system. The Geneva Conventions rely on a protective power system,[22] but the system has not been a success in

[13] Convention I, article 49–50; Convention II, article 50; Convention III, articles 126–8; Convention IV, articles 142–7.
[14] Cf. above, p. 168, and below, p. 325.   [15] Article 80.
[16] Cf. United States, A/C.6/37/SR.19, 5, para. 16.
[17] Forsythe, 'Legal management of internal war', 294.
[18] Article 80.   [19] Article 1 and above, p. 107.   [20] Above, p. 12.
[21] Article 84. See, further, Abi-Saab, 'Le mécanisme demise en oeuvre du droit humanitaire', 177.
[22] See Convention I, article 8–11; Convention II, articles 8 and 11; Convention II, articles 8 and 11, and Convention IV, articles 9 and 12.

practice. It has been used only twice, in Suez and in the Goa affairs in 1956 and 1971 respectively.[23] In the 1971 Bangladesh crisis Switzerland was nominated as a protective power, but the nomination was not accepted by India.[24]

Protocol I mentions protective powers in various contexts,[25] and it is clear that a system similar to that of the Geneva Conventions has been adopted. By the definitions in the Protocol[26] it is clear that a neutral State, or a State not party to the conflict, may be appointed as protecting power and can carry out functions under the Protocol. An 'impartial' body can presumably also undertake this task if the parties so agree.[27]

At the Conference there was a specific offer by the Sovereign Order of Malta to this effect and the representative underlined that the Order would be glad to co-operate with the ICRC, a body which, of course, is of great importance in this context.

There had been an attempt to secure an automatic appointment of the ICRC if other protective powers failed to be nominated.[28] The confidence of States in the ICRC was repeatedly assured,[29] but the article failed to be adopted.

The Protocol 'missed the opportunity of making an advance in the system of implementation of humanitarian law' by not making an offer to act as protective power compulsory.[30]

However, it was made clear that other organisations would also be prepared to assist as protective powers if so requested, for example the Organisation of African States.[31]

b. Fact finding commissions

The 1929 Convention on the Wounded and the Sick[32] provided for inquiries to be instituted in the case of alleged violations of the Con-

---

[23] Also before the Geneva Conventions there had been problems in appointing an *ad hoc* protective power, for example to supervise the treatment of prisoners of war in enemy territory. For instance, a request for such an appointment by Finland in the Winter War was refused by the Soviet Union, see Wulff, *Handbok i folkrätt under krig*, 241. On the traditional right of belligerents to select a protecting power to safeguard their interests when diplomatic relations have been suspended, see Rousseau, *Conflits armés*, 36–52.

[24] See Forsythe, *Humanitarian Politics*, 166.

[25] Articles 2, 5, 6(1), 11, 33, 45, 60(2), 78(1) and 84.   [26] Article 2(c).

[27] Cf. resolutions of the Institut de Droit International, on Conditions of Application of Humanitarian Rules of Armed Conflict to Hostilities in which the United Nations Forces may be Engaged, and Bindschedler-Robert, *Reconsideration*.

[28] E.g. Greece, CDDH/SR.37, vol. 6, 78.   [29] E.g. Belgium, CDDH/SR.47, vol. 6, 76.

[30] Egypt, *ibid.*, 77.   [31] Nigeria, *ibid.*, 80.   [32] Above, p. 275.

vention. The ICRC was called on, in this context, in the Italy–Abyssinian War in 1936 and in connection with the Katyn Affair in 1943.[33]

The Geneva Conventions also include some provisions on inquiries.[34] Although called upon under the relevant articles to inquire into alleged use of bacteriological weapons in the Korean War in 1952, the ICRC showed reluctance to carry out any investigations as it 'would be a first step of a judicial procedure which does not lie within its purview. Moreover, by assuming that role [of a body responsible for inquiries] the ICRC would find its neutrality called in question by at least one of the parties, to the detriment of the unquestionably useful humanitarian activities carried out on that party's territory.'[35] The United Nations Secretariat sometimes dispatches an inquiry team to verify compliance with the laws of war. Thus, a mission of the Secretary General was requested in 1985 to report on treatment of prisoners of war in the Iran–Iraq War.[36] The ICRC had suspended its protection activities in Iran in 1983 as a result of continuing difficulties due to which the ICRC found itself unable to fulfil its obligations under the Geneva Convention.[37]

Under Protocol I of 1977 an international Fact Finding Commission will be established if not less than 20 States accept its competence.[38] Only if States make an Optional Declaration, modelled on the Optional Clause of the Statute of the International Court of Justice, will they be bound by the findings of the Commission. This compromise was reached after some discussion and may show how sensitive States still are to allowing inspection groups in their territory. It must also be noted that the prospective Commission was not even granted any powers of decision but can only make recommendations.

The Commission, once established, will have the power to 'make enquiries' into alleged grave breaches of Protocol I and restore, through its good offices, respect for humanitarian values.[39] Its Chambers may invite parties to a conflict to produce evidence and it will

---

[33] ICRC, *Action by the ICRC in the Event of Breaches of International Humanitarian Law*, Geneva, 1981, 5.
[34] Geneva I, article 52; II, article 53; III, article 132, and IV, article 149.
[35] ICRC, *Action by the ICRC*, 5.   [36] S/16962, 19 February 1985.
[37] ICRC, *Second Memorandum of the ICRC to State Members Parties to the Geneva Convention of 1949 Concerning the Conflict between the Islamic Republic of Iran and the Republic of Iraq*, 10 February 1984; cf. CICR, *Appel*, 7 May 1983.
[38] Article 90(1)(b).   [39] Article 90(2)c ii.

'seek' other evidence as it finds appropriate. All evidence will be disclosed to the parties[40] but will not be made public.[41]

The Commission will, to some extent, be institutionalised, having special administrative facilities granted by Switzerland[42] and will be financed by contributions.[43]

The working of the Commission may well prove to be valuable and more effective than the 'condemning' practice of the General Assembly of the United Nations.[44]

c. Mediation

Mediation may prove a useful method of settling an armed conflict once it has commenced.[45] The ICRC has played an important role in mediation. This study has often referred to the role of the ICRC[46] and the functions of the ICRC may be underlined further in the context of mediation in armed conflicts as such mediation provides a means to ensure the application of humanitarian rules. In a paradoxical statement one commentator has summed up the role of the ICRC stating that 'The ICRC is too weak to be feared and that is the source of its strength.'[47] The ICRC may prove valuable as mediator to ensure the application of Protocol I and may also, unofficially, contribute as mediator for Protocol II. It has mediated in numerous hijacking and kidnapping incidents[48] and has experience of mediating in Indo-China, both during the French phase[49] and during the American phase.[50] It also mediated in Algeria.[51]

The reason for the success of the services of the ICRC in wars is undoubtedly that it is considered to be 'above the battle'. It was, for example, the only relief organisation able to assist in the Hungarian Revolution in 1956.[52] It was also the ICRC which, after the Suez débâcle in 1956, provided the first airliner between Israel and Egypt since the beginning of the war in Palestine in 1948.[53]

The ICRC is empowered under its own Statutes to take 'cognizance' of complaints regarding alleged breaches of the humanitarian Conventions,[54] but has also in practice intervened on its own initiative.[55] There is perhaps a distinction to be made between the intervention by the ICRC in some instances after reports of violation and

[40] Article 90(4)(b).　[41] Article 90(5)(c).　[42] Article 90(1)(f).
[43] Article 90(7).　[44] See Kalshoven, 'Reaffirmation and development', 122.
[45] Above, p. 97.　[46] See above, p. 124.　[47] Forsythe, *Humanitarian Politics*, 248.
[48] *Ibid.*, 29.　[49] *Ibid.*, 144ff.　[50] *Ibid.*, 152ff.　[51] *Ibid.*, 47ff.
[52] Joyce, *Red Cross International and the Strategy of Peace*, 167.　[53] *Ibid.*, 148.
[54] Article 6(4).　[55] ICRC, *Action by the ICRC*, 2–3.

in cases where the ICRC more clearly sets out to mediate between the parties to a conflict. But both types of action can be subsumed under a wide heading of mediation if this is construed to include all efforts to achieve compliance with the humanitarian Conventions.

One advantage of the ICRC mechanism is possibly the 'discretion' principle, which reassures States that no evidence will be disclosed to the outside world. The ICRC has often shown that it would not communicate any facts on alleged violations of the European Conventions of Human Rights, for example to the Council of Europe in the Greek case, although prompted to do so by the Scandinavian States.[56] There may have been, in that instance, a formal agreement between the ICRC and the Greek Government.[57] but even if there had been none States could rely on the discretion of the ICRC. Red Cross officials have certainly proved impartial in practice and have been devoid of any allegiance to particular States.[58]

The ICRC is not always able to visit detainees and prisoners of war when it wishes,[59] but may contribute towards solutions of problems by good offices if allowed to engage in full discussions.

The recognition by the ICRC of certain national Red Cross groups has great importance for the claimed statehood of certain factions,[60] but this issue must not be confused with its potential function as mediator between established States and liberation movements under Protocol I.

d. The role of individuals

Various treaties on the Law of War grant rights and protection to individuals. Certain duties are also imposed in that rebels, too, must wage only certain types of warfare and grant combatants and civilians the level of treatment stipulated. On the other hand, the mechanisms of execution of certain instruments of the Law of War, especially the Geneva Conventions and the Protocols of 1977, also depend on the assistance of individuals, as is expressly acknowledged by these treaties.

The Martens clause figured in the Preamble of the 1899 Conven-

[56] *Ibid.*, 43.   [57] *Ibid.*
[58] Some officials carry a Swiss passport in addition to the Red Cross *laissez passer*. See further Boissier, *Histoire du Comité International de la Croix-Rouge*; Huber, *The Red Cross, Principles and Problems*; H. G. Knitel, *Les délégations du CIRC*, IHEI, Geneva, 1967.
[59] On the difficulties of visiting Palestinian prisoners, see PLO-Observer, A/C.6/37/SR.19, 6, para. 19.
[60] See further *ibid.*, 16ff.

tions and the Fourth Hague Convention of 1907. The clause is named after the Russian negotiator at the Hague Conferences and is highly illustrative of the differences between the Law of War and other parts of international law. The clause has a supplementing function:

Until a more complete code of the laws of war has been issued, the High Contracting Parties deem it expedient to declare that in cases not included in the Regulations adopted by them, the inhabitants and the belligerents remain under the protection and the rule of the principles of the law of nations, as they result from the usages established among civilized peoples, from the laws of humanity, and the dictates of public conscience.

Thus, the clause would supply the necessary norms for cases where there was no textual support in the Convention or the annexed Regulations. But the Convention and the Regulations were concerned only with land warfare and the other Conventions concluded at the Hague in 1907[61] on, for example, naval warfare did not contain the clause. However, it was soon recognised that the clause covered all types of warfare and that it would supply valuable guidance in unregulated cases.

The Martens clause was upgraded in Protocol I of 1977 to form part of the substantive text. It is inserted among basic obligations,[62] such as the duty not to mutilate prisoners of war or not to carry out medical experiments on such persons or on civilians. The substance of the Martens clause provides that, in cases not covered by international agreements, civilians and combatants 'remain under the protection and authority of the principles of International Law derived from established custom, from the principles of humanity and from the dictates of public conscience'.[63] It has been suggested that the essence of the Martens clause rests on four principles: necessity, discretion, proportionality and humanity.[64] Others claim that the clause could be used for new developments in the sense of supplementing the law. The clause could be used for any change in, for example, combatant status.[65]

It may be simpler than that. The Martens clause probably covers the most basic rights and acts as a counter-weight to literally interpreted law. The Martens clause explains the existence of law which underlies the Convention although it has not been incorporated or

[61] Above, p. 97.   [62] Article 11.   [63] Protocol I 1977, article 1(2).
[64] R. Falk, 'Law and responsibility in warfare, the Vietnam experience', in P. D. Trooboff (ed.), *Law and Responsibility in Warfare, the Vietnam Experience*, Chapel Hill, North Carolina, 1975, 103ff.
[65] G. I. A. D. Draper, 'The legal classification of belligerent individuals', 149.

spelt out in the text. This might also mean that the impact of that law goes beyond the circle of the contracting parties. For if the law that can be discerned through the Martens clause exists, behind the textual world of treaties, it may be that its underlying obligation is derived from international law in general.[66] In that case States not bound by treaties in question might well be bound, albeit on another ground, by another mechanism or by another source of obligation, that which is entrenched in general international law. This is the line that certain courts have taken in trials concerning the treatment of persons in war. In one case it was, for example, held that the rules on the treatment of prisoners of war in the Hague Regulations applied to Germany even in the absence of ratification, as such rules form part of international law.[67] In another case it was considered 'irrelevant' whether or not the Soviet Union had adhered to the Geneva Convention of 1929; its provisions were binding in any event.[68]

What then is this conscience? States do not have a conscience, nor do groups. Who does? Individuals, combatants and those who actually fight the wars do. Is it not reasonable to think that it is they who in the unregulated cases will have to do their best to assess what the law might be, assuming at all times that the law itself must be reasonable?

Members of armed forces are sometimes instructed on the limits of their mission set in relation to the law. For example, British soldiers are issued with yellow cards indicating both their precise mandate and the limits of the law. By making the level of the mandate considerably more limited than the limits of the law, the soldier thus has a good latitude for personal errors of judgment. But the case may arise when he is unguided in his decision for action. Is he then not best equipped himself to decide what he must do? It seems that the Martens clause is merely an application of the rule of common sense in a practical situation.

In a sense, then, individuals are subjects of this limited part of international law which, sometimes, requires their assistance for its application.[69]

There was considerable discussion at the Diplomatic Conference

[66] Cf. above, pp. 134 and 259 on underlying obligations.
[67] See *Prisoner-of-War (Germany) Case*, (1919), *AD*, 1919–22, 433 (before the Leipzig Supreme Court).
[68] The Great War Criminals Case, IMT, 1.10.1946.
[69] Pictet, *Humanitarian Law and the Protection of War Victims*, 22; J. H. Schmid, *Die völkerrechtliche Stellung Partisanen im Kriege*, Zurich, 1956, 82.

on the ICRC Draft of 1973, as this Draft referred to the principles of humanity and the dictates of public conscience as a source outside international law.[70] The Martens clause was adopted in the final version and inserted in the main text in its original form which indicates that, in the opinion of the Conference, such principles and dictates form part of international law.

On the other hand, decisions are expected to be so difficult to take at times for the individuals involved in the execution of the Protocols that they will be expected to have legal advisers at hand to advise the military leaders on the 'appropriate level of application' of Protocol I.[71]

e. Dissemination

New rules cannot be implemented unless they are known. The Protocols provide that their contents are disseminated.[72] States have been urged by the Secretary General of the United Nations and by the ICRC to organise reunions to better understand and learn the contents of humanitarian rules.[73]

However, it may be noted that the laws of war do not form part of courses on international law in numerous universities and do not form part of any of the modern standard textbooks on international law.

[70] On the Draft see above, p. 157.   [71] Article 82.
[72] Protocol I, article 83; Protocol II, article 19.   [73] See *AFDI*, 1982, 686.

A. DENUNCIATION

The Weapons Conventions contain drastic rights of denunciation. The Biological Weapons Convention[1] of 1972 thus provides that 'Each State Party to the Convention shall in exercising its national sovereignty have the right to withdraw from the Convention if it decides that extraordinary events, related to the subject matter of the Convention, have jeopardised the supreme interests of its country.'[2] Such a provision clearly leaves great latitude to States in deciding subjectively[3] what their 'supreme interests' are. However, the adjectives 'extraordinary' and 'supreme' both convey some heightened obligation States have to show that objective circumstances warrant their subjective assessment. The provision appears to be an escape clause which leaves a loophole for States in case unusual action has to be taken. The way the clause reads, it also suggests that it may have to be a question of an emergency caused by some overhanging and immediate threat. But considering that the Convention deals mainly with the destruction of biological weapons stock,[4] it is difficult to visualise a situation where States would feel justified in safeguarding their 'supreme interests' by taking up further production of biological weapons. But the organisation of production of new biological weapons would involve some time, and this time element is difficult to reconcile with such a decision in an implied situation of emergency.

Similar clauses of denunciation have been included in the two major recent drafts of a Chemical Weapons Convention.[5] The United Kingdom Draft of 1976 thus refers to denunciation for 'supreme' national interests[6] and the United States 1984 Draft refers

---

[1] Above, p. 219.   [2] Article XIII(2).
[3] Cf. above, pp. 234, 236 and 238 on subjective criteria.
[4] See further above, p. 219.   [5] Above, p. 222.   [6] Article V.

to a State's right to withdraw from the Convention 'if it decides that extraordinary events, related to the subject matter of the Convention, have jeopardized the supreme interests of its country'.[7] The State must notify other States and the Security Council of the United Nations what such extraordinary events involve.[8]

The Conventional Weapons Convention of 1981[9] lays down a time limit for denunciation, a method which is not uncommon in treaty technique,[10] but which has a special significance to a weaponry treaty. The treaty allows specifically that it may be denounced by a party,[11] but it also stipulates that such denunciation will only take effect one year after receipt of notification of the denunciation.[12] Furthermore, the Convention will continue to apply to any war or armed conflict, and these situations include liberation wars,[13] in which a party is 'engaged' at the expiry of the one-year period. Such obligation to be bound by the Convention continues

until the end of the armed conflict or occupation and, in any case, until the termination of operations connected with the final release, repatriation or re-establishment of the person protected by the rules of International Law applicable in armed conflict, and in the case of any annexed Protocol containing provisions concerning situations in which peace-keeping, observation or similar functions are performed by United Nations forces or missions in the area concerned, until the termination of those functions.[14]

The application of the Convention is thus lengthened to make it difficult for States to denounce the Convention because of any actual involvement in war. The State would remain bound until the end of that war. It is to be noted that the Convention applies both to wars and to liberation wars[15] and it may be suggested that the only time a State would find it politically expedient and legally possible to denounce the Convention because of actual armed conflict would be in the situation of an internal war which did not qualify as a liberation war.

It is interesting that the Weaponry Convention prolongs its own application after denunciation even up to the stage of repatriation of prisoners of war, which usually takes place after the end of hostilities.[16] But if hostilities have ceased, the need for weapons will also have discontinued and the regulation of their use seems chronologically unwarranted. It may be that the phrase 'repatriation' was

[7] Article XVI(2).   [8] *Ibid.*   [9] Above, p. 180.   [10] See my *Essays*, 87.
[11] Article 9(1).   [12] Article 9(2).   [13] Above, p. 182.   [14] Article 9(2).
[15] Above, p. 158.   [16] Above, p. 298.

chosen to indicate what is normally held to be the final phase of termination of war.[17]

Another matter which should be clarified is the ambiguous reference in the denunciation clause to the United Nations forces or missions. The way the article reads suggests that these forces or missions have been given specific functions under the Protocols and that such functions also could lengthen the application of the Convention. But this is not so. The only Protocol that refers at all to the UN forces and missions is Protocol II on Treacherous Weapons,[18] which provides for enhanced protection of such forces and missions in a mined or booby-trapped area: the reason for the presence of such missions and forces lies outside the Protocol. But indirectly this means that it is ultimately the Security Council, or in exceptional cases the General Assembly,[19] that will have the power to decide that the Conventional Arms Convention will continue to apply in a war after the engaged State party has denounced the treaty, by prolonging the mandate of the United Nations forces or missions in the area.

The Geneva Conventions, as well as the Protocols of 1977, can be denounced by mere unilateral declarations.[20]

B. BREACH

Reasons for violating rules of war are often put forward as 'justifications' of breaches.[21]

i. *Ground for deviations*

a. *Military necessity*

The existence of military necessity was recognised in treaty law in the St Petersburg Declaration of 1868,[22] which established that there are 'technical limits at which military necessities ought to yield to the requirements of humanity'. By implication, there are thus cases when such limits will not yield. On the other hand, the defence plea of military necessity has sometimes been rejected completely as one 'condemned by the civilized world'.[23] There is no need to emphasise

[17] Above, p. 297.   [18] Above, p. 183.
[19] Under the Uniting for Peace Resolution, see my *Law Making*, 38–9.
[20] Geneva I, article 63; Geneva II, article 62; Geneva III, article 142; Geneva IV, article 158.   [21] Protocol I, article 99; Protocol II, article 25.
[22] 18 NRGT 1, série 474, and above, p. 135.
[23] *The Rauter Case*, (1948) *AD*, 1949, 543.

that it is a dangerous and harmful doctrine,[24] providing as it does a
loophole, an excuse, for every conceivable situation. There are end-
less cases where the defence plea has been raised to justify the suspension of virtually every rule of the Law of War. The concept is usually
known as military necessity but also *Kriegsraison*[25] or military security.[26] Military necessity suspends the criminal character of certain
war 'crimes' and converts them into legitimate acts. But military
necessity is a vague concept, often relying on a presumption that the
principle *vae victis* will pre-empt investigation as to justifications of
acts of the victor in a war after the end of hostilities.

There is great difficulty in reconciling any humanitarian rules of
warfare with 'military necessity'. On the one hand, a State already
engaged in a war is doing its utmost to win the war but, on the other
hand, this objective may be more easy to attain if the State resorts to
inhumane warfare. The elusive blanket phrase 'military necessity'
may undermine any advances made in the humanitarian field since,
again, it is a matter for the subjective assessment of the State whether
such necessity exists. Yet, there appeared to exist a core of identifiable
needs which determined whether a belligerent may take certain action and which made it possible to ascertain at least drastic ex-
cesses.[27]

The question of military necessity becomes most acute if there is a
question of shortening the war as a whole. Some have mentioned
Churchill's 'abhorrence' of liquidating German officers on a large
scale even if it would have shortened the war.[28] Some may, at the
same time, defend the dropping of the atom bomb on Japan during
the Second World War, as the decision had been taken 'in acute
tension'.[29]

In terms of the Law of War, the decision to use the Hiroshima–
Nagasaki atom bomb on a largely civilian population appears to be
questionable even if it was 'effective' in the sense that it shortened the
war. With regard to the 'tension' in which the decision-makers found

[24] W. G. Downey, 'The law of war and military necessity', 47 *AJIL* 1953, 251.
[25] Above, p. 34.
[26] E.g. *The Mannstein or Lewinski Case*, (1949) *AD*, 1949, 509 has been used to cover
similar ground.
[27] Cf. the allegation at the Nuremberg trials that some German generals had confused military necessity with convenience, e.g. *United States* v. *List et al.*, XI *Nuremberg
Trials of War Criminals*, 1252–5.
[28] K. J. Holsti, *International Politics, a Framework for Analysis*, 4th edn, Englewood
Cliffs, 1983, 381.
[29] *Ibid.*

themselves, a sharp distinction must be made between such a deliberate act, put into effect relatively slowly and involving the co-operation of numerous persons, and the overwhelming necessity that hallmarks any right to self-defence, or legitimate acts of necessity.

There arises, in any armed conflict, a question of balance between principles of humanity and demands of military necessity. At the Hague Conferences in 1907 there were arguments suggesting that too strict application of the laws of war would lead to military disadvantage, particularly with regard to stringent rules for treatment of prisoners of war.[30] Equally, retreats from a campaign often entailed, for military reasons, the burning of civilian property, which the withdrawing forces would set alight to safeguard themselves. At sea, it is often difficult for a vessel engaged in strategic operations to abandon its planned pursuits to rescue shipwrecked people.

The Hague Conventions recognised the conflict between military necessity and strict application of humanitarian rules and admitted certain exceptions to the Conventions. Hague Convention IV[31] thus stipulates that 'it is especially forbidden ... (g) to destroy or seize the enemy's property, unless such destruction or seizure be imperatively demanded by the necessities of war'.

The 1929 Convention on Prisoners of War also contained provisions which recognised military necessity as a means of mitigating strict application of the Convention. Thus, the Convention allows derogations due to military necessity until a taken person has reached a prisoner of war camp.[32]

The Geneva Conventions of 1949 contain several limitations, such as 'The Party to the conflict which is compelled to abandon wounded or sick to the enemy shall, as far as military considerations permit, leave them with a part of its medical personnel and material to assist in their care'.[33] There are numerous other examples in the Geneva Conventions[34] and Convention IV even contains an escape clause

---

[30] Cf. the reservations to the 1907 Conventions with regard to interrogation of prisoners of war, above, p. 286.

[31] Article 23.   [32] Article 1.   [33] Geneva Convention I, article 12.

[34] Convention I, article 42 concerning obligations to make emblems of medical units visible to the enemy (similar rules on identification are contained in Convention IV, article 18 on civilian hospitals); Convention III, article 8(3) on the duty of protecting powers to take into account such necessity; article 23 on prisoner of war camps; article 76(3) on rights of correspondence; article 126(2) on visits to prisoners; Convention IV, article 83 on camps of internment; Convention IV, article 49 on mass forcible transfers; *ibid.*, article 78 on 'assigned residence' and internment of civilians; Convention III, article 126 concerning restrictions of visits of protecting powers to prisoner of war

wide enough to exempt all protected persons under its aegis. The Convention thus prescribes that 'the Parties to the conflict may take such measures of control and security in regard to protected persons as may be necessary as a result of war'.[35]

Military necessity may also justify, in terms of the Geneva Conventions, destruction of civilian property,[36] and a similar exception clause was inserted in the Hague Convention of 1954 on the Protection of Cultural Property.[37] Cultural property, in general, may be attacked in case of military necessity[38] and even specially protected property[39] may be attacked in case of 'unavoidable' military necessity. Geneva Convention IV on Civilians also permits derogations from the rights of the protecting power over food supplies and medicines.[40]

The escape clauses in the Geneva Conventions even made some writers doubt whether 'the equipoise thus sought to be established between the principles of military necessity and humanity is realistically a durable one'.[41] It may be that any derogation from the Conventions must be substantiated as compelling military necessity as no one can be held to do the impossible.[42] However, at the root of the difficulty doubtless lies the uncertainty as to what exactly military necessity implies: it cannot be the global aim of 'overpowering the enemy',[43] which is a definition so wide as to be useless.[44]

Any wide definition of necessity would wholly undermine the network of laws of war. Indeed, the equation of military necessity and the purpose of war reiterates the condemned[45] German theory of primacy of *Kriegsraison* over *Kriegsmanier*, i.e. the doctrine that any 'reason' or 'necessity' of war displaces provisions on the customs of war.[46] Thus, even the military success of an individual operation may be subsumed under such a wide definition.[47]

camps; Convention IV, article 55 on verification of the state of food and medical supplies by protecting powers; *ibid.*, article 16 concerning search for the killed and wounded.
[35] Article 27, *in fine*.   [36] Convention IV, article 53.
[37] 249 UNTS 240.   [38] Article 4.   [39] Above, p. 250.   [40] Article 55.
[41] M. S. McDougal and F. P. Feliciano, *Law and Minimum World Public Order: the Legal Regulation of International Coercion*, New Haven, 1961, 684.
[42] Cf. ICRC, *Report on 1947 Conference of Government Experts*, 114, and Diplomatic Conference, II A, 323, and II B, 280.
[43] Oppenheim thus equates military necessity with the purpose of war, 2 Oppenheim 1952, 232.
[44] McDougal and Feliciano, *Law and Minimum World Public Order*, 1038–9.
[45] See Stone, *Legal Controls*, 353.
[46] 2 Oppenheim 1952, 232 argues in the same vein that the laws of war are not suspended, merely its usages.
[47] Meurer, 2 *Kriegsrecht* 1907, 14.

Such a wide concept of military necessity is no longer accepted, as is shown in ample case law. In the *Peleus Case* it was emphasised that the proper way for a submarine to avoid detection after sinking a ship is to depart as quickly as possible rather than to shoot all survivors under a cloak of military necessity.[48] Thus, if there is an alternative course of action the plea will not be accepted; and there is usually some such course, albeit affording less effective and immediate military advantage. These restrictive rules also apply to any plea of military necessity to help the 'war effort', such as when German Armaments Minister Speer ordered civilians from occupied territories to work in munitions factories.

Similarly, the use of anticipatory force to destroy property in an occupied State to prevent incursions by enemy forces has been condemned.[49] General Jodl ordered the destruction of real property in northern Norway to make the advance of Soviet troops more difficult. The Court held that such destruction could not be warranted by any military necessity as the Soviet troops had not yet crossed the border. Thus, military necessity cannot afford protection in cases where the imminent danger of attack has not yet materialised.

The Protocols of 1977 mark an advance on the previous pattern of exception clauses insofar as there are comparatively few such clauses. However, if there is 'imperative military necessity' a party to a conflict may be entitled, under Protocol I, to destroy foodstuffs or agricultural areas for example, although these may be 'indispensable to the survival of the civilian population'.[50] Such a provision was included to enable a party to use the 'scorched earth' technique of withdrawing forces to defend their own national territory from attack. There were protests at the anti-humanitarian formulation, but it was the 'most demanding standard that would be acceptable' to States.[51] Activities of relief personnel may be limited in case of imperative military necessity[52] and for similar reasons civil defence personnel may be restrained in their tasks.[53]

The denunciation clauses in the Weapons Conventions can also be thought to be an expression of the military necessity doctrine. Here, it is not actual necessity in combat which suspends the treaties but the

[48] 1 *War Crimes Report*, 1946, 1.
[49] *The Jodl Case*, UK, *Trial of Major German War Criminals*, London, 1948, 413.
[50] Article 54(5) and (2).
[51] CDDH/407/Rev. 1, 51, and Bothe, Partsch and Solf, *New Rules on Victims of War*, 342.
[52] Article 71(3) of Protocol I.   [53] Article 62(1).

general overall political or military threat to State 'security'. In the operation to bring about the suspension of otherwise valid treaties the doctrine of military necessity and the theory of necessity of State[54] come near to one another.

It is not only treaties and conventions that may be suspended in their application by dubious claims of military necessity, but also general uncodified rules on methods, including rules on targets and humanitarian rules. The legal position today, after a considerable body of case law has developed, appears to be that rules of the Law of War must be suspended only in case of 'clear' military necessity; that the burden of proof is increased for the suspension of any rules exempting targets from attack; and an especially enhanced burden of proof applies in the case of suspension from humanitarian rules. The degree of military necessity is also increased in proportion to violation of these three groups; the presumption exists that no military necessity can justify violations of rules of the Law of War.

b. Anterior breach

Most treaties can be denounced if there is a substantial breach on the part of one of the co-contracting parties.[55] The rules in this respect, followed for a very long time indeed, were codified in the Vienna Convention on the Law of Treaties of 1961.[56] However, a curious exception was made in the article to treaties of a 'humanitarian' character: a breach by another party would, according to the Vienna Convention, not entitle a party to denounce a 'humanitarian' Convention.[57] Which are these 'humanitarian' Conventions? Are they *all* the treaties bearing on the Law of War? If that is so, how is the loss of right to 'denounce' a treaty for breach compatible with the right to 'denounce' for even less than that, without there having been a breach, a right entrenched in most of the Conventions on the Law of War?[58] It does seem difficult to reconcile these two positions and serious questions arise as to the nature of the legal obligation of the treaties of the Law of War and the problem of reciprocity.[59]

c. Repression of breaches

The Geneva Conventions provide rules as to what a party may do when there is an alleged breach of the Convention.[60] There is no

[54] Above, p. 304.   [55] See my *Essays*, 91.   [56] Article 60.
[57] Article 60(5).   [58] Above, p. 330.   [59] Below, p. 339.
[60] Geneva I, article 52; Geneva II, article 53; Geneva III, article 132; and Geneva IV, article 149.

existing framework for the solution of disputes on breaches, but States have undertaken to proceed to *in casu* settlement. If such discussions do not lead to amicable understanding the parties shall appoint arbitrators.[61] There are few undertakings by contracting parties to repress breaches of the Weapons Conventions by internal legislation.[62] On the other hand, the Geneva Conventions have a detailed network of rules for duties of contracting parties both to implement relevant rules in national leglislation and to 'search' for persons who have committed violations of substantive provisions.[63] Special provisions are made for punishment of certain 'grave' breaches.[64]

The contracting parties bind themselves to repress breaches of the Geneva Conventions,[65] Protocol I,[66] but not of Protocol II. Certain breaches shall, under Protocol I, be considered as 'grave'[67] and, as such, warrant special repression. Among such 'grave' breaches are violations of the rights which figure in the catalogue of fundamental rights in the two Protocols.[68]

Although not systematically presented, it appears that Protocol I relies on the *aut dedere aut punire* method adopted by the hijacking Conventions.[69] But the system is relying on an assumption that it is individuals under the control of a State who are guilty and who must be found and prosecuted. There is a real possibility that it is the State itself, or rather persons in charge of the State, for example members of the government, who may be guilty and, for such cases, the Conventions and the Protocols do not offer any mechanisms for complaints.

With regard to the individual responsibility of persons covered by the Protocols it appears that Protocol I recognises the possibility of such personal responsibility. Until the Second World War only States had been held responsible under international law, but due to the growth of rights accruing to individuals under this system, symmetric duties also developed. Thus individuals are protected, but they also have duties not to infringe the rights which they themselves enjoy.

---

[61] Cf. J. Patrogic, 'Control of the application of humanitarian conventions', *RDPMDG*, 1966, 405.

[62] On general problems of transformation, above, p. 163.

[63] Geneva I, articles 49–51; Geneva II, articles 50–2; Geneva III, articles 129–31; Geneva IV, articles 142–8.

[64] *Ibid.*   [65] Above, p. 12, note 69.   [66] Article 85.

[67] Article 85(3).   [68] Above, pp. 273 and 274.

[69] The Hague Convention, 1970, 860 UNTS 105; cf. the Montreal Convention, 1973, 10 *ILM* 1151.

Protocol I states emphatically that a soldier may not avail himself of the *respondeat superior* defence.[70] On the other hand, the responsibility of superior authorities may be engaged as well to the extent they had knowledge, or constructive knowledge, of any breaches of the Protocol. There will therefore be cases of double responsibility under Protocol I. Such double responsibility is rare under international law and should probably cover only proper 'war crimes'.[71]

It may therefore go beyond the limits of present international law to impose personal responsibility for apartheid and to equate such acts, at any level, with war crimes. Yet one may understand the attitudes of developing countries and their ambition of including apartheid among the grave breaches of the Protocol. However, in practice, inclusion may create certain problems.

A provision on compensation which is a normal consequence of responsibility is somewhat dislocated in an article organically separated from other rules on responsibility.[72] Under this article only a 'party' to a conflict may be required to pay compensation. In other words, individual responsibility cannot be coupled with any obligation to pay such compensation. On the other hand, a liberation movement may conceivably be liable for such compensation as it, and a State, may be party to an armed conflict.

ii. *The problem of reciprocity*

The requirements for combatant and belligerent status have been discussed at length earlier in this work.[73] Certain questions are incidental to such status and concern the nature of the legal obligation; some of these questions are specific to the nature of the Law of War and present problems which are not acute in other parts of international law.

a. *General principles*

Reciprocity is at the root of the international legal system itself,[74] although it is a notion which cannot explain the existence of all rules.[75] It is a concept which is particularly important to the Law of

---

[70] Article 86(2) and see further below, p. 357.

[71] See my 'Foreign warships', 70.   [72] Article 91.   [73] Above, p. 103.

[74] Cf. A. Verdross and B. Simma, *Universelles Völkerrecht, Theorie und Praxis*, Berlin, 1967, 63; M. Virally, 'Le principe de réciprocité dans le droit international contemporain', 122 *RCADI* 1969.

[75] For a theory on reciprocity as reinforcing the basis of obligation, see my *Concept*.

War. Reciprocity affects the Law of War in many ways. In one sense a war-waging party must always consider what effects his actions will have and what reciprocal actions his adversary may take once he is in a position to counteract. Such actions may be delayed until peace-time and may not themselves violate international law, but merely represent the resentment created by the practices in a previous war.[76]

In this sense reciprocity will always be important to the behaviour of parties in armed conflicts. But reciprocity can be used in another sense, that of explaining whether a mutual element of obligation is necessary for States to be bound by any particular rules. Some still view the restriction of war and the rules of behaviour in armed conflicts as based on reciprocity,[77] whereas others claim that such rules do not rest on any such principle.[78]

There has certainly for long been, and perhaps still is, a reluctance to allow the existence of any obligations without strict reciprocity. This is, some claim, at least a partial basis of obligation of international law as a whole.[79] It is also often true as regards the substantive *quid pro quo* which a party to a treaty claims to be the reason for adhering to a convention.[80] It is even true for the way international acts are construed: for example, decisions by international organisations have been claimed to constitute 'disguised' treaties and attempts to explain the activity as a unilateral regulatory function are not common.[81]

There is in any treaty a presumption of such reciprocity and the violation by one party of substantive provisions is normally a ground for denunciation or breach.[82] One could even suggest that reservations to treaties regarding reciprocity, i.e. stipulating that the treaty will apply only on such basis, are unnecessary.

The legal obligation is not as clear as one might first assume. The

[76] Cf. I. Kant, *Zum ewigen Frieden*, Königsberg, 1795, sec. 1, art. 6 'Es soll sich kein Staat im Kriege mit einem anderen solche Feindseeligkeiten erlauben, welche das wechselseitige Zutrauen im künftigen Frieden unmöglich machen müssen.'

[77] E.g. Rosas, *The Legal Status of Prisoners of War*, 17, 52.

[78] E.g. M. Bothe, 'Conflits armés et droit international humanitaire', *RGDIP*, 1978, 93.

[79] See, for example, Verdross and Simma, *Universelles Völkerrecht*, 63; Virally, 'Le principe de réciprocité dans le droit international contemporain'.

[80] On unequal treaties, see my *Independent State*, 195, and my 'Problem of unequal treaties', 1069.

[81] But see my *Law Making, passim*.

[82] Cf. Vienna Convention on the Law of Treaties, 1961, 63 *AJIL* 1969, 875, article 60(5); cf. GAOR, 1st sess., 1968, 354–60; *ibid.*, 1969, 112–15; cf. E. Schwelb, in *Archiv des Völkerrechts*, 1973, 14–27.

1899 and 1907 Hague Conventions are multilateral conventions with relatively few reservations.[83] The Conventions stipulate that they apply only to the parties and also contain the *si omnes* clause, implying that they apply only if all parties to a conflict are bound by the Conventions.[84] But sometimes strict reciprocity is factually impossible: that was the case with Serbia, which had ratified the maritime Conventions although she had no sea border. But such factual circumstances, of which the contracting parties had been well aware, could not influence the application of the Conventions.[85]

The violation of the Hague Conventions of 1899 and 1907 by Germany during the Second World War raised the question whether such substantial breaches released other belligerents from their obligations.[86] It may be that flagrant violations, construed as repudiation, give rise to a right to accept that repudiation. But unless that acceptance is coupled with a certain behaviour, the relevant Convention will still be binding and a party will not be released from its obligations under the instrument.[87]

The numerous reservations of this type made to the Geneva Gas Protocol[88] restrict the application of the treaty regime.[89] But they cannot affect rules which already form part of international law. If the Protocol states only what is already binding in international law,[90] reservations do not affect the operation of such rules.

Yet reservations to the Geneva Protocol provide that a State will consider itself released from its obligations if there are violations by the enemy.[91] On the other hand, some of the States making such reservations assume, at the same time, that provisions of the Protocol are binding on third parties by virtue of forming part of general international law. But these two attitudes are incompatible: either the obligations are binding between parties alone, on the basis of reciprocity, or, if third parties are bound, this indicates that the root of obligation is not to be found in the treaty, but in general international law, in which case the ambit of the rules is beyond amendment by a single State.

In the field of weapons restrictions there have been efforts to dis-

---

[83] But see above, p. 286.   [84] Below, p. 348.
[85] Cf. *The Blonde*, (1922) AC 313.   [86] Colombos, *Law of Prize*, 8.
[87] *The Blonde*, (1915) P. 129, 176; *The Germania*, (1916) P. 5.
[88] See for list Schindler and Toman, *Documents*, 2nd edn, 115ff.
[89] See my *Essays*, 49.   [90] Above, p. 134.
[91] E.g. reservation by France; cf. H. Meyrowitz, *Les armes biologiques et le droit international*, Paris, 1968, 64.

pense with reciprocity. The Conventional Weapons Convention[92] thus stipulates[93] that 'when one of the parties to a conflict is not bound by an annexed Protocol, the parties bound by this Convention and that annexed Protocol shall remain bound by them in their mutual relations' and thus suggests that a State is bound only on the basis of strict reciprocity.[94] Under the Weaponry Convention of 1981, a State can consider itself released[95] from any obligations under the Convention as soon as, for example, a liberation movement in the conflict ceases to apply the Geneva Convention and/or the Weaponry Convention.[96]

Reliance on common rules would, say some, explain the difficult question why a rebel movement can be legally bound by the assumption of certain obligations by the State which the movement opposes.[97] It has been said that when States adhere to the Geneva Conventions their undertakings do not concern the 'interchange of benefits' which may be normal in treaty relations, but lay down 'guarantees to which every human being is entitled'.[98] A unilateral undertaking to apply certain rules may not be unknown,[99] but the whole system of a set of rules to which States adhere without any requirement of reciprocity is new. And it has been claimed that everyone must apply the rules as binding regardless of reciprocity.[100] The rules would even amount to *jus cogens*.[101]

Some statements have suggested emphatically that this is not so.[102] Others have widened the issue and claimed that rules in general for the protection of persons in war do not rest on any strict principle of reciprocity.[103] But when the principle of reciprocity is refuted it is done in terms of arbitrary practical considerations, rather than by the more obvious reasoning based on treaty technique. The state-

---

[92] Above, p. 182.   [93] Article 7(1).   [94] Above, p. 180.
[95] Under article 7(4)(b). See above, p. 370 on the system of indirect obligation of this Convention.
[96] J. A. Ruach, 'Certain conventional weapons conventions: arms control or humanitarian law?' 105 *Mil LR* 1984, 3 at 26.
[97] Cf. ICRC, CDDH/I/SR.59, vol. 9, 239. Cf. Forsythe, *Humanitarian Politics*, 156.
[98] 13 *IRRC* 1973, 640.
[99] For example, Japan had undertaken to apply the 1929 Convention on Prisoners of War *mutatis mutandis*, although it was not a party to the Convention, see ICRC, *Report on Activities during the Second World War*, 1948, vol. 1, 229.
[100] Pictet, *Humanitarian Law and the Protection of War Victims*, 19: cf. Pictet in the 1983 and 1985 editions.
[101] A. de la Pradelle, 18 *Annales de droit international médical*, 1968, 9; cf. R. J. Wilhelm, 'Problèmes relatifs à la protection de la personne humaine', 367.
[102] Rosas, *Legal Status*, 17, 52.   [103] Bothe, 'Les conflits', 93.

ment in the Geneva Conventions that the obligations assumed under them will be binding 'in all circumstances' is not necessarily any indication that the condition of reciprocity is abandoned. Any treaty may stipulate that its provisions will be binding 'in all circumstances', but this does not necessarily mean that conditions of reciprocity are abandoned.

The Nuremberg Tribunal acknowledged that the Hague Conventions of 1907 apply to non-signatories, and that Czechoslovakia, for example, was bound although it had never ratified.[104] Even those who hold that parties to a conflict can agree to 'keep the situation outside the application of the Geneva Conventions'[105] in certain limited military operations would agree that if the situation escalates and constitutes an armed conflict in a 'sociological and objective way' the relevant Geneva Convention will enter into operation even for parties to a conflict who have not adhered to the Convention in question. The reason this is so is that it can be deduced from the obligation to refrain from reducing rights under the Convention[106] by special agreement; such further agreement must not 'adversely affect' rights granted by the Convention.

The 1977 Protocols are even less dependent on such reciprocity in non-international conflicts as it is 'a question of respecting, with regard to one's own nationals, a few basic humanitarian rules'.[107]

b. Application to third parties

First of all, contracting parties to a treaty cannot make that treaty bind third States. To such third States the treaty is legally not binding, for it is a transaction between others, a *res inter alios acta*.[108]

Secondly, we have seen that some guerilla groups will be bound by the provisions of a treaty by the fact that the treaty so provides.[109] Other guerilla groups may be bound on the basis of equality if they are combatants in a war.[110]

---

[104] Judgment 1, October 1946, IMT, 54. Cf. the Military Tribunal for the Far East, in the *Hirota Case*, (1948) *AD*, 1948, 365.
[105] Rosas, *The Legal Status of Prisoners of War*, 233. The Geneva Convention in the event was Convention III.
[106] In the event of prisoners of war, Rosas, *The Legal Status of Prisoners of War*, 234.
[107] ICRC, CDDH/I/SR.59, vol. 9, 240. But see below, p. oo on the interpretation of article 96 by certain authorities.
[108] See my *Essays*, 100ff.
[109] Like the Conventional Weapons Convention in certain circumstances, see above, p. 186; or the Protocols of 1977, above, p. 154.
[110] Above, p. 4 on equality and p. 103 on requirements for combatant status.

Thirdly, nationals of a State may well be bound by virtue of inter-nal application of the Law of War.[111] There may also be rights enjoyed by nationals under a treaty, at least as far as some protection of the person is concerned. The United States clarified at the Diplo-matic Conference for the 1977 Additional Protocols that persons pro-tected under Protocol I include a State's own nationals.[112] But the matters under discussion in that context concerned the most basic rights, such as the right not to be subjected to mutilations or medical experiments.[113] There were some proposals on the application of the Conventional Weapons Conventions to third parties.[114] But who are these third parties? Are they other States or are they guerilla groups? Or are they even individuals inside the territory of a State?

c. Application to non-States

With regard to the 'intra-State' Protocol II of 1977, where is the basis of obligation? How can an insurgent group be bound by the acts of its own government against which it has risen in arms?[115] Some suggest that ratification by a State also binds emerging subjects on its terri-tory at least 'provisionally'.[116]

Some commentators have questioned whether rebels will respect the rules of the Law of War.[117] However, the instruments on the Law of War, of which the 1977 Protocols and the Conventional Weapons Convention accord special status to rebels, are more designed to stimulate rather than to preclude such respect.

Must both parties apply common article 3 of the Geneva Conven-tions? Reciprocity may not have been made an express condition for the application of the standards of this article.[118] Some claim that a party is released from certain obligations under the Geneva Conven-tion if an adversary has violated their provisions.[119] Yet in practice considerations of reciprocity may still be decisive.

The question concerning the standing of non-State belligerents

---

[111] Above, p. 163.   [112] CDDH/SR.37, vol. 6, 81.

[113] *Ibid.* and Protocol I, article 11.

[114] A/CONF.95/WG/L.9 (1979) (Netherlands). Cf. *ibid.*, L/6.

[115] Cf. Bothe, 'Conflits armés', 92.

[116] Ph. Bretton, 'La Convention du 10 avril 1981 sur l'interdiction ou la limitation d'emploi de certaines armes classiques qui peuvent être considerées comme produisant des effets traumatiques excessifs ou comme frappant sans discriminations', *AFDI*, 1981, 92; cf. E. Lattmann, *Schutz Kulturgüter bei bewaffneten Konflikten*, Zurich, 1974, 96 for similar construction of the 1954 Hague Convention on Cultural Property; cf. above, p. 249.   [117] Dinstein, 'The new Geneva Protocols', 268.

[118] Zorgbibe, 'De la théorie', 91–2.   [119] Cf. Draper, *The Red Cross Conventions*, 12.

leads, on the one hand, to such units being recognised today as belligerents.[120] But if they do not, at the same time, assume duties under the Law of War, the State will be unilaterally bound *vis-à-vis* belligerent insurgents or guerilla groups: the non-State party to the conflict will not be bound. This is so, say some writers, because only States, and possibly certain international organisations, can be subjects of international law and only States and such organisations can therefore be parties to treaties. This may be true for international law in general and is specifically entrenched in the Vienna Convention on the Law of Treaties of 1961, supplemented by the Convention on Treaties by International Organizations, drafted by the International Law Commission.[121] But there has, in some quarters, been unrest for some time about this classification and especially about the fact that non-State entities conclude agreements of very similar substance, and with very similar effects, to traditional treaties.[122] It has already been shown that ample provisions exist in the field of the Law of War today by which non-States can also adhere to treaties.[123] This is true not only for rules on warfare methods or humanitarian rules under which individuals derive certain specific benefits. But there are also a number of treaties, as there are many general uncodified rules, under which individuals assume considerable duties of behaviour.

Are non-State parties bound as well although they have not been able to accede to treaties as State parties?

Not so long ago dissident forces were denied the status of belligerents in the Spanish Civil War, and therefore deprived of the application of the laws of war.[124] On the other hand, in other situations, resistance movements have been recognised as enjoying rights under the Law of War, although they did not fulfil the requirements for combatant status at the time. For example, in the *Rauter Case* before a Special Criminal Court in the Hague in 1948 it was held that the Dutch resistance movement would be recognised as legitimate combatants, even though they had operated clandestinely, as the occupying power was in flagrant violation of international law.[125] In other words, the violation of law by an adverse party improved the standing of a group as combatants.

---

[120] Above, p. 35.   [121] See P. Reuter, 'Report', 1 *ILC Yearbook* 1985.
[122] See my *Concept* and my *Law Making*, 319ff.   [123] Above, p. 154.
[124] See Padelford, *International Law and Diplomacy in the Spanish Civil Strife*, 18; Ch. Rousseau, *La non-intervention en Espagne*, Paris, 1939, 511.
[125] (1948) *AD*, 1949, 526 at 530; cf. *Sansolini* v. *Bentivegna*, *RivDI*, 1958, 129; *ILR* 1959, 986.

Now guerillas and liberation movements are capable of adhering as contracting parties to several international treaties. But the actual application of rules of the Law of War by guerillas in both international and internal conflicts has become a real problem. Protocols I and II enhance the possibility of such application.

The ICRC proposed at the Stockholm Conference in 1948 that resistance movements should 'act in obedience to the laws and customs of warfare; and in particular that they should treat nationals of the occupying Power who may have fallen into their hands according to the provisions of the [Geneva] Convention'.[126] But the formula was abandoned at the 1949 Conference for the Geneva Conventions as the conference decided to adopt a common formula for resistance movements and independent militia and volunteer corps and to re-state in this formula the four traditional conditions[127] of the Brussels Declarations and the Hague Regulations[128]

Normally only States can take full part in diplomatic conferences and only States can sign the official text of treaties.[129] At the same time, it is claimed that non-State parties to conflict have no rights or standing under treaties and no corresponding duties. But how can the notion of reciprocity explain the lop-sided situation when different rights accrue on both sides? If, on the one hand, guerilla groups are considered to be belligerents, they too should be bound by the Law of War. But this cannot be achieved on the basis of reciprocity as such reciprocity cannot be entrenched in treaties where only States are parties.

The General Assembly has repeatedly argued that captured combatants on both sides should be given prisoner of war status.[130] It is obviously a crucial question whether rebels will obey similar rules to those binding the State.[131] Both anti-governmental and governmental forces need protection; it must not always be assumed that government forces are superior in war.[132]

It is this lack of reciprocity in standing that is the reason for a sharp distinction that many writers make between the Law of the Hague

---

[126] ICRC, *Projects on the Revised or New Conventions*, Geneva, 1948, 54; ICRC, *Report on the 1947 Conference of Government Experts*, Geneva, 1947, 108.
[127] Above, p. 103.
[128] Federal Political Department of Switzerland, *Final Record of the Diplomatic Conference*, vol. 2 A, 414, 465, 477.
[129] CDDH/SR.57, vol. 7, 278 (Spain).
[130] GAOR, 13th sess., 1st Committee, 1022 mtg, 374.
[131] Dinstein, 'The new Geneva Protocols', 278.
[132] Cf. CDDH/II/SR.33, vol. 11, 341 (USSR).

and the Law of Geneva insofar as they state that the former set of rules is really for the international law subjects who have a *jus bellandi*.[133] But one might also suggest that it is precisely the circle of the subjects entitled to *jus bellandi* that has changed[134] and that, therefore, the hazy limit between the two 'laws' remain and, with that, also the distinction in the requirement of reciprocity of standing. It was quite understandable that delegations at the conference for negotiation of the 1977 Protocols were anxious to ensure that if government forces were prepared to abide by certain rules *vis-à-vis* guerillas, so should dissident forces.[135]

It would appear reasonable to argue that rebels are also bound by the provisions in, for example, the Protocols of 1977, since they also derive benefits from them. Many delegates at the Diplomatic Conference emphasised that rebels are bound as well as State parties.[136]

The Weaponry Convention, too, will be applied to all parties, even to non-State parties, by the novel technique of indirect application.[137] Article 96 of Protocol I indicates that it is applicable only between those parties which accept and apply the instrument. In relation to a third party a State only has to apply general international law. Some have deduced a far-reaching principle of reciprocity and claim that a party would no longer be legally obliged to apply such general international law if the other party does not respect such rules.[138] But this also leads to the conclusion that the non-State party, which most international lawyers insist is no 'subject' of international law, is not bound to apply any specific rules *vis-à-vis* a third party. This attitude certainly undermines the very concept of humanitarian law and it is of little consequence that such statements are coupled with comments to the effect that such suspension of general rules will not be 'recommended'.[139]

---

[133] Bindschedler-Robert, *Reconsideration*; cf. Bindschedler-Robert, *Cours introductif*, IHEI, Geneva, 1975–6, 15.

[134] Above, p. 127.

[135] E.g. USSR, CDDH/II/SR.33, vol. 11, 341: both sides need protection; Federal Republic of Germany, CDDH/I/SR.23, vol. 8, 220.

[136] CDDH.1/SR.23, vol. 8, 220 (West Germany); cf. CDDH/SR.36, vol. 6, 63 (New Zealand).

[137] Above, p. 186.   [138] SOU 1984: 56, 68; cf. 20 and 54.

[139] SOU 1984: 56, 20; cf. 70. The Swedish Committee on the International Laws of War suggested that even *vis-à-vis* a State which has ratified the Protocol application would depend on 'actual' implementation by the other side: for a while therefore a State would be entitled to delay or suspend application until it has been verified whether the adversary complies with the rules.

One cannot on the one hand maintain a criterion of reciprocity in internal war, and on the other hand deny that groups may be subjects, in limited respects, to the same rules. But if one abandons the condition of reciprocity there is little remedy for a State party to a conflict if the insurgent group resorts to practices which violate the Law of War.[140]

It is not reciprocity on which the obligation relies. It is equality. It may be correct to question whether it is just to place an aggressor on the same footing as his victim,[141] but this need not affect what could be called 'forensic equality', i.e. the capacity to assume rights and obligations.[142] In this sense all belligerents are equal.[143] And, therefore, the obligations under both the Weapons Conventions, the Geneva Conventions and the Protocols of 1977, are in their essence binding upon two parties to a conflict. Either the non-State party has to be recognised and is then under similar duty as the State party, or, if it is not given that right, it cannot be bound by any duties under these instruments.

d. A general or contractual basis of obligation?

The 1899 Conventions were only binding between the contracting states in wars between two or more of these parties.[144] The Hague Conventions of 1899 contained[145] a provision that the obligations of the Conventions would only be binding between contracting parties in wars between two or more of them.

The 1907 Hague Conventions contained an even more limiting formula, stipulating that the Conventions would only apply to the contracting parties in a war between them, and then only if all the belligerents were parties to the Conventions.[146] This was the famous *clausula si omnes* stipulating that the provisions of the Conventions would be activated only if all the parties to the conflict were bound by the Convention in question.

Some suggest that the original element of reciprocity in the Hague Conventions has been gradually displaced as more and more rules

---

[140] See above on guerilla warfare.
[141] Bindschedler-Robert, *Reconsideration*, ch. 50.
[142] See my article 'The problem of unequal treaties'.
[143] Rousseau, *Conflits armés*, 24–6.
[144] For reference, above, p. 97.   [145] Article 2(5).
[146] Hague IV, article 2; Hague V, article 20; Hague VI, article 6; Hague VII, article 7; Hague VIII, article 8; Hague IX, article 8; Hague X, article 18; Hague XI, article 9; Hague XIII, article 28.

from these instruments became absorbed in general international law.[147]

The Geneva Conventions, for example, contain no clause on reciprocity and this development, some writers claim, breaks new ground as the Geneva Conventions are regarded as applicable, imposing, as it were, unilateral obligations without any requirement of reciprocity.

Common Article 1 of the Geneva Conventions stipulates that the contracting parties 'undertake to respect and to ensure respect for the present Convention in all circumstances'. This provision makes, say many,[148] the whole Convention mandatory without any condition of reciprocity. At the Diplomatic Conference of the Additional Protocols it was also emphasised that article 1 of the Geneva Conventions had 'broken new ground' in 1949 by introducing the idea of a unilateral obligation not subject to reciprocity.[149] The Geneva Gas Protocol 1925 also referred to prohibitions being 'universally accepted as a part of international law, binding alike the conscience and the practice of nations'.

The Institut de Droit International decided in a Resolution of 1971 that the Geneva Conventions have become part of general international law, binding even in their details on all, even on non-contracting parties.[150] Some members argued in their replies to a questionnaire from the Institut that only the principles, but not the details, of the Conventions had become part of general law.[151] But the Institut found that the Conventions *in toto* had become incorporated in the system of international law. It would therefore bind even non-parties.[152]

But it is only the most basic rights and duties that have been incorporated into general international law. That this is the case is shown also by the recurrent entrenchment of these very basic rights in other specific international agreements on human rights.[153] Among the basic rights referred to in this context may be the 'alleviation of

---

[147] SOU 1984: 56, *Folkrätten i Krig*, 55.
[148] E.g. Hinz, *Das Kriegsgefangenenrecht*, 15; Pictet, *Humanitarian Law and the Protection of War Victims*, 21; Pictet, *Développements et principes du droit international humanitaire*, Geneva, 1983; Pictet, *International Humanitarian Law*; cf. H. Coursier, *Lessons on the Geneva Conventions*, Geneva, 1963, 25.
[149] CDDH/1/SR.4, para. 35 (Nigeria).
[150] Resolution, 54 Annuaire 1971, ii, 465.   [151] 54 *Annuaire* 1971, i, 113.
[152] Such non-parties may include United Nations forces, see *ibid.*, ii, 240 (Seyersted).
[153] Above, p. 130.

massive suffering' which, according to some writers, is an implied goal of the Charter of the United Nations.[154]

This goal forms part of protection of basic human rights[155] and part of the right to protection against genocide,[156] but it also has its own, separate justification as an objective of the United Nations.[157] The Courts often stated that, since law is not to be interpreted literally, the defendants should have known that they were bound by law as understood under the Martens clause. The Martens clause was relied on in the trials of war criminals[158] to rebut any defence plea on *nullum crimen sine lege.*

The Geneva Conventions contain special provisions to the effect that denunciation of the Conventions will not have effect only for the denouncing power. The Conventions then go on to stipulate that the denunciation 'shall in no way impair the obligations which the Parties to the conflict shall remain bound to fulfil by virtue of the principles of nations, as they result from the usages established among civilized people, from the laws of humanity and the dictates of public conscience'.[159] It is unclear whether there is a disjunction between the first statement about the limited effect of a denunciation for the denouncing party alone, and the second statement, which appears to apply to all parties to a conflict, even to the denouncing party. The 1977 Protocols have been interpreted both to provide general rules[160] and to include a degree of reciprocity.[161] Special problems arise in connection with the 1977 Protocols, although they really only concern the application of 'a few basic humanitarian rules' in non-international conflicts.[162]

The standards imposed by the relevant Conventions, as supplemented by the Martens clause, also involve rights given to individuals which the individuals themselves may even be able to validly renounce.[163] Views on the basis of obligation will vary according to views on international ethics as a separate set of rules which can be assessed and determined.

[154] Schachter, 'The United Nations and internal conflict', 408ff.
[155] Cf. above, p. 203.   [156] Cf. above, p. 130.
[157] Schachter, 'The United Nations and internal conflict', 408.
[158] E.g. *Von Leeb Case,* (1948) *AD,* 1948, 377 (before IMT); *Rauter Case,* (1949) *AD,* 1949, 542 (before a Dutch Special Court).
[159] Geneva I, article 63; Geneva II, article 62; Geneva III, article 142(4); and Geneva IV, article 158.
[160] Above, p. 134.   [161] Above, p. 339.
[162] ICRC, CDDH/I/SR.59, vol. 9, 240, and above, p. 273.
[163] E.g. Geneva III, articles 7, 78, 54(2), 68 and 109(3).

Could one argue that such very rules of international law must be suspended or adapted to the case when an adversary violates rules of international law and, for example, resorts to unlawful weapons[164] or unlawful use of weapons?[165]

The issue centres on two problems: one concerns the right to resort to counter-measures, like reprisals[166] when rules are violated; the other question concerns the very standing of non-State belligerents in the problem of reciprocity.

To comment on the first question first, it is clear that Geneva Convention III expressly forbids reprisals,[167] as did the earlier 1929 Geneva Convention.[168] Does this mean that whatever measures a belligerent may decide to take, they must not include reprisals? Or is a belligerent free from all obligations under the Geneva Convention so that even reprisals against innocent civilians can be used? But the victims of the retaliation will not even have the same identity[169] as the perpetrators of the violations. Therefore, it would seem reasonable to refuse this proposition.[170]

Some have claimed that international ethics will be violated in the case of any serious infringement of the Universal Declaration of Human Rights.[171] Ethics, or similar concepts, may well be a useful bridge between theological and secular spheres and between divergent cultural traditions provided it is understood as sufficiently broad to cover and sufficiently specific to identify common values across boundaries.[172] It may be that some rules in international society are of such essential importance that they must be upheld.[173]

But there are still considerable problems. Some still argue that a State can prevent, by the mechanism of article 2(3), the Geneva Convention from 'becoming applicable'.[174] However, to the extent that rules form part of 'general ethics' and to the extent they are identified by 'conscience' they cannot be subject to denunciation[175]

[164] Above, p. 176. [165] Above, p. 232. [166] Above, p. 254.
[167] Article 13(3). [168] Article 2(3).
[169] Cf. the situation in terrorism when threat or force is applied against a third party, above, p. 23.
[170] But Egypt considered a similar provision in Protocol I of 1977, article 20, to be binding only on the basis of reciprocity: CDDH/SR.37, vol. 6, 77.
[171] J. Castaneda, 'La valeur juridique des résolutions des Nations Unies', 129 *RCADI* 1970, 205.
[172] Cf. J. Turner-Johnson, *Just War Tradition and the Restraint of War, a Moral and Historical Inquiry*, Princeton, 1981, 117–18.
[173] On the nature of 'prophylactic' rules according to a new theory, see my *Concept*, 53.
[174] Rosas, *The Legal Status of Prisoners of War*, 242; cf. 101. [175] Above, p. 336.

either unilaterally or after anterior breach. But suspension of various rules of the Law of War is envisaged by certain specific provisions in relevant treaties that lay down rules for this law. Thus, civilians in general and medical units will forfeit their privileges if they resort to perfidy by shielding military targets.[176] This means that the effect of certain rules can be suspended by previous breach. But there seem to be other rules which must never be violated. These concern the most fundamental rights to evade indiscriminate attack, torture or other inhuman treatment.

There thus appear to be several layers of rules pertaining to the rules of war, some of which are subjected to ordinary requirements of reciprocity and others, of a rather more fundamental type, which are exempt from denunciation and which do not seem to be subject to reciprocity.

C. RESPONSIBILITY FOR BREACHES

i. State responsibility

Violations of the Law of War engage the international responsibility of a State.[177] Yet war crimes perpetrated, at a higher level, by the high command or by politicians may only lead to trials by a victor State at the end of a war.[178] There is certainly a clear application of the *vae victis* principle in the field of war crimes. Some have questioned the lack of symmetry when no officers of the Allies were prosecuted for acts amounting to war crimes.[179] Furthermore, the imbalance has been further criticised in view of the fact that the War Crimes Court was flawed by procedural inadequacies.[180] But rudi-

---

[176] Above, p. 352.
[177] Hague Regulations, article 3; Protocol I of 1977, article 9. See Verdross, *Die völkerrechtwidrige Kriegshandlung*; and J. W. Garner, 'Punishment of offenders against the laws and customs of war', *AJIL*, 1920, 70. On responsibility in general see the ILC *Yearbook*, 1963 onwards. On the importance of the notion of imputation see my *Concept*, 62; *contra*, Brownlie, *Responsibility*, 35.
[178] Cf. K. Zemanek, 'Das Kriegs- und Humanitärrecht', in *Handbuch des Völkerrechts*, Vienna, 1983, no. 2129 at 394.
[179] R. A. Falk, G. Kolko and R. J. Lifton, *Crimes of War, a Legal, Political–Documentary and Psychological Inquiry into the Responsibility of Leaders, Citizens and Soldiers for Criminal Acts in War*, New York, 1971, 141; A. M. de Zayas, *Die Wehrmachtuntersuchungsstelle, Deutsche Ermittlungen über Alliirte Völkerrechtverletzungen im Zweiten Weltkrieg*, Munich, 1980, *passim*.
[180] Cf. R. H. Minear, *Victors' Justice, the Tokyo War Crimes Trial*, Princeton, 1971. On the right to a 'fair' trial see the High Command Case, 12 *Nuremberg* 63.

mentary sanctions by a victor State are probably better than a situation where war criminals feel themselves exempt from any future prosecution.[181]

Interesting questions are raised by the status of liberation movements and guerilla groups. Do they have collective responsibility, as States do, or is it in their case always a question of individual responsibility? The answer may be that, should they not win their fight, they will, as a group, be dissolved by the State and in this sense there will remain no bearer of collective responsibility; then, in all likelihood, the individuals concerned will be prosecuted for their part in any crimes. And if they do win their fight, they will emerge as States: although they would then be able to assume collective responsibility under international law, they are, in practice, as victors, likely to escape such responsibility.

ii. Individual responsibility

a. Identification of war crimes

Above the collective responsibility of States and potentially collective responsibility of guerillas, a normal consequence of any violation of international rules, there is also in some cases individual responsibility for certain 'war crimes'. That such responsibility exists in certain circumstances was already shown in the provisions of the Versailles Treaty declaring Kaiser Wilhelm guilty of crimes against 'international morals' and the 'sanctity of treaties',[182] and furthermore stipulating that war criminals had to be surrendered by Germany to the Allies.[183] New efforts in the field of individual responsibility were made by the Declarations of London in 1942, of Moscow in 1943 and of Berlin in 1945.[184] But the substantial development of detailed rules in the field of individual responsibility probably came with the Nuremberg trials[185] and the Far East trials.[186]

But war crimes still occur.[187] The development of individual re-

---

[181] Zemanek, 'Das Kriegs- und Humanitärrecht', 394.
[182] Article 227.   [183] Articles 228–30.
[184] See Rousseau, *Conflits armés*; cf. UN, *History of United Nations War Crimes Commission* London, 1948.
[185] R. Woetzel, *The Nuremberg Trials in International Law with a Postlude on the Eichmann Trial*, 2nd edn, New York, 1962.
[186] See P. S. Dull and M. T. Unemura, *The Tokyo Trials*, University of Michigan, 1962; B. V. A. Roling, 'The Tokyo trials and the development of international law', *Indian LR*, 1953, 4.
[187] E.g. on My Lai see Committee on Armed Services, House of Representatives, 91st

sponsibility has been codified in the Geneva Conventions of 1949 and in the Protocols of 1977.

The Nuremberg Tribunals and the Tribunal for the Far East enumerated 'war crimes' in their Charters[188] but this classification has not been entirely adopted in the doctrine.[189] Many consider that the notion 'crimes against peace' is too vague to imply a war crime in the technical sense[190] and that the Charters thus employed a notion of war crime that is too wide.[191]

Some have suggested that the list of war crimes should be enlarged by including the use of nuclear weapons[192] as a new war crime.[193] Others have assumed that misuse of conventional weapons, or the use of forbidden such weapons, will qualify as war crimes even though the Conventional Weapons Convention itself is silent on this point.[194]

The traditional war crime included from the earliest inception of rules on the Law of War probably concerned illegitimate violence

Congress, 2nd sess., Hearings of the Armed Services Investigating Subcommittee, *Investigation of the My Lai Incident*, 1976; W. Peers, *The My Lai Inquiry*, Washington, DC, 1979 and cf. *The Peers Report, First Report of the Department of the Army Review of the Preliminary Investigation into the My Lai Incident*, 1970; *US* v. *Calley*, (1973) 46 CMR 1131; cf. *Koster* v. *US*, (1982) 685 F 2nd 407; cf. P. C. Warnke, 'Individual responsibility in warfare', in P. D. Trooboff (ed.), *Law and Responsibility in Warfare, the Vietnam Experience*, Chapel Hill, North Carolina, 1975, 187ff; on Shatila and Sabra, see W. D. Burnett, 'Command responsibility and a case study of the criminal responsibility of Israeli military commanders for the pogrom at Shatila and Sabra', 107 *MilLR* 1985, 71; on the massacre at Kafr-Kassem in 1947 see Ch. Rousseau, 'Chronique des faits internationaux', *RGDIP*, 1959, 513; International Organisation for the Elimination of All Forms of Racial Discrimination (ed.), *Witness of War Crimes in Lebanon, Testimony Given to the Nordic Commission in Oslo, October 1982*, London, 1983, 20ff, also on the Red Cross not being respected.
[188] UN Doc. A/1316 1950; The relevant provisions are reproduced in my 'Foreign warships', 68.
[189] See discussion in the International Law Commission for the 1954 Draft on Code of Offences Against the Peace and Security of Mankind, *Yearbook*, ii, 1954, 149.
[190] Cf. Zemanek, 'Kriegs- und Humanitärrecht', 394.
[191] Cf. P. R. Piccagallo, *The Japanese on Trial, Allied War Crimes Operations in the East 1945–1951*, Dallas, 1979, 212.
[192] See above, p. 201 on legality of use.
[193] C. van den Wijngaert, 'Les euromissiles et le droit pénal international', in Actes du Colloque, October 1984, *Les consequences juridiques de l'installation éventuelle de missiles cruises et pershing en Europe*, Brussels, 1984, 111; A. Andries, 'L'emploie de l'arme nucléaire est un crime de guerre', *La revue nouvelle*, 1983, 315. On the importance of moral–legal condemnation of the use of nuclear weapons, see Bindschedler-Robert, *Reconsideration*, 11–12.
[194] J. A. Rauch, 'Certain Conventional Weapons Convention: arms control or humanitarian law?' 105 *MilLR* 1984, 58.

and the rights of prisoners of war.[195] The rules on treatment of
prisoners of war[196] may have fallen into some disrespect after the First
World War.[197] However, after the Second World War inhuman treatment of prisoners of war was clearly condemned as a war crime.[198]
Other typical offences would be murder and devastation not justified
by military necessity.[199] Numerous convictions in the Nuremberg
trials thus concerned atrocities against civilians. For example, von
Leeb was held personally responsible for partaking in the 'Barbarossa
Order' to shoot civilians on mere suspicion of certain acts.[200] Also in
the Far East trials war crimes often concerned violations of rules
protecting civilians, in the *Case of Yamashita*, for example, involving
atrocities against the civilian population in the Philippines.[201] Other
war crimes include the killing of enemy soldiers who have surrendered.
This is a practice condemned in the early textbooks, although it is often
coupled there with exceptions for military necessity,[202] reprisals[203] or
even for the case where the surrendered soldier is himself guilty of a
crime.[204] The last case is still catered for in the Geneva Convention on
Prisoners of War.[205] Under this article certain persons will still be
exempt from the privileges of being treated as a prisoner of war.[206] The
effect of this provision, however, may be mitigated by the extended
protection granted by Protocol I of 1977.[207] However, the reservations
to the relevant article of Protocol I will bring back much to the level of
the Third Geneva Convention.[208]

War crimes, especially certain practices in the Second World War,
have been thought to be so abhorrent that they belong to a different
class from other violations of international law. They are so serious
that many suggest there should be no limitation period,[209] almost

[195] E.g. Special Commission Established by the Peace Conference in 1919, Commission on the Responsibility of the Authors of the War and on the Enforcement of
Penalties, 14 *AJIL* 1920, 95.
[196] Above, p. 281.
[197] C. Mullins, *The Leipzig Trials*, London, 1921; Rousseau, *Conflits armés*, 99.
[198] *The Great War Criminals Case*, *AD*, 1946, 216; *The Hirota Case*, Tribunal for the Far
East (1949), *AD*, 1948, 366.
[199] Above, p. 322.   [200] *The von Leeb Case*, 11 *Nuremberg* 554, 560.
[201] *The Yamashita Case*, UN War Crimes Commission, 4 *Law Reports of the Trials of War
Criminals*, 1948, 3.
[202] Above, p. 332.   [203] Above, p. 254.
[204] G. F. Martens, *Précis du droit des gens moderne de l'Europe*, 2nd edn, Paris, 1864, Bk.
VIII, ch. 4, para. 272 at 232.
[205] Geneva III, article 85.   [206] Above, p. 281.   [207] See above, p. 170.
[208] See above, p. 282.
[209] P. Mertens, 'L'imprescriptibilité des crimes des guerre et contre l'humanité, in

forgetting that rules on limitation normally apply to secure accuracy of evidence rather than necessarily reflecting the severity of crimes. There are still proceedings for war crimes forty years after the end of the Second World War. Many States have introduced special regulations to prolong the possibility of bringing prosecutions for war crimes,[210] but a time of forty years exceeds most provisions in national legislation[211] on prosecution for murder or other serious crimes. Some such extending provisions in national legislation were adopted as measures to implement a special Convention on the Non-Applicability of Statutory Limitations to War Crimes and Crimes Against Humanity concluded in 1968.[212] Some demands, like the one for Klaus Barbie from Bolivia,[213] may have become defunct, not because they were successful, but because a State in other ways came to claim jurisdiction. There are still outstanding demands[214] for the extradition of war criminals such as Mengele from Paraguay[215] and G. F. Wagner from Brazil.[216]

With regard to another aspect of prosecution, we have seen[217] that protection under Geneva Convention III may not be available to perpetrators of war crimes. This is, in the opinion of some courts,[218] a question of 'interpretation' of the Convention and thus a specific reservation to the Convention is not necessary to deprive war criminals of the benefits of the Convention with regard to treatment of prisoners of war.

b. Right of prosecution for war crimes

As there is no permanent international criminal court,[219] each State undertakes to punish those who have violated the Law of War. This way of using national machinery for the implementation of rules of international law is an application of the doctrine of 'dedoublement fonctionnel'[220] and indicates that national organs can provide the institutional machinery when the international legal system lacks adequate structural bodies.[221]

Université de Bruxelles (ed.), *Etude de droit international et de droit pénal comparé*, Brussels, 1974, 226: to allow limitation would be to normalise genocide.

[210] *Ibid.*, 25ff.   [211] Note that not all countries have such statutory provisions.
[212] 8 *ILM* 68.   [213] *RGDIP, Chronique*, 1972, 135.
[214] See, further, Rousseau, *Conflits armés*, 182–3.   [215] *RGDIP*, 1980, 411.
[216] *Ibid.*, 355.   [217] Above, under prisoners of war, p. 281.
[218] On the Italian case concerning Via Rasella, above, p. 255.
[219] Cf. E. Thorneycroft, *Personal Responsibility and the Law of Nations*, The Hague, 1961.
[220] G. Scelle, *Traité de droit international*, Paris, 1929.
[221] For the application, see my *Law Making*, 117.

Some have suggested that any flagrant disrespect for human rights gives rise to universal jurisdiction and that, therefore, war criminals can be tried anywhere.[222] Such acts would thus give rise to universal jurisdiction and allow any State or, as Robespierre said, 'all'[223] to take action against the party at fault. Universal jurisdiction has always existed with regard to pirates, who are by tradition *hostes gentium* or the enemies of all. The system of such universal jurisdiction has also been adopted by the Geneva Conventions, based on the maxim *aut dedere aut punire*, i.e. either a State must extradite a war criminal or make sure that he is punished in its own criminal proceedings.[224] A similar system has been adopted in later treaties on hijacking and other forms of terrorism.[225] With regard to chronology, it may be added that the right to prosecute subsists for a considerable time period.

c. *The doctrine of* respondeat superior

The plea of *respondeat superior*[226] as a defence in proceedings concerning responsibility is derived from the very organisation of the armed forces. They are highly stratified, depending at every level on order, discipline and the accurate and speedy execution of orders. All military codes contain detailed regulation of the effects of disobeying orders, providing in many cases for proceedings by a court martial. They are often supplemented with emergency measures, entitling even summary executions of members of the armed forces if orders are disobeyed in the face of the enemy.

If, then, a member is under such strict discipline in most armed forces, it is natural that only the responsibility of those giving the orders should be engaged. Therefore, the application of the doctrine *respondeat superior* can be suspended only in extreme situations.

---

[222] Robespierre, quoted by J. Basdevant, *La révolution française et le droit de la guerre continentale*, Paris, 1901, 165: 'Ceux qui font la guerre à un peuple pour arrêter les progrès de la liberté et aréantir les droits de l'homme doivent être poursuivis par tous, non comme des ennemis ordinaires mais comme des assassins et des brigands rebelles.'
[223] See quotation in the previous note.
[224] See Geneva I, article 49; Geneva II, article 50; Geneva III, article 129; and Geneva IV, article 146.
[225] Above, p. 19.
[226] See, e.g. L. C. Green, *Superior Orders in National and International Law*, Leiden, 1976; E. Muller-Rappard, *L'ordre supérieur militaire et la responsabilité pénale du subordonné*, Paris, 1965; C. Eustathiades, 'Quelques aspects de la jurisprudence concernant les criminels de guerre, l'exception des ordres reçus et autres moyens de defense similaires', in 2 *Festschrift Laun*, 1953, 395; cf. my 'Foreign warships', 70.

But for the trial of war crimes the doctrine was not fully accepted and it was thought suitable to allow its operation to mitigate a sentence but not to exclude responsibility. The Treaty of London of 8 August 1945[227] contained a clause stating: 'The fact that the Defendant acted pursuant to order of his Government or of a superior shall not free him from responsibility but may be considered in mitigation of punishment if the Tribunal determines that justice so requires.'[228]

Yet, as a rule, and in view of the importance of military discipline and of the unquestioned execution of orders, the principle must operate to exclude responsibility except in exceptional circumstances. Such situations are those where the execution of an order would involve a grave breach of the Law of War, including all humanitarian rules. The Geneva Conventions exemplify such grave breaches by a list of examples.[229] Protocol I of 1977 makes this category of 'grave' breaches even clearer.[230] On the other hand, the Protocol does not contain the article which existed in the Draft, which had provided that no one would be punished for obeying orders, even if an act committed in the execution of such orders constituted a grave breach,[231] unless the person executing the order knew his act would constitute a grave breach.[232] Some felt that combatants would face a dilemma if they had to decide whether they should obey or question an order as contrary to international law.[233] But the final text of the Protocol expressly excludes any defence under the doctrine.[234] In practice it has also often been held that superior orders constitute no effective defence for certain grave violations of the Law of War, for example by the sinking of a hospital ship: this was aptly illustrated in the *Llandovery Castle Case*.[235] But the doctrine will still, in all likelihood, be applied by courts in mitigation of a sentence if it does not altogether exclude liability; on the other hand, the doctrine may operate as a defence for all but the gravest of acts.

A member of the armed forces may, if prosecuted for a war crime, resort to the usual defences, for example self-defence or necessity, to

[227] 59 Stat 1544.   [228] Article 8.   [229] E.g. above, p. 338.
[230] Article 85(3)–(5).
[231] Article 77(1) of the Draft, CDDH/SR.45, vol. 6, 334.
[232] Article 77(2) of the Draft, *ibid.*
[233] *Ibid.* But the United States considered that the draft article did not go far enough, *ibid.*, 339. Cf. D. Matthei, 'Befehlserweigerung aus humanitären Grunden', *RDPMDG*, 1980, 257.
[234] Article 86(2).
[235] *Germany* v. *Dithmar & Boldt.* in L. Friedman (ed.), 1 *The Law of War: a Documentary History*, New York, 1972, 868.

exclude liability. A sentence may be mitigated if the defendant thought he was in greater danger than he actually was. However, other subjective defences, like being ignorant of the contents of international law,[236] are no longer allowed,[237] bringing the traditional principle *ignorantia juris nocet* into full operation.

That means that the defence *nullum crimen sine lege* will be defeated since the *lex* does contain rules of which no one must be ignorant. But the argument that there had been no legal prohibitions was certainly at the centre of pleadings on the part of the defence both in the international war trials and in national courts.[238]

A superior officer is, as described above, normally liable for war crimes committed by persons under his command, on the condition that he gave the relevant order, or that he knew of a planned act and refrained from preventing it from being committed. The Genocide Convention[239] failed to regulate these matters but Protocol I of 1977 now clarifies the position.[240] Similar rules were applied in the Nuremberg trials, where personal responsibility was incurred for subordinates,[241] including neglect by their inaction.[242] These rules were accepted in the doctrine as being an expression for general international law[243] and were also applied in the My Lai investigation,[244] where it was held that General Westmoreland had taken adequate precautions and should therefore be acquitted.[245]

A commanding officer may also be personally responsible after the event if he knew of a committed act and did not institute proceedings against the perpetrator.[246] In practice superior officers have been held responsible for war crimes committed by persons they commanded although the officers had not authorised the acts.[247]

---

[236] Cf. above, p. 329 on dissemination of knowledge and education of the armed forces.
[237] Cf. Zemanek, 'Kriegs- und Humanitärrecht', no. 2134 at 395.
[238] For Belgium, where the defence of *nullum crimen sine lege* was partly accepted in municipal cases, see A. Beirlaen, *De vervolging van oorlogsmisdadigers in Belgie na de Tweede Wereldoorlog in de bestraffing van inbreuken tegen het oorlogs- en het humanitair recht*, Brussels, 1980, 67.
[239] Above, p. 45.   [240] Protocol I, articles 86 and 87.
[241] *The List Case*, 11 Nuremberg 1259; cf. *The Roques Case*, ibid., 632; *The Reinecke Case*, ibid., 651; and *The Woeler Case*, ibid., 683.
[242] *The Kucheler Case*, 11 Nuremberg 565; *The Salmuth Case*, ibid., 617.
[243] W. H. Parks, 'Command responsibility for war crimes', 62 *MilLR* 1963; R. Campbell, *Military Command Liability for Grave Breaches of War and International Law: Absolute or Limited?*, London, 1974.
[244] On sources, above, p. 353, note 187.   [245] *The Peers Report*, 7.
[246] Protocol I, articles 86–7.   [247] *In Re Yamashita*, US 1945 672.

CONCLUSIONS: EVALUATION OF THE CONTEMPORARY LAWS OF WAR

War may be technically outlawed; but wars still occur. Practices in war have become even more cruel and indiscriminate now that States pretend that there are no wars but that conflicts on their territories are a matter for their concern alone. It is important to show that far from being withdrawn from the rules of the Law of War, intra-State conflicts, just as much as inter-State wars, are subject to the Law of War.

This means that it is not only States that are bound but also, on the basis of equality, or in a sense of belligerency, liberation movements and guerilla groups.

The pattern of war has changed. Nowadays States do not attack other States outright because of any open policy of expansion which has to be implemented by action. The State which used to go to attack in war now takes quite a different position: it is often from various internal movements that the violence first comes, after the State has denied them the right of self-determination or other rights that they seek. When their claims are denied they often resort to arms. The State then takes violent counter-measures and suppresses, or seeks to suppress, the movements. Often a larger State is called on for further help. These powerful outside States spread their activities in a more sophisticated way into areas which they consider come under their hegemony. And if they are not called upon to help the government, if that government is of a different political shade, they often intervene by supporting internal strife against that government of whose policies they do not approve. So wars spiral by outside support and intervention from all sides. Yet many still pretend that conflicts are merely internal and the Law of War is irrelevant.

The territorial State is worried about insurgents on its territory; they often seek to usurp power to the detriment of that State. There are some new contenders for the power of States: the liberation movements and the guerilla groups, which attack States and hope themselves to achieve statehood by warfare. Since States have absorbed the territories of the globe, liberation movements and guerillas must necessarily seek their own terrritory at the expense of existing States; their claims will inevitably encroach on the territorial sovereignty of States.

The way that liberation movements and guerilla groups are treated in State practice and, in particular, with respect to the Law of War, raises serious misgivings whether the 'fundamental' principles on which international law, according to most writers, is said to rest, are correct. A close scrutiny of the Law of War thus seems to suggest that it is not true that States (and intergovernmental organisations) are the only subjects of international law; it is not true that only States (and organisations) conclude treaties; it is not true that only States wage wars; it is not true that international law does not apply, without transformation, in the internal sphere of States; finally, it is not true that 'customary law', which in the field of the Law of War is of a prevailing negative nature, relying as it does on non-action rather than action of belligerents, furnishes any valid legal foundation of relevant rules.

Liberation movements and guerillas have become, alongside States, important units in the international community, highlighting the fragile structure of States. An increasing fragmentation of States has taken place, first by decolonisation under the rule of self-determination, but then by further splitting off by subsequent claims to autonomy.

It could be questioned whether the world is on a path back towards the conditions in the sixteenth and seventeenth centuries before the strong nation State arose to quell the constant civil wars. But situations are different today: now, wars are fought within fairly consolidated States, which often merely provide a venue for a confrontation of two outside supporting States who feed either side with financial or material support. Yet, the anarchical trends that can be discerned today, with a constant undermining of State power, might lead to a reaction that an even stronger bloc building or superstructural network will result.

Now missile strategy reverts more and more to the 'catapult' technique of the Romans. The distinction between the laws of warfare on land, in the air or at sea is eroded because of the overriding impact of missile warfare. But missile weapons can rarely comply with some basic tenets of the Law of War: they do not discriminate between civilian population and military targets, and their force is rarely proportionate to the need. Such lack of discrimination, together with disproportionality, indicates the illegality of many such weapons.

It is fictitious to justify the application of the Law of War in certain internal conflicts by claiming that conflicts are 'internationalised', for example by holding that liberation movements are belligerents in 'international wars' under Protocol I of 1977 regardless of outside support or objective circumstances justifying such qualification. It appears more reasonable to claim that the same Law of War is applicable in all wars.

Some commentators claim that questions of disarmament do not form part of the Law of War. However, in practice, disarmament on a partial or limited basis operates to regulate wars: certain weapons are prohibited; others may not be used except in a specific way; others may be used only provided their effects are not of a prohibited nature. The trend to prohibit weapons at, or even before, the research stage is important, as it is more difficult to eliminate weapons which are manufactured and deployed. Further detailed rules on weapons, including aspects of the arms trade and methods of warfare, coupled with humanitarian rules, form the important body of the Law of War.

In spite of some disagreement, particularly on the part of the United States with regard to incendiary weapons, the Weapons Conventions have already been treated, in large part, as binding international law. The provisions they contain concern weapons whose legality is already questionable under international law. Although there have been assertions to the contrary by the United States and France, the first (and possibly also the second) use of nuclear weapons is a violation of international law. In the field of protection of individuals from certain warfare methods and in the field of humanitarian law there is even greater agreement that international law now incorporates numerous provisions in unratified treaties. For example, a book devised for military commanders of various levels in Sweden to ascertain applicable rules of international law in war includes references to rules on personal protection under the Additional Protocols of 1977 as if they were already part of general international law.[1]

---

[1] Wulff, *Handbok i folkrätt under krig*, passim.

This is probably the correct position, although there will be an area of doubt about the rules on certain indiscriminate weapons. The position in law will obviously be strengthened by further accession to the Protocols, especially in view of probable further adherence by States like the United Kingdom to the Protocols.

The Law of War is remarkably consolidated. It does not consist of any elusive 'customary' rules, but rather more of universally evident rules, binding by common recognition.[2] The Law of War is well accepted to be binding on all belligerents and combatants and in great part rules are not subject to unilateral abrogation as was shown in the war crimes trials. There are certain standards from which no one must deviate and in this respect also the Law of War presents different characteristics from international law in general. The Law of War has the individual as its exclusive focus and the rationale of all rules can be derived from a common agreement to keep compulsory standards of behaviour. There is no doubt that the use of any indiscriminte weapon is illegal, as no weapon must be used that is not adequately aimed at military targets. There is no doubt that weapons that cause unnecessary suffering are forbidden. There is no doubt that the civilian population and all who are *hors de combat* must at all times be exempt from attack and given necessary medical assistance.

The Law of War may rely on a few basic and simple principles. But, on the other hand, the ambit of these is not as narrow as some have made out. Rules on weapons, methods and humanitarian treatment are all clearly relevant.

After having accepted such rules and after claiming that the rules of war bind all, even third parties, it is hypocritical for States, at the same time, to seek to safeguard their national interests by clauses on denunciation. Such clauses are incompatible with any claim that rules are 'generally binding'. And how can the supplementary rules, which are found in everyone's 'conscience', be denounced? There is a constant contradiction between the interests of the States and the interests of the individual. But for the most part, there is an overwhelming presumption, well supported in case law, that States, groups and individuals are bound by the core of the Law of War in its totality and they cannot denounce the general rules.

When we say 'in its totality' no doubt many will argue that there will always be refinements and details by which not all States can be

---

[2] See my *The Concept of International Law*, 104 (cf. 112, 56).

bound in the absence of specific consent. Yet the core of the Law of War consists of less than that and it is only the totality of the 'core' by which parties are bound. The basic rules are very simple and have been stated above as rules concerning exemption from attack of civilians and those *hors de combat*; prohibition of indiscriminate weapons, a rule which really only follows from the first; and a rule on assistance to those who are wounded or in need of help, partly based on the rudimentary principle of reciprocity.

But it is not only States which are bound. By the reason of equality of belligerence liberation movements and guerillas are also bound. States have feared that any such admission would give such groups an undeserved 'standing' which could lead to dangers to the security of the State. But this is misconceived. It is the Law of War that would impose far-reaching duties on such belligerents as liberation movements and guerillas and it is in the interest of States to allow for formalisation of accession to treaties on the Law of War. This has already been achieved in the field of the Conventional Weapons Convention and Protocol I of 1977. That individuals are bound is clearly shown in the war trials and in this field, too, there is a sharp contrast between the Law of War and other parts of international law.

The more rules that are laid down and codified, the more they will crystallise a pattern of behaviour for States and groups. At the time of their adoption the Hague Regulations of 1907 may have represented a major advance on existing international law. But by 1939, i.e. within 32 years, they were held to have become binding upon all members of the international community, even those who had not adhered to them, as they were 'declaratory of the laws and customs of war'.[3]

The tendency to consider conventions on the Law of War as absorbed in 'general' international law binding even on non-parties to the treaties is also reflected in the adoption of certain resolutions of the General Assembly, pronouncing on the state of law as it stands. Certainly, the basic tenets of the Law of War on discrimination between military and civilians, the rules of proportionality and the rule of humanity to victims of war form part of general international law, binding on States, liberation movements and individuals alike. The application of these principles inevitably leads to questions of

---

[3] See the Statute of the Military Tribunal at Nuremberg, *AJIL*, 1947, 249.

legality about the use of nuclear weapons and other weapons of mass destruction: such weapons violate all these time-honoured principles and, like the First World War gas methods, may even pose a danger to the attacking State in adverse wind conditions, even if there is no counter-attack.

The Biological Weapons Convention of 1972, the En-Mod Convention of 1979 and the Weaponry Conventions of 1981, together with the Protocols of 1977 to the Geneva Conventions of 1949, present, in spite of escape clauses like the one we have called the 'jungle exception', a formidable network of rules which is clearly acceptable to States and individuals alike. The rules clarify several hazy areas and define many concepts which give a new focus of application of similar terms in older Conventions. The new instruments furthermore advance on previous protection by extending to some hitherto unprotected groups. For these reasons, the Conventions will also contribute to a clearer identification of rules applicable in armed conflicts both on the international and internal scale, even to parties which do not adhere to these treaties.

The Law of War has also had considerable impact on the law of treaties, seriously questioning whether States and organisations are the only entities endowed with treaty-making power. New methods widen the circle of partners by allowing units such as liberation movements to deposit signatures and 'ratifications' to treaties. Other treaties, like the Conventional Weapons Convention, provide explicitly for the treaty-making power of liberation movements, peculiarly ignored by textbooks, although this development represents one of the most significant changes in international society.

Another area of great change in international law and international relations is the new impact of the articles forbidding force in the United Nations Charter, particularly article 2(4). The Charter forbids the aggressive use of force, but only between States: force against or by insurgents is not prohibited. There is a tentative development of international law, possibly extending the application of the prohibition of force, to restrain use of force *against* insurgents on the basis of human rights. This development would, for example, explain certain attitudes to the events in South Africa. There is a corresponding growth of sympathy for insurgents who, if not representing the majority, have considerable popular support or represent a definable minority, and are receiving gradual protection by international law: by human rights, which restrain the type and intensity of force used against them, or by the emerging rule of democracy which legitimises certain claims for autonomy or independence.

All these trends indicate a shifting of focus in international society, from States to groups and individuals, both insofar as protection of interests and rights are concerned and as regards obligations of such subjects. Thus, in the Law of War, the increased concern about treatment of civilians, prisoners of war and detainees of regular or irregular forces is coupled with increasing duties on the part of such individuals to comply on their side with the rules of the Law of War. By clinging to the State paradigm in a war situation, and by alleging that liberation movements are not 'subjects' of the system, one will only reach the result that States, but not liberation movements, are bound to respect rules of ethics and basic rules of warfare. The time has come to recognise that all parties in any war, whether States or not, are bound by the basic tenets of the Law of War.

SELECT BIBLIOGRAPHY*

Abi-Saab, G., 'Wars of national liberation and the laws of war', 3 *Annals of International Studies* 1972
Histoire législative de l'article 3 commun aux quatre Conventions de Genève, Geneva, 1973
'Les guerres de libération nationale', in *Proceedings of the International Symposium on Humanitarian Law*, Brussels, 1974
'Wars of national liberation and the development of humanitarian law', in R. J. Akkerman, P. J. van Krieken and C. O. Pannenborg (eds.), *Declarations on Principles, a Quest for Universal Peace*, Leiden, 1977
'Les mécanismes de mise en oeuvre du droit humanitaire', 82 *RGDIP* 1978, 103
Adachi, S., *A Process to Reaffirmation to International Humanitarian Law, a Japanese View*, n.p., 1984
Ago, R., 'Le délit international', 68 *RCADI* 1939, ii, 415
Agrawala, S. K., 'An approach to arms control in outer space', *ZaöRVR*, 1984, 497
Ahmed, M. S., 'The neutrals and the test ban negotiations', *Carnegie Occasional Papers*, no. 4, New York, 1964
Albrecht, A. R., 'War reprisals in the war crime trials and the Geneva Conventions of 1949', 47 *AJIL* 1953, 590
Albrecht, E., 'Requisitionen von neutralen Privateigentum inbesondere von Schiffen', 6 *ZaöRVR*, Suppl., 1912, *Kriegs-und Neutralrecht*, 244
Alexander, Y., 'Limitations on chemical and biological warfare beyond those of the Geneva Protocol', in Carnegie Endowment (ed.), *The Control of Chemical and Biological Weapons*, New York, 1971
Alexander, Y. and Gleason, J. M., *Behavioural and Quantitative Perspectives on Terrorism*, Oxford, 1981
Alexander, Y. and Myers, K. A. (eds.), *Terrorism in Europe*, London, 1982
Alexander, Y. and O'Day, A., *Terrorism in Ireland*, London, 1984
Alexander, Y. *et al.* (eds.), *Terrorism: Theory and Practice*, Boulder, Colorado, 1979
Alford, J. (ed.), *The Future of Arms Control*, London, 1979
Alibert, C., *Du droit de se faire justice dans la société internationale depuis 1945*, Paris, 1983

* Additional references on war and armed conflict are to be found in my *Bibliography of International Law*, New York and London, 1976, 397–449

Almond, H. H., 'Deterrence and a policy oriented perspective on the legality of nuclear weapons', in A. S. Miller and M. Feinrider (eds.), *Nuclear Weapons and Law*, Westport, 1984, 57

American Society of International Law, 'Should weapons of dubious legality be developed?' *Proceedings*, 1978

Anand, R. P., 'Pakistan prisoners-of-war and international law', 28 *India Quarterly* 1972, 107

Anderson, O., 'Some further light on the inner history of the Declaration of Paris', 76 *LQR* 1960, 379

Andrassy, J., 'Quelques réflexions sur le problème des opérations de maintien de la paix', *Hommages Guggenheim*, 1968, 773

Andries, A., 'L'emploi de l'arme nucléaire est un crime de guerre', *La revue nouvelle*, 1983, 315

Ansart, P., *Les idéologies politiques*, Paris, 1974

Ansprenger, F., *Die SWAPO, Profil einer afrikanischen Befreiungsbewegung*, Mainz, 1984

Anzilotti, D., 'Effetti della guerra sui trattati internazionali', 12 *Rivista* 1918, 53

Armanazi, N., *Les principes islamiques et les rapports internationaux en temps de paix et de guerre*, Paris, 1929

Arnold, T., *Der revolutionäre Krieg*, Pfaffenhofen, 1961

Aron, R., *Paix et guerre entre les nations*, Paris, 1962
   Penser la Guerre: Clausewitz, Paris, 1976

Aroneanu, E., *La définition de l'agression, exposé objectif*, Paris, 1958

Arzinger, R., *Das Selbsbestimmungsrecht im allgemeinen Völkerrecht*, Berlin, 1966

Asprey, R. B., *War in the Shadows, the Guerilla in History*, New York, 1975

Atala, C. and Groffier, F., *Terrorisme et Guerilla*, Ottawa

Azcarraga, L. J., *El derecho actual de la guerra maritima*, Valladolid, 1961
   El derecho de angaria, Madrid, 1965

Baccino-Astrada, A., *Manual on the Rights and Duties of Medical Personnel in Armed Conflicts*, Geneva, 1982

Baenziger, J., *Die Repressalien im Völkerrecht*, Freiburg, 1925

Bailey, S., *Prohibitions and Restraints in War*, Oxford, 1972
   The Making of Resolution 242, Doordrecht, 1985

Baird, J. W. (ed.), *From Nuremberg to My Lai*, Lexington, 1972

Baker, S. B. and Dodd, W. E., *War and Peace, Presidential Messages, Addresses and Public Papers 1917–1924 of Woodrow Wilson*, New York, 1927

Balladore Pallieri, G., *Diritto bellico*, 2nd edn, Padua, 1954

Balladori Pallieri, M. G., 'The concept of "war" and the concept of "combatant" in modern conflicts', 10 *RDMDG* 1971, 339

Ballis, W. B., *The Legal Position of War: Changes in its Practice from Plato to Vattel*, The Hague, 1973

Barendon, P., *Le système juridique de la Société des Nations pour la prévention de la guerre*, Geneva, 1933

Barker, A. J., *Prisoners-of-War*, New York, 1975

Barnaby, F. and Thomas, G., *The Nuclear Arms Race*, London, 1982

Barnet, R. J. and Falk, R. A., *Security in Disarmament*, Princeton, 1965

Barrett, P. W. and Nurick, L., 'Legality of guerilla forces under the laws of war', *AJIL*, 1949, 563

Barton, J. H. and Weiler, L. D., *International Arms Control, Issues and Agreements*, Stanford, 1976

Bastid, S., *Droit des gens, le droit des crises internationales*, Paris, 1959–69

Batounkov, G., *La protection des biens culturels, monuments historiques et oeuvres d'art en cas de conflit*, Paris, 1977

Baxter, R. R., 'The duty of obedience to the belligerent occupant', 27 *BYIL* 1950, 235

'So-called unprivileged belligerency: spies, guerillas and saboteurs', 28 *BYIL* 1951, 322

'Constitutional forms and some legal problems of international military command', 29 *BYIL* 1952, 335

'Asylum to prisoners-of-war', 30 *BYIL* 1953, 489

'The Privy Council on the qualification of belligerents', 63 *AJIL* 1969, 290

'Criteria of prohibition of weapons in international law', *Festschrift Ulrich Scheuner*, Berlin, 1973

'*Jus in bello interno*, the present and future law', in J. N. Moore (ed.), *Law and Civil War in the Modern World*, Baltimore, 1974

'The Geneva Conventions of 1949 and wars of national liberation', 57 *Rivista* 1974, 193

'Humanitarian law or humanitarian politics?' 16 *Harvard International LJ*, 1975, 1

'Modernizing the law of war', 78 *MLR* 1977, 165

Baxter, R. R. and Buergenthal, T., 'Legal aspects of the Geneva Protocol of 1925', *AJIL*, 1970, 853

Beaton, L., *The Spread of Nuclear Weapons*, London, 1962

Beaufre, A., *Dissuasion et stratégie*, Paris, 1964

La guerre révolutionnaire, Paris, 1972

Bechhoefer, B. G., *Postwar Negotiations for Arms Control*, Washington, DC, 1961

Becker, A. S., *Military Expenditure Limitations for Arms Control*, Cambridge, Massachusetts, 1977

Becker, H. D., *Die Dreizehn Gebote der Kriegskunst*, Munich, 1972

Bedjaoui, M., *Law and the Algerian Revolution*, Brussels, 1961

Beer, F. A., *How Much War in History*, Beverly Hills, 1974

Behuniak, T. E., 'The law of humanitarian intervention by armed force, a legal survey', 79 *MilLR* 1978, 157

Beirlaen, A., *De vervolging van oorlogsmisdadigers in Belgie na de Tweede Wereldoorlog in de bestraffing van inbreuken tegen het oorlogs- en het humanitair recht*, Brussels, 1980

Beirlaen, A., Dockx, S., de Haan, K. and van den Wijngaert, C., *De Bestraffing van Inbreuken tegen het oorlogs- en het Humanitair Recht*, Antwerp, 1970

Belkherroubi, A., 'Essai sur une théorie juridique des mouvements de libération nationale', 28 *Revue égyptienne de droit international* 1972, 20

La naissance et la reconnaissance de la République algérienne, Brussels, 1972

Bellany, I. and Blacker, C. D. (eds.), *The Verification of Arms Control Agreements*, London, 1983

Bello, E. G., *African Customary Humanitarian Law*, Geneva, 1980

Benedek, W., 'Die Anerkennung der PLO durch Österreich', 40 *ZaöRVR* 1980, 841

Bennouna, M., *Le consentement à l'ingérence militaire dans les conflits internes*, Paris, 1974

Berber, F., *3 Lehrbuch des Völkerrechts, Kriegsrecht*, Munich, 1977

Berger, J. F., *L'action du CICR en Indochine 1946–1954*, Montreux, 1982

Bergier, J. and Delaban, J. P., *L'espionnage stratégique*, Paris, 1973

Bernard, H., *Historie de la résistance européenne*, Verviers, 1968

Bernard, I., *War and its Causes*, New York, 1944

Bernard, J., 'The sociological study of conflict', in J. Bernard, I. H. Pear and R. Aron (eds.), *The Nature of Conflict: Studies of the Sociological Aspects of International Tensions*, Paris, 1957

Bertram, C., *Mutual Force Reductions in Europe*, London, 1972
　　Strategic Deterrence in a Changing Environment, London, 1982
　　Third World Conflict and International Security, London 1982

Bertschy, *Die Schutzmacht im Völkerrecht*, Fribourg, 1952

Beshir, M. O., *The Mercenaries and Africa*, Khartoum, 1972

Best, G., *Humanity in Warfare*, London, 1980

Betts, R. K., *Soldiers, Statesmen and Cold War Crises*, Cambridge, Massachusetts, 1977

Bidwell, S., *Modern Warfare: a Study of Men, Weapons and Theories*, London, 1971

Bierzanek, R., 'Le statut juridique des partisans et des mouvements de résistance armée', in *Mélanges offerts à Juraj Andrassy*, The Hague, 1968

Bindschedler, R., 'Die Neutralität im modernen Völkerrecht', 17 *ZaöVR* 1956–7, 1
　　'Die Unterscheidung zwischen Zivilbevölkerung und bewaffneten Kräften', in *Festschrift Verdross*, 1971, 58
　　'Frieden, Krieg und Neutralität im Völkerrecht der Gegenwart', in *Festschrift Wilhelm Wengler*, 1973, 27

Bindschedler-Robert, D., 'Les commissions neutres instituées par l'armistice de Corée', *ASDI*, 1953, 80
　　A Reconsideration of the Law of Armed Conflict, Geneva, 1969
　　'Problems of the law of armed conflict', in M. Bassiouni and V. Nanda (eds.), 1 *International Criminal Law*, Springfield, Illinois, 1973
　　'Les bons offices dans la politique étrangère de la Suisse', in A. Riklin, H. Haug and H. C. Binswanger (eds.), *Handbuch der Schweizerischen Aussenpolitik*, Berne, 1975, 679
　　'Actions of assistance in non-international conflicts, article 18 of Protocol II', in *European Seminar on Humanitarian Law*, Geneva, 1980

Birkett, J., 'International legal theories evolved at Nuremberg', 32 *International Affairs* 1947

Black, C. E. and Thornton, T., *Communism and Revolution*, Princeton, 1964

Blacker, C. D. and Duffy, G. (eds.), *International Arms Control, Issues and Agreements*, 2nd edn, Stanford, 1984

Blanco Gaspar, V., *La agresion internacional: intentos de definicion*, Madrid, 1975

Blechman, B. M., *The Control of Naval Armaments*, Washington, DC, 1975

Bleckmann, A., 'Die Wiederanwendung deutscher Vorkriegsverträge', *ZaöRVR*, 1973, 607

Blix, H., 'When are the laws of war and neutrality applicable?' *Revue égyptienne de droit international public*, 1976, 125
　　'Aerial bombardment, rules and reasons', *BYIL*, 1978, 31

Bloch, I. S., *Modern Weapons and Modern War*, London, 1900, lxiii

Bluntschli, J. C., *Das moderne Kriegsrechts der zivilisierten Staaten*, 2nd edn, Nordlingen, 1874

Boals, K., 'The relation of international law to the internal war in Yemen', in R. A. Falk (ed.), *The International Law of Civil War*, Baltimore, 1971, 306

Bobbio, N. *et al.*, *La guerre et ses théories*, Paris, 1970

Bock, I., *Die Entwicklung des Minenrechts von 1900–1960*, Hamburg, 1963

Bockhoff, F., 'Begriff und Wirklichkeit des Neutralität', *ZaöRVR*, 1939

Bogdanov, O. V., 'Outlawry of war and disarmament', 133 *RCADI* 1971, ii, 15

Bogouslavsky, M. M., *La protection internationale des biens culturels*, Moscow, 1979

Boissier, P., *L'epée et la balance*, Geneva, 1953
  Histoire du Comité International de la Croix-Rouge, de Solférino à Tsoushima, Paris, 1963

Bond, B., *War and Society in Europe, 1870–1970*, London, 1984

Bond, J. E., *The Rules of Riot, Internal Conflict and the Law of War*, Princeton, 1974

Bonnet, C., *La guerre révolutionnaire au Viet-Nam*, Paris, 1969

Borchard, E., 'War and peace', 27 *AJIL* 1933
  'Was Norway delinquent in the case of the *Altmark*?' *AJIL*, 1940, 289

Born, W., *Die offene Stadt, Schützzonen und Guerillakämpfer, Regelungen zum Schütze der Zivilbevölkerung in Kriegszeiten*, Berlin, 1978

Bosli, I. E., *Development in Disarmament Law with Particular Reference to the Biological Weapons Convention of 1972*, Leiden, 1973

Botero, G., *Della Ragione di Stato*, Turin, 1948

Bothe, M., *Le droit de la guerre et les Nations Unies*, Geneva, 1967
  Streitkräfte internationaler Organisationen, Cologne, 1968
  Das völkerrechtliche Verbot des Einsatzes chemischer und bakteriologischer Waffen, Cologne, 1973
  'Rechtsprobleme humanitärischer Hilfsaktionen zugunsten der Zivilbevölkerung bei bewaffneten Konflikte', in P. Fleck (ed.), *Beiträge zur Weiterentwicklung des humanitärischen Völkerrechts für bewaffnete Konflikte*, Hamburg, 1973
  'Die Erklärung der Generalversammlung der Vereinten Nationen über die Definition der Aggression', 18 *JIR* 1975, 127
  'Aspekte des Angola Konfliktes', 37 *ZaöRVR* 1977, 590
  'Le statut de la profession médicale en temps de conflit armé', *Annales de droit international médical*, 1979, 52

Bothe, M., Ipsen, K. and Partsch, K. J., 'Die Genfer Konferenz und das humanitäres Völkerrecht', *ZaöRVR*, 1978, 31

Bothe, M., Partsch, K. J. and Solf, W. A., *New Rules on Victims of War*, The Hague, 1982

Bottie, E., *Essai sur la génèse et l'évolution de la notion de neutralité*, Paris, 1937

Bourdoncle, R., *De l'influence des ruses sur l'évolution du droit de la guerre*, Paris, 1958

Bouthoul, G., *La guerre. Eléments de polémologie*, Paris, 1971, 6th edn, 1978

Boutros-Ghali, B., *Les conflits de frontières en Afrique*, Paris, 1972

Bowett, D., 'Collective self-defence under the charter of the United Nations', *BYIL*, 1955–6

Self-defence in International Law, Manchester, 1958

'Reprisals involving recourse to armed force', 66 *AJIL* 1972, 1

Bowett, D. W., *United Nations Forces: a Legal Study of United Nations Practice*, London, 1964

Boye, T., 'Quelques aspects du développement des règles de la neutralité', 64 *RCADI* 1938, ii, 157

Brandweiner, H., 'Das Partisanenproblem und die Genfer Konventionen von 12. August 1949', 72 *Juristische Blätter* 1950, 261

Brau, J. L., *Les armés de guerilla*, Paris, 1972

Brauch, H. G. and Clarke, D. L., *Decision Making for Arms Limitation: Assessments and Prospects*, Cambridge, Massachusetts, 1983

Brennan, D. G. (ed.), *Arms Control, Disarmament and National Security*, New York, 1961

Bretton, Ph., *Le droit de la guerre*, Paris, 1970

'De quelques problèmes de la guerre dans le conflits indo-pakistanais', *AFDI*, 1972, 201

'Problèmes actuels de l'élaboration du droit des conflits armés', in Colloque de Toulouse, *L'élaboration du droit international public*, Paris, 1975

'Le problème des "méthodes et moyens de guerre ou de combat" dans les Protocols additionnels aux Conventions de Genève du 12 août 1949', *RGDIP*, 1978, 43

'La Convention du 10 avril 1981 sur l'interdiction ou la limitation d'emploi de certaines armes classiques qui peuvent être considerées comme produisant des effets traumatiques excessifs ou comme frappant sans discriminations', *AFDI*, 1981, 92

Bretton, Ph. and Chaudet, J. P., *La coexistence pacifique*, Paris, 1971

Breuker, J., 'La réserve des nécessités militaires dans la Convention de la Haye sur la protection des biens culturels', *RBDI*, 1975, 255

Bridge, J. W., 'The case for an international court of criminal justice and the formulation of international criminal law', *ICLQ*, 1964

Brière, Y., 'Evolution de la doctrine et de la pratique en matière de ressailles', *RCADI*, 1928, ii, 241.

Brierly, J. L., 'International law and the resort to armed force', 4 *Cambridge LJ* 1932

Bright, F., 'Nuclear weapons as a lawful means', *MilLR*, 1965

Brines, R., *The Indo-Pakistani Conflict*, London, 1968

Broms, B., *The Definition of Aggression in the United Nations*, Åbo, 1968

'The definition of aggression', 154 *RCADI* 1977, i, 299

Brown, F. J., *Chemical Warfare: a Study in Restraint*, Princeton, 1968

Brown, H. and Luce, D., *Hostages of War, Saigon's Political Prisoners*, Washington, DC, 1973

Brown, T. D., 'World prize law applied in a limited war situation: Egyptian restrictions on neutral shipping with Israel', 50 *Minnesota LR* 1965–6, 849

Brown-Barclay, R. J., 'Guerre et paix', 49 *Revue de droit international et des science diplomatiques et politiques* 1971, 110

Brownlie, I., 'Volunteers and the Law of War and neutrality', *ICLQ*, 1956, 570
'International law and the activities of armed bands', *ICLQ*, 1958, 712
International Law and the Use of Force by States, Oxford, 1963; reprinted 1982
'Some legal aspects of nuclear weapons', 14 *ICLQ* 1965, 437
'Humanitarian intervention', in J. N. Moore (ed.), *Law and Civil War in the Modern World*, Baltimore, 1974, 217
Bruel, E., '*Altmark* affaeren', *NordTIR*, 1949, 249
Bruha, T., *Die Definition der Aggression*, Berlin, 1980
Bruneau, J., *La ruse dans la guerre sur mer*, Paris, 1938
Brungs, B. J., 'The status of biological warfare in international law', *MilLR*, 1964
Bruns, P., *Über die Wirkung der Bleispitzgeschosse 'Dum Dum'*, Tübingen, 1898
Brzoska, M. and Ohlson, T., *Arms Production in the Third World*, London (SIPRI), 1985
Buchan, A., *War in Modern Society: an Introduction*, London, 1966
Change without War: the Shifting Structures of World Power, London, 1974
Buchan, A. and Windsor, P., *Arms and Stability in Europe*, London, 1963
Buhse, K.-H., *Der Schutz von Kulturgut im Krieg unter besonderer Berucksichtigung der Konvention zum Schutz des Kulturguts im Fall eines bewaffnetes Konflikts vom 14. Mai 1954*, Hamburg, 1959
Bujard, D., 'The Geneva Convention of 1864 and the Brussels Conference of 1874', 14 *IRRC* 1974, 527
Bull, H., *The Control of the Arms Race, Disarmament and Arms Control in the Missile Age*, London, 1961, New York, 1965
'War and International order', in J. Alan (ed.), *The Bases of International Order*, Oxford, 1973
(ed.), *Intervention in World Politics*, New York, 1984
Burckler-Guissani, L., *Die rechtliche Stellung der Rotkreuzformationen nach schweizerischen Recht und nach Völkerrecht*, Zurich, 1979
Burmester, H., 'The recruitment and use of mercenaries in armed conflicts', 72 *AJIL* 1978, 37
Burnett, W. D., 'Command responsibility and a case study of the criminal responsibility of Israeli military commanders for the pogrom at Shatila and Sabra', 107 *MilLR* 1985, 71
Burns, A. L. and Heathcote, N., *Peace-keeping by United Nations Forces*, New York, 1963
Burns, R. D. (ed.), *Arms Control and Disarmament*, War and Peace Bibliography Series, vol. 6, Santa Barbara, 1977
(ed.), *Peace and War*, War and Peace Bibliography Series, vol. 16, Santa Barbara, 1983
Burrows, B. and Edwards, G., *The Defence of Western Europe*, London, 1982
Burt, R., *New Weapons Technologies*, London, 1976
(ed.), *Arms Control and Defense Problems in the 1980s*, Boulder, Colorado, 1982
Butenko, A. P., *Voina i revolutsiya*, Moscow, 1961
Cable, J., *Gunboat Diplomacy 1919–1979: Political Applications of Limited Naval Force*, London, 1981
Cable, L. E., *Conflict of Myths, the Development of American Counterinsurgency Doctrine and the Vietnam War*, New York and London, 1986

Cahen-Salvador, G., *Les prisonniers de guerre 1914–1919*, Paris, 1929

Calogerospoulos-Stratis, A. S., *Droit humanitaire de droits de l'homme, la protection de la personne en periode de conflit armé*, Geneva, 1980

Campbell, A. F., *Guerillas, a History and Analysis*, London, 1967

Campbell, R., *Military Command Liability for Grave Breaches of War and International Law: Absolute or Limited?*, London, 1974

Cansacchi, G., *Nozioni di diritto internazionale bellico*, Turin, 1968

Capotorti, F., *L'occupazione nel diritto de guerra*, Naples, 1949

'L'extinction et la suspension des traités', 134 *RCADI* 1971, iii, 554–5

Carey, J. (ed.), *When Battle Rages How Can Law Protect?*, New York, 1971

Carlisle, G. E., 'The interrelationship of international law and United States naval operations in South East Asia', 22 *JAG Journal of US Navy* 1967, 11

Carlton, D., *The Dynamics of the Arms Race*, London, 1975

Carlton, D. and Schaerf, C. (eds.), *Reassessing Arms Control*, London, 1985

Carnahan, B. M., 'The law of land mine warfare, Protocol II to the UN Convention', 105 *MilLR*, 1984, 73

Carnegie, A. R., 'Jurisdiction over violations of the laws and customs of war', 29 *BYIL* 1963

Carnegie Endowment for International Peace (ed.), *The Control of Chemical and Biological Weapons*, New York, 1971

Chemical Weapons and Chemical Arms Control, New York, 1978

Carrillo Salcedo, J. A., 'Consideraciones sobre el fundamento, naturaleza y significado de la operaciones de la Naciones Unidas destinadas al mantenimiento de la paz', *REDI*, 1965

Casanovas la Rosa, O., 'La reglementacion internacional de los conflictos armados', in D. de Velasco (ed.), 1, *Derecho internacional publico*, n.p., 1980

Casas, V., 'El estatuto juridico–internacional de los mercenarios', 77 *REDI* 1977, 143

Cassese, A., 'Means of warfare, the present and the emerging law', 12 *RBDI* 1976, 143

'The prohibition of indiscriminate means of warfare', in R. J. Akkerman, P. J. van Krieken and C. O. Pannenborg (eds.), *Declarations on Principles, a Quest for Universal Peace*, Leiden, 1977

'Mercenaries, lawful combatants or war criminals?' *ZaöRVR*, 1980, 1

Castberg, F., *Noitralitet*, n.p., n.d.

'Folkerrettslige spörsmål omkring den spanske borgerkrig', *NordTIR*, 1938, 160

Postliminium, Uppsala, 1944

'La neutralité aérienne', *ZaörVR*, 1951, 120

Borgerkrig og revolusjon, Oslo, 1952

Soldater, partisaner og franktirörer, Oslo, 1954

'Neutralität', *AVR*, 1955, 21

Castrén, E., *The Present Law of War and Neutrality*, Helsinki, 1954 'La protection juridique de la population civile dans la guerre moderne', *RGDIP*, 1955, 13

Cavaglieri, A., 'Belligeranza, neutralità e posizioni giuridiche intermedie', *Rivista*, 1919

Centre Henri Rolin (ed.), *Droit humanitaire et conflits armés*, Brussels, 1970
Cesner, R. E. and Brant, J. W., *Law of the Mercenary*, London, 1968
Chalfont, A., *Star Wars, Suicide or Survival*, London, 1985
Chalian, G. (ed.), *Stratégie de la Guérilla*, Paris, 1979
Chaliand, G., *Terrorisme et guérillas*, Paris, 1985
Chandler, D. C., *The Art of Warfare on Land*, London, 1974
Charlier, R. E., 'Questions soulevées pour l'évolution de la science atomique', 91 *RCADI* 1957, i, 213
Charmatz, J. and Wit, H. M., 'Repatriation of prisoners of war and the 1949 Geneva Convention', 62 *Yale LJ* 1952–3, 391
Chatterjee, P., *Arms, Alliances and Stability*, New Delhi, 1975
Chaturvedi, S. C., 'The proposed trial of Pakistani war criminals', *Indian Journal of International Law*, 1971, 645
Chaumont, Ch., 'Nations Unies et neutralité', 89 *RCADI* 1956, i, 59
Ch'en, J., *Mao Papers*, London, 1970
Chiviam, E. *et al.* (eds.), *Last Aid, the Medical Dimension of Nuclear War*, San Francisco, 1982
Christol, C. Q. and Davies, C. R., 'Maritime quarantine: the naval interdiction of offensive weapons and associated material to Cuba, 1962', 57 *AJIL* 1963, 525
Clark, G., 'The English practice with regard to reprisals by private persons', 27 *AJIL* 1933, 694
Clarke, D. L., *Politics of Arms Control: the Role and Effectiveness of the US Arms Control and Disarmament Agency*, London, 1979
Clarke, M. and Mowlam, M., *Debate on Disarmament*, London, 1982
Clarke, R., *We All Fall Down, the Prospect of Biological and Chemical Warfare*, London, 1968
Clausewitz, C. von, *Vom Kriege*, 1834, 18th edn, Bonn, 1972
  On War, ed. M. Howard and P. Paret, Princeton, 1976
CLBV, 'La personalité juridique de l'OTAN', *AFDI*, 1955
Clutterbuck, R., *Guerillas and Terrorists*, London, 1977
Colard, D., *Le désarmement*, Paris, 1972
Colbert, E. S., *Retaliation in International Law*, New York, 1948
Coll, A. R. and Arend, A. C. (eds.), *The Falkland War*, Winchester, Massachusetts, 1985
Colombos, C. J., *A Treatise on the Law of Prize*, London, 1926
Constantinides, J. S., *La réquisition des navires étrangers*, Marseilles, 1942
Constantopoulos, D. S., 'Guerra justa et guerra legal', *REDI*, 1950, 6
Cookson, J. and Nottingham, J., *A New Perspective on War, Chemical and Biological Warfare*, Newcastle upon Tyne, 1968
  A Survey of Chemical and Biological Warfare, London, 1969
Cordnides, W. and Volle, H., *Die internationale Verhandlungen über die Schaffung der Europäischen Verteidigungsgemeinschaft*, 1952
Cornelissen, A. J. M., *De strijd om de moderne staatsidee*, Nijmwegen, 1946
Cosentini, F., *Code international de la paix et de la guerre*, Paris, 1937
Cosyns-Verhaegen, R., *Des armées irrégulières dans l'évolution des Etats et de la société*, 2nd edn, Brussels, 1961
Cot, J. P., *La conciliation internationale*, Paris, 1968

Cotton, J. R., 'The right of mercenaries as prisoners-of-war', 77 *MilLR* 143

Coursier, C., 'L'accession des nouveaux Etats africains aux Conventions de Genève', 7 *AFDI* 1961

Coursier, H., 'L'évolution du droit international humanitaire', 99 *RCADI* 1960, i, 357
   Lessons on the Geneva Conventions, Geneva, 1963

Courteix, S., *Exportation nucléaire et non-prolifération*, Paris, 1978

Cox, A. M., *The Dynamics of Detente*, New York, 1976

Cros, L., *Condition et traitement des prisonniers*, Montpellier, 1900

Cross, M., 'Passage through the Suez Canal of Israeli bound cargo and Israeli ships', 51 *AJIL* 1957, 530

Crozier, B., 'Terrorism: the problem in perspective', in United States, Department of State, *Conference on International Terrorism*, Washington, DC, 1976

Cruden, J. C., 'The war making process', *MilLR*, 1975

Curtis, R. E., 'The law of hostile military expeditions as applied by the United States', *AJIL*, 1914, 1

Dabrowna, S., 'A mi-chemin de la codification du droit international des conflits armés', 5 *Polish Yearbook of International Law* 1972–3, 115

Dahlitz, J., *Nuclear Arms Control*, London, 1983

Dahm, G., *Zur Problematik des Völkerstrafrechts*, Göttingen, 1956
   'Das Verbot der Gewaltanwendung nach Art. 2(4) der UNO-Charta und die Selbsthilfe gegenüber Völkerrechtsverletzungen die keinen Angriff enhalten', 10 *JIR* 1962, 48

Datner, S., *Crimes against Prisoners of War, Responsibility of the Wehrmacht*, Warsaw, 1964

David, E., *La protection des populations civiles pendant les conflits armés*, Strasbourg, 1977
   Mercenaires et volontaires internationaux en droit des gens, Brussels, 1978

Davidon, B., *Frihetskampen i Guinea-Bissau*, Boras, 1969

Davie, M. R., *The Evolution of War, a Study of its Role in Early Societies*, New Haven, 1929
   La guerre dans les sociétés primitives, Paris, 1931

Davis, M., *Civil Wars and the Politics of International Relief*, New York, 1975

Dean, A. H., *Test Ban and Other Disarmament: the Path of Negotiations*, New York, 1966

Deane-Drummons, A., *Riot Control*, London, 1975

Debray, R., *La critique des armes*, Paris, 1974

de Breukner, J., 'La Déclaration de Bruxelles de 1874 concernant les lois et coutumes de la guerre', 27 Chronique de politique étrangère, 1974

Deffarge, C. and Troeller, G., *Yemen 1962–1969, De la révolution sauvage à la trêve des guerriers*, Paris, 1969

de la Pradelle, A., 'Des hostilités sans déclaration de guerre', *RDP*, 1904

de la Pradelle, P., 'Le droit humanitaire des conflits armés', *RGDIP*, 1978, 28

Delbez, L., 'La notion étique de la guerre', 52 *RGDIP* 1952–3, 193

Delcoigne, G. and Rubinstein, G., *Non prolifération des armes nucléaires et systèmes de control*, Brussels, 1970

Delf, G., *Humanizing Hell, the Law v. Nuclear Weapons*, London, 1985

Delivanis, J., *La légitime défense en droit international public moderne, le droit international face à ses limites*, Paris, 1971

Delmas, C., *La guerre révolutionnaire*, Paris, 1959

de Mulinen, F., 'Law of War and armed forces, in Société Internationale de Droit Pénal Militaire et Droit de la Guerre, *Forces armées et développement du droit de la guerre*', Brussels, 1982

den Beer Poortugael, J. C., *Het internationaal maritiem recht*, Breda, 1888

de Sainte-Croix, L., *La déclaration de guerre et ses effets immédiats*, Paris, 1892

d'Estefano, M. A., 'La Cuarantina y el derecho internacional', *Politica Internacional*, no. 4, Havana, 1963

Detrez, C., *Les mouvements révolutionnaires en Amérique latine*, Brussels, 1972

Detter (De Lupis), Ingrid, *Law Making by International Organisations*, Stockholm, 1965

    'The problem of unequal treaties', ICLQ, 1966, 1069

    Essays on the Law of Treaties, London, 1967

    Bibliography of International Law, New York and London, 1976

    Finance and Protection of Investments in Developing Countries, 2nd edn, London 1987

    'Foreign warships and immunity for espionage', *AJIL*, 1984

    International Law and the Independent State, 2nd edn, London, 1987

    The Concept of International Law, Stockholm, 1987

Deventer, H. W. v., 'Mercenaries at Geneva', 70 *AJIL* 1976, 811

DeVisscher, Ch., *La protection des monuments et oeuvres d'art en temps de guerre*, Paris, 1939

    Problèmes de confins en droit international public, Paris, 1969

DeVisscher, F., 'La Convention relative à la non-fortification et à la neutralité des Iles d'Åland', *RDILC*, 1921, 568

de Zayas, A. M., *Die Wehrmachtuntersuchungsstelle, Deutsche Ermittlungen über Aliirte Völkerrechtverletzungen im Zweiten Weltkrieg*, Munich, 1980

Diallo, Y., *Traditions africaines et droits humanitaires*, Geneva, 1976

Diaz Martinez, A., *Manuel de derecho internacional publicao, privado, humanitario*, Bogota, 1977

Dickmann, F., *Friedensrecht und Friedenssicherung*, Göttingen, 1971

Dinstein, Y., *The Defence of Obedience to Superior Orders in International Law*, Leiden, 1965

    'Belligerent occupation and human rights', 8 *IYHR* 1971, 107

    'Another step in codifying the laws of war', *YWA*, 1974, 288

    'The new Geneva Protocols: a step forward or backward?' *YWA*, 1979, 267

Dixon, A. C. and Heilbrunn, O., *Partisanen, Strategie und Taktik des Guerillakrieges*, Frankfurt, 1956

Dobson, C., *The Falkland Conflict*, London, 1982

Dollot, R., 'Essai sur la neutralité permanente', 67 *RCADI* 1939, i, 1

Dominicé, C., 'La notion de caractère ennemi des biens privés dans la guerre sur terre', diss., Geneva, 1961

    'Observations sur les droits de l'Etat victime d'un fait internationalement illicite', in IHEI (ed.), 2 *Droit international*, Paris, 1981–2

    'La personnalité juridique internationale du CICR', in *Etudes Pictet*, Geneva, 1984, 663

Domke, M., *Trading with the Enemy in World War II*, New York, 1943; *Trading with the Enemy and the Control of Alien Property*, New York, 1947
'The War Claims Act of 1962', *AJIL*, 1963, 354
Donelan, M., 'Grotius and the Image of War', 12 *Millennium* 3, Autumn 1983
Dorandeu, H., *La fin de l'état de guerre sans traité de paix*, Montpellier, 1965
Dougherty, J. E., *Arms Control and Disarmament, the Critical Issues*, 1966
Douglas, J. J., 'Counter insurgency: a permitted intervention?' *MilLR*, July 1964
Downey, W. G., 'Captured enemy property, booty of war and seized enemy property', 44 *AJIL* 1950, 488
'The law of war and military necessity', 47 *AJIL* 1953, 251
Draper, G. I. A. D., *The Red Cross Conventions*, London, 1958
'Penitential discipline and public wars in the Middle Ages', 1 *IRRC* 1961, 4
'The legal limitations upon the employment of weapons by the United Nations Force in the Congo', 12 *ICLQ* 1963, 387
'The Geneva Conventions of 1949', 114 *RCADI* 1965, i, 57
'The interaction of Christianity and chivalry in the historical development of the Law of War', 5 *IRRC* 1965, 3
'The legal classification of belligerent individuals', in Centre Henri Rolin (ed.), *Le droit humanitaire et conflits armés*, Brussels, 1970, 149
'The relationship between the human rights regime and the law of armed conflict', 1 *YHR* 1971, 193
'The status of combatants and the question of guerilla warfare', 45 *BYIL* 1971, 173
'Combatant status, the historical perspective', 2 *RDPMDG* 1972, 135
'The People's Republic of China and the Red Cross', in A. Cohen (ed.), *China's Practice of International Law: Some Case Studies*, Cambridge, Massachusetts, 1972
'The implementation and enforcement of the Geneva Convention of 1949 and the two Additional Protocols of 1977', *RCADI*, 1979, 9
Dubner, B. H., *The Law of International Sea Piracy*, The Hague, 1980
Duculeco, V., 'Effet de la reconnaissance de l'état de belligérance par les tiers, y compris les organisations internationales, sur le statut juridique des conflits armés a caractère non international', 79 *RGDIP* 1975, 125
Dull, P. S. and Unemura, M. T., *The Tokyo Trials*, University of Michigan, 1962
Dunbar, N. C. H., 'Military necessity in war crimes trials', *BYIL*, 1952, 442
Duner, B., *Military Intervention in Civil Wars*, Stockholm, 1985
Military Intervention in Civil Wars, the 1970's, London, 1985
Dunshee de Abranches, C. A., *Prosericao das armas nucleares*, Rio de Janeiro, 1964
Dupuy, R. J., 'Agression indirecte et intervention sollicité à propos de l'affaire libanaise', *AFDI*, 1959, 431
Dupuy, R. J. and Leonetti, A., 'La notion de conflit armé à caractère non international', in A. Cassese (ed.), *The New Humanitarian Law of Armed Conflict*, Naples, 1979
Dupuy, T. N. and Hammerman, G. M. (eds.), *A Documentary History of Arms Control and Disarmament*, New York, 1973

Durand, A., *Histoire du Comité International de la Croix Rouge, de Sarajevo à Hiroshima*, Geneva, 1978

Eagleton, C., 'The attempt to define war', *IC*, 1930, 599

'The form and function of the declaration of war', *AJIL*, 1938, 19

Egner, D. O., Shank, E. B., Wargovitch, M. J. and Tiedemann, A. F., *A Multidisciplinary Approach to the Evaluation of Less Lethal Wars*, Maryland, 1973

Ehrhardt, A., *Kleinkrieg, geschichtliche Erfahrungen und künftige Mögligkeiten*, Potsdam, 1935

Eide, A., 'Indre uroligheter og innblandning utenfra', *Tidskrift for Retsvitenskap*, 1965, 1

'Humanitet i vaepnet kamp? Krigets folkrerett under revisjon', *Internasjonal Politikk*, 1973, 341

Eide, A. and Marek, T., *Problems of Contemporary Militarism*, London, 1980

Einhorn, R. J., *Negotiation from Strength: Leverage in US–Soviet Arms Control Negotiations*, New York, 1985

El Hinnawi, E. E., *Nuclear Energy and the Environment*, Oxford, 1980

Ellis, J., *A Short History of Guerilla Warfare*, London, 1975

Elman, S., 'Prisoners-of-war under the Geneva Conventions, based on *Public Prosecutor* v. *Koi* and associated appeals', 18 *ICLQ* 1969, 178

Epstein, W., *The Last Chance: Nuclear Proliferation and Arms Control*, London, 1976

Epstein, W. and Feld, B. T., *New Directions in Disarmament*, New York, 1981

Erich, R., 'La question des zones demilitarisés', *RCADI*, 1929, i, 591

Några folkrättsliga synpunkter hänförande sig till sanktionsproblemet, Uppsala, 1936

Eroglu, *La représentation internationale en vue de protéger les intérêts des belligérants*, Neuchâtel, 1949

Esgain, A. and Solf, W. A., 'The 1949 Geneva Conventions relative to the treatment of prisoners-of-war', 41 *North Carolina LR* 1963, 537

Eudes, D., *Les Kapetanios, la guerre civile grecque 1943–1949*, Paris, 1979

Euler, A., *Die Atomwaffe im Luftkriegsrecht*, Cologne, 1960

Eustathiades, C., 'Quelques aspects de la jurisprudence concernant les criminels de guerre, l'exception des ordres reçus et autres moyens de défense similaire', in 2 *Festschrift Laun*, 1953, 395

'La définition de l'agression adoptée aux Nations Unies et la legitime défense', *Revue héllenique de droit international*, 1975, 1

Evans, A. and Murphy, J. F., *Legal Aspects of International Terrorism*, Lexington, 1978

Evrard, E., 'OMS: Médicin militaire et Conventions de Geneve', *RDPMDG*, 1972, 15

'Le nouveau statut protecteur des transports sanitaires par voie aérienne en temps de conflit armé', *RGDIP*, 1978, 234

Eysinga, W. E. van, 'La guerre chimique et le movement pour sa repression', 16 *RCADI* 1927, i, 347

Fahl, G. (ed.), *Internationales Recht der Rüstungsbeschränkung*, 3 vols., Berlin, 1975

Falk, R. A., *Law, Morality and War in the Contemporary World*, New York, 1963
  'The Shimoda Case, a legal appraisal of the atomic attacks upon Hiroshima and Nagasaki', 59 *AJIL* 1965, 759
  'World law and human conflict', in E. B. McNeil and C. Englewood (eds.), *The Nature of Human Conflict* New York, 1965
  (ed.), *The Vietnam War and International Law*, Princeton, 1969
  'International law aspects of repatriation of prisoners-of-war during hostilities', 67 *AJIL* 1971, 465
  The International Law of Civil War, Baltimore, 1971
  'Law and responsibility in warfare, the Vietnam experience', in P. D. Trooboff (ed.), *Law and Responsibility in Warfare, the Vietnam Experience*, Chapel Hill, North Carolina, 1975
  'Toward a legal regime for nuclear weapons' in A. S. Miller and M. Feinrider (eds.), *Nuclear Weapons and Law*, Westport, 1984, 107
Falk, R. A. and Barnet, R. J., *Security in Disarmament*, Princeton, 1965
Falk, R. A., Kolko, G. and Lifton, R. J., *Crimes of War, a Legal, Political–Documentary and Psychological Inquiry into the Responsibility of Leaders, Citizens and Soldiers for Criminal Acts in War*, New York, 1971
Falk, R. A., Meyrowitz, L. and Sanderson, J., *Nuclear Weapons and International Law*, Princeton, 1981
Farer, T. J., 'The humanitarian laws of war in civil strife: towards a definition of "international armed conflict"', 7 *RBDI* 1971, 29
Fawcett, J. E. S., 'Intervention in international law: a study of some recent cases', *RCADI*, 1961, ii
Feilchenfeld, E. H., *The International Economic Law of Belligerent Occupation*, Washington, DC, 1942
Feld, M. D., *The Structure of Violence*, Beverly Hills, 1977
Fenwick, C. G., 'Intervention: individual and collective', *AJIL* 1945
  'Intervention and the inter-American rule of law', *AJIL*, 1959
  'The issues at Punta del Este: non-intervention v. collective security', *AJIL*, 1962
  'The Quarantine against Cuba, legal or illegal?' 57 *AJIL* 1963, 588
  'Is neutrality still a term of present law?' *AJIL*, 1969
Ferencz, B., 'Defining aggression', *AJIL* 1972, 491
  Defining International Aggression, the Search for World Peace, a Documentary History and Analysis, New York, 1975
Fernandez-Flores, J. L., *Del derecho de la guerra*, Madrid, 1982
Firmage, E. B., 'The war of national liberation and the Third World', in J. N. Moore (ed.), *Law and Civil War in the Modern World*, Baltimore, 1974
Fisch, J., *Krieg und Frieden im Friedensvertrag*, Stuttgart, 1979
Fischer, G., 'Les armes chimiques et bactériologiques', *AFDI*, 1967, 127
  The Non-Proliferation of Nuclear Weapons, 2nd edn, London, 1971
  'Les accords sur la limitation des armements stratégiques', *AFDI*, 1972, 9
Fischer, G. and Vignes, D., *L'inspection internationale*, Brussels, 1976
Fischer, H., *Der Einsatz von Nukleärwaffen nach Artikel 51 des I. Zusatzprotokolles zu den Genfer Konventionen von 1949, Völkerrecht zwischen humanitären Anspruch und Militärpolitischer Notwendigkeit*, Berlin, 1983

Fischer, J. B., *Incendiary Warfare*, New York, 1945

Fitzmaurice, G., 'Some aspects of modern contraband control and the law of prize', *BYIL*, 1945, 73

'The juridical clauses of the Peace Treaties', 73 *RCADI* 1948, ii, 255

Fleck, D., 'Die rechtliche Garantien des Verbots von unmittelbaren Kampfhandlungen gegen Zivilpersonen', *RDPMDG*, 1966, 97–8

(ed.), *Beiträge zur Weiterentwicklung des humanitärischen Völkerrechts für bewaffnete Konflikte*, Kiel, 1973

'Ruses of war and prohibition of perfidy', *Revue du droit de la guerre*, 1974, 269

Flory, M., *Le statut international des gouvernements réfugiés et le cas de la France libre 1939–1945*, Paris, 1952

'Vers une nouvelle conception du prisonnier de guerre', 59 *RGDIP* 1954, 67

'Algérie et le droit international', *AFDI*, 1959, 817

Algérie algérienne et le droit international, *AFDI*, 1960, 973

'Négotiation ou dégagement en Algérie', *AFDI*, 1961, 836

Flory, W. E. S., *Prisoners of War, a Study in the Development of International Law*, Washington, DC, 1942

Forndran, E., *Rüstungskontrolle, Friedensicherung zwischen Abschreckung und Abrüstung*, Bonn, 1977

Forsythe, D. P., 'The 1974 diplomatic conference on humanitarian law: some observations', 69 *AJIL* 1975, 77

'Who guards the guardian? Third parties and the law of armed conflict', 70 *AJIL* 1976, 41

Humanitarian Politics, the ICRC, Baltimore, 1977

'Legal management of internal war', 72 *AJIL* 1978, 272

Franck, T. and Rodley, N., 'After Bangladesh: the law of humanitarian intervention by military force', *AJIL*, 1973, 275

François, J. P., 'L'égalité d'application des règles du droit de la guerre aux parties à un conflit armé', *AFDI*, 1963

Franklin, W. M., 'Municipal property under belligerent occupation', *AJIL*, 1944, 383

Freedman, L., 'Britain and the arms trade', *International Affairs*, July 1978

Britain and Nuclear Weapons, London, 1980

Arms Control in Europe, London, 1981

The Evolution of Nuclear Strategy, London, 1981

Arms Control, Management or Reform?, London, 1986

Freeman, A. V., 'General note on the law of war booty', *AJIL*, 1946, 795

'Responsibility of states for unlawful acts of their armed forces', 88 *RCADI* 1955, ii, 267

Frei, D., 'The regulation of warfare, a paradigm to the legal approach to the control of international conflict', in International Political Science Association (ed.), *IX World Congress*, Montreal, 1973

Frey, H. K., *Die disziplinärische und gerichtliche Bestrafung von Kriegsgefangene*, Vienna, 1948

Freymond, J., 'Aid to the victims in the civil war in Nigeria', 19 *IRRC* 1970, 65

'Confronting total war, a "global" humanitarian policy', 67 *AJIL* 1973, 672

Guerre, révolutions, Croix Rouge, réflexions sur le rôle du CICR, Geneva, 1976

Guerres, révolutions, Croix-Rouge, Geneva, 1976

Fried, H. E., 'International law prohibits the first use of nuclear weapons', *RBDI*, 1981–2, 1, 33

Friedmann, L., *The Law of War: a Documentary History*, New York, 1972

Frohwein, J., 'Völkerrechtliche Aspekte des Vietnam-Konfliktes', *ZaöRVR*, 1967, 1

Fuller, J. F. C., *War and Western Civilization 1832–1932*, London, 1932

Armament and History. A Study of the Influence of Armaments on History from the Dawn of Classical Warfare to the Second World War, London, 1946, 62

The Conduct of War 1789–1961, London, 1961

Furet, M. F., *Le désarmement nucléaire*, Paris, 1972

Le discours de la guerre, Paris, 1979

Furet, M. F., Martinez, J. C. and Dorandeau, M., *La guerre et le droit*, Paris, 1979

Galtung, J., *Fredsforskning*, Halmstad, 1969

Galula, D., *Counter-insurgency Warfare, Theory and Practice*, New York, 1964

Gann, L., *Guerillas in History*, Stanford, 1971

Garcia Arias, L., 'El concepto de guerra y la denominada guerra fria' and 'Sobre la legalidad de la guerra moderna', in *La guerra moderna y sa organizacion internacional*, Madrid, 1962

Garcia, L. R., 'La poblacion civil y la guerra moderna', *REDI*, 1953, 325

Garcia-Mora, M. R., *International Law and Asylum as a Human Right*, Washington, DC, 1956

Garcia Robles, A., 'The Treaty for the prohibition of Nuclear Weapons in Latin America (Treaty of Tlatelolco)', *SIPRI Yearbook*, 1969/70, 218

Gardot, A., 'Le droit de la guerre dans l'oeuvre des capitaines français du XVIe siècle', 72 *RCADI* 1948, i, 393

Garner, J. W., 'Some questions of international law in the European war, blockades', *AJIL*, 1915

'Punishment of offenders against the laws and customs of war', *AJIL*, 1920, 70

International Law and the World War, 2 vols., London, 1929

'Violation of maritime law by the Allied Powers during the World War', 25 *AJIL* 1931, 26

Garnett, J. (ed.), *Theories of Peace and Security*, London, 1970

Gathings, J. A., *International Law and American Treatment of Alien Enemy Property*, Washington, DC, 1940

Gavelle, J. F., 'The Falkland (Malvinas) Islands: an international law analysis of the dispute between Argentina and Great Britain', 107 *MilLR* 1985, 5

Genot, G., 'Quelques garanties nouvelles offertes au combattant capturé', 13 *RBDI* 1977, 298

George, A. *et al.*, *The Limits of Coercive Diplomacy*, Boston, 1971

Germany, Bundesministerium für Verteidigung, *Völkerrechtliche Grundsätze der Landkriegsführung*, Bonn, 1961

Gervais, A., 'Le droit des prises maritimes dans la seconde guerre mondiale', *RGDIP*, 1948, 88; 1949, 201; 1950, 251; 1951, 481

'La jurisprudence italienne des prises maritimes durant la seconde guerre mondiale', *RGDIP*, 1950, 251ff, 433ff

'La jurisprudence allemande des prises maritimes durant la seconde guerre mondiale', *RGDIP*, 1951, 481

'Les armistices palestiniens, coréens et indochinois et leurs enseignements', *AFDI*, 1956, 97

Gervasi, T., *Arsenal of Democracy, American Weapons Available for Export*, New York, 1977

Ghionda, F., *Il diritto d'angheria*, Rome, 1948

Gialdino, A. C., *Gli effetti della guerra sui trattati*, Milan, 1959

Giap, V. V., *La guerre de libération nationale au Vietnam*, Hanoi, 1970

Gibson, R., *African Liberation Movements*, London, 1972

Gihl, T., 'Om krigets natur och det ekonomiska kriget', *Svensk Tidskrift*, 1930, 454

Folkrätt under krig och neutralitet, Stockholm, 1941

'Svensk neutralitetsrättslig praxis under de båda världskrigen', *Jus Gentium*, 1949

Gilks, A. and Segal, G., *China and the Arms Trade*, London, 1985

Gilmore, W., *The Grenada Intervention*, London, 1984

Ginsburgs, G., 'The Soviet Union, the neutrals and international law in World War II', *ICLQ*, 1962, 171

Giraud, E., 'La théorie de la légitime défense', *RCADI*, 1934, iii, 858

'L'interdiction du recours à la force, la théorie et la pratique des Nations Unies', 67 *RGDIP* 1963, 501

Glahn, G. v., *The Occupation of Enemy Territory: a Commentary on the Law and Practice of Belligerent Occupation*, London, 1957

Glaser, S., 'La protection internationale des prisonniers de guerre et la responsabilité pour les crimes de guerre', 31 *RDPC* 1950–1, 897

'La Convention de Genève et les criminels de guerre', 32 *RDPC* 1951–2, 517

'Responsabilité pour la participation à une guerre-crime. Les soldats qui y prennent part, encourent-ils une responsabilité pénae?' 24 *RSCDPC* 1969, 593

Glass, H. B., 'The biology of nuclear war', in C. A. Barker (ed.), *Problems of World Disarmament*, Boston, 1963

Glasstone, S. and Doland, P. J. (eds.), *The Effects of Nuclear Weapons*, 3rd edn, Washington, DC, 1977

Glucksmann, A., *Le discours de la guerre*, Paris, 1979

Glueck, S., *The Nuremberg Trial and Aggressive War*, New York, 1946, reprint, 1966

Goldblat, J., *Agreement for Arms Control, a Critical Survey*, London, 1982

Gompert, D. C. *et al.* (eds.), *Nuclear Weapons and World Politics*, New York, 1977

Gonsalves, E. L., 'De Protocollen van Geneve en de verbetende bescherming van gewonden, zicken en gemeeskundige diensten', 17 *Militair Rechtelijk Tijdschrift*, 1978, 1

Gooch, J. P., *Armies in Europe, Military Organization and Society*, London, 1980

Goodwin, G., *Ethics and Nuclear Deterrence*, London, 1982

Gordon, E., 'La visite des convois neutres', *RGDIP*, 1934, 566

Gotlieb, A., *Disarmament and International Law*, Toronto, 1965

Gowing, M., *Independence and Deterrence, Britain and Atomic Energy 1945–1952*, London, 1964

Graven, J., 'Les crimes contre l'humanité', 76 *RCADI* 1950, i, p. 433

Green, L. C., *Superior Orders in National and International Law*, Leiden, 1976
Essays on the Modern Law of War, New York, 1985

Greenberg, E. C., 'Law and the conduct of the Algerian revolution', 11 *Harvard International LJ* 1970, 37

Greenspan, M., *Modern Law of Land Warfare*, London, 1959

Grenander, D. K., *Om de folkrättsliga villkoren for ratt att i krig betraktas som soldat*, Stockholm, 1877

Grob, O., *The Relativity of War and Peace, a Study in Law, History and Politics*, New Haven, 1949
Das Recht der Kriegsgefangen und Zivilpersonen nach der Genfer Konvention vom 12.8.1949, Hamburg, 1952

Groffier, E., *Terrorisme et guerilla, la révolte armée devant les nations*, Ottawa, 1973

Gros Espiel, H., 'La signature du Traité de Tlatelolco par la Chine et la France', *AFDI*, 1973, 13

Gross, L., 'Voting in the Security Council and the PLO', 70 *AJIL* 1976, 470

Guettard, J., 'Les conditions d'intervention du CICR avant belligérance', *AFDI*, 1956, 353

Guevara, Ernesto ('Che'), *La guerra de guerillos*, Havana, 1960
(trans. V. Ortiz) *Reminiscences of the Cuban Revolutionary War*, London, 1968
Guerilla Warfare, London, 1969
Pasajes de la guerra revolucionaria, Mexico, 1969

Guggenheim, P., 'La securité collective et le problème de la neutralité', *ASDI*, 1945

Guillaume, C. and Levasseur, G., *Terrorisme international*, Paris, 1977

Gurlt, E., *Zur Geschichte der internationalen und freiwilligen Krankenpflege im Kriege*, Leipzig, 1873

Gutteridge, J., 'The Geneva Conventions of 1949', 26 *BYIL* 1949, 294
'The rights and obligations of an occupying power', *YWA*, 1952, 152
'The repatriation of prisoners-of-war', 2 *ICLQ* 1953, 207

Guttinger, P., 'Réflexions sur la jurisprudence des prises maritimes de la seconde guerre mondiale', *RGDIP*, 1975, 25

Haggenmacher, P., *Grotius et la doctrine de la guerre juste*, Paris, 1983

Hahlweg, W., *Guerilla: Krieg ohne Fronten*, Stuttgart, 1968
Lehrmeister des kleinen Krieges, Von Clausewitz bis Mao Tse Tung und Che Guevara, Darmstadt, 1968

Halperin, M. H., *Limited War in a Nuclear Age*, New York, 1963

Hambro, E., 'Das Neutralitätsrecht der nordischen Staaten', *ZaöRVR*, 1938, 32
'Ideologie und Neutralität', *ZaöRVR*, 1939

Hanrieder, W. F., *Arms Control and Security, Current Issues*, Boulder, Colorado, 1979

Hanslian, R., *Der chemische Krieg*, Berlin, 1937

Harris, R. and Paxman, J., *A Higher Form of Killing: the Secret Story of Gas and Germ Warfare*, London, 1982

Hartley, J. E., 'The law of angary', 13 *AJIL* 1919, 290
Harvey, F., *Air Warfare, Vietnam*, New York, 1967
Haug, H., *Rotes Kreuz*, Stuttgart, 1966
Hazan, E. T., *L'état de nécessité en droit pénal interétatique et international*, Paris, 1949
Hecht, B., *Perfidy*, New York, 1961
Herczegh, T., 'Recent problems in international humanitarian law', in G. Haraszti (ed.), *Questions of International Law*, Budapest, 1977
Herezegh, G., 'La protection de l'environnement et le droit humanitaire', in *Pictet Etudes*, Geneva, 1984, 725
Herrioit, C. E., 'Biological warfare', in C. A. Barker (ed.), *Problems of World Disarmament*, Boston, 1963
Hersh, S. M., *Chemical and Biological Warfare*, New York, 1968
Herzog, J. B., 'Les principes juridiques de la répression des crimes de guerre', 60 *Schweizerische Zeitschrift für Strafrecht* 1946, 282
Heydte, A. v. d., *Die Geburtsstunde des souveränen Staats*, Frankfurt, 1952
 'Atomäre Kriegführung und Völkerrecht', 9 *AVR* 1961-2, 162
 'Grundbegriffe des modernen Kriegsrechts', 56 *Die Friedenswarte* 1961-6, 333
 'Le problème que pose l'existence des armes de destruction massive et la distinction entre objets militaires et non-militaires', Rapport in Institut de Droit International, 52 *Annuaire* 1967, i
 'Humanisierung des Kriegsrechts? Kritische Bemerkungen zu den Genfer Vertragsentwurf von 1977', 26 *Europäische Wehrkunde* 1977, 550
Heyns, H., *Die Anwendung von militärischen Repressalien*, Kiel, 1938
Hiebel, J. L., *Les droits humains de l'assistance spirituelle dans les conflits armés*, Strasbourg, 1976
Higgins, P. A., 'Submarine warfare', *BYIL*, 1920–1, 149
 'Ships of war as prize', *BYIL*, 1925, 103
 'Visit search and detention', *BYIL*, 1926, 43
 'The treatment of mails in time of war', *BYIL*, 1928, 31
Higgins, R., 'International law and civil conflict', in E. Luard (ed.), *International Regulation of Civil Wars*, London, 1972
 'Intervention and international law', in H. Bull (ed.), *Intervention in World Politics*, New York, 1984
Higham, R. D. S., *Civil War in the Twentieth Century*, Lexington, 1972
Hingorami, R. C., *Prisoners-of-War*, Bombay, 1963
Hinz, J., *Das Kriegsgefangenenrecht*, Berlin, 1955
 Kriegsvölkerrecht, 2nd edn, Cologne, 1960
Hinz, J. and Rauch, E., *Kriegsvölkerrecht*, Cologne, 1984
Hoffman, S., 'The problem of intervention', in H. Bull (ed.), *Intervention in World Politics*, New York, 1984
Holland, T., *The Laws of War on Land*, Oxford, 1908
Holtzoff, A., 'Some phases in the law of blockade', *AJIL*, 1916, 53
Hoopes, T., *The Limits of Intervention*, New York, 1969
Horelick, A. L., *Perspectives on the Study of Comparative Military Doctrines*, Santa Monica, 1973
Horlemann, J., *Modelle der kolonialen Konterrevolution*, Frankfurt, 1968

Howard, M. (ed.), *Studies in War and Peace*, London, 1970
   (ed.), *Restraints on War*, Oxford, 1979
   War in European History, Oxford, 1976
   War and the Liberal Conscience, Oxford, 1978
   The Causes of War and Other Essays, London, 1983
Hsia, C. L., *War and Use of Force in International Law*, New York, n.d.
Huber, M., *The Red Cross, Principles and Problems*, Geneva, n.d.
   'Kriegsrechtlichen Verträge und die Kriegsraison', *ZVR*, 1913, 351
Hudson, M. O., 'Seizures in land and naval warfare distinguished', *AJIL*,
   1922, 483
   'A soldier's property in war', *AJIL*, 1932, 340
Hurst, C. J. B., 'The effect of war on treaties', *BYIL*, 1921–2, 37
Hussain, M., 'New developments in international humanitarian law', in First
   Asian Seminar (ed.), *Humanitarian Law*, Kuala Lumpur, 1978
Hyde, C., 'Japanese execution of American aviators', *AJIL*, 1943, 480
Hyde, D., *On Roots of Guerilla Warfare*, London, 1968
ICRC, *La protection des populations civiles contre les bombardements, consultations
   juridiques*, Geneva, 1930
   (ed. J. Pictet), *Les Conventions de Genève de 1949, Commentaire*, 4 vols., Geneva,
   1958
   *Respect for and Development of International Humanitarian Law, from Manila (1981)
   to Geneva (1986), Interim Assessment and Future Prospects*, Geneva, 1985
Iglesias Buigues, J. L., 'La prohibicion general del recurso de la fuerza y las
   resoluciones descoloniazadoras de la Asamblea General de la Naciones
   Unidas', *REDI*, V, XXIV-1
Ijalaye, D. A., 'Was "Biafra" at any time a state in international law?' 65
   AJIL 1971, 551
Independent Commission for Disarmament and Security Issues, *Common Se-
   curity, Programme for Disarmament, the Palme Report*, London, 1982
Inglis, D. R., 'Nuclear warfare', in C. A. Barker (ed.), *Problems of World
   Disarmament*, Boston, 1963
Institut Henri Dunant and UNECSO (ed.), *Les dimensions internationales du
   droit humanitaire*, Paris, 1984
Institute for the Study of Conflict (ed.), *Annual of Power and Conflict, a Survey of
   Political Violence and International Influence*, London, 1976–7
International Institute for Peace and Conflict Research (ed.), *The Problems of
   Chemical and Biological Warfare*, New York, 1971
International Institute for Strategic Studies, *New Conventional Weapons and
   East–West Security*, 2 parts, London, 1978
International Organisation for the Elimination of All Forms of Racial Dis-
   crimination (ed.), *Witness of War Crimes in Lebanon, Testimony Given to the
   Nordic Commission in Oslo, October 1982*, London, 1983
Ipsen, K., 'Die Kampfführungsbestimmungen des I. Protokolls unter beson-
   dere Berücksichtigung des Kombattantenstatus', 21 *NZWR* 1979, 98
Irving, D., *The Destruction of Dresden*, London, 1963
Izquierdo, E., *Apuntes de derecho internacional humanitario*, Quito, 1983
Jakovljevic, B., *New International Status of Civil Defence as an Instrument for
   Strengthening the Protection of Human Rights*, The Hague, 1982

Janner, *La puissance protectrice en droit international*, Basle, 1948

Jasani, B., *Space Weapons: the Arms Control Dilemma*, London (SIPRI), 1984

Jennings, R. Y., '*The Caroline and McLeod Case*', *AJIL*, 1938
    'Open towns', 22 *BYIL* 1945, 258

Jescheck, H. H., *Die Verantwortlichkeit der Staatsorgane nach Völkerstrafrecht*, Bonn, 1952

Jessup, P., 'A belligerent occupant's power over property', *AJIL*, 1944, 457

Jessup, P., Deak, F. and Reede, A. H., *Neutrality, its History, Economics and Law*, 4 vols., New York, 1935–6

Jobst, V., 'Is the wearing of the enemy's uniform a violation of the laws of war?' 35 *AJIL* 1941, 435

Johann, H., *Begriff und Bedeutung des Ultimatums im Völkerrecht*, Berlin, 1967

Johnson, C., *Revolution and the Social System*, Stanford, 1964
    Revolutionary Change, London, 1966
    Autopsy on People's War, London, 1973

Johnson, J. T., *Just War Tradition and the Restraint of War, a Moral and Historical Inquiry*, Princeton, 1981
    Can Modern Wars be Just?, London, 1984

Joyce, J. A., *Red Cross International and the Strategy of Peace*, New York, 1959

Kalshoven, F., *Belligerent Reprisals*, Leiden, 1971
    The Laws of Warfare, Leiden, 1973
    'The Conference of Government Experts in the Use of Certain Conventional Weapons, 2nd session, Lugano 1976', *NedTIR*, 1976, 199
    'The reaffirmation and development of international humanitarian law applicable in armed conflicts, the Diplomatic Conference in Geneva 1974–1977', 8 *NedTIR* 1977, 122
    'Belligerent reprisals in the light of the 1977 Geneva Protocols', in *European Seminar on Humanitarian Law*, Geneva, 1980

Kant, I., *Zum ewigen Frieden*, Königsberg, 1795

Katevenis, G., 'The law of maritime war, considerations on the law of prize jurisdiction over the enemy's ships in time of war', 4 *RDPMDG* 1965, 359

Keen, M., *The Laws of War in the Later Middle Ages*, Oxford, 1965

Kegel, G., Rupp, H. and Zweigert, K., *Die Einwirkung des Krieges auf Vertrage*, Berlin, 1941

Keliher, J. G., *The Negotiations on Mutual and Balanced Force Reductions*, New York, 1980

Kelly, J. B., 'Gas warfare in international law', 9 *MilLR* 1960
    'Legal aspects of military operations in counterinsurgency', 21 *MilLR* 1963

Kelly, W. A. and Miller, L. R., *Internal War and International Systems*, New York, 1973

Kelsen, H., 'Unrecht und Unrechtsfolge im Völkerrecht', *ZaöRVR*, 1932, 270
    'È possibile e desiderabile definire l'aggressione?' in 2 *Scritti in onore di Tomaso Perassi*, Milan, 1957, 3

Khadduri, M., *War and Peace in the Law of Islam*, Baltimore, 1955

Khare, S. C., *Use of Force under UN Charter*, New Delhi, 1985

Khushlana, Y., *Dignity and Honour of Women and Basic Fundamental Human Rights*, The Hague, 1982

Kimminich, O., *Völkerrecht im Atomzeitalter, der Atomsperrvertrag und seine Folgen*, Freiburg, 1965

Humanitäres Völkerrecht – Humanitäre Aktion, Munich, 1972

Schutz der Menschen in bewaffneten Konflikten: Zur Fortentwicklung des humanitärischen Völkerrechts, Munich, 1979

'Der Einfluss des humanitären Völkerrechts und auf die Kriegswaffenfrage', in I. v. Munch (ed.), *Festschrift Schlochauer*, Berlin, 1981, 407

Kincade, W. H. and Porro, J. D. (eds.), *Negotiating Security: an Arms Control Reader*, New York, 1979

Kischlat, W. D., *Das Übereinkommen über das Verbot der Entwicklung, Herstellung und Lagerung bakteriologischer (biologischer) Waffen und von Toxin-Waffen sowie über die Vernichtung solcher Waffen*, Frankfurt, 1976

Klawkowski, A., 'Les formes de cessation de l'état de guerre en droit international', *RCADI*, 1976, i, 217

Les formes de cessation de l'état de guerre en droit international, Leiden, 1977

Kleen, R., *De la contrabande de guerre*, Paris, 1893

Krigets historia ur folkrättslig synpunkt, Stockholm, 1906

Röda Korset enligt konventionerna, Stockholm, 1906

Kodifierad handbok i krigets lagar till lands och till sjöss enligt aftal och vedertagen sedvänja bland hyfsade folkslag, Stockholm, 1909

Klein, E., 'Nationale Befreiungkampfe und Dekolonisierungspolitik der Vereinten Nationen', 36 *ZaöRVR* 1976, 618

Klimmeck, H. D., *Die Zulässigkeit von staatlichen Sanktionen im heutigen Völkerrecht*, Cologne, 1968

Knorr, L., *On the Uses of Military Power in the Nuclear Age*, Princeton, 1966

Kolodkin, A. L., 'Morskaya blokada i sovremennoe mezhdunarodnoe pravo', *Sovetskoe gosudarstvo i pravo*, Moscow, 1963, no. 4, 92

Kolodziej, E., 'France and the arms trade', *International Affairs*, January 1980

Komarnicki, T., 'The place of neutrality in the modern system of international law', 80 *RCADI* 1952, i, 395

Komarnicki, W., 'La définition de l'agresseur dans le droit international moderne', 75 *RCADI* 1949, ii, 1

Korovine, E., 'La guerre chimique et le droit international', 36 *RGDIP* 1929

Kotzsch, L., *The Concept of War in Contemporary History and International Law*, Geneva, 1956

Krafft, A., 'The present position of the Red Cross Geneva Conventions', 37 *TransGrotSoc* 1951, 146

Krass, A. S., *Verification: How Much is Enough?*, London (SIPRI), 1983

Krepon, M., 'Weapons potentially inhuman: the case of cluster bombs', in R. Falk (ed.), 4 *The Vietnam War and International Law*, Princeton, 1976, 266

Kreuger-Sprengel, F., 'The concept of proportionality in the context of the law of war', in *VIII Congress of the International Society for Military Law and the Law of War*, Ankara, 1979

Krippendorff, E., *Staat und Krieg*, Frankfurt, 1985

Kuhlman, J. A. (ed.), *Strategies, Alliances and Military Power*, Leiden, 1977

Kunz, J. L., *Gaskrieg und Völkerrecht*, Vienna, 1927

Kriegsrecht und Neutralitätsrecht, Vienna, 1935

'British prize cases 1939–1941', 36 *AJIL* 1942, 204

'British prize law', *Law Quarterly Review*, 1945, 49

'The Geneva Conventions of August 12 1949', in *Hommages Kelsen*, Los Angeles, 1953

'*Bellum iustum* and *bellum legale*', 45 *AJIL* 1956, 528

'The laws of war', 50 *AJIL* 1956, 317

'Die neuen amerikanischen Flotteninstruktionen über Seekriegsrecht', 8 *ÖZöR* 1957, 270

'The chaotic status of the laws of war and the urgent necessity for their revision', in J. Kunz *The Changing Law of Nations, Essays on International Law*, Chicago, 1968

Kunzmann, K. H., 'Militärisches Objekt und unverteidigte Stadt', *RDPMDG*, 1965

Kurtzer, D. C., *Palestine Guerilla and Israeli Counter Insurgency Warfare*, New York, 1976

Labrousse, A., *Die Tupamaros, Stadtguerilla in Uruguay*, Munich, 1971

Lachs, M., 'La nouvelle fonction des armistices contemporains', *Mélanges Basdevant*, Paris, 1960

Lalive, J. F., 'Quelques nouvelles tendances de la neutralité', *Die Friedenswarte*, 1940, 1

'International organization and neutrality', *BYIL*, 1947, 72

Lamberti Zanardi, P., *La legitima difesa nel diritto internazionale*, Milan, 1972

Lapidoth, R., 'Qui a droit au statut de prisonnier de guerre?' *RGDIP*, 1978, 170

Laqueur, W., *Guerilla, a Historical and Critical Study*, London, 1977

Lasala Samper, F. M., *La proteccion de los heridos, enfermos y naufragos de la fuerzas armadas en campana*, Zaragoza, 1964

Laun, R., *Die Haager Landkriegsordnung vom 18.10.1907*, 3rd edn, Hanover, 1947

Lauterpacht, H., 'The limits of the operation of the laws of war', 30 *BYIL* 1953, 206

Lazarus, C., 'Le statut des mouvements de libération nationale à l'ONU', *AFDI*, 1974, 173

Le Fur, L., *Des répressailles en temps de guerre, répressailles et réparation*, Paris, 1919

Leiden, C. and Schnitt, K. (eds.), *The Politics of Violence: Revolution in the Modern World*, Englewood Cliffs, New Jersey, 1968

Le Quang, G., *La guerre d'Indochine 1964–1973*, Paris, 1973

Levie, H. S., 'Employment of prisoners-of-war', 57 *AJIL* 1963, 318

'Some major inadequacies in the existing law relating to the protection of individuals during armed conflict', in D. T. Fox (ed.), *The Cambodian Incursion*, New York, 1971

'Legal aspects of the continued detention of Pakistani prisoners of war by India', *AJIL*, 1973, 512

Protection of War Victims, Protocol I to the Geneva Conventions, 4 vols., New York, 1979–81

Mine Warfare and International Law, US Naval War College, Newport, 1980

Lew, D. H., 'Manchurian booty and international law', *AJIL*, 1946, 584

Liddell Hart, B. H., *The Revolution in Warfare*, London, 1946

Strategy, the Indirect Approach, London, 1967

Littauer, R. and Uphoff, N., *The Air War in Indochina*, Boston, 1972
Little, R., *Intervention, External Involvement in Civil Wars*, Totowa, New Jersey, 1975
Livingston, M. H., Kress, L. B. and Wanck, M. G. (eds.), *International Terrorism in the Contemporary World*, London, 1978
Lodemann, E., 'Die Genfer Abkommen vom 12. August 1949', *AVR*, 1953, 72
Lodge, J. (ed.), *Terrorism: A Challenge to the State*, Oxford, 1981
Lombardi, A. V., *Bürgerkreig und Völkerrecht*, Berlin, 1976
Loverdo, C., *Les macquis rouges des Balkans 1941–1945*, Paris, 1967
Luard, E., *Conflict and Peace in the International System*, Boston, 1968
  The International Regulation of Civil War, London, 1972
  War in International Society, a Study in International Sociology, London, 1986
Luck, E. C. (ed.), *Arms Control: The Multilateral Alternative*, New York, 1983
Lumsden, M., *From the Dum Dum to Napalm, the Struggle against Inhumane Weapons*, London, 1980
Lussu, E., *Théorie de l'insurrection*, Paris, 1971
McCuen, J. J., *The Art of Counter-revolutionary War*, Harrisburg, 1966
McDougal, M. S., 'The Soviet Cuban Quarantine and self-defence', 57 *AJIL* 1963, 597
McGrath, M. E. E., 'Nuclear weapons, a crisis of conscience', 107 *MilLR* 1985, 191
Machiavelli, *Il Principe*, XVIII (ed. Vertelli), Milan, 1960
McLachlan, K., *The Gulf War, a Survey of Political Issues and Economic Consequences*, Special Report no. 176, The Economist Intelligence Unit, London, 1984
McNair, A. D., 'The legal meaning of war and the right to reprisals', 11 *TransGrotSoc*, 1926
  'Les effets de la guerre sur les traités', 49 *RCADI* 1937, i, 527
McNair, A. D. and Watts, D. V., *The Legal Effects of War*, 4th edn, Cambridge, 1966
McNemar, D. W., *International Law and Internal War, the Congo and the United Nations*, Princeton, 1971
McNulty, J. F., 'Blockade, evolution and expectation', in US Naval War College (ed.), *International Law Situations*, Newport, 1980, 172
Maigret, M., *La guerre psychologique*, Paris, 1956
Mailler, A., *De la distinction des combattants et non combattants comme base du droit de guerre*, Paris, 1916
Mainar, H. L., *Ensayo de un derecho de la guerra*, Buenos Aires, 1954
Malintoppi, A., *La protection dei beni culturali in caso di conflito armato*, Milan, 1966
Malkin, H. W., 'Blockade in modern conditions', *BYIL*, 1922–3, 483
  'The inner history of the Declaration of Paris', *BYIL*, 1927, 1
Mallein, J., *La situation juridique des combattants dans les conflits armés non internationaux*, Grenoble, 1978
Mallison, W. T., 'Limited naval blockade or quarantine interdiction, national and collective defence claims valid under international law', 57 *AJIL* 1963, 592

Submarines in General and Limited Warfare, US Naval War College, Newport, 1968

Mallison, W. and Mallison, S., 'The juridical status of privileged combatant under the Geneva Protocol of 1977', 42 *Law and Contemporary Problems* 1978, 4

Mangold, P., *Superpower Intervention in the Middle East*, London, 1978

Mangoldt, H. v., 'Das Kriegsverbrechen und seine Verfolgung in der Vergangenheit und Gegenwart', 1 *Jahrbuch für internationales und ausländisches öffentliches Recht*, 1948–9, 283

Mao Tse Tung People's Publishing House (ed.), 1 *Selected Works of Mao Tse Tung*, Peking, 1977

Maresca, A., 'Gli articoli comuni delle convenzioni di Ginevra del 12 agosto 1949', *Rivista*, 1953, 108

La protezione internazionale dei combatatenti e dei civili, Milan, 1965

Marin Lopez, A., *El desarme nuclear*, Granada, 1974

Marin, M. A., 'The evolution and present status of the laws of war', 92 *RCADI* 1957, ii, 629

Marks, S., 'Les principes et normes des droits de l'homme applicables en periode d'exception', in K. Vasak (ed.), *Les dimensions internationales des droits de l'homme*, Paris, 1978

Marosy Megele, D., 'Los "crimes contre la paz" y el derecho internacional', *REDI*, 1950, 1

Martens, G. F., *Nouveau Recueil Général de Traités et autres actes relatifs aux rapports de droit international*, Göttingen (Leipzig from vol. XXII), 1ère série, 1843–75; 2ème série, 1876–1908; 3ème série, 1915–44

Martin, A., *Legal Aspects of Disarmament*, London, 1963

Martin, L. (ed.), *Strategic Thought in the Nuclear Age*, London, 1980

Martin, O. P. M., *Le conflit israeli–arabe, recherches sur l'emploi de la force en droit international public positif*, Paris, 1973

Martinez, J. C., 'Le droit international et le commerce des armes', in Colloque de Montpellier, *Le droit international et les armes*, Paris, 1982

Massourides, P. A., *Le principe de non-intervention en droit international moderne*, Athens, 1968

Massu, J., *La vraie bataille d'Algers*, Evreux, 1971

Matekalo, I., *Les dessous du terrorisme international*, Paris, 1973

Matthei, D., 'Befehlserweigerung aus humanitären Grunden', *RDPMDG*, 1980, 257

Mayda, J., 'The Korean repatriation problem and international law', 47 *AJIL* 1953, 414

Mayer, R., *Vers le désarmement*, New York, 1976

Mayer-Tasch, P. C., *Guerillakrieg und Völkerrecht*, Baden-Baden, 1972

Meeker, L., 'Defensive quarantine and the law', 57 *AJIL* 1963, 515

Mehrish, B. N., *War Crimes and Genocide, the Trial of Pakistani Criminals*, New Delhi, 1972

Meinecke, F., *Die Idee der Staatsraison in der Geschichte*, 4th edn, Berlin, 1957

Melzer, Y., *Concepts of Just War*, Leiden, 1975

Menon, P. K., 'Legal limitation on the use of certain conventional weapons', *RDPMDG*, 1979, 9

Menzel, F., *Legalität oder Illegalität der Anwendung von Atomwaffen*, Tübingen, 1960

Mercier, Vega, L., *Guerillas in Latin America*, New York, 1969

Merglen, A., *La guerre de l'inattendu, opérations subversives*, Paris, 1966

Merle, M., *Le procès de Nuremberg et le châtiment des criminels de guerre*, Paris, 1949

Mertens, P., 'L'impréscriptibilité des crimes de guerre et contre l'humanité', in Université de Bruxelles (ed.), *Etude de droit international et de droit pénal comparé*, Brussels, 1974

Mesa Garrido, R., 'Guerra civil y guerra internacional, el conflicto de Vietnam', *REDI*, V, XXI–3

Meselson, M. (ed.), *Chemical Weapons and Chemical Arms Control*, New York, 1978

Meuli, H., 'De la neutralité du personnel sanitaire au cours des hostilités', *RICR*, 1956, 377

Meyer, A., *Völkerrechtliche Schutz friedlicher Personen und Sachen gegen Luftangriffe*, Königsberg, 1935

Meyrowitz, H., 'Les armes psychochimiques et le droit international', *AFDI*, 1964, 81

'Le droit de la guerre dans le conflit de Vietnam', *AFDI*, 1967, 153

Les armes biologiques et le droit international, Paris, 1968

'The Law of War in the Vietnamese conflict', in R. A. Falk (ed.), 2 *The Vietnam War and International Law*, Princeton, 1969, 567

'La guérilla et le droit de la guerre', in Centre Henri Rolin (ed.), *Droit humanitaire et conflits armés*, Brussels, 1970

Le principe d'égalité des belligérants devant le droit de la guerre, Paris, 1970

'La guérilla et le droit de la guerre', *RBDI*, 1971

'La stratégie nucléaire et le Protocole additionnel I aux Conventions de Genève de 1949', *RGDIP*, 1979, 905

'Problèmes juridiques relatifs à l'arme à neutron', *AFDI*, 1981, 87

'Le Protocole additonnel I aux Conventions de Genève de 1949 et le droit de la guerre maritime', *RGDIP*, 1985, 294

Miaja de la Muela, A., *La emancipacion de los peublos coloniales y el derecho internacional*, Madrid, 1968

Miatello, A., *La responsabilité internationale encourue en raison des activités liées à l'utilisation de l'énergie nucléaire*, Geneva, 1985

Michel, M., *La seconde guerre mondiale*, Paris, 1977

Midlarsky, M., *On War, Political Violence in the International System*, New York, 1975

Migliorino, L., *Fondi marini e armi di distruzione massiva*, Milan, 1980

Miksche, F. O., *Secret Forces, the Technique of Underground Movement*, London, 1950

Miller, A. S. and Feinrider, M. (eds.), *Nuclear Weapons and the Law*, London, 1984

Miller, L. B., *World Order and Local Disorder: the United Nations and Internal Conflicts*, Princeton, 1967

Miller, N. and Aya, R. (eds.), *National Liberation, Revolution in the Third World*, New York, 1971

Miller, R., *The Law of War*, Lexington, 1975

Miller, R. H., 'The Convention on the non-applicability of statutory limitations to war crimes and crimes against humanity', *AJIL*, 1971, 476

Miller, S. E., *Strategy and Nuclear Deterrence*, Princeton, 1984

Minear, R. H., *Victors' Justice, the Tokyo War Crimes Trial*, Princeton, 1971

Ming-Min-Peng, 'Le bombardement aérien et la population civile depuis la seconde guerre mondiale', *Revue général de l'air*, 1952, 302

Miramanoff, J., *La Croix Rouge et les armes biologiques et chimiques*, Geneva, 1970

Miyazaki, S., 'The Martens Clause and international humanitarian law', in *Etudes Pictet*, Geneva, 1984, 433

Mockler, A., *The Mercenaries*, London, 1970

Monaco, R., 'La sospensione delle norme giuridiche internazionali in tempo de guerra', *Jus*, 1941, 236

Mondlande, E., *The Struggle for Moçambique*, London, 1969

Montealegre, H., *La seguridad de estado y los derechos humanos*, Santiago, 1979

Moore, J. N., 'The lawfulness of military assistance to the Republic of Vietnam', 61 *AJIL* 1967, 1

'Ratification of the Geneva Protocol on Gas and Bacteriological Warfare, a legal and political analysis', 3 *Virginia LR* 1972, 419

(ed.), *Law and Civil War in the Modern World*, Baltimore, 1974

Moreillon, J., *Le Comité international de la Croix-Rouge et la protection des détenus politiques*, Lausanne, 1973

Morgan, W. J., *Spies and Saboteurs*, London, 1955

Morgenstern, F., 'Validity of the acts of the belligerent occupant', *BYIL*, 1951, 291

Mosler, H., *Die Grossmachtstellung im Völkerrecht*, Heidelberg, 1949

Moss, R., *Urban Guerillas*, London, 1972

Mulinen, F., 'Les "villes ouvertes"', *RMS*, 1973, 362

'Das Kriegsrecht und die Streitkräfte', *RICR*, 1978

The Laws of War and the Armed Forces, Geneva, 1981

Muller-Rappard, E., *L'ordre supérieur militaire et la responsabilité pénale du subordonné*, Paris, 1965

Munch, F., 'Das Völkerrecht der militärischen Besetzung vor nationalen Gerichten', in I. V. Münch (ed.), *Festschrift Schlochauer*, Berlin, 1981, 457

Murphy, J. F., *The United Nations and the Control of International Violence*, Manchester, 1983

Myers, D. P., 'The legal basis of the rules of blockade in the Declaration of London', *AJIL*, 1910, 571

Myrdal, A., *The Game of Disarmament*, New York, 1976, rev. edn, New York, 1982

Nahlik, S. E., 'Droit dit "de Genève" et droit dit "de la Haye": unité ou dualité', *AFDI*, 1978, 9

'Le problème des répresailles à la lumière des travaux de la Conférence diplomatique sur le droit humanitaire', *RGDIP*, 1978, 130

'L'extension du statut de combattant à la lumière du Protocole I de Genève de 1977', 164 *RCADI* 1979, iii, 171

'The role of the 1977 Geneva Protocols in the progress of the law of armed conflict', in *European Seminar on Humanitarian Law*, Geneva, 1980

Neinast, W. H., 'United States use of biological warfare', 24 *Military Law Journal* 1964, 27
    'Biological warfare. Two views', 24 *MilLR*, 1965
Neuhold, H., *Internationale Konflikte*, Vienna, 1977
Neuman, S. G. (ed.), *Arms Transfers in the Modern World*, New York, 1979
Nguyen, K. V. (ed.), *Chemical Warfare*, Hanoi, 1971
Niezing, J. (ed.), *Urban Guerilla Studies on the Theory, Strategy and Practice of Political Violence in Modern Societies*, Rotterdam, 1974
Nkrumah, K., *Handbook of Revolutionary Warfare*, London, 1968
Northedge, F. S., *The Use of Force in International Relations*, London, 1974
Northedge, F. S. and Donelan, M. D., *International Disputes: the Political Aspects*, London, 1971
Norway, Utriksdepartementet, St. meld. nr. 102 (1978–9), *Om Norges deltakelse på Diplomatkonferansen om menneskerettigheter i vaepnade konflikter*, Oslo, 1979
Nurick, L., 'Aerial bombardment, theory and practice', *AJIL*, 1945, 689
    'The distinction between combatant and non-combatant in the law of war', *AJIL*, 1945, 680
Nutting, A., *Disarmament: an Outline of the Negotiations*, London, 1959
Nys, E., *Le droit de la guerre et les précurseurs de Grotius*, Brussels, 1882
Oakeshott, R. E., *The Archaeology of Weapons, Arms and Armour from Prehistory to the Age of Chivalry*, London, 1960
Obradovic, K., 'La protection de la population civile dans les conflits armés internationaux', in A. Cassese (ed.), *The New Humanitarian Law of Armed Conflict*, Naples, 1971
O'Brien, W. V. O., 'Biological and chemical warfare' and the international law of war', *Georgetown Law Journal*, 1962, 5
O'Connell, D. P., 'Contemporary naval operations', 44 *BYIL* 1970, 27
    Influence of Law on Sea-Power, Manchester, 1975
O'Connor Howe, J. (ed.), *Armed Peace: the Search for World Security*, London, 1984
Oglesby, R. R., *Internal War and the Search for Normative Order*, The Hague, 1971
Ogston, A., 'The Peace Conference and the dum-dum bullets', *British Medical Journal*, 1899, 278
Oppenheim (ed. H. Lauterpacht), 2 *International Law, War and Neutrality*, 7th edn, London, 1952
Oppenheimer, M., *Urban Guerilla*, London, 1970
Oraison, A., 'Quelques réflexions critiques sur la concession française du droit des peuples à disposer d'eux-mêmes à la lumière du différend franco–comorien sur l'île de Mayotte', *RBDI*, 1983
Osgood, R. E. and Tucker, R. W., *Force, Order and Justice*, Baltimore, 1967
Ottawa Faculty of Law (ed.), *International Terrorism*, Ottawa, 1974
Ottensooser, D., 'Termination of war by unilateral declaration', *BYIL*, 1952, 435
Ottmuller, R., *Die Anwendung von Seekriegsrecht in militärischen Konflikten seit 1945*, Hamburg, 1978
Overweg, A. B., *Die chemische Waffen und das Völkerrecht*, Berlin, 1937

Ozerden, K., *Le sort des militaires belligéréants, victimes de la guerre debarqués dans un port neutre, d'après la Convention de Genève*, Paris, 1971

Padelford, R. J., *International Law and Diplomacy in the Spanish Civil Strife*, New York, 1939

Paret, P., *French Revolutionary Warfare from Indochina to Algeria*, London, 1964
Clausewitz and the State, Oxford, 1976

Paret, P. and Shy, J. W., *Guerillas in the 1960's*, New York, 1962

Parfond, P., *Le droit de prise et son application dans la marine française*, Paris, 1955

Paskins, B. and Dockrill, M., *The Ethics of War*, London, 1979

Paston, D. G., *Superior Orders as Affecting Responsibility for War Crimes*, New York, 1946

Paust, J. J., 'Weapons regulation, military necessity and legal standards: are contemporary Department of Defense "Practices" inconsistent with legal norms?' 4 *Denver Journal of International Law and Policy* 1974, 229
'Non-protected persons or things', in A. E. Evans and J. F. Murphy (eds.), *Legal Aspects of Terrorism*, Lexington, 1978

Peterson, H. A., Reinhardt, C. C. and Conger, E. E. (eds.), *The Role of Airpower in Counterinsurgency and Unconventional Warfare*, Symposium, Santa Monica, 1963

Phillipson, C., *Termination of War and Treaties of Peace*, London, 1916

Philonenko, A., *Essais sur la philosophie de la guerre*, Paris, 1976

Piccagallo, P. R., *The Japanese on Trial, Allied War Crimes Operations in the East 1945–1951*, Dallas, 1979

Picchio, L. F., *La sanzione nel diritto internazionale*, Padua, 1974

Pictet, J., 'La Croix Rouge et les Conventions de Genève', *RCADI*, 1950, i, 5
'The new Geneva Conventions for the protection of war victims', 45 *AJIL* 1951, 462 at 472
La Convention de Genève pour l'amélioration du sort des blessés et des malades dans les forces armées en campagne, Geneva, 1952
La Convention de Genève pour la protection des personnes civiles en temps de guerre, Geneva, 1956
Les principes du droit international humanitaire, Geneva, 1967
Le droit humanitaire et la protection des victimes de guerre, Leiden, 1973
Humanitarian Law and the Protection of War Victims, Leiden, 1975
Les principes fondamentaux de la Croix-Rouge, Geneva, 1979
Développements et principes du droit international humanitaire, Geneva, 1983
Une institution unique en son genre, Le CICR, Geneva, 1983
International Humanitarian Law, Geneva, 1985

Pillet, A., *Les Conventions de la Haye du 29 juillet et du 18 octobre 1907, étude juridique et critique*, Paris, 1918

Pilloud, C., *Reservations to the Geneva Conventions of 1949*, vol. 1, Geneva, 1958, vol. 2, Geneva, 1965

Pinto, R., 'Les règles du droit international concernant la guerre civile', 114 *RCADI* 1965, i, 451
'L'évolution de la nature juridique du conflit armé au Vietnam', in *Mélanges Marcel Bridel*, Lausanne, 1968

Piradow-Starnscheko, 'Das Prinzip der Nichteinmischung im modernen

Völkerrecht', in Arzinger (ed.), *Gegenwartsprobleme des Völkerrechts*, Berlin, 1962

Plassman, C., *Das Kriegsgefangenenrecht und seine Reform*, Berlin, 1928

Plattner, D., *Protection of Children in International Humanitarian Law*, ICRC, Geneva, 1984

Poidevin, R., *Les origines de la première guerre mondiale*, Paris, 1975

Pokstefl, J. and Bothe, M., 'Entwicklungen und Tendenzen des Kriegsrecht seit den Nachkriegskodifikation', *ZaöRVR*, 1975, 547

Politis, N., 'L'avenir de la médiation', *RGDIP*, 1910, 130

'Les commissions internationales d'enquête', *RGDIP*, 1912, 149

Polmar, N., *Strategic Weapons: an Introduction*, New York, 1982

Pompe, C. A., *Aggressive War, an International Crime*, The Hague, 1953

Potter, P. B., 'Repatriation of prisoners-of-war', *AJIL*, 1952, 568

Prentiss, A. M., *Civil Defense in Modern War*, New York, 1961

Preuss, L., 'International responsibility for hostile propaganda against foreign states', *AJIL*, 1934, 649

Prokosch, E., *The Simple Act of Murder, Antipersonnel Weapons and their Development*, Philadelphia, 1972

Proudhon, P. J., *La guerre et la paix. Recherches sur le principe et la constitution du droit des gens*, Paris, 1927

Prugh, G. S., 'The code of conduct for the armed forces', 56 *ColLR* 1956, 678

Pustay, J. S., *Counterinsurgency Warfare*, New York, 1965

Quenéudec, J., 'Les zones denucléarisées', in Colloque de Montpellier (ed.), *Le droit international et les armes*, Paris, 1982

Quester, G. H., *Sea Power in the 1970's*, New York, 1975

Quintano Ripolles, A., 'Tecnicismo penal internacional de la delincuencia de guerra', *REDI*, 1950

Tratado de derecho penal internacional, Madrid, 1955

Rabus, W. G., 'A new definition of the *levée en masse?*' 24 *NedTIR* 1977, 232

Radley, K. N., 'The Palestinian refugees, the right to return in international law', 72 *AJIL* 1978, 586

Rambaud, P., 'La définition de l'agression par l'Organisation des Nations Unies', *RGDIP*, 1976, 835

Ramcharan, B. G., *Humanitarian Good Offices in International Law, the Good Offices of the United Nations Secretary General in the Field of Human Rights*, The Hague, 1983

Randelshofer, A., 'Flächenbombardement und Völkerrecht', *Festschrift van der Heydte*, 1977, 471

Ranger, R., *The Canadian Contribution to the Control of Chemical and Biological Warfare*, Toronto (Canadian Institute of International Affairs), 1976

Ränk, R., *Einwirkung des Krieges auf die nicht-politischen Staatsverträge*, Uppsala, 1949

'Modern war and validity of treaties', 38 *Cornell LQ* 1952–3, 312

Rauch, E., 'The Protocol Additional to the Geneva Conventions for the Protection of Victims of International Armed Conflicts and the United Nations Conventions on the Law of the Sea, repercussions on the law of naval warfare', *Report to the International Society for Military Law and Law of War*, Berlin, 1984

Reimann, M., *Quasi-konsulärische und schützmächtähnliche Funktionen des Internationalen Komitees vom Roten Kreuz ausserhalb bewaffneter Konflikte*, Geneva, 1971

Reisman, M. and McDougal, M. S., 'Humanitarian intervention to protect the Ibos', in R. B. Lillich (ed.), *Humanitarian Intervention and the United Nations*, Charlottesville, 1973

Rejai, M. (ed.), *Mao on Revolution and War*, Garden City, 1969

Reuter, P., 'Le droit de la guerre maritime et les juridictions internationales temporaires issues des Traités de paix de la grande guerre', *RDI*, 1934, 375

    'La personnalité juridique internationale du Comité internationale de la Croix Rouge', in *Etudes Pictet*, Geneva, 1984, 783

Revel, G., 'Rôle et caractère des commissions de conciliation', *RGDIP*, 1931, 564

Richards, E., 'The British prize courts and the war', *BYIL*, 1920–1, 11

    'Contraband', *BYIL*, 1922–3, 1

Riche, D., *La guerre chimique et biologique*, Paris, 1982

Roach, J. A., 'Certain conventional weapons conventions: arms control or humanitarian law?' 105 *MilLR* 1984, 3

Roberts, A., 'What is military occupation?' *BYIL*, 1984, 249

    Nations in Arms: the Theory and Practice of Territorial Defence, 2nd edn, London, 1986

Roberts, A. and Guelff, R., *Documents on the Laws of Law*, Oxford, 1982

Robertson, A. H., 'Human rights as the basis of international humanitarian law', *Acte du congrès international de droit humanitaire*, San Remo, 1970

Robinson, J. P., *The Effects of Weapons on Ecosystems, UNEP*, Oxford, 1979

    Chemical Warfare Arms Control: a Framework for Considering Policy Alternatives, London (SIPRI), 1985

Rohwer, J., *Superpower Confrontation on the Seas, Naval Development and Strategy since 1945*, Beverly Hills, 1975

Rolin, A., *Le droit moderne de la guerre*, 3 vols., Brussels, 1920

Röling, B. V. A., 'The Tokyo trials and the development of international law', *Indian LR*, 1953, 4

    'The question of defining aggression', *Symbolae Verzijl*, The Hague, 1958

    'The law of war and national jurisdiction since 1945', 100 *RCADI* 1960, ii, 428

    'Die Definition der Aggression', in *Festschrift Eberhard Menzel*, 1975, 387

    'The significance of the laws of war', in A. Cassese (ed.), *Current Problems of International Law*, Milan, 1975

    'Aspects of the criminal responsibility for violations of the laws of war', in A. Cassese (ed.), *The New Humanitarian Law of Armed Conflict*, Naples, 1979

Ronzitti, N., *La guerra di liberazione nazionale e il diritto internazionale*, Paisa, 1974

    'Wars of national liberation, a legal definition', *RivDI*, 1975, i, 192

Rosas, A., *The Legal Status of Prisoners of War*, Helsinki, 1976

Rose, S. (ed.), *Chemical and Biological Warfare*, Boston, 1969

Rosecrance, R., *International Relations: Peace or War*, New York, 1973

Rosenau, J. N., *International Aspects of Civil Strife*, Princeton, 1964

Rosenblad, E., *International Humanitarian Law of Armed Conflict, Some Aspects of the Principle of Distinction and Related Problems*, Geneva, 1979

Rotter, M., *Die dauernde Neutralität*, Berlin, 1981

Rougier, A., *Les guerres civiles et le droit des gens*, Paris, 1903

Rousseau, Ch., 'Le conflit italo-éthiopien', *RGDIP*, 1937, 692
　La non-intervention en Espagne, Paris, 1939
　Le droit des conflits armés, Paris, 1983

Rowen, D., *The Quest for Self-determination*, New Haven, 1979

Rowson, S. W. D., 'Italian prize law 1940–1943', *BYIL*, 1946, 282
　'Modern blockade, some legal aspects', *BYIL*, 1946, 346

Rozakis, C., 'Terrorism and the internationally protected persons in the light of the ILC's Draft Articles', *ICLQ*, 1974, 32

Ruegger, P., 'L'organisation internationale de la Croix Rouge sous ses aspects juridiques', *RCADI*, 1953, i, 377

Ruiz Moreno, I., *Guerra terrestre y aeria*, Buenos Aires, 1926

Rumpf, H., *The Bombing of Germany*, New York, 1962

Russell, D. E. H., *Rebellion, Revolution and Armed Force*, London, 1974

Rybakov, Y. N., *Voorozhennaya agressia, tiagchaishe mezhdunarodnoe prestuplennge*, Moscow, 1980

Rydichi, T., *The Right of Self Defence in International Law*, Lusaka, 1978

St Jorre, J., *The Nigerian Civil War*, London, 1972

Sandford, R., 'Evolution du droit de la guerre maritime et aérienne', 68 *RCADI* 1939, 555

Sandoz, Y., *Des armes interdites en droit de la guerre*, Geneva, 1975
　'La place des Protocoles additionnels aux Conventions de Genève du 12 août 1949 dans le droit humanitaire', 12 *RDH* 1979, 135
　'Localités et zones sous protection spéciale', in Institut Henri Dunant (ed.), *Quatre études du droit international humanitaire*, Geneva, 1985, 35

Saussure, H., 'Recent developments in the law of air warfare', *Annuaire canadien de droit aérien*, 1978, 33
　'Belligerent air operations and the 1977 Geneva Protocol I', *Annuaire canadien de droit aérien*, 1979, 459

Scelle, G., 'De l'influence de l'état de guerre sur le droit conventionnel', *JDI*, 1950, 26
　'*Jus ad bellum*', 6 *NedTIR* 1959, 292

Schachter, O., 'The United Nations and internal conflict', in J. N. Moore (ed.), *Law and Civil War in the Modern World*, Baltimore, 1974, 409

Schapiro, L. B., 'Repatriation of deserters', *BYIL*, 1952, 310

Schätzel, W., *Der Krieg als Endigungsgrund von Verträgen*, Berlin, 1911
　'Die Annexion im Völkerrecht', 2 *AVR* 1950, 1

Scheidl, F., *Die Kriegsgefangenenrecht von den ältesten Zeiten bis zur Gegenwart*, Berlin, 1943

Schelling, T. C., 'The military use of outer space, bombardment satellites', in J. M. Goldsen (ed.), *Outer Space and World Politics*, New York, 1963

Scheuner, U., 'Die Annexion im modernen Völkerrecht', 49 *Die Friedenswarte* 1949, 81
　'Die kollektive Sicherheit des Friedens im gegenwärtigen Völkerrecht', *Berichte der Deutschen Gesellschaft für Völkerrecht*, 1958, ii, 1

'Krieg und Bürgerkrieg in der Staatenwelt der Gegenwart', in *Festschrift Friedrich Berber*, 1973

'Entwicklungen im Seekriegsrecht seit dem zeiten Weltkrieg', *Festschrift Rolf Stödter*, 1979

Schindler, D., 'Die Anwendung der Genfer Rotkreuzabkommen seit 1949', 22 *ASDI* 1965, 75

'Aspects contemporains de la neutralité', 121 *RCADI* 1967, ii, 221

'The different types of armed conflicts according to the Geneva Conventions and Protocols', 163 *RCADI* 1979, ii, 117

Schindler, D. and Toman, J., *The Law of Armed Conflict, a Collection of Conventions, Resolutions and Other Documents*, Leiden, 1973, 2nd edn, 1983

Schlochauer, H. J., 'Die Einwirkung des Krieges auf den Bestand völkerrechtlicher Verträge', 1 *Deutsche Rechtszeitschrift* 1946, 161

Schlosser, R., *Das völkerrechtliche Problem des Partisanenkrieges*, Mainz, 1939

Schmid, J. H., *Die völkerrechtliche Stellung Partisanen im Kriege*, Zurich, 1956

Schmidt, D. A., *Yemen: the Unknown War*, London, 1968

Schmitt, C., *Theorie der Partisanen*, Berlin, 1963

Schmitt, J., *Die Zulässigkeit von Sperrgebieten im Seekrieg*, Hamburg, 1966

Schmitz, E., 'Die offene Stadt im geltenden Kriegsrecht', 10 *ZaöRVR*, 1940–1, 618

Schonholzer, J. P., 'Le soldat sanitaire n'est pas un combattant', *RICR*, 1955, 245

Schröder, A. H., *Das Angarienrecht, die Beschlagnahmne von Handelsschiffen im Kriege*, Kiel, 1965

Schücking, W., *Das völkerrechtliche Institut der Vermittlung*, Kristiania, 1923

Schwarzenberger, G., *The Legality of Nuclear Weapons*, London, 1958

2 *International Law as Applied by International Courts and Tribunals, the Law of Armed Conflict*, London, 1968

Schwebel, S. M., 'Aggression, intervention and self-defence in modern international law', 135 *RCADI* 1972, ii, 411

Schweisfurth, T., 'Operation to rescue nationals in third states involving the use of force in relation to the protection of human rights', 23 *GYIL* 1980, 159

Sciso, E., 'L'aggressione indiretta nella definizione dell'Assemblea Generale delle Nazioni Unite', *RivDI*, 1983, 253

Sereni, A. P., 'Italian prize courts 1966–1942', 37 *AJIL* 1943, 248

Servier, J., *Le terrorisme*, Paris, 1979

Setalvad, M., 'Nuclear weapons and international law', *Indian Journal of International Law*, 1963, 383

Seyersted, F., *United Nations Forces in the Law of Peace and War*, Leiden, 1966

Shaker, M. I., *The Nuclear Non-proliferation Treaty, Origins and Implementation, 1959–1979*, 3 vols., New York, 1980

Shamgar, M., *Military Government in the Territories Administered by Israel 1967–1980*, Jerusalem, 1982

Shapiro, H., 'The repatriation of deserters', *BYIL*, 1952, 310

Shearer, I. A., 'International humanitarian law and naval operations', in Institut Henri Dunant (ed.), *Quatre Etudes du droit international humanitaire*, Geneva, 1985

Shields Delessert, C., *Release and Repatriation of Prisoners-of-War at the End of Active Hostilities*, Zurich, 1977

Sico, L., *Toute prise doit être jugée, il giudizio delle prede nel diritto internazionale*, Naples, 1971

Silvanie, H., *Responsibility of States for Acts of Unsuccessful Insurgent Governments*, New York, 1939

Simma, B., 'Zur bilateralen Durchsetzung verträglich verankerte Menschenrechte', in C. Schreuer (ed.), *Autorität und internationale Ordnung*, Berlin, 1979, 129

Simpson, J. L. and Fox, H., *International Arbitration: Law and Practice*, London, 1959

Sims, N., *Approaches to Disarmament: an Introductory Analysis*, 2nd edn, London, 1979

'Chemical weapons, control or chaos?' *Faraday Discussion Paper No. 1*, London (Council for Arms Control), 1984

'Biological and toxin weapons: issues in the 1986 Review Conference', *Faraday Discussion Paper No. 7*, London (Council for Arms Control), 1986

Singh, B. and Ko-Wang, M., *Theory and Practice of Modern Guerilla Warfare*, London, 1971

Singh, N., *Nuclear Weapons and International Law*, London, 1959

Siotis, J., *Le droit de la guerre et les conflits armés d'un caractère non-international*, Paris, 1958

SIPRI, *The Problem of Chemical and Biological Warfare, a Study on the Historical, Technical, Military, Legal and Political Aspects of CBW and Possible Disarmament Measures*, 6 vols., Stockholm, 1971–8

(ed.), *Incendiary Weapons*, Stockholm, 1975

(ed. Marek Thee), *Armaments and Disarmament in the Nuclear Age, a Handbook*, London, 1976

(ed.), *The Law of War and Dubious Weapons*, Stockholm, 1976

(ed.), *Weapons of Mass Destruction and the Environment*, Stockholm and London, 1977

(ed.), *Anti-Personnel Weapons*, Stockholm, 1978

Chemical Weapons, Destruction and Conversion, London, 1980

(ed. J. Goldblatt), *Agreements for Arms Control*, London, 1982

Armament or Disarmament, Stockholm, 1983

Skubiszewski, K., 'Use of force by states, collective security, law of war and neutrality', in M. Sörensen (ed.), *Manual of International Law*, London, 1968

Smith, H. A., 'Booty of war', *BYIL*, 1946, 227

The Law and Custom of the Sea, London, 1959

Smith, M. J., *The Soviet Air and Strategic Rocket Forces, 1939–1980, a Guide to Sources in English*, Oxford, 1981

Snow, D. M., *Nuclear Strategy in a Dynamic World*, University of Alabama, 1981

Sobel, L. A., *Political Terrorism*, vol. 1, New York, 1975, vol. 2, New York, 1979

Söderhjelm, J. O., *Démilitarisation et neutralisation des Iles d'Aland en 1856 et 1921*, Helsinki, 1928

Solf, W. A., 'Human rights in armed conflicts', in H. H. Han (ed.), *Challenges to Human Rights*, Washington, DC, 1979
Spaight, J. M., *War Rights on Land*, London, 1911
   Air Power and the Cities, London, 1930
   Air Power and War Rights, London, 1933, 3rd edn, London, 1947
Spetzler, E., *Luftkrieg und Menschlichkeit*, Göttingen, 1965
Spiers, E. M., 'The ruse of dum dum bullets in colonial warfare', 4 *Journal of Imperial and Commonwealth History* 1975
   Chemical Warfare, London, 1986
Spinnler, P., *Das Kriegsgefangenrecht in Korean Konflikt*, Zurich, 1976
Spiropoulos, J., 'Sur l'existence de l'état de guerre entre la Grèce et l'Albanie', 1 *RHDI* 1948, 375
Stahel, C. R., *Die Blockade im Kriegsvölkerrecht*, Basle, 1972
Stein, A. A., *The Nature of War*, Baltimore, 1981
Stein, E., 'Impact of new weapons technology on international law', 133 *RCADI* 1971, iii, 222
Steinecke, D., *Das Navicertsystem*, 2 vols., Hamburg, 1966
   Handelsschiffahrt und Prisenrecht, Hamburg, 1973
Steinert, M. G., *Les origines de la seconde guerre mondiale*, Paris, 1974
Stephen, J., *War in Disguise or the Fraudes of the Neutral Flags*, London, 1805, reprinted by Sir Francis Piggott, London, 1917
Stokes, R., 'External liberation movements', in I. Robertson and P. Whitten, *Race and Politics in South Africa*, Brunswick, New Jersey, 1978
Stone, J., *Aggression and World Order, Critique of United Nations Theories of Aggression*, London, 1958
   Legal Controls of International Conflict, Sydney, 1954, 2nd edn, New York, 1973
   'Hope and loopholes in 1974 definition of aggression', *AJIL*, 1977, 226
   'Legal problems of espionage in conditions of modern conflict', in R. J. Stabger *et al.* (eds.), *Essays on Espionage and International Law*, Columbus, Ohio, 1982
Stowell, E. C., 'The laws of war and the atomic bomb', 39 *AJIL* 1945, 784
Stracey, J., *On the Prevention of War*, London, 1962
Strebel, H., 'Die strafrechtliche Sicherung humanitärer Abkommen', 15 *ZaöRVR* 1953–4, 31
   'Die Haager Konventionen zum Schutze der Kulturgüter im Faller eines bewaffneten Konfliktes', 16 *ZaöRVR* 1955, 35
   'Die Genfer Abkommen vom 12. August 1949, Fragen des Anwendungbereichs', 13 *ZaöRVR* 1959, 12
Stremlau, J. J., *The International Politics of the Nigerian Civil War 1967–1970*, Princeton, 1977
Strupp, K., *Das internationale Landkriegsrecht*, Frankfurt, 1914
Sullivan, C. D., Eliot, G. F., Gayle, G. D. and Corson, W. R., *The Vietnam War*, Washington, DC, 1968
Sun Tse, *The Art of War*, ed. and trans. S. B. Griffiths, Oxford, 1963
Suter, K. D., 'An inquiry into the meaning of the phrase "Human Rights in Armed Conflicts"', 15 *RDPMDG* 1976, 393

An International Law of Guerilla Warfare, London, 1984

Peaceworking: the United Nations and Disarmament, Sydney, 1985

Sweden, Committee on International Law, *Folkrätten i krig, Rättsregler under väpnade konflikter – tolkning, tillämpning och undervisning*, Sveriges offentliga utredningar (SOU), 1984: 56, 82

Switzerland, Federal Political Department, *Diplomatic Conference on the Reaffirmation and Development of International Humanitarian Law Applicable in Armed Conflict, Geneva 1974–1977, Official Records*, 17 vols., Berne, 1978

Taber, R., *The War of the Flea, a Study of Guerilla Warfare*, London, 1970

Tallow, A. A., *Command Responsibility*, Manila, 1965

Tamkoc, H., *International Civil War*, Ankara, 1967

Tanham, G., *Communist Revolutionary Warfare*, New York, 1961

Taoka, R., *The Right of Self-defence in International Law*, Osaka, 1978

Tapias, Salinas, L., *Cuestiones de derecho aeronautico de guerra*, Madrid, 1942

Taubenfeld, H. J., 'The applicability of the laws of war in civil war', in J. N. Moore (ed.), *Law and Civil War in the Modern World*, Baltimore, 1974

Tchirkovitch, S., 'Les nouvelles conventions internationales de Genève du 12 août 1949', *RGDIP*, 1950, 97

Thomas, A. V. and Thomas, A. J., *Non-intervention*, Dallas, 1956

The Concept of Aggression in International Law, Dallas, 1972

Chemical and Biological Weapons, New York, 1982

Thomas, C., *New States, Sovereignty and Intervention*, London, 1985

Thomas, H., *The Spanish Civil War*, London, 1961

Thomas, M., *Terrorisme et guerilla*, Ottawa, 1973

Thompson, R., *Revolutionary War in World Strategy 1945–1969*, New York, 1970

Thorn, C., *The Issue of War*, London, 1985

Thorneycroft, E., *Personal Responsibility and the Law of Nations*, The Hague, 1961

Toman, J., 'La conception soviétique des guerres de libération nationale', in A. Cassese (ed.), *Current Problems of International Law*, Milan, 1975

Tomaon, E., *Kriegsbegriff und Kriegsrecht der Sowjetunion*, Berlin, 1979

Tomuschat, C., 'Gewalt und Gewaltverbot als Bestimmungsfaktoren der Weltordnung', 36 *Europa Archiv* 1981, 325

Tooke, J. D., *The Just War in Aquinas and Grotius*, London, 1965

Torriani, A., *Posizione giuridica dei partigiani e franchi tiratori nel diritto internazionale bellico vigente per gli eserciti in campagna con speciale considerazione dei problemi imposti dalla IIa guerra mondiale*, Basle, 1950

Tosenau, N. J., *International Aspects of Civil Strife*, Princeton, 1964

Trainin, I. P., 'Voprosy partizanskoi voiny v meshdunarodnom prave', in *Izvestija Akademii Nauk SSSR*, 1945, 4, 1

'Questions of guerilla warfare in the law of war', 40 *AJIL* 1946, 534

Trials of the Major War Criminals before the International Military Tribunal, Nuremberg, 1947

Tromm, J., 'Open Steden', 59 *Militair-rechtelijk Tijdschrift* 1966, 321

Trooboff, P. D., *Law and Responsibility in Warfare, the Vietnam experience*, Chapel Hill, North Carolina, 1975

Tucker, R. C., *The Marxian Revolutionary Idea: Essays on Marxist Thought and its Impact on Radical Movements*, Norton, 1969

Tucker, R. W., *The Law of War and Neutrality at Sea*, Naval War College, Washington, DC, 1957
  Force, Order and Justice, Baltimore, 1967
Tunkin, G., *Sila i pravo v mezhdunarodnoe sisteme*, Moscow, 1983
  (Tounkine), 'L'installation des missiles américaines en Europe viole le droit international', in *Les conséquences juridiques de l'installation éventuelle de missiles cruises et pershings en Europe, Acte du Colloque*, Bruxelles, 1–2 octobre 1982, Brussels, 1984, 107
Turlington, E., 'Treatment of enemy property in the United States before the World War', *AJIL*, 1928, 270
Turner-Johnson, J., *Just War Tradition and the Restraint of War, a Moral and Historical Inquiry*, Princeton, 1981
Tuscher, H. P., *Die völkerrechtliche Regelung des Loses des Kriegsopfer vor dem Abschluss der Genfer Konvention von 1964*, Zurich, 1969
Twitchett, K. J., 'Strategies for security, some theoretical considerations', in K. J. Twitchett (ed.), *International Security, Reflections on Survival and Stability*, Oxford, 1971
Umozurike, O., *Self-determination in International Law*, Hamden, Connecticut, 1972
Undén, O., 'Om krigets kriminalisering', *Uppsala Universitets Arsskrift*, 1924, 22
  'Quelques observations sur la notion de guerre d'agression', *RDILC*, 1931, 3
United Kingdom, *Trial of Major German War Criminals*, London, 1948
United States, *Strategic Bombing Survey, the Effect of Bombing on Health and Medical Care in Germany*, Washington, DC, 1945
  Strategic Bombing Survey, the Effects of Strategic Bombing on Japan's War Economy, Washington, DC, n.d.
  Committee on Foreign Relations, 'Nuclear weapons and foreign policy', *Hearings before the Subcommittee on United States Security Agreements*, Washington, DC, 1974
  Committee on Foreign Relations, 'Prohibition of chemical and biological weapons', *Hearings before the 93rd Congress*, 2nd sess., Washington, DC, 1974
  Committee on International Relations, 'First use of nuclear weapons', *Hearings before the 94th Congress*, 2nd sess., Washington, DC, 1976
  Department of State, *Licences for Export of Arms to Foreign Police Forces*, 2 vols., Washington, DC, 1976
  Department of the Air Force, *International Law, the Conduct of Armed Conflict and Air Operation*, Washington, DC, 1976
  Department of the Army, *Jungle Training and Operations, Field Manuals No. 31–30, 1965; 31–35, 1969*
  Naval War College, *The Use of Force, Human Rights and General International Legal Issues*, 62 International Legal Studies, Newport, 1980
  Naval War College, *Documents on Prisoners-of-War*, 60 International Legal Studies, Newport, 1979
Vagts, A., *A History of Militarism*, London, 1959
Verdross, A., *Die völkerrechtwidrige Kriegshandlung und der Strafanspruch der Staaten*, Vienna, 1920

Vernant, J. (ed.), *Les refugiés dans l'après guerre*, Geneva, 1951

Verri, P., Considérations sur l'application dans les conflits modernes des articles 3 et 4 des Conventions de Genève de 1949', 11 *RDPMDG* 1972, 93

Verwey, W. D., *Riot Control Agents and Herbicides in War*, Leiden, 1977

Verzijl, J. H., *Le droit des prises de la grande guerre*, Leiden, 1924

Veuthey, M., 'Règles et principes de droit international humanitaire applicable dans la guérilla', 7 *RBDI* 1971, 505

    'Comportement et statut des combattants', 12 *RDPMDG* 1973, 47

    'Guerre de libération et droit humanitaire', 7 *RDH* 1974, 93

    'Les conflits armés de caractère non international et le droit humanitaire', in A. Cassese (ed.), *Current Problems of International Law*, Milan, 1975

    Guérilla et droit humanitaire, Geneva, 1976, 2nd edn, Geneva, 1983

Vinal Casas, A., 'La conferencia diplomatica de Ginebra sobre reaffirmacion y el desarollo del derecho internacional humanitario aplicable en los conflictos armados', 19 *REDI* 1976, 86

    'El estatudo juridico internacional de los mercenarios', *REDI*, 1977

Vincent, R. J., *Non-intervention and International Order*, Princeton, 1974

Violle, J., *L'espionnage militaire en temps de guerre*, Paris, 1903

Vitta, E., 'Le azioni internazionali di soccorso umanitario', *Studi in onore di Balladori Pallieri*, Milan, 1978, 658

Waldock, C. H. M., 'The release of *The Altmark*'s prisoners', *BYIL*, 1947, 216

    'The regulation of the use of force by individual states and international law', *RCADI*, 1952, ii, 455

Walters, R. E., *Sea Power and the Nuclear Fallacy*, New York, 1975

Walzer, M., *Just and Unjust Wars*, London, 1978

Wannow, M., *Das Selbstbestimmungsrecht im sowjetischen Völkerrechtsdenken*, Göttingen, 1965

Warnke, P. C., 'Individual responsibility in warfare', in P. D. Trooboff (ed.), *Law and Responsibility in Warfare, the Vietnam Experience*, Chapel Hill, North Carolina, 1975, 187

Wayda, A. P., *War in Ecological Perspective*, New York, 1976

Webber, G. J., *The Effect of War on Contracts*, London, 1940

Weber, H., *Der Vietnam Konflikt – Bellum Legale? Die Rechtspflichten der Staaten unter dem Gewaltgebot der UN-Charta*, Hamburg, 1970

Weber, M., 'Legitimacy, politics and the state', in H. Gerth and C. W. Mills (eds.), *From Max Weber: Essays in Sociology*, New York, 1958, 77; reprinted in W. E. Connolly (ed.), *Legitimacy and the State*, Oxford, 1984

Webster, C. and Frankland, N., *The Strategic Air Offensive against Germany 1939–1945*, 4 vols., London, 1961

Wehberg, H., *Seekriegsrecht*, Stuttgart, 1915

    'Guerre civil et droit international', in *Crise mondiale*, Zurich, 1938

    'La guerre civile et le droit international', 63 *RCADI* 1938, ii, 127

    'König Gustav Adolf und das Problem der Annexion besetzten feindlichen Gebiete', *Liber amicorum Algot Bagge*, Stockholm, 1956

    'Die Vergleichkommissionen im modernen Völkerrecht', in *Festgabe Makarov*, Stuttgart, 1958, 551

Weiler, H., *Vietnam*, Montreux, 1969

Weill, G., *Théories sur le pouvoir royal en France pendant les guerres de religion*, Paris, 1892

Weizsacker, C. F. (ed.), *Kriegsfolgen und Kriegsverhütung*, n.p., 1971

Weller, J., *Weapons and Tactics*, London, 1966

Wells, D. A., *War Crimes and Laws of War*, New York, 1981

Werner, G., 'Les prisonniers de guerre', 21 *RCADI* 1928, i, 1

Westing, A. H., *Weapons of Mass Destruction and the Environment*, London, 1977

Westman, C. G., *Folkratten och den neutrala handeln*, Stockholm, 1924

White, G. (ed.), *The Environmental Effects of Nuclear War*, Washington, DC, 1984

Wijngaert, C. v. d., 'Les euromissiles et le droit pénal international', in Actes du Colloque, October 1984, *Les conséquences juridiques de l'installation éventuelle de missiles cruises et pershing en Europe*, Brussels, 1984, 111

Wilhelm, R. J., 'Problèmes relatifs à la protection de la personne humaine par le droit international dans les conflits armés ne présentant pas un caractère international', 137 *RCADI* 1972, iii, 311

Williams, S., *The International and National Protection of Movable Cultural Property, a Comparative Study*, Dobbs Ferry, 1978

Wilson, W., 'Non-belligerency in relation to the terminology of neutrality', *AJIL*, 1941, 362

Wiseberg, L. S., *The Nigerian Civil War 1967–1970, a Case Study in the Efficiency of International Law as a Regulator of Intrastate Violence*, Santa Monica, 1972

Woetzel, R. K., *The Nuremberg Trials in International Law*, New York, 1960; *The Nuremberg Trials in International Law, with a Postlude on the Eichmann Trial*, 2nd edn, New York, 1962

Wolf, E., *Peasant Wars in the Twentieth Century*, London, 1971

Wolf, U., 'Le statut des prisonniers de guerre dans les luttes de libération nationale', *RIDC*, 1984, 33

Woolsey, L. H., 'The forced transfer of property in enemy occupied territory', *AJIL*, 1943, 282

Wright, Q., 'When does war exist?' 26 *AJIL* 1932, 362

    'The law of the Nuremberg trial', *AJIL*, 1947

    'The outlawry of war and the Law of War', 47 *AJIL* 1953, 38, 365

    'The new law of war and neutrality', in *Varia Juris Gentium Liber Amicorum J. P. A. François*, Leiden, 1959

    'United States intervention in the Lebanon', *AJIL*, 1959, 112

    'Subversive intervention', *AJIL*, 1960, 22

    'The Goa incident', *AJIL*, 1962, 24

    'The Cuban Quarantine', 57 *AJIL* 1963, 546

    A Study of War, 2nd edn, Chicago, 1965

    'Legal aspects of the Vietnam situation', 60 *AJIL* 1966

Wulff, T., *Krig och humanitet*, Stockholm, 1975

    Handbok i folkrätt under krig, neutralitet och ockupation, 3rd edn, Stockholm, 1980

    Barriers against Weapons, Development of Weapons and Restrictions on their Use, Roda Korset, Stockholm, 1984

xxx, 'La notion juridique de la guerre, le critérion de la guerre', 57 *RGDIP* 1953, 177

Yakemchouk, R., 'Les transferts internationaux d'armes de guerre, Paris, 1980

Yingling, R. T. and Ginnane, R. W., 'The Geneva Conventions of 1949', 46 *AJIL* 1952, 393

Zacklin, R., 'International law and the protection of civilian victims of non international armed conflicts', in *Essays on International Law in Honour of Krishna Rao*, Leiden, 1976

Zemanek, K., 'Das Kriegs- und Humanitärrecht', in *Handbuch des Völkerrechts*, Vienna, 1983, no. 2129

Zimmer, G., *Gewaltsame territorielle Veränderungen und ihre völkerrechtliche Legitimation*, Berlin, 1971

Zoller, E., *Peacetime Unilateral Remedies, an Analysis of Countermeasures*, New York, 1984

Zorgbibe, C., 'De la théorie classique de la reconnaissance de belligérance à l'article 3 des Conventions de Genève', in Centre Henri Rolin (ed.), *Droit humanitaire et conflits armés*, Brussels, 1970

  La guerra civil, Barcelona, 1975

  La guerre civile, Paris, 1975

  Le risque de guerre, Paris, 1981

Zorn, A., *Das Kriegsrecht zu Lande in seiner neuesten Gestaltung*, Berlin, 1966

Zourek, J., 'La définition de l'agression en le droit international, Développements récents de la question', 92 *RCADI* 1957, ii, 755

  'Enfin une définition de l'agression', *AFDI*, 1974, 9

  L'interdiction de l'emploie de force en droit international, Leiden, 1974

  'La lutte d'un peuple en vue de faire prévaloir son désir d'auto-détermination constitue-t-elle au regard du droit international un conflit interne ou un conflit de caractère international?' in 1 *Studi in onore di Manlio Udina*, Milan, 1975, 895

Index